BOOK DESIGN BY **MARK CORDELL HOLMES**

IMAGE COMICS, INC.
Erik Larsen - *Publisher*
Todd McFarlane - *President*
Marc Silvestri - *CEO*
Jim Valentino - *Vice-President*
Eric Stephenson - *Executive Director*
Jim Demonakos - *PR & Marketing Coordinator*
Mia MacHatton - *Accounts Manager*
Traci Hui - *Administrative Assistant*
Joe Keatinge - *Traffic Manager*
Allen Hui - *Production Manager*
Jonathan Chan - *Production Artist*
Drew Gill - *Production Artist*
www.imagecomics.com

AFTERWORKS, VOL. 2. 2006. PUBLISHED BY IMAGE COMICS, INC., OFFICE OF PUBLICATION: 1942 UNIVERSITY AVENUE, SUITE 305, BERKELEY, CALIFORNIA 94704.

AFTERWORKS™ 2

for
joe
ranft

2

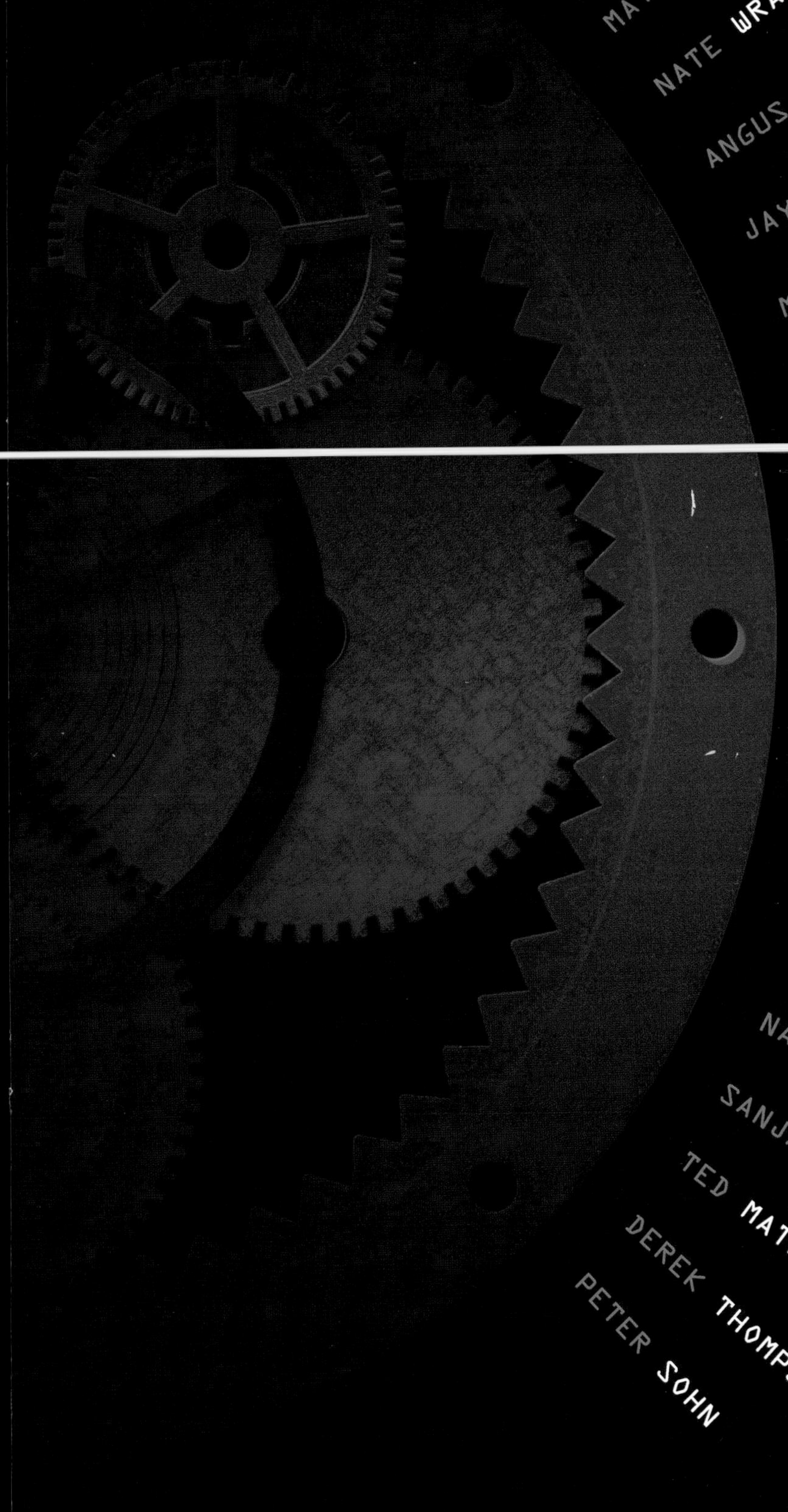

BILL PRESING
MATT PETERS
NATE WRAGG
ANGUS MACLANE
JAY BOOSE
MARK ANDREWS
SCOTT MORSE
JEFF PIDGEON
JOSH COOLEY
ANTHONY WONG
JENNIFER CHANG
LOUIS GONZALES
BRIAN LARSEN
ROB GIBBS
NATE STANTON
SANJAY PATEL
TED MATHOT
DEREK THOMPSON
PETER SOHN

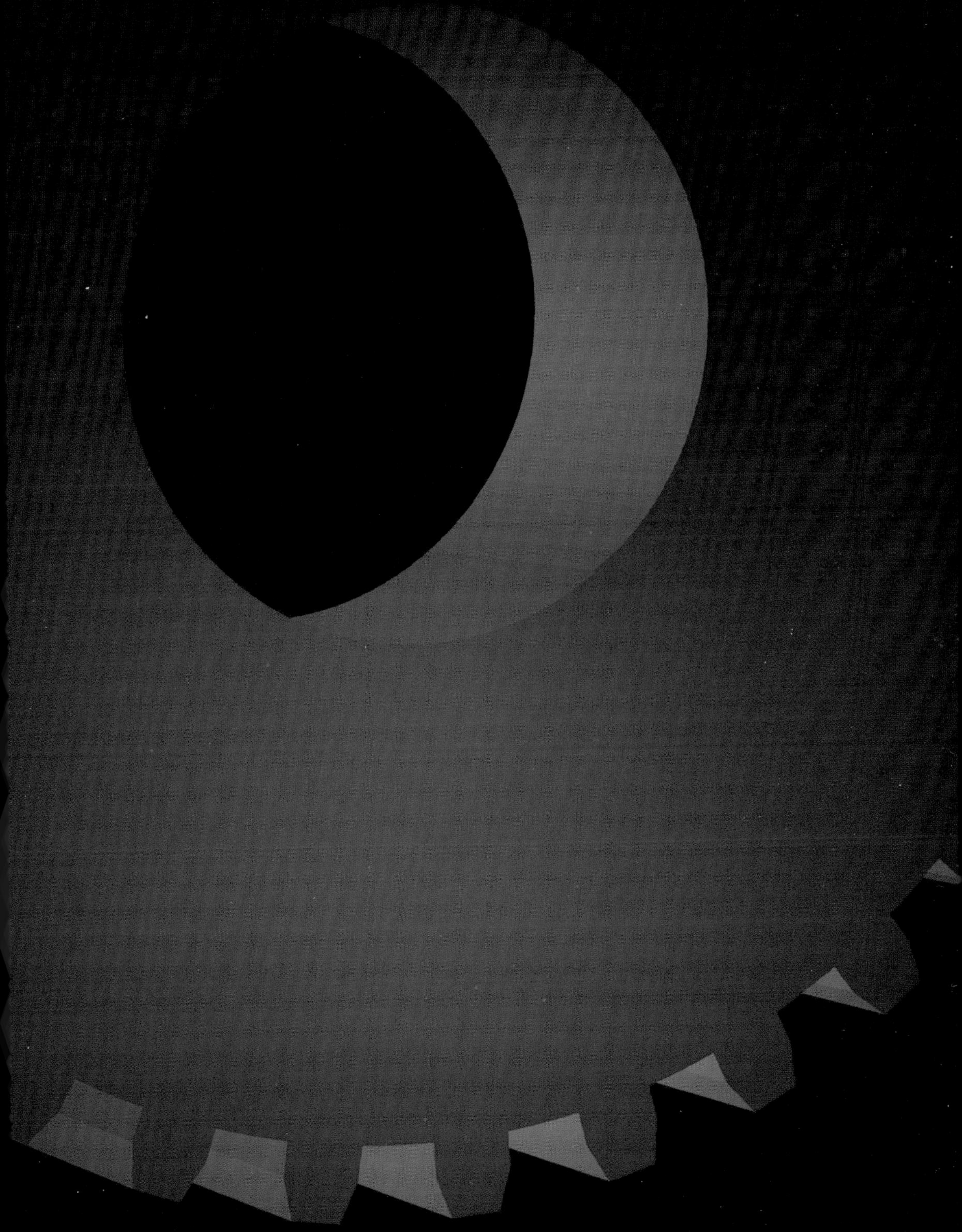

BILL PRESING
MATT PETERS

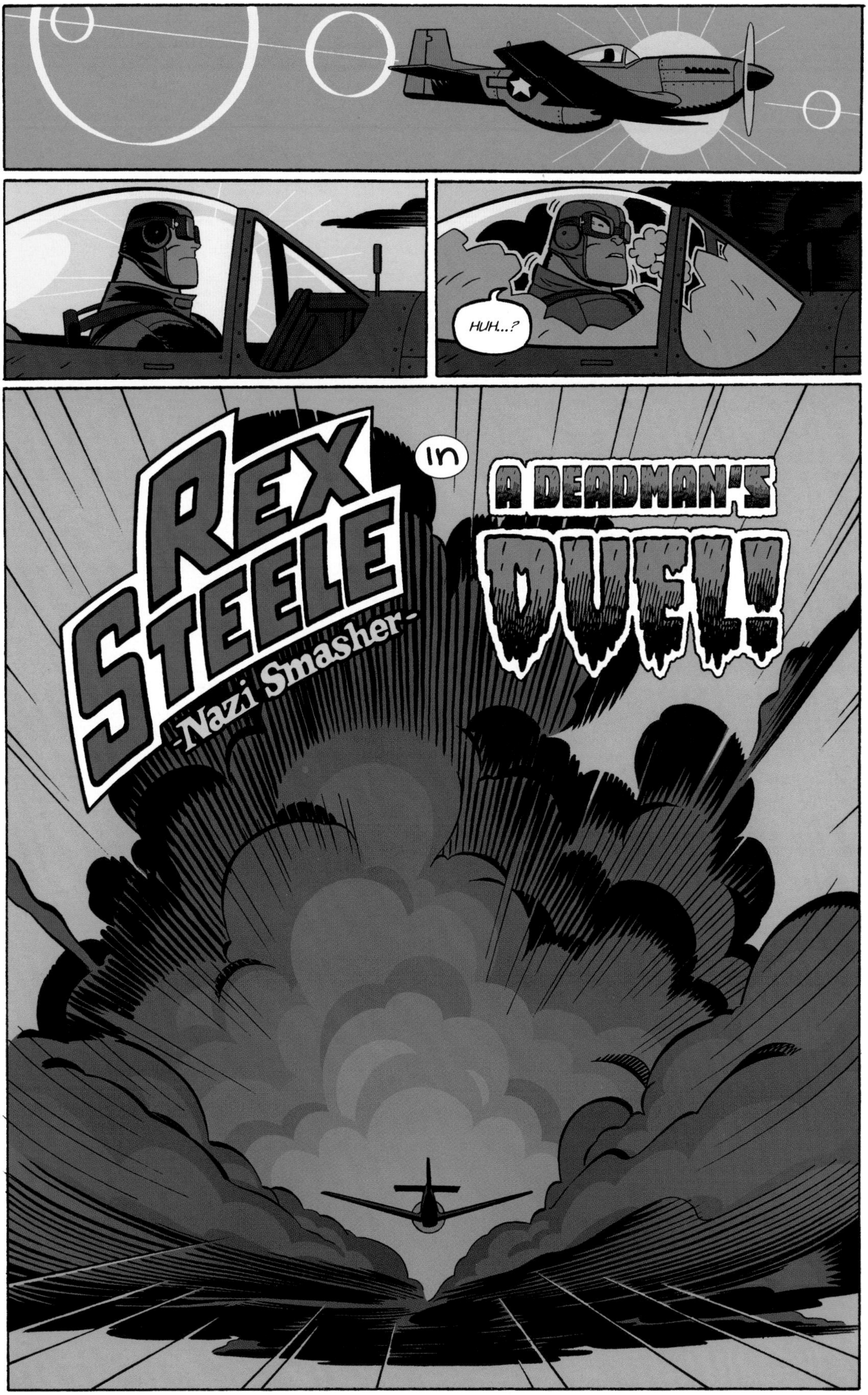
HUH...?
REX STEELE
-Nazi Smasher-
in
A DEADMAN'S
DUEL!

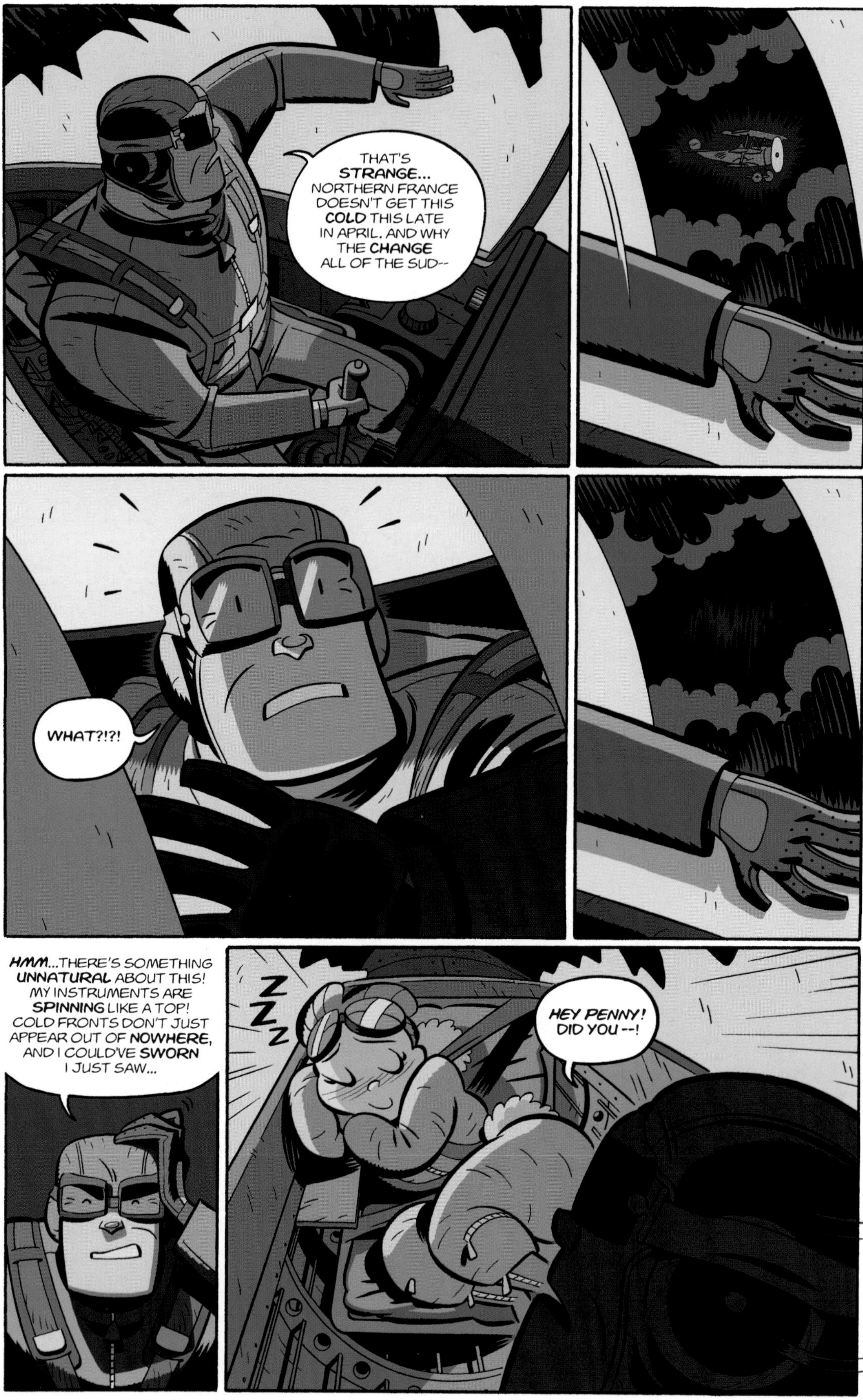
THAT'S STRANGE... NORTHERN FRANCE DOESN'T GET THIS COLD THIS LATE IN APRIL. AND WHY THE CHANGE ALL OF THE SUD--
WHAT?!?!
HMM...THERE'S SOMETHING UNNATURAL ABOUT THIS! MY INSTRUMENTS ARE SPINNING LIKE A TOP! COLD FRONTS DON'T JUST APPEAR OUT OF NOWHERE, AND I COULD'VE SWORN I JUST SAW...
ZZZ
HEY PENNY! DID YOU --!

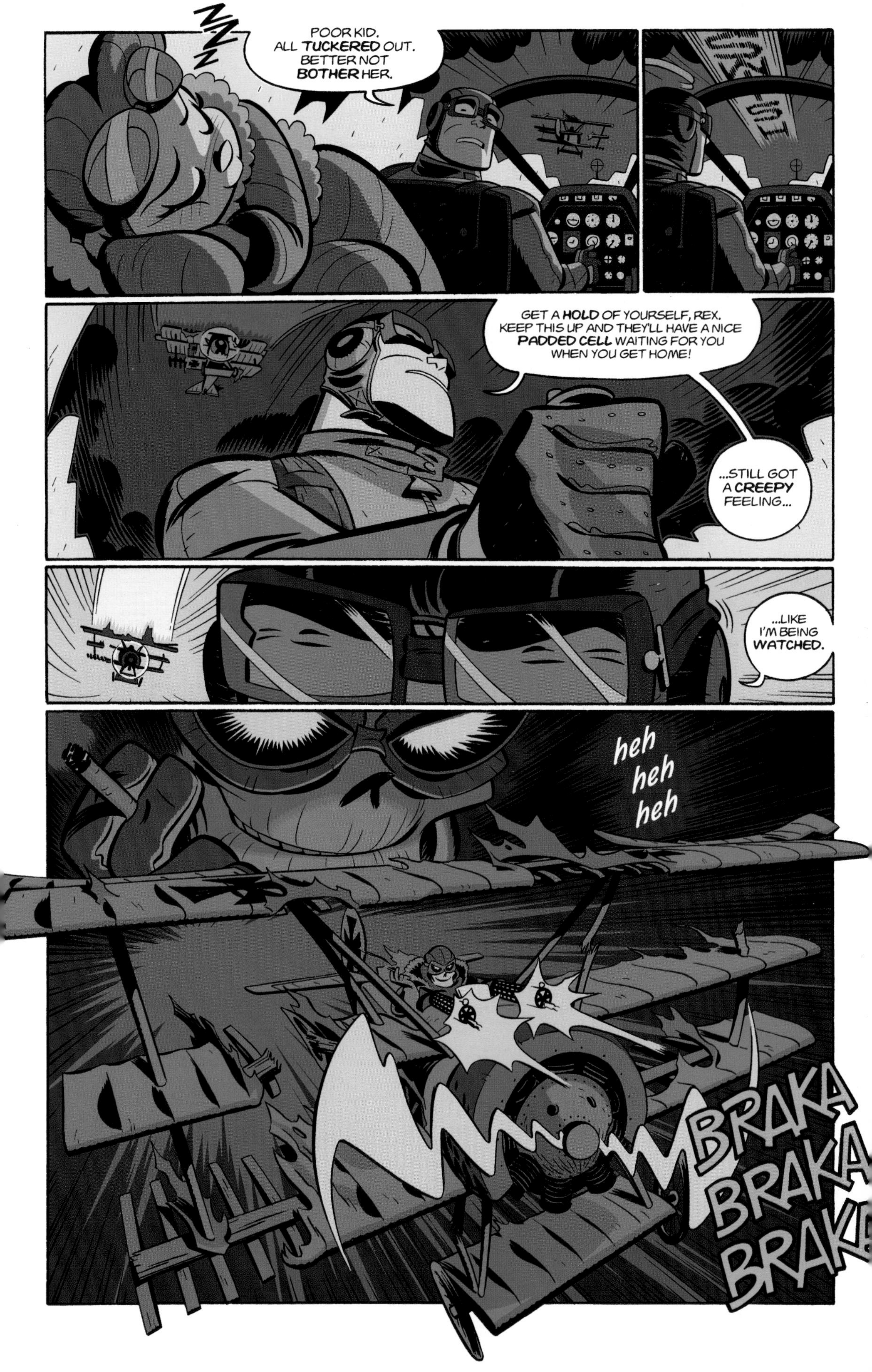

ZZZ
POOR KID. ALL TUCKERED OUT. BETTER NOT BOTHER HER.
GET A HOLD OF YOURSELF, REX. KEEP THIS UP AND THEY'LL HAVE A NICE PADDED CELL WAITING FOR YOU WHEN YOU GET HOME!
...STILL GOT A CREEPY FEELING...
...LIKE I'M BEING WATCHED.
heh heh heh
BRAKA BRAKA BRAK!

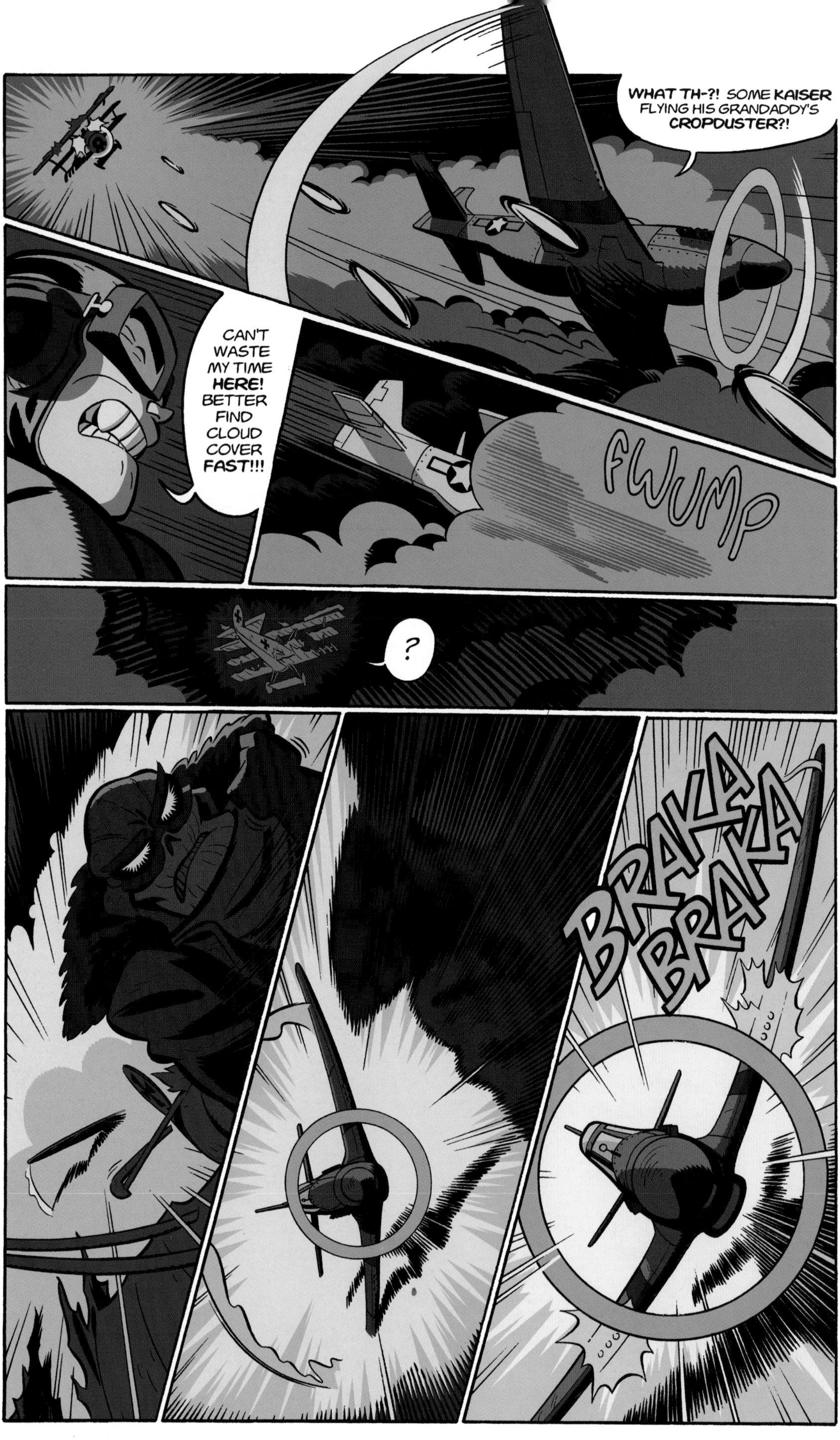
WHAT TH-?! SOME KAISER FLYING HIS GRANDADDY'S CROPDUSTER?!
CAN'T WASTE MY TIME HERE! BETTER FIND CLOUD COVER FAST!!!
FWUMP
?
BRAKA BRAKA

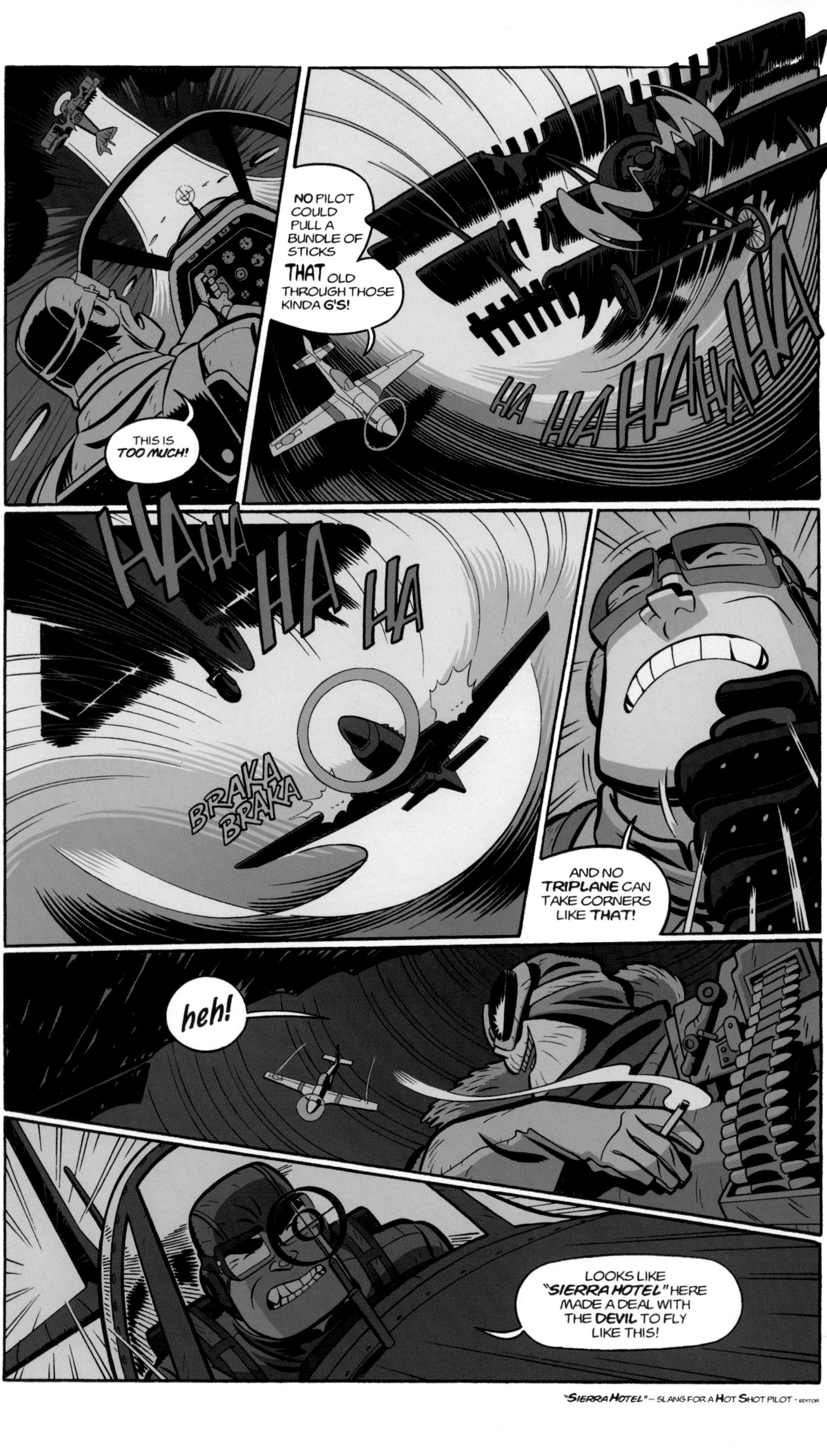
THIS IS TOO MUCH!
NO PILOT COULD PULL A BUNDLE OF STICKS THAT OLD THROUGH THOSE KINDA G'S!
HA HA HA HA HA HA
HA HA HA HA
BRAKA BRAKA
AND NO TRIPLANE CAN TAKE CORNERS LIKE THAT!
heh!
LOOKS LIKE "SIERRA HOTEL" HERE MADE A DEAL WITH THE DEVIL TO FLY LIKE THIS!

"SIERRA HOTEL" -- SLANG FOR A HOT SHOT PILOT - EDITOR

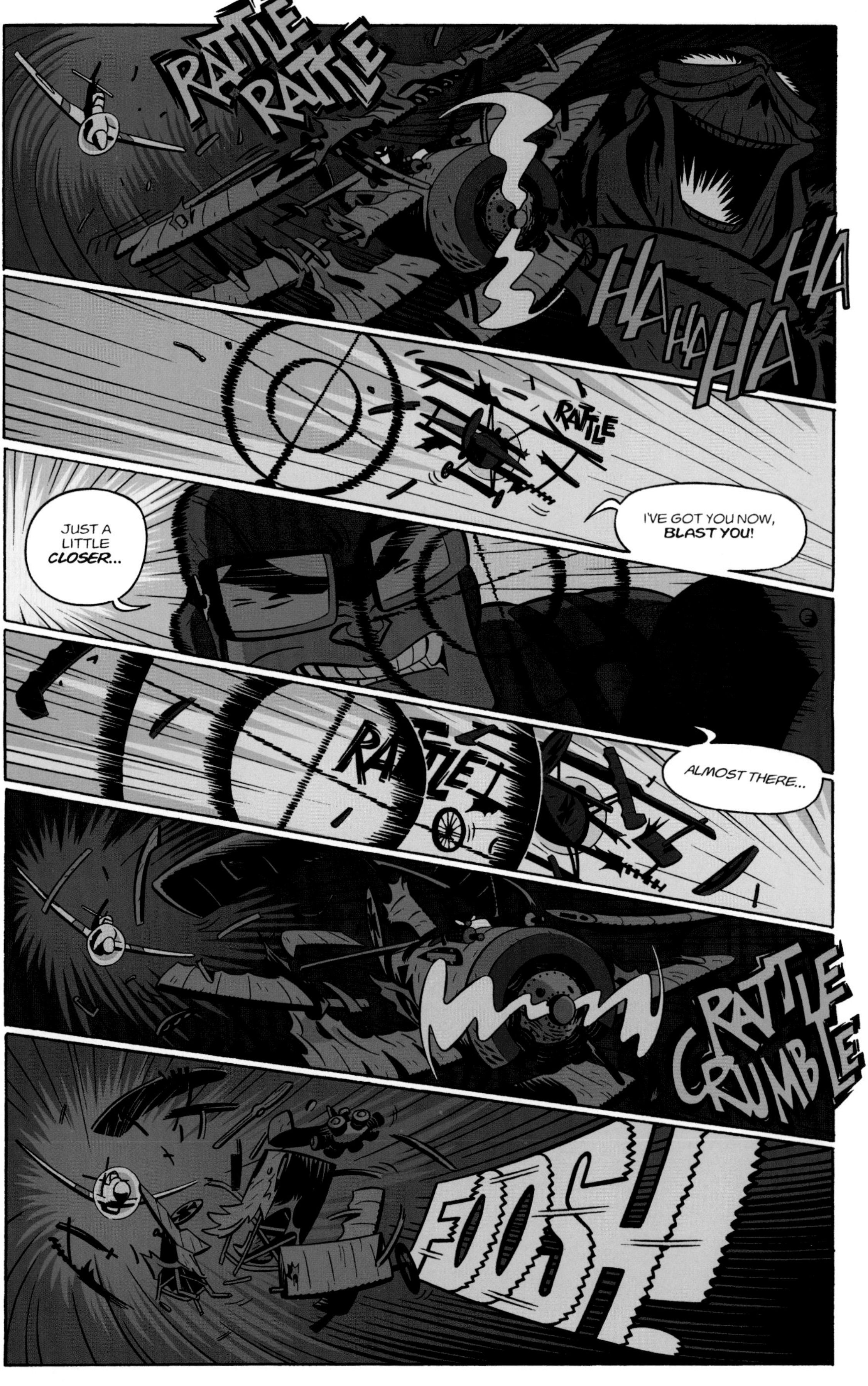
RATTLE RATTLE
HA HA HA HA HA
RATTLE
JUST A LITTLE CLOSER...
I'VE GOT YOU NOW, BLAST YOU!
RATTLE
ALMOST THERE...
RATTLE CRUMBLE
FOOSH!

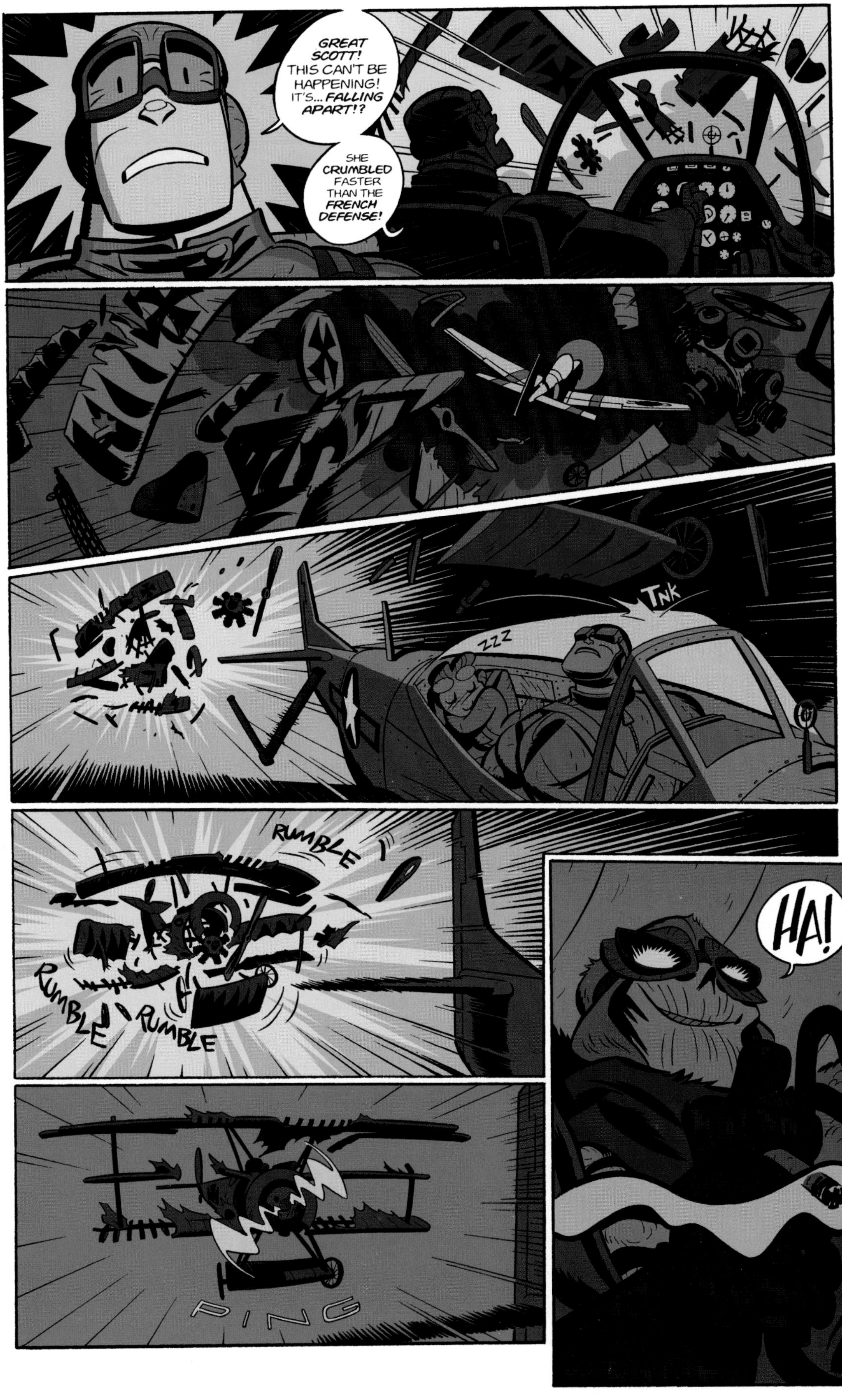
GREAT SCOTT! THIS CAN'T BE HAPPENING! IT'S... FALLING APART!?
SHE CRUMBLED FASTER THAN THE FRENCH DEFENSE!
TNK
ZZZ
RUMBLE
RUMBLE
RUMBLE
HA!
PING

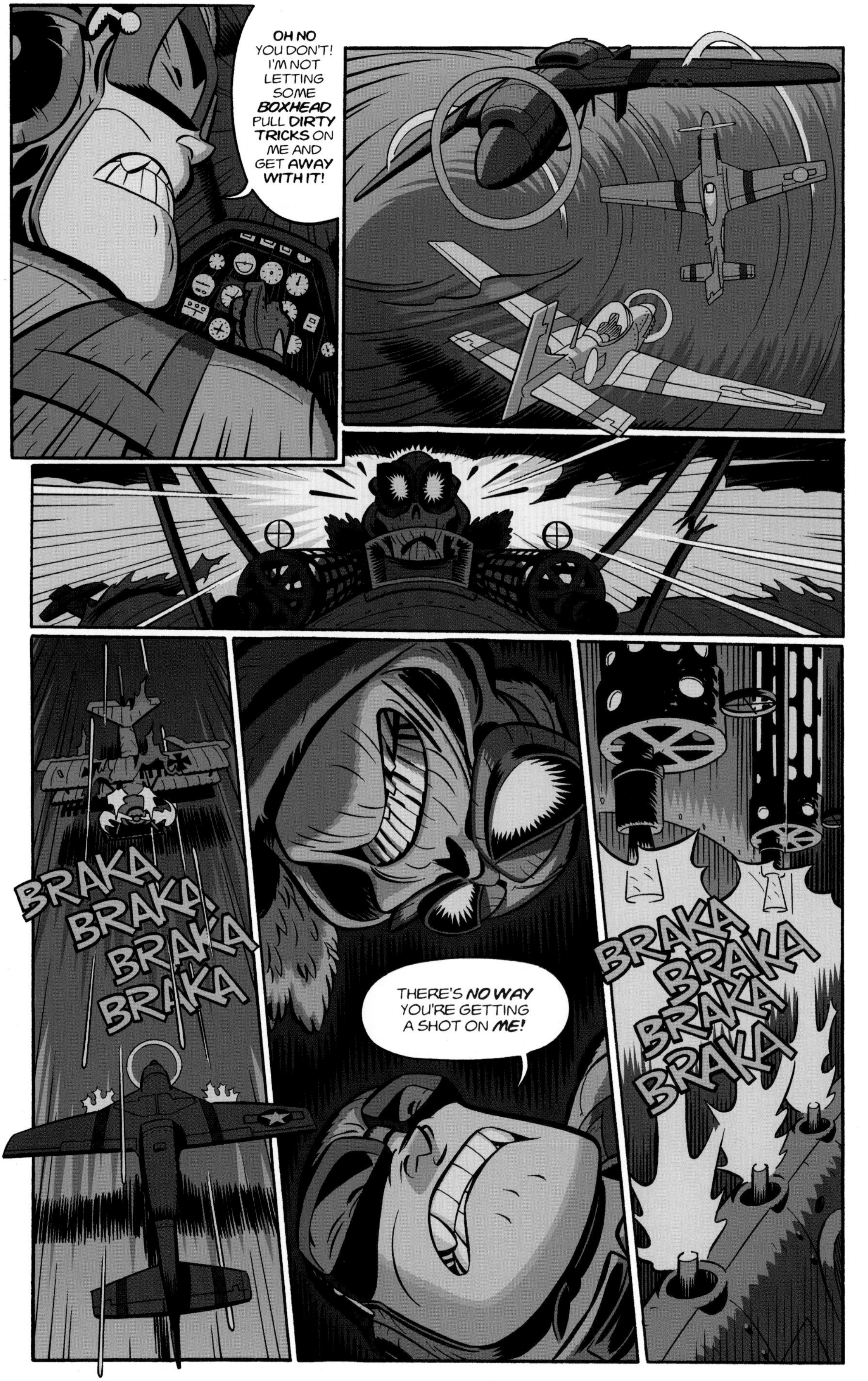
OH NO YOU DON'T! I'M NOT LETTING SOME BOXHEAD PULL DIRTY TRICKS ON ME AND GET AWAY WITH IT!
BRAKA BRAKA BRAKA BRAKA
THERE'S NO WAY YOU'RE GETTING A SHOT ON ME!
BRAKA BRAKA BRAKA BRAKA BRAKA

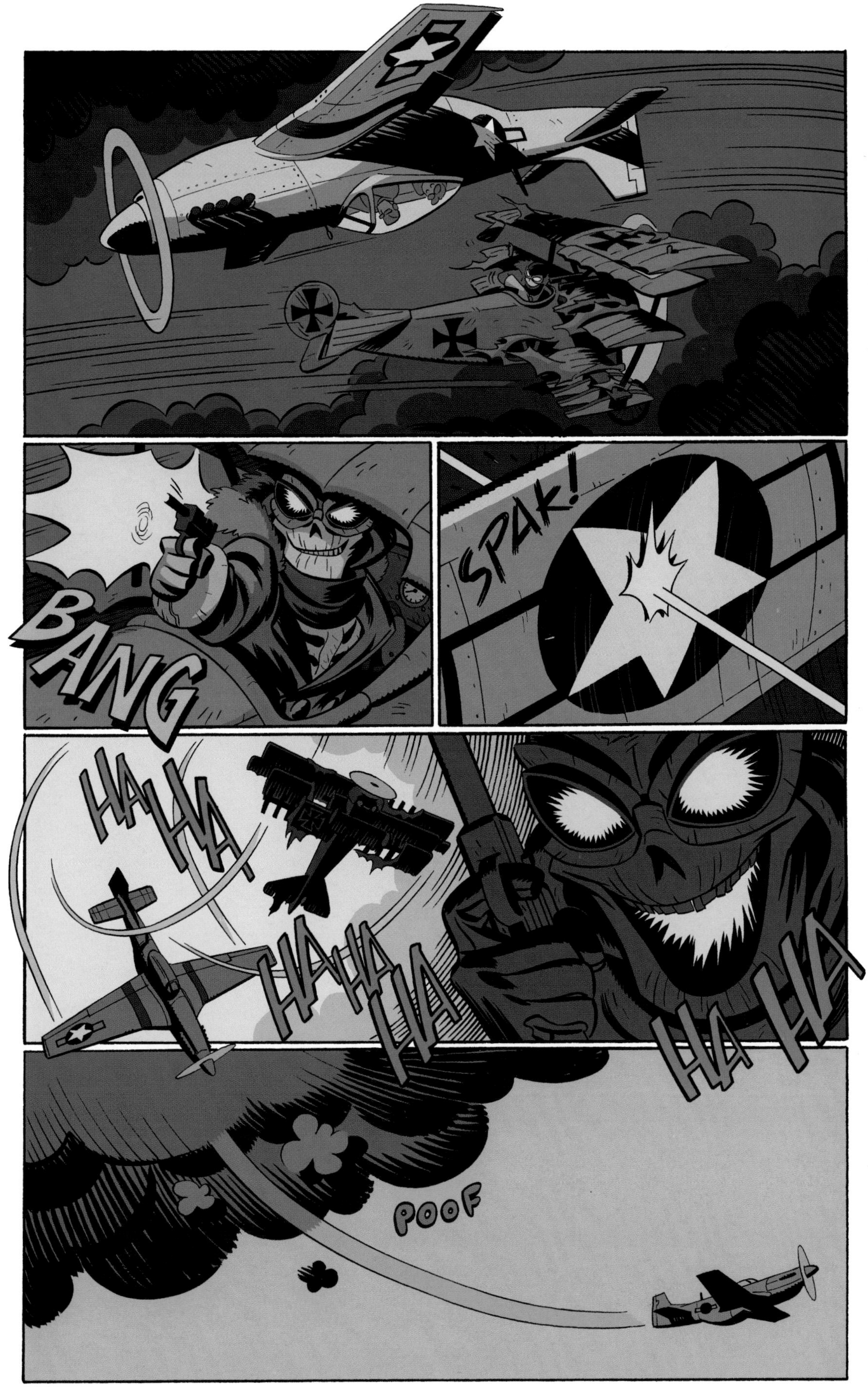
BANG
SPAK!
HA HA
HA HA HA
HA HA
POOF

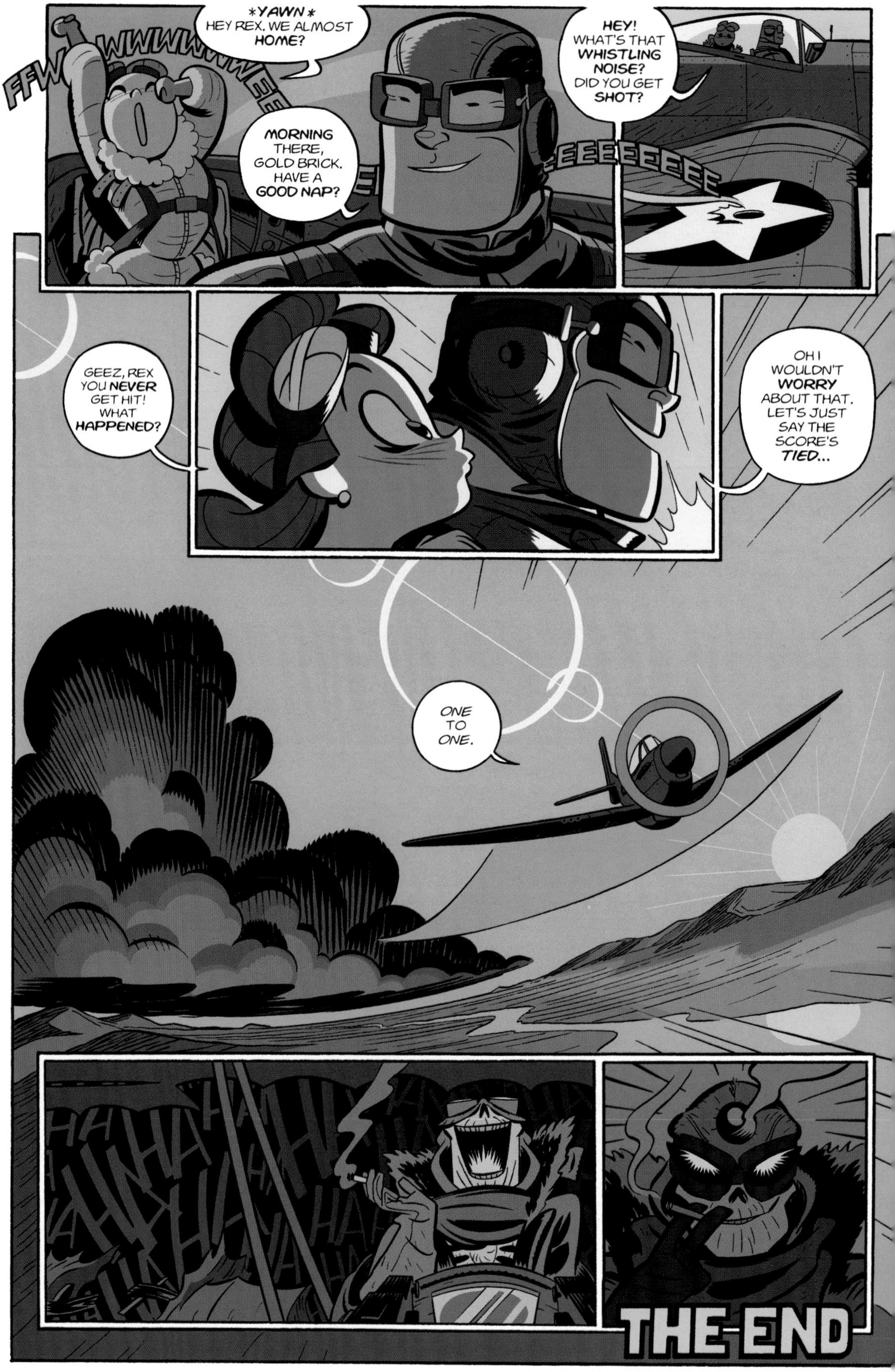

YAWN
HEY REX. WE ALMOST HOME?
FFWWWWWWWWEEEEEEEEEEEE
MORNING THERE, GOLD BRICK. HAVE A GOOD NAP?
HEY! WHAT'S THAT WHISTLING NOISE? DID YOU GET SHOT?
GEEZ, REX YOU NEVER GET HIT! WHAT HAPPENED?
OH I WOULDN'T WORRY ABOUT THAT. LET'S JUST SAY THE SCORE'S TIED...
ONE TO ONE.
THE END

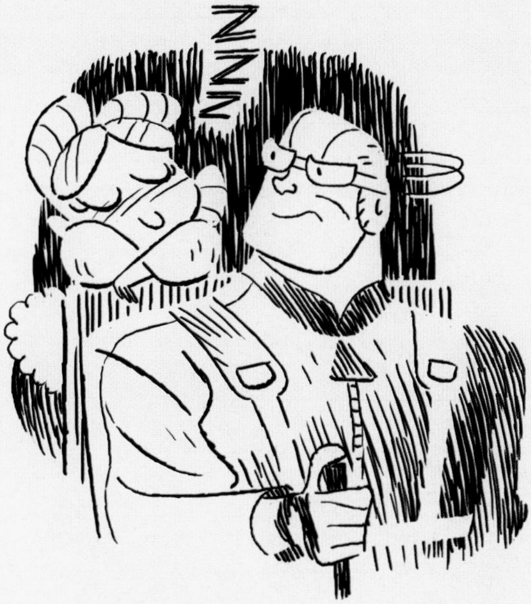
ZZZZ

A VERY SPECIAL THANKS TO **IKUMI MORIYA** AND **ALEX WOO** FOR HELPING TO COLOR THIS STORY. WE WOULDN'T HAVE MADE IT IN TIME WITHOUT YOU.

AND THANKS ALSO TO **"SMASHING" SIMON DUNSDON** FOR PROVIDING HIS ACTION PACKED PIN UP ON THE FOLLOWING PAGE.

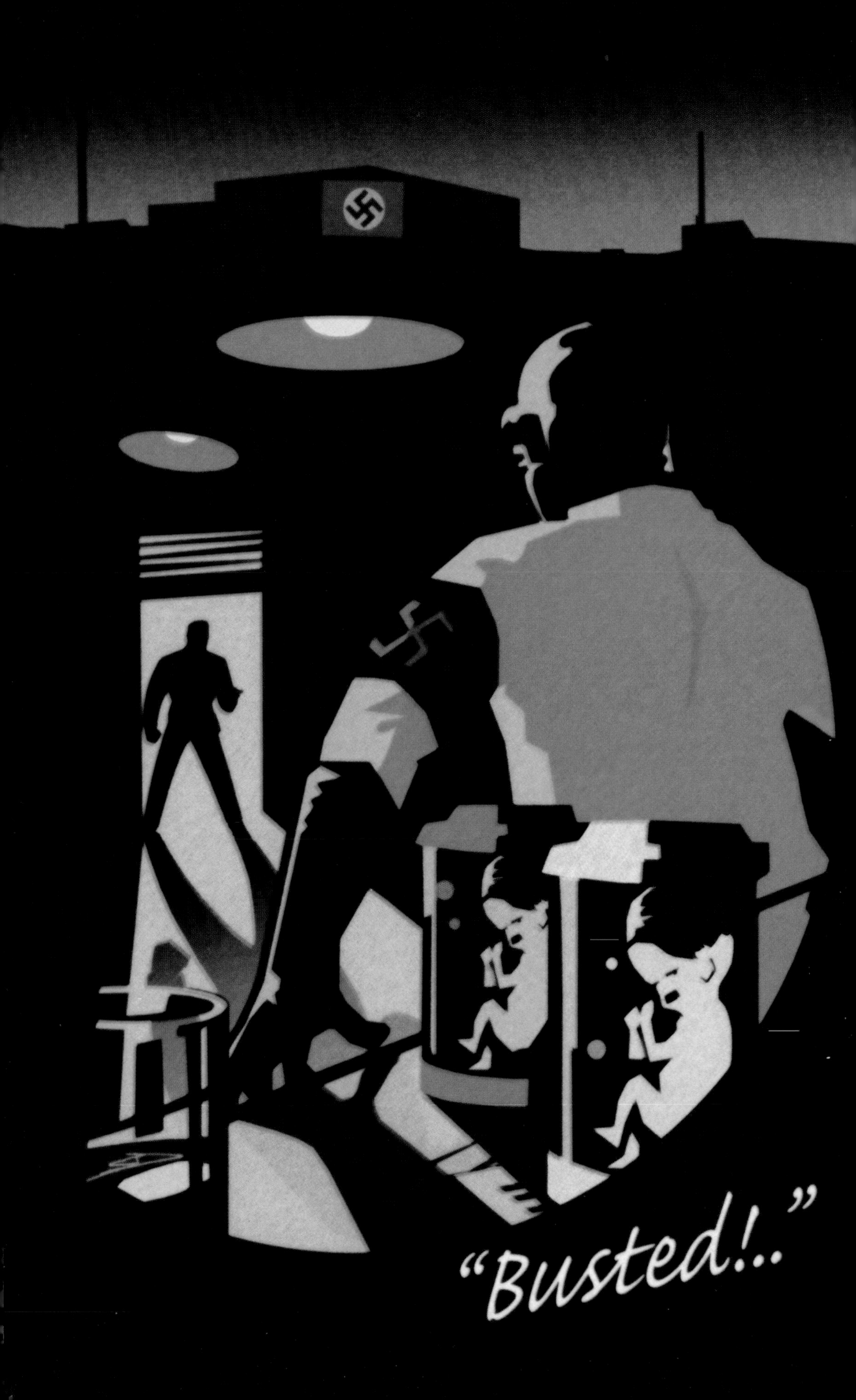
"Busted!.."

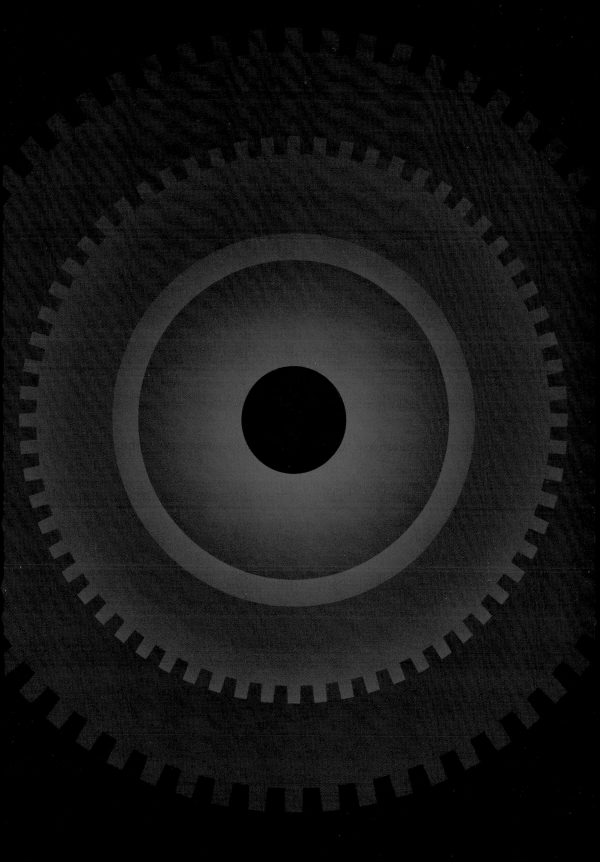

NATEWRAGG

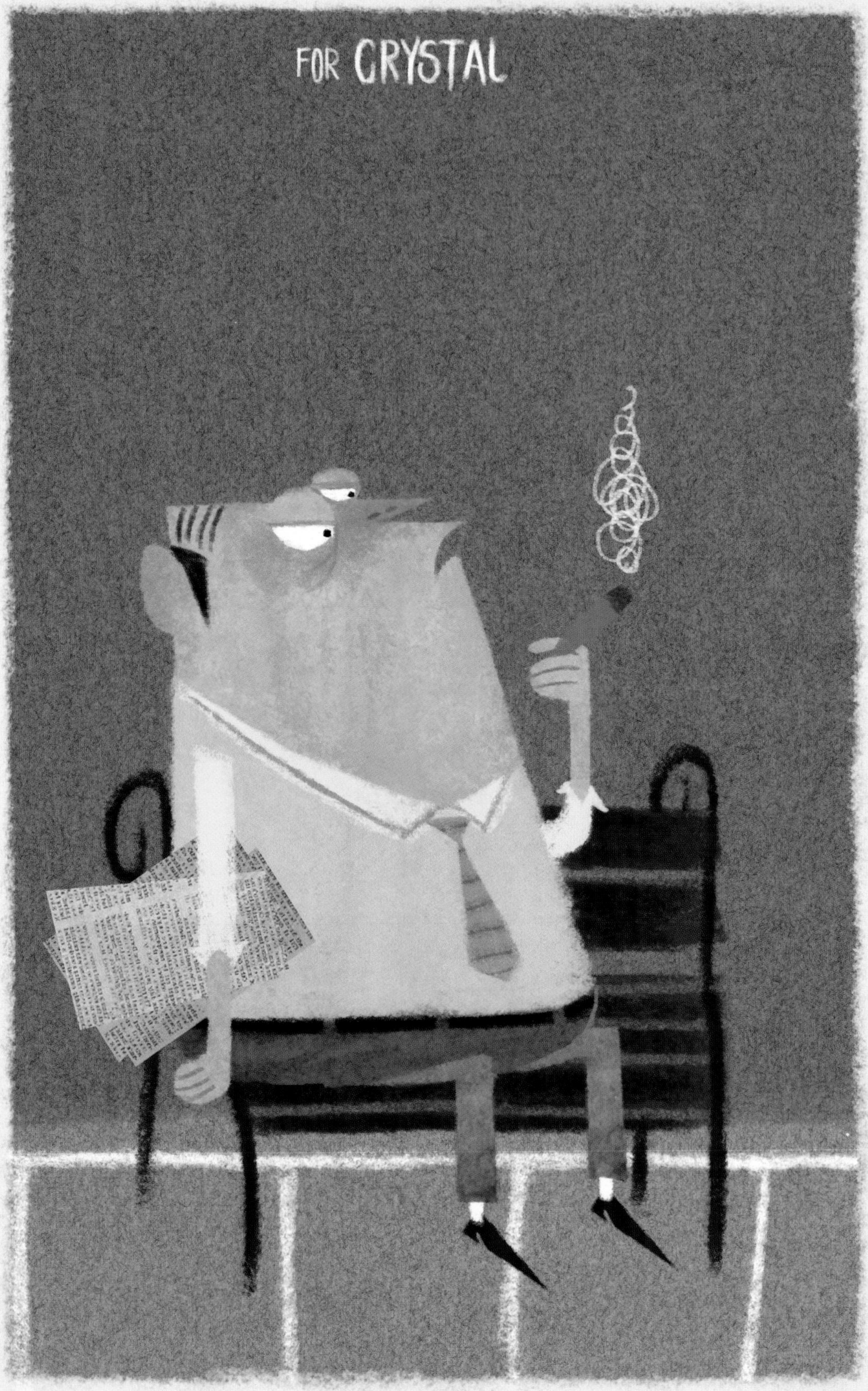
FOR CRYSTAL

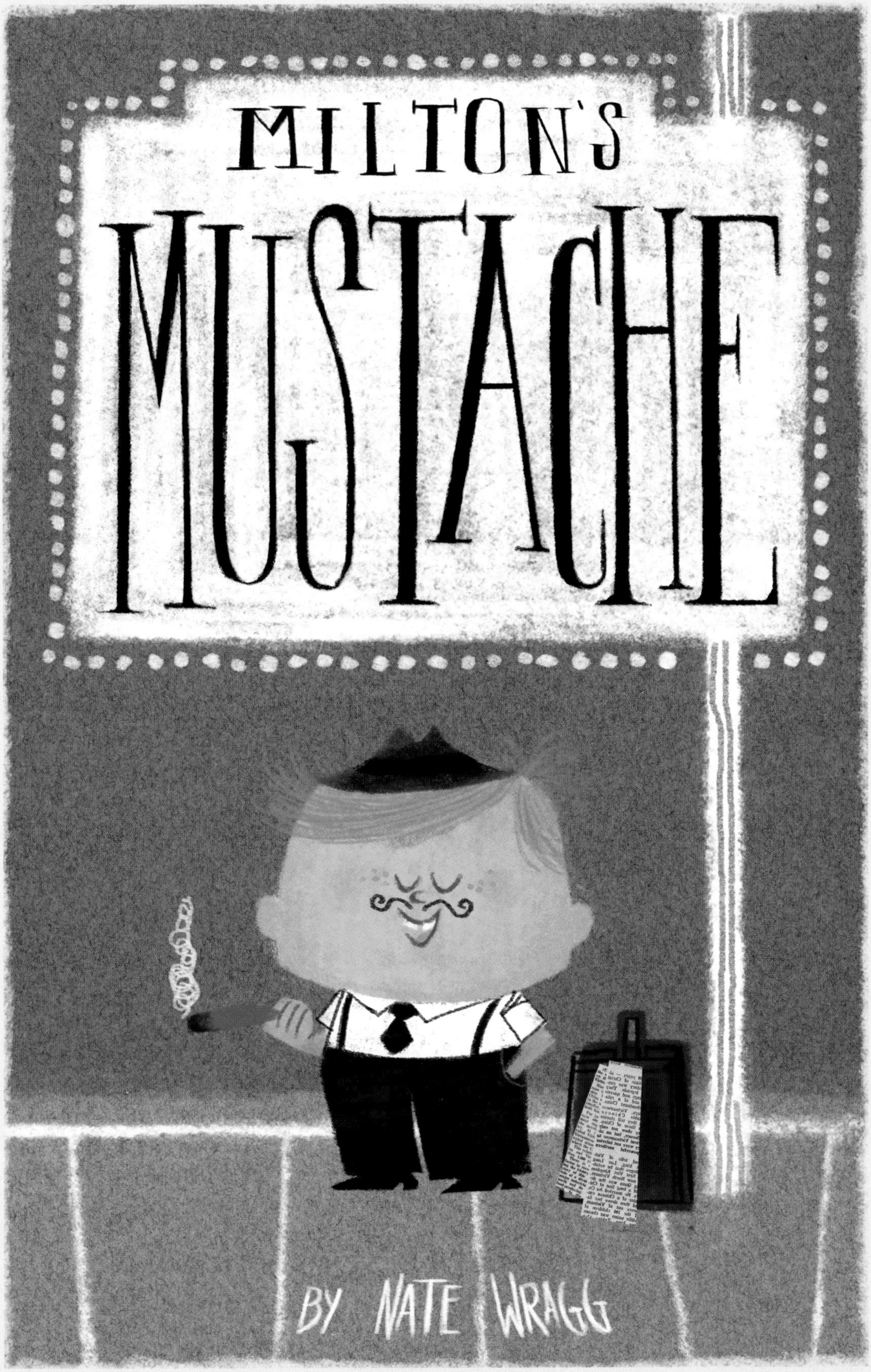
MILTON'S
MUSTACHE
BY NATE WRAGG

The morning started out just like every other morning for Milton. He woke up, and walked into the bathroom to wash up and get ready for 1st grade. Only to Milton's surprise, this morning was very different. It appeared that while he had slept through the night, Milton had grown his very first mustache.

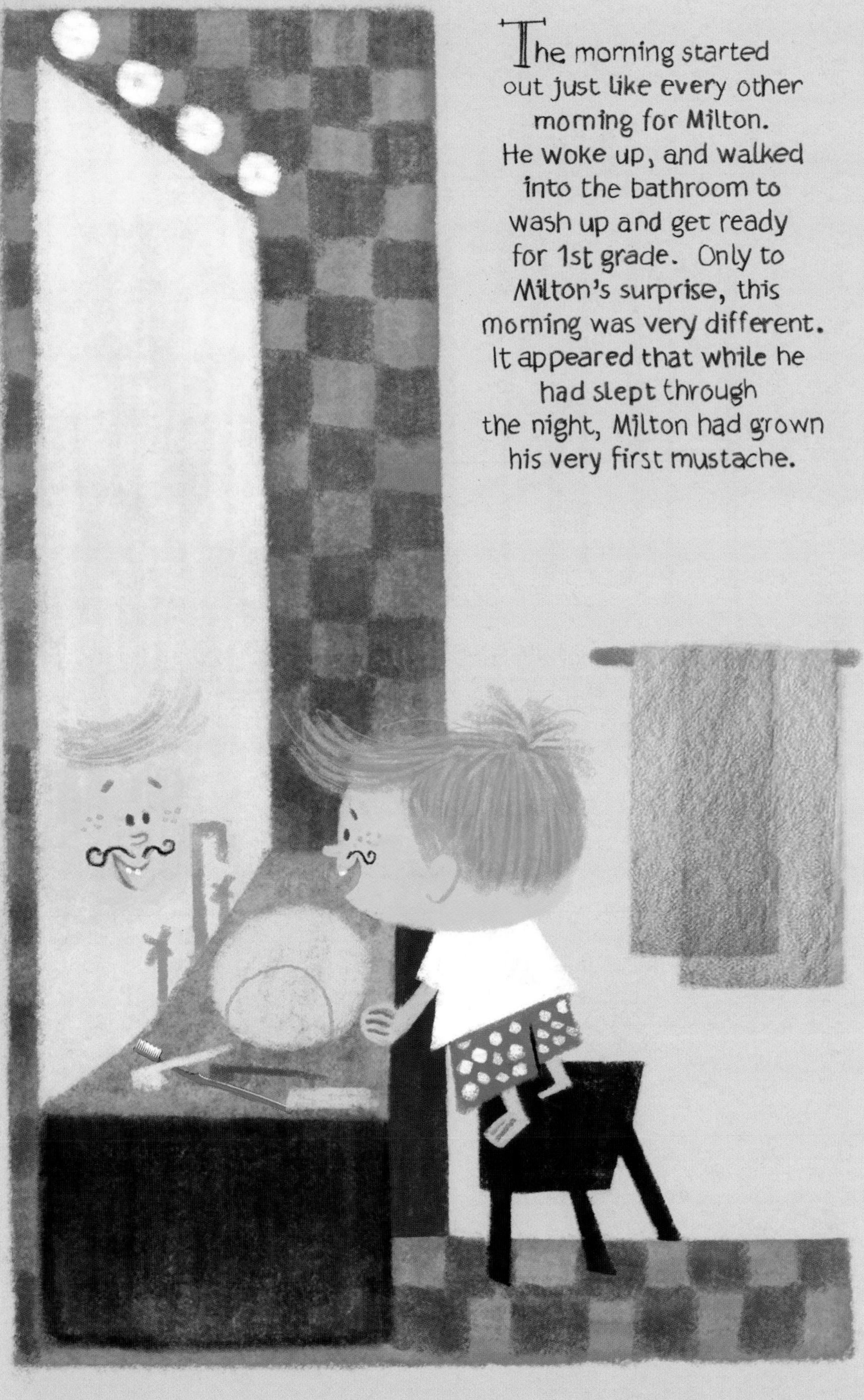

When Milton's father noticed the difference in Milton, he couldn't have been happier. "Now that's my boy," he said. "You know Milton, I remember when I got my first mustache. I wasn't as lucky as you are to get such a gift so young, but god damn if it wasn't the best thing that ever happened to me!"

Milton's father takes a cigar out of his pocket and give's it to Milton. "Here, try this on for size....look at that, it's a perfect fit, it's a good look for you son. Here, what do you say, you go put on one of your best suits and come into the city and work with me today. I'll show you the ropes, just don't tell your mother, she won't have it. She'll say you're too young and you're not ready for a mustache, but that's bullshit. You're a man now, and it's time to put that Mustache to work!"

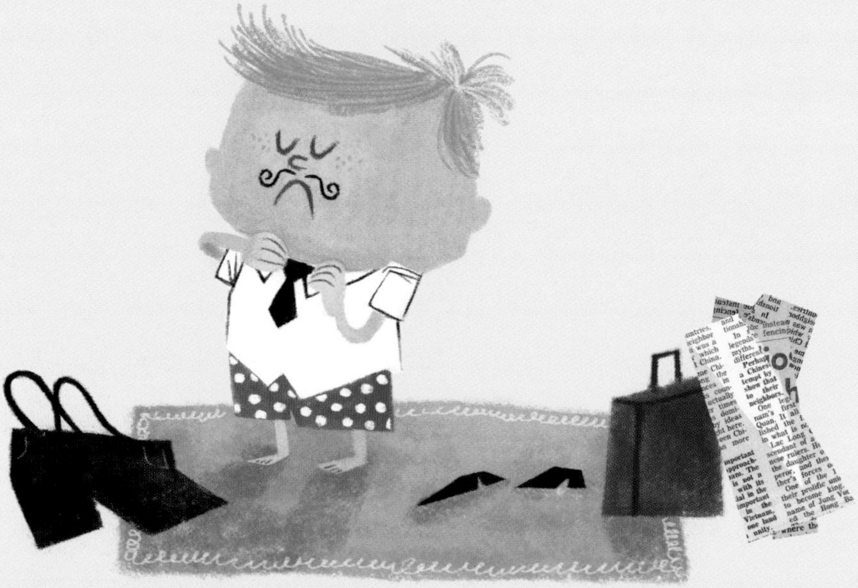

So Milton quickly ran up to his room and got out his finest suit. It was time to get ready for his first day on the job.

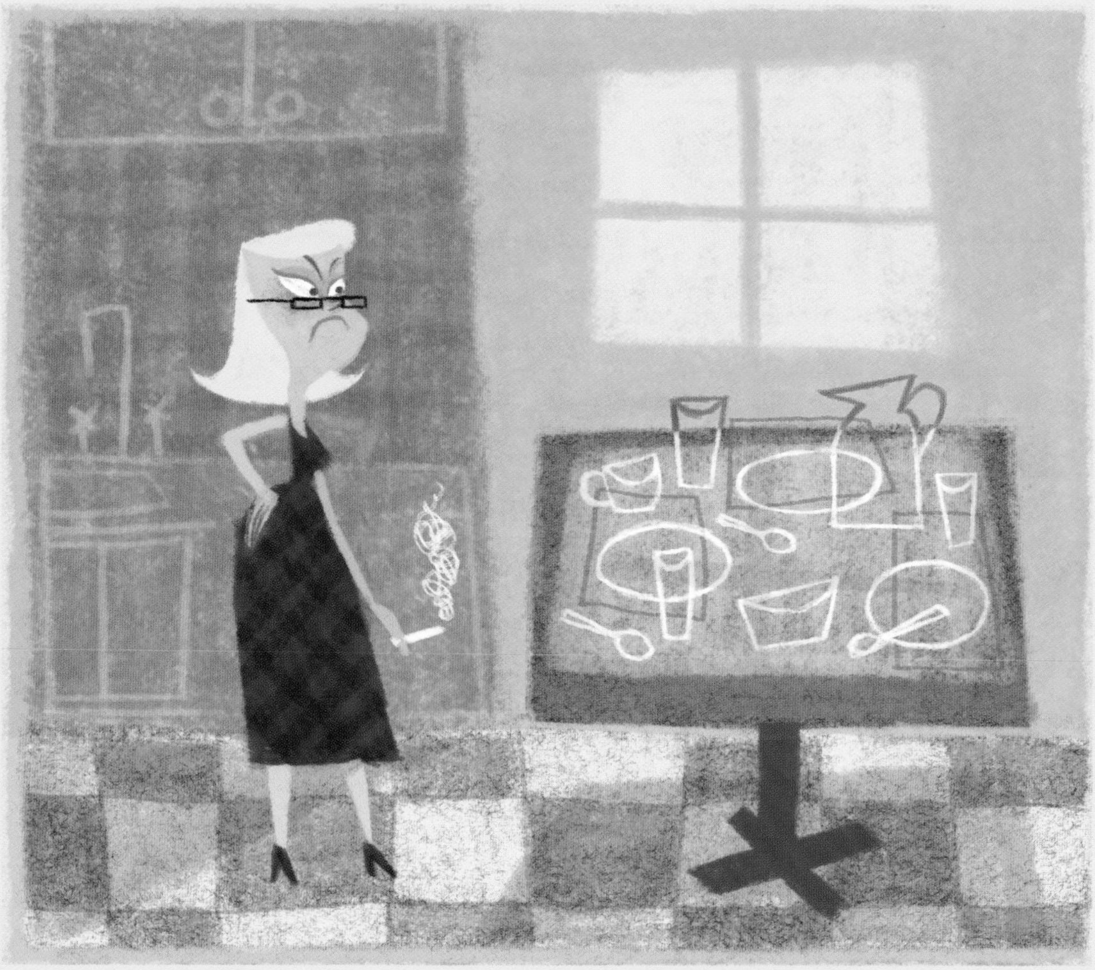

"Sorry, honey, but we don't have time for breakfast this morning,"
Milton's father said to Milton's Mother.

"Well, where are you guys going in such a
hurry, and why is Milton wearing a suit?" Milton's mother asked.

"Like I said sweetie, no time to chat. I'll drop Milton off at school
on my way to work. See you later," Milton's father replied,
and the two were out the door.

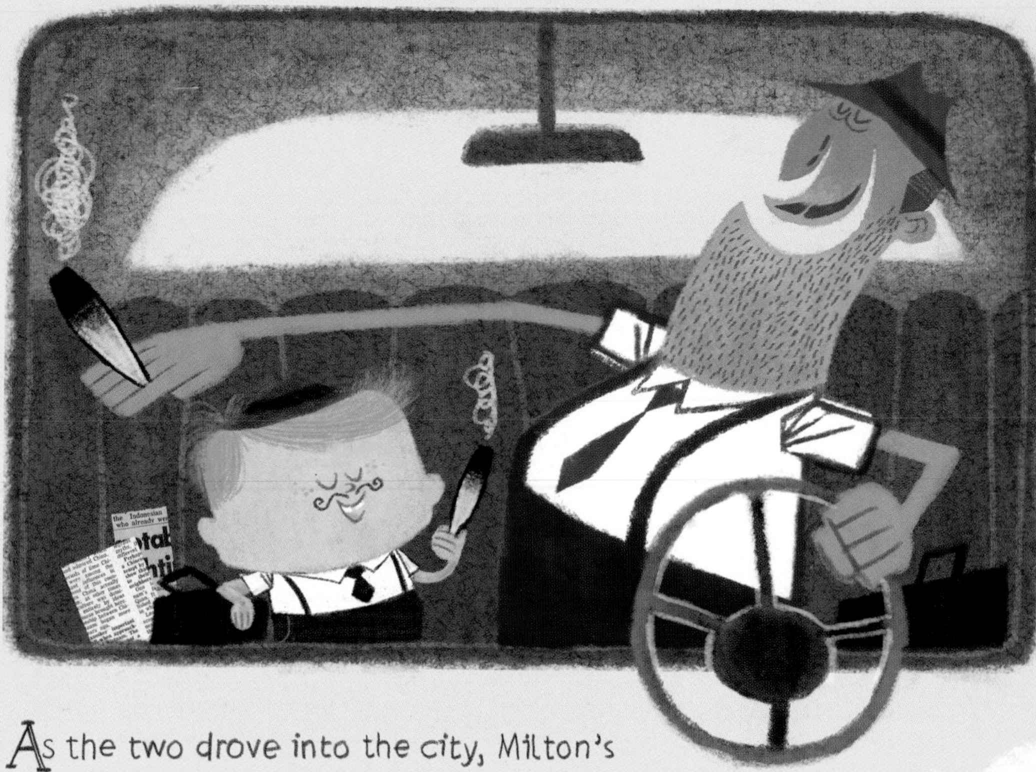

As the two drove into the city, Milton's father lit up two cigars and eased into his seat. "Milton," he said, "I just want to let you know that I'm damn proud of you. It's a wonderful thing to see you follow in my footsteps."

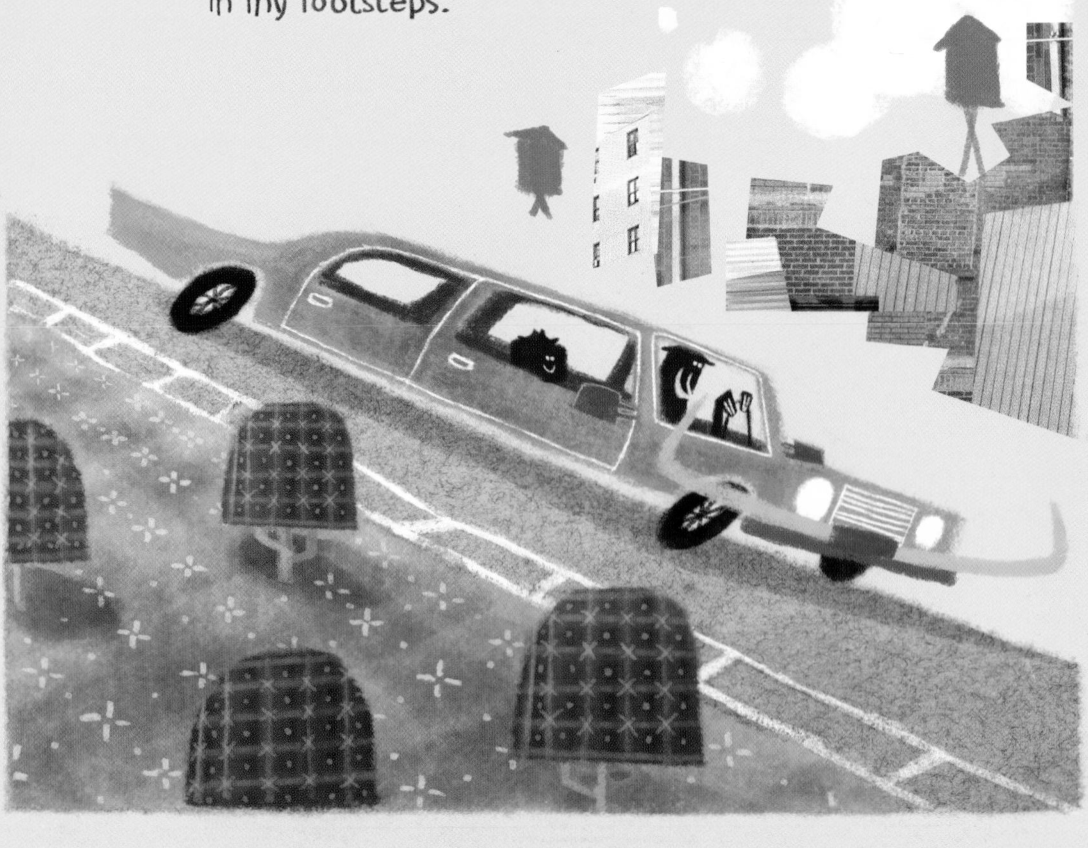

"This is it son, now how 'bout we go make us some money!"

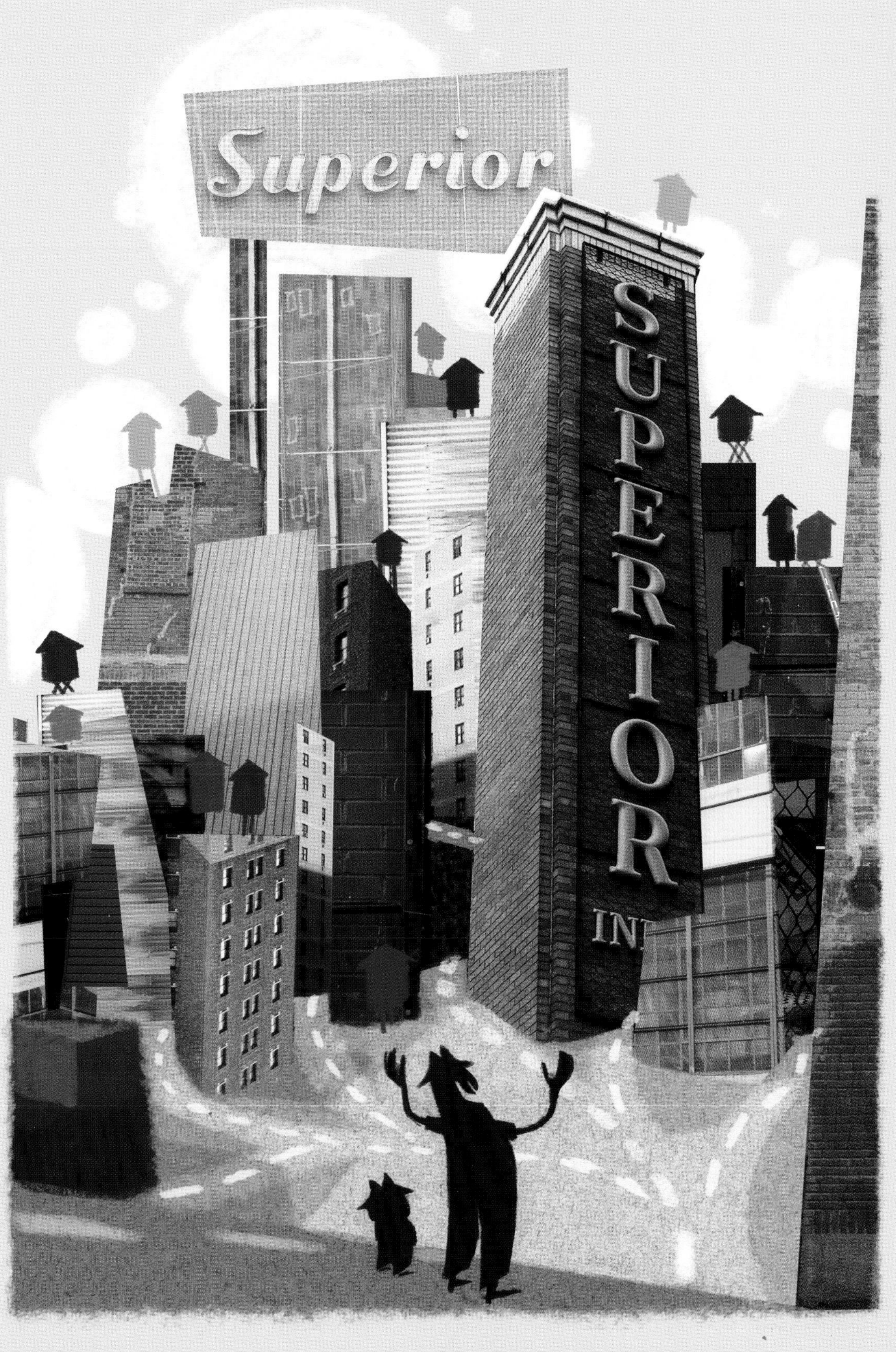
Superior
SUPERIOR
INI

"Now Milton, I'm going to be honest with you. This is when things get serious," his father says as they walk into the building where his father works. "If you want to be successful, then you can't waste your time standing around at the bottom of the corporate ladder. You have to watch the market, influence the financial standings, buy low and sell high and let that mustache take you to to the top of the charts!"

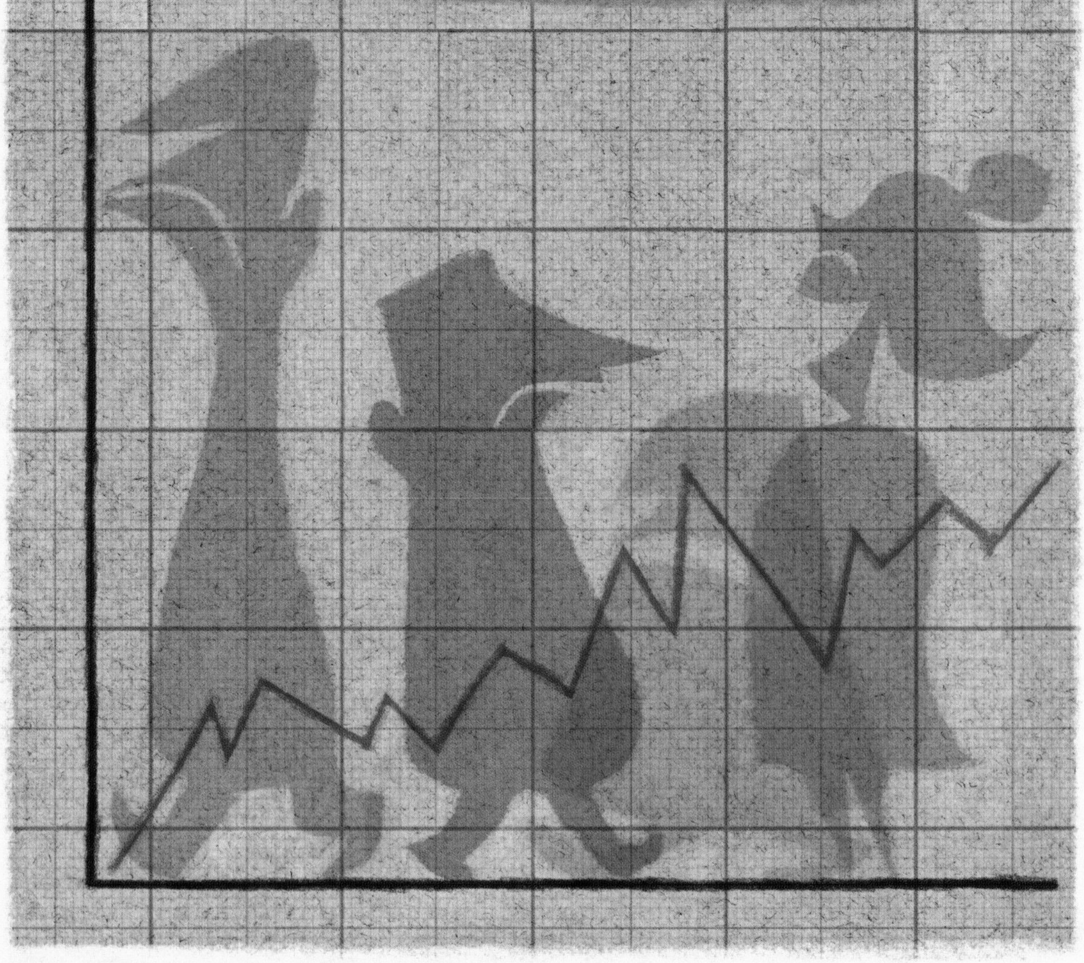

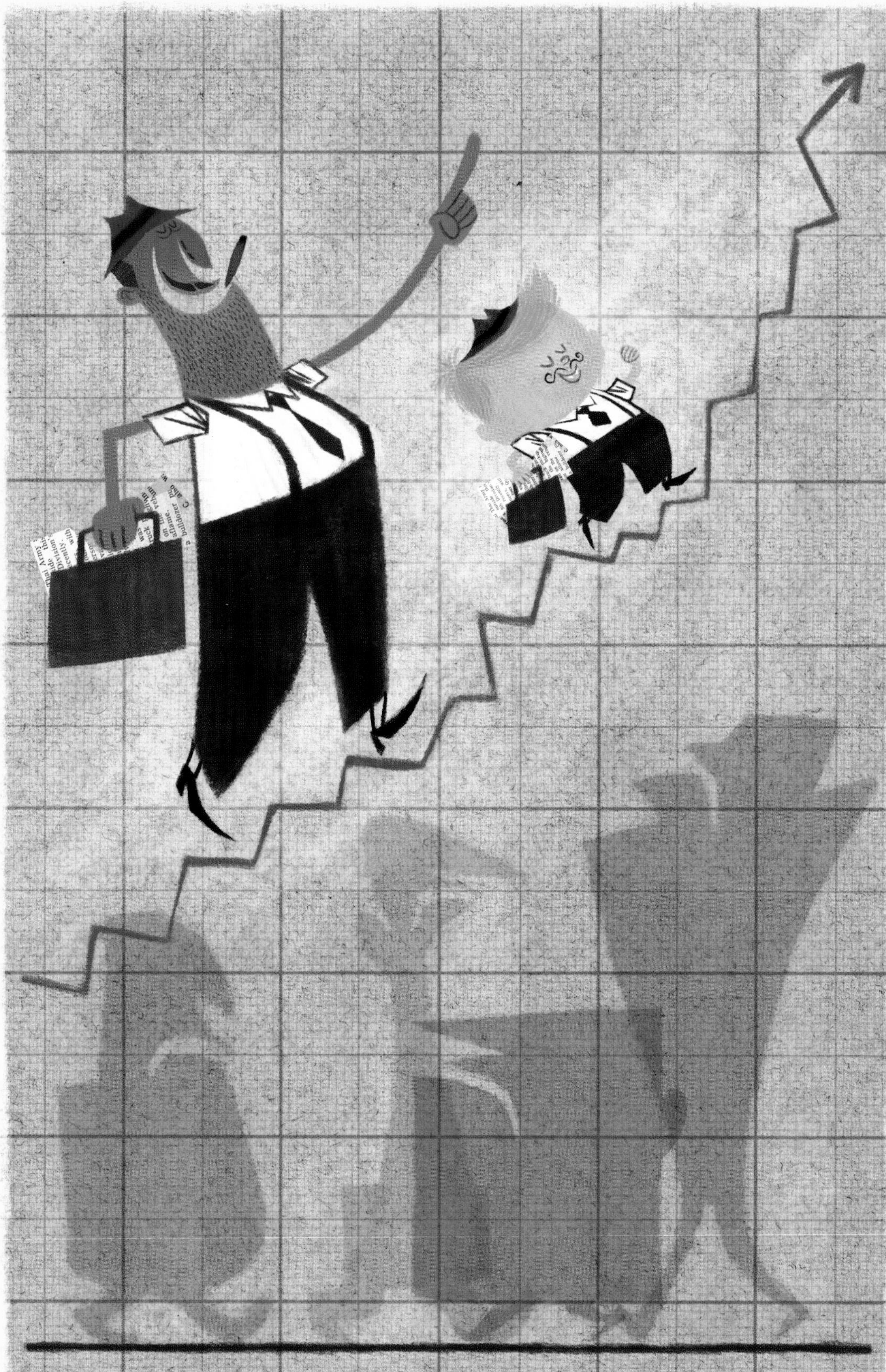

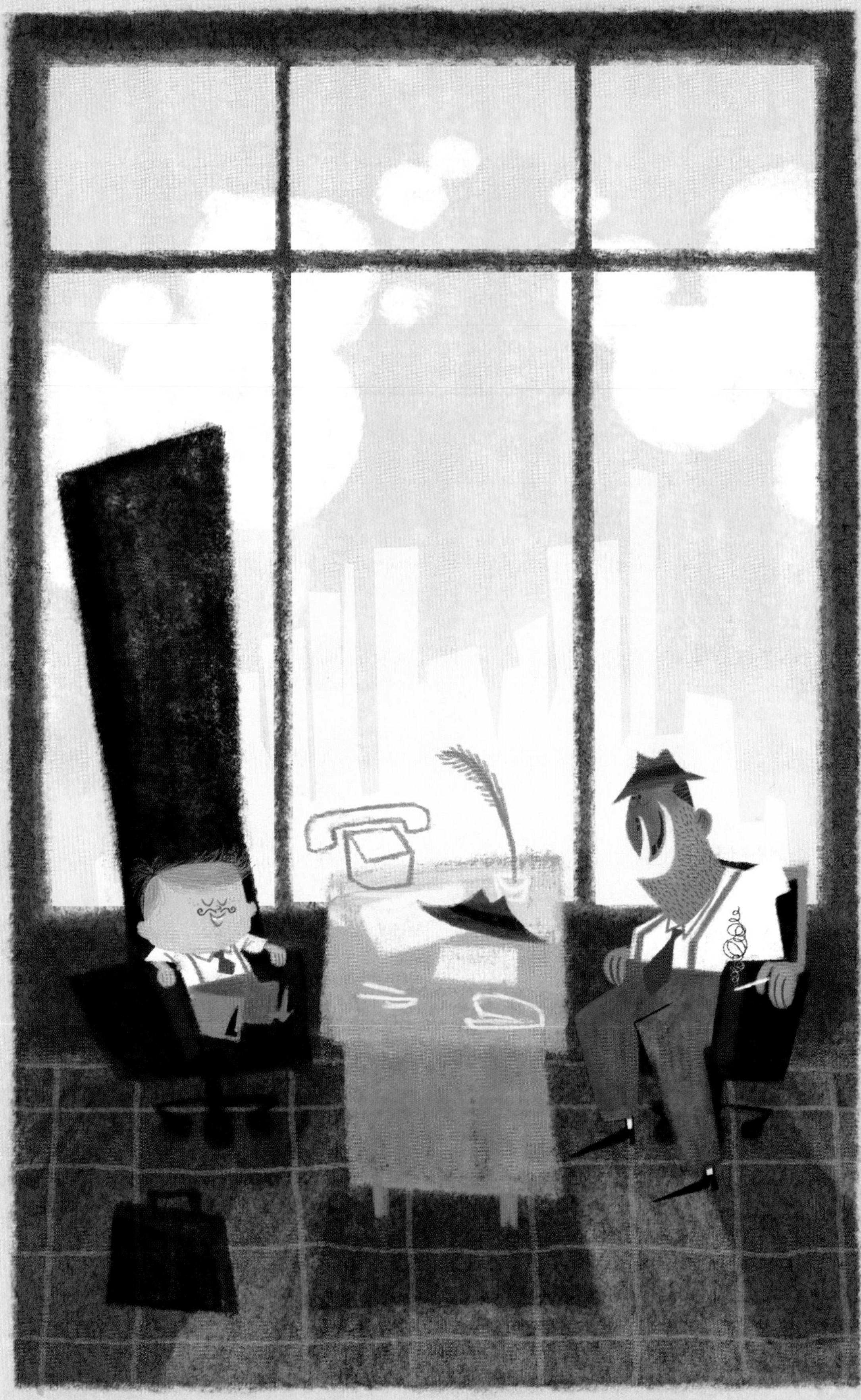

Milton's father showed him to his very own top floor office, got him all set up, and then let the boy get to work. And that's exactly what Milton did, he got on the phones and started making things happen. He was getting new clients and closing out deals before lunch. In fact, as word of Milton's success was going around the office, a few of the guys thought it would be nice to take Milton out after work.

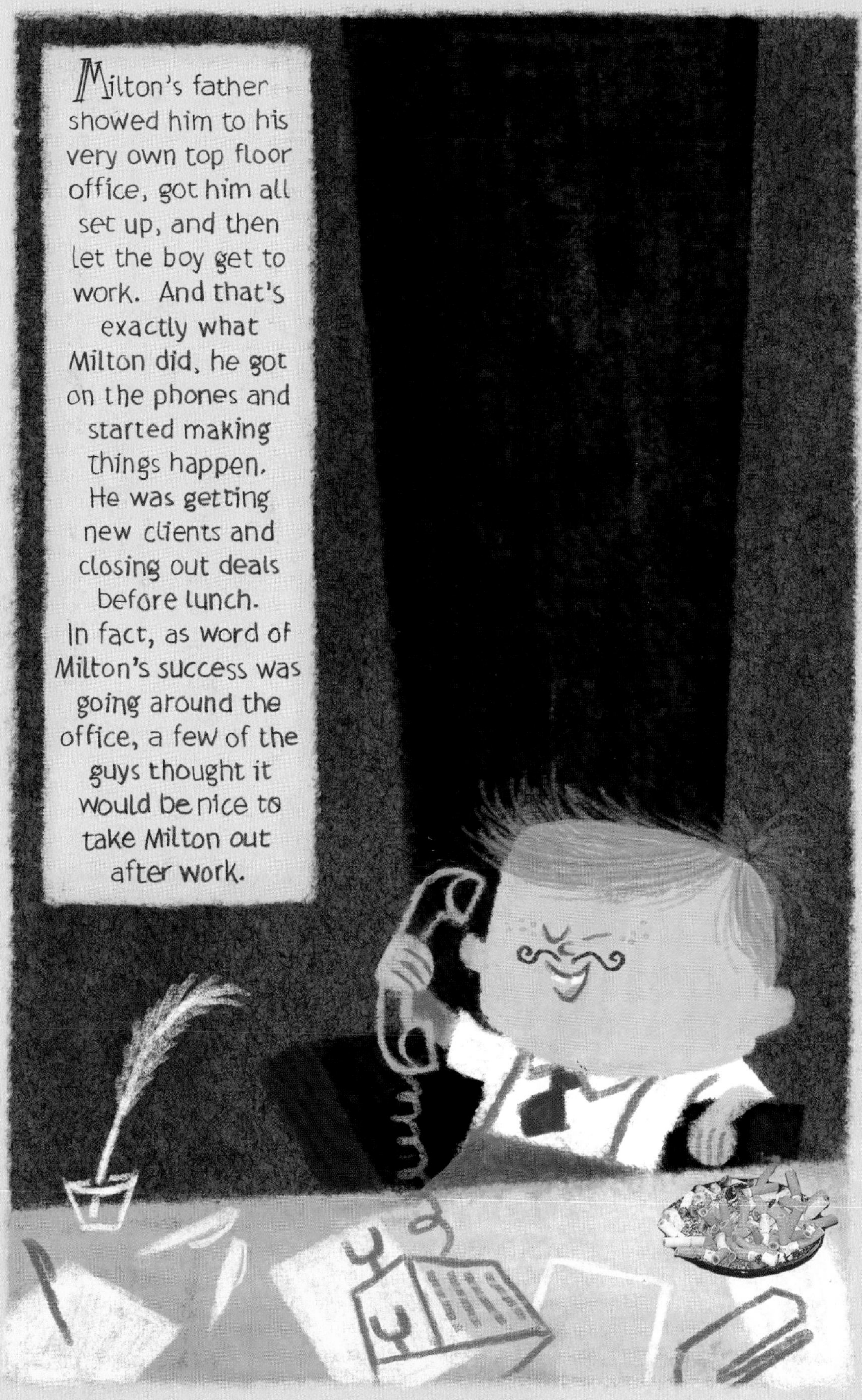

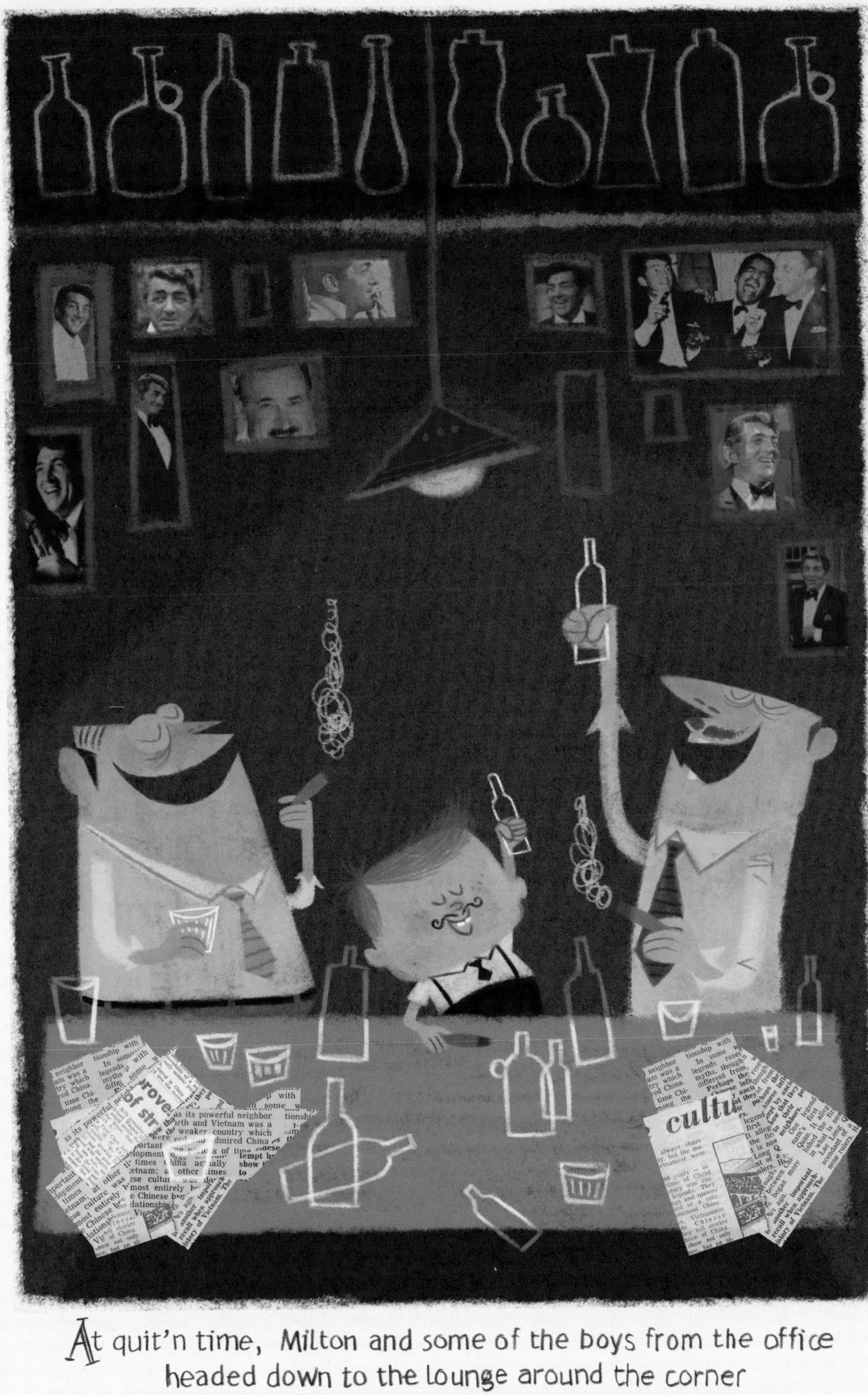

At quit'n time, Milton and some of the boys from the office
headed down to the lounge around the corner
for a few drinks to toast Milton's quick success.

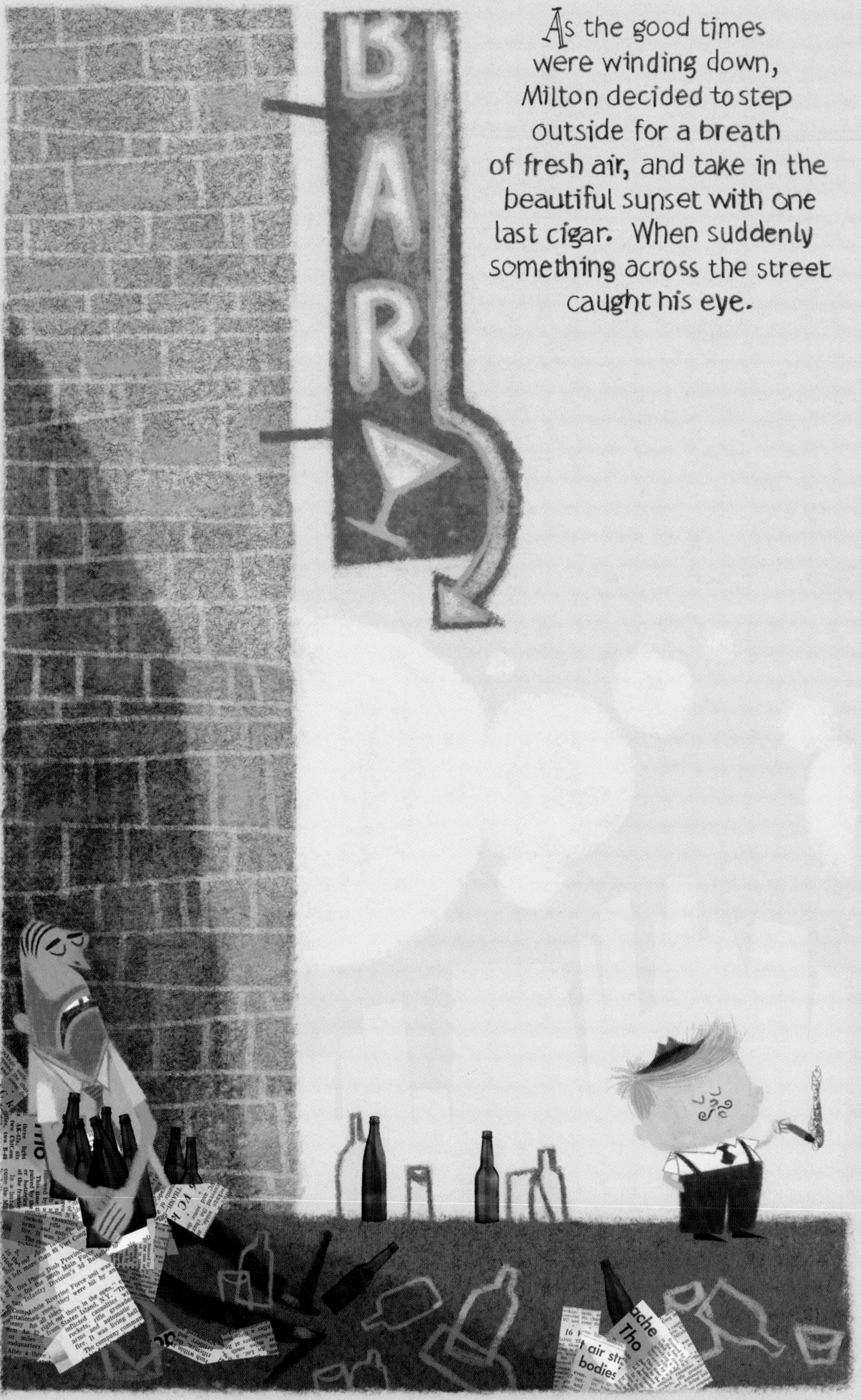
BAR

As the good times were winding down, Milton decided to step outside for a breath of fresh air, and take in the beautiful sunset with one last cigar. When suddenly something across the street caught his eye.

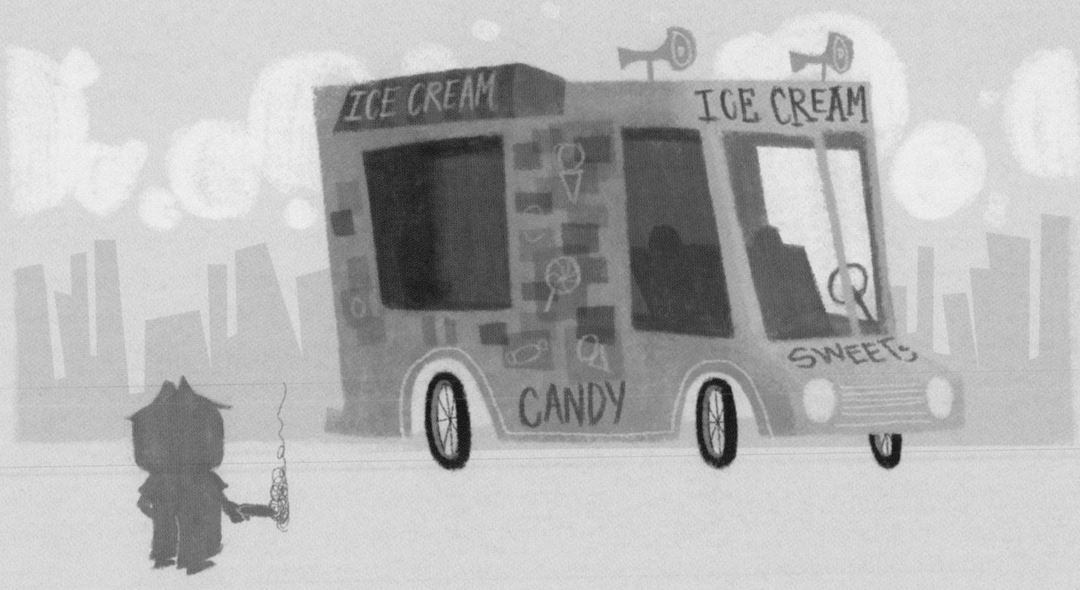
ICE CREAM
ICE CREAM
SWEETS
CANDY

It was an ice cream truck. Now Milton had tasted many other riches during the day, cigarettes, scotch, you name it.

But now it was the mint chip ice cream that had caught his eye, something no six year old could resist, so Milton approached the truck and signaled as to what he wanted.

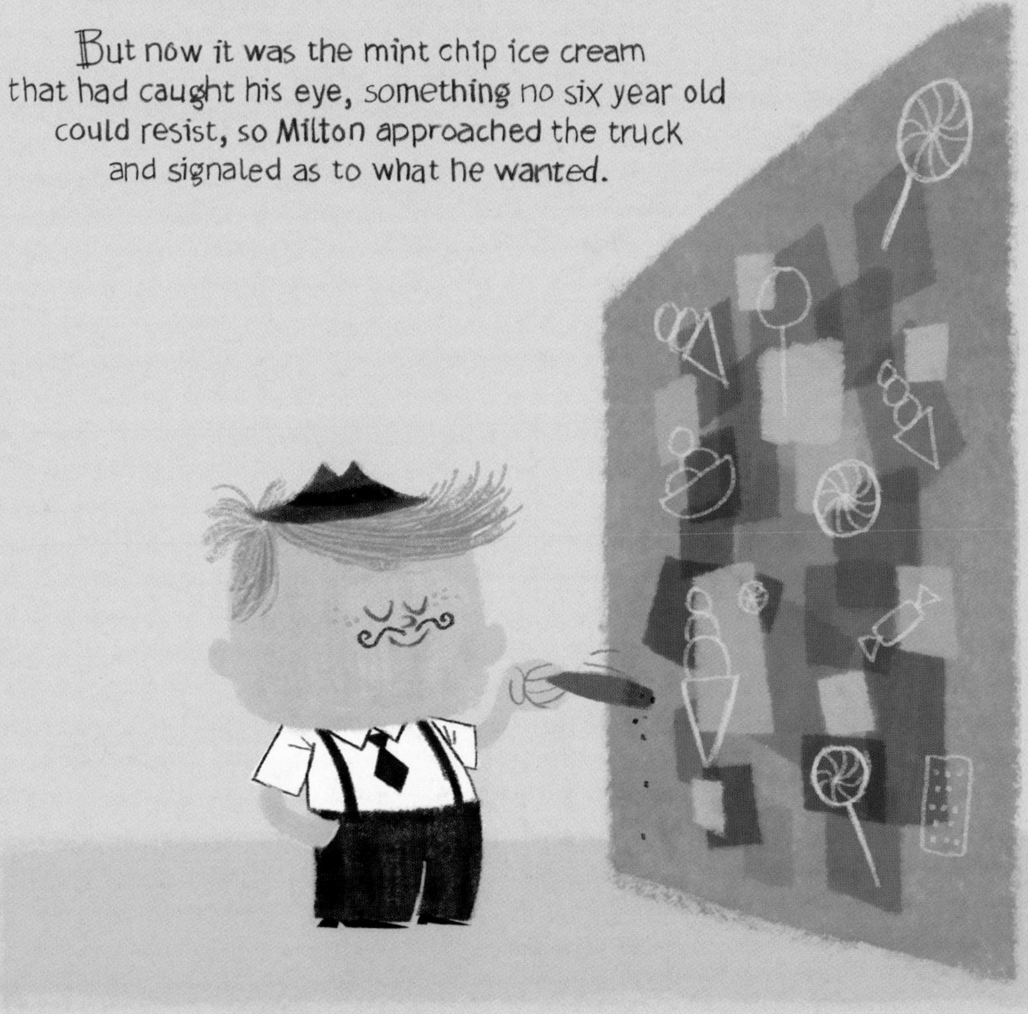

The ice cream man peeked his head out of the truck and looked at Milton. "Ha ha, very funny. You know how many drunks roll out of that bar, stumble over here, and scare off

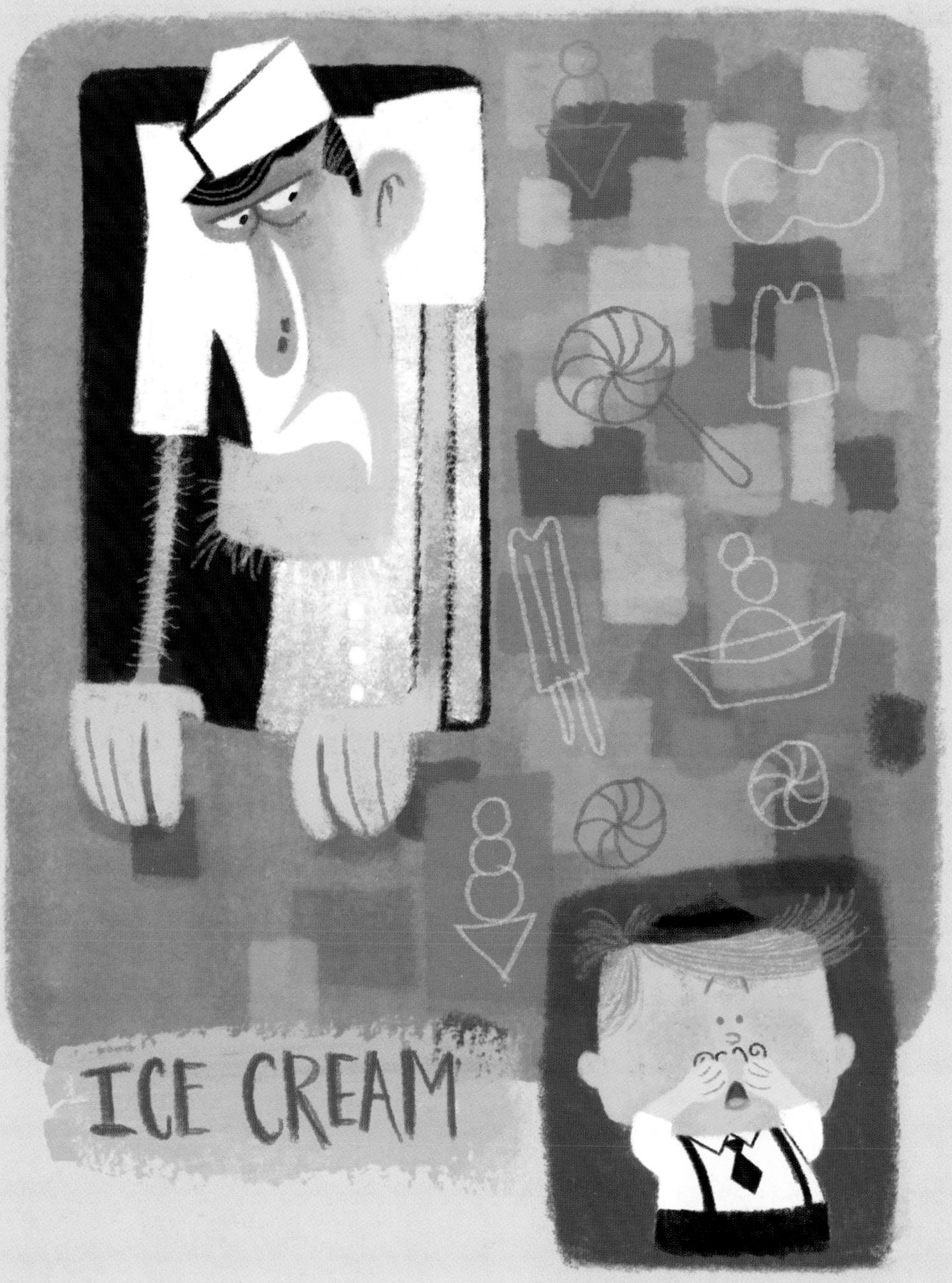
ICE CREAM

all the little kids who actually want ice cream? Do me a favor and get the hell out of here. I don't need you passing out next to my truck and freaking out my real customers. Milton tried to explain his situation. "No sir, I'm just a kid. Look at how short I am, can't you tell?" The ice cream man replies, "Listen buddy. you're not slippin' one past me, OK? You think I don't see that mustache on your face? Now get the hell out of here.

After his scary run-in with the ice cream man, Milton decided he had had enough of being an adult.

While he did enjoy the high stakes of city life, chasing the Yankee dollar, drinking with the boys and all the perks that came along with having a mustache, in some ways, life for Milton was better without one.

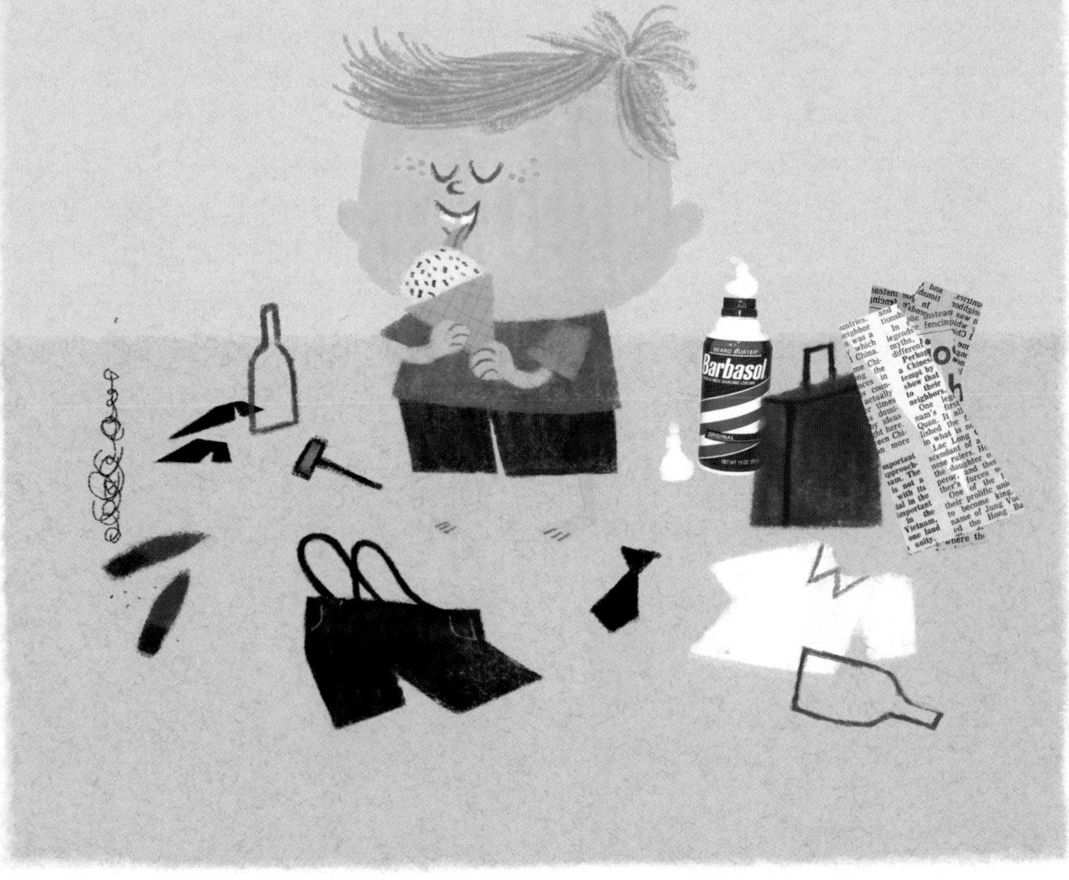
Barbasol

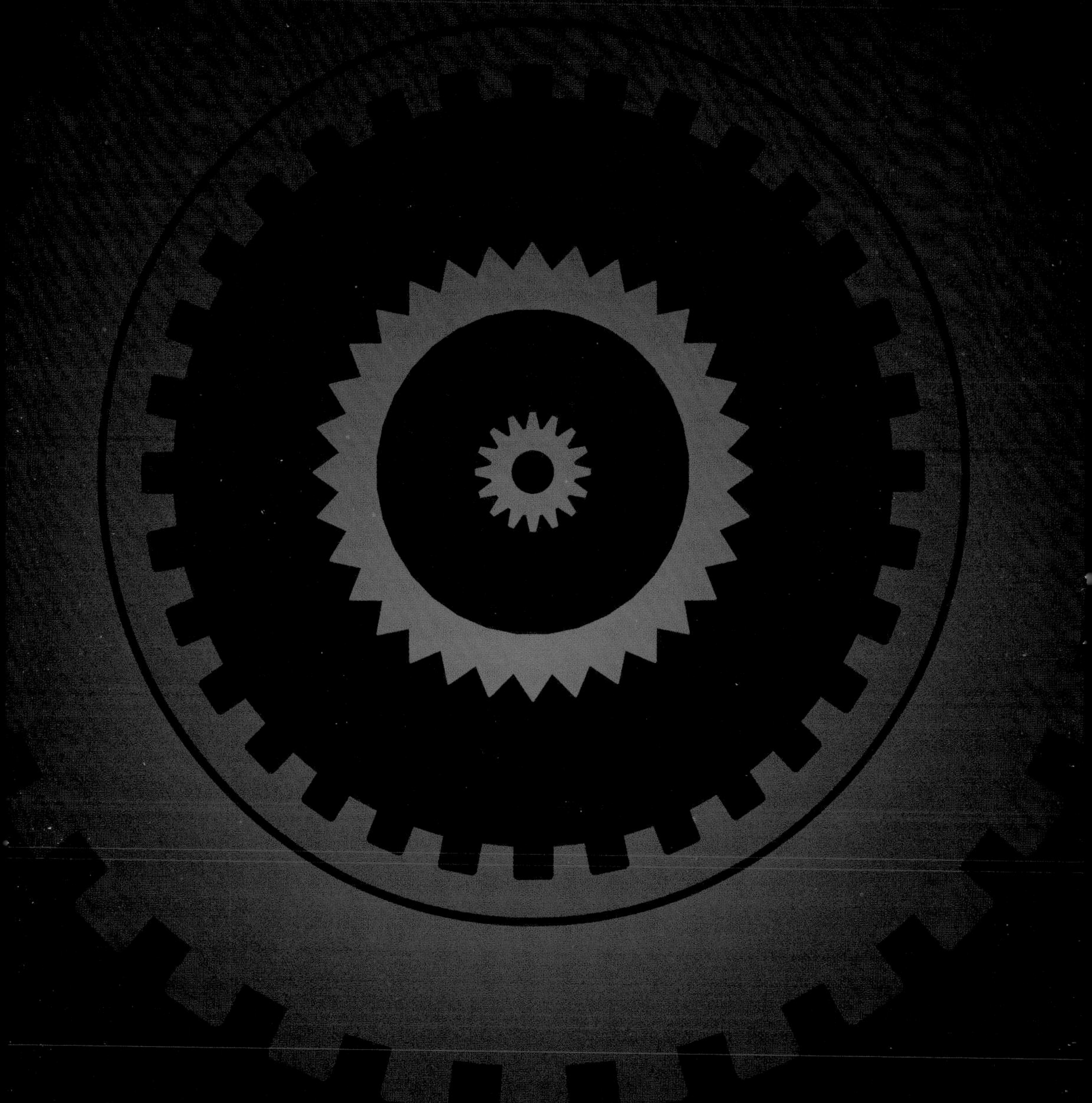

ANGUS MACLANE

PARTY TIME!!!!
Rockin SF railroad flat apt. house party. I'm psyched. I hope there's some hotties there. Should be up here on the next block. Sure glad we walked–parking woulda sucked big time. Number 343 here it is. Hello? Oh it's open. Sure is a lotta dudes here. Dammit what a Sausagefest. Well let's finish this beer then we can go roll the 500 Club. 415-555-2000

TELEMARKETING OPPERTUNITY
Be instantly hated by people you've never met. No Exp. Needed. Don't call us we'll call you. Send us your # ASAP-Colma

ATTENTION EVERYONE TODAY'S HOT LUNCH
Will be... Chicken Fried Steak, Mashed Potatoes and Gravy, Fruit Cup, Roll, Milk. Don't forget that friday is opposite day so wear you pants backwards like Daddy Mack.

C O N F E S S I O N
Sometimes I don't read all of the fine print in Chris Ware's many p u b l i c a t i o n s .

ADVICE TO YOUNG ARTISTS
Keep drawing. Find people you trust to give you useful feedback. Draw from life. Go to the Zoo and draw animals. I didn't and that's why my animal drawings suck. There's other stuff you should know about... like Sculpey is different than plasticine clay. Plasticine will never harden in the oven, okay? It makes a bad smell. Trust me.

RSVP PLEASE- What's the deal? Just because people wear sweatpants to work means that you don't have to let me

RIO RANCHO Properties. I'm here to do good for you and me. Call Grace and put me on the board. (414) GLN-ROSS

Golf Caddy- Got an old set of golf clubs that need to be carried around for a while. prior exp. req. Call ASAP. Day or night. salary+ bnfts. Act now!!!?

HOFF BRAU MEAT Carver-Min 2 yrs Knife exp. needed. 24 hr shifts req. Emeryville

Hi/Yo Industries- Many positions to fill ASAP! No Exp needed.Call 510-555-3181.

SUPPORT FOR THIS ENDEAVOR
was provided by many kind and talented individuals. First and foremost thanks to my loving and supportive wife, Tashana.

Thanks are in order for: Mom, Dad, Chelsea, Mark Andrews, Scott Clark, Andrew Gordon, Jeremy Lasky, Aaron Lopresti, Ted Mathot, Scott Morse, Ray Nelson Jr., Nathan Stanton, Suzy Zuckert, The fine folks at Pixar Animation Studios and everyone else who supported me.

LODGING NEEDED ASAP-
SAN DIEGO-July I forgot to book my hotel for the con and now I gotta stay at the HoJo's at Sea World. I'll crash on you sofa.

HATS OFF TO BEAVERS here we come. Beavers are fighters every one. Beavers will conquer any foe, we will go go go, Lets hear a cheer for the beavers watch them score, knocking on victory's door Something something- we will win to-night

LLER NEEDED- Major
w has seats that need
g. Min. 5 shows exp.
and insurance req'd.
ne to 555-1001

KEY needed for loud
nnoying? Bad taste in
u're hired. ex. 77645

NEEDED
comic book reader to
time to actually read
. So thorough they
ad the stuff in the
e book (I don't know
al term) Let me
re are any typos. THX

- 10x10 Trampoline
have knee pads too.
00 O.B.O. On site
. CALL 160-KRSTY

CED Turnsignalist
drive in front of me
urs/no pay or bnfts

u an Artist?
awaiting your talent
o on some plastic
et's get to sculpting
piece. $5-$6/hour
mby bnfts. Call
510-NDS-SNDYS.

DOORPERSON
let the dogs out.
should be able to
er mouth shut.

WICH avail. now at
e. Help yourself.
it's got plenty of
Pt. Richmond area.

CK NEEDED for
k. Only expensive
need apply. Call
15) KL5-3000

online dating time? Join the Club.
www.wrcrftrulesmylife.com

RESTAURANT STAFF Waitperson- $10-$17 hourly. Surly, bitter attitude a plus. No exp? No Prob. Just show up, you'll do. Oh- and dress like a rockstar. Emeryville 94608.

SALT & BATTERY
(well mostly Battery) star in a short comic adventure. The story is called

WORKING BATTERY

ANGUS MacLANE

ANIMATRONICS Technician. $10-$12/hr w/o bnfts. Rodent Band in desperate need of repair. Prior experience helpful but not required. Must provide own air compressing unit. Apply at 441 E Jungle Blvd.

EXPERIENCED DISTRIBUTOR Playing cards mostly. Flex sched. No claustrophobics please. Fax resume: 510-555-3181www.lucky7.com

ADVERTISING EXECUTIVE P/T or F/T Needed To make everyone's life more difficult. Bad ideas and no outlet for expression? This is the job for you. Are you up for the challege? Bad taste, a plus. Please Call 6175-559-33421

D.I.Y. BOY BAND, Start crooning today!!! Write for free informative pamphlet.

OSTRICH FARMER??

CAPS LOCK STUCK
COMPUTER????!!!! Loc
your left hand. There
you should press. F

HIGH FINANCE
Looking for a cupla
help me out on one la
risk, big reward. Look
motivated individual w
tools and flexible mon
$45000-$56000/hr c
at extension 555-432

FRESH GAME, seek
gazelle, antelope or w
a quick meal ASAP. C
cougar 415-555-629

FETCHPERSON
There is a cold be
fridge. Could you get
I just sat down.
bunch. ex. 33455

FLEXIBLE HOURS, Lo
little to no benefits. P
will be wasted and sou
crushed. Why not call
Free Training and coffe
at $2-$4/hour Refrerer
must. Fax Resume to (
555-8892

HIP SIDEKICK NEEDE
CGI trainwreck. Only exp
celebrities need apply. C
today (415) KL5-3000

POGS 4 SALE- Act No
your faves are here. set
5600. just $400. C'mo
people. Help me out.

BLAH BLAH BLAH, Bla
Blee Blee Blah Blah Blah
Salary,bnfts. Blah Blah
Call now Blah Blah Blah-

GET A GRIP- of cash th
Many positions avail! No

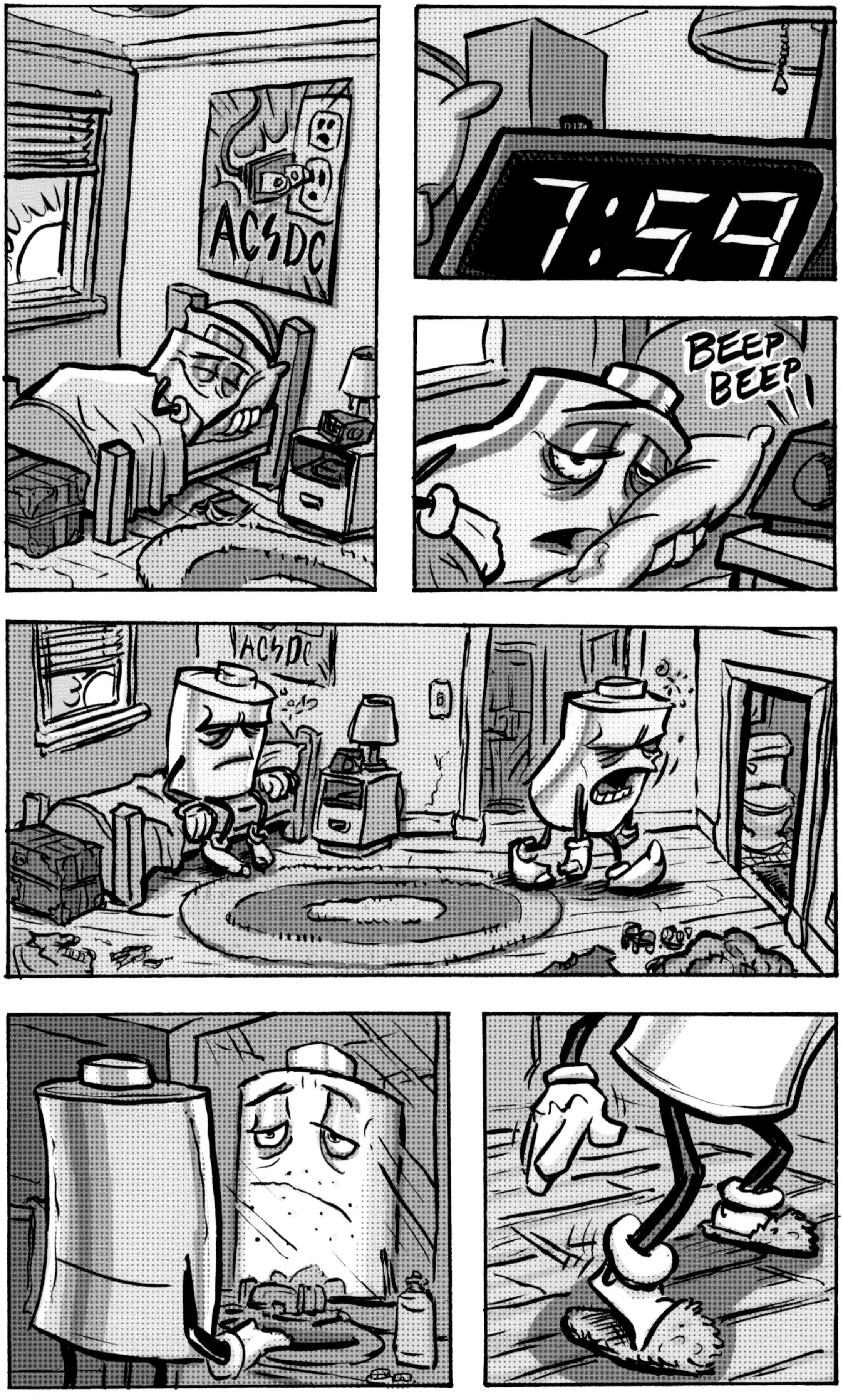
ACϟDC
7:59
BEEP
BEEP

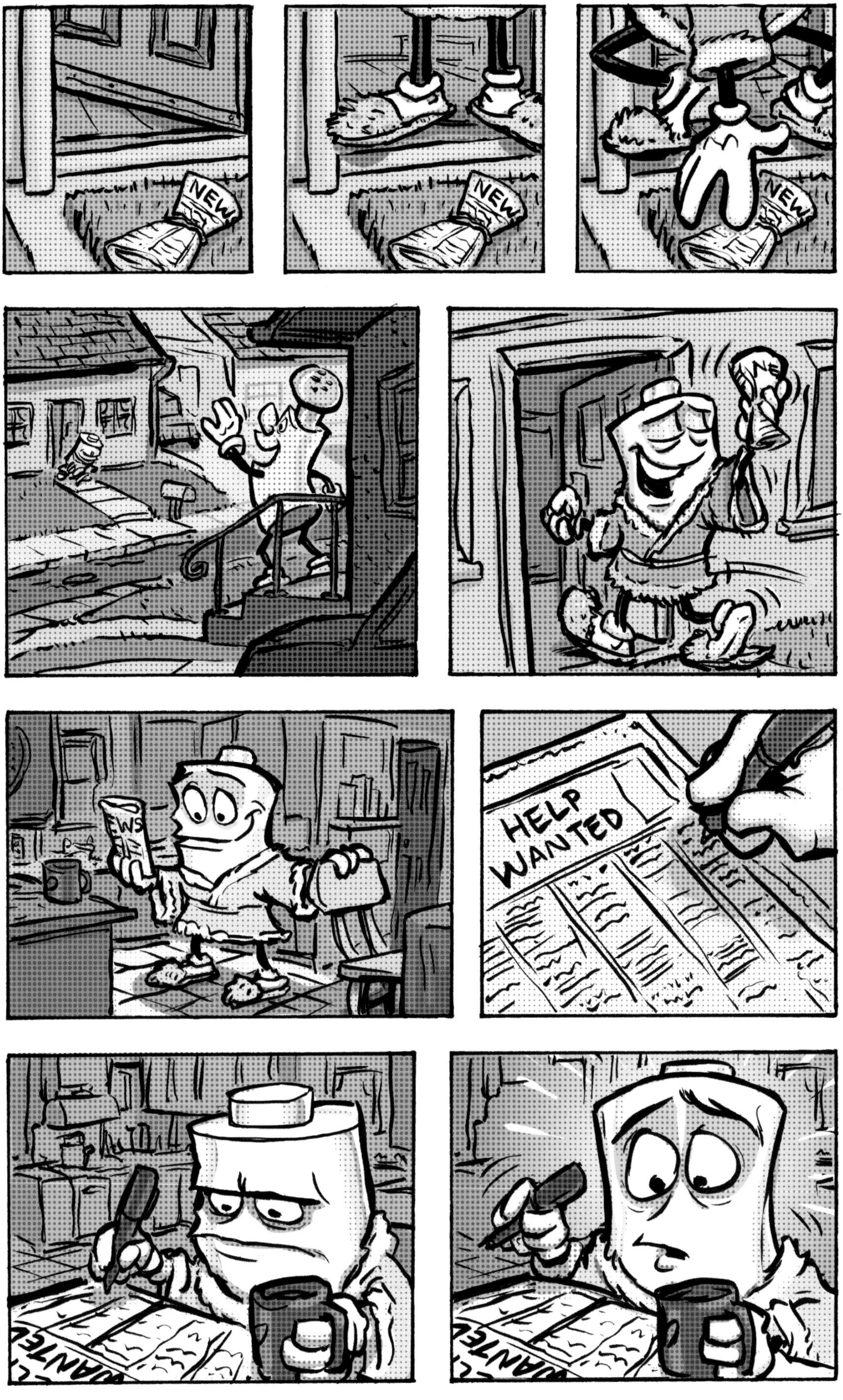
NEW
NEW
NEW
EWS
HELP WANTED
WANTED
WANTED

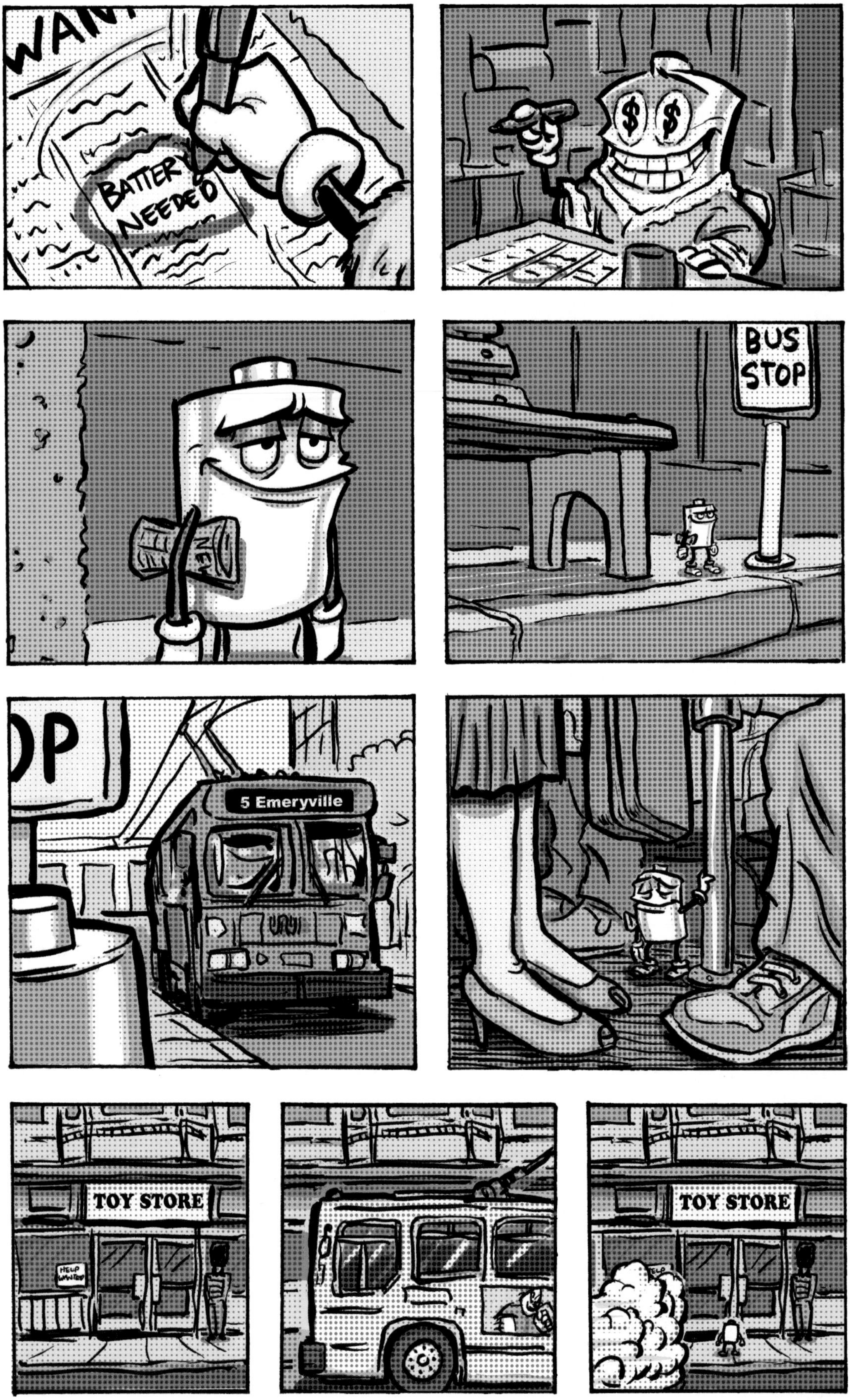
BATTERY NEEDED
BUS STOP
5 Emeryville
TOY STORE
HELP WANTED
TOY STORE

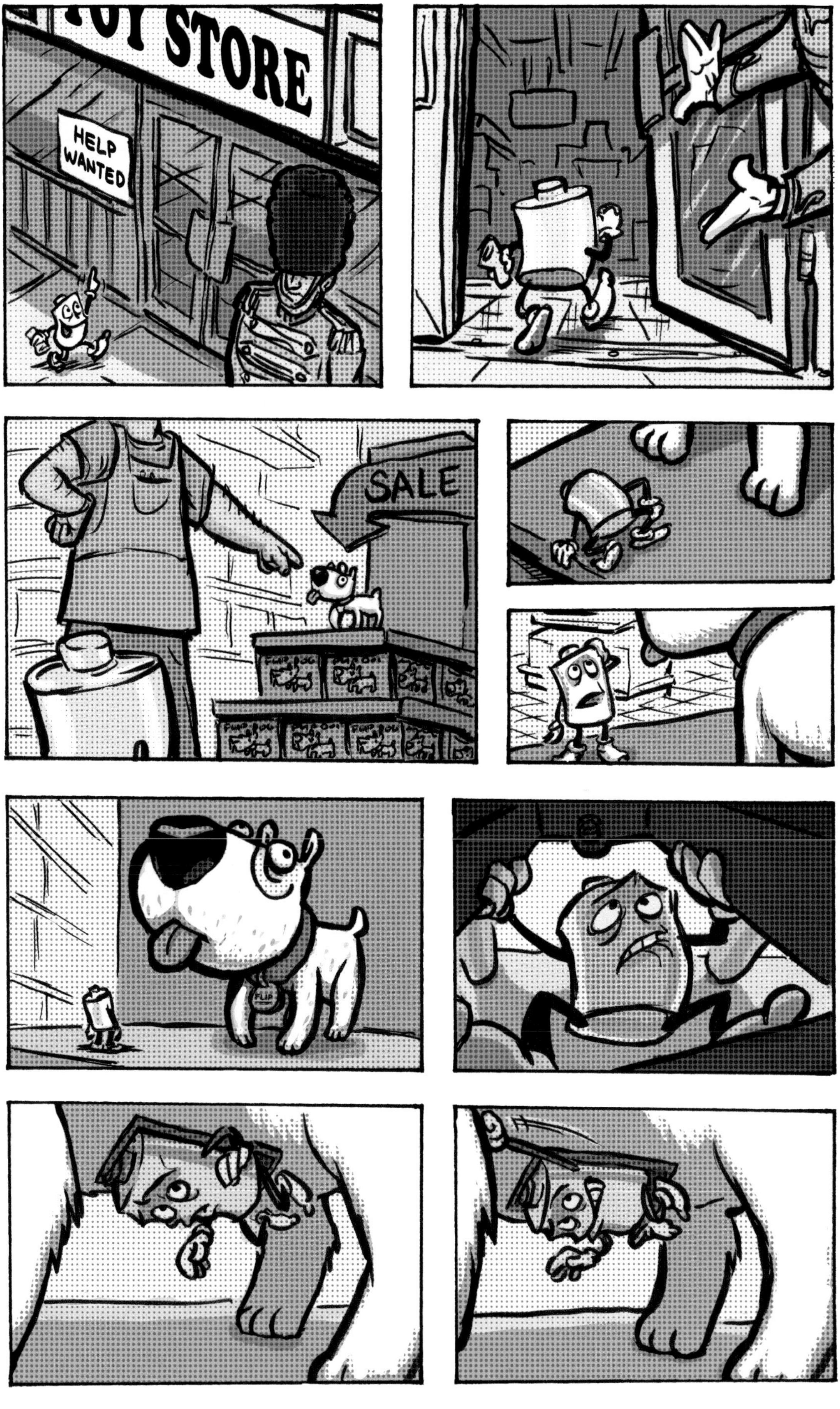
TOY STORE
HELP WANTED
SALE
FLIP

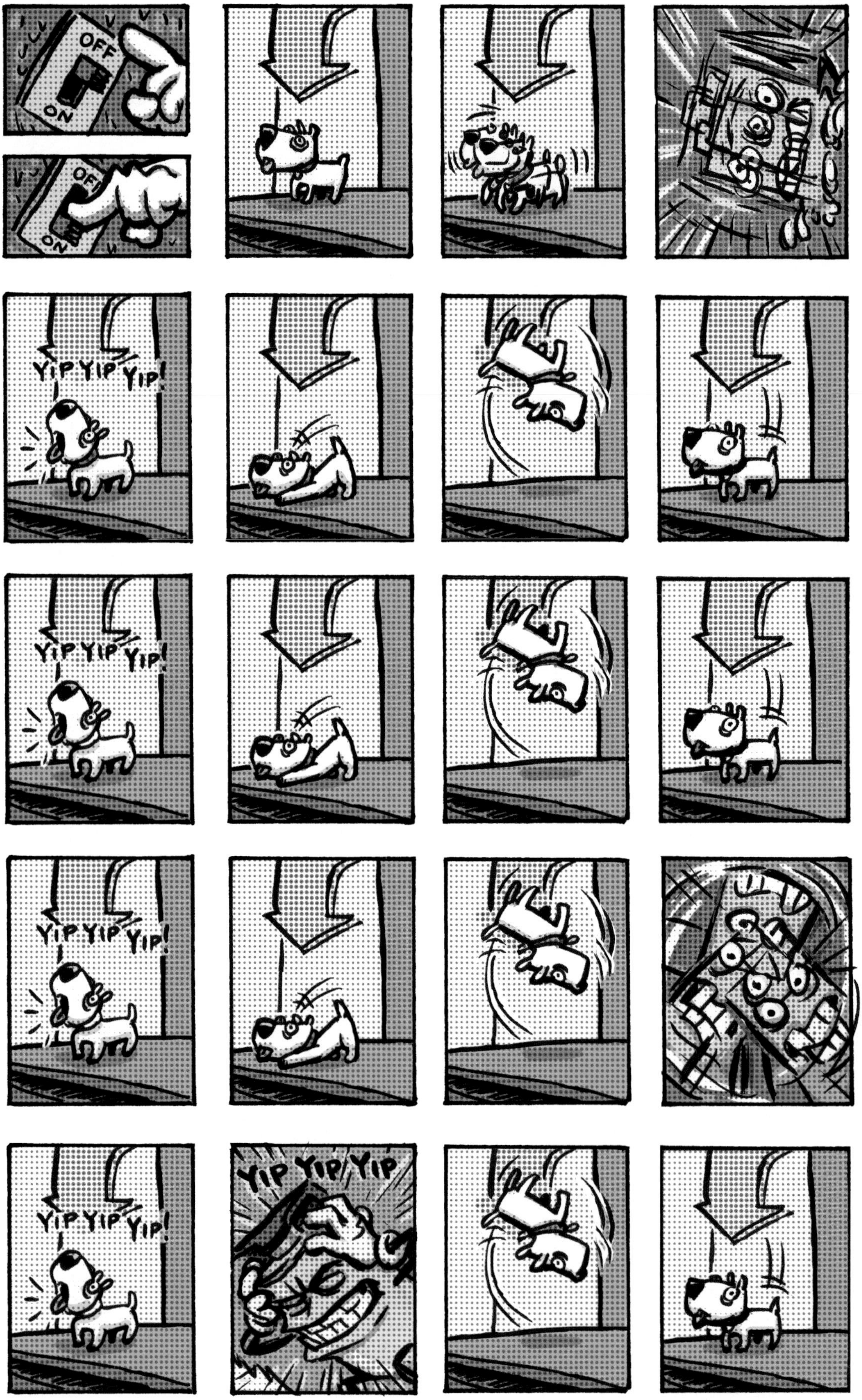

OFF
ON
ON
YIP YIP YIP!
YIP YIP YIP!
YIP YIP YIP!
YIP YIP YIP!
YIP YIP YIP

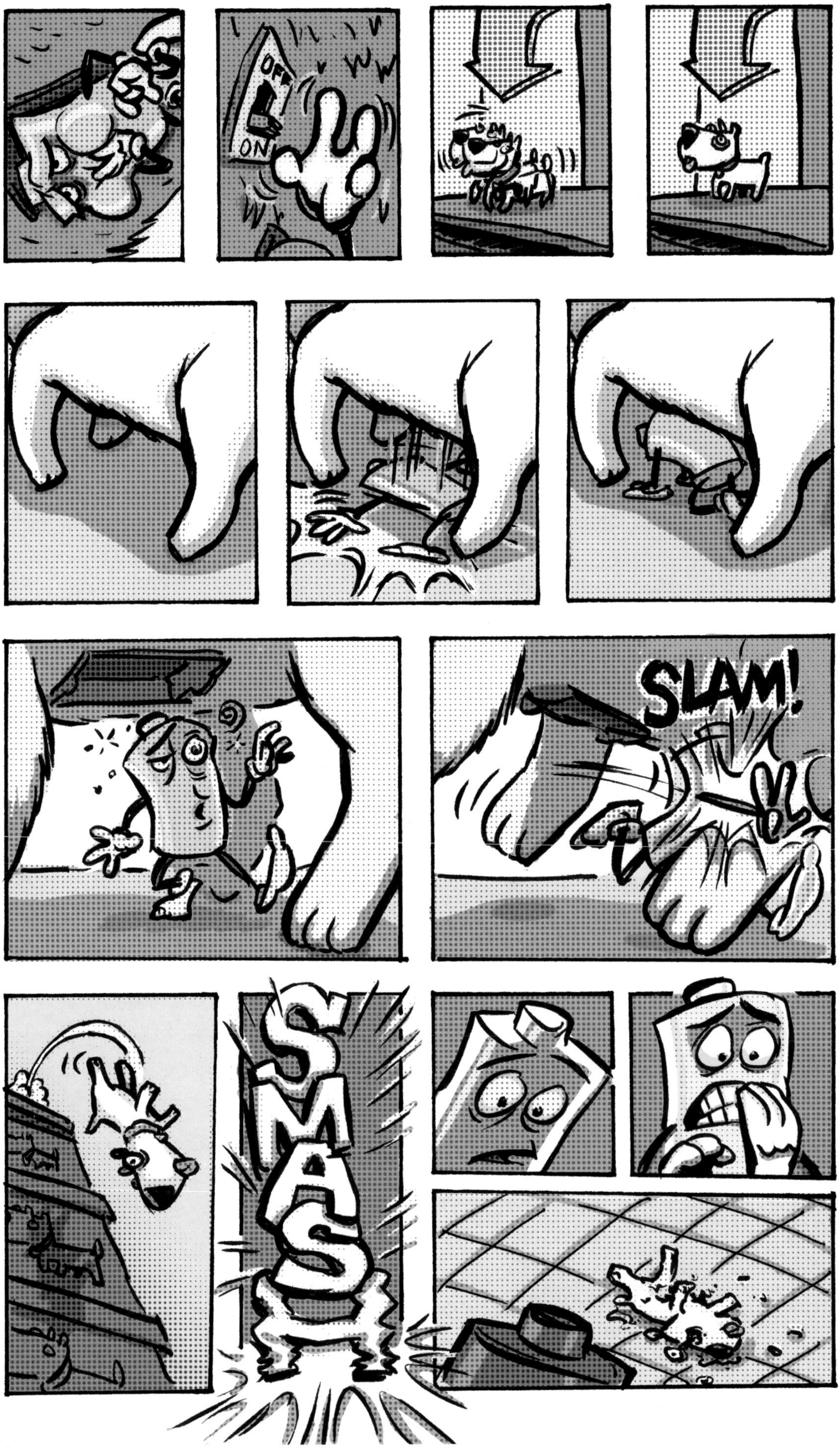
OFF
ON
SLAM!
SMASH

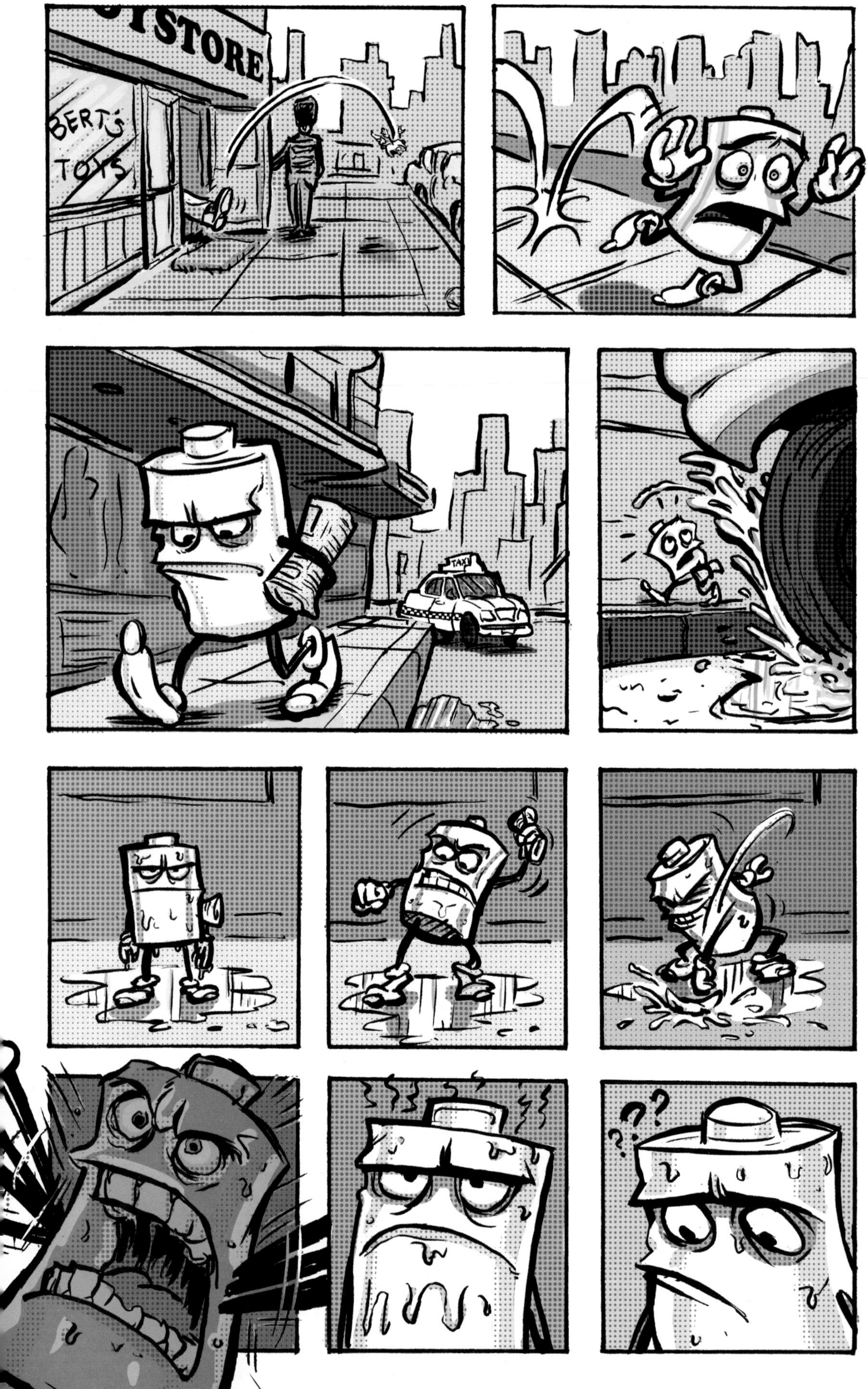

YSTORE
BERT'S
TOYS
TAXI

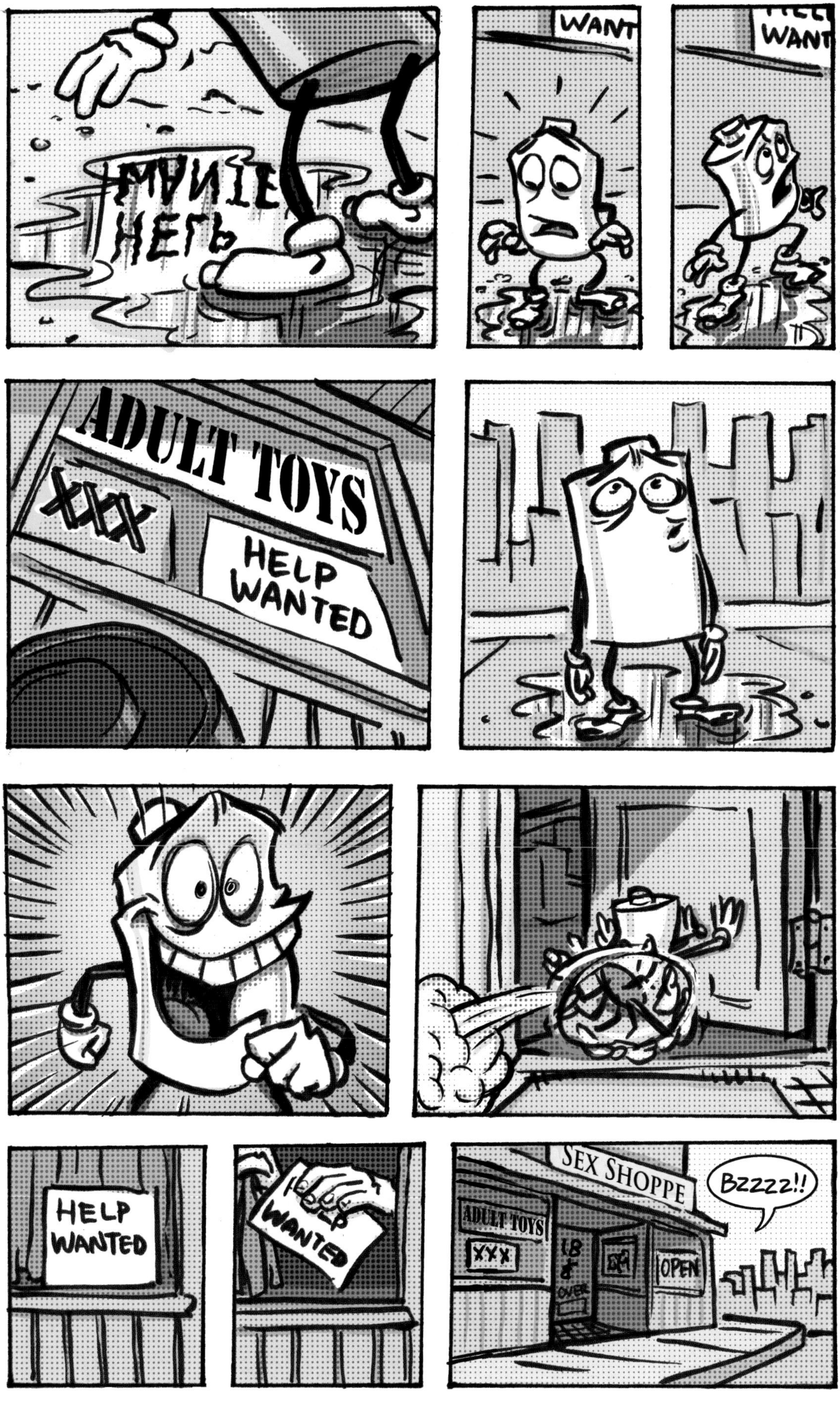

WANT
WANT
ADULT TOYS
XXX
HELP WANTED
HELP WANTED
WANTED
SEX SHOPPE
ADULT TOYS
XXX
18 & OVER
OPEN
Bzzzz!!

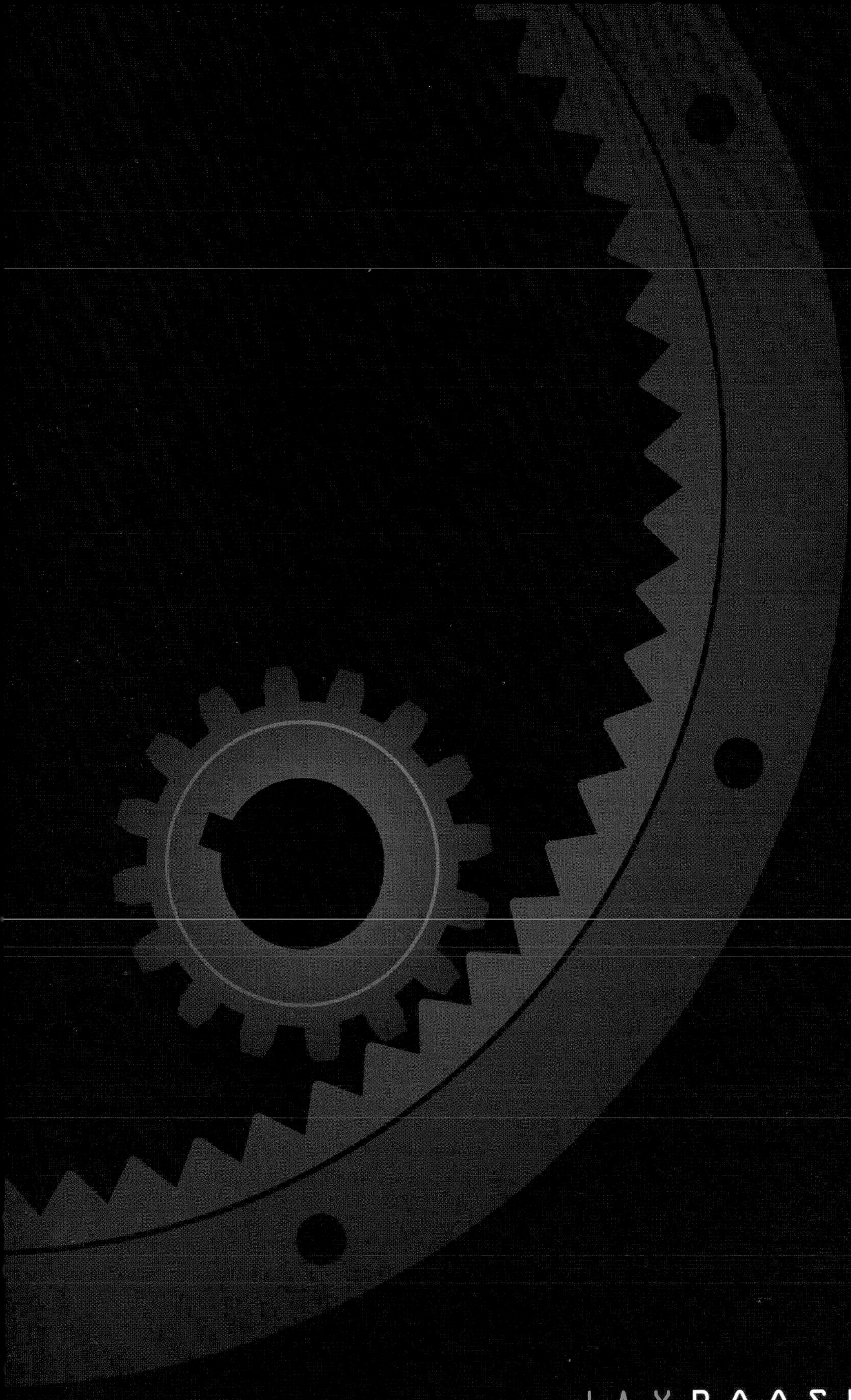

JAY BOOSE

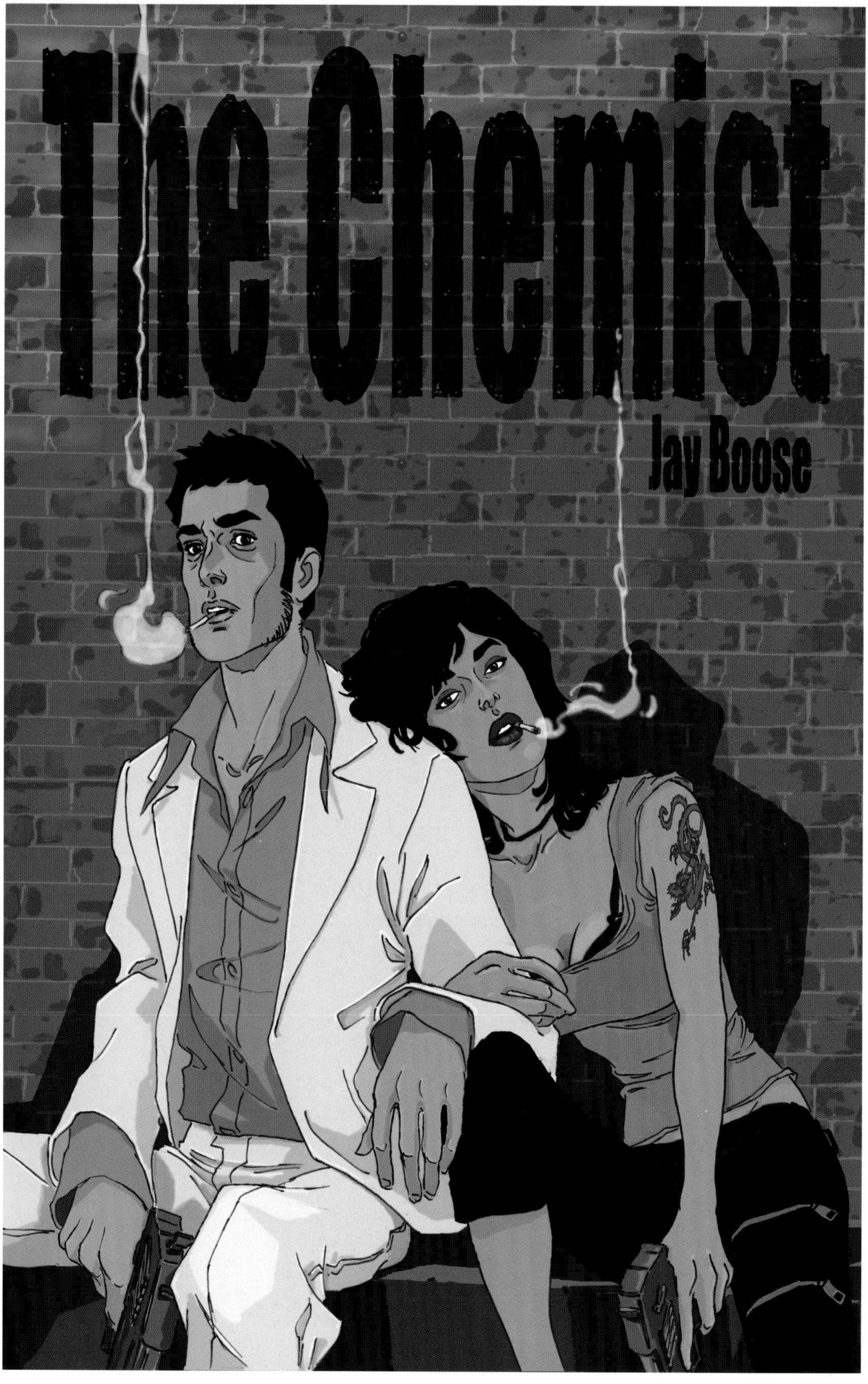
The Chemist
Jay Boose

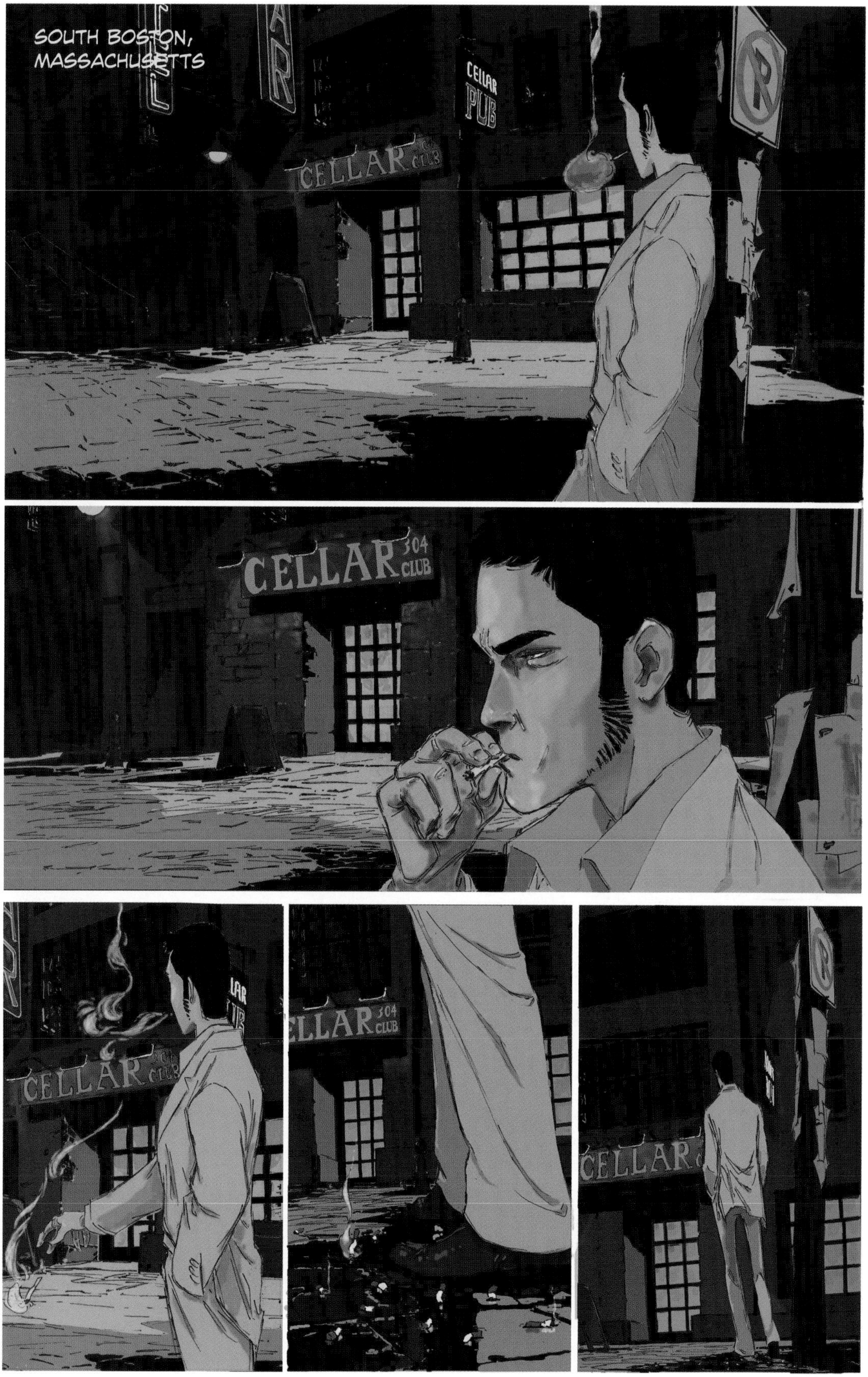
SOUTH BOSTON, MASSACHUSETTS
CELLAR PUB
CELLAR CLUB
CELLAR 304 CLUB

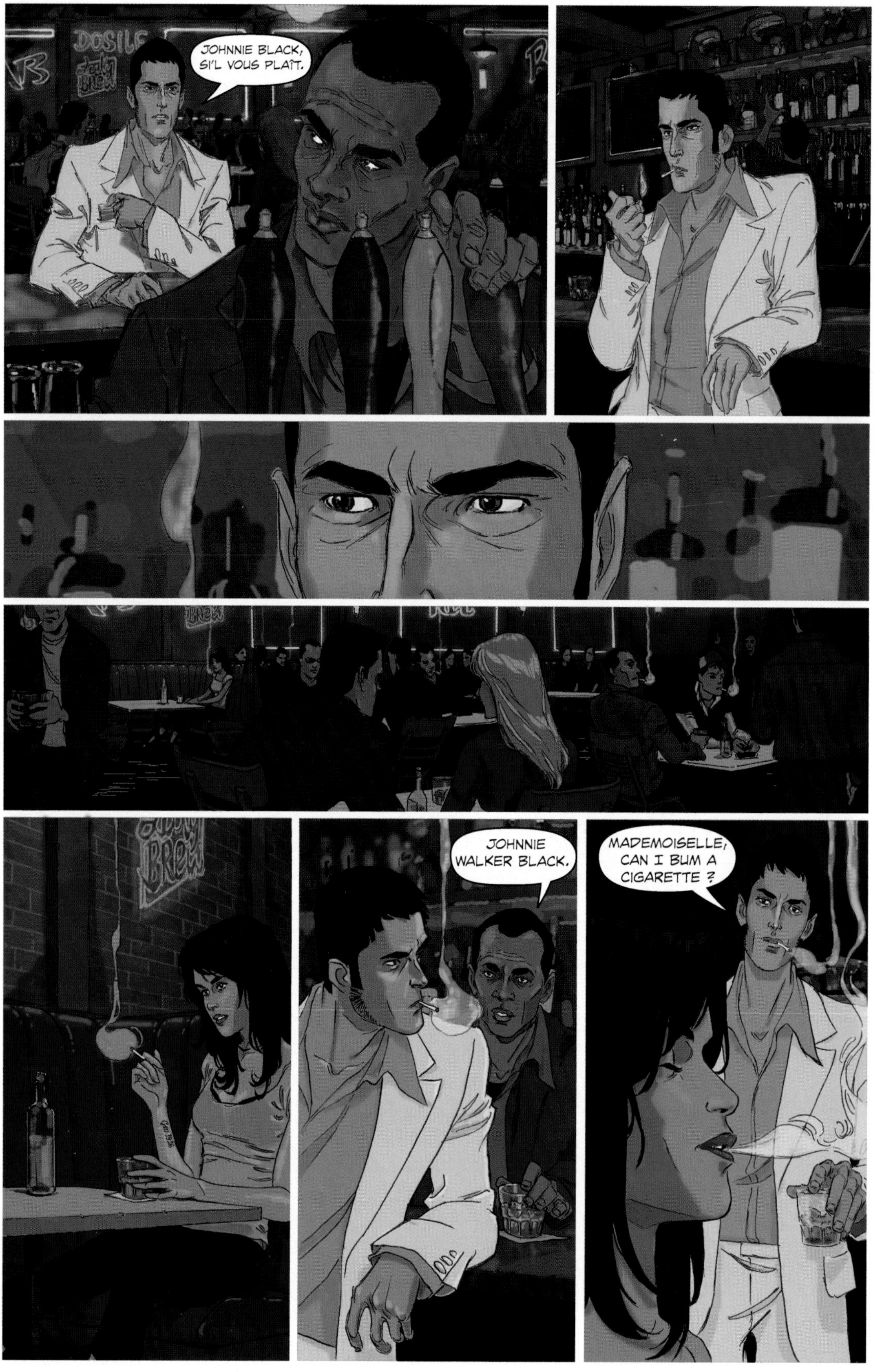
JOHNNIE BLACK, SI'L VOUS PLAÎT.
DOSILE
JOHNNIE WALKER BLACK.
MADEMOISELLE, CAN I BUM A CIGARETTE ?

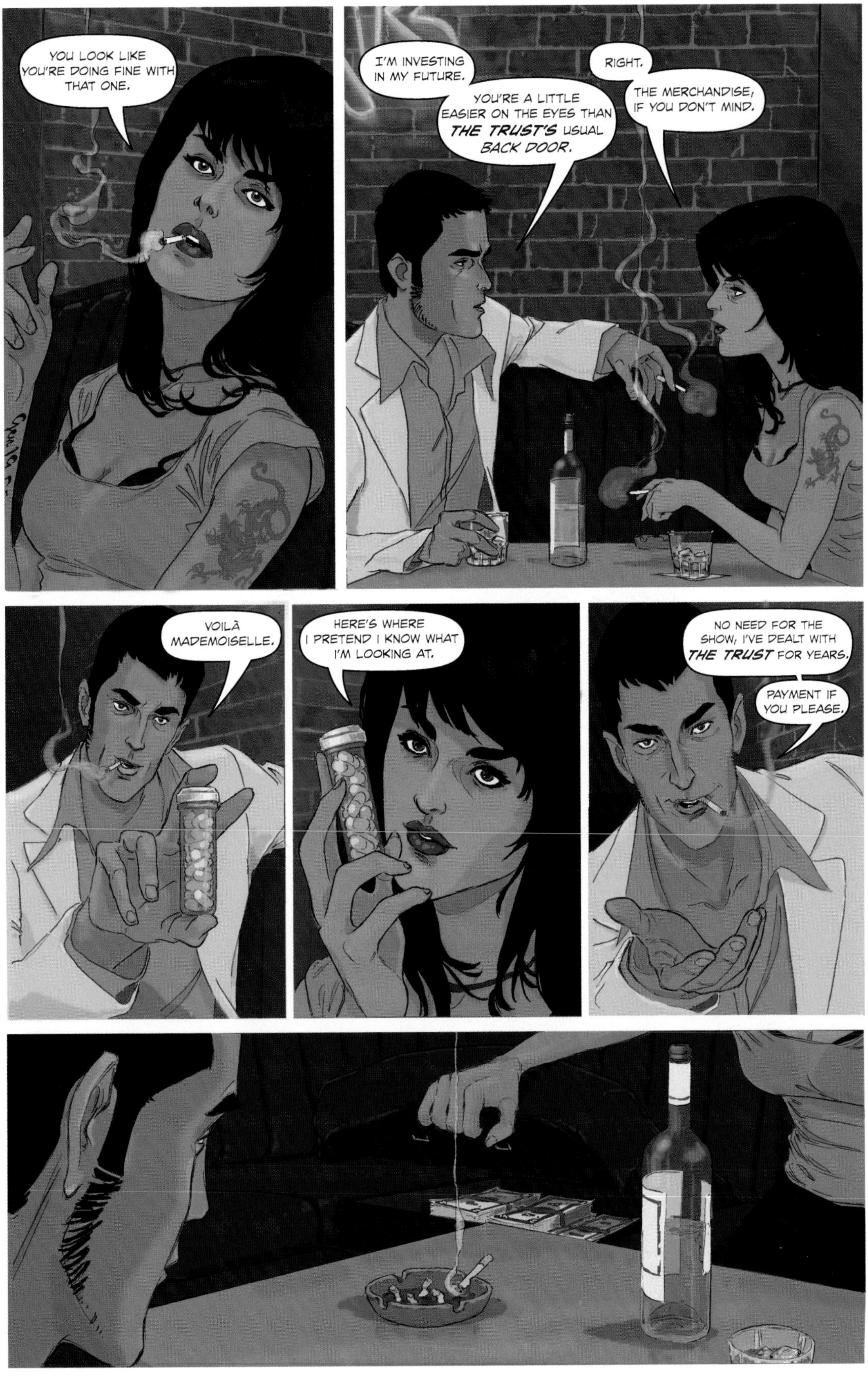
YOU LOOK LIKE YOU'RE DOING FINE WITH THAT ONE.
I'M INVESTING IN MY FUTURE.
YOU'RE A LITTLE EASIER ON THE EYES THAN ***THE TRUST'S*** USUAL BACK DOOR.
RIGHT.
THE MERCHANDISE, IF YOU DON'T MIND.
VOILÀ MADEMOISELLE.
HERE'S WHERE I PRETEND I KNOW WHAT I'M LOOKING AT.
NO NEED FOR THE SHOW; I'VE DEALT WITH ***THE TRUST*** FOR YEARS.
PAYMENT IF YOU PLEASE.

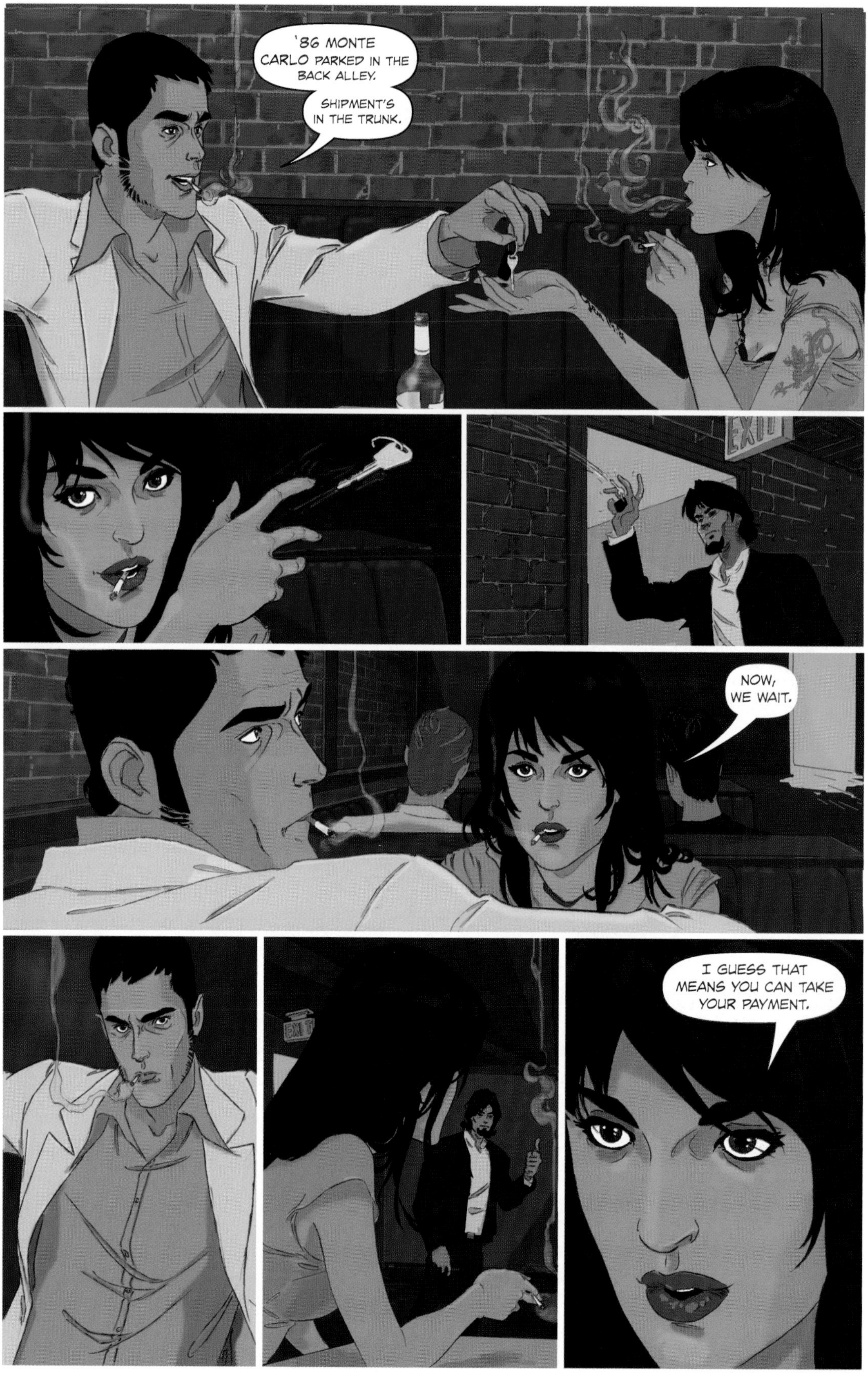
'86 MONTE CARLO PARKED IN THE BACK ALLEY.
SHIPMENT'S IN THE TRUNK.
EXIT
NOW, WE WAIT.
I GUESS THAT MEANS YOU CAN TAKE YOUR PAYMENT.

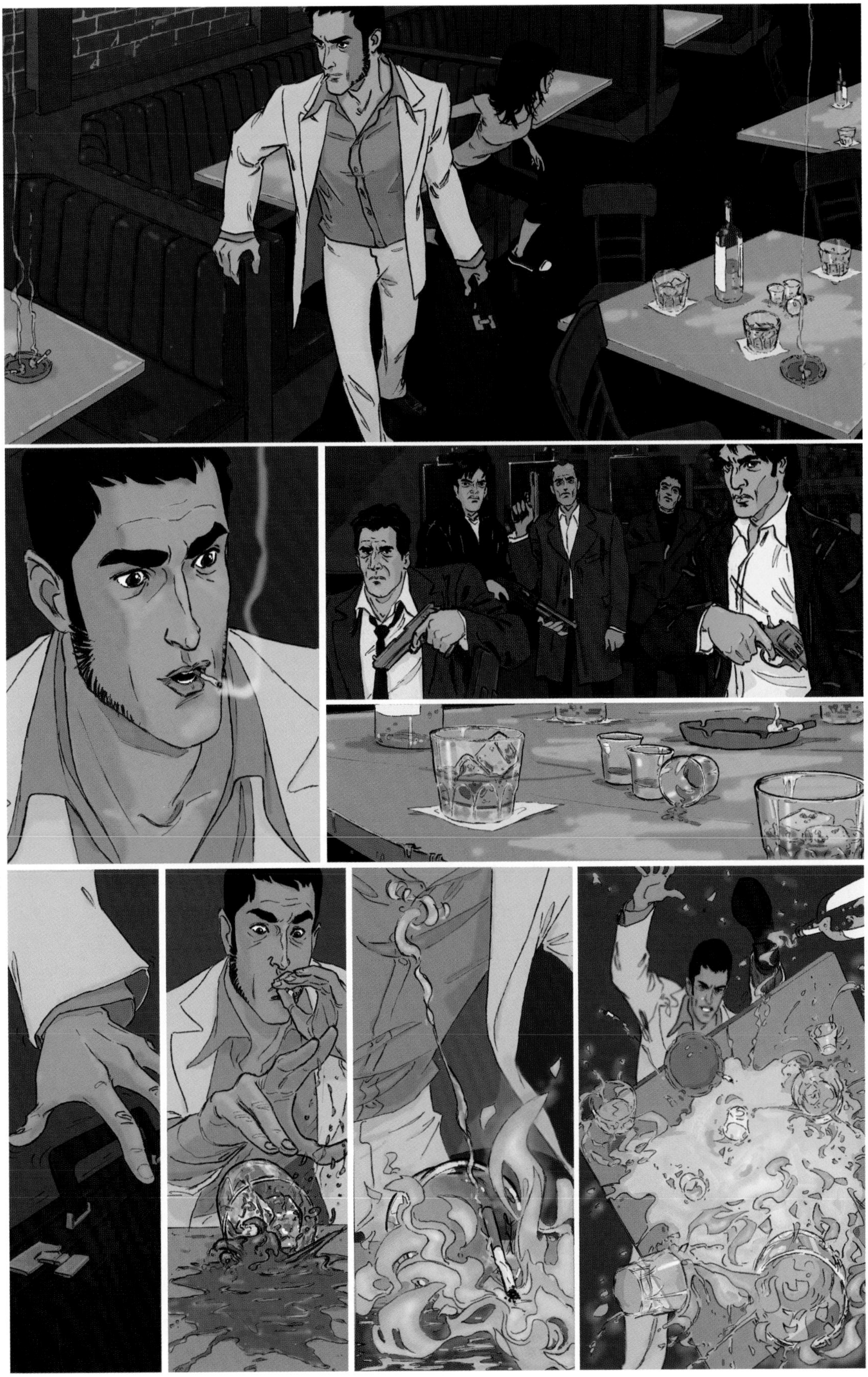

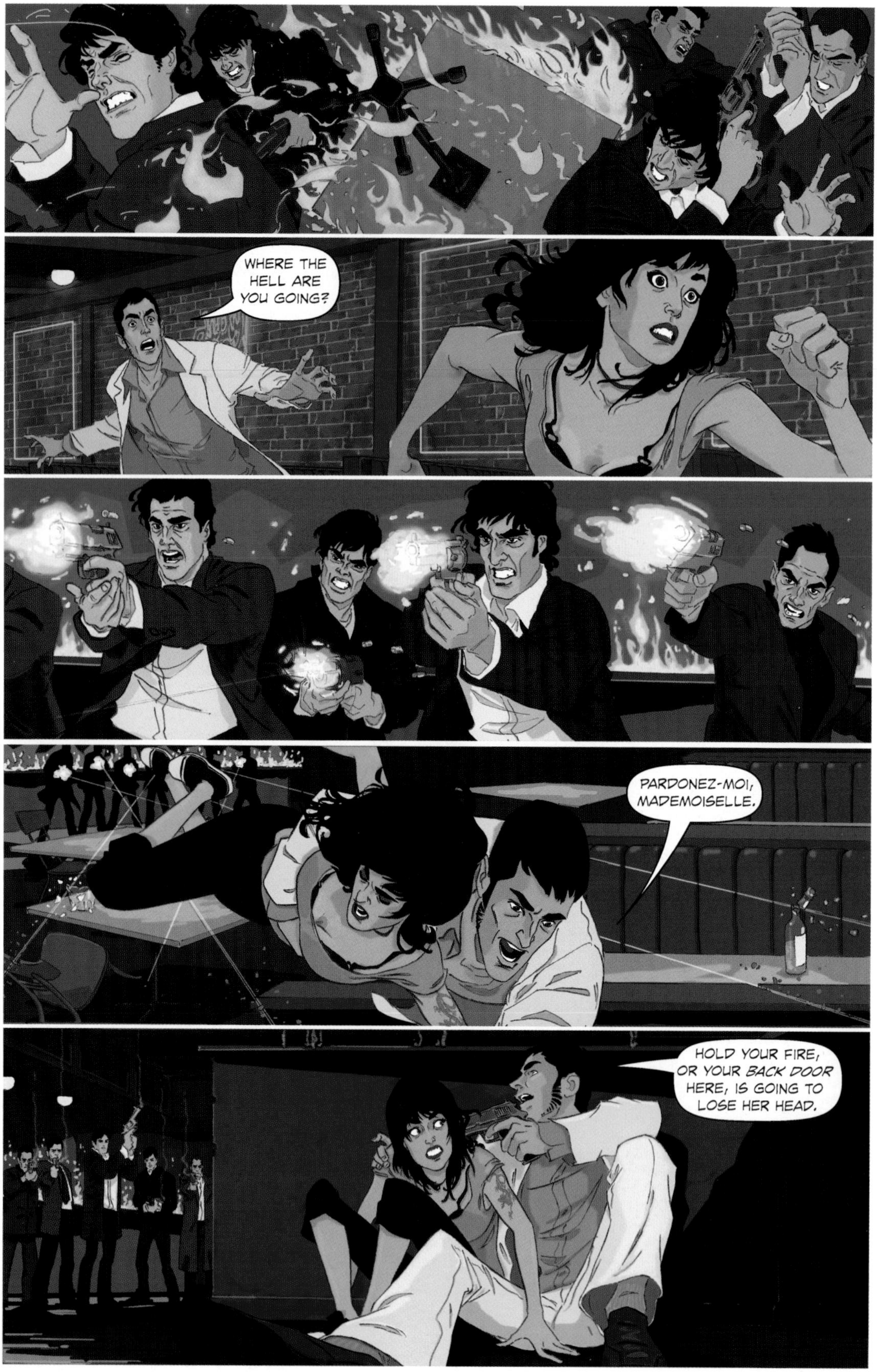
WHERE THE HELL ARE YOU GOING?
PARDONEZ-MOI, MADEMOISELLE.
HOLD YOUR FIRE, OR YOUR *BACK DOOR* HERE, IS GOING TO LOSE HER HEAD.

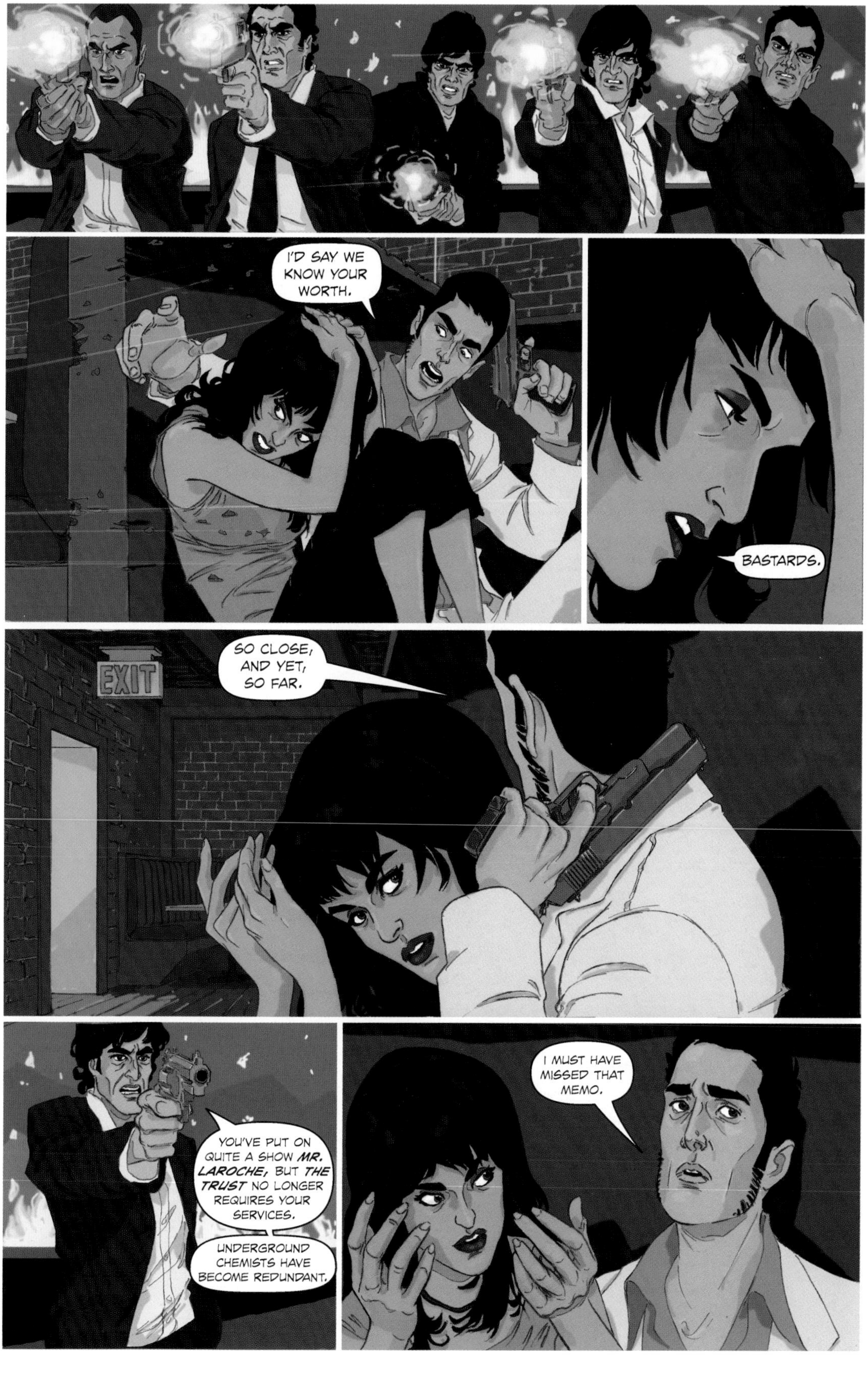
I'D SAY WE KNOW YOUR WORTH.
BASTARDS.
SO CLOSE, AND YET, SO FAR.
EXIT
YOU'VE PUT ON QUITE A SHOW MR. LAROCHE, BUT THE TRUST NO LONGER REQUIRES YOUR SERVICES.
UNDERGROUND CHEMISTS HAVE BECOME REDUNDANT.
I MUST HAVE MISSED THAT MEMO.

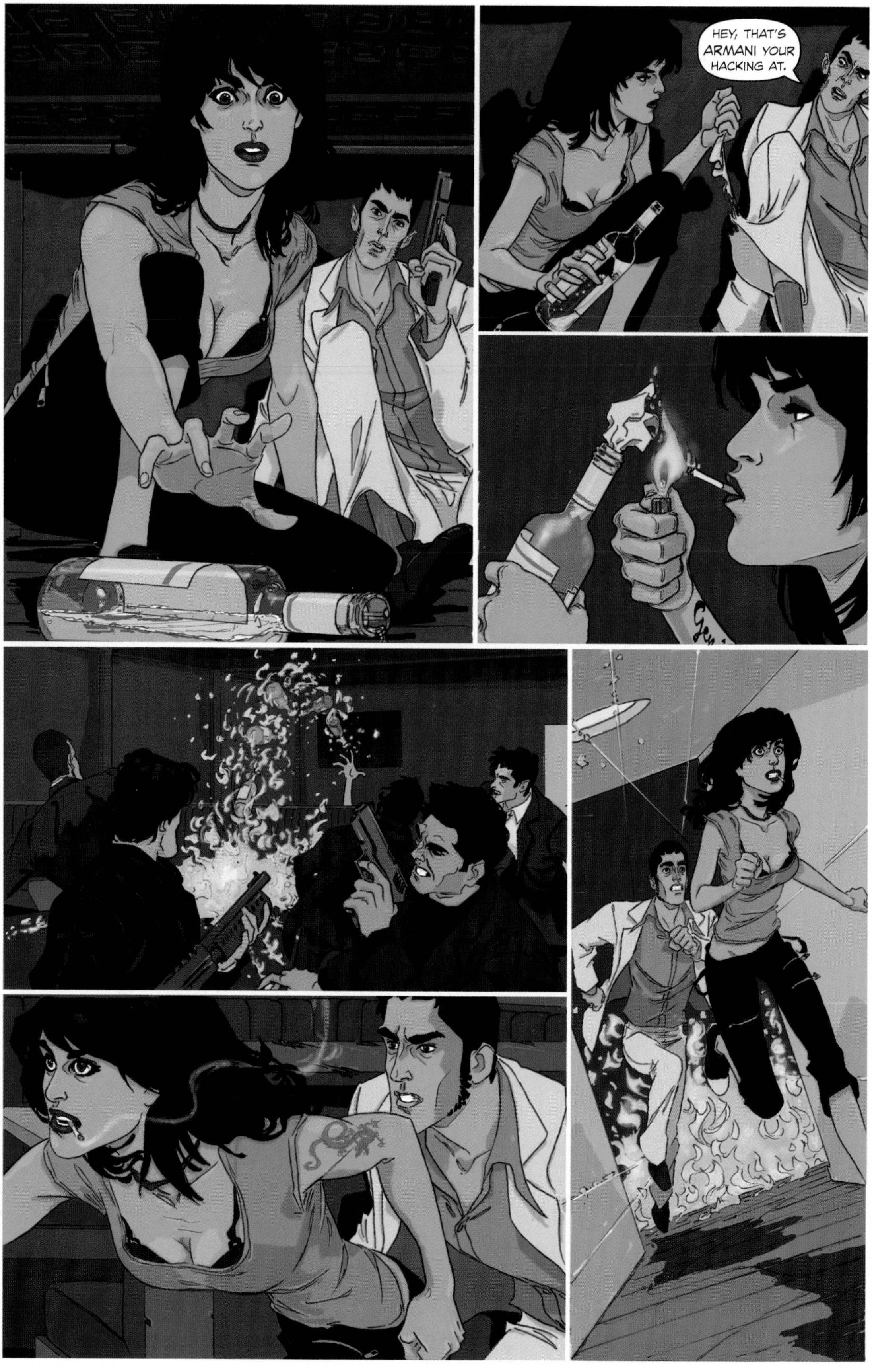
HEY, THAT'S ARMANI YOUR HACKING AT.

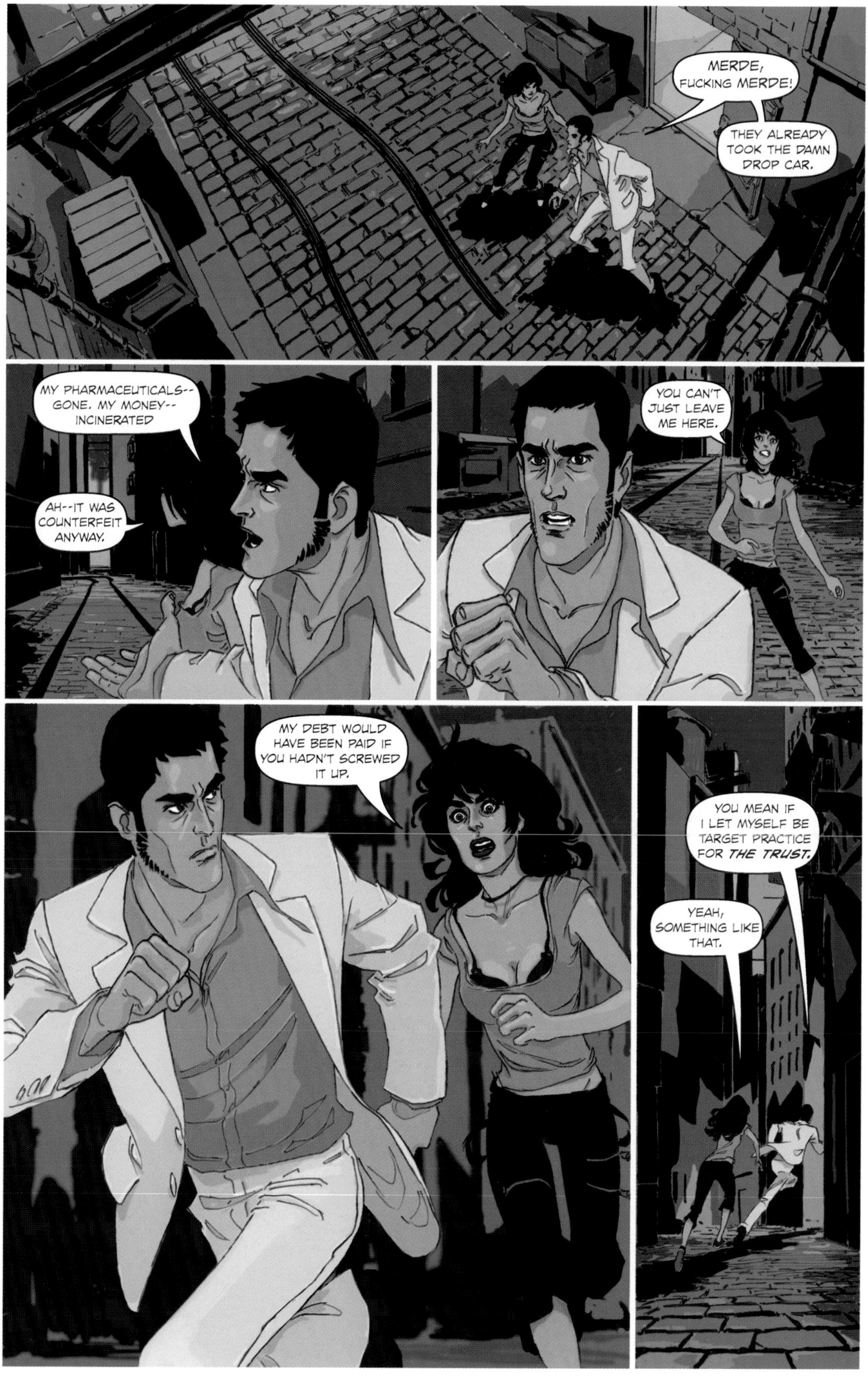
MERDE, FUCKING MERDE!
THEY ALREADY TOOK THE DAMN DROP CAR.
MY PHARMACEUTICALS-- GONE. MY MONEY-- INCINERATED
AH--IT WAS COUNTERFEIT ANYWAY.
YOU CAN'T JUST LEAVE ME HERE.
MY DEBT WOULD HAVE BEEN PAID IF YOU HADN'T SCREWED IT UP.
YOU MEAN IF I LET MYSELF BE TARGET PRACTICE FOR *THE TRUST.*
YEAH, SOMETHING LIKE THAT.

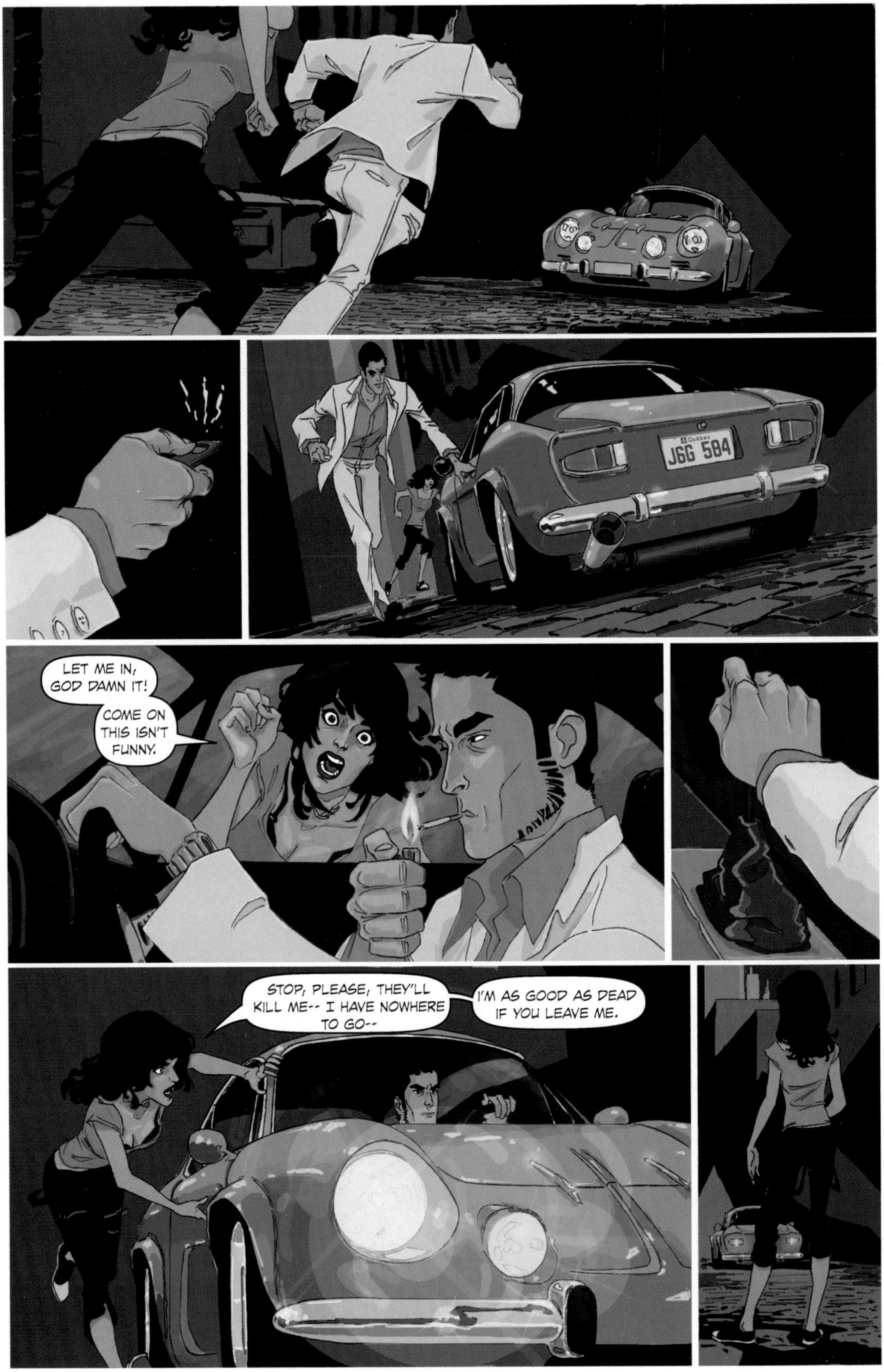

Québec
J6G 584
LET ME IN, GOD DAMN IT!
COME ON THIS ISN'T FUNNY.
STOP, PLEASE, THEY'LL KILL ME-- I HAVE NOWHERE TO GO--
I'M AS GOOD AS DEAD IF YOU LEAVE ME.

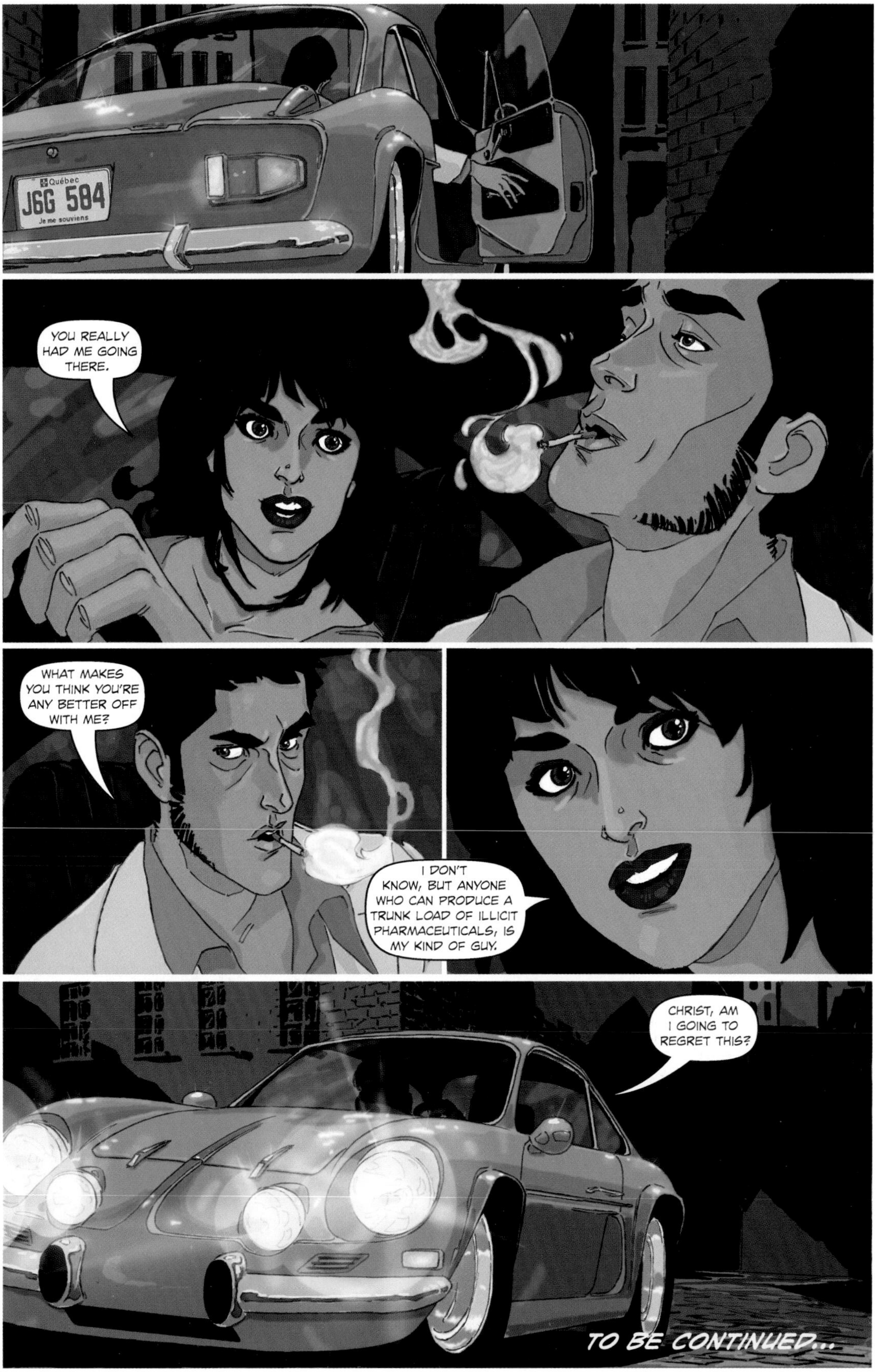
Québec
J6G 584
Je me souviens
YOU REALLY HAD ME GOING THERE.
WHAT MAKES YOU THINK YOU'RE ANY BETTER OFF WITH ME?
I DON'T KNOW, BUT ANYONE WHO CAN PRODUCE A TRUNK LOAD OF ILLICIT PHARMACEUTICALS, IS MY KIND OF GUY.
CHRIST, AM I GOING TO REGRET THIS?
TO BE CONTINUED...

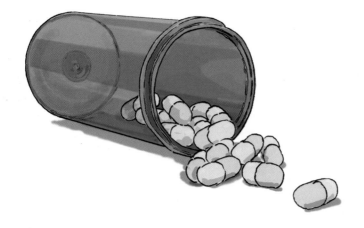

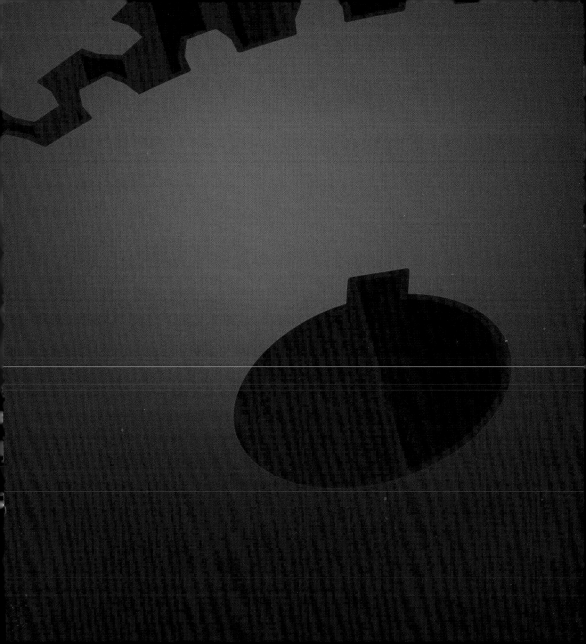

FALLUJAH

by

MANDREWS

color

KONDO

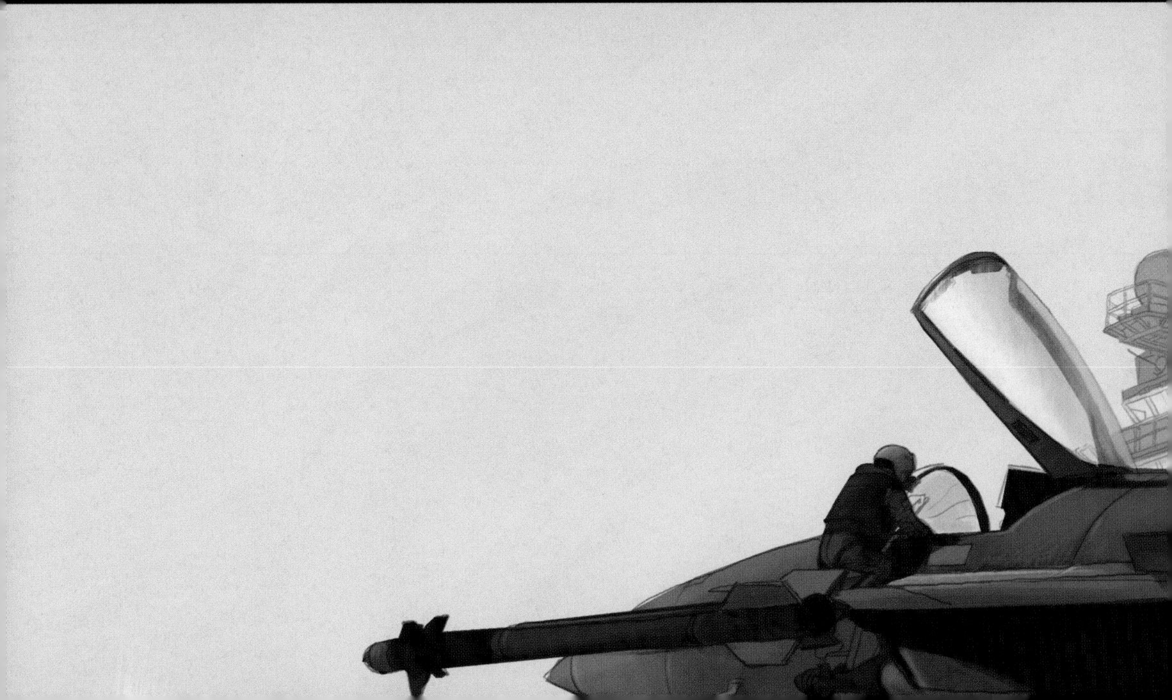

Inspired by actual events

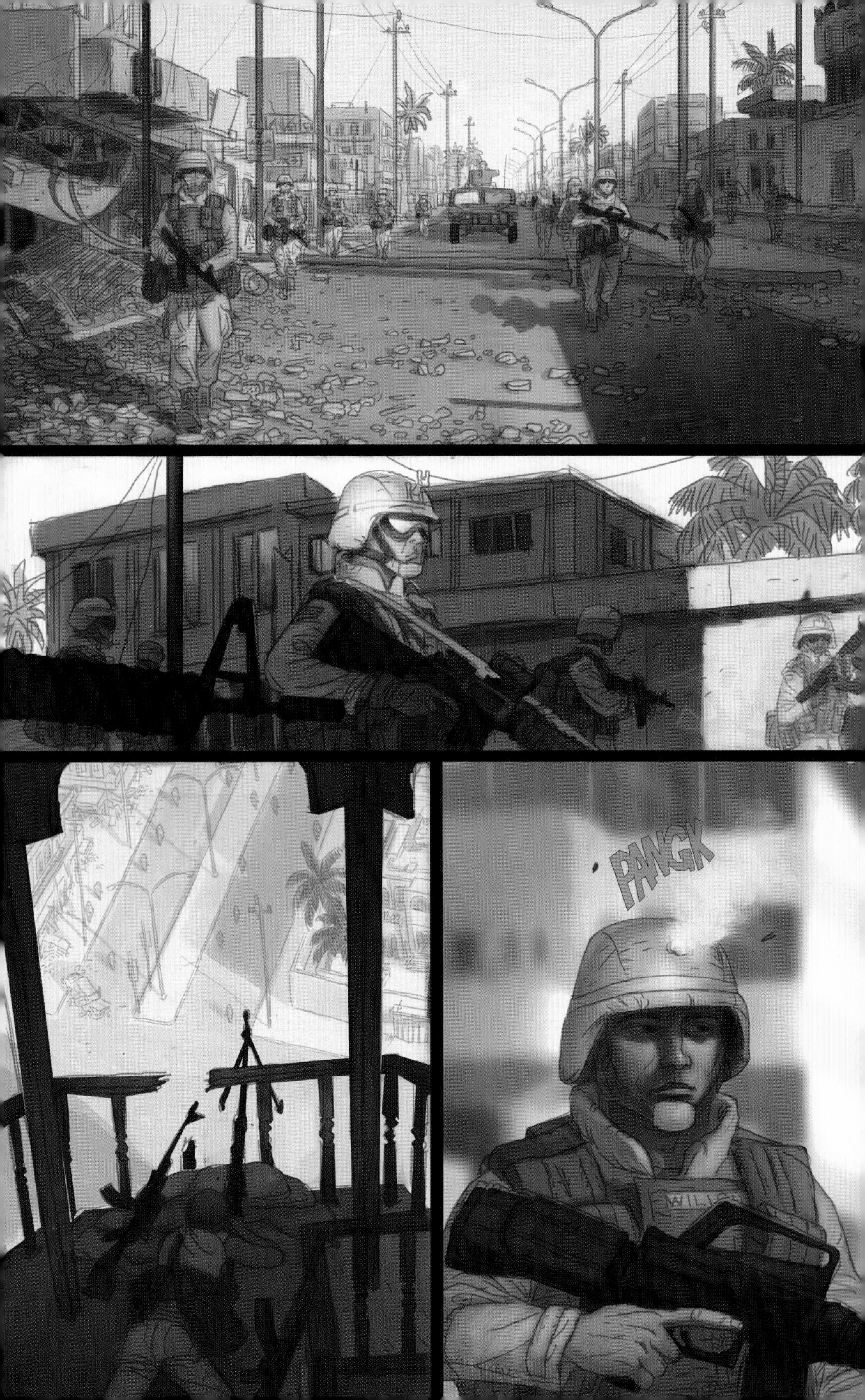
PANGK

SNIPER!

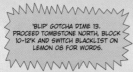

'CLICK' WARHAWK, DIME 13
CHECKING IN. UP AS FRAGGED, 1XAGM-65,
2X GBU-12, 500 ROUNDS 20MM.
PLAYTIME O + 50.

'BLIP' GOTCHA DIME 13.
PROCEED TOMBSTONE NORTH, BLOCK
10-12'K AND SWITCH BLACKLIST ON
LEMON O8 FOR WORDS.

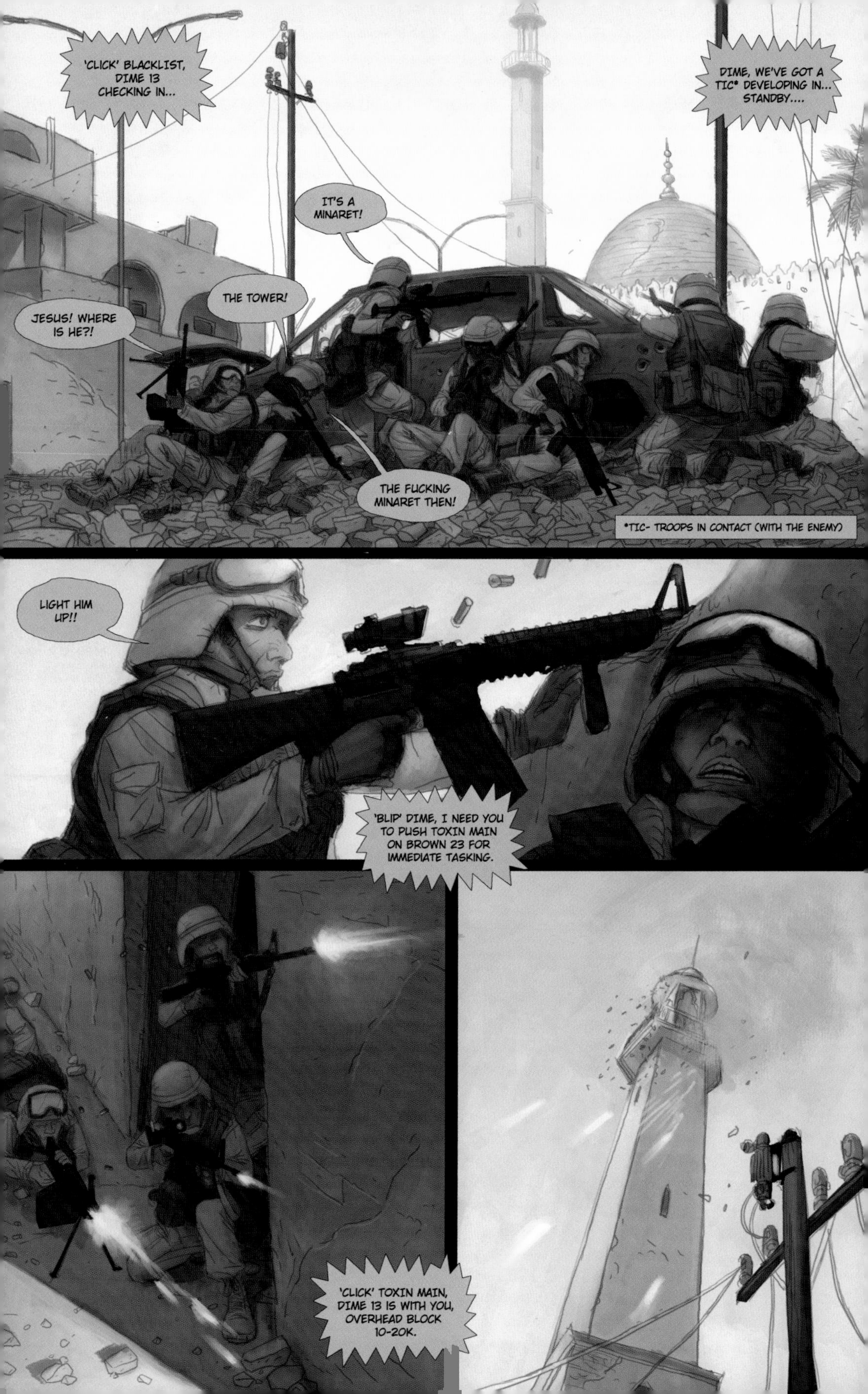

'CLICK' BLACKLIST, DIME 13 CHECKING IN...
DIME, WE'VE GOT A TIC* DEVELOPING IN... STANDBY....
IT'S A MINARET!
THE TOWER!
JESUS! WHERE IS HE?!
THE FUCKING MINARET THEN!
*TIC- TROOPS IN CONTACT (WITH THE ENEMY)
LIGHT HIM UP!!
'BLIP' DIME, I NEED YOU TO PUSH TOXIN MAIN ON BROWN 23 FOR IMMEDIATE TASKING.
'CLICK' TOXIN MAIN, DIME 13 IS WITH YOU, OVERHEAD BLOCK 10-20K.

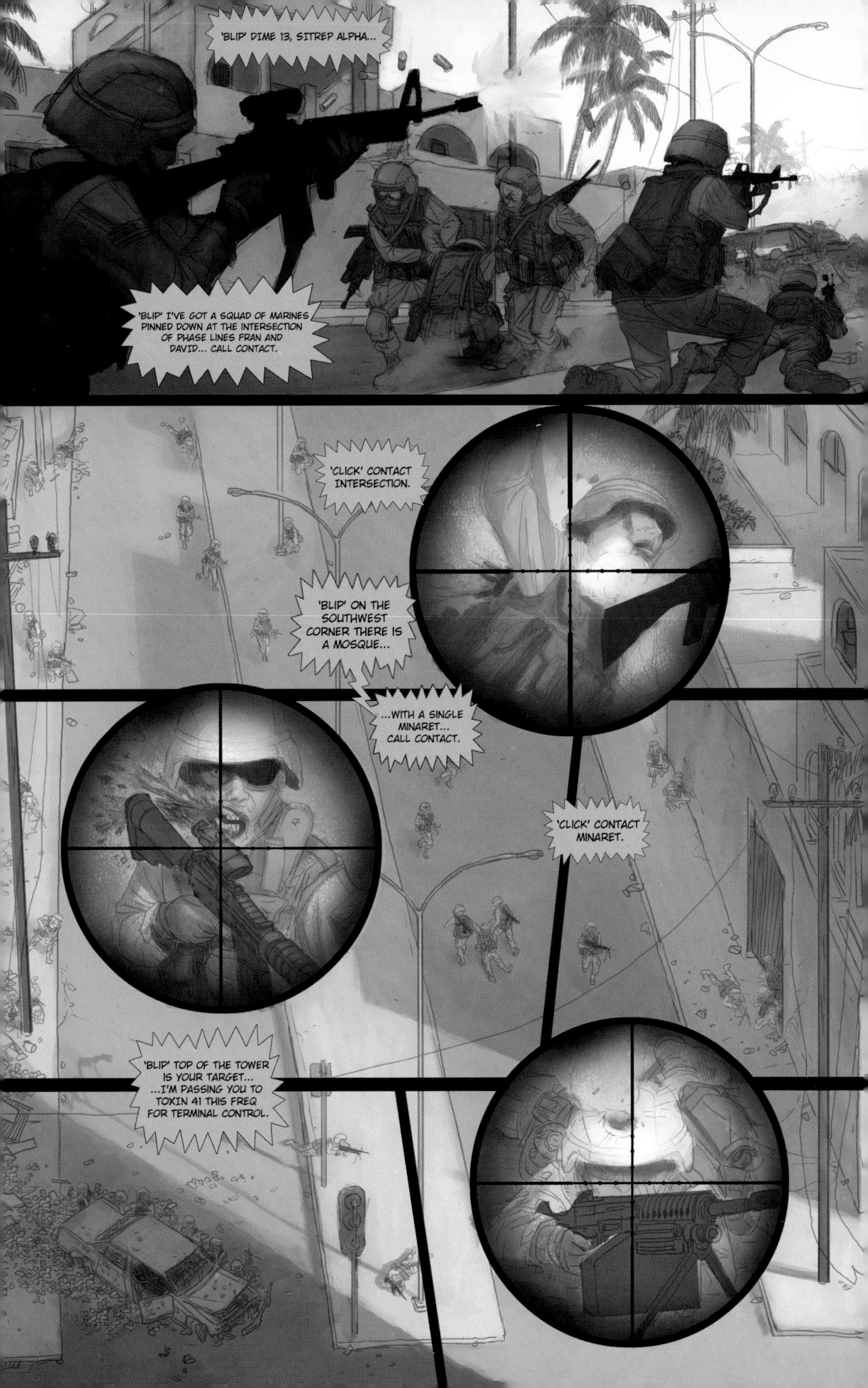
'BLIP' DIME 13, SITREP ALPHA...
'BLIP' I'VE GOT A SQUAD OF MARINES PINNED DOWN AT THE INTERSECTION OF PHASE LINES FRAN AND DAVID... CALL CONTACT.
'CLICK' CONTACT INTERSECTION.
'BLIP' ON THE SOUTHWEST CORNER THERE IS A MOSQUE...
...WITH A SINGLE MINARET... CALL CONTACT.
'CLICK' CONTACT MINARET.
'BLIP' TOP OF THE TOWER IS YOUR TARGET... ...I'M PASSING YOU TO TOXIN 41 THIS FREQ FOR TERMINAL CONTROL.

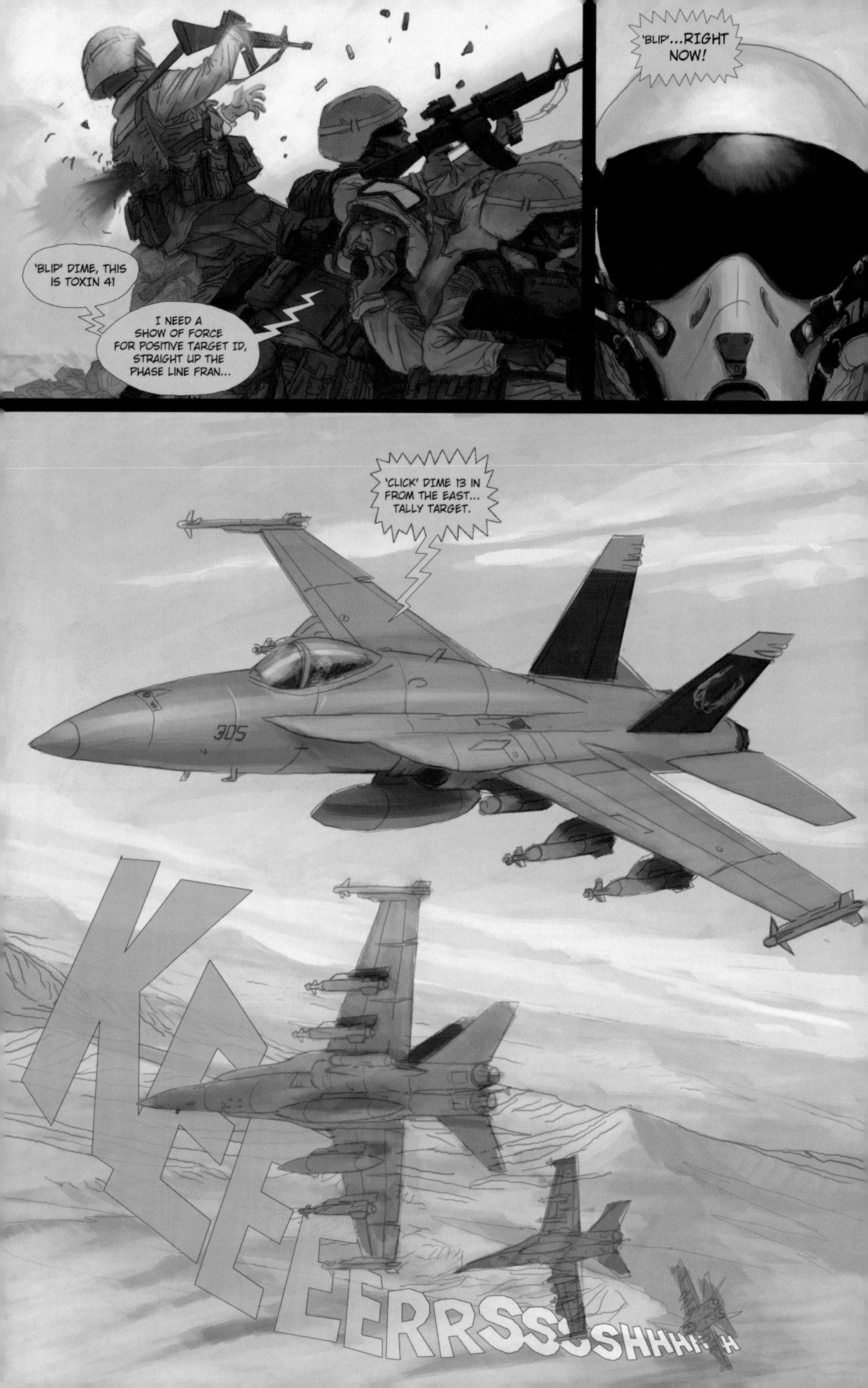
'BLIP' DIME, THIS IS TOXIN 41
I NEED A SHOW OF FORCE FOR POSITIVE TARGET ID, STRAIGHT UP THE PHASE LINE FRAN...
'BLIP'...RIGHT NOW!
'CLICK' DIME 13 IN FROM THE EAST... TALLY TARGET.

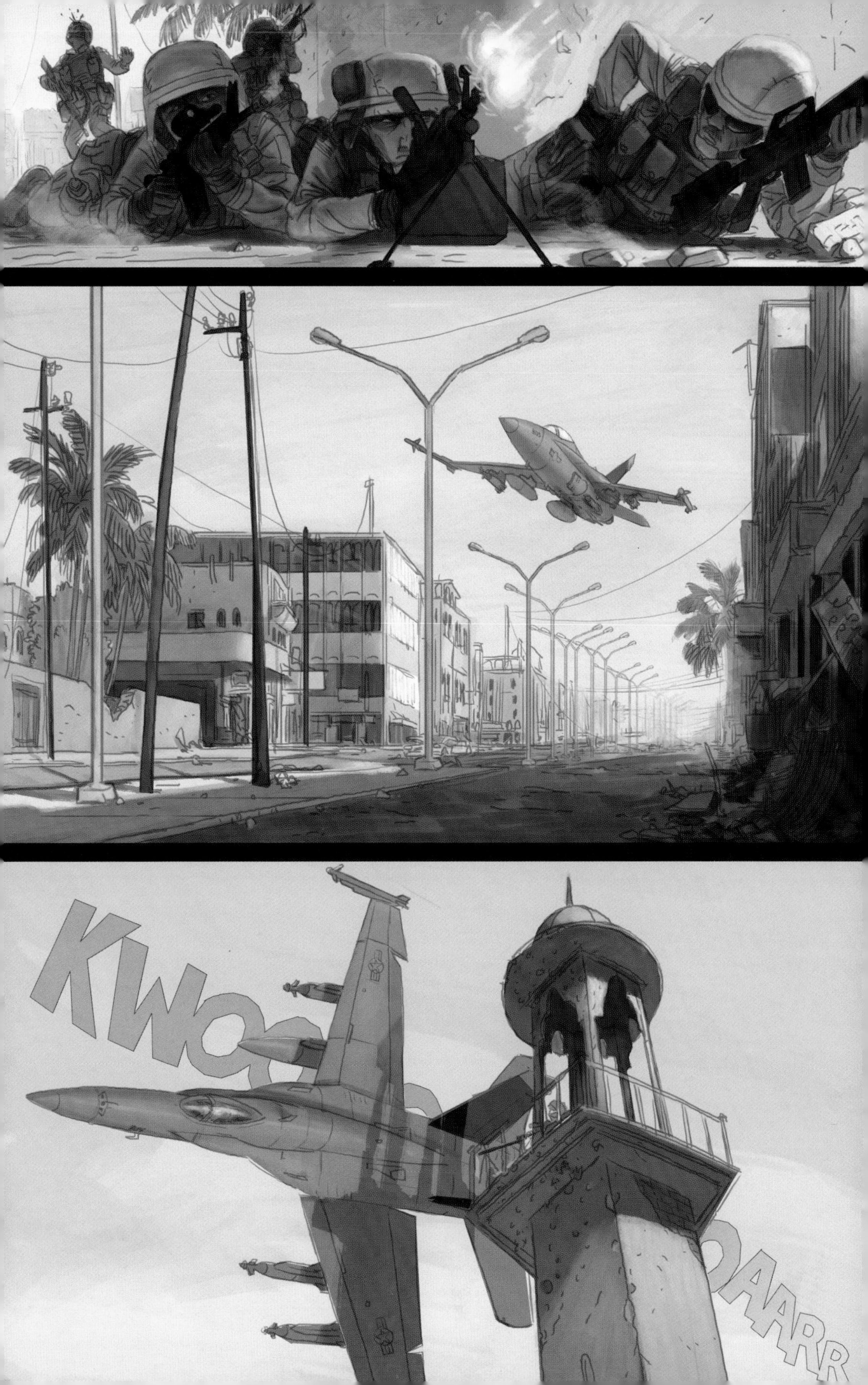
KWO
OAARR

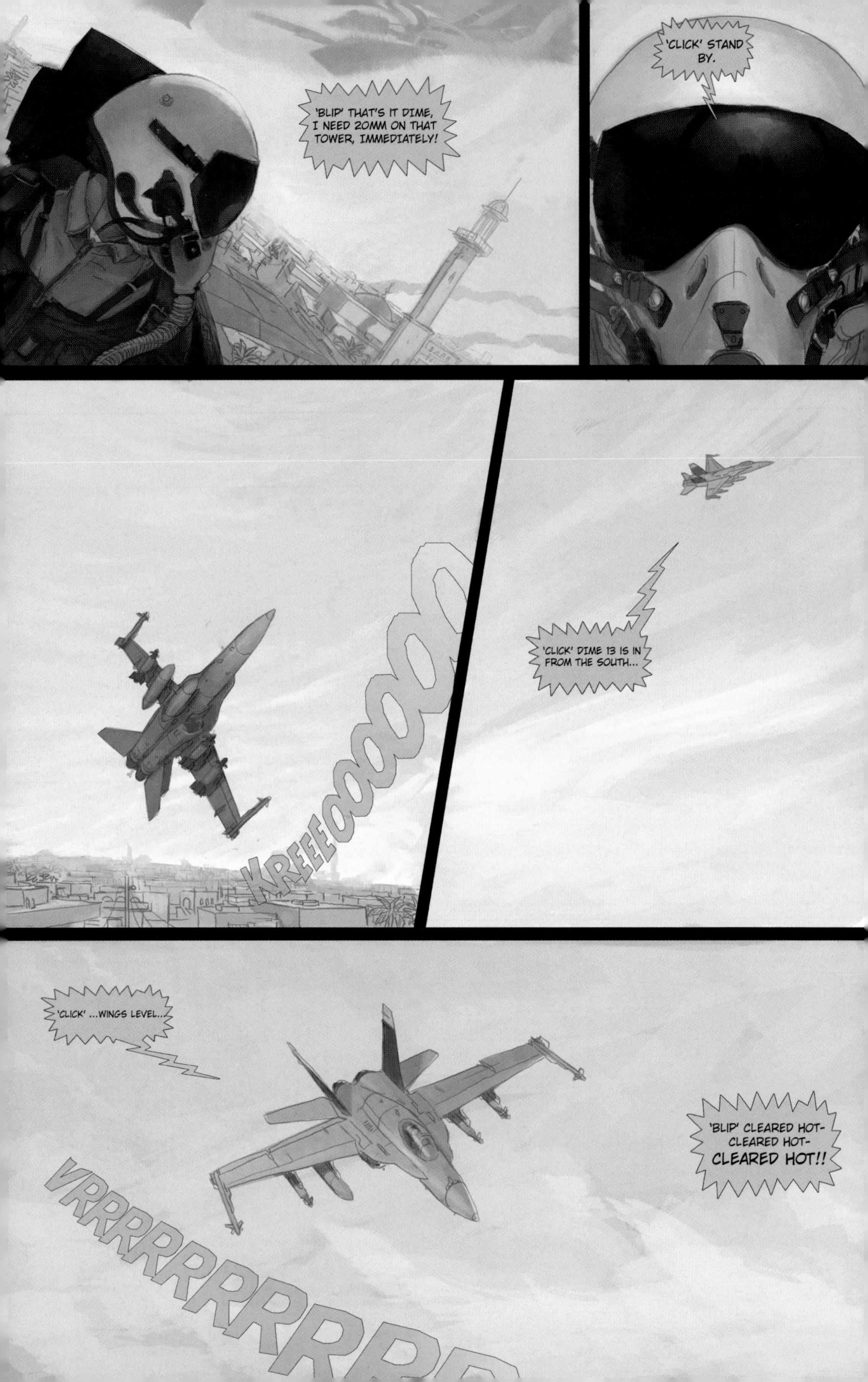
'BLIP' THAT'S IT DIME, I NEED 20MM ON THAT TOWER, IMMEDIATELY!
'CLICK' STAND BY.
KREEEOOOOOOO
'CLICK' DIME 13 IS IN FROM THE SOUTH...
'CLICK' ...WINGS LEVEL...
'BLIP' CLEARED HOT- CLEARED HOT- CLEARED HOT!!
VRRRRRRRRRRR

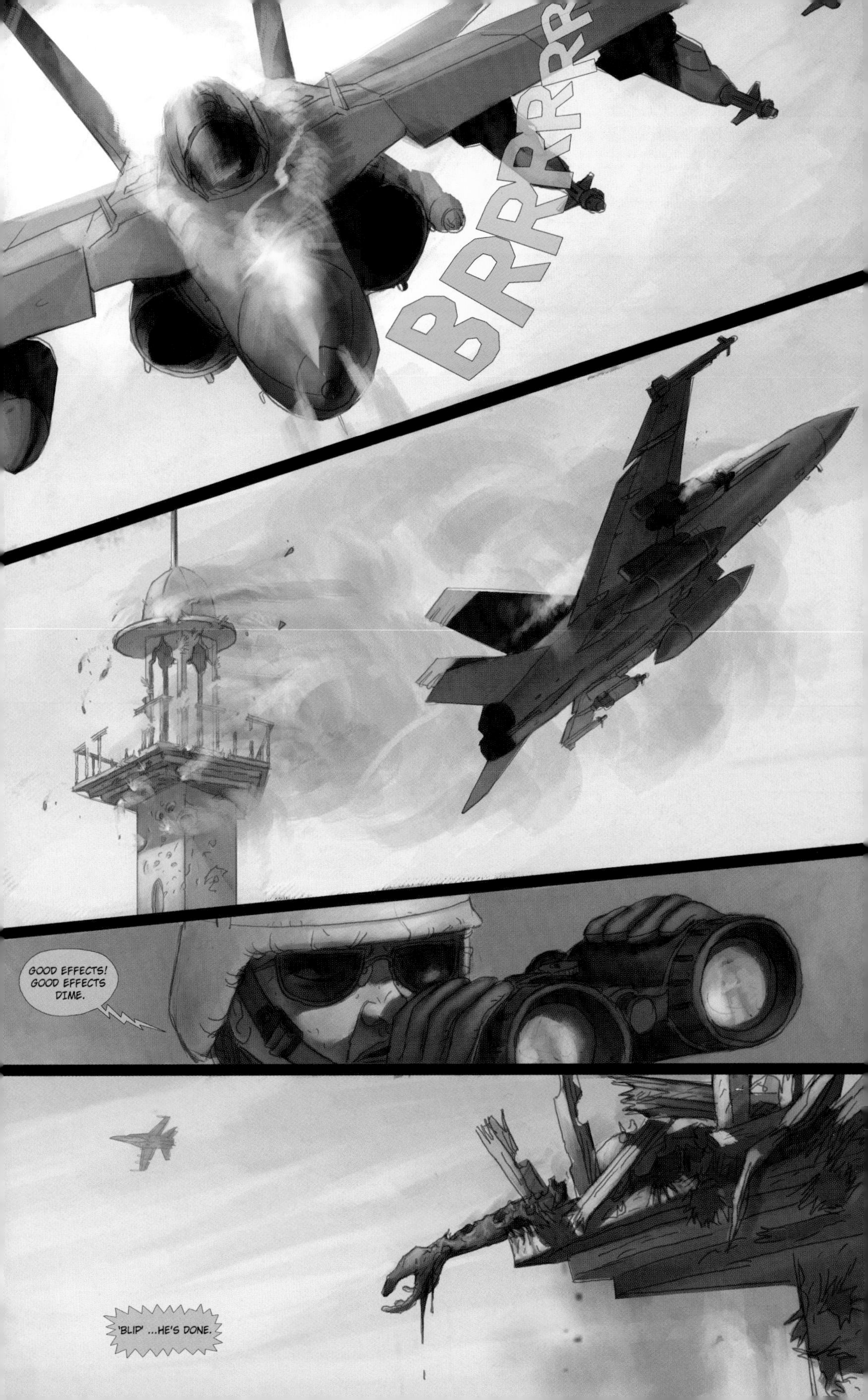
BRRRRRRRR
GOOD EFFECTS! GOOD EFFECTS DIME.
'BLIP' ...HE'S DONE.

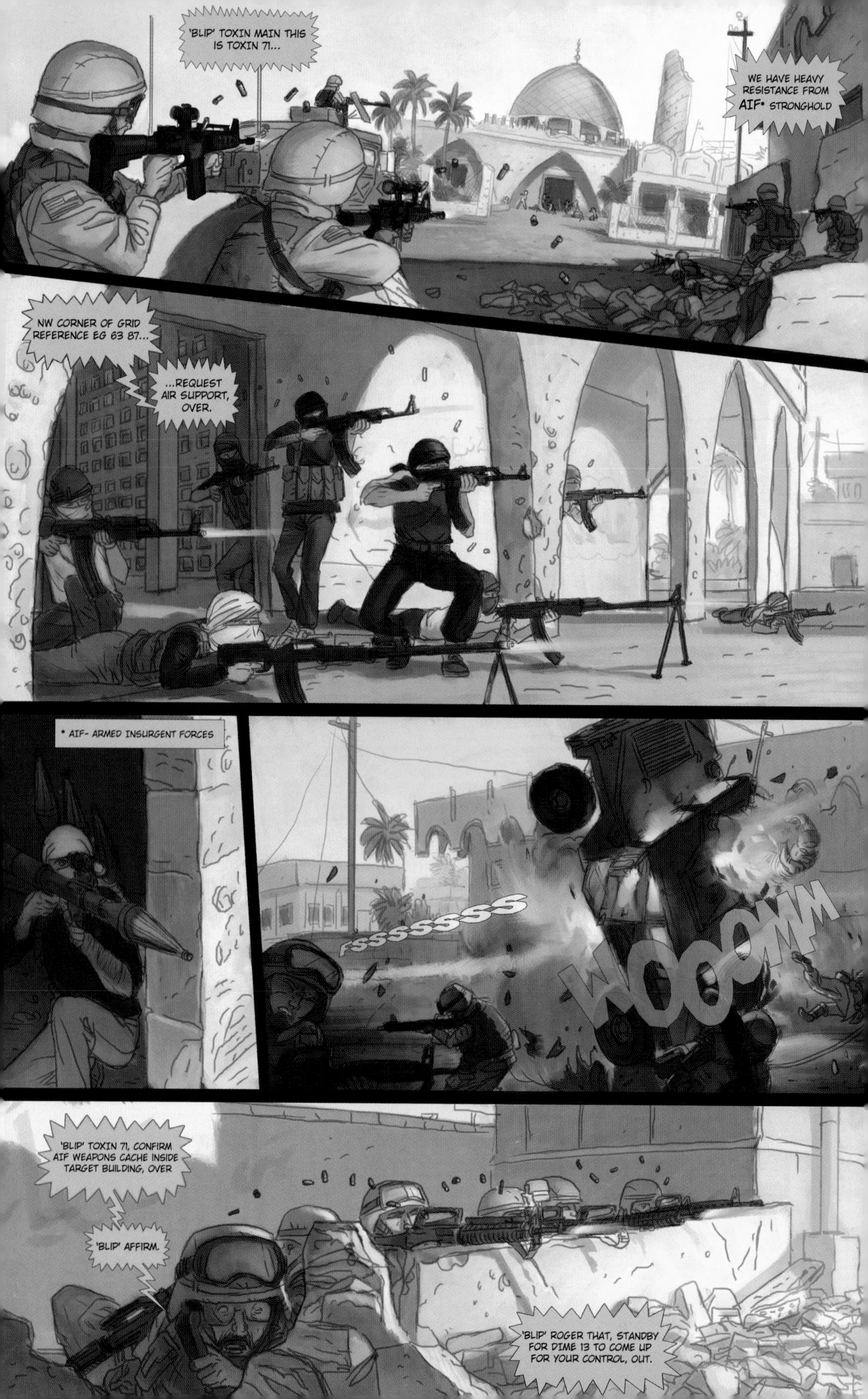
'BLIP' TOXIN MAIN THIS IS TOXIN 71...
WE HAVE HEAVY RESISTANCE FROM AIF* STRONGHOLD
NW CORNER OF GRID REFERENCE EG 63 87...
...REQUEST AIR SUPPORT, OVER.
* AIF- ARMED INSURGENT FORCES
FSSSSSSSS
WOOOMM
'BLIP' TOXIN 71, CONFIRM AIF WEAPONS CACHE INSIDE TARGET BUILDING, OVER
'BLIP' AFFIRM.
'BLIP' ROGER THAT, STANDBY FOR DIME 13 TO COME UP FOR YOUR CONTROL, OUT.

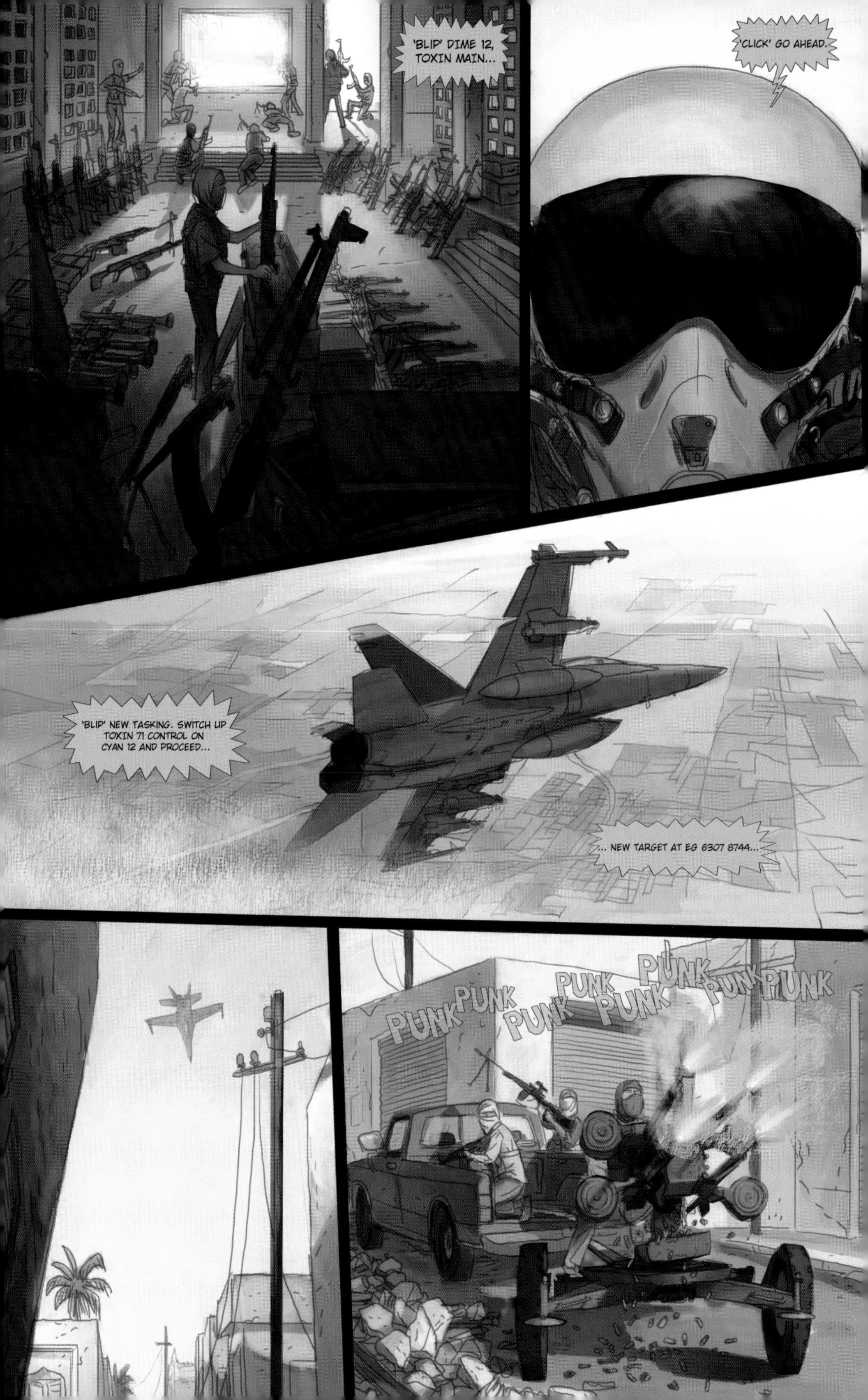
'BLIP' DIME 12, TOXIN MAIN...
'CLICK' GO AHEAD.
'BLIP' NEW TASKING. SWITCH UP TOXIN 71 CONTROL ON CYAN 12 AND PROCEED...
... NEW TARGET AT EG 6307 8744...
PUNK PUNK PUNK PUNK PUNK PUNK PUNK PUNK

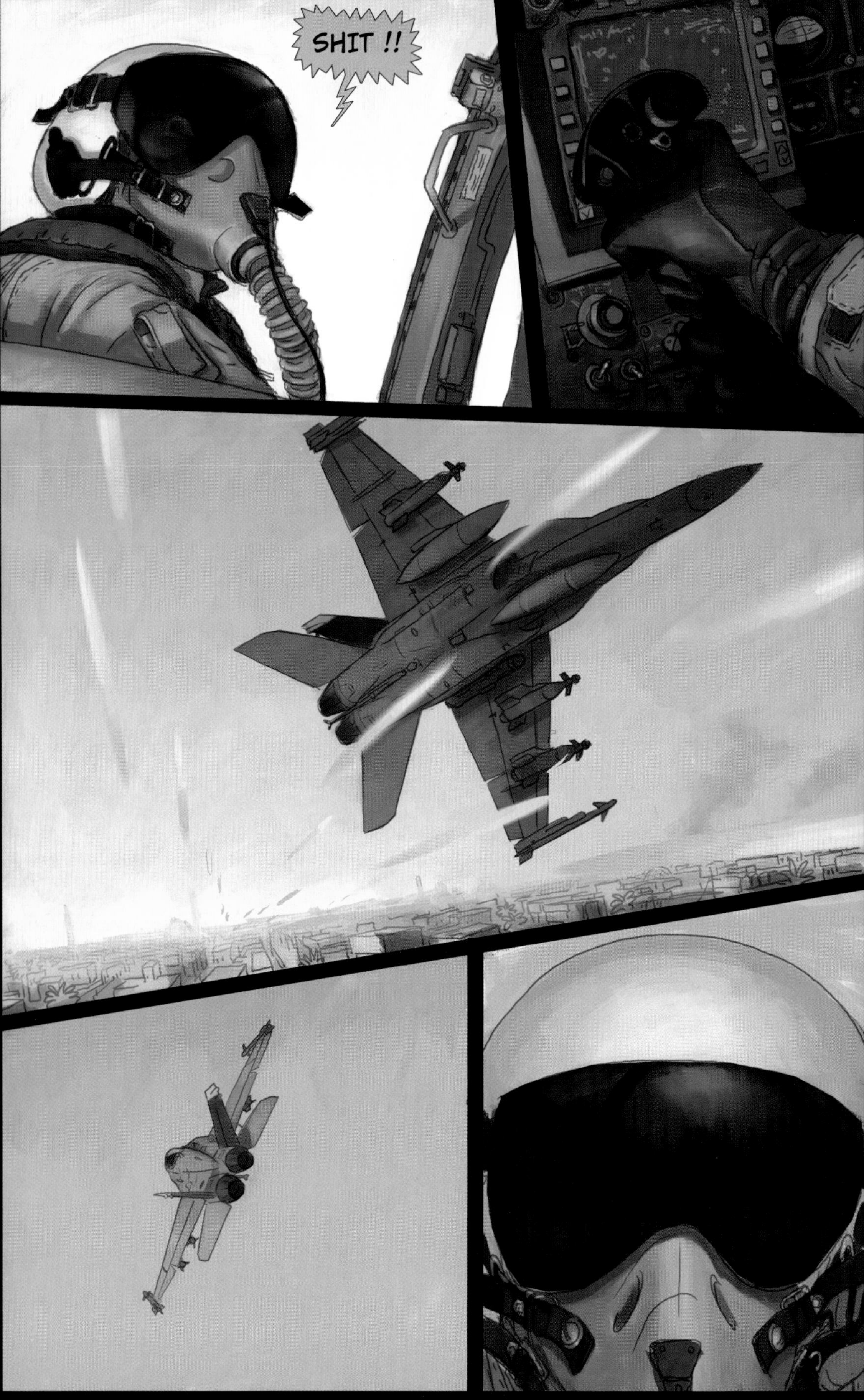
SHIT !!

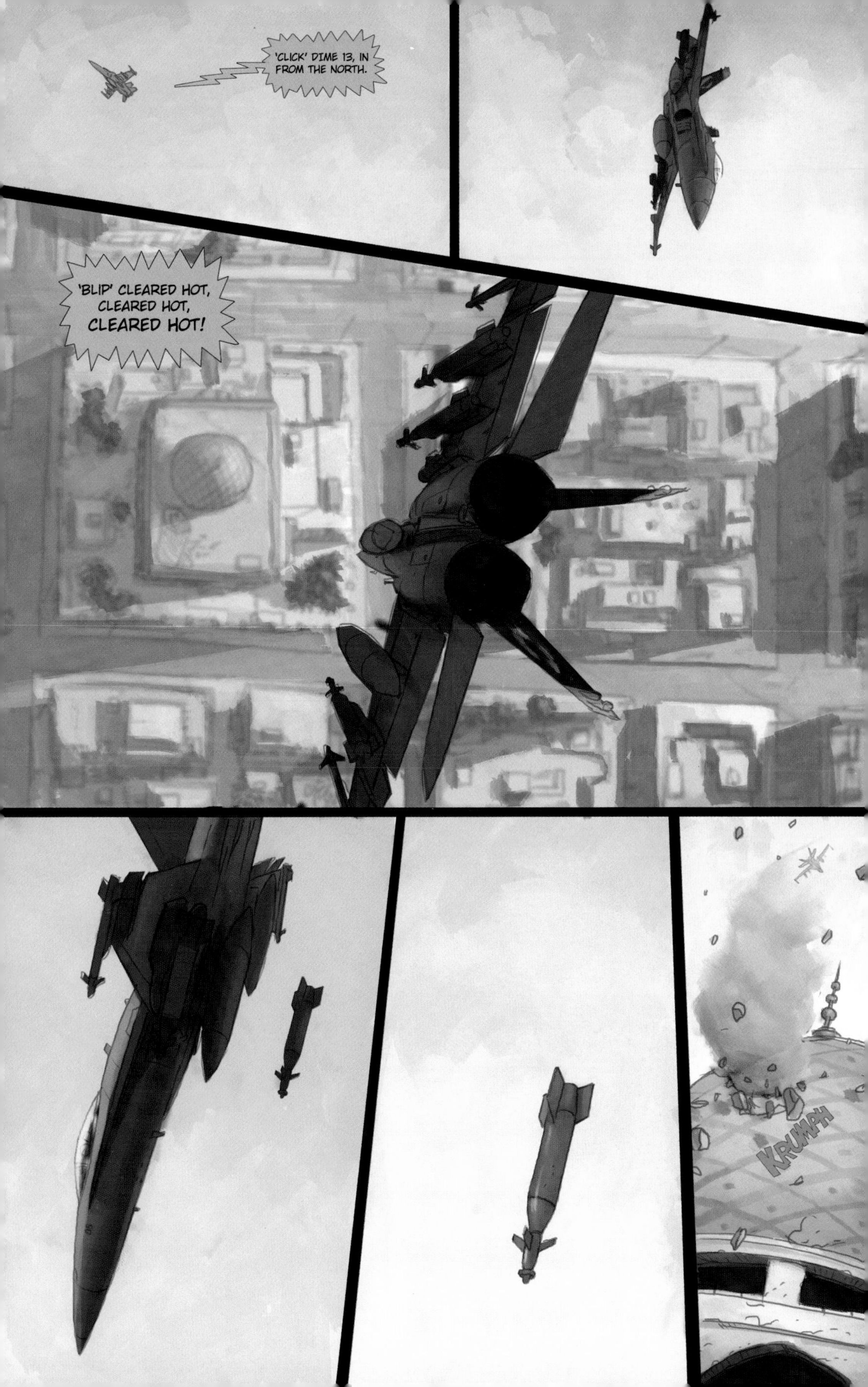
'CLICK' DIME 13, IN FROM THE NORTH.
'BLIP' CLEARED HOT, CLEARED HOT, CLEARED HOT!
KRUMPH

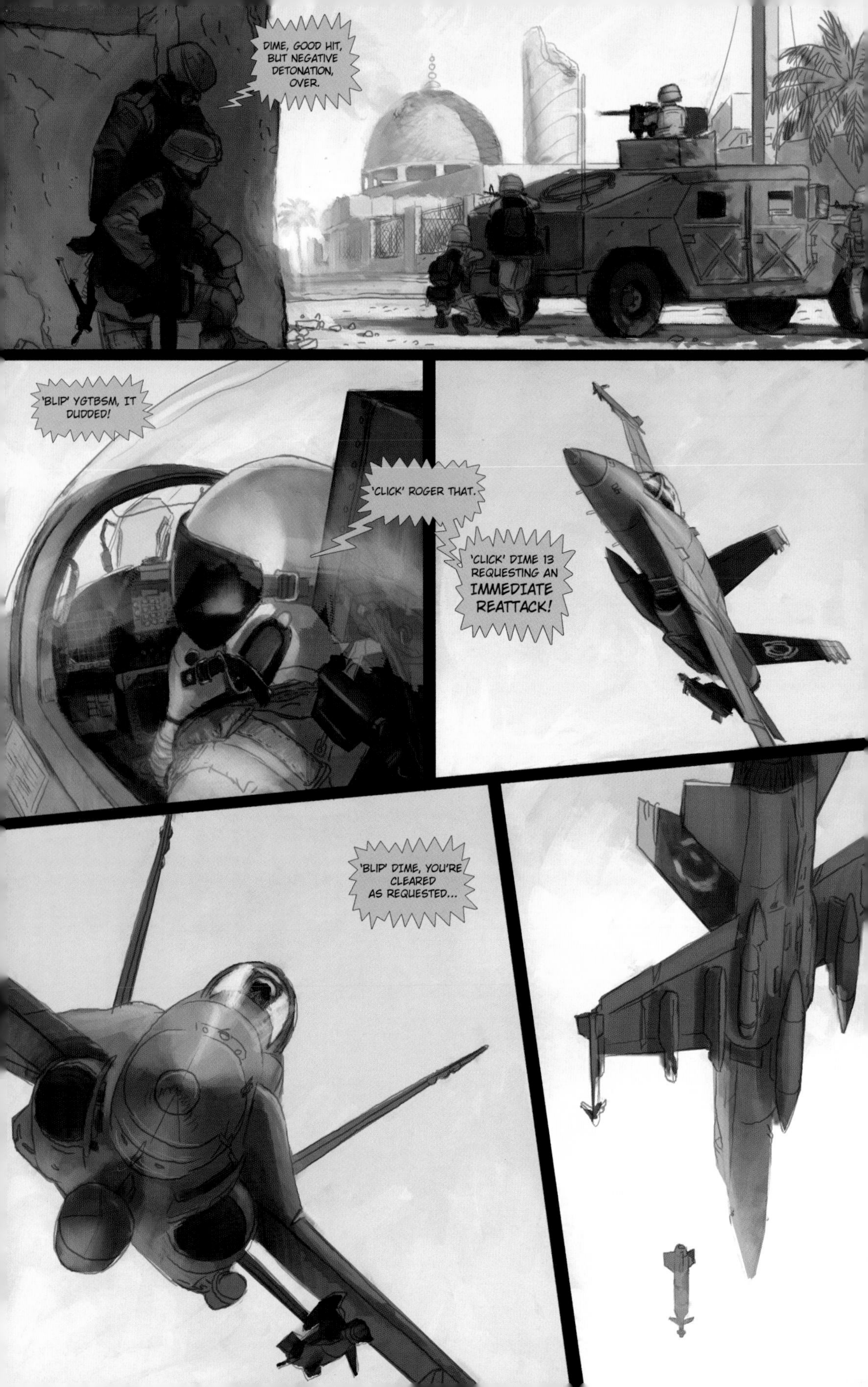
DIME, GOOD HIT, BUT NEGATIVE DETONATION, OVER.
'BLIP' YGTBSM, IT DUDDED!
'CLICK' ROGER THAT.
'CLICK' DIME 13 REQUESTING AN IMMEDIATE REATTACK!
'BLIP' DIME, YOU'RE CLEARED AS REQUESTED...

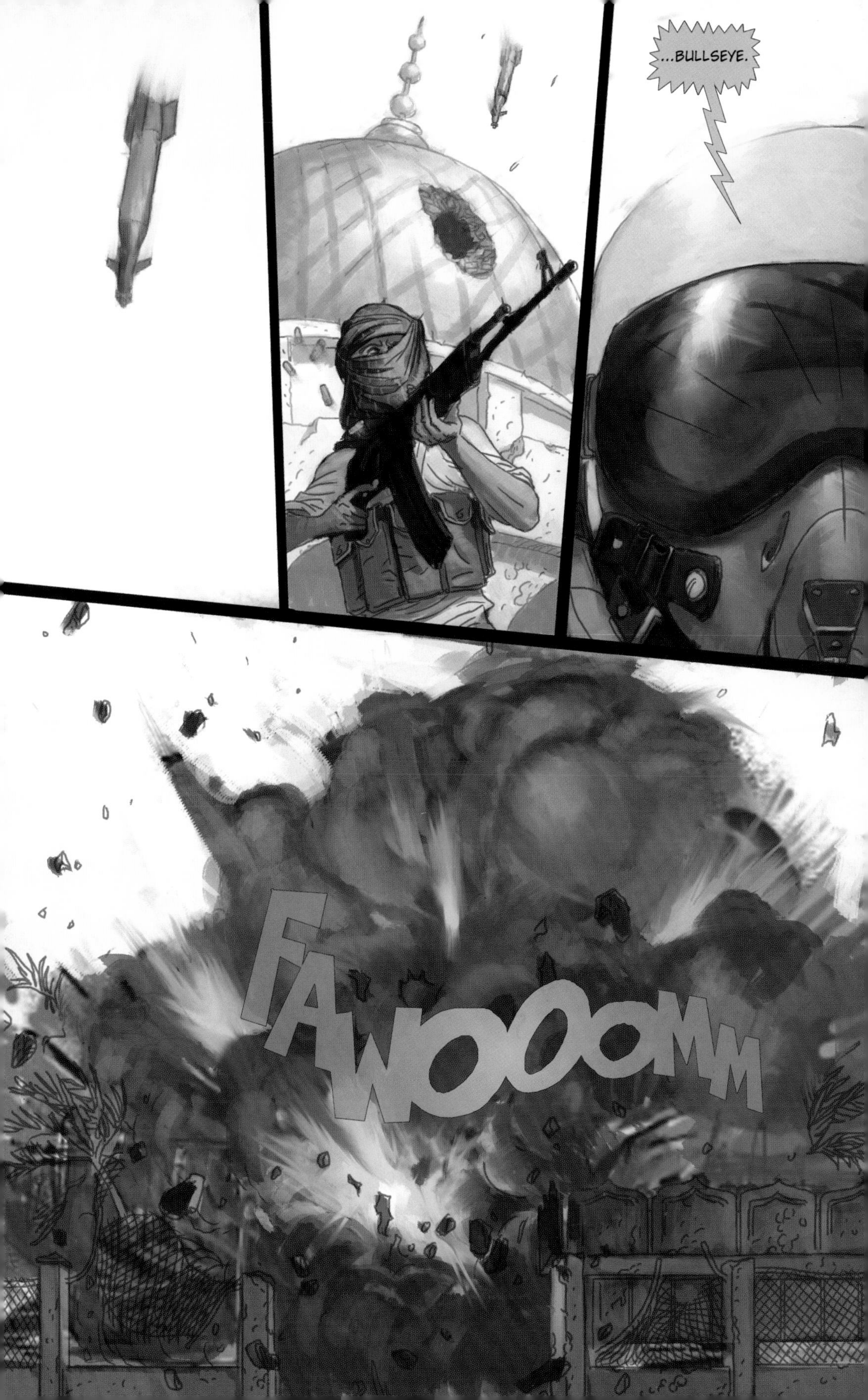
...BULLSEYE.
FAWOOOMM

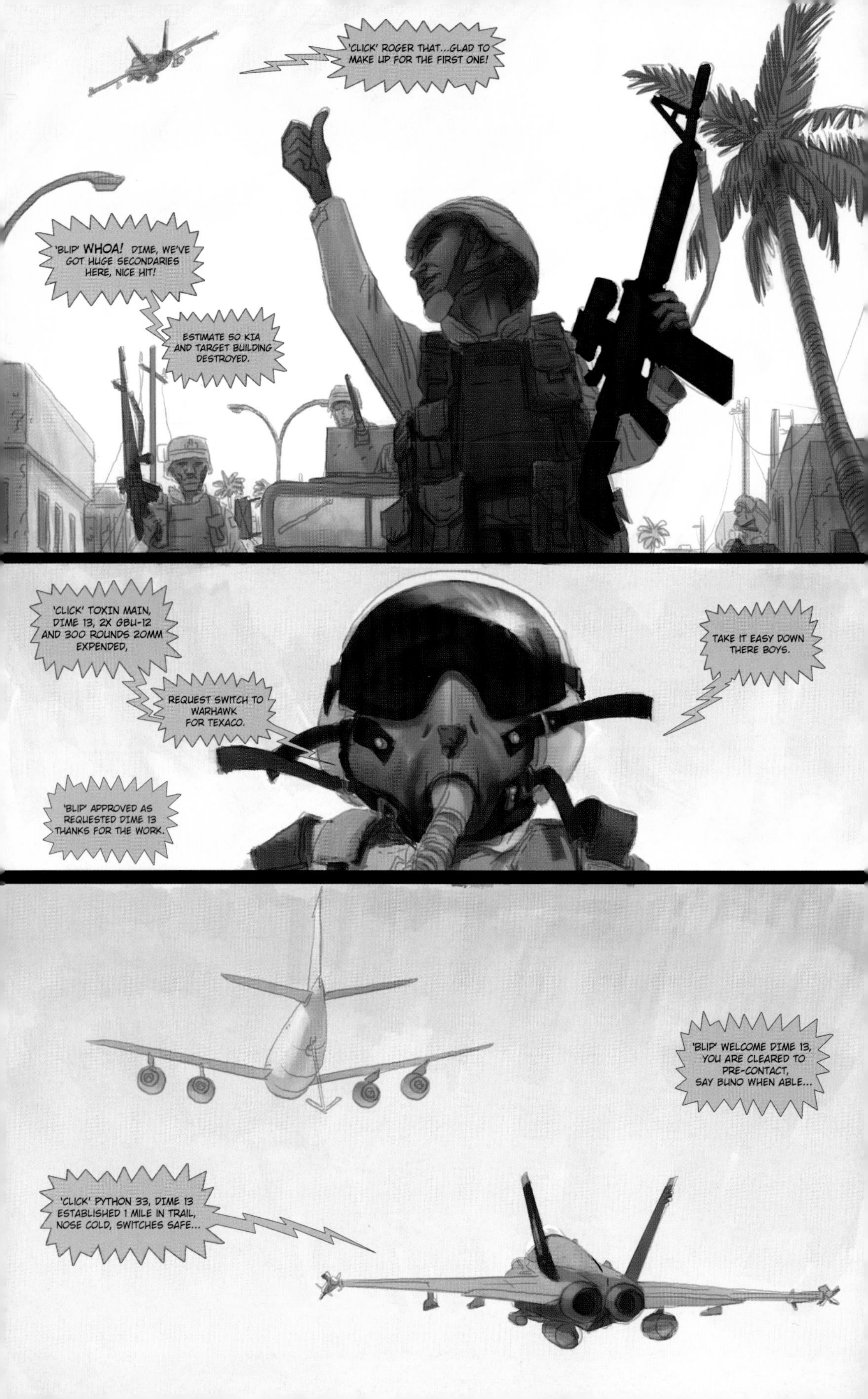
'CLICK' ROGER THAT...GLAD TO MAKE UP FOR THE FIRST ONE!
'BLIP' WHOA! DIME, WE'VE GOT HUGE SECONDARIES HERE, NICE HIT!
ESTIMATE 50 KIA AND TARGET BUILDING DESTROYED.
'CLICK' TOXIN MAIN, DIME 13, 2X GBU-12 AND 300 ROUNDS 20MM EXPENDED,
REQUEST SWITCH TO WARHAWK FOR TEXACO.
TAKE IT EASY DOWN THERE BOYS.
'BLIP' APPROVED AS REQUESTED DIME 13 THANKS FOR THE WORK.
'BLIP' WELCOME DIME 13, YOU ARE CLEARED TO PRE-CONTACT, SAY BUNO WHEN ABLE...
'CLICK' PYTHON 33, DIME 13 ESTABLISHED 1 MILE IN TRAIL, NOSE COLD, SWITCHES SAFE...

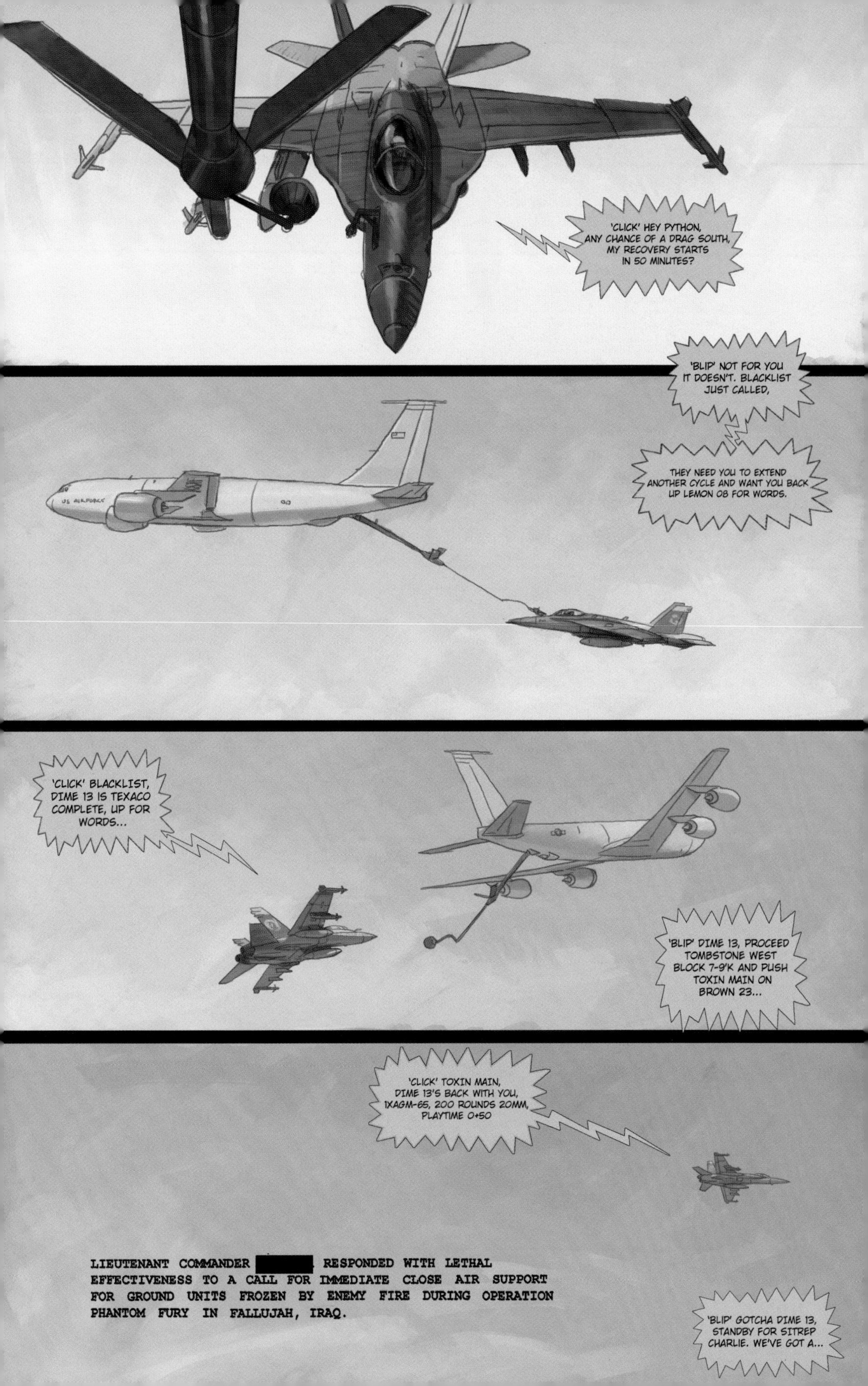
'CLICK' HEY PYTHON, ANY CHANCE OF A DRAG SOUTH, MY RECOVERY STARTS IN 50 MINUTES?
'BLIP' NOT FOR YOU IT DOESN'T. BLACKLIST JUST CALLED,
THEY NEED YOU TO EXTEND ANOTHER CYCLE AND WANT YOU BACK UP LEMON 08 FOR WORDS.
'CLICK' BLACKLIST, DIME 13 IS TEXACO COMPLETE, UP FOR WORDS...
'BLIP' DIME 13, PROCEED TOMBSTONE WEST BLOCK 7-9'K AND PUSH TOXIN MAIN ON BROWN 23...
'CLICK' TOXIN MAIN, DIME 13'S BACK WITH YOU, 1XAGM-65, 200 ROUNDS 20MM, PLAYTIME 0+50
LIEUTENANT COMMANDER [redacted] RESPONDED WITH LETHAL EFFECTIVENESS TO A CALL FOR IMMEDIATE CLOSE AIR SUPPORT FOR GROUND UNITS FROZEN BY ENEMY FIRE DURING OPERATION PHANTOM FURY IN FALLUJAH, IRAQ.
'BLIP' GOTCHA DIME 13, STANDBY FOR SITREP CHARLIE. WE'VE GOT A...

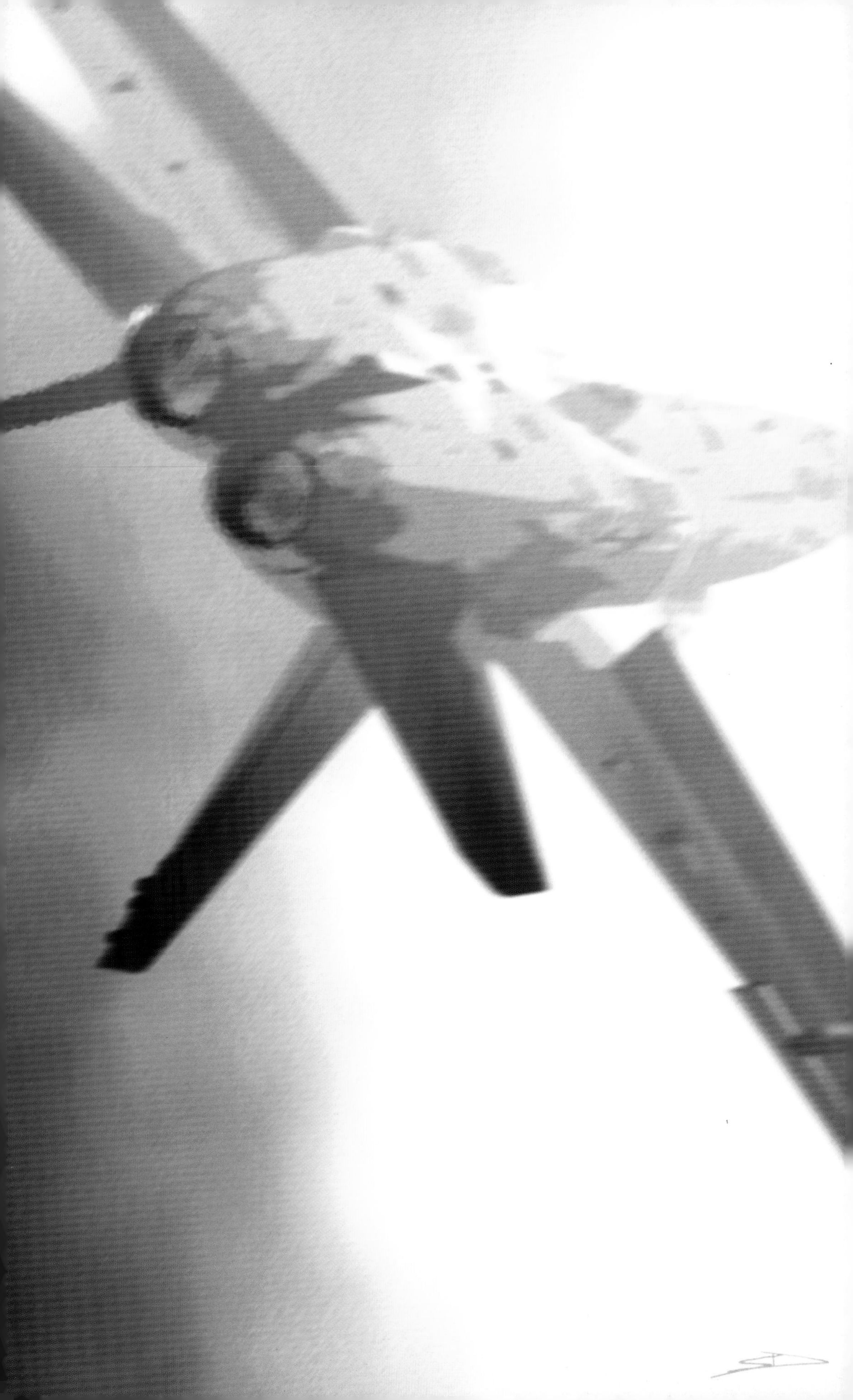

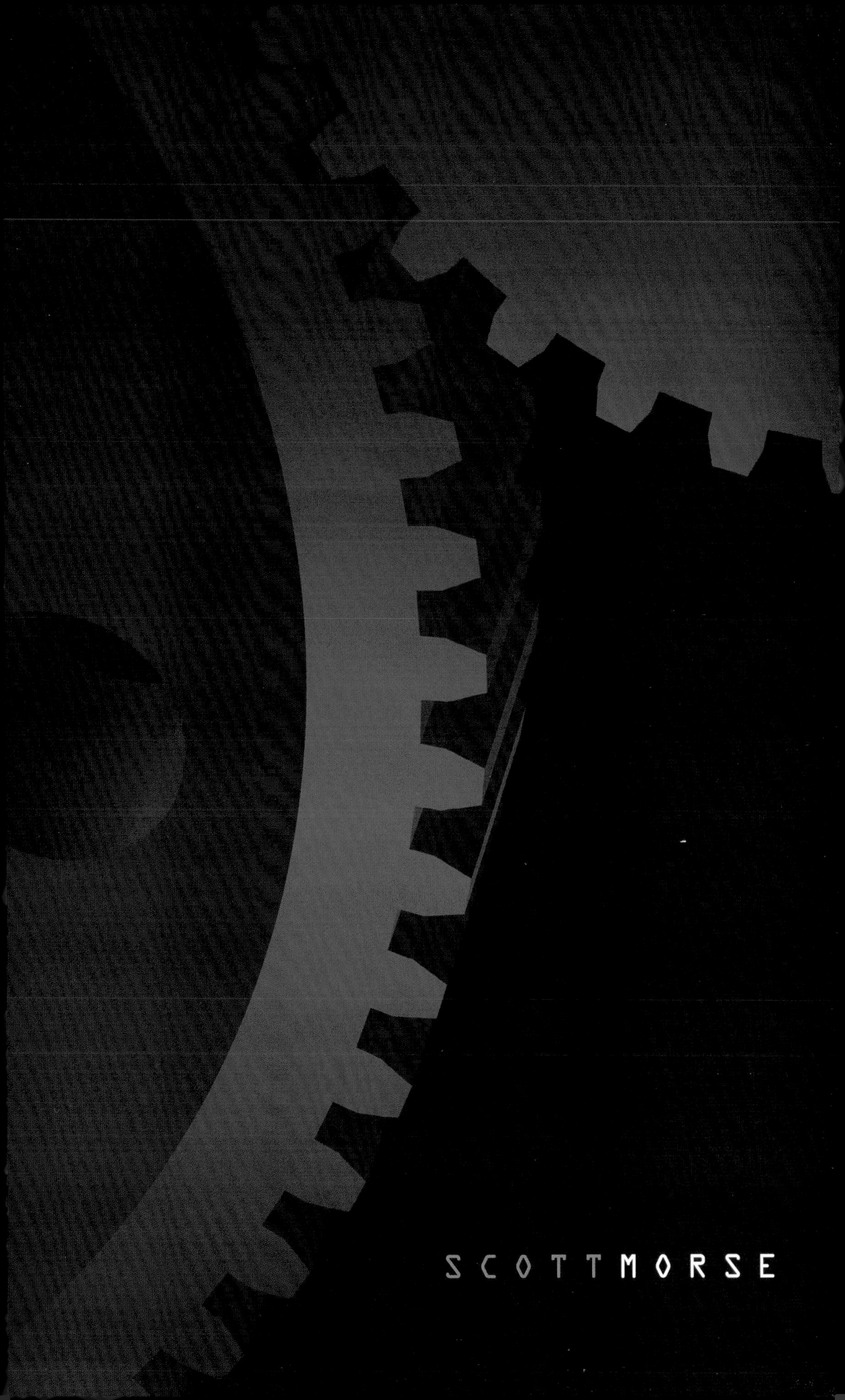
SCOTT MORSE

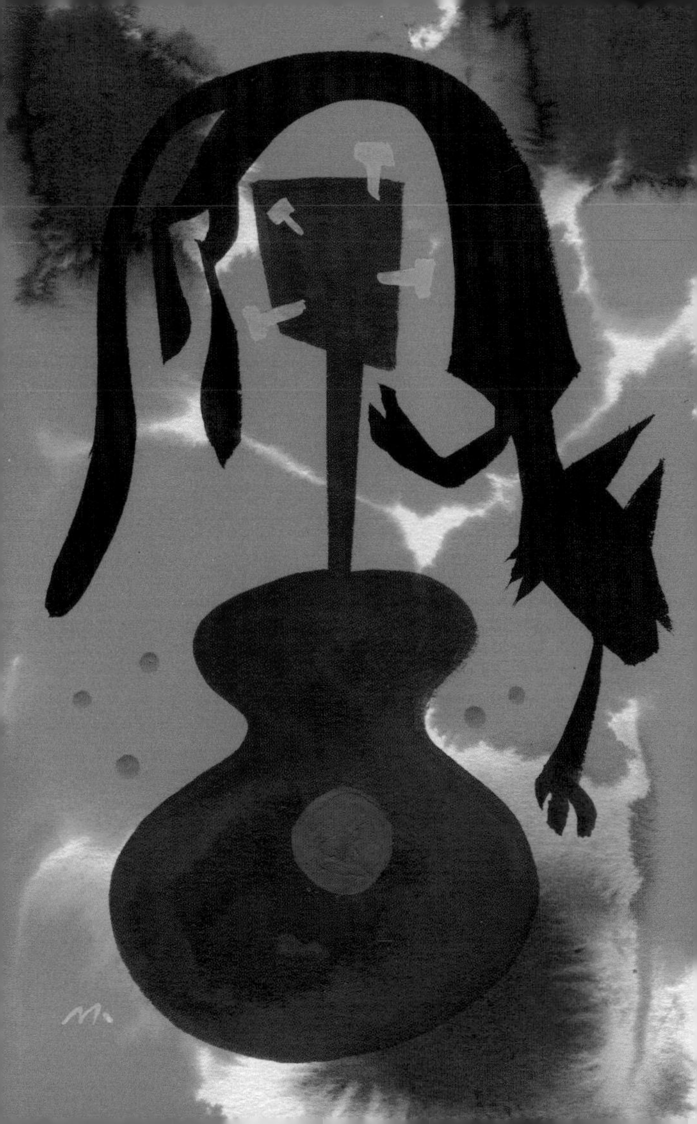

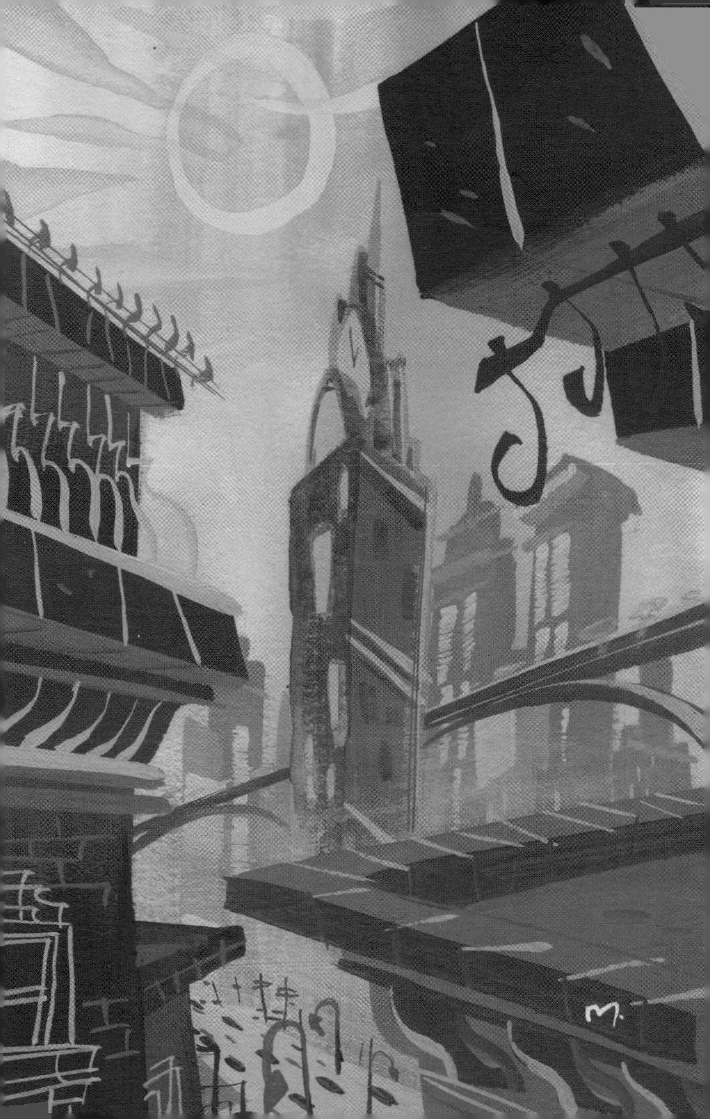
M.

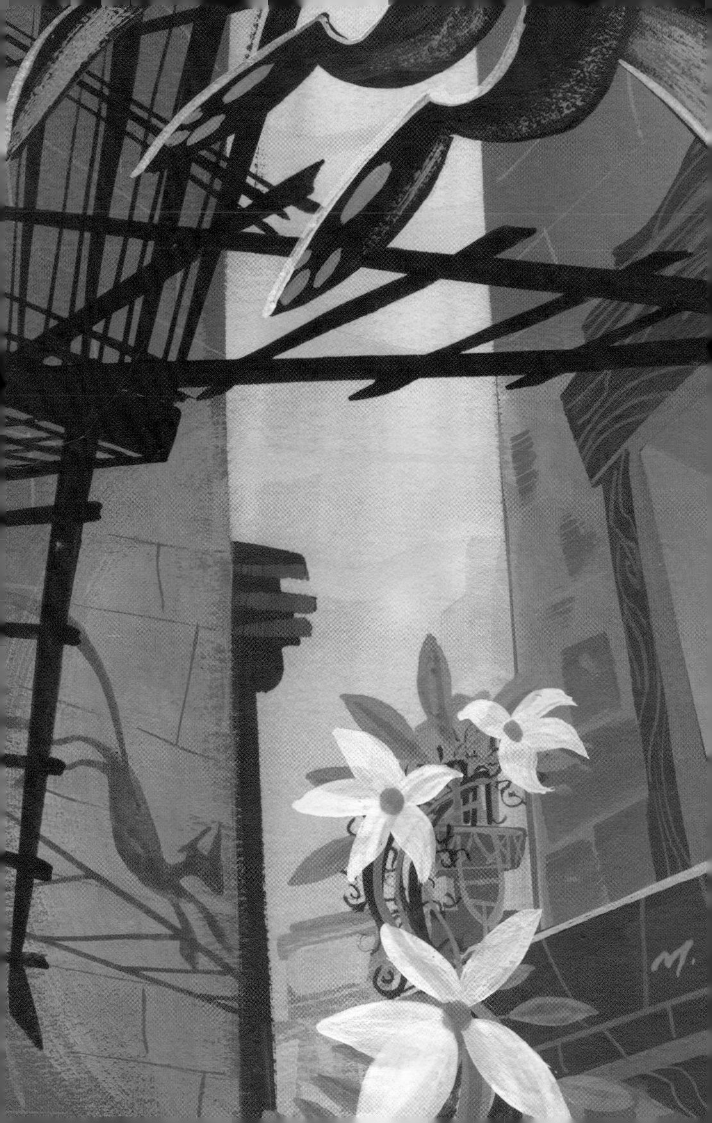

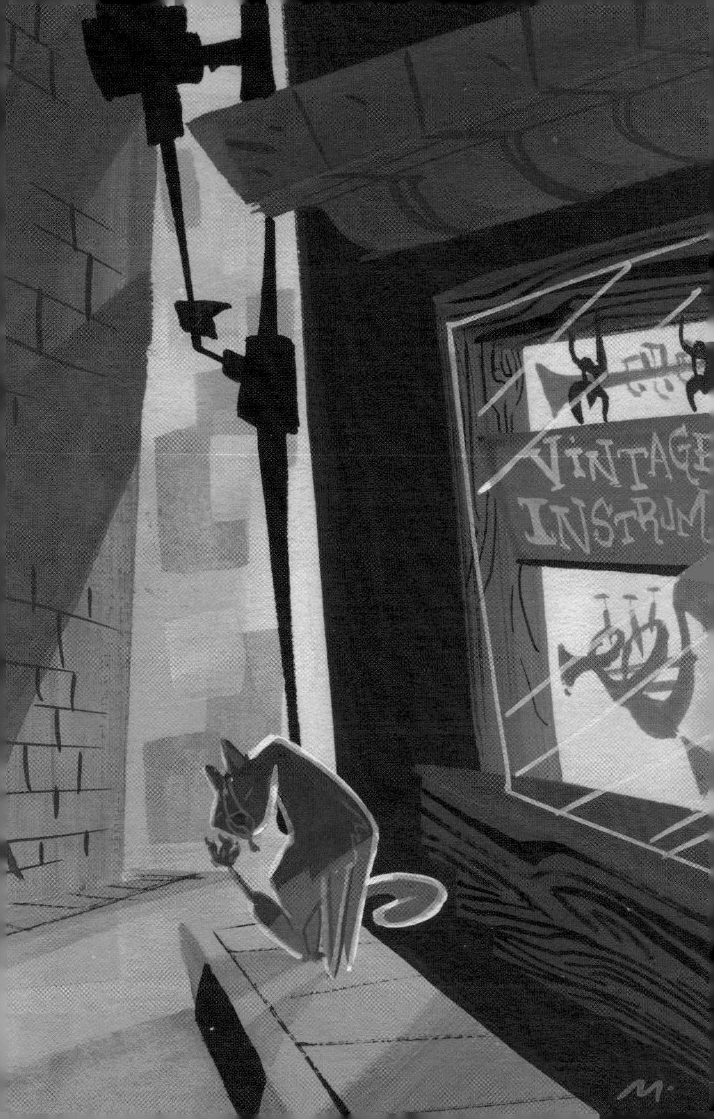
VINTAGE
INSTRUM

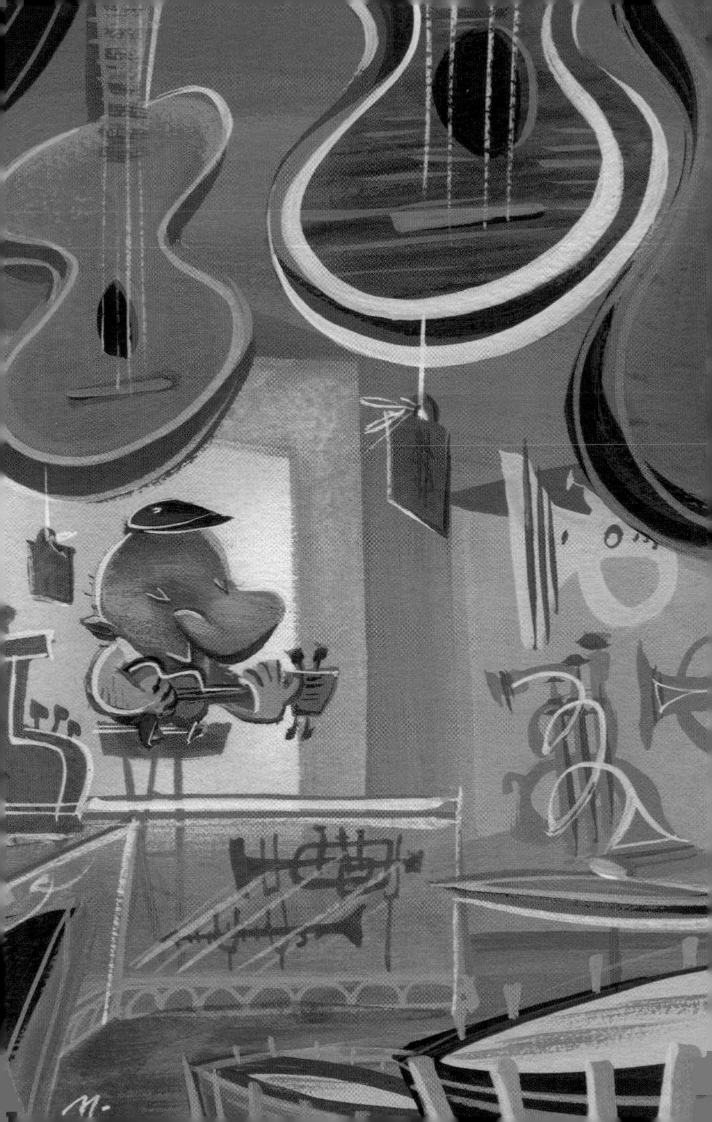

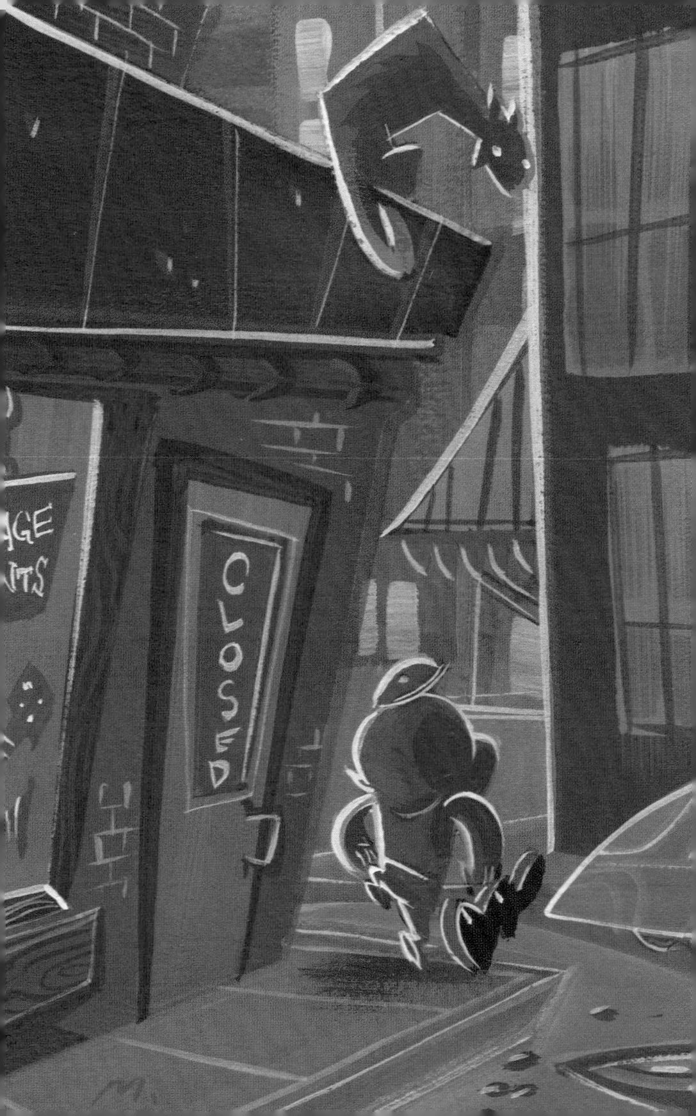
CLOSED

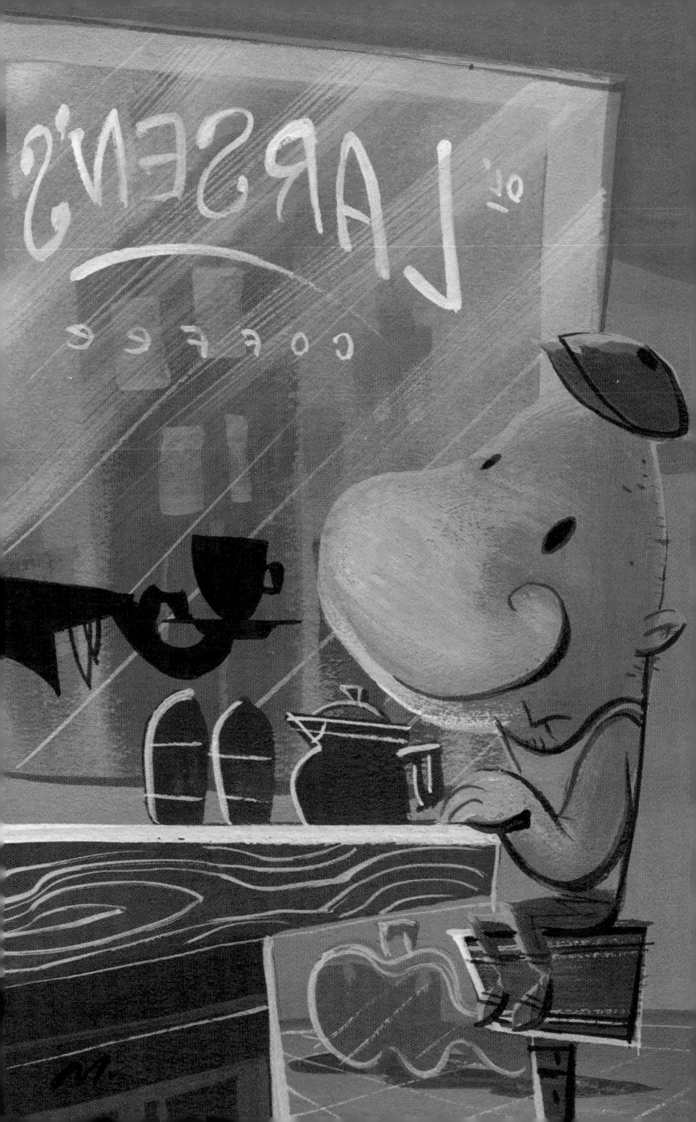
LARSEN'S
COFFEE

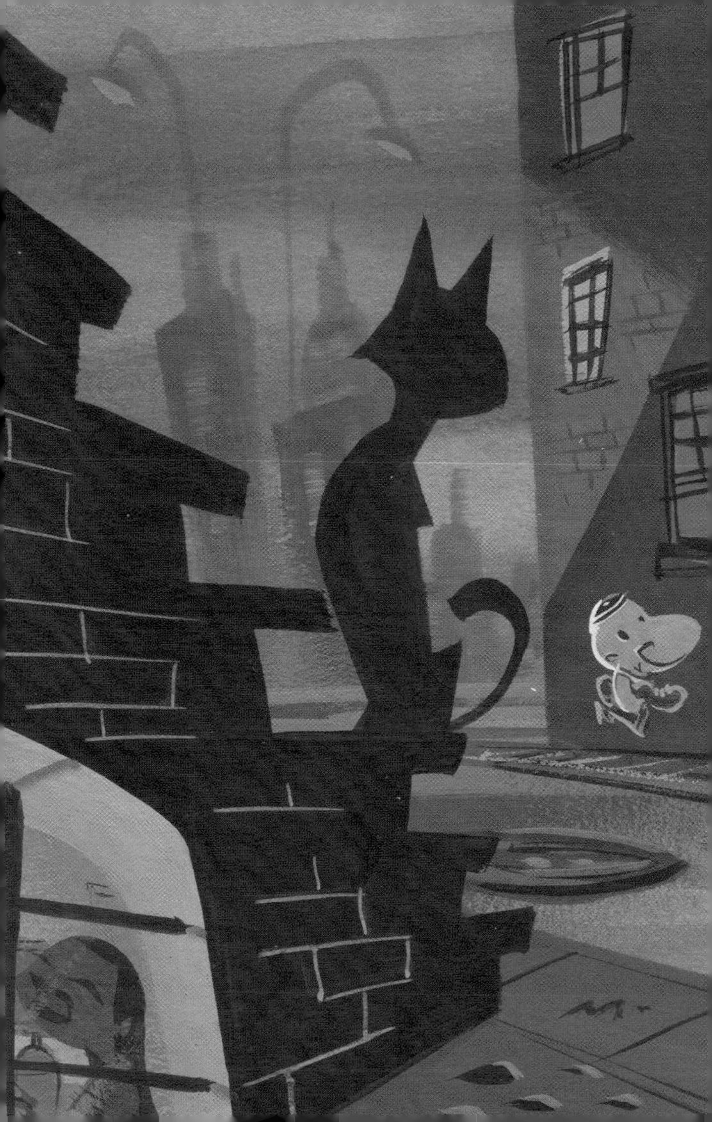

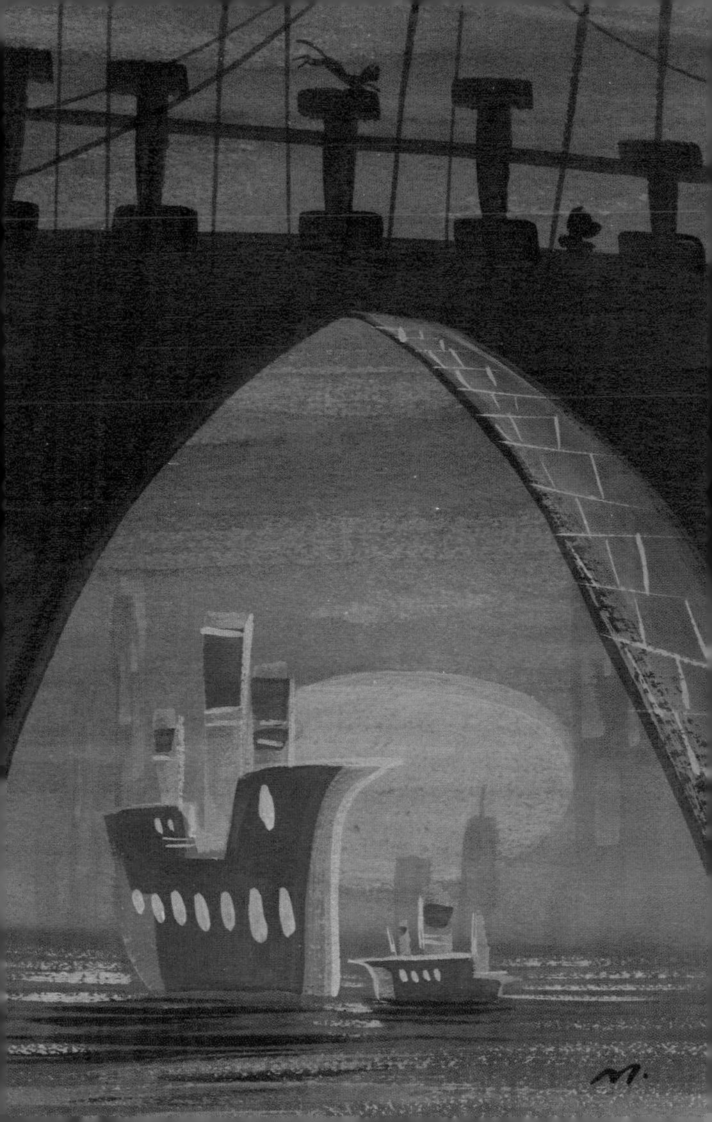

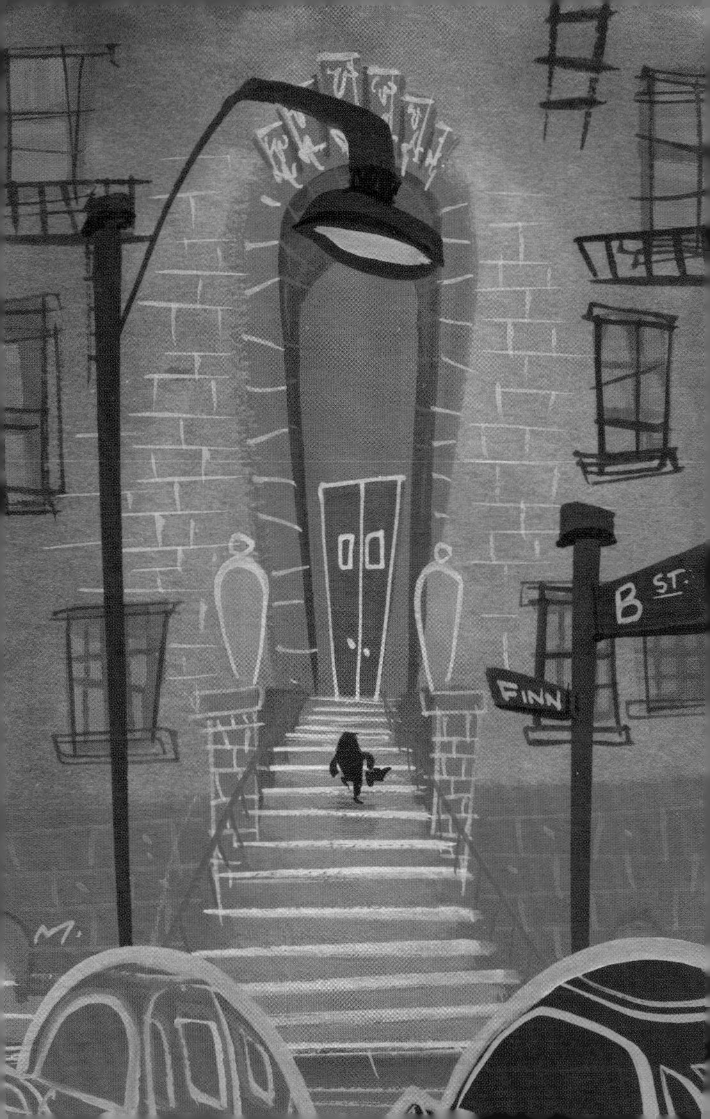
B ST.
FINN

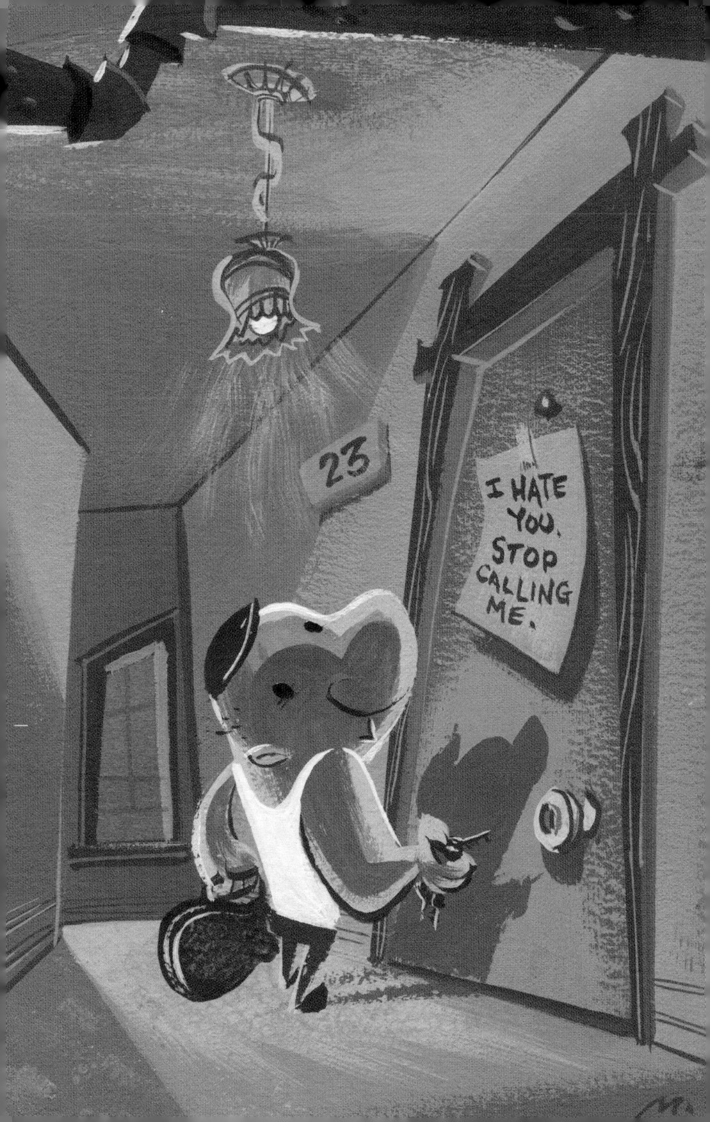
23
I HATE YOU. STOP CALLING ME.

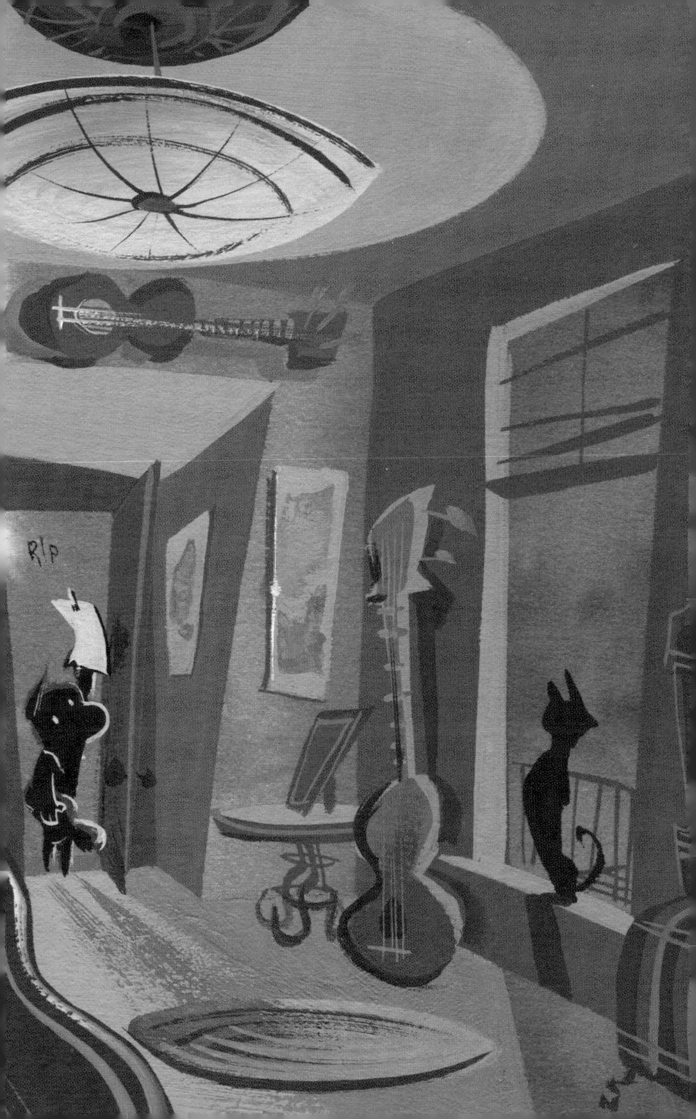
RIP

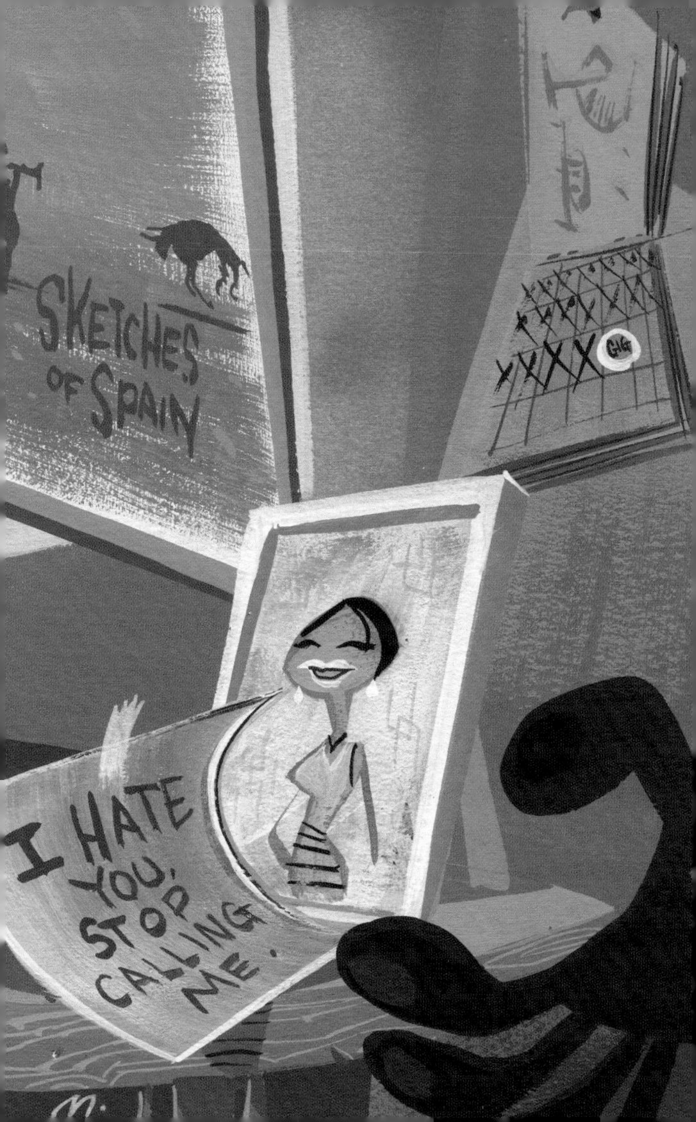
SKETCHES OF SPAIN
GIG
I HATE YOU, STOP CALLING ME.

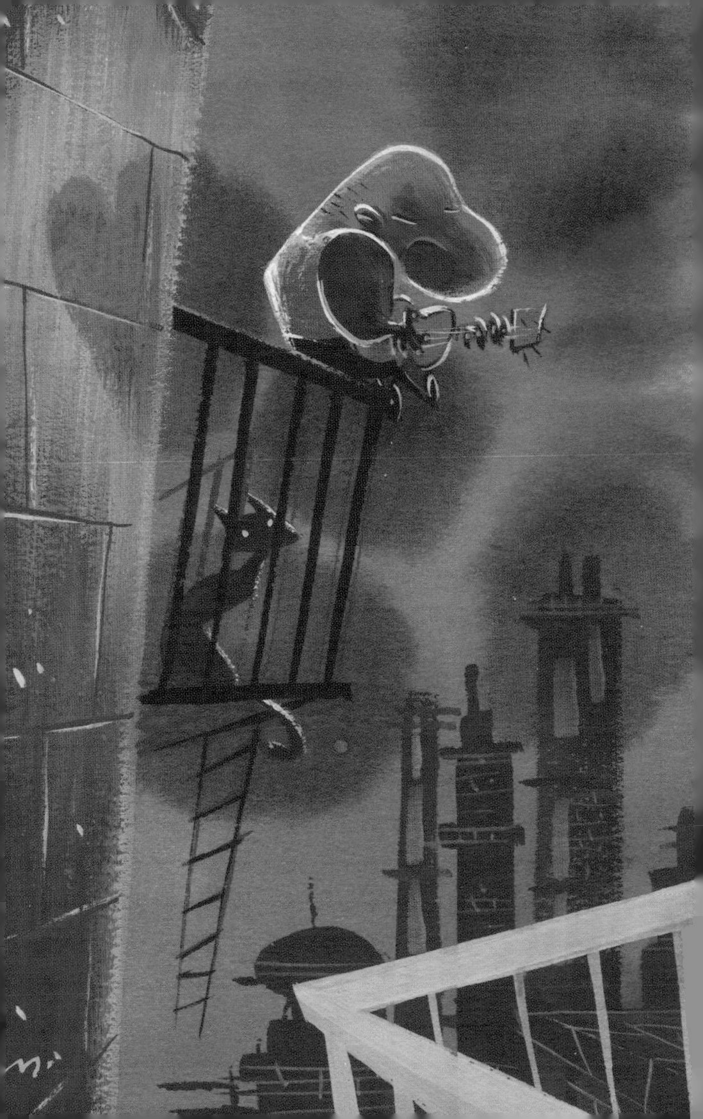

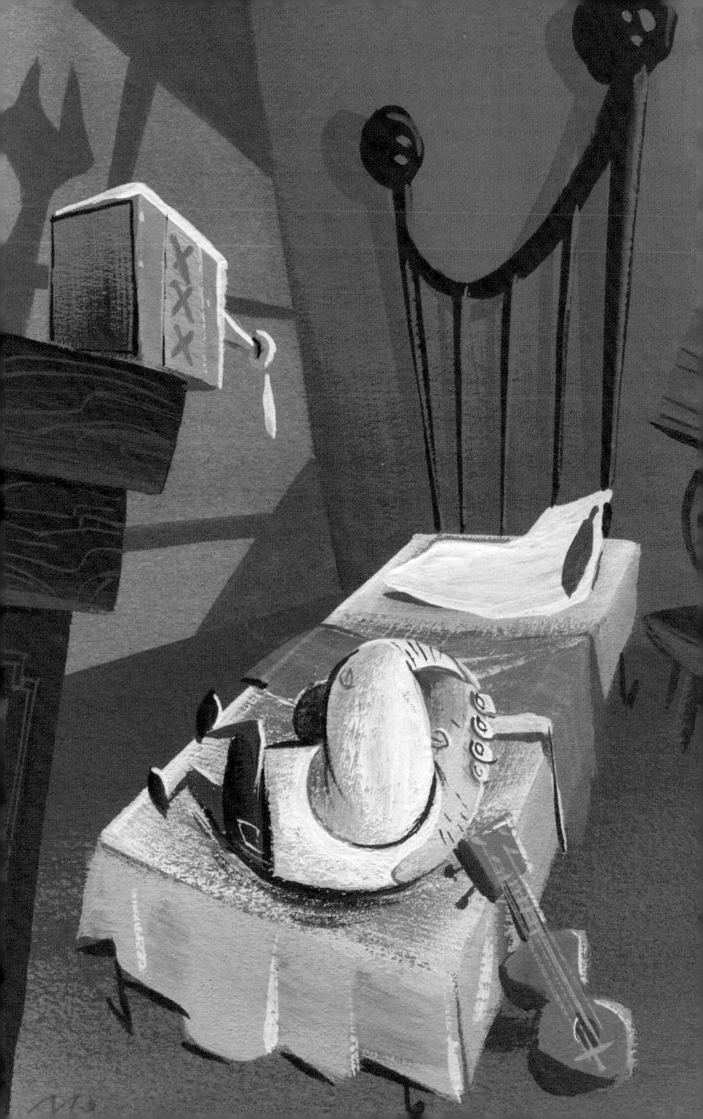

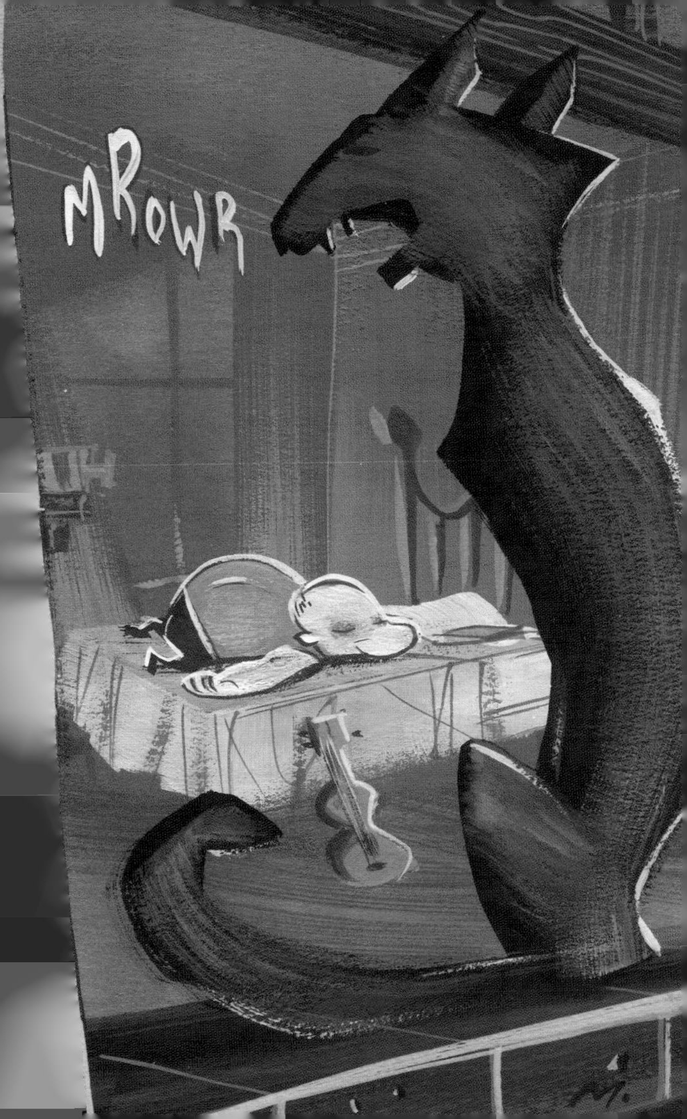
MROWR

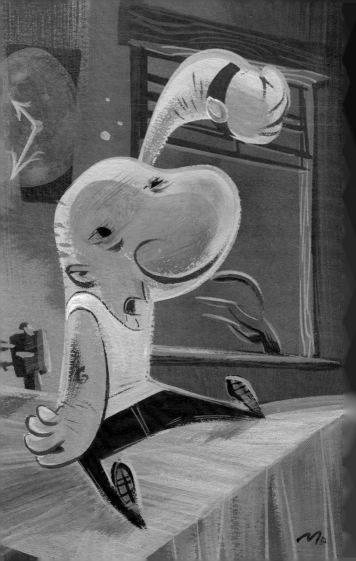

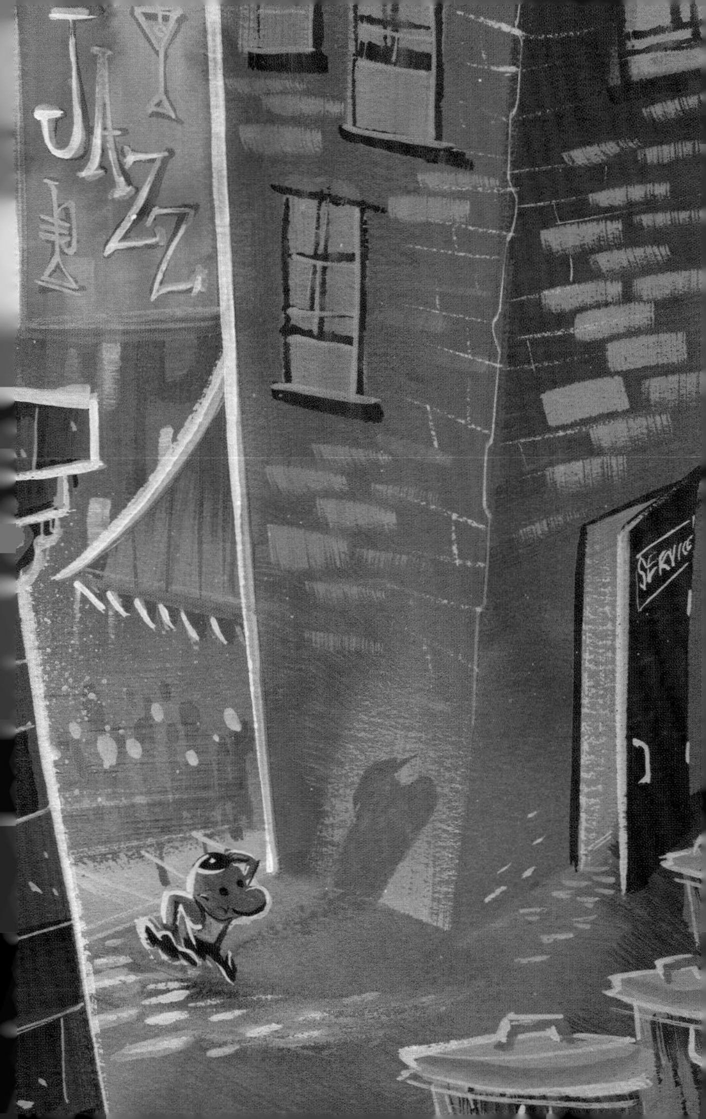
JAZZ
SERVICE

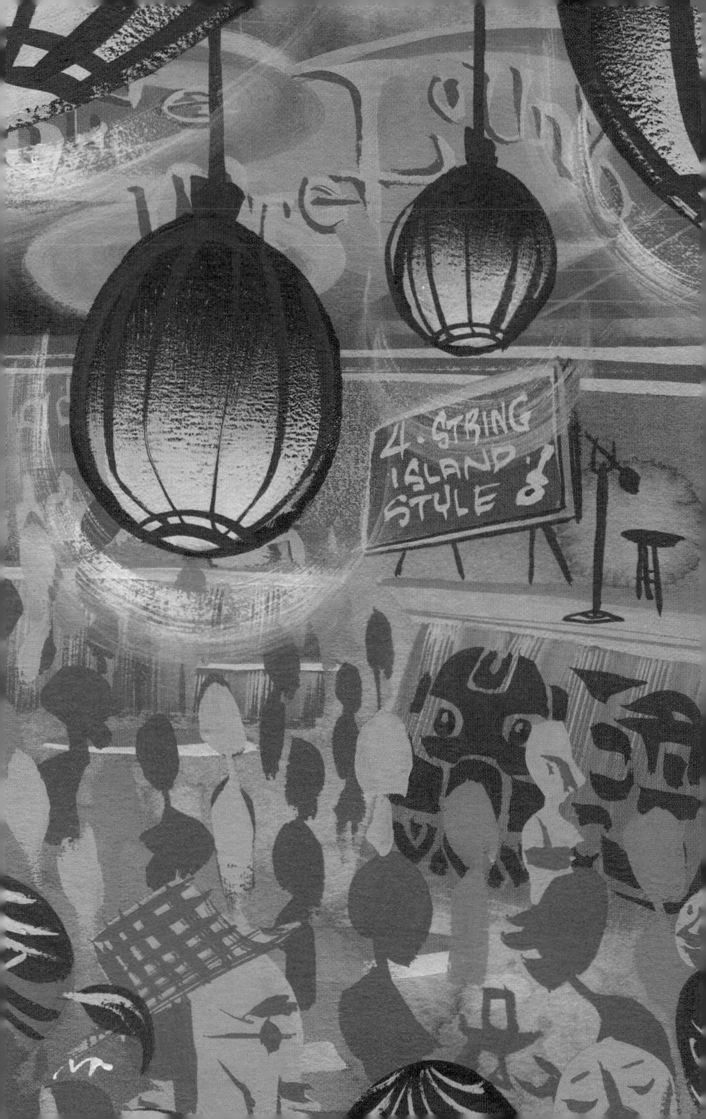
4 · STRING
ISLAND
STYLE

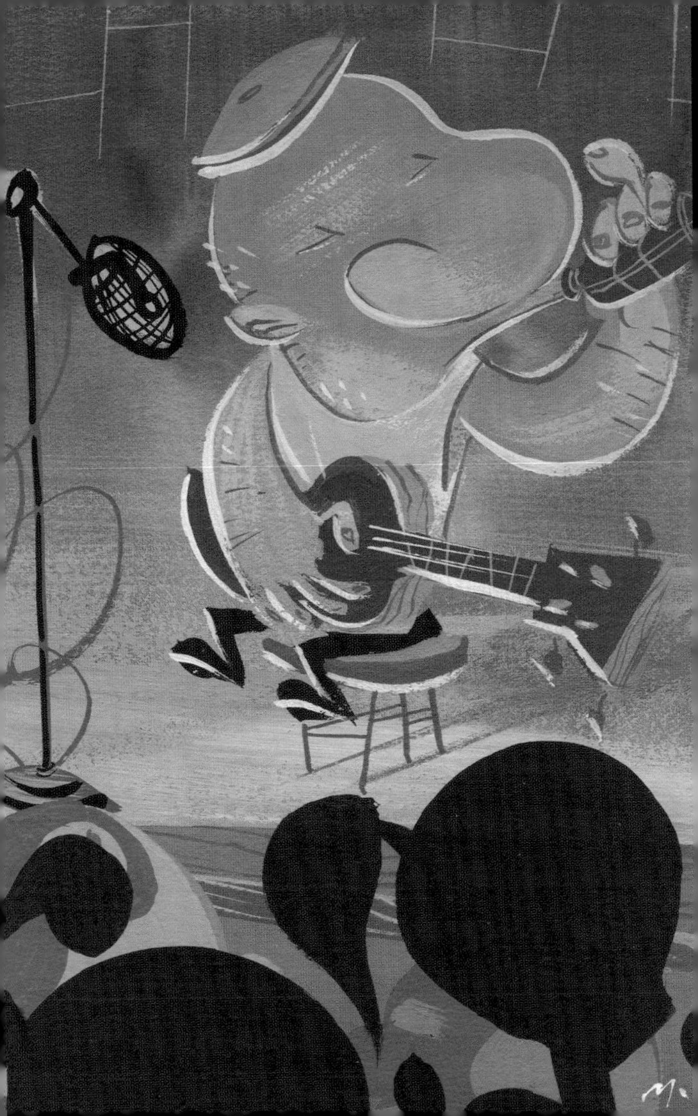

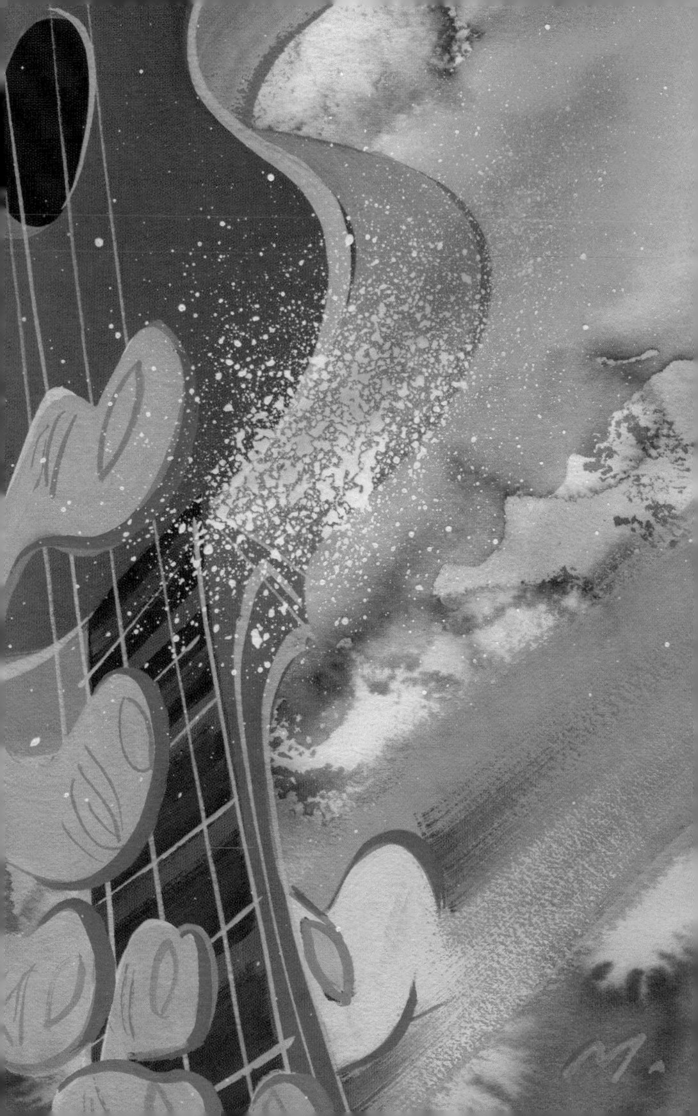

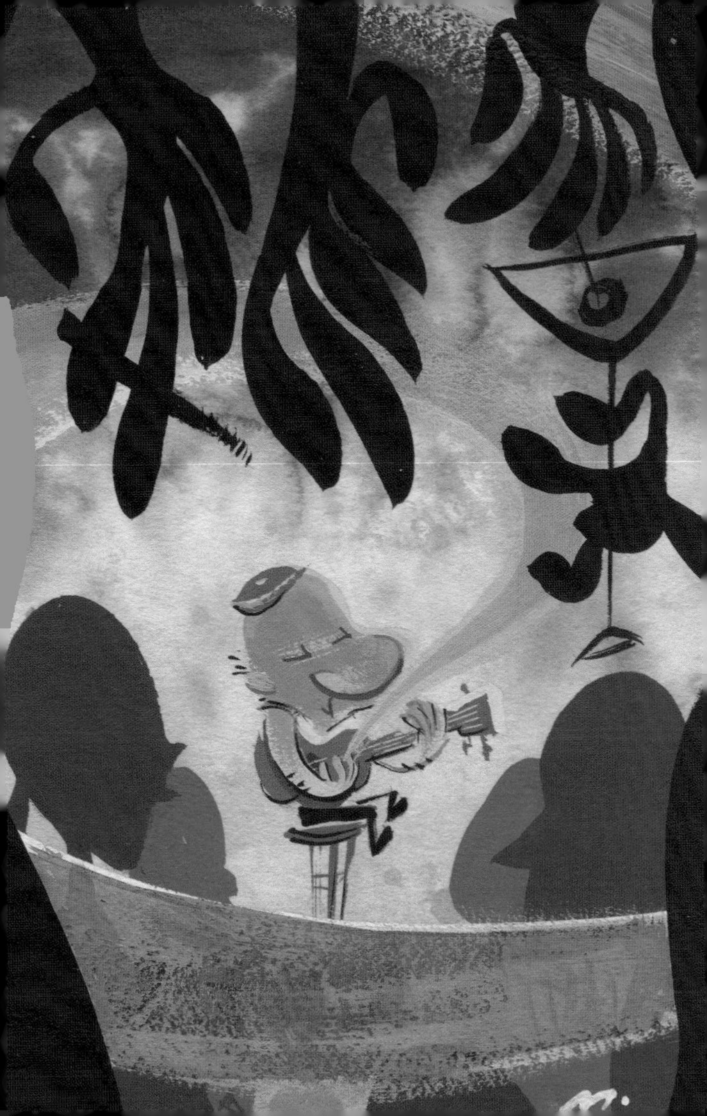

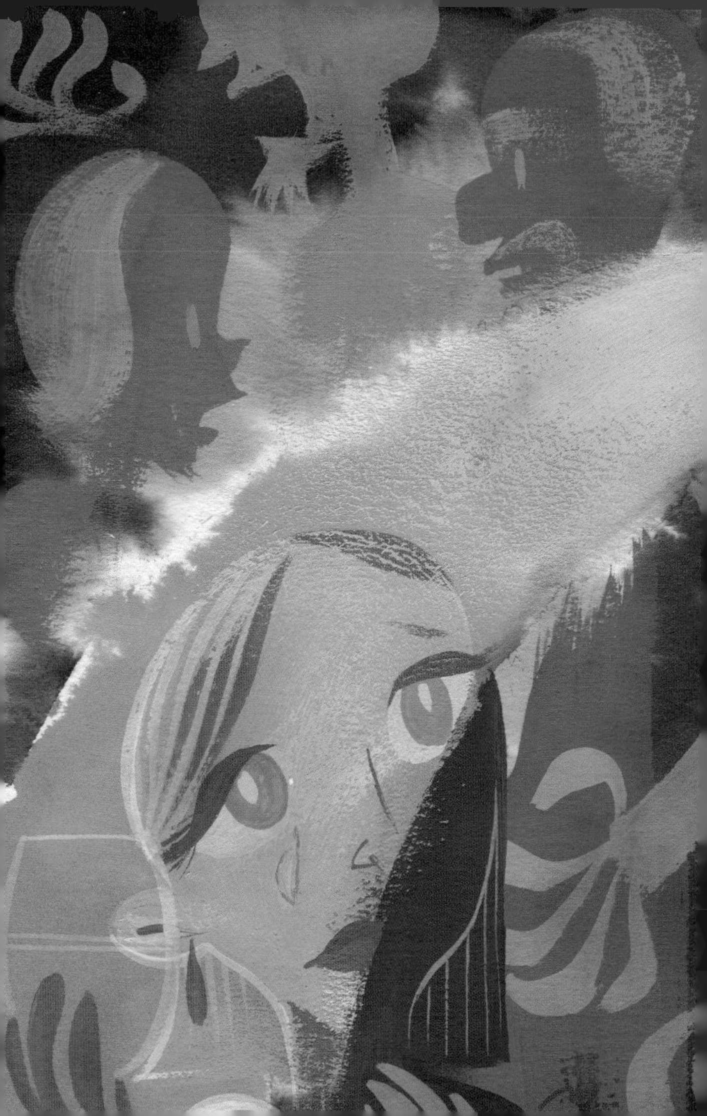

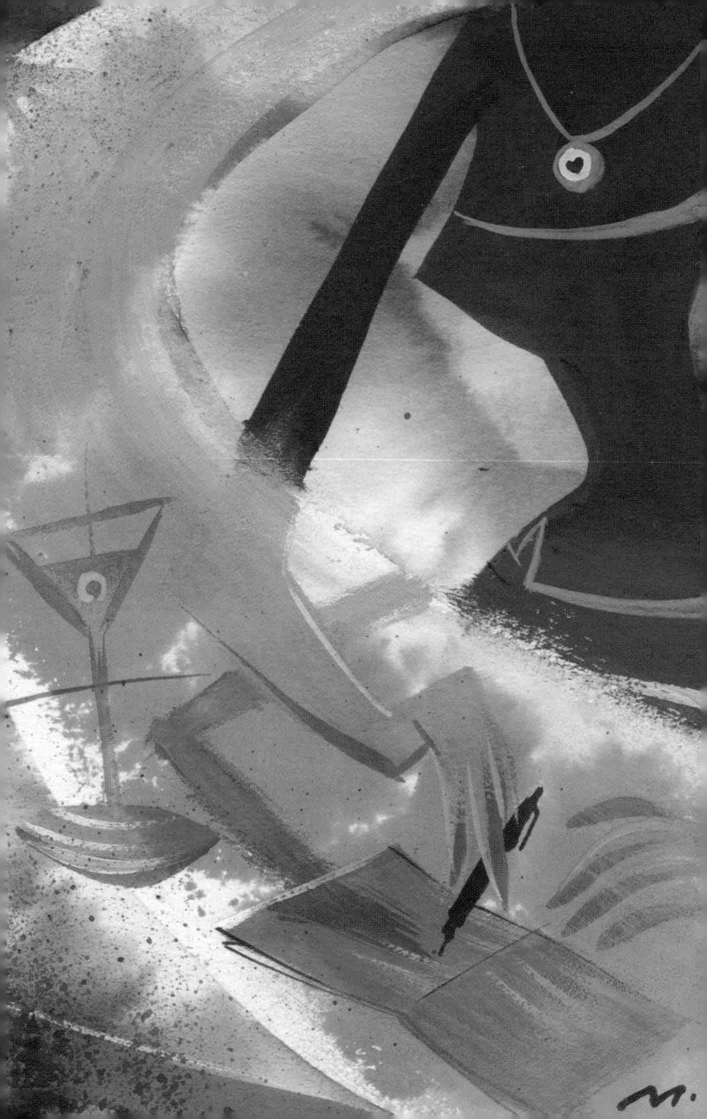

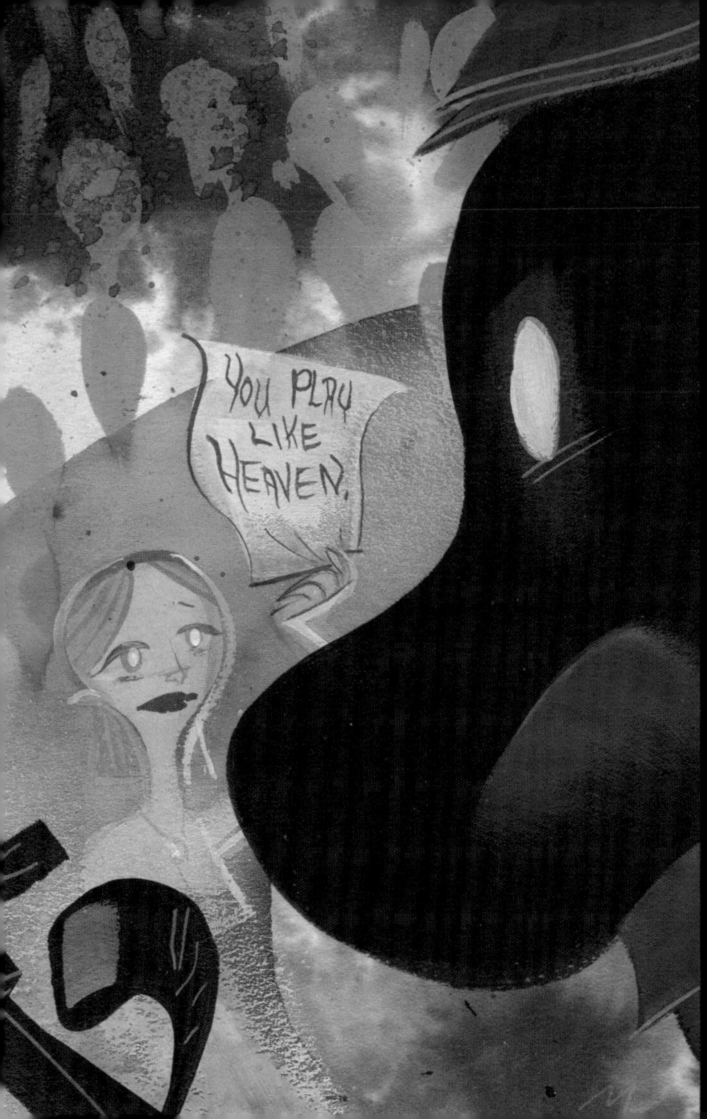
YOU PLAY LIKE HEAVEN.

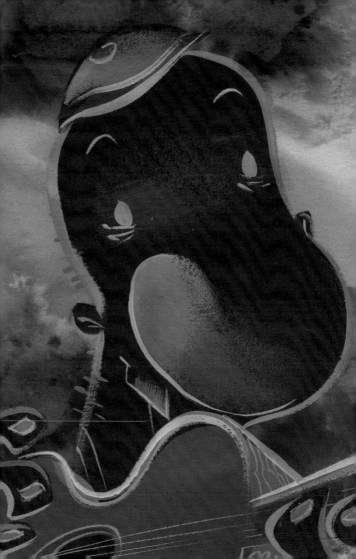

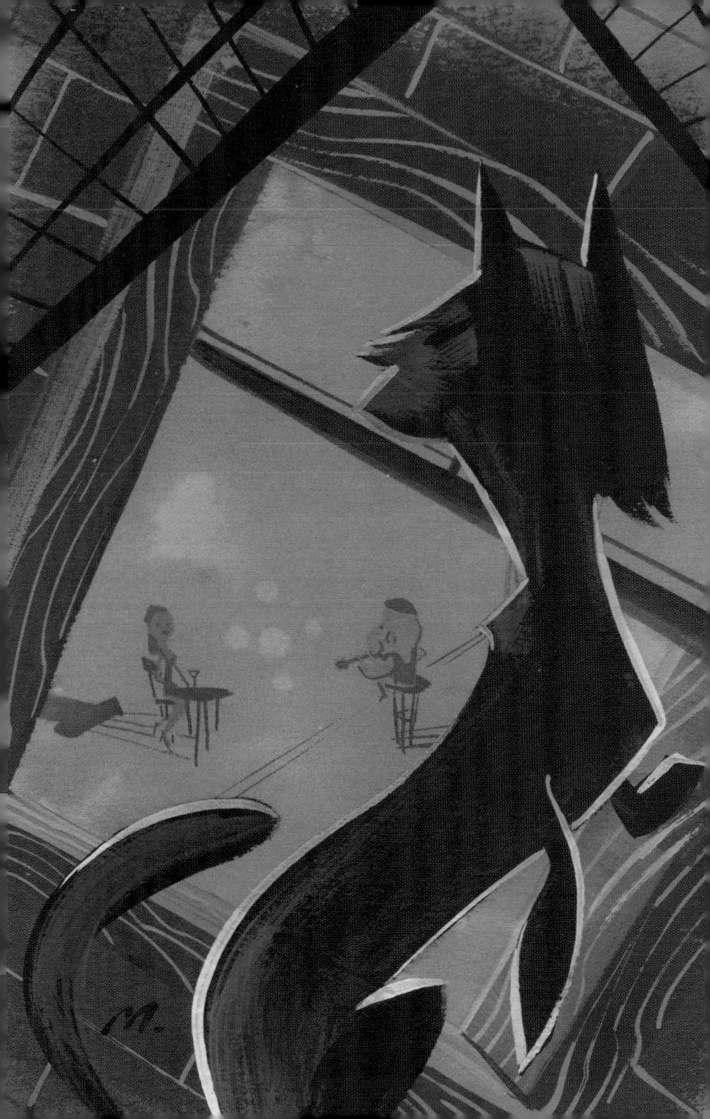

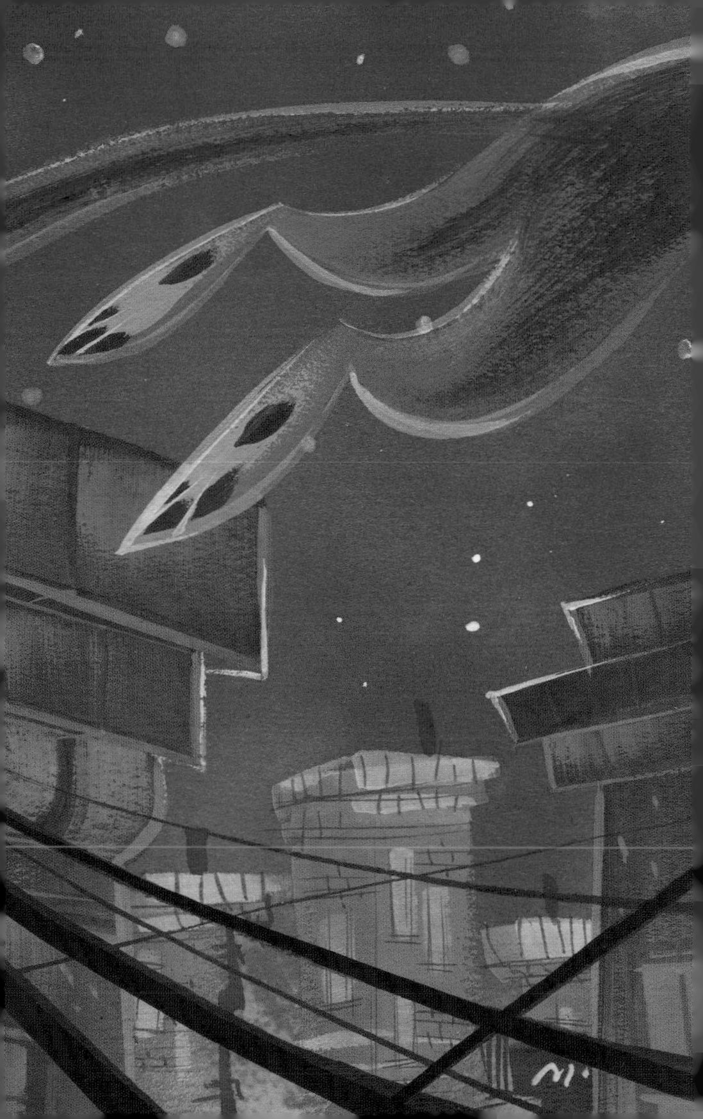

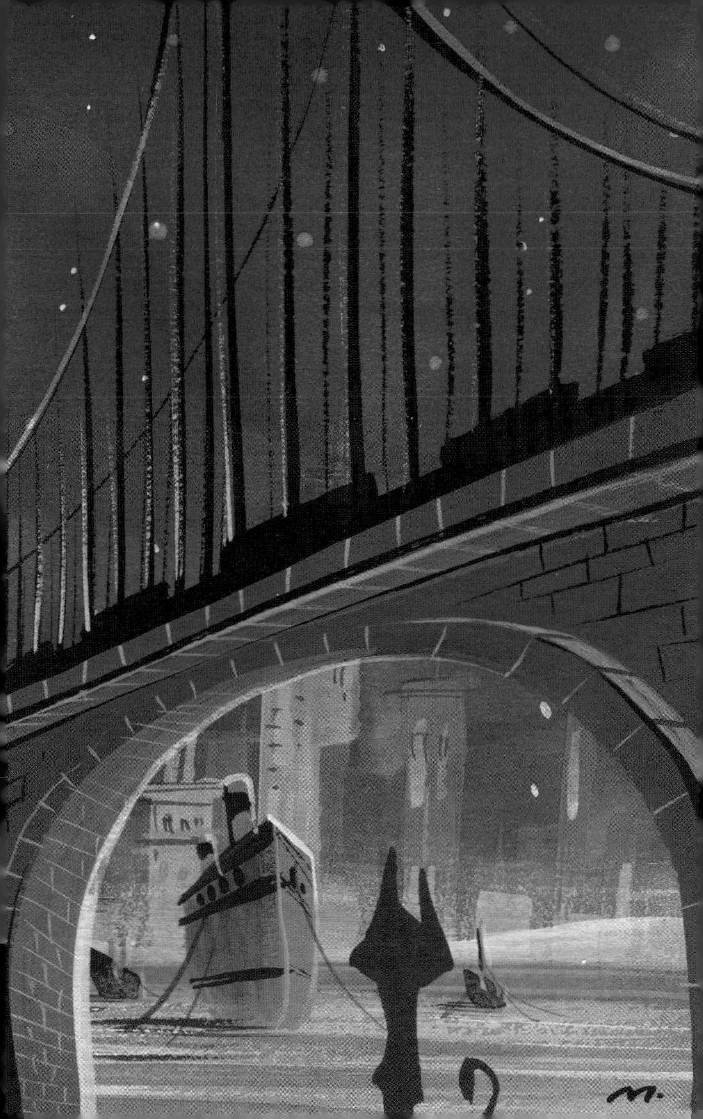

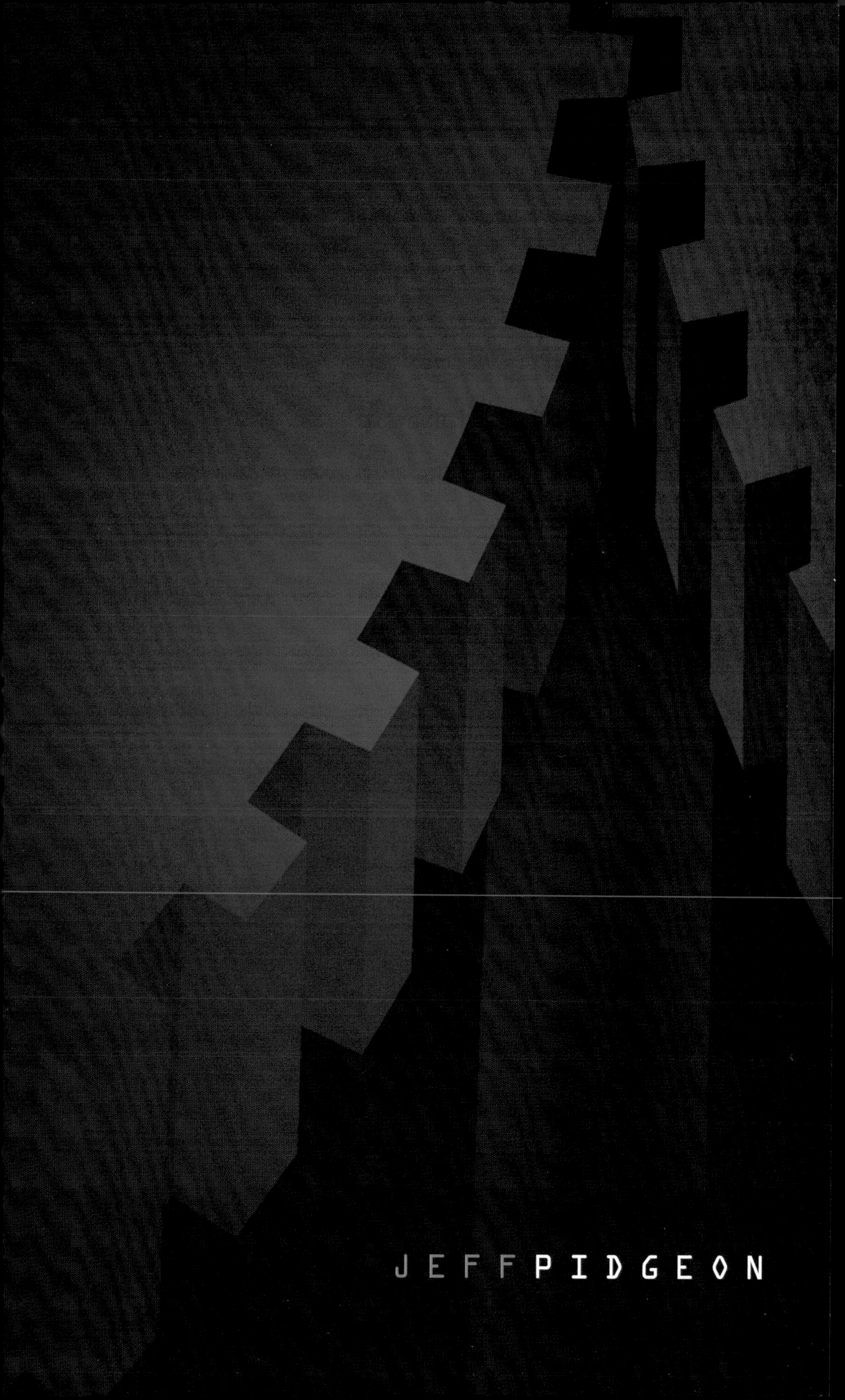
JEFF PIDGEON

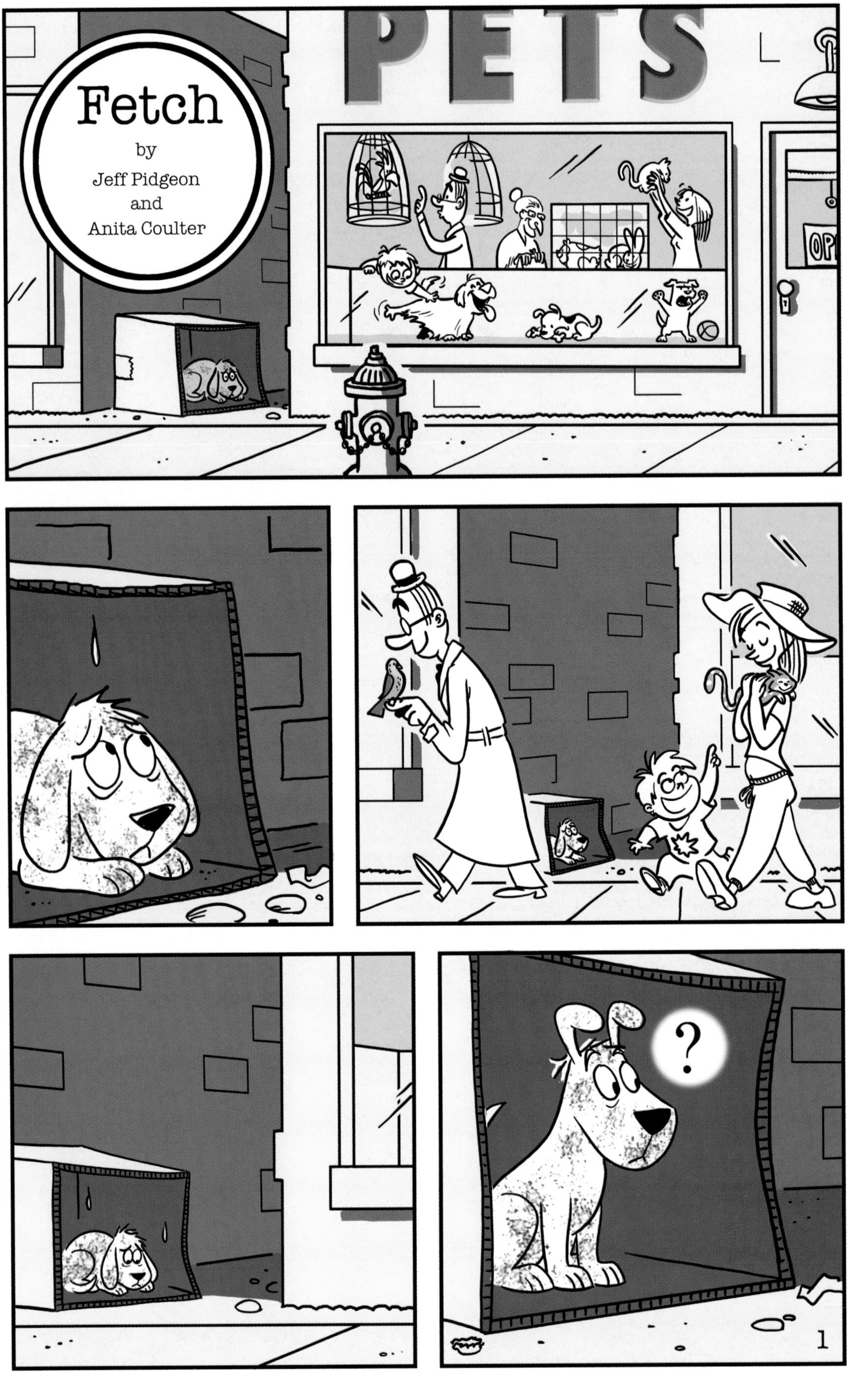
Fetch
by
Jeff Pidgeon
and
Anita Coulter
PETS
?

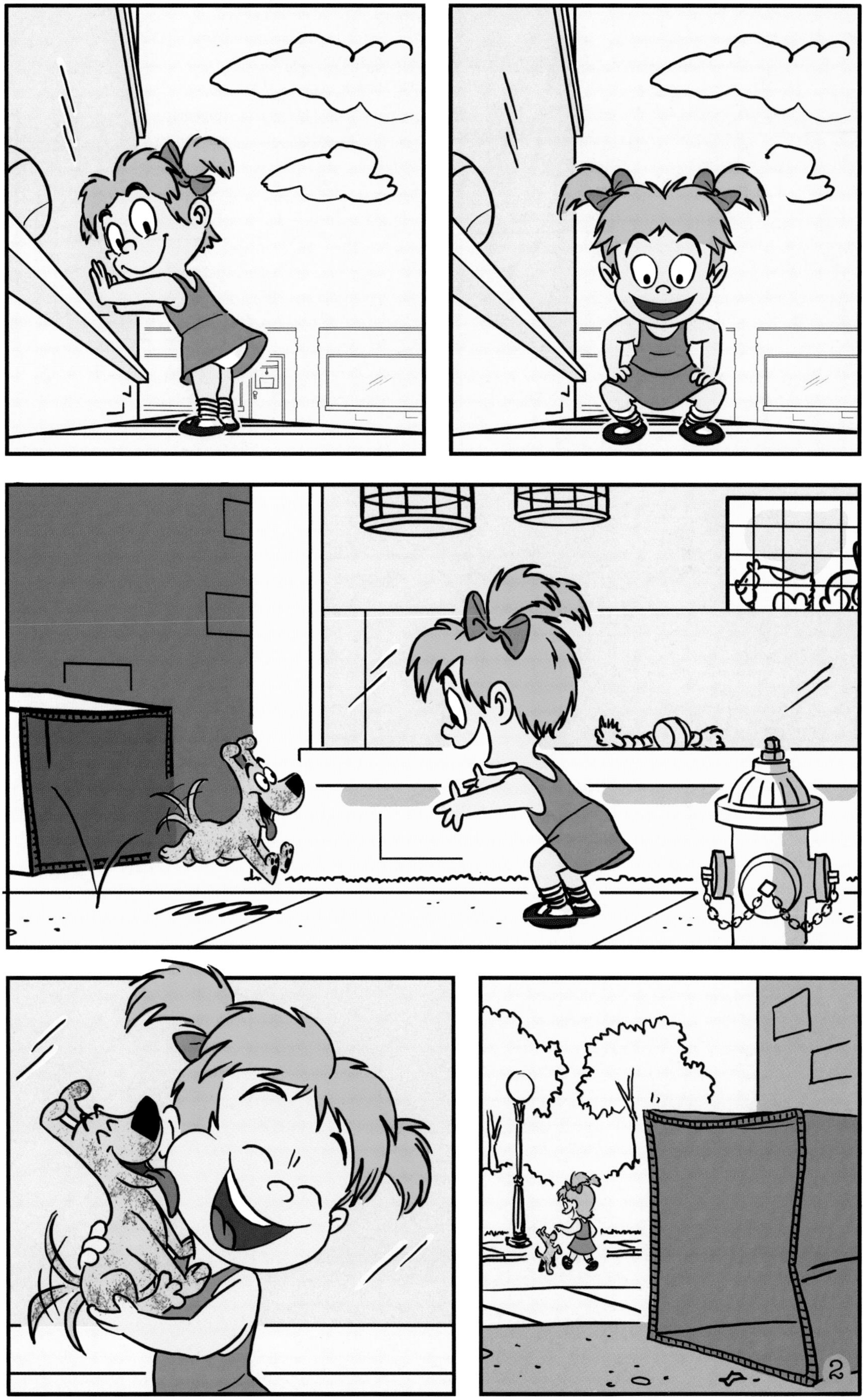
2

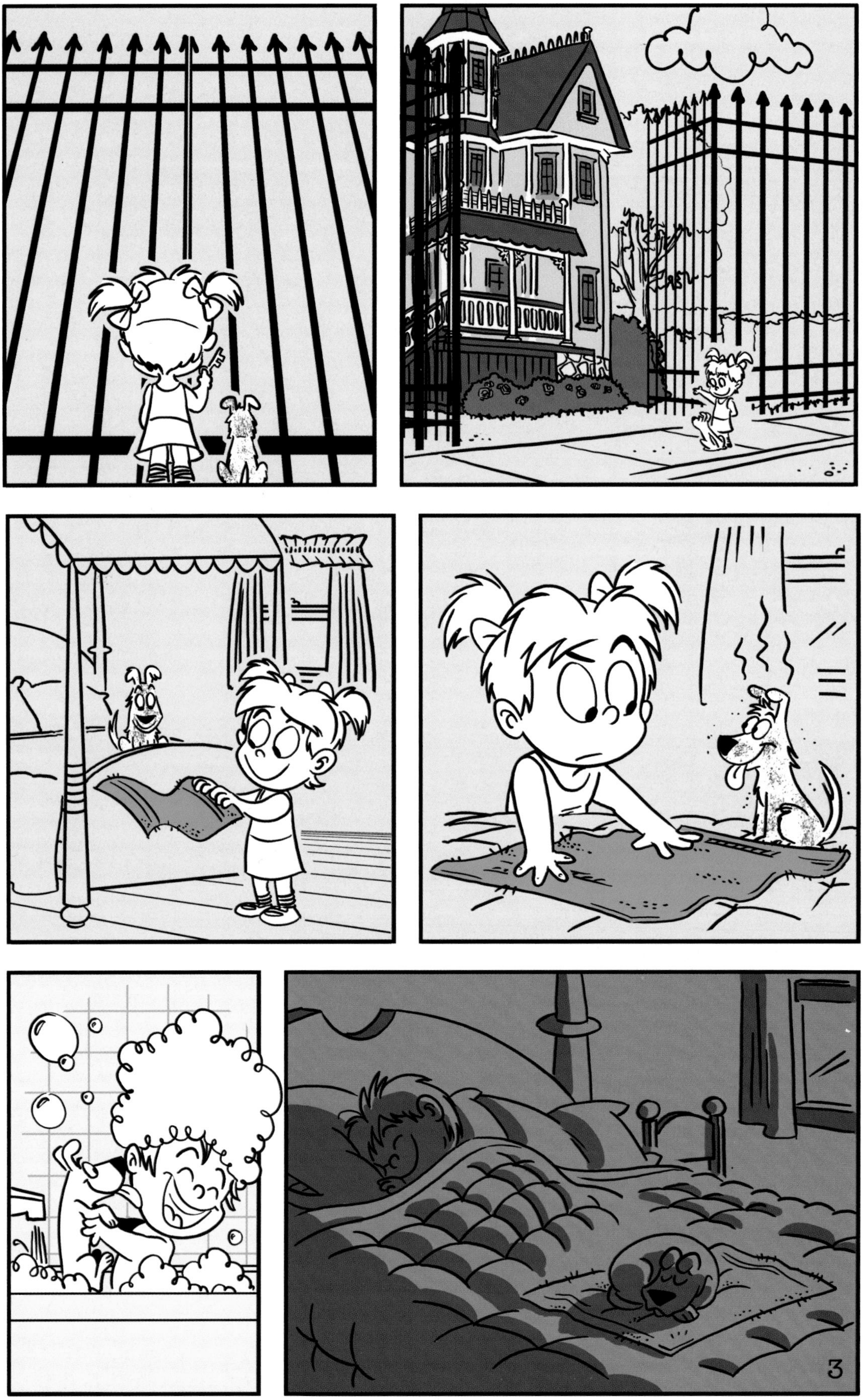

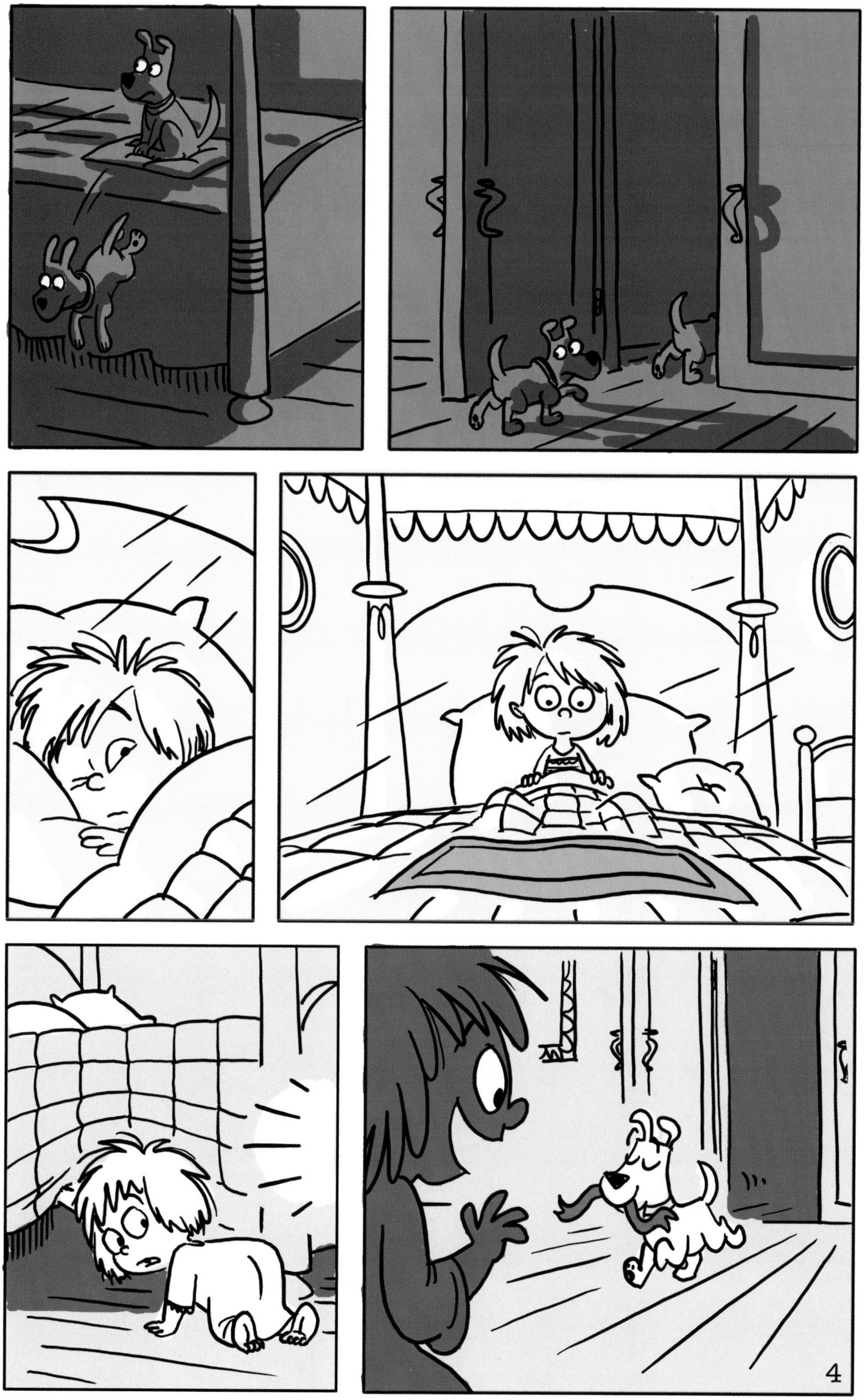

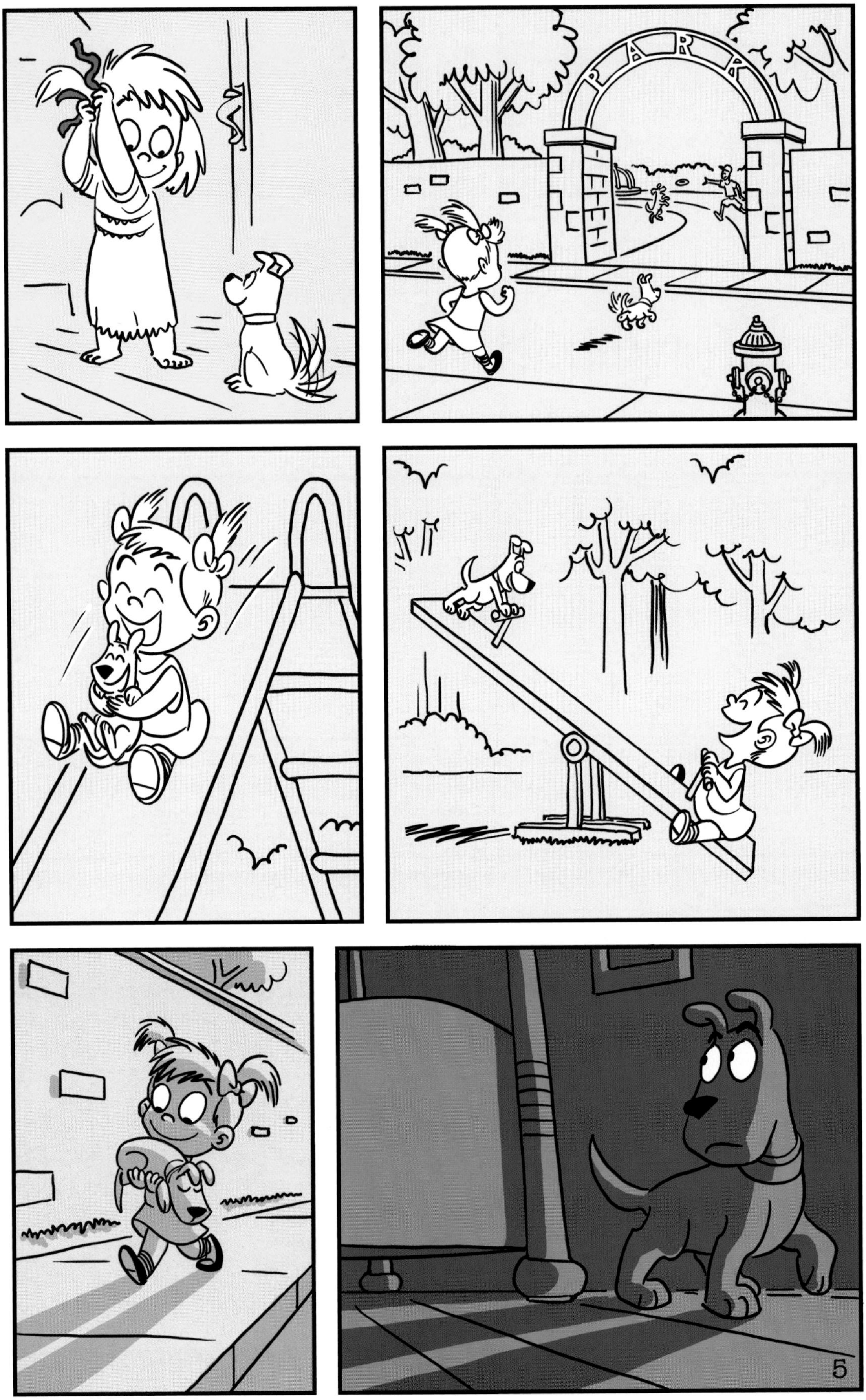
PARK

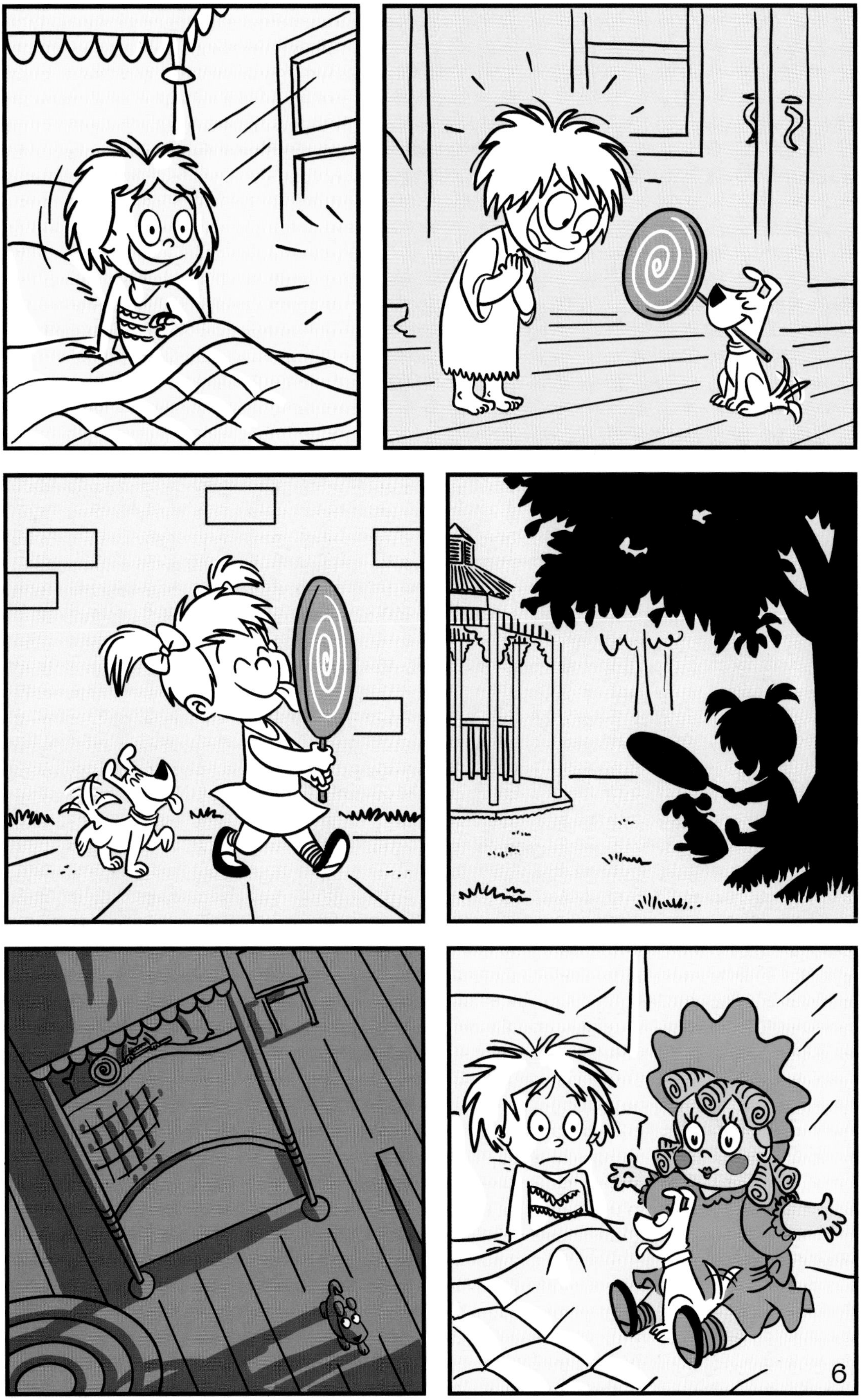

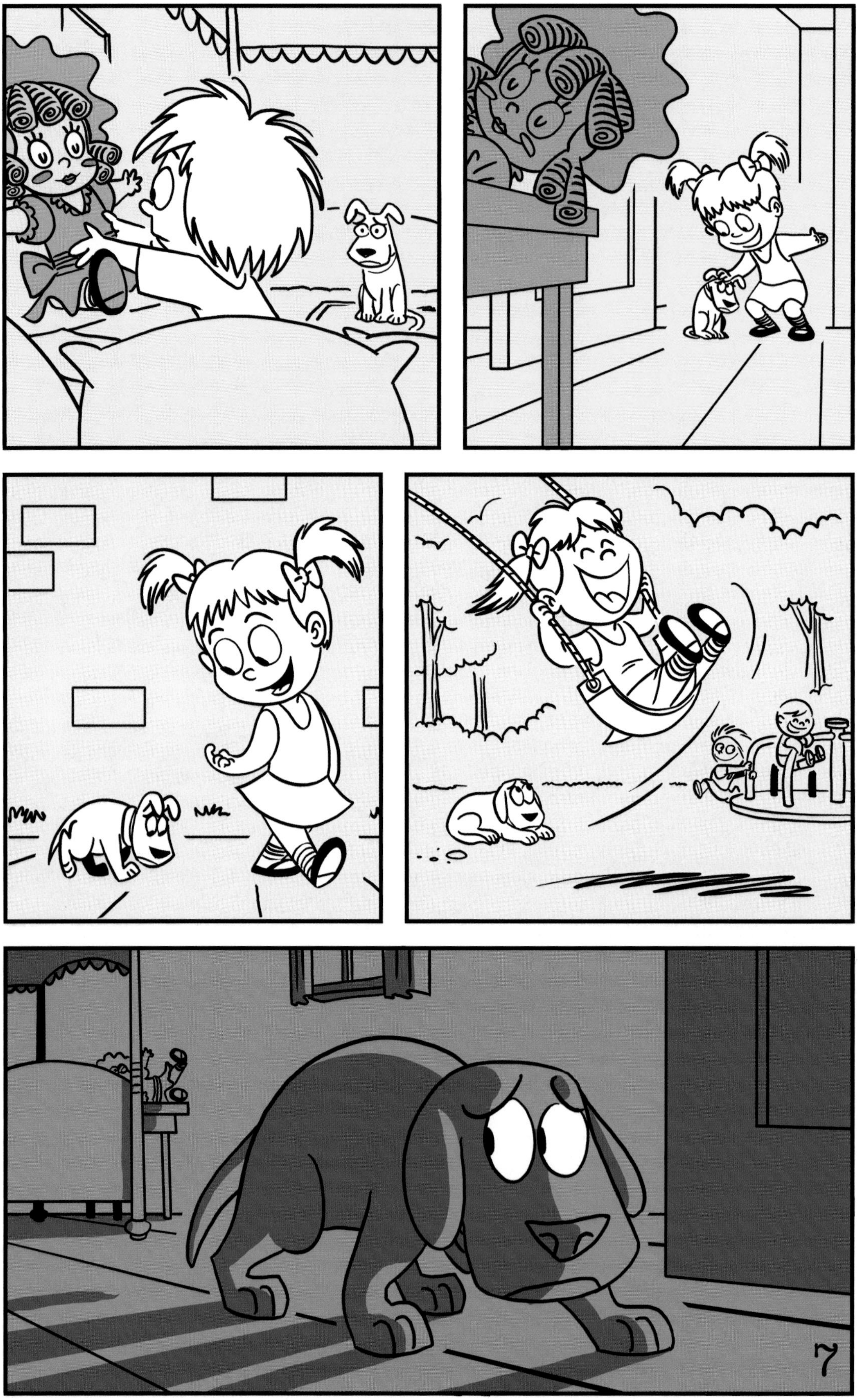

7

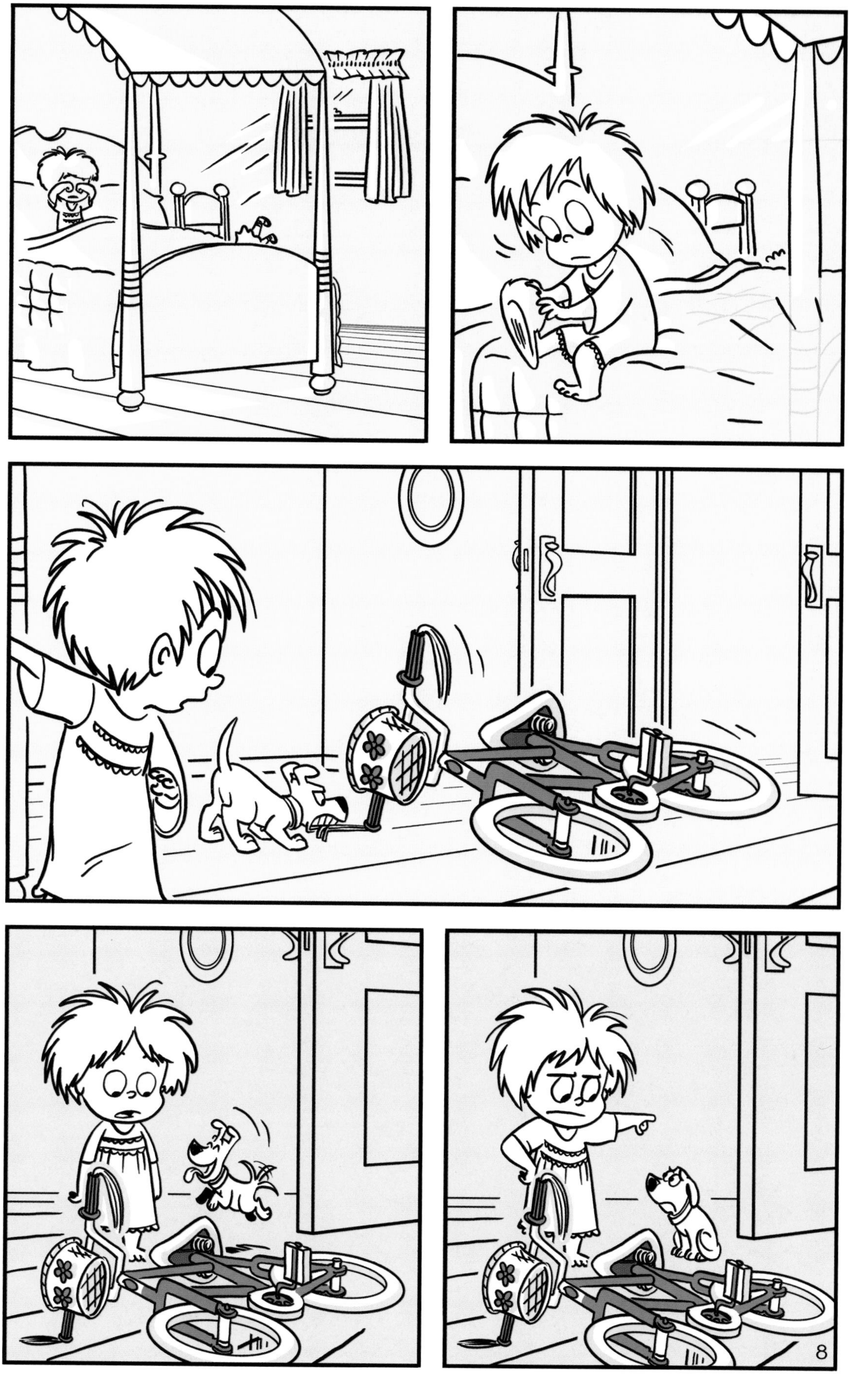

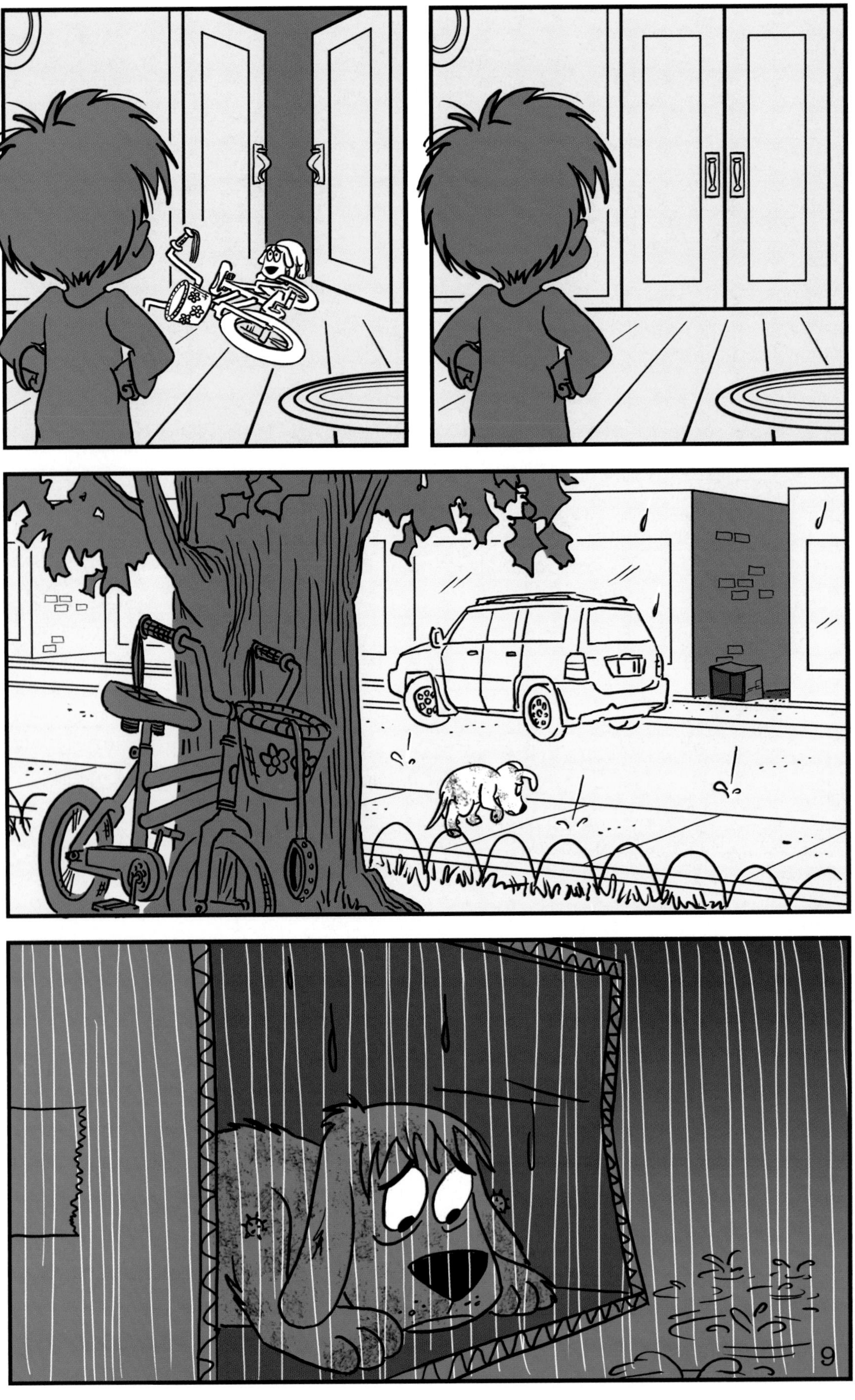

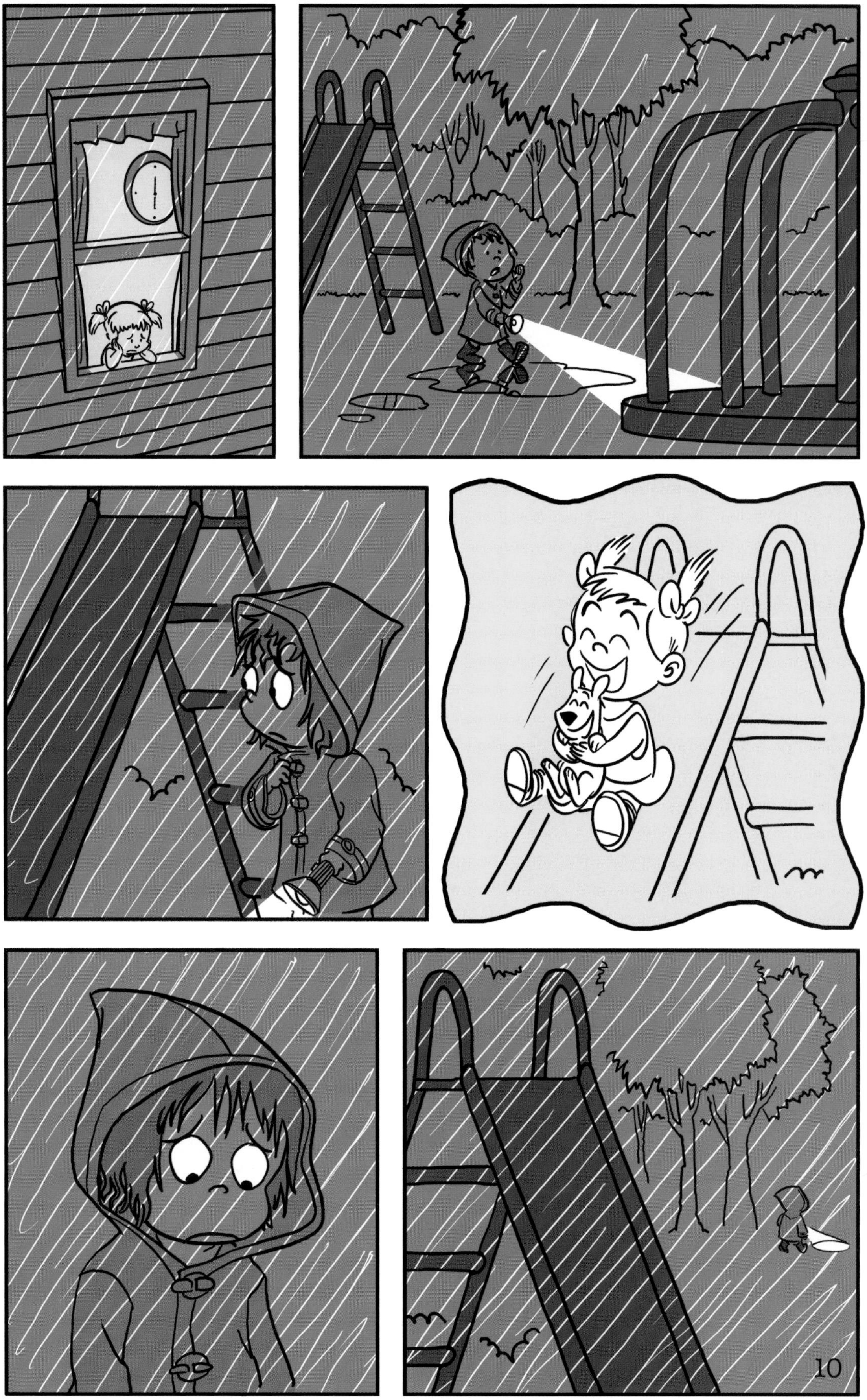

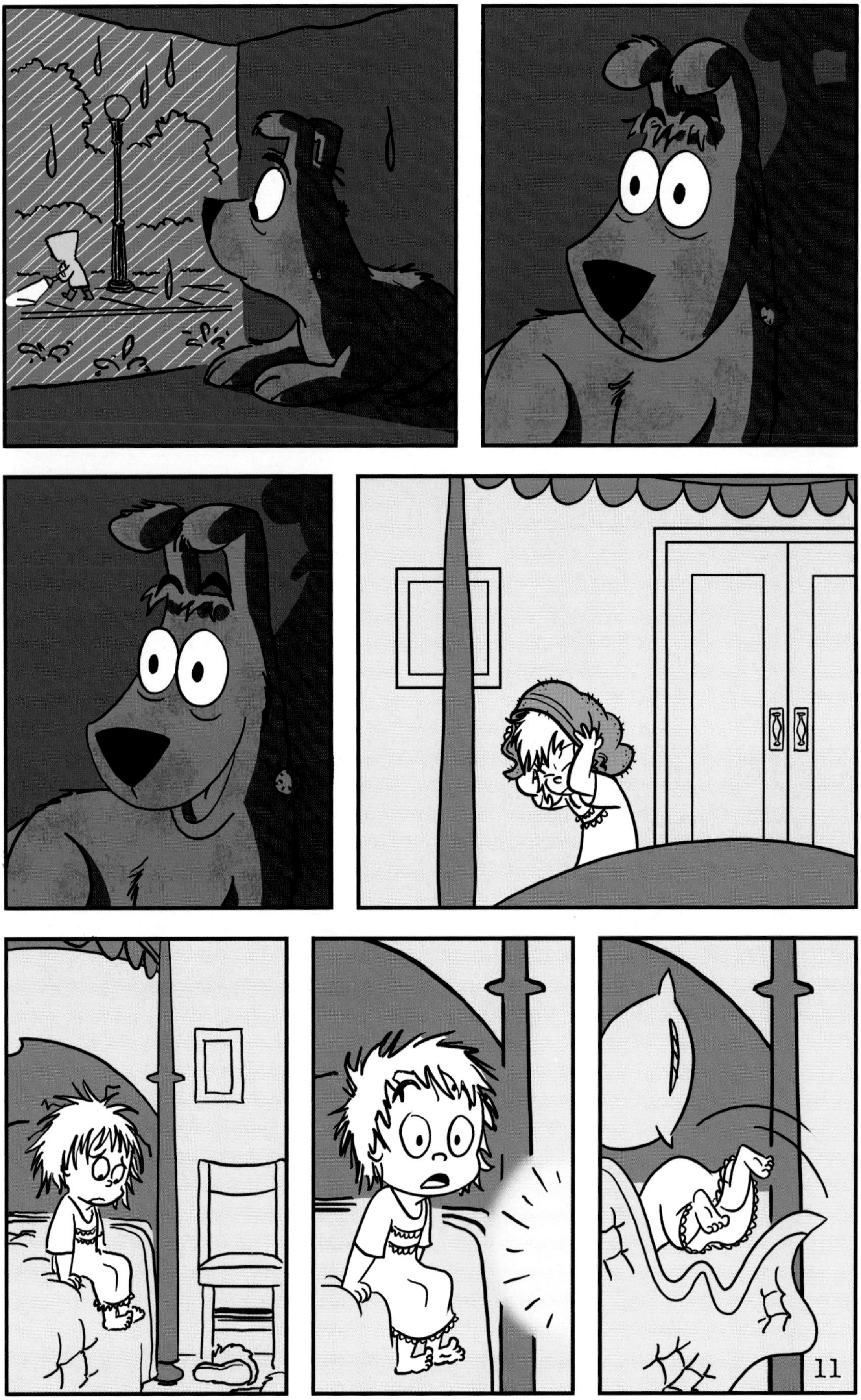

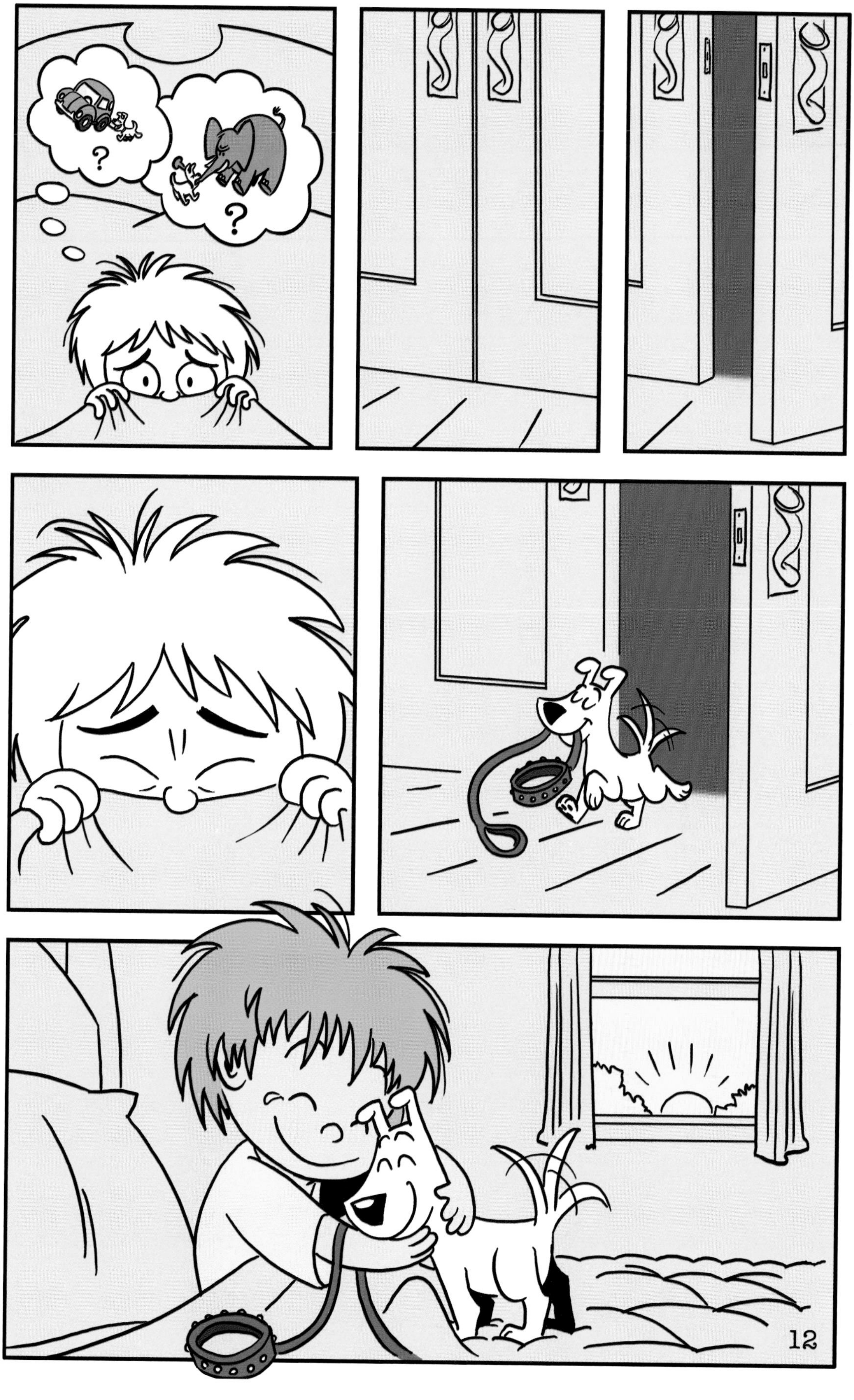

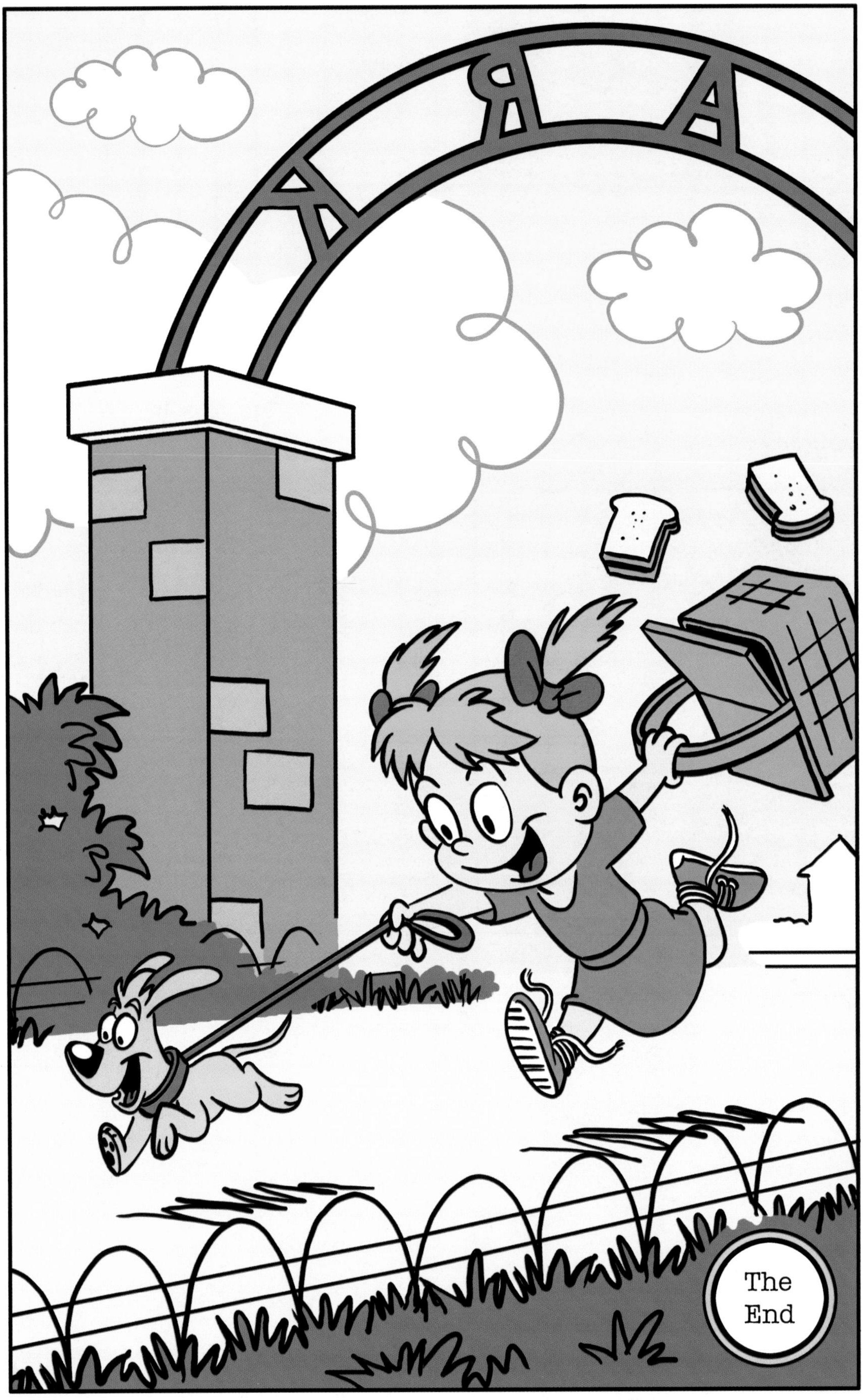
The
End

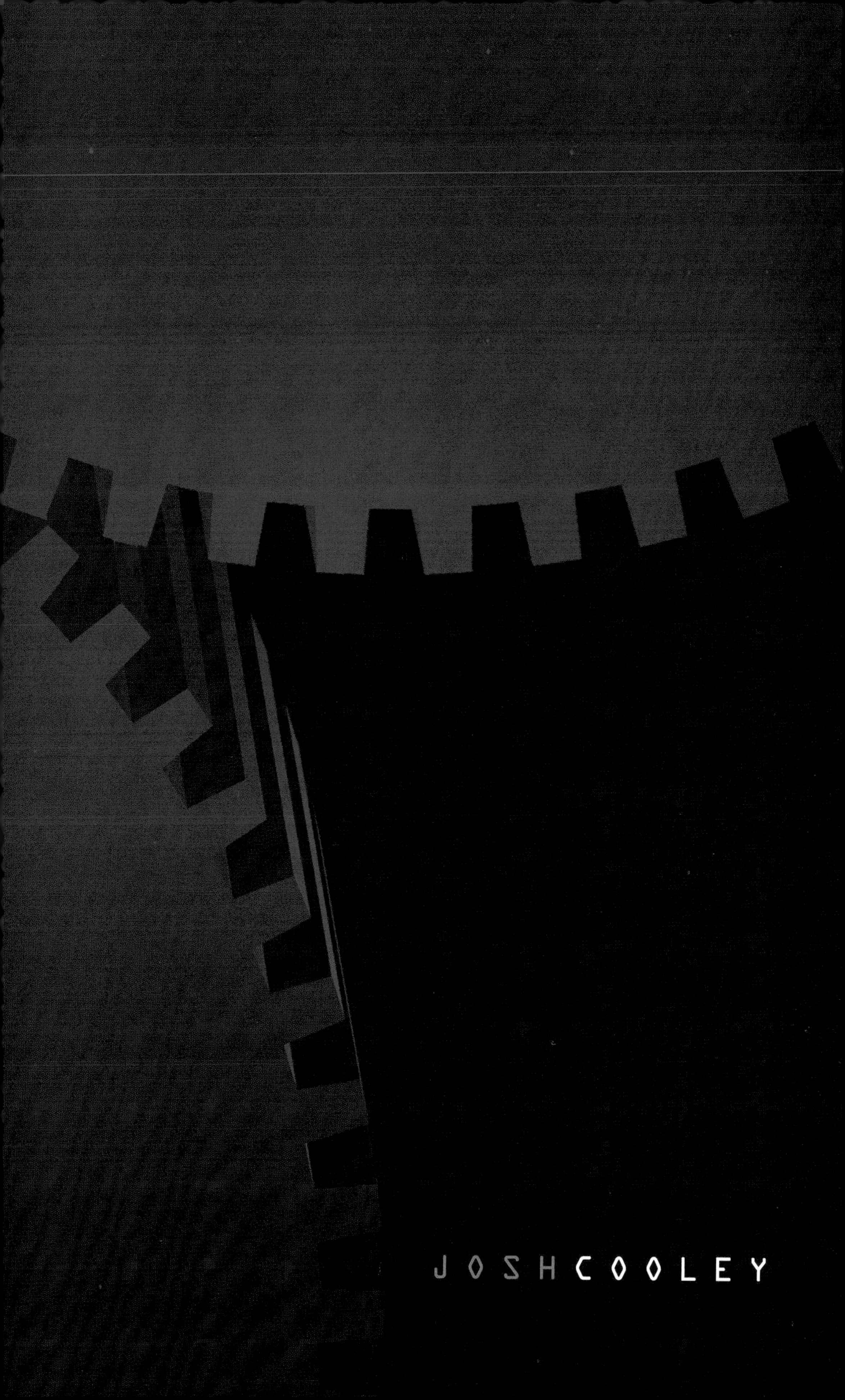
JOSH COOLEY

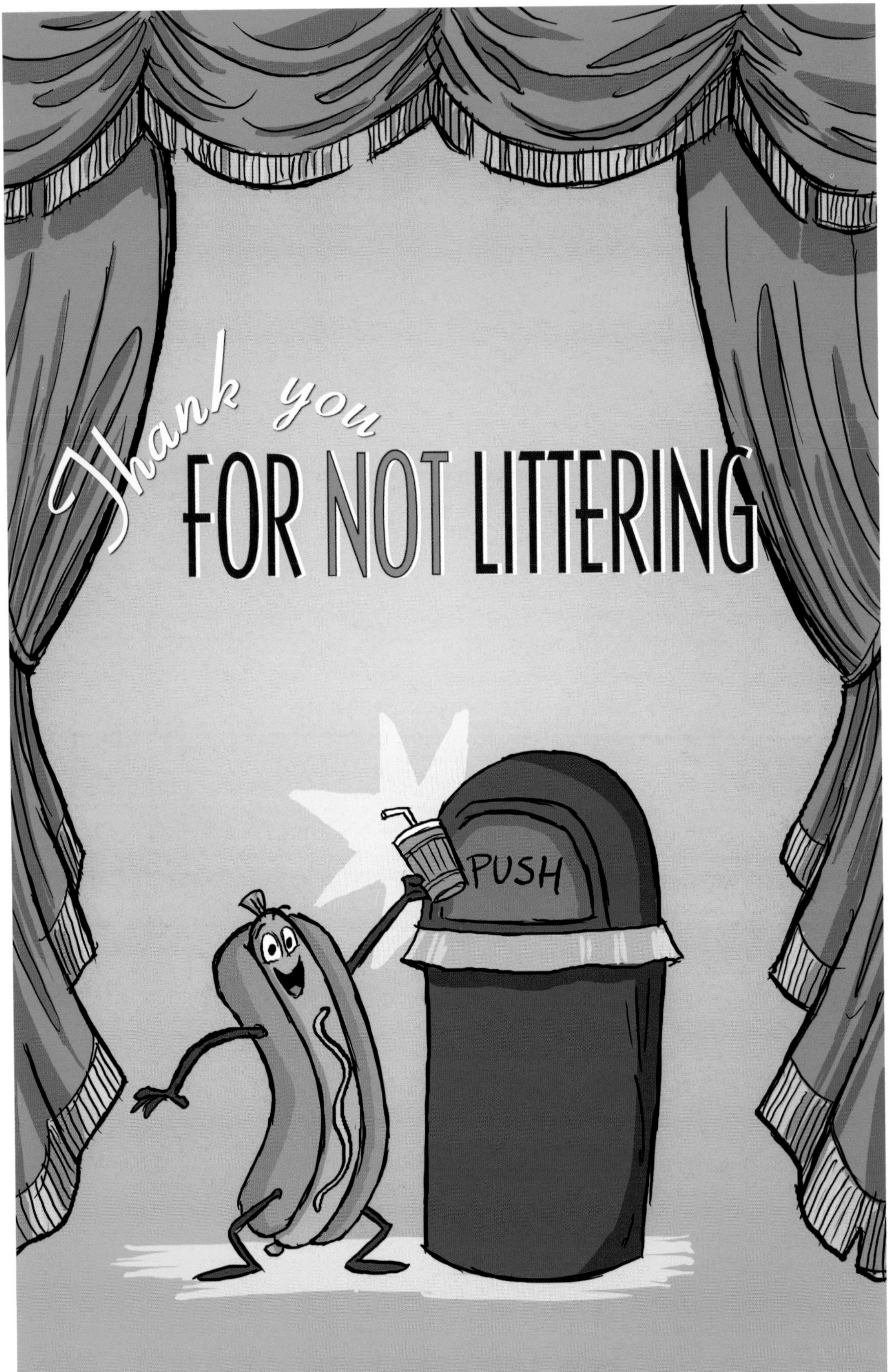
Thank you
FOR NOT LITTERING
PUSH

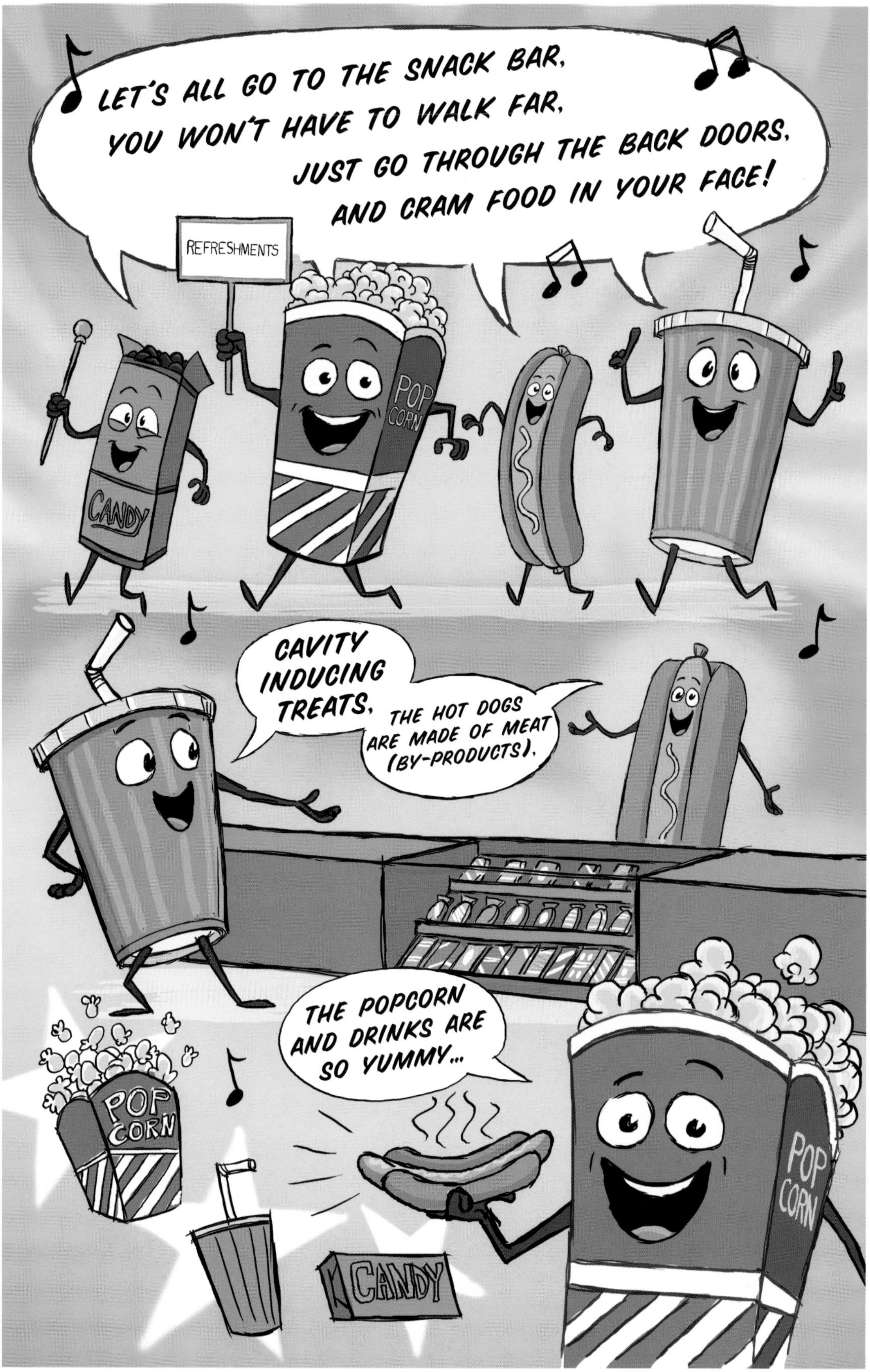
LET'S ALL GO TO THE SNACK BAR,
YOU WON'T HAVE TO WALK FAR,
JUST GO THROUGH THE BACK DOORS,
AND CRAM FOOD IN YOUR FACE!
REFRESHMENTS
POP CORN
CANDY
CAVITY INDUCING TREATS,
THE HOT DOGS ARE MADE OF MEAT (BY-PRODUCTS),
THE POPCORN AND DRINKS ARE SO YUMMY...
POP CORN
CANDY
POP CORN

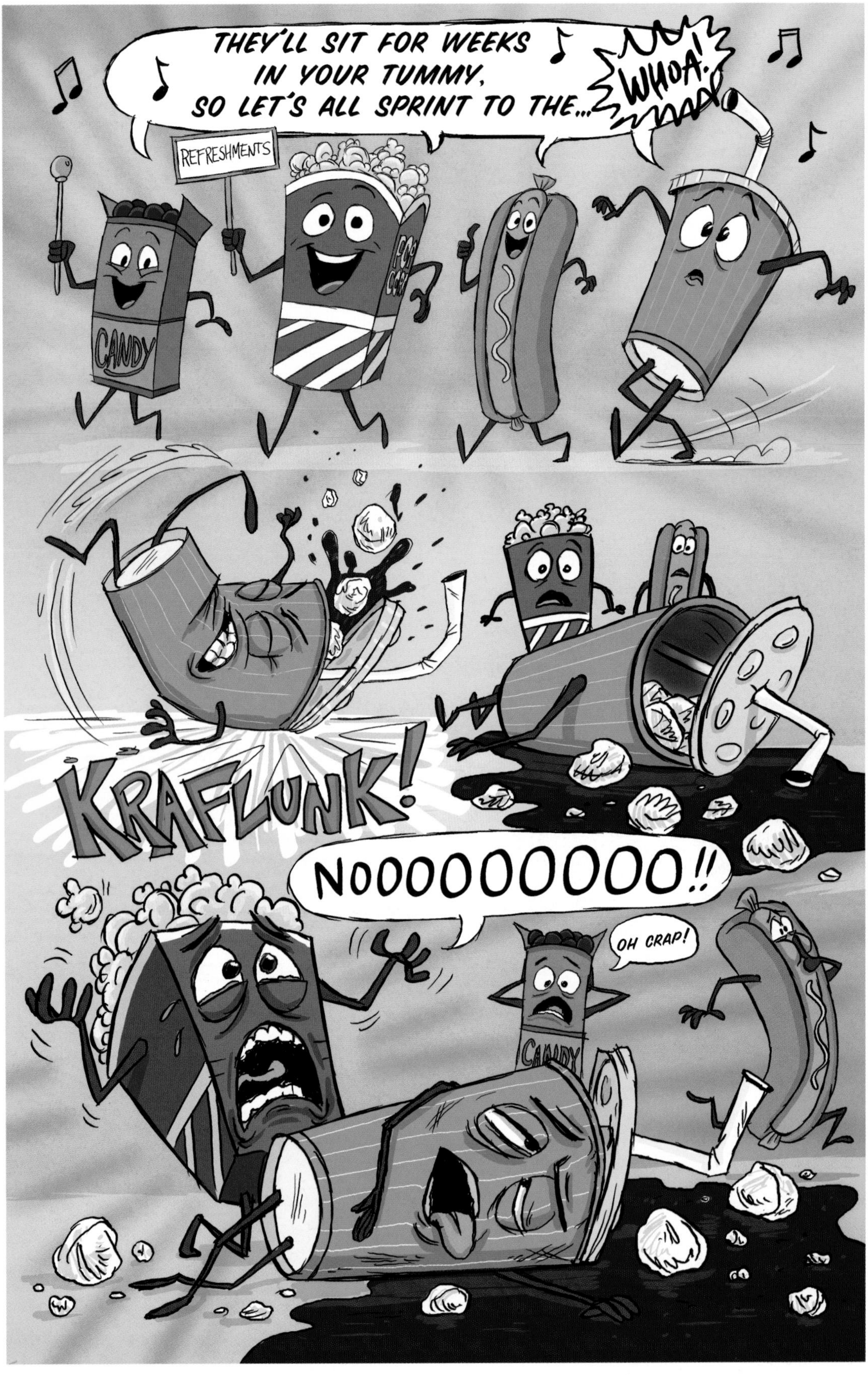
THEY'LL SIT FOR WEEKS IN YOUR TUMMY, SO LET'S ALL SPRINT TO THE...
WHOA!
REFRESHMENTS
CANDY
KRAFLUNK!
NOOOOOOOOOO!!
OH CRAP!
CANDY

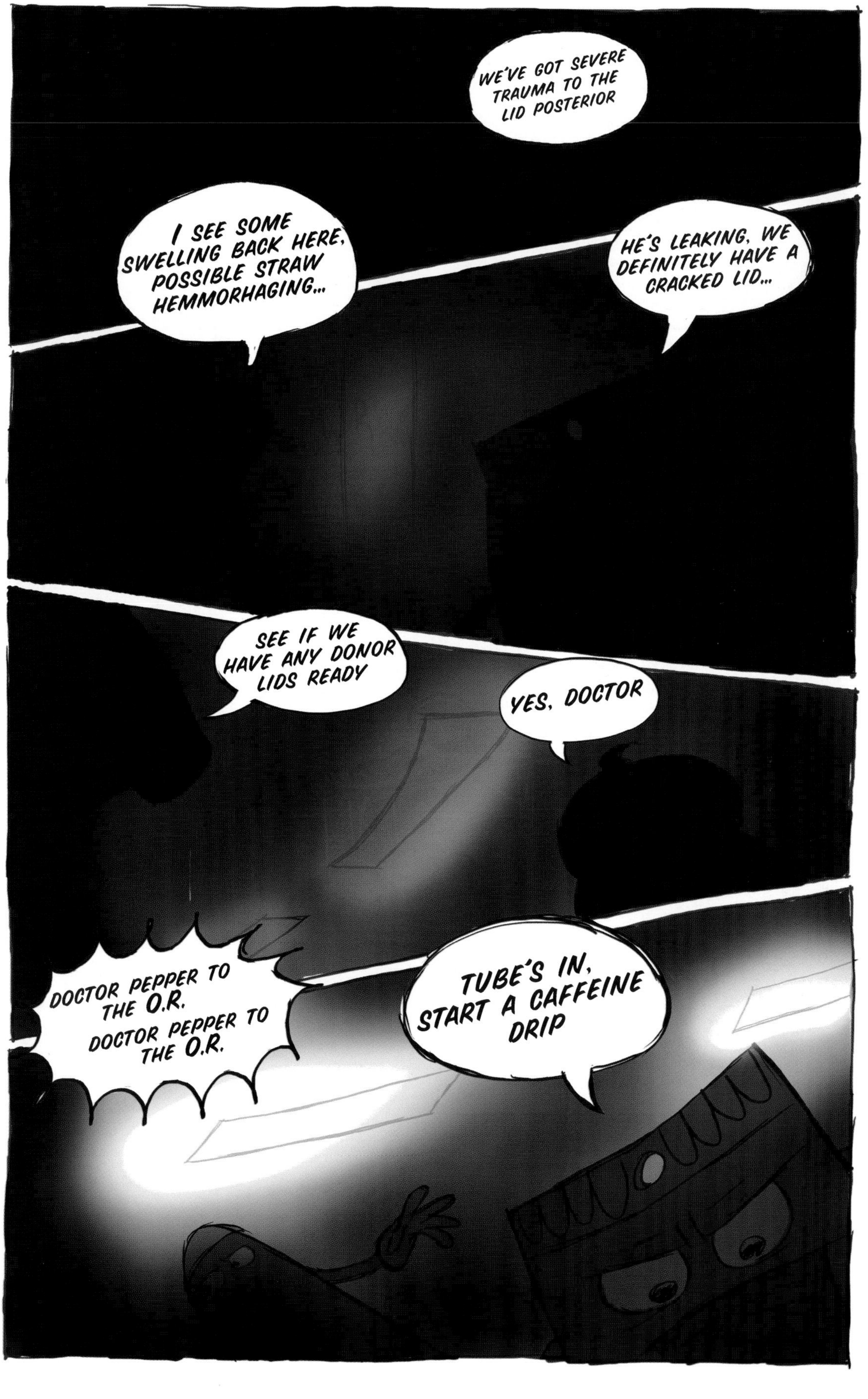
WE'VE GOT SEVERE TRAUMA TO THE LID POSTERIOR
I SEE SOME SWELLING BACK HERE, POSSIBLE STRAW HEMMORHAGING...
HE'S LEAKING, WE DEFINITELY HAVE A CRACKED LID...
SEE IF WE HAVE ANY DONOR LIDS READY
YES, DOCTOR
DOCTOR PEPPER TO THE O.R. DOCTOR PEPPER TO THE O.R.
TUBE'S IN, START A CAFFEINE DRIP

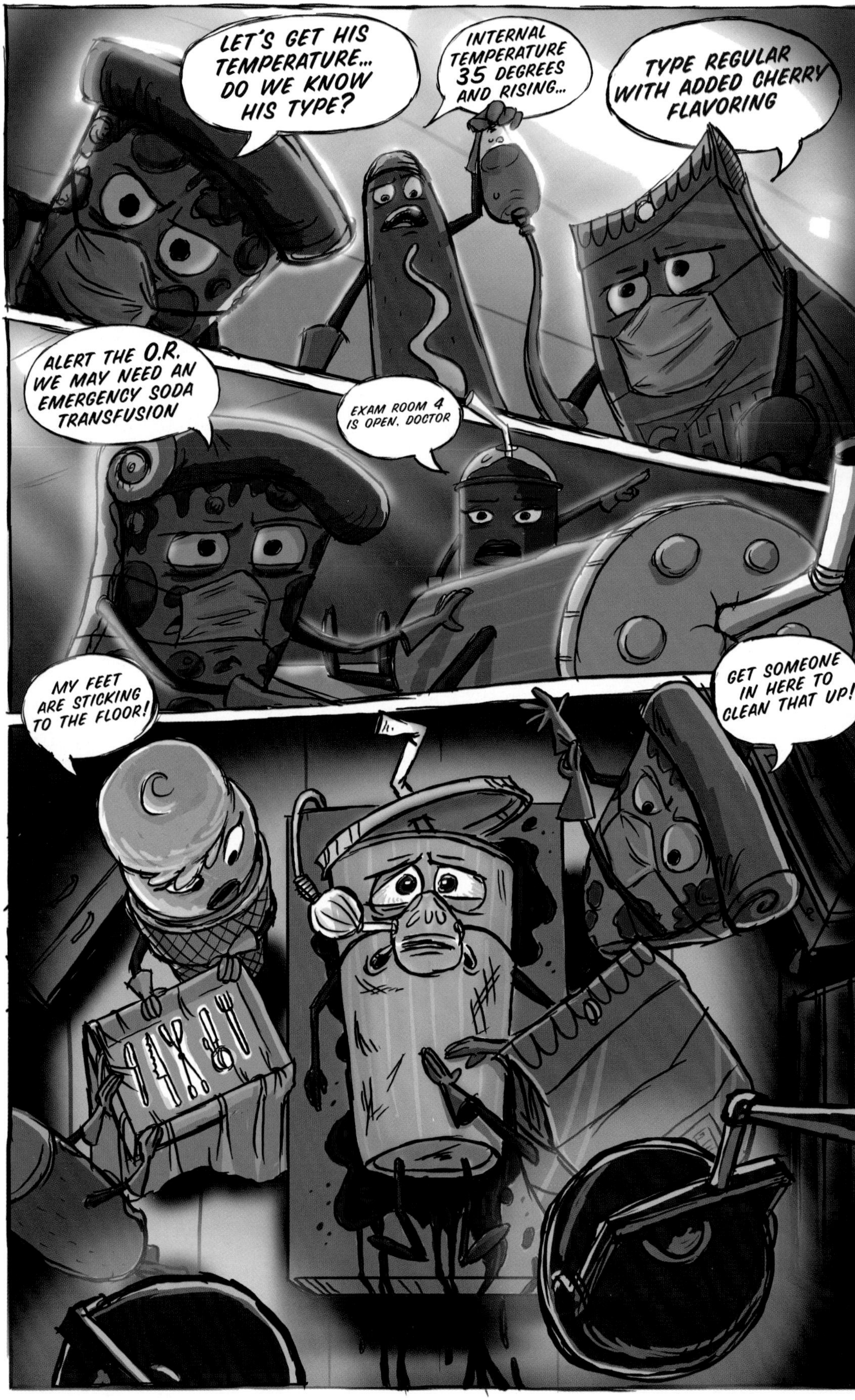
LET'S GET HIS TEMPERATURE... DO WE KNOW HIS TYPE?
INTERNAL TEMPERATURE 35 DEGREES AND RISING...
TYPE REGULAR WITH ADDED CHERRY FLAVORING
ALERT THE O.R. WE MAY NEED AN EMERGENCY SODA TRANSFUSION
EXAM ROOM 4 IS OPEN, DOCTOR
MY FEET ARE STICKING TO THE FLOOR!
GET SOMEONE IN HERE TO CLEAN THAT UP!

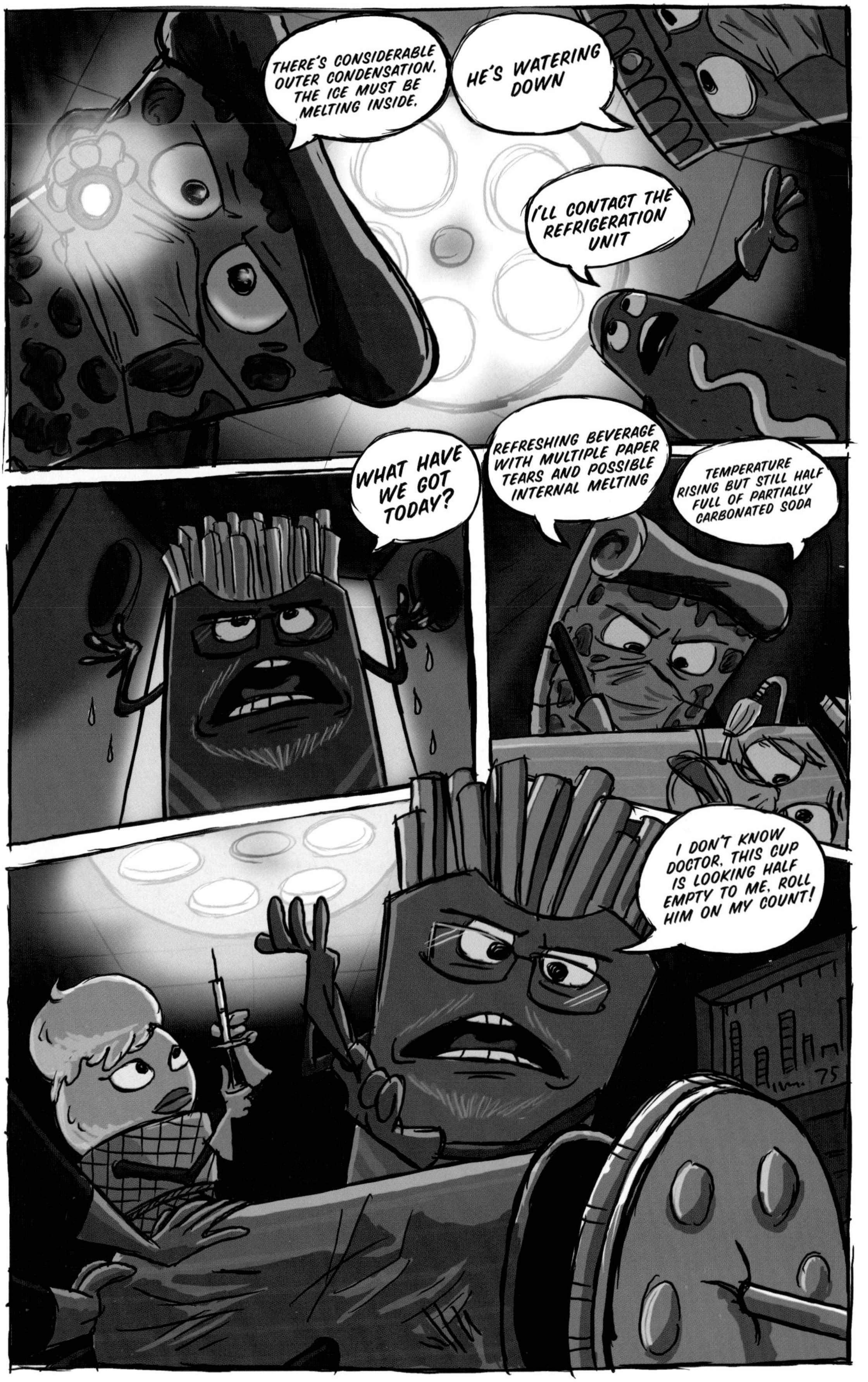
THERE'S CONSIDERABLE OUTER CONDENSATION. THE ICE MUST BE MELTING INSIDE.
HE'S WATERING DOWN
I'LL CONTACT THE REFRIGERATION UNIT
WHAT HAVE WE GOT TODAY?
REFRESHING BEVERAGE WITH MULTIPLE PAPER TEARS AND POSSIBLE INTERNAL MELTING
TEMPERATURE RISING BUT STILL HALF FULL OF PARTIALLY CARBONATED SODA
I DON'T KNOW DOCTOR, THIS CUP IS LOOKING HALF EMPTY TO ME, ROLL HIM ON MY COUNT!
75

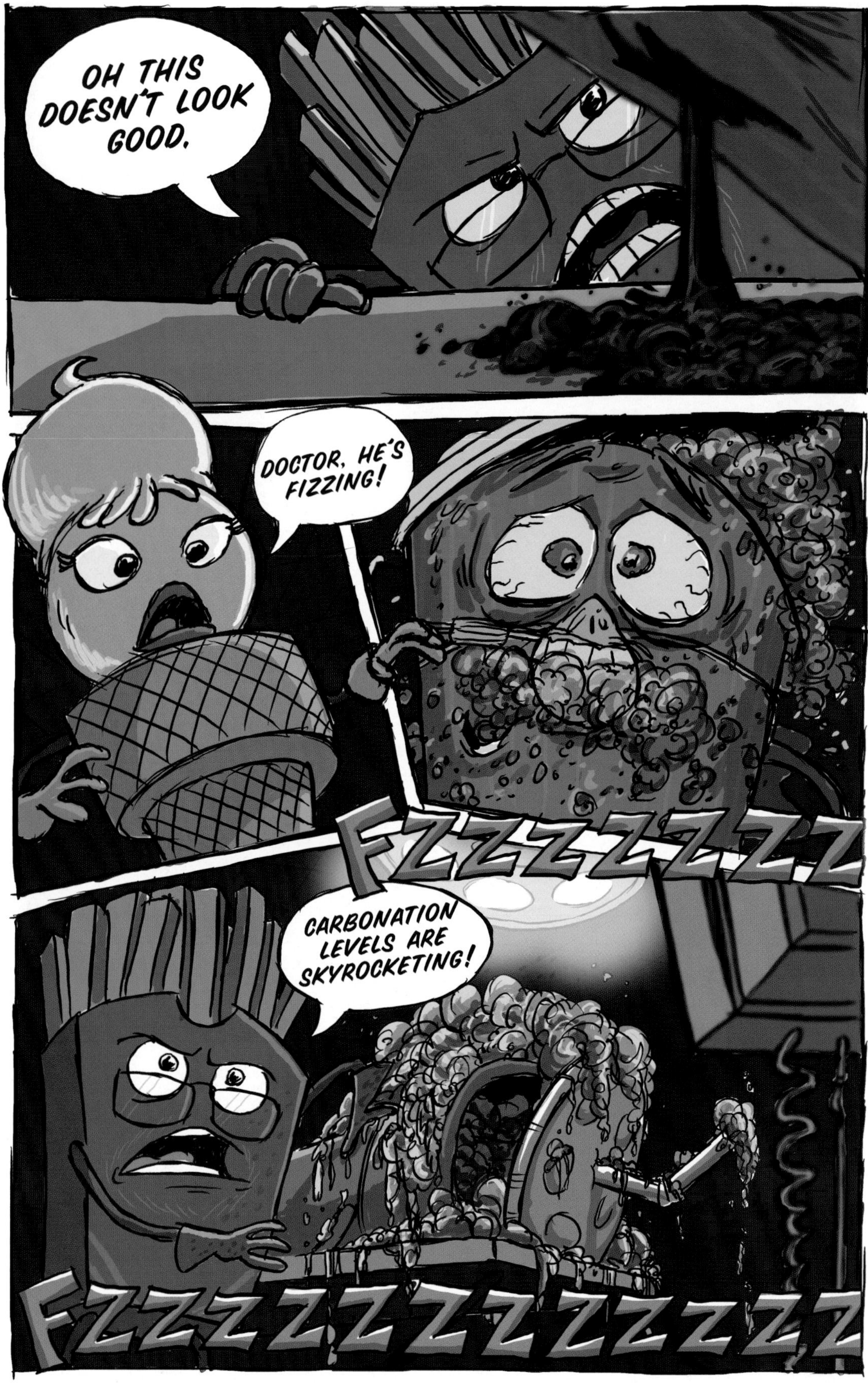
OH THIS DOESN'T LOOK GOOD.
DOCTOR, HE'S FIZZING!
FZZZZZZZZ
CARBONATION LEVELS ARE SKYROCKETING!
FZZZZZZZZZZZZZZZZ

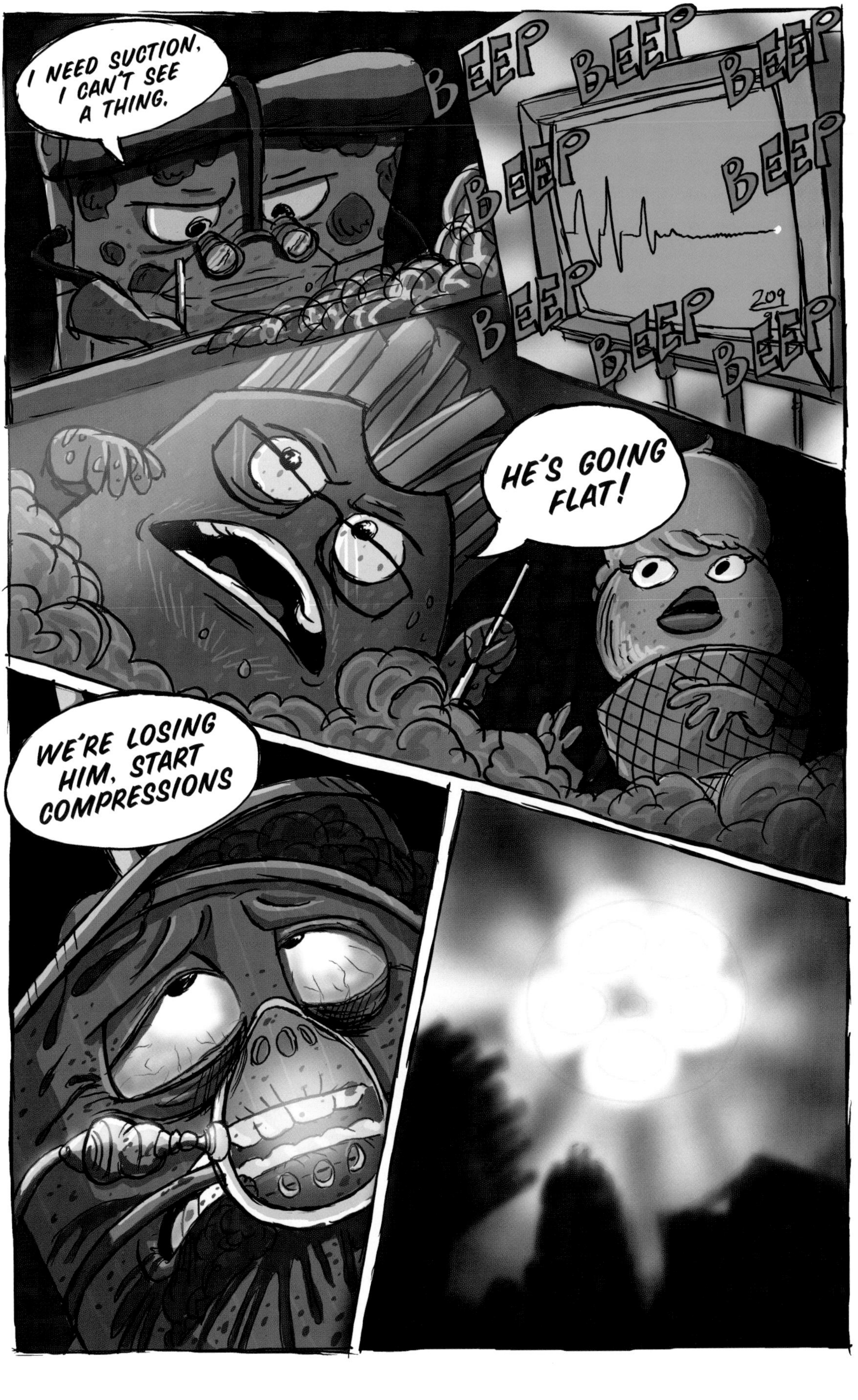
I NEED SUCTION, I CAN'T SEE A THING.
BEEP BEEP BEEP BEEP BEEP BEEP BEEP BEEP
HE'S GOING FLAT!
WE'RE LOSING HIM, START COMPRESSIONS

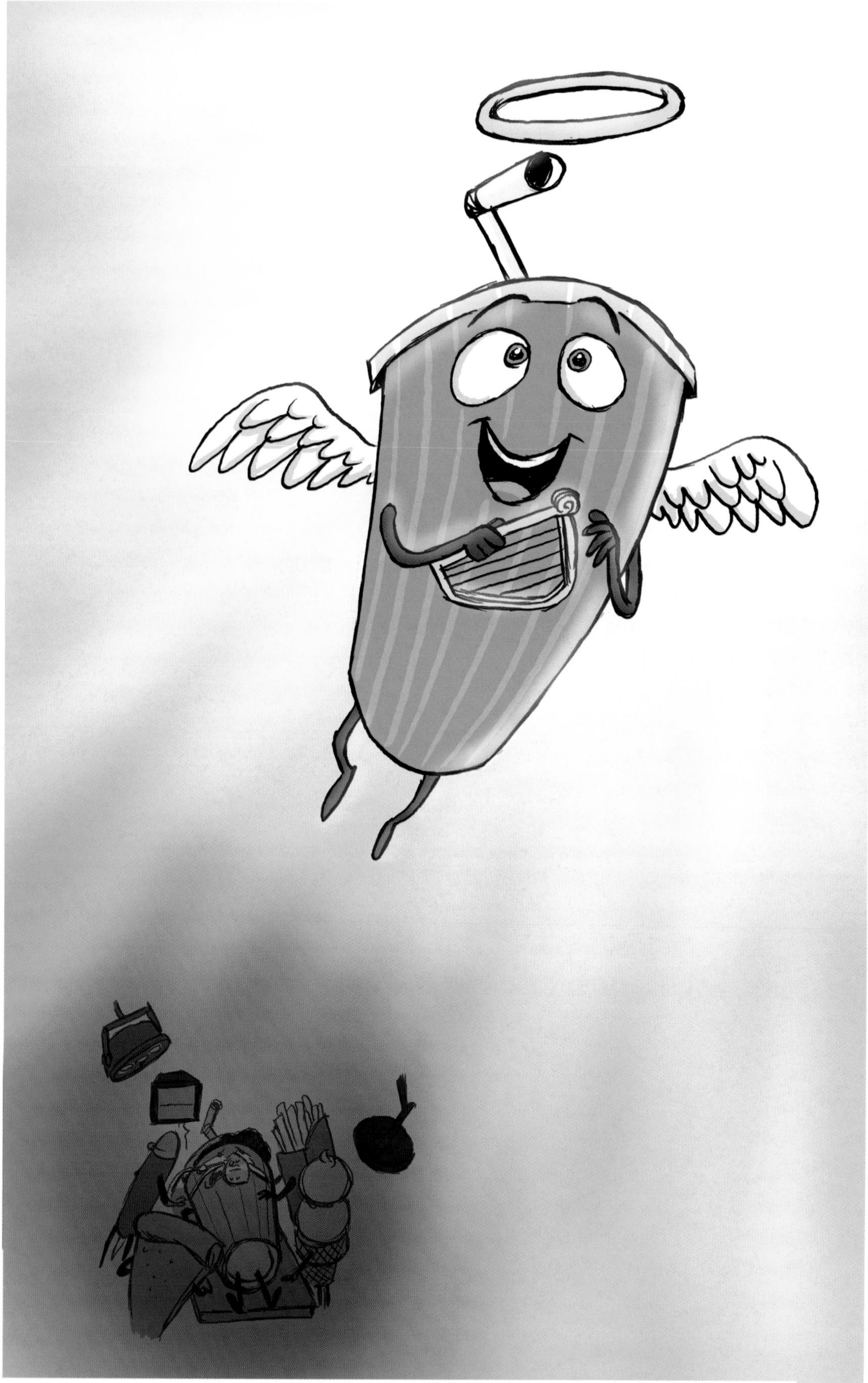

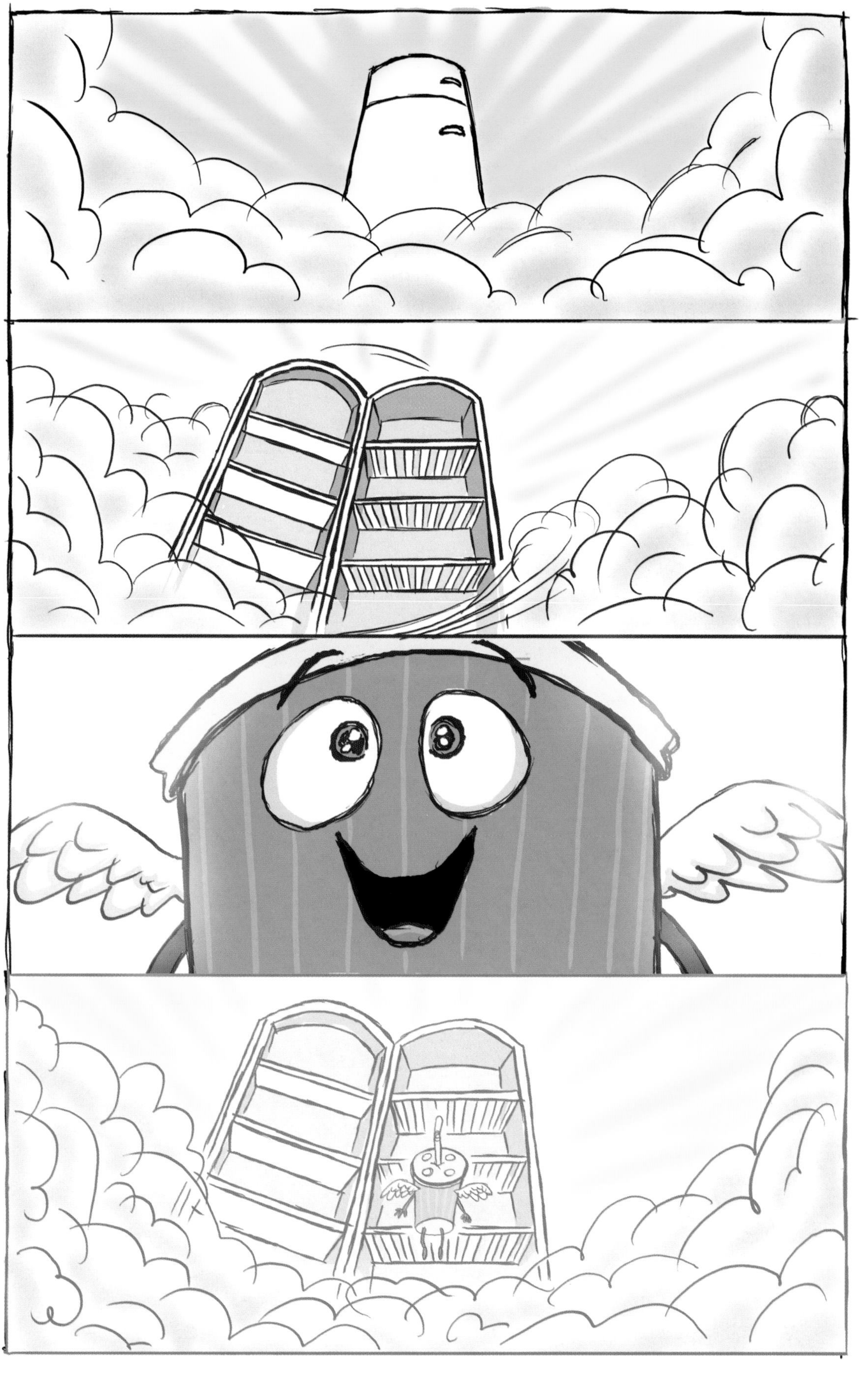

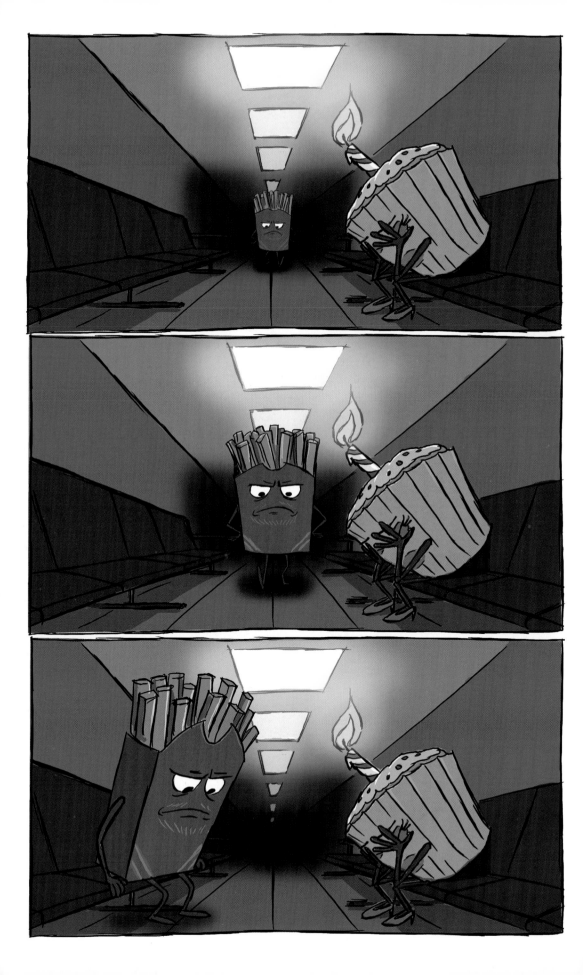

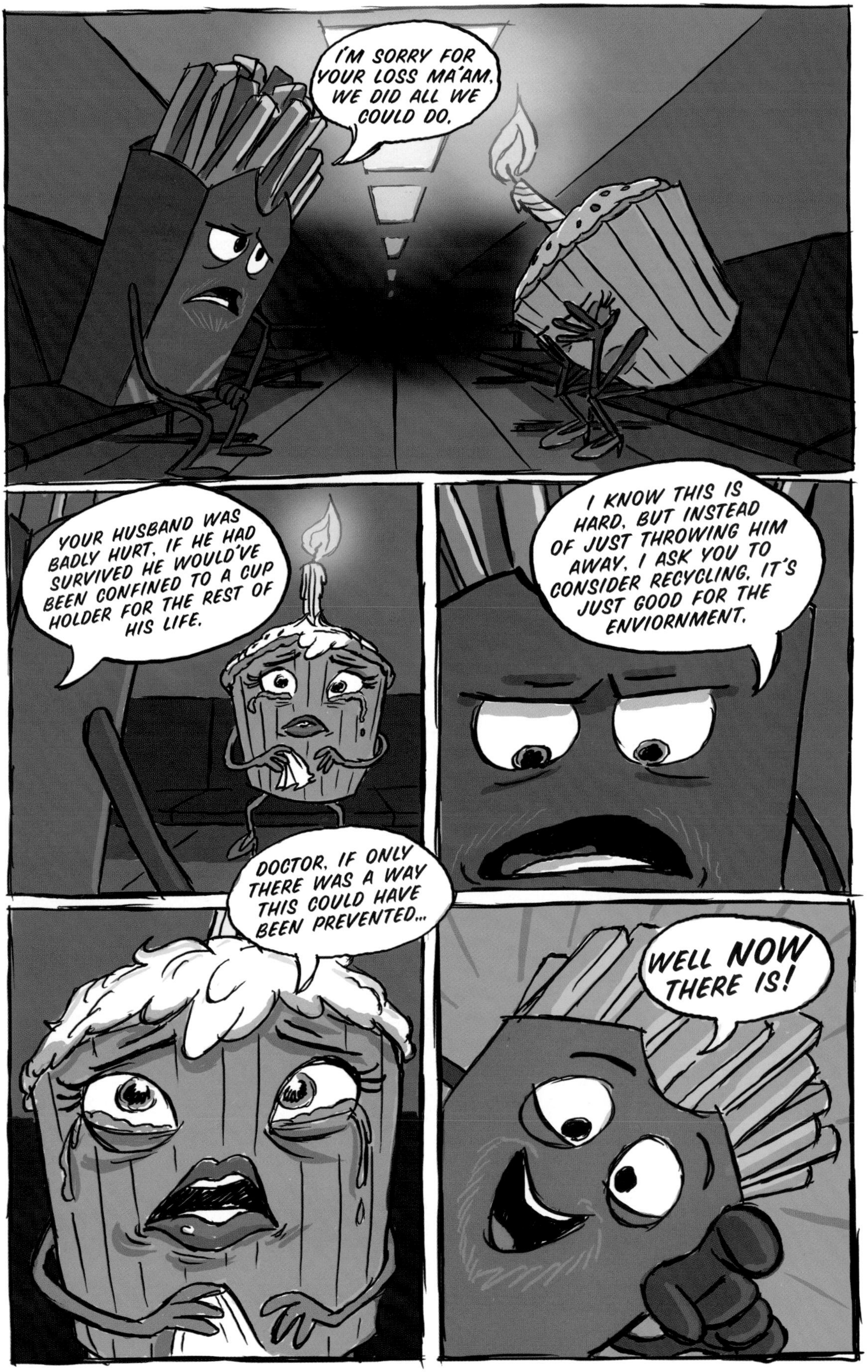
I'M SORRY FOR YOUR LOSS MA'AM. WE DID ALL WE COULD DO.
YOUR HUSBAND WAS BADLY HURT. IF HE HAD SURVIVED HE WOULD'VE BEEN CONFINED TO A CUP HOLDER FOR THE REST OF HIS LIFE.
I KNOW THIS IS HARD, BUT INSTEAD OF JUST THROWING HIM AWAY, I ASK YOU TO CONSIDER RECYCLING. IT'S JUST GOOD FOR THE ENVIORNMENT.
DOCTOR, IF ONLY THERE WAS A WAY THIS COULD HAVE BEEN PREVENTED...
WELL NOW THERE IS!

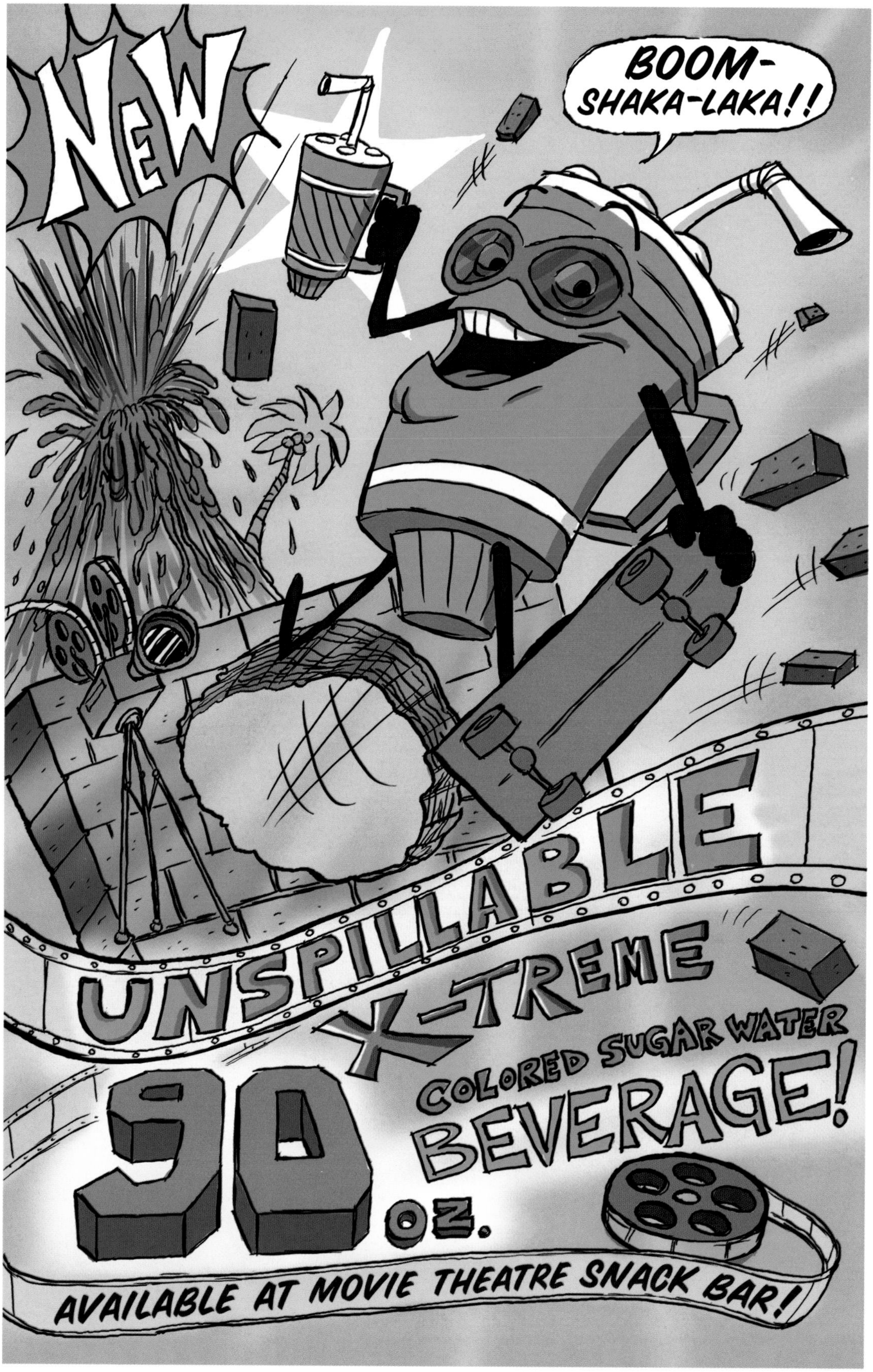
NEW
BOOM-SHAKA-LAKA!!
UNSPILLABLE
X-TREME
COLORED SUGAR WATER
BEVERAGE!
90 OZ.
AVAILABLE AT MOVIE THEATRE SNACK BAR!

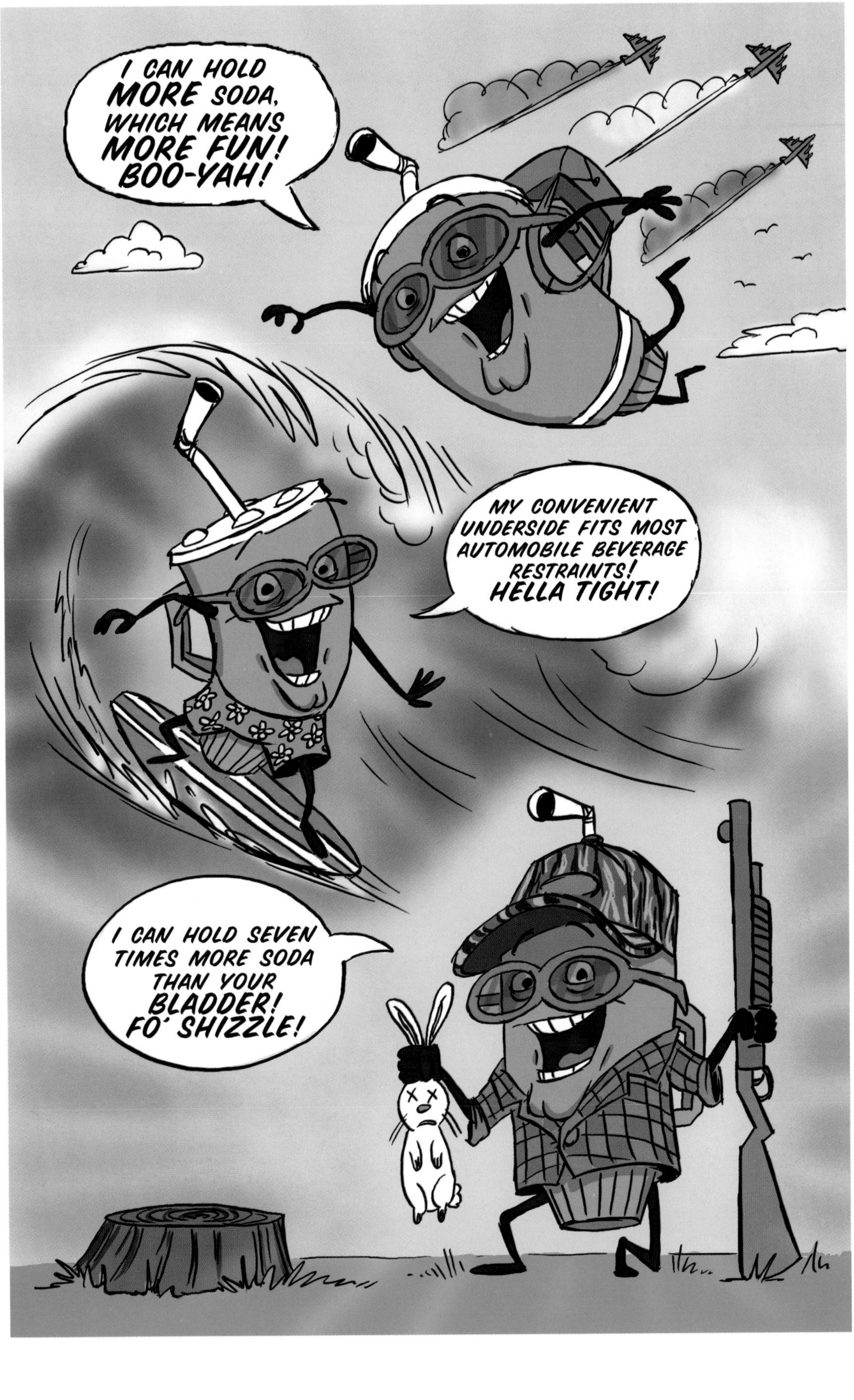
I CAN HOLD MORE SODA, WHICH MEANS MORE FUN! BOO-YAH!
MY CONVENIENT UNDERSIDE FITS MOST AUTOMOBILE BEVERAGE RESTRAINTS! HELLA TIGHT!
I CAN HOLD SEVEN TIMES MORE SODA THAN YOUR BLADDER! FO' SHIZZLE!

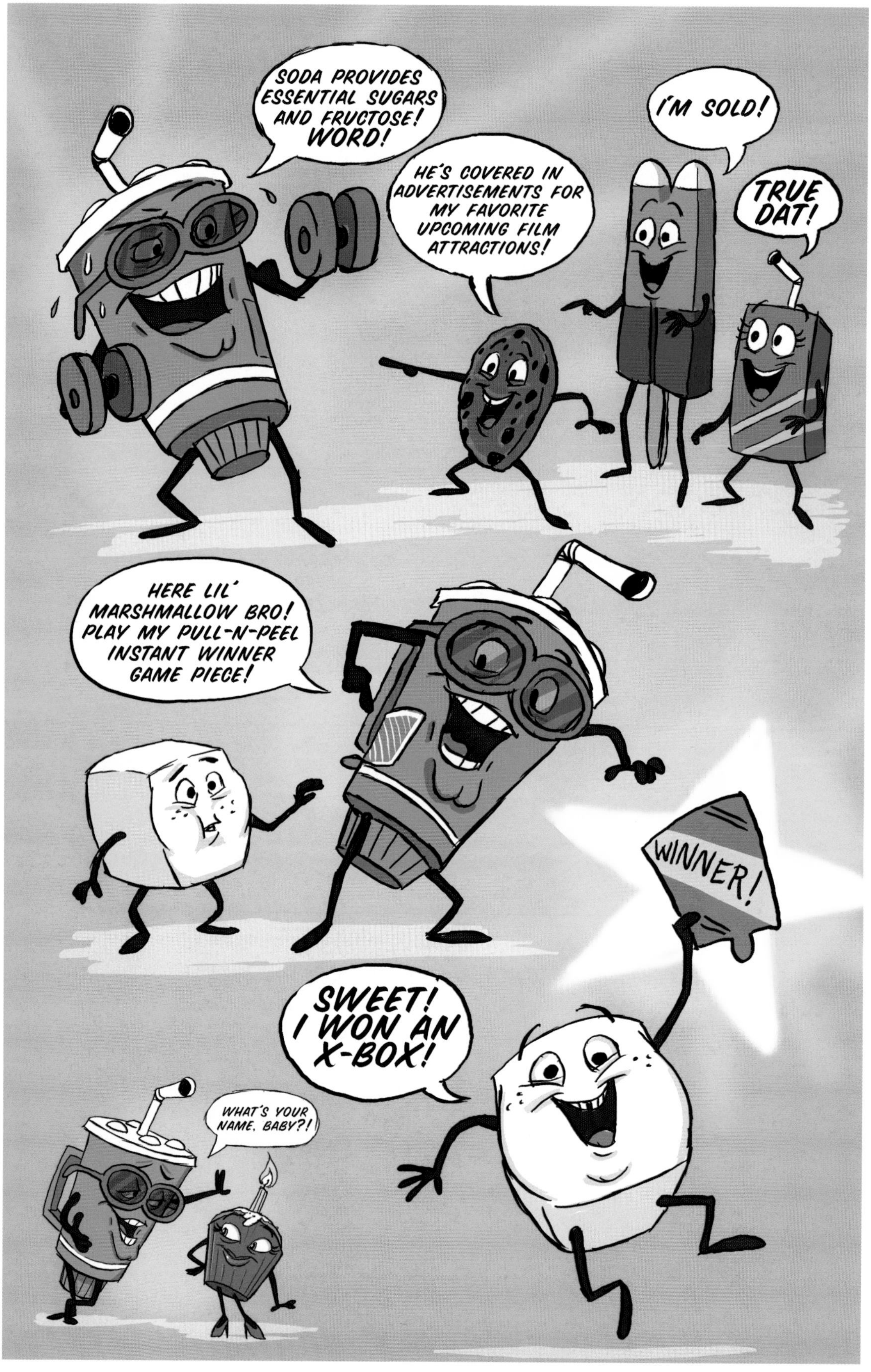

SODA PROVIDES ESSENTIAL SUGARS AND FRUCTOSE! WORD!
HE'S COVERED IN ADVERTISEMENTS FOR MY FAVORITE UPCOMING FILM ATTRACTIONS!
I'M SOLD!
TRUE DAT!
HERE LIL' MARSHMALLOW BRO! PLAY MY PULL-N-PEEL INSTANT WINNER GAME PIECE!
WINNER!
SWEET! I WON AN X-BOX!
WHAT'S YOUR NAME, BABY?!

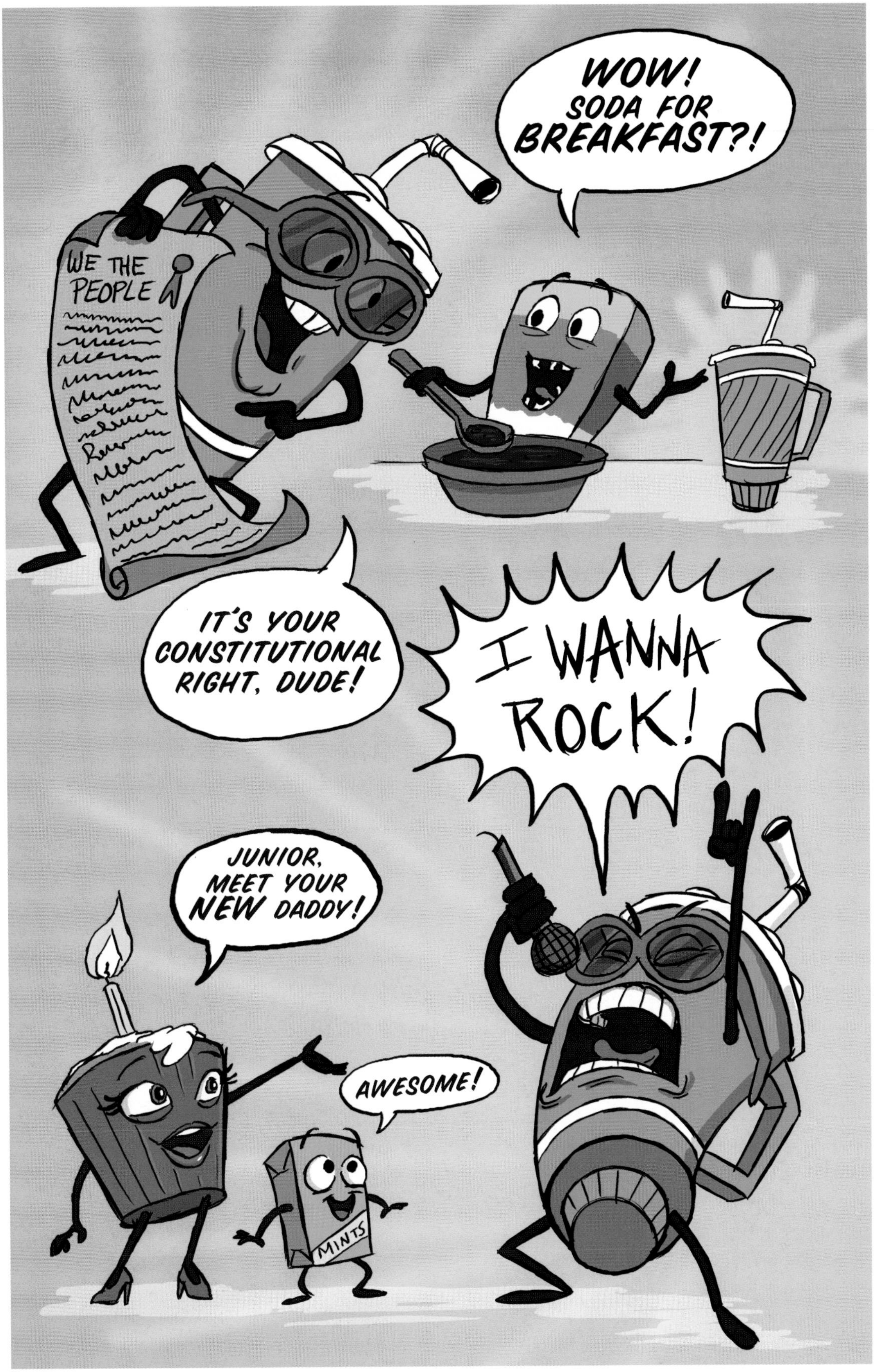
WE THE PEOPLE
WOW! SODA FOR BREAKFAST?!
IT'S YOUR CONSTITUTIONAL RIGHT, DUDE!
I WANNA ROCK!
JUNIOR, MEET YOUR NEW DADDY!
AWESOME!
MINTS

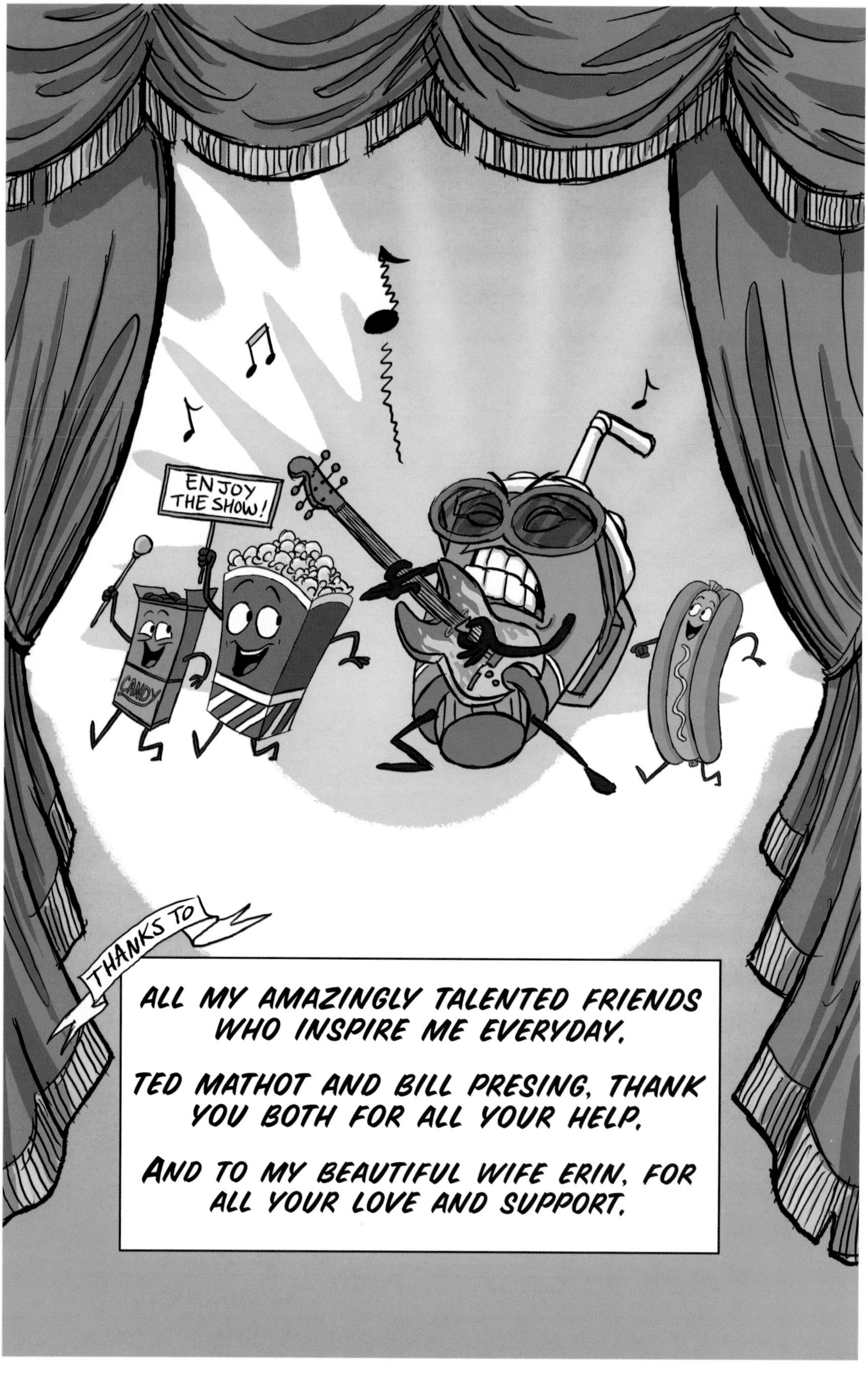
ENJOY THE SHOW!
CANDY
THANKS TO
ALL MY AMAZINGLY TALENTED FRIENDS WHO INSPIRE ME EVERYDAY.
TED MATHOT AND BILL PRESING, THANK YOU BOTH FOR ALL YOUR HELP.
AND TO MY BEAUTIFUL WIFE ERIN, FOR ALL YOUR LOVE AND SUPPORT.

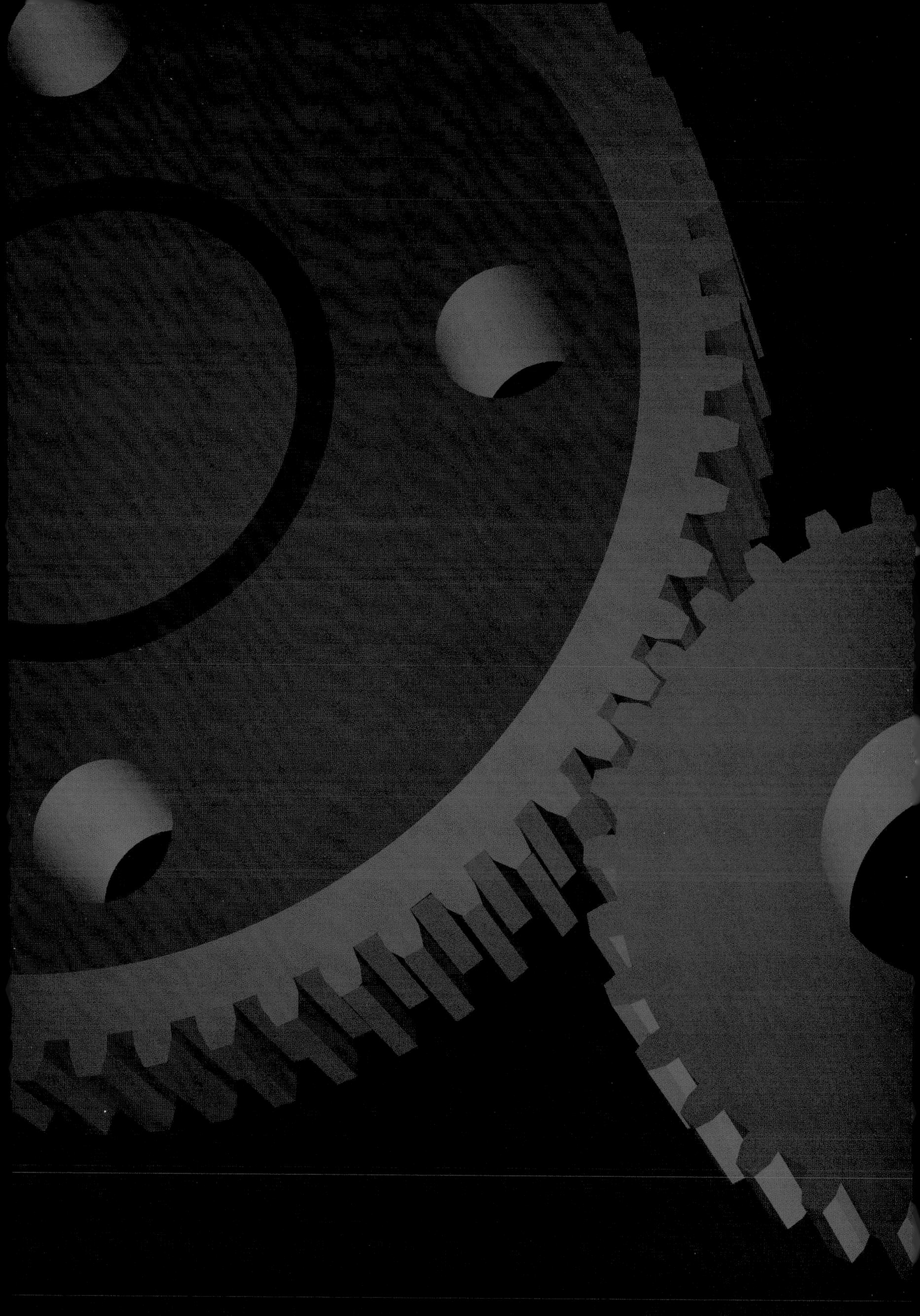

ANTHONY WONG

Story 1

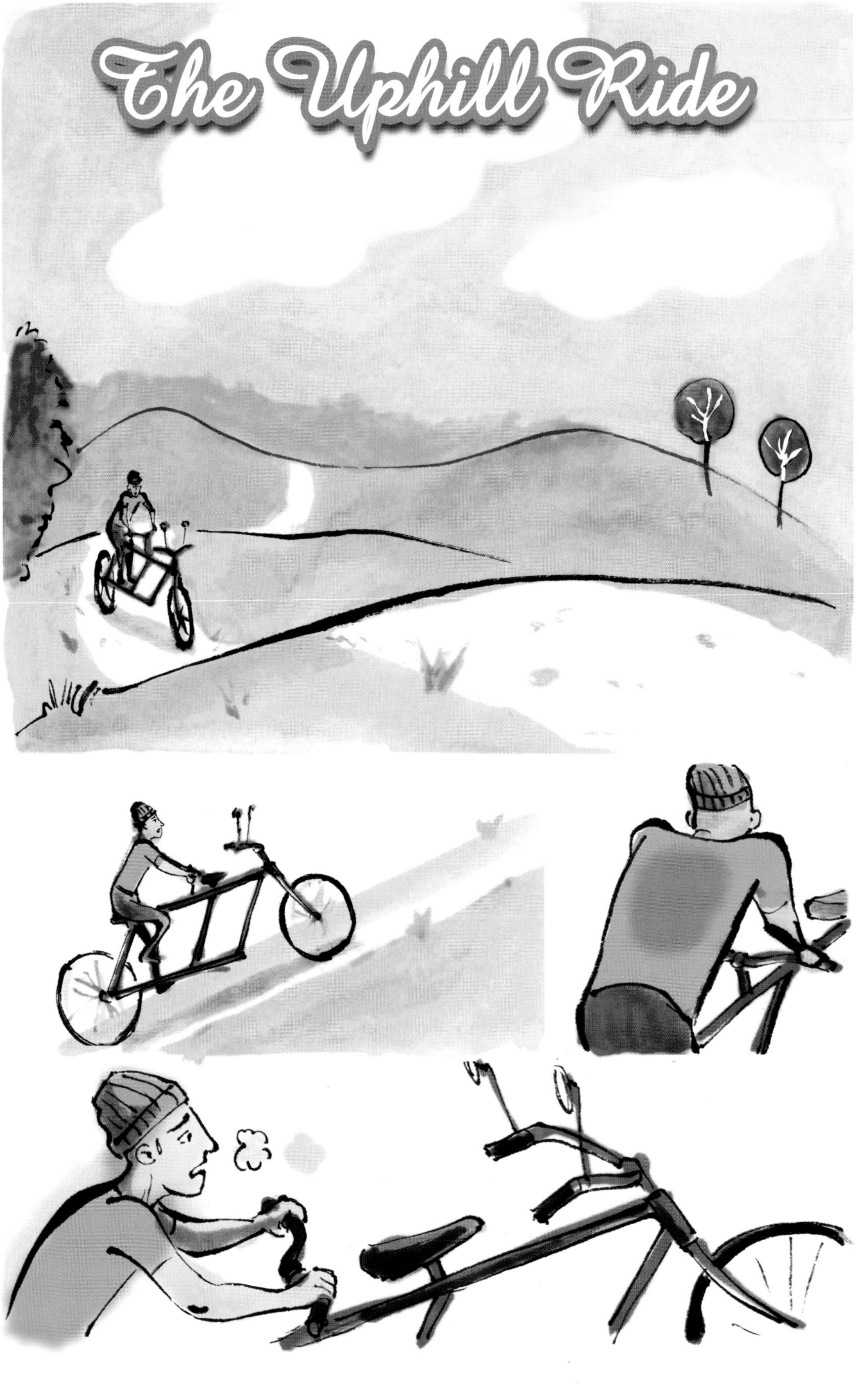
The Uphill Ride

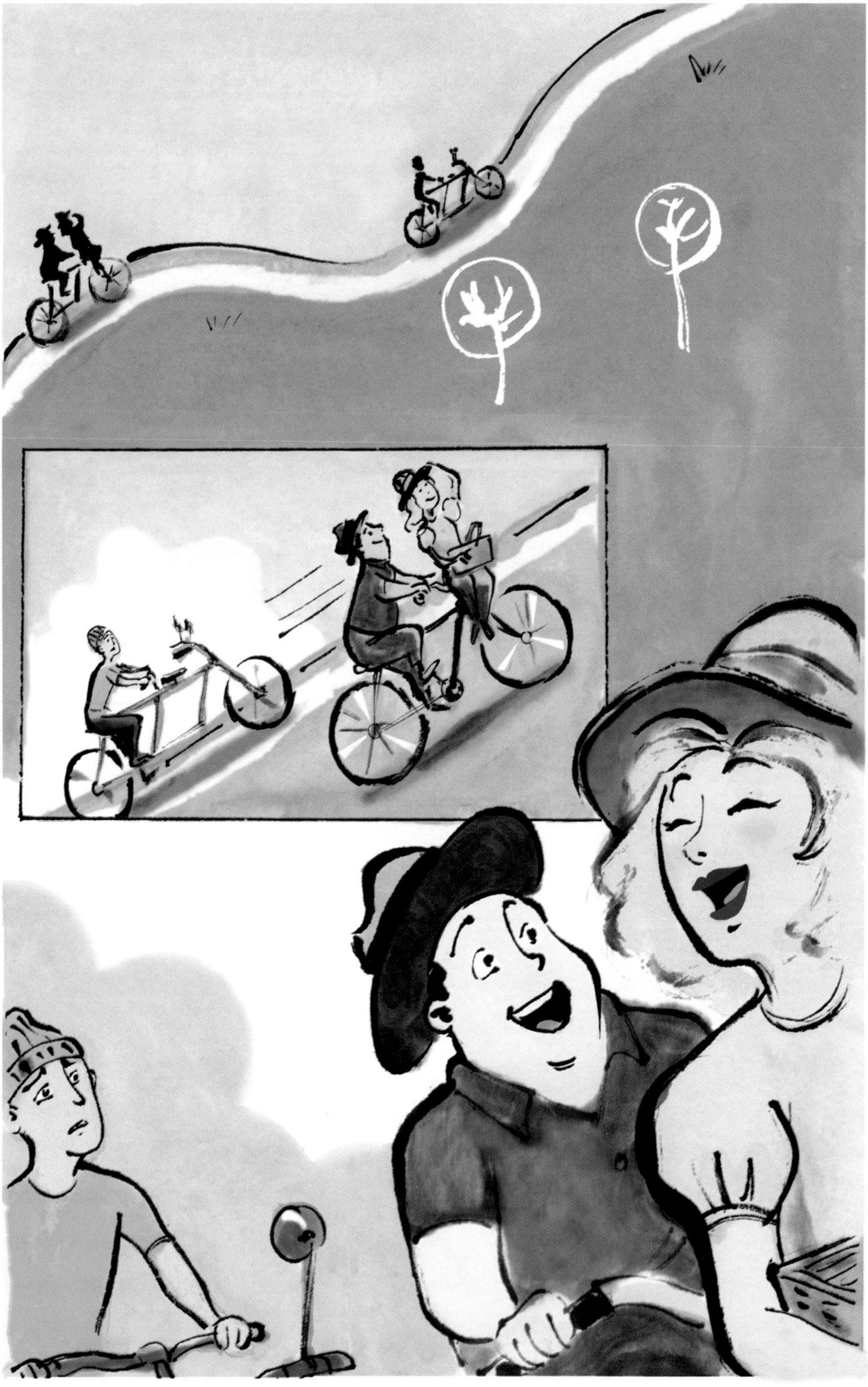

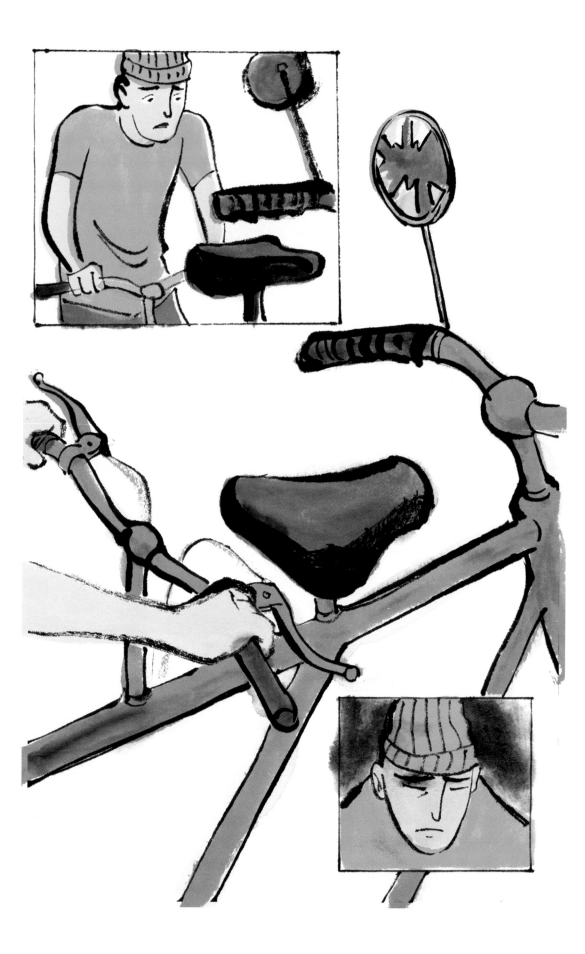

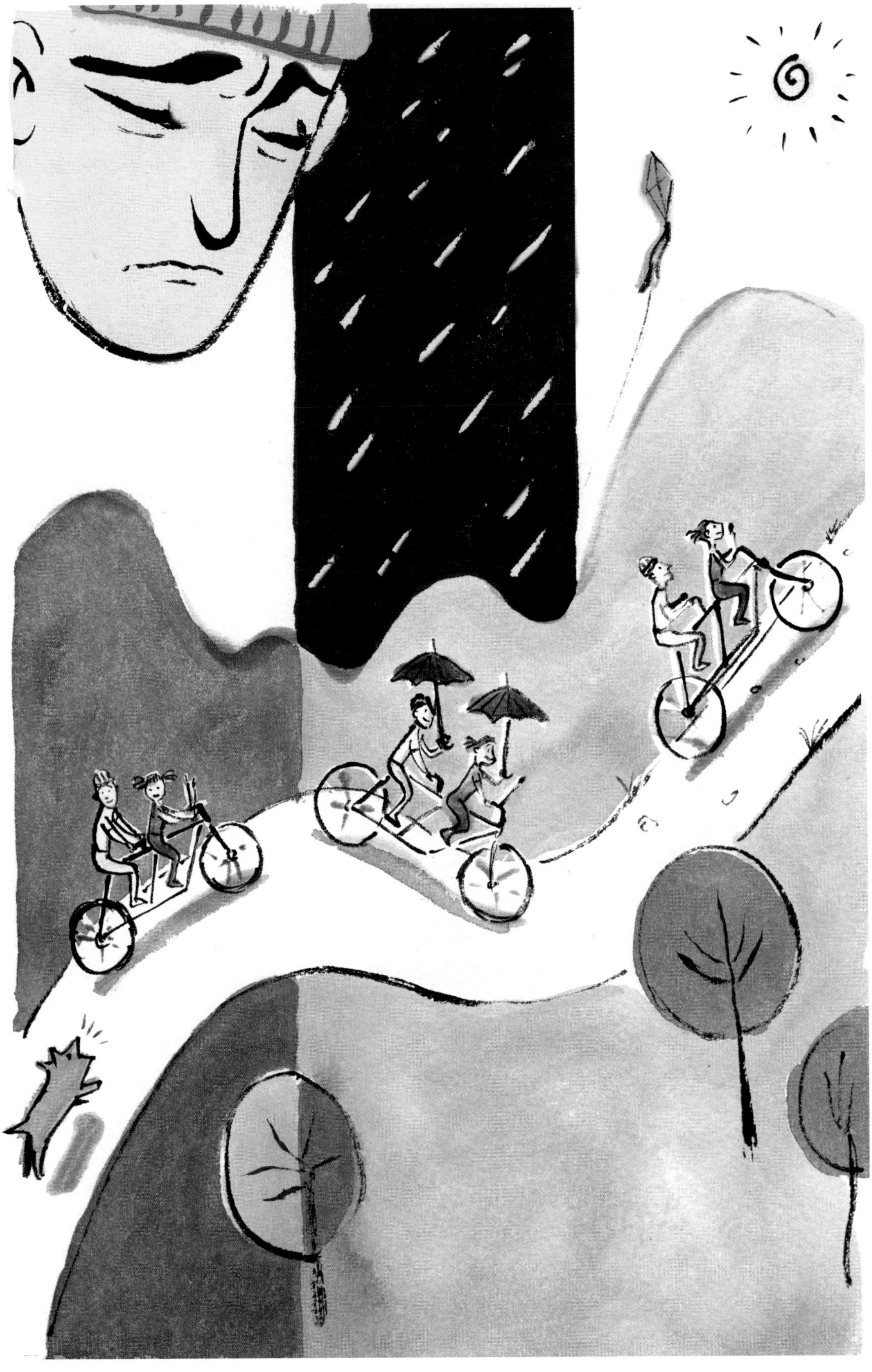

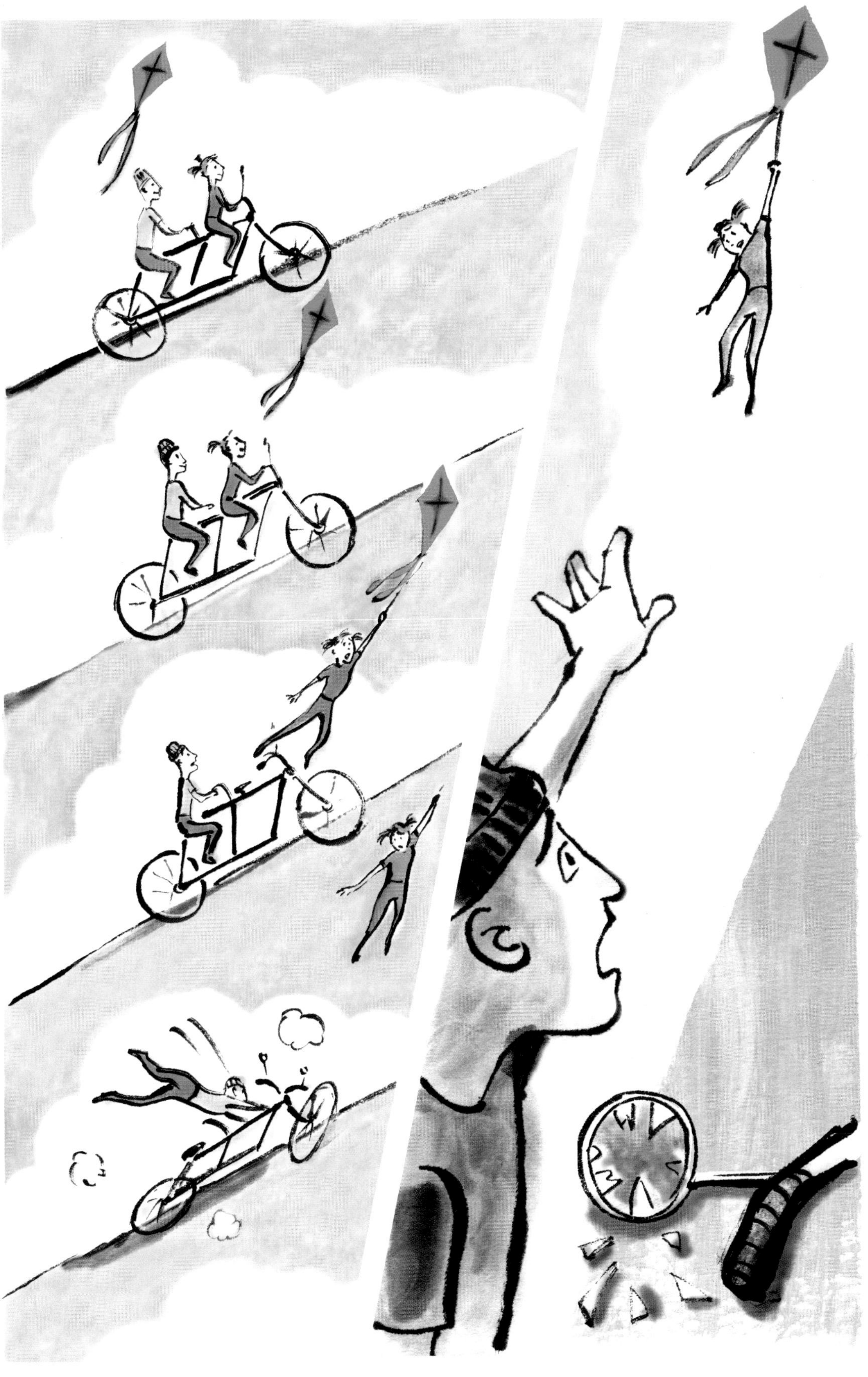

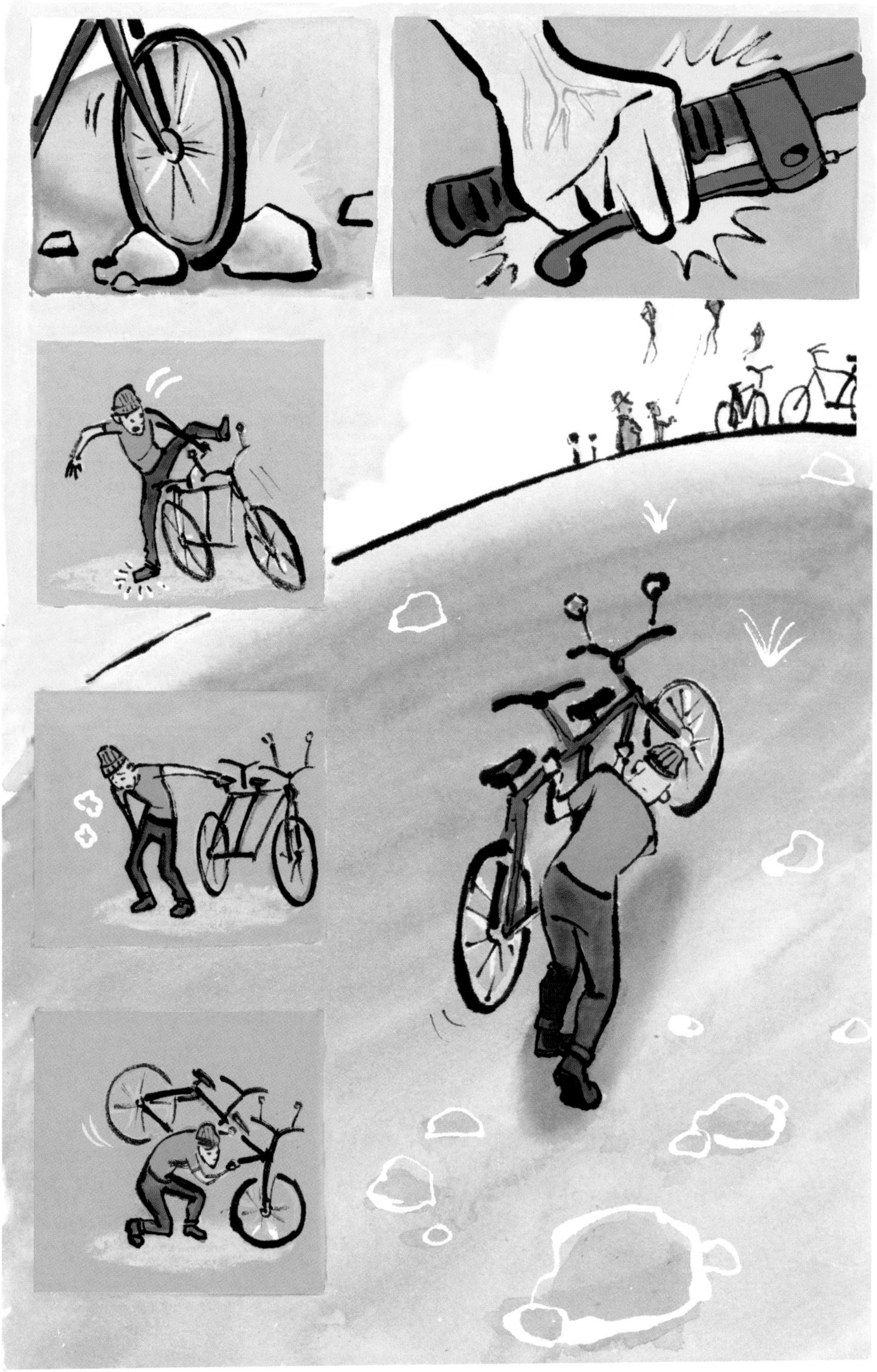

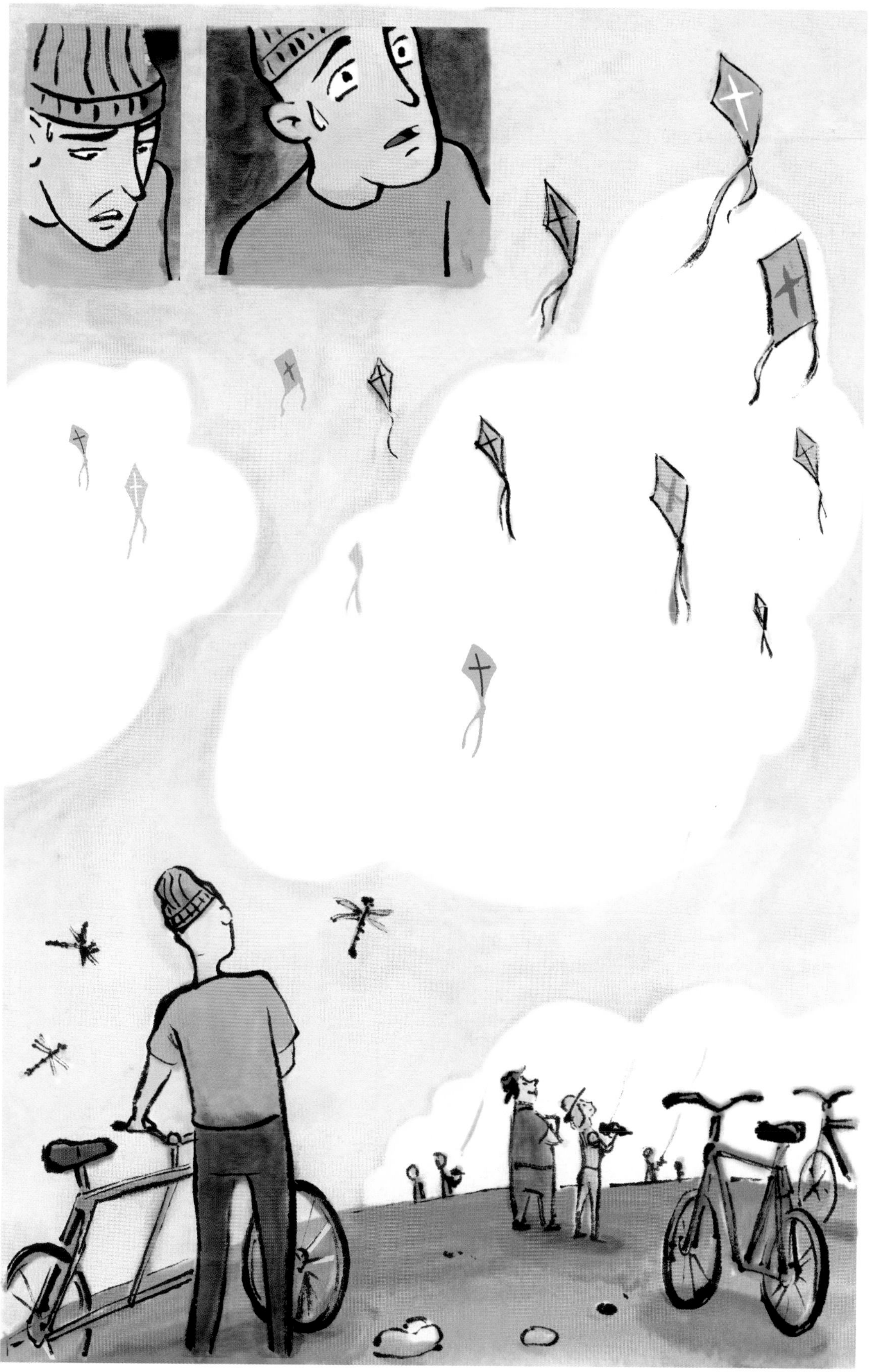

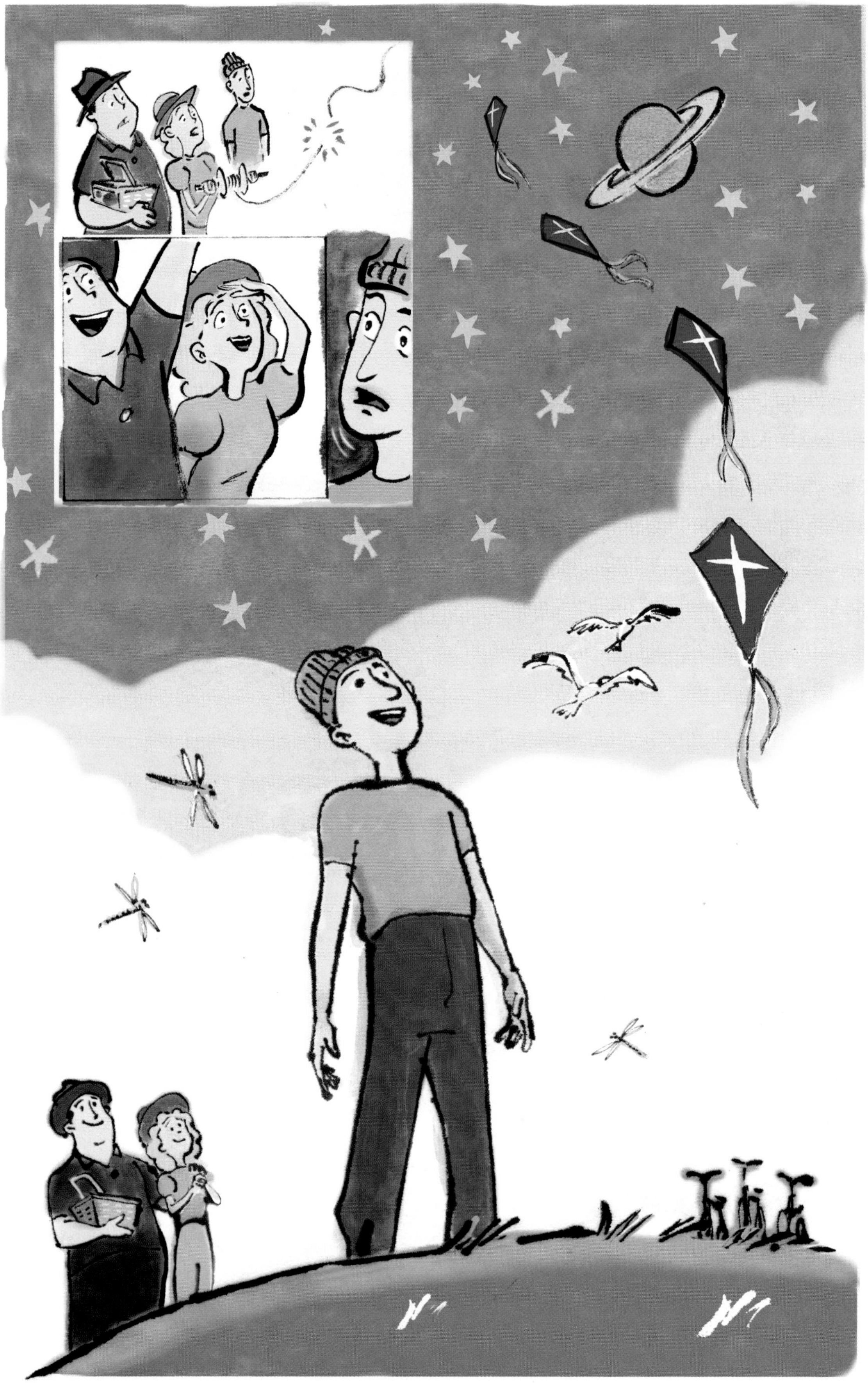

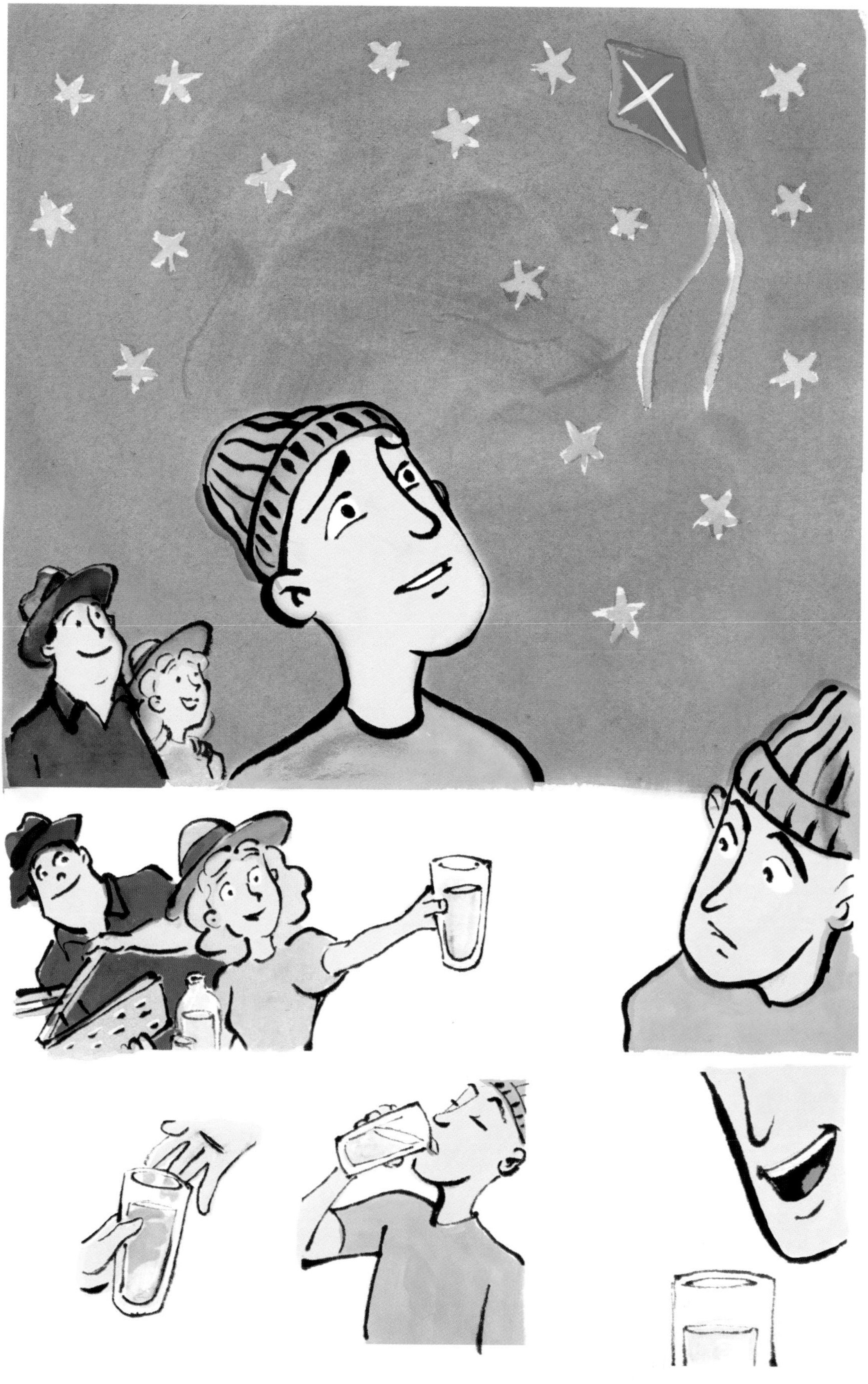

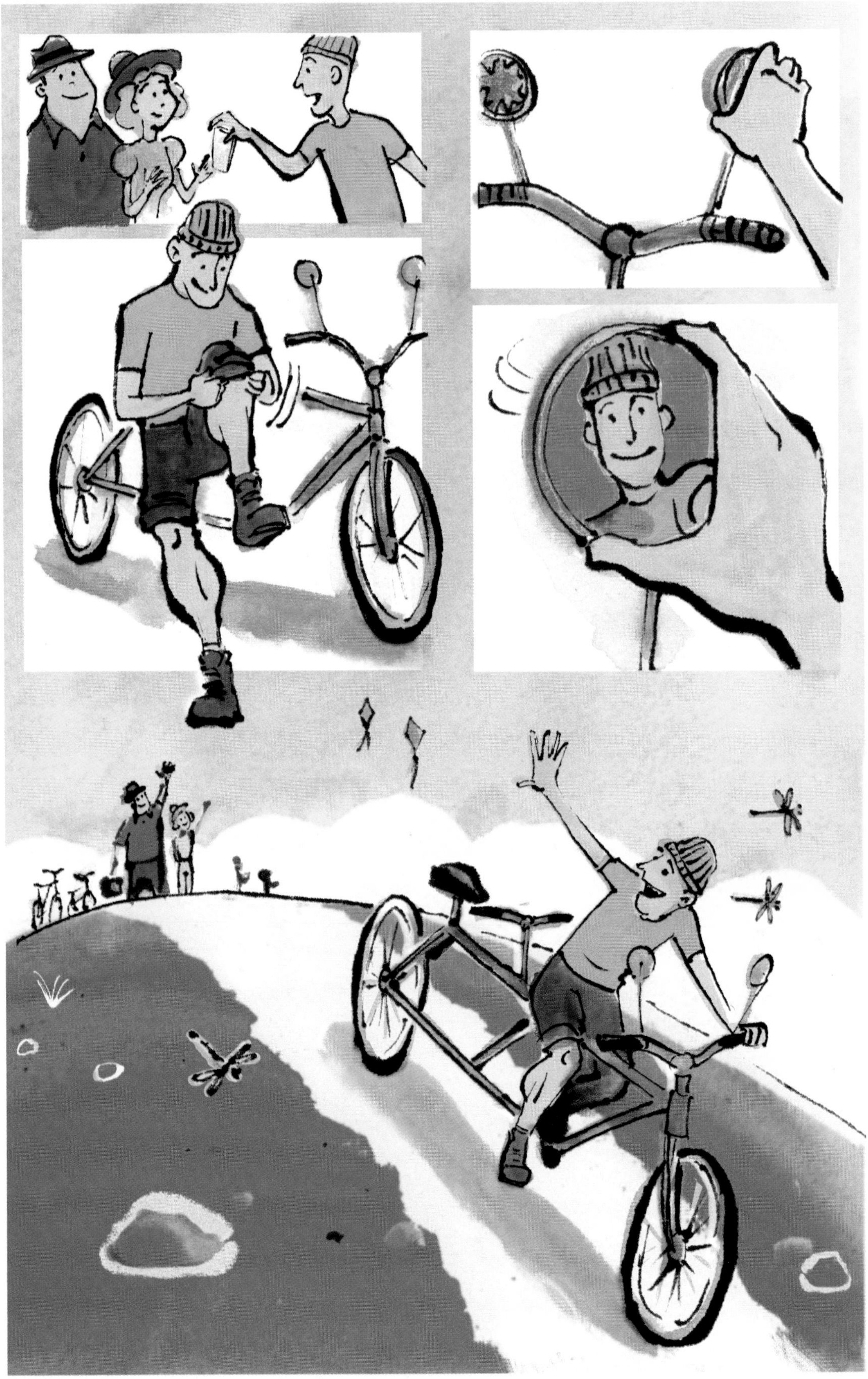

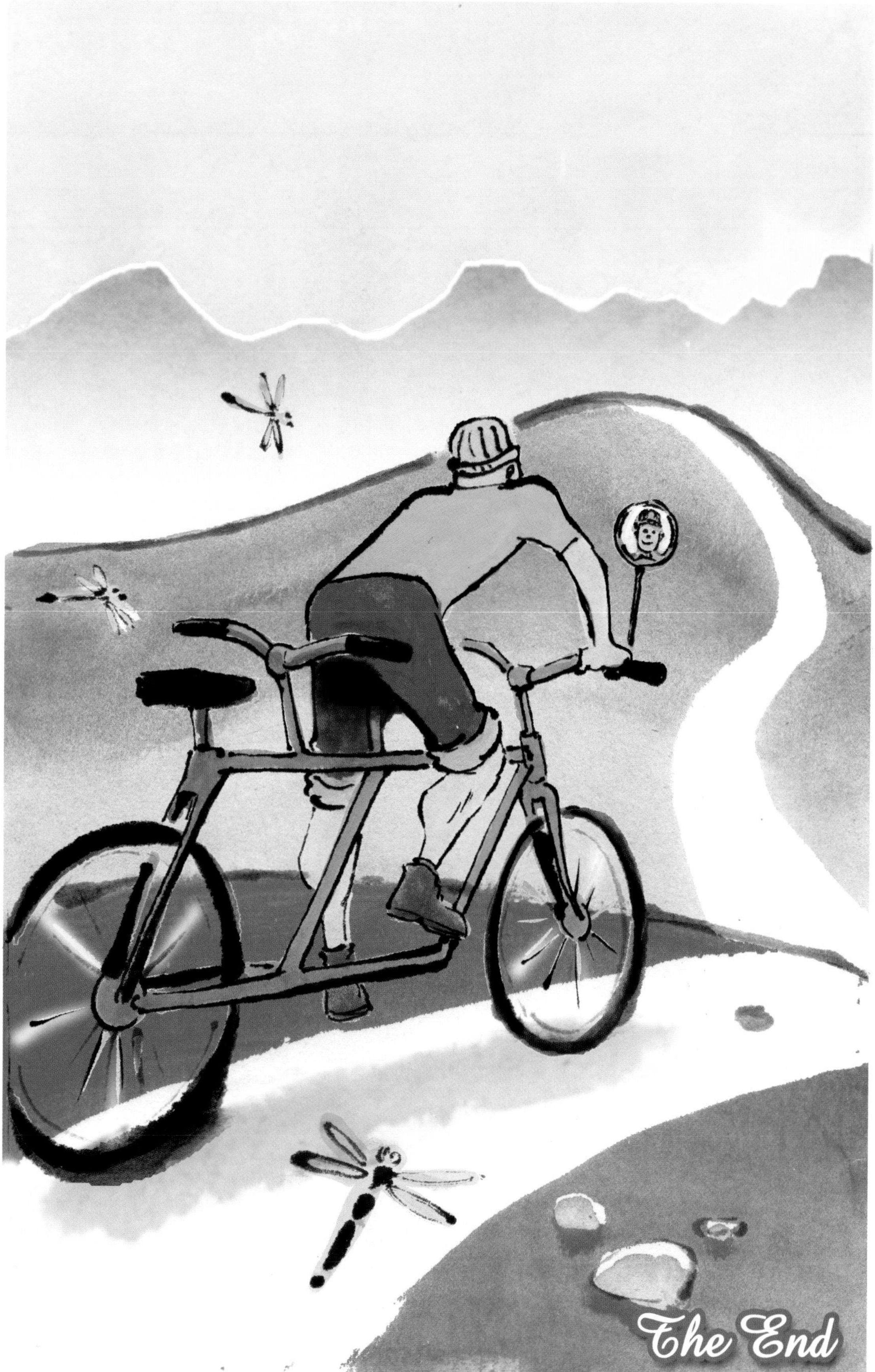
The End

Story 2

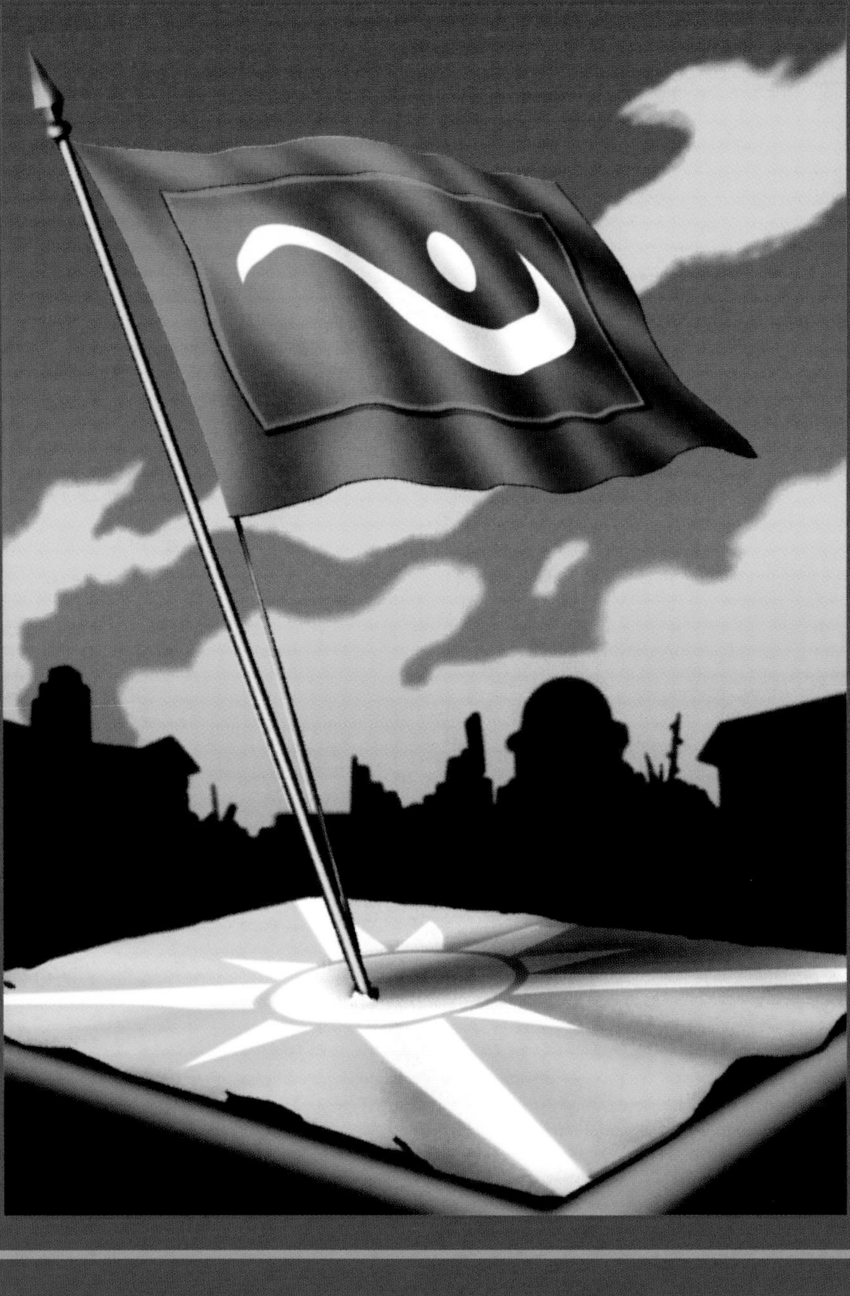

THE IMAGES OF GLORY

Chronicle

Tuesday, March 26th | 25122114

NEW WAR HERO CAPTAIN BRAVERMAN

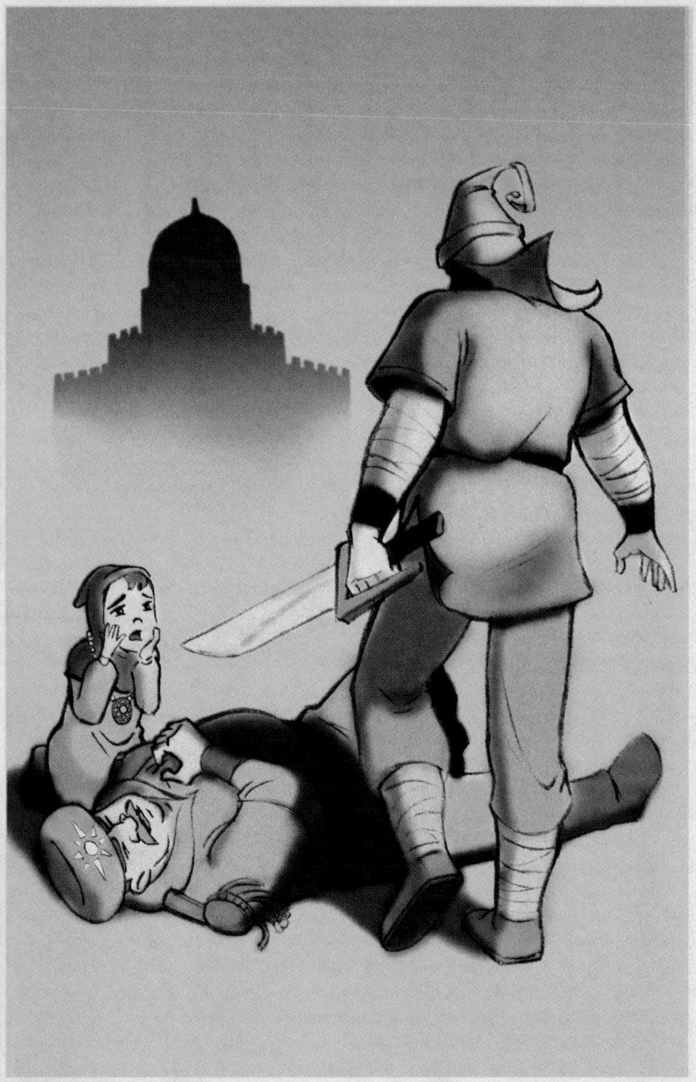

Capt. Braverman slaying the evil Emperor outside Tajuk capital. The princess seen in the photo has been reported missing since this incident.

WAR REPORT

Preemptive Strike Accomplished:

Captain honored in slaying Enemy Emperor

By Joe Authur
CHRONICLE STAFF WRITER

Tajuk City -- The 15 months invasion was declared successful when the enemy Emperor was slain last Sunday outside his capital city.

Capt. Braverman, 35, of the 23rd Division of the Army was responsible for this historic moment.

Capt. Braverman will be honored with the Golden Flag Medal Monday. The award ceremony will be broadcast so the whole country can see her new hero. He is the perfect role model for all citizens of our great nation.

Our preemptive strike claimed 3466 military causalties and cost $12 billion. The administration denies that the invasion is about the precious resources in Tajuk.

Continues on Page A2

30,000 civilians died during preemptive invasion

Debate over justifications of invasion continues

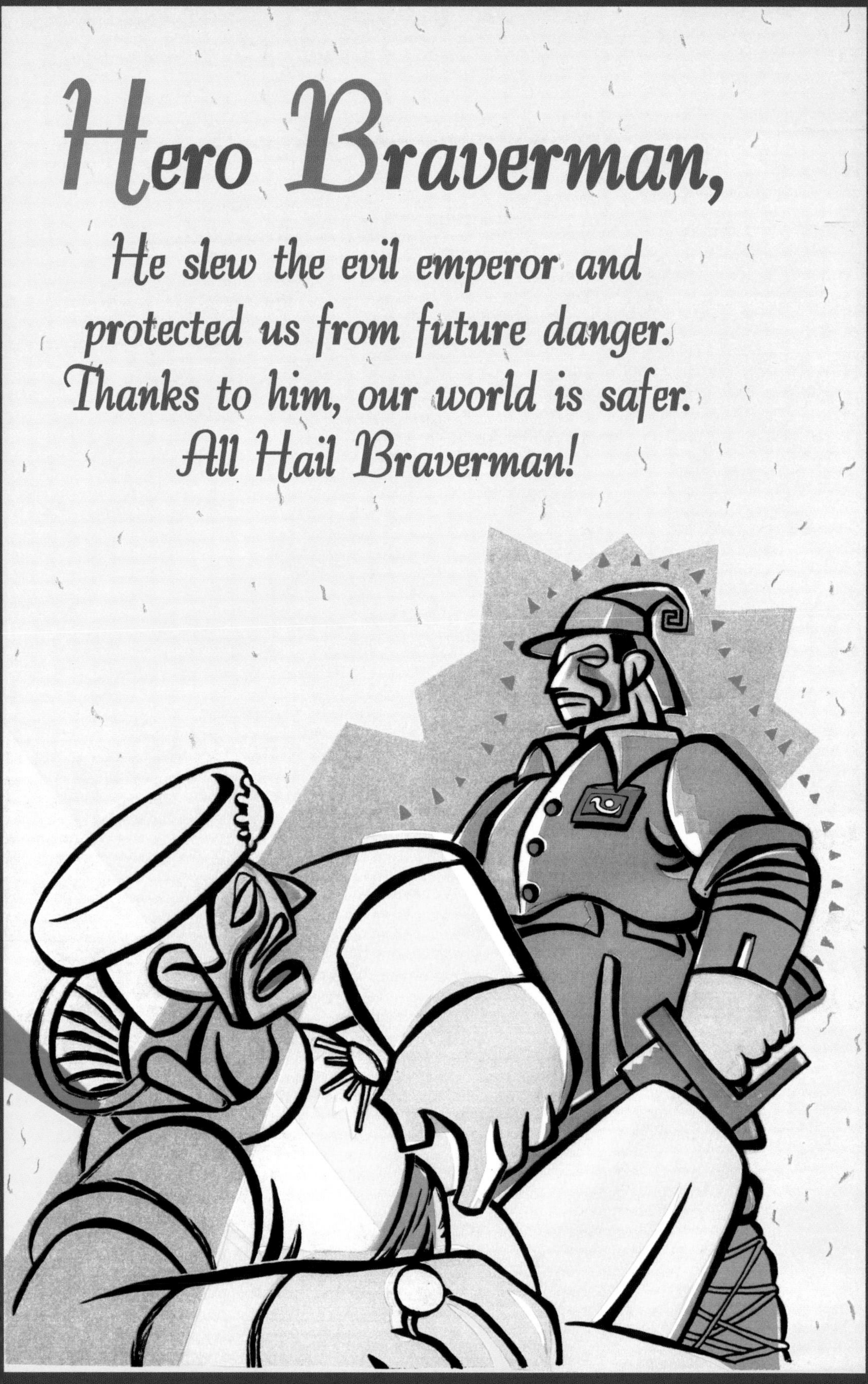

Hero Braverman,
He slew the evil emperor and
protected us from future danger.
Thanks to him, our world is safer.
All Hail Braverman!

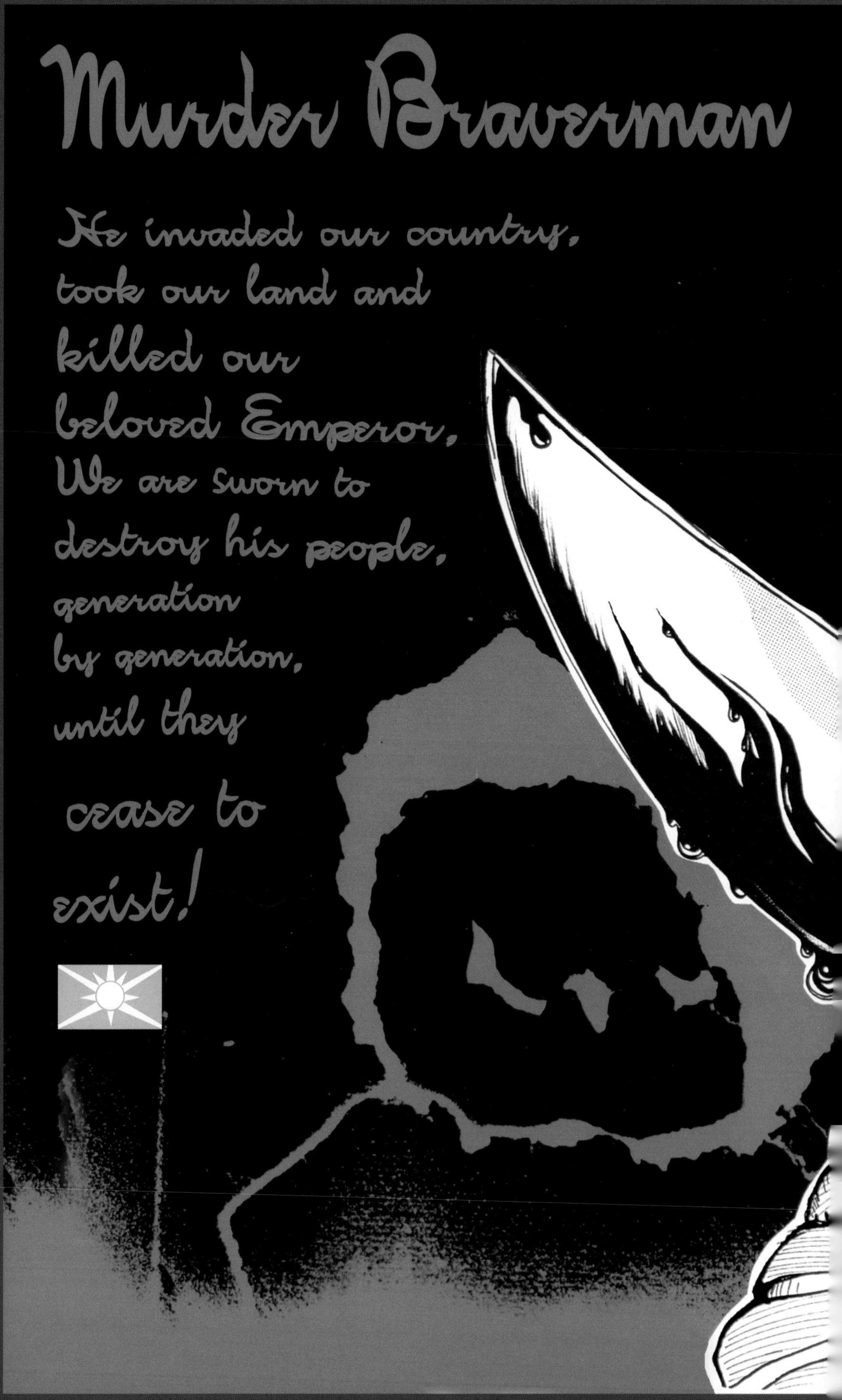
Murder Braverman
He invaded our country,
took our land and
killed our
beloved Emperor.
We are sworn to
destroy his people,
generation
by generation,
until they
cease to
exist!

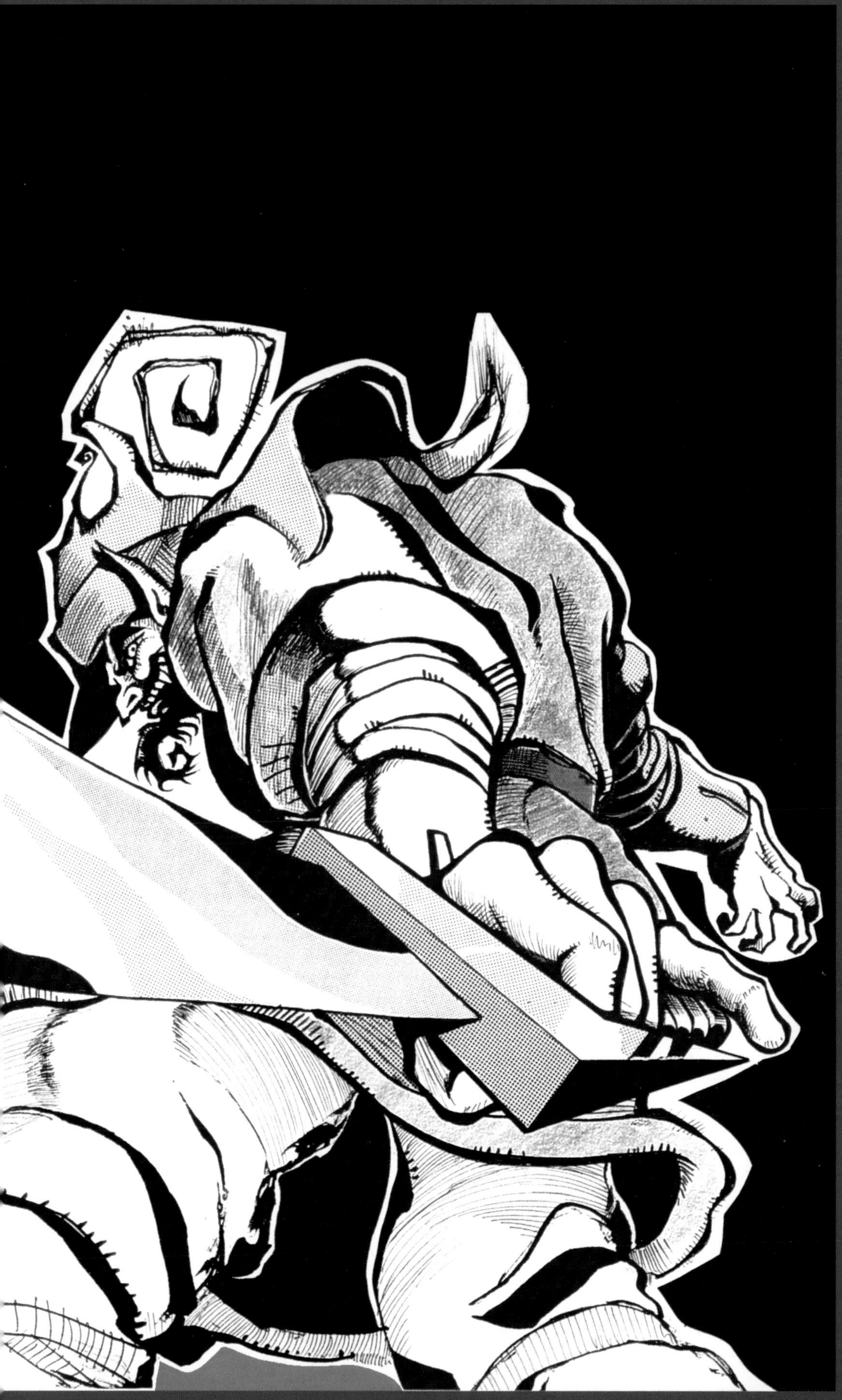

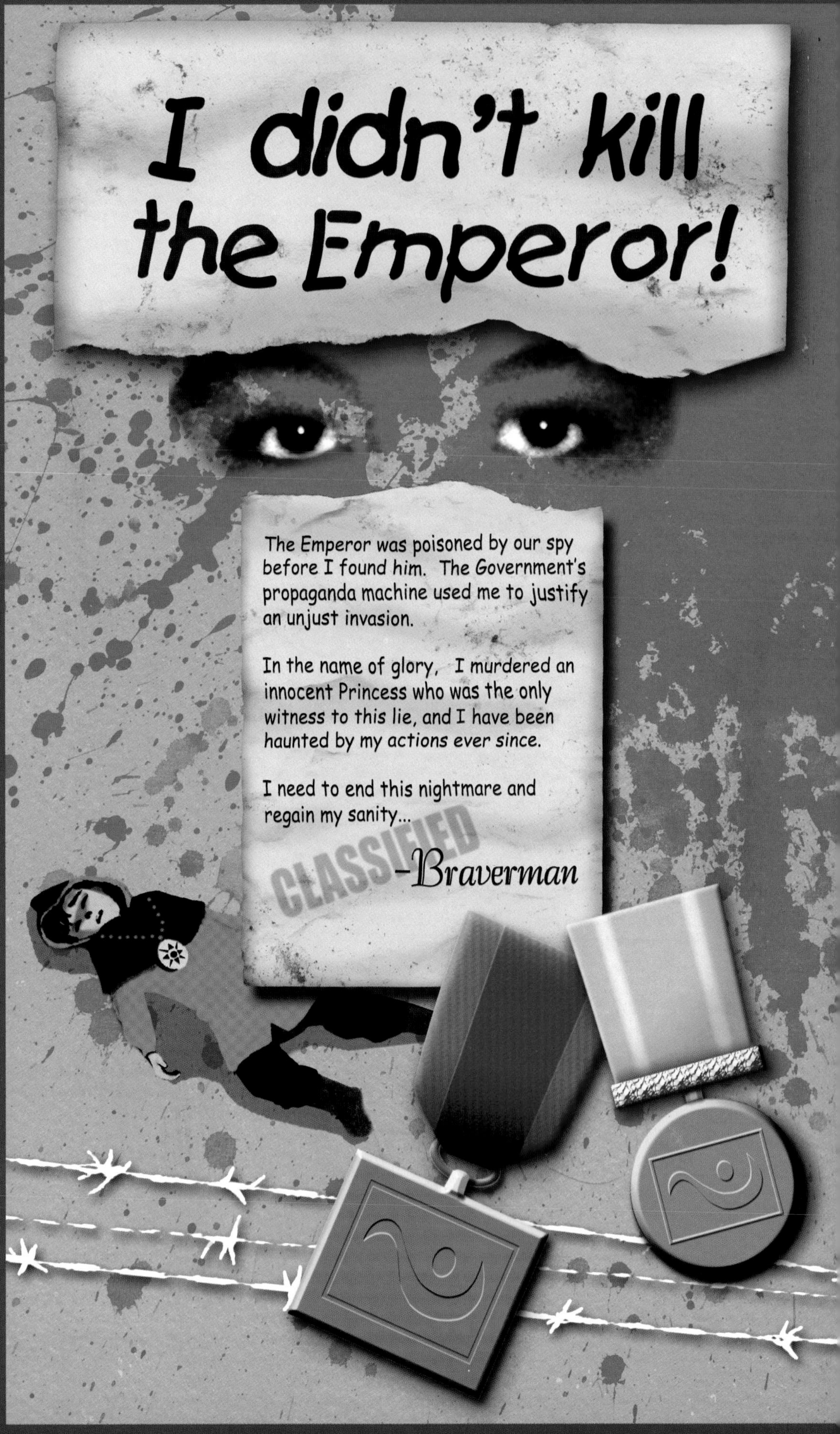
I didn't kill the Emperor!
The Emperor was poisoned by our spy before I found him. The Government's propaganda machine used me to justify an unjust invasion.
In the name of glory, I murdered an innocent Princess who was the only witness to this lie, and I have been haunted by my actions ever since.
I need to end this nightmare and regain my sanity...
CLASSIFIED
-Braverman

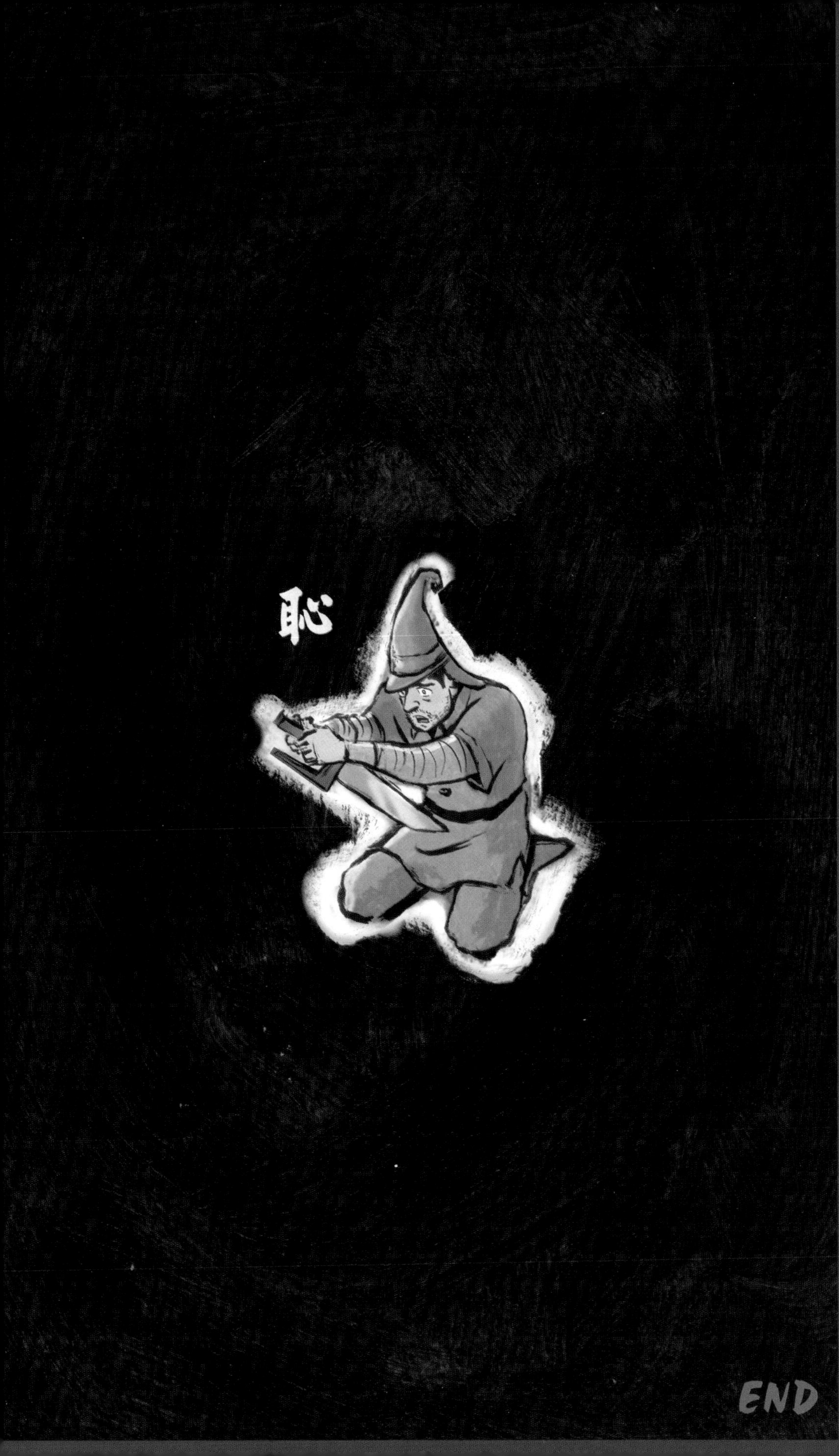
恥
END

$\mathcal{D}$edicated to my wonderful wife Ellen Yao who is always so supportive and inspiring.

$\mathcal{S}$pecial thanks to Brian Kindregan who, despite his busy schedule, served as the editor of my work.

$\mathcal{T}$hanks to Nathan Stanton and Ted Mathot for their support, and to those who make project Afterworks2 possible.

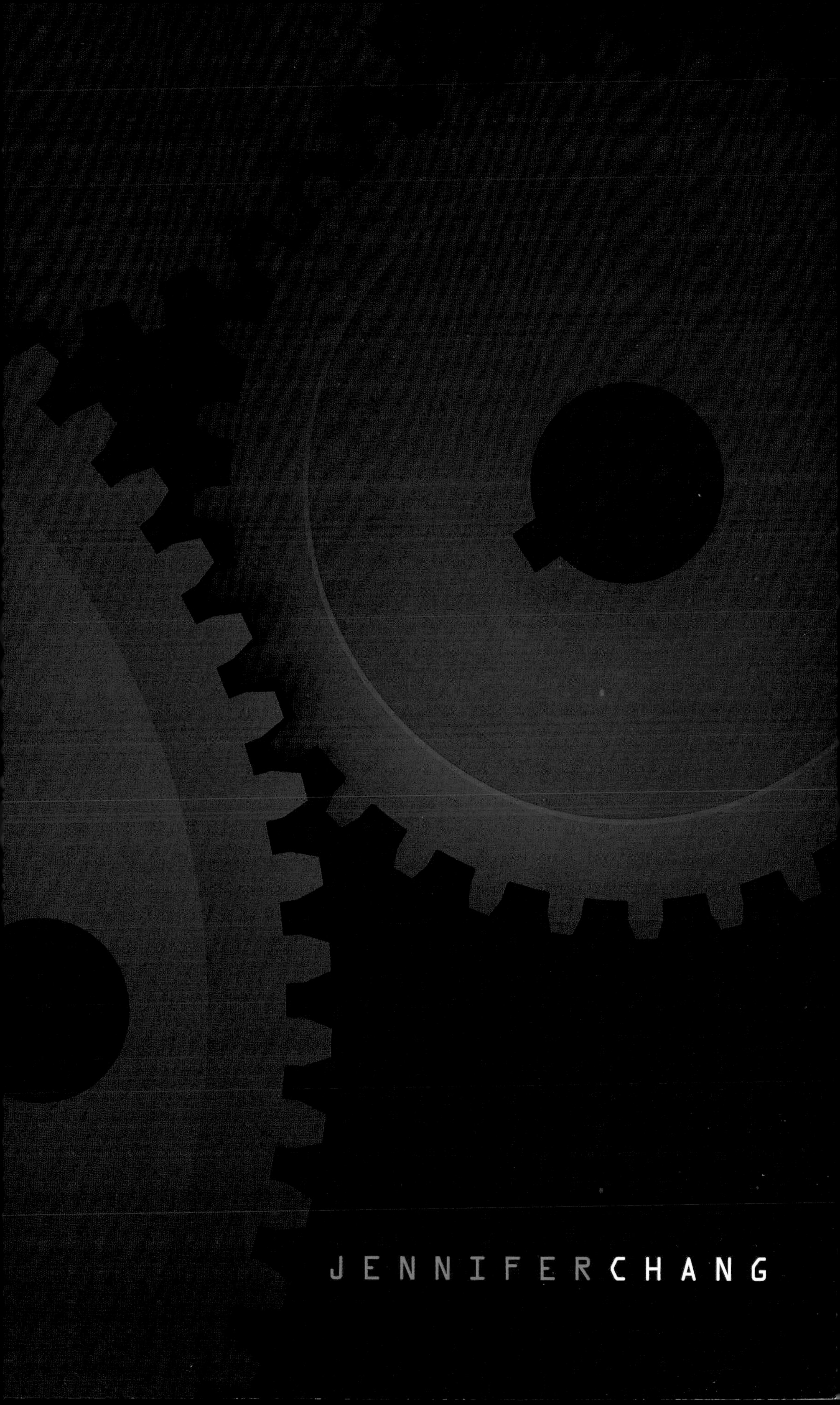
JENNIFER CHANG

Kitosan, Fruit 果

二〇〇六冬

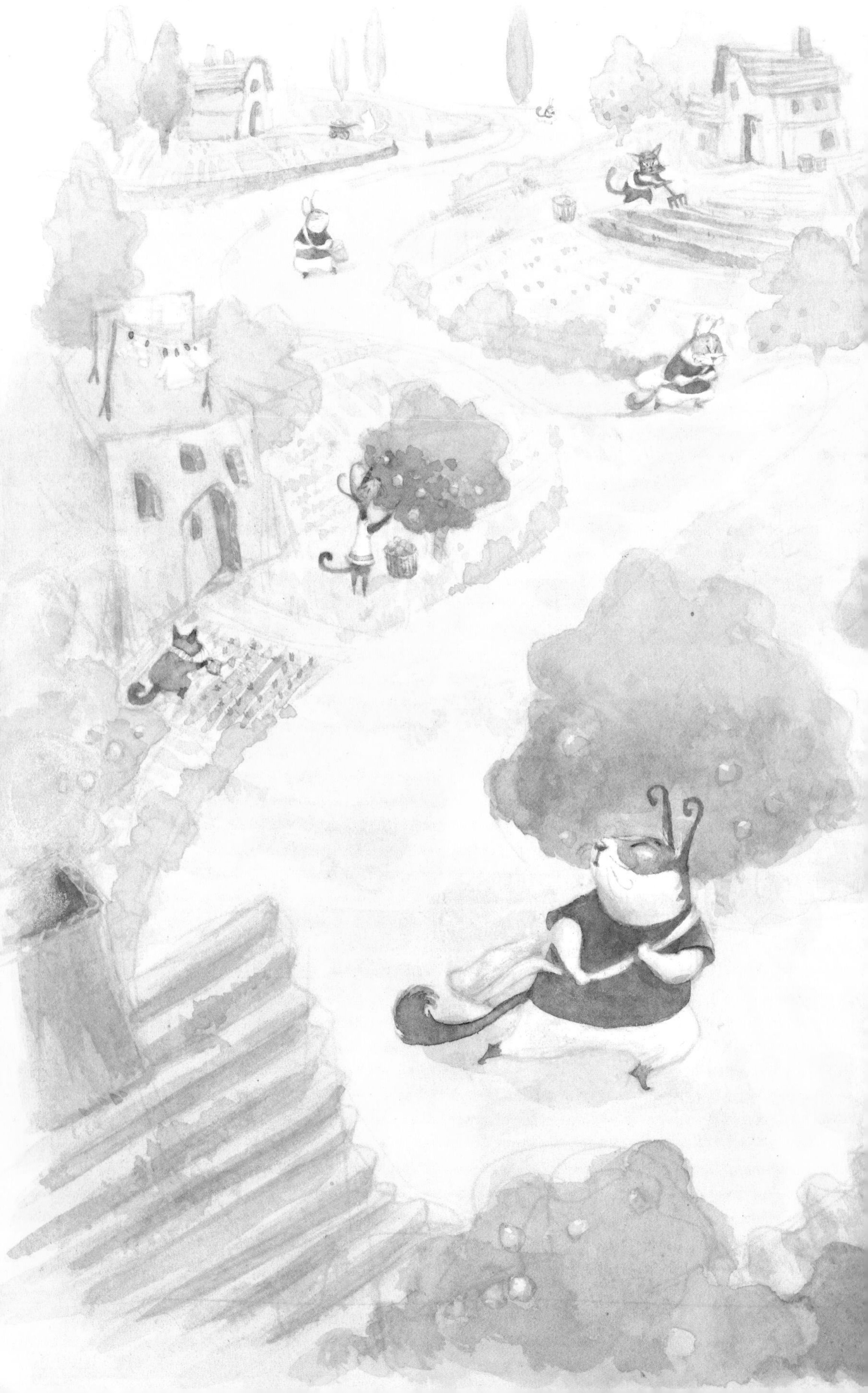

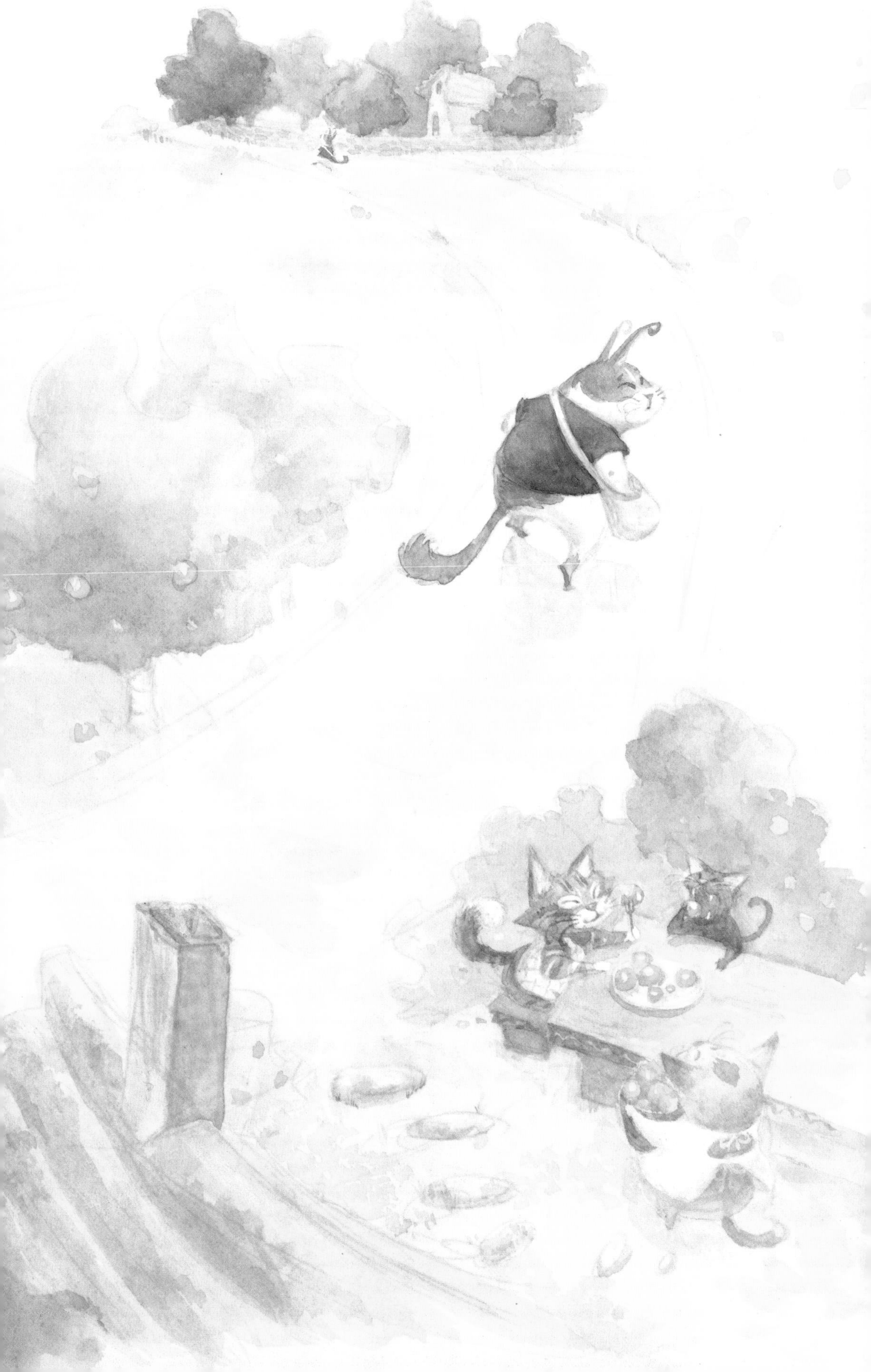

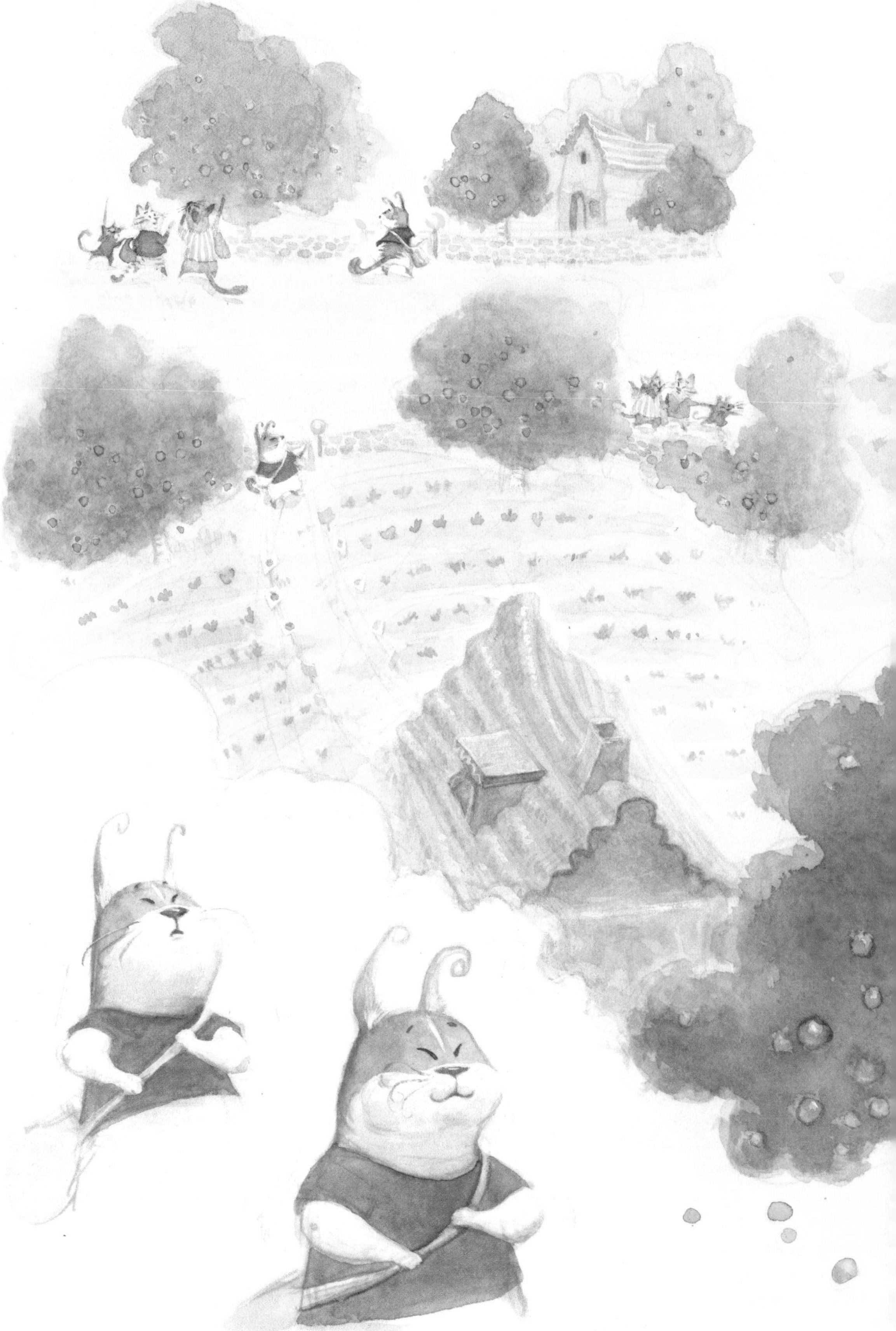

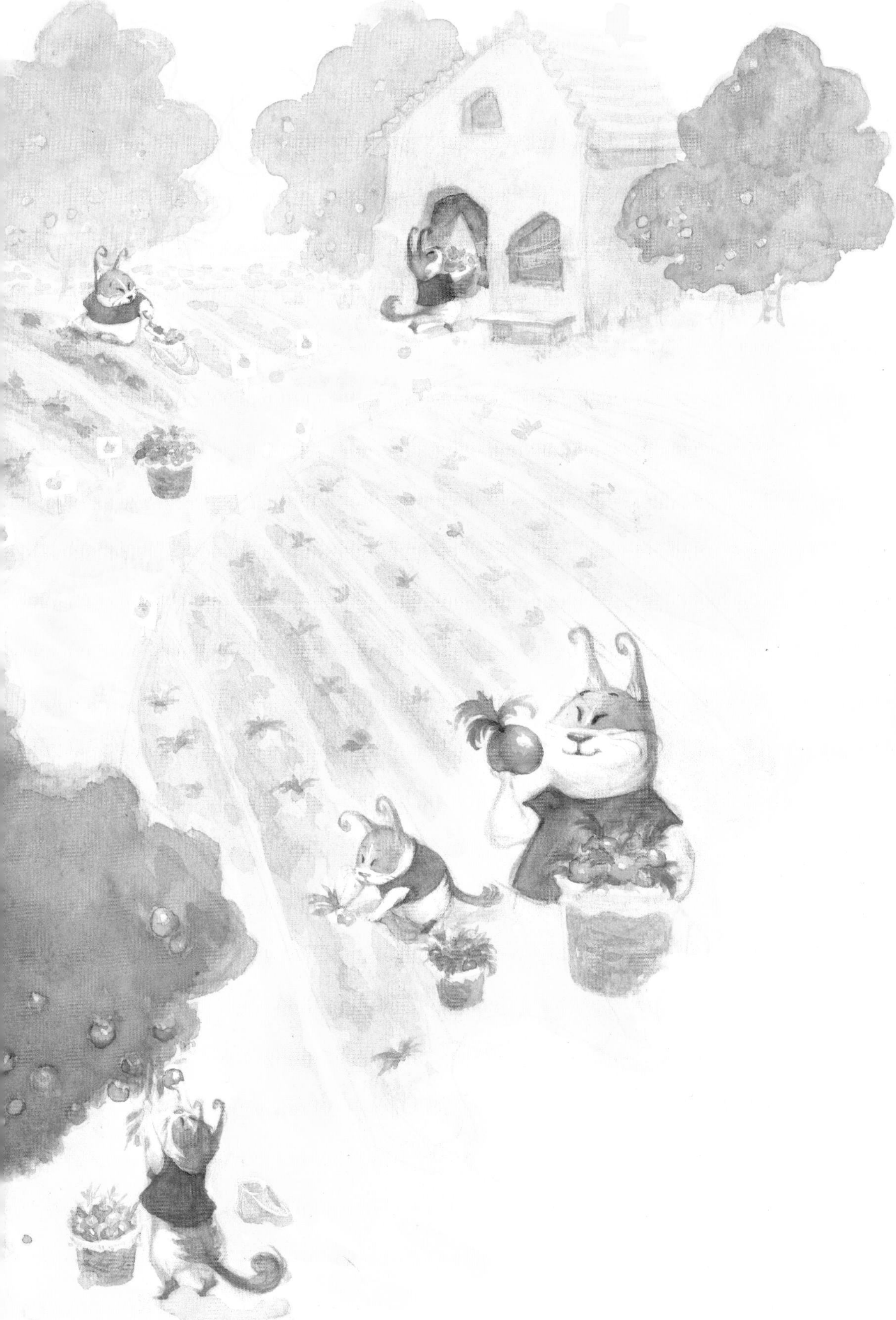

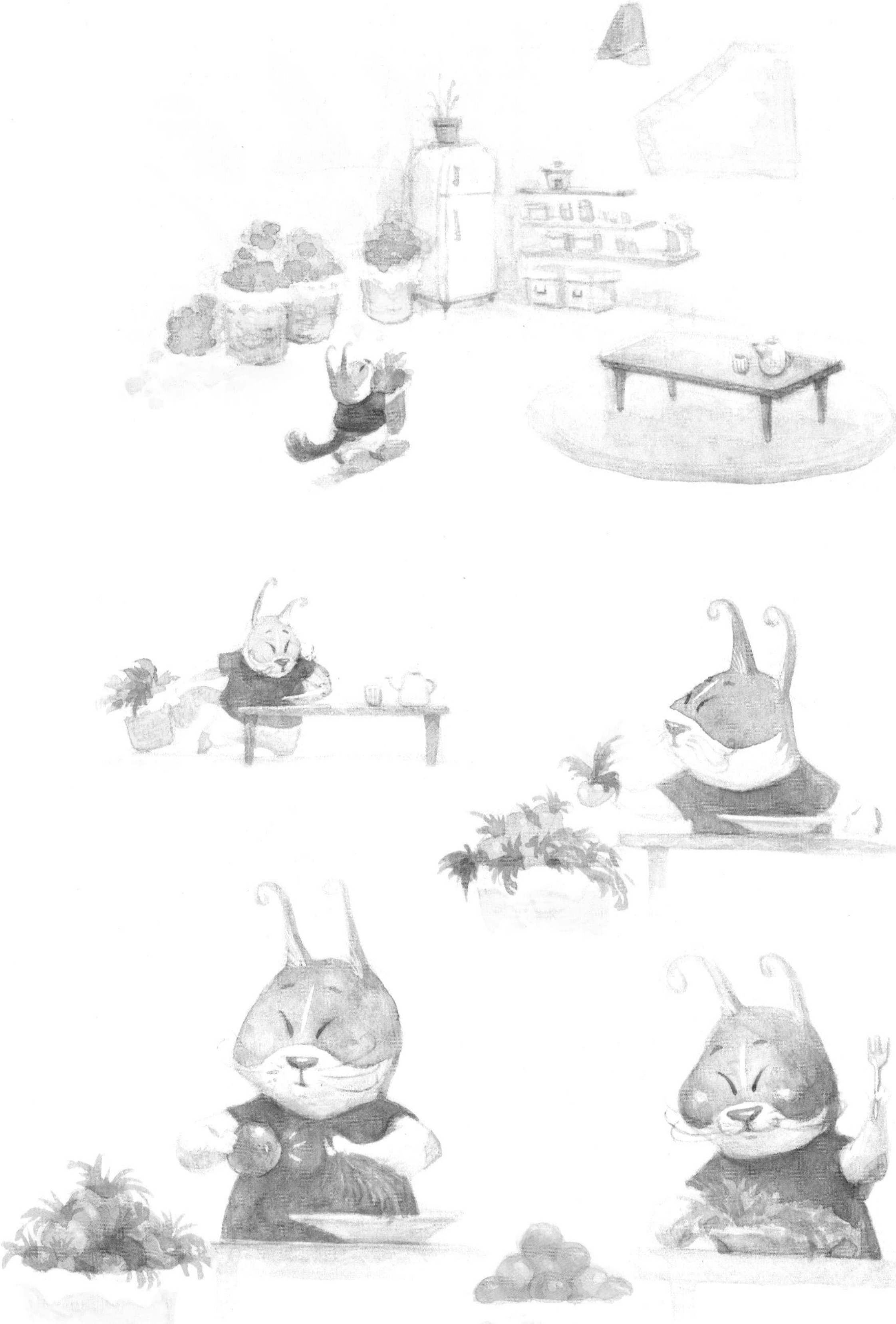

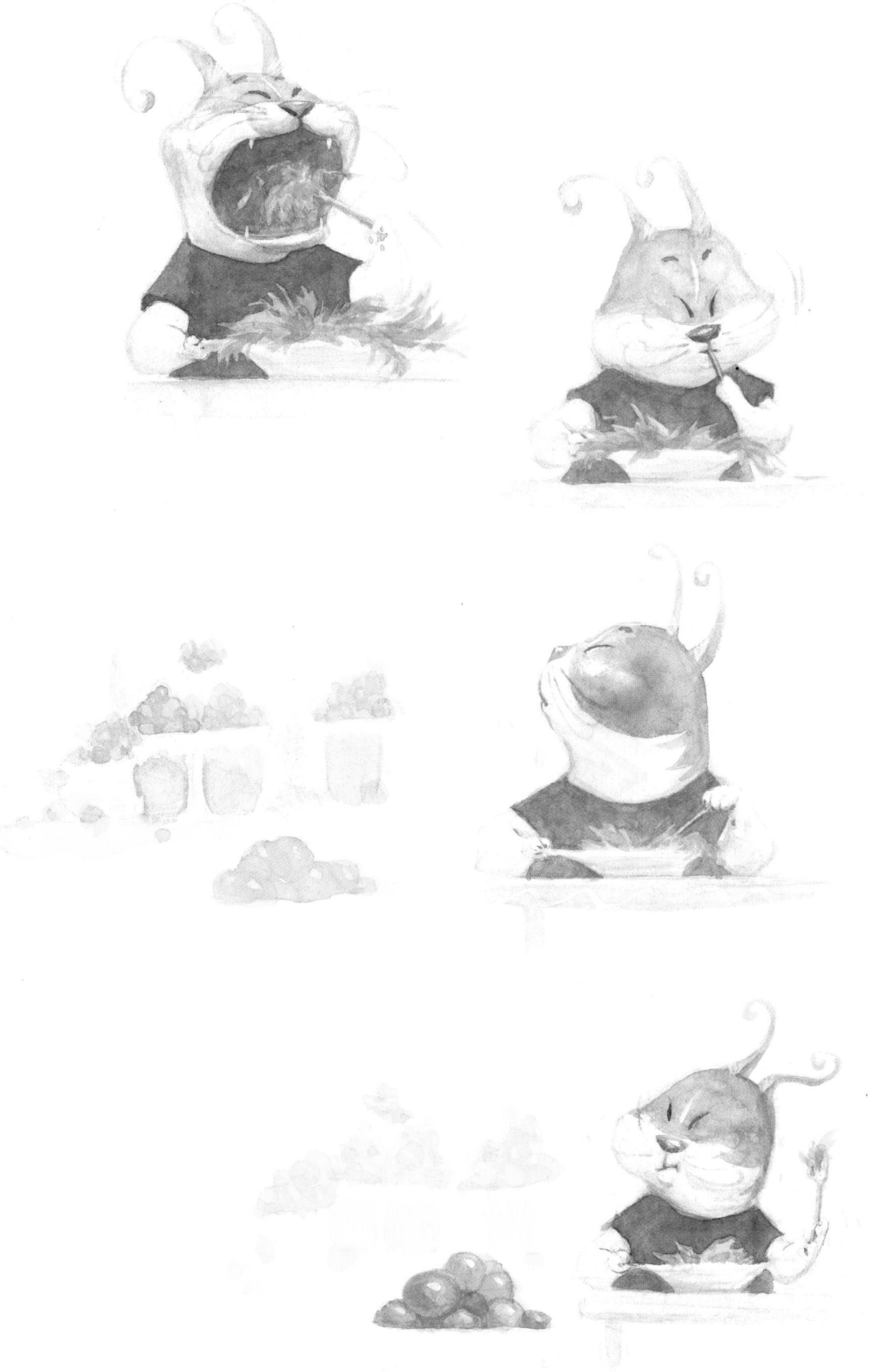

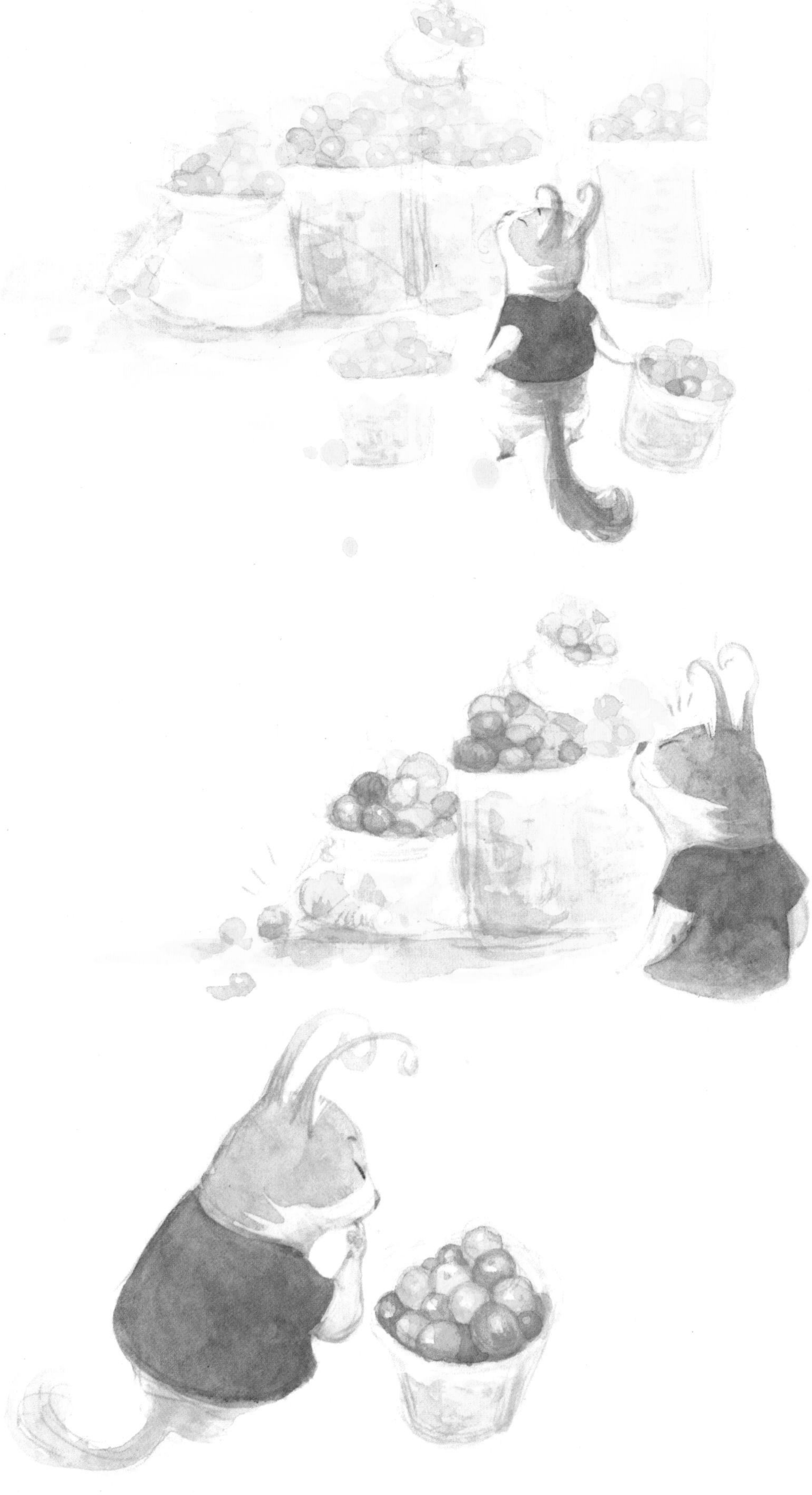

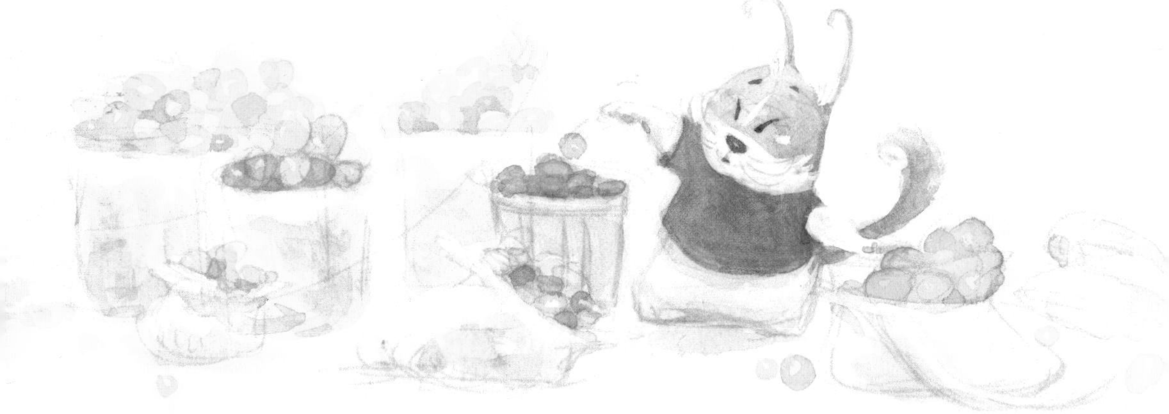

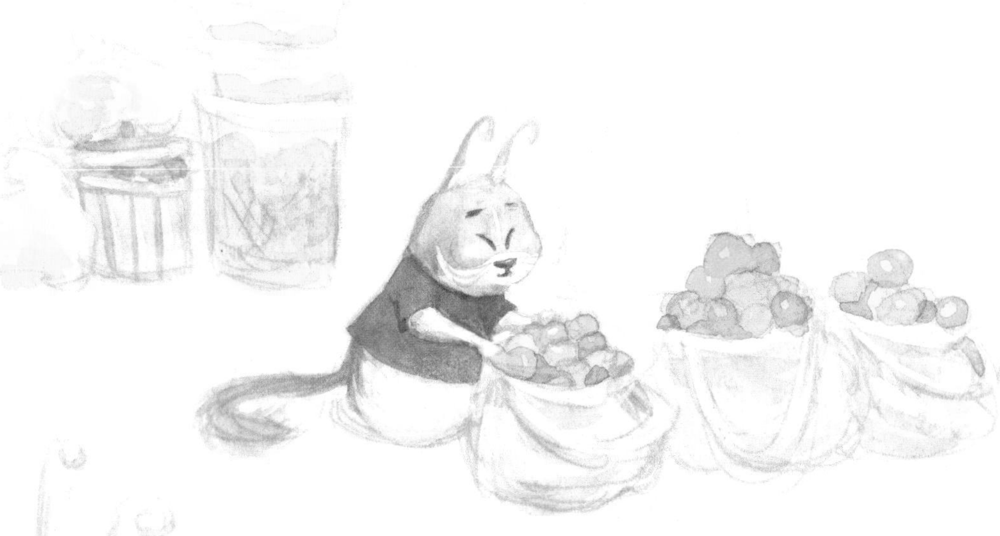

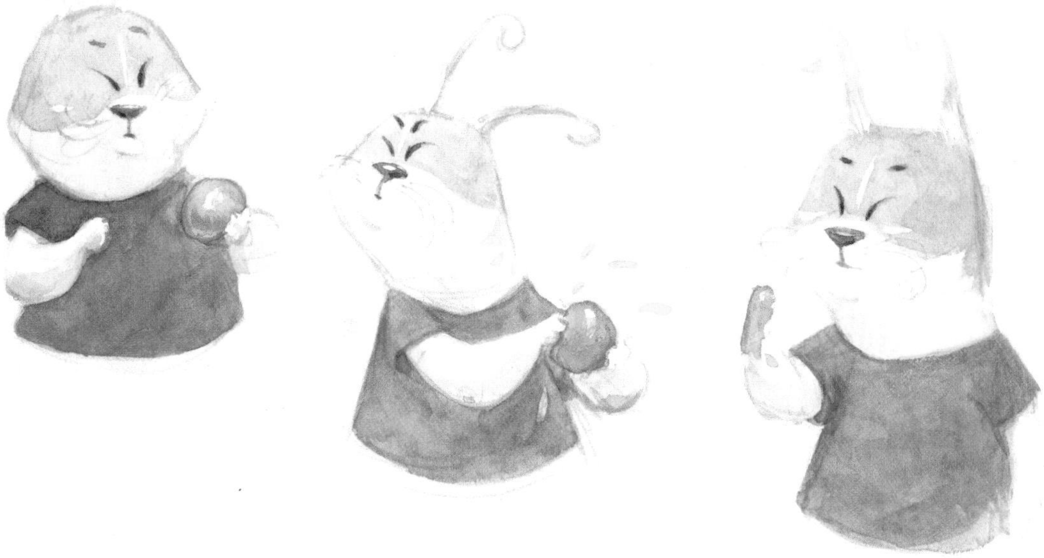

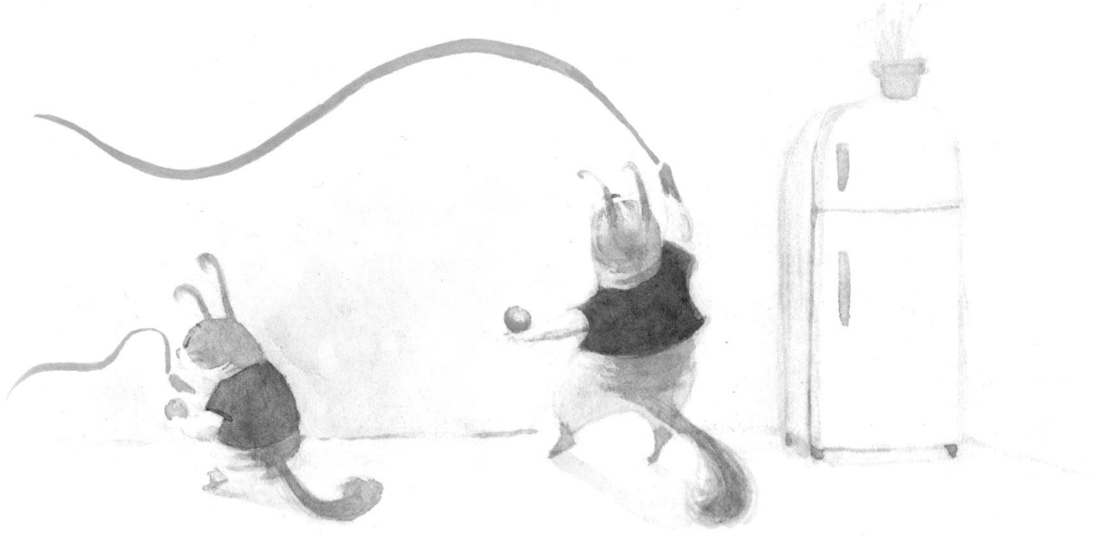

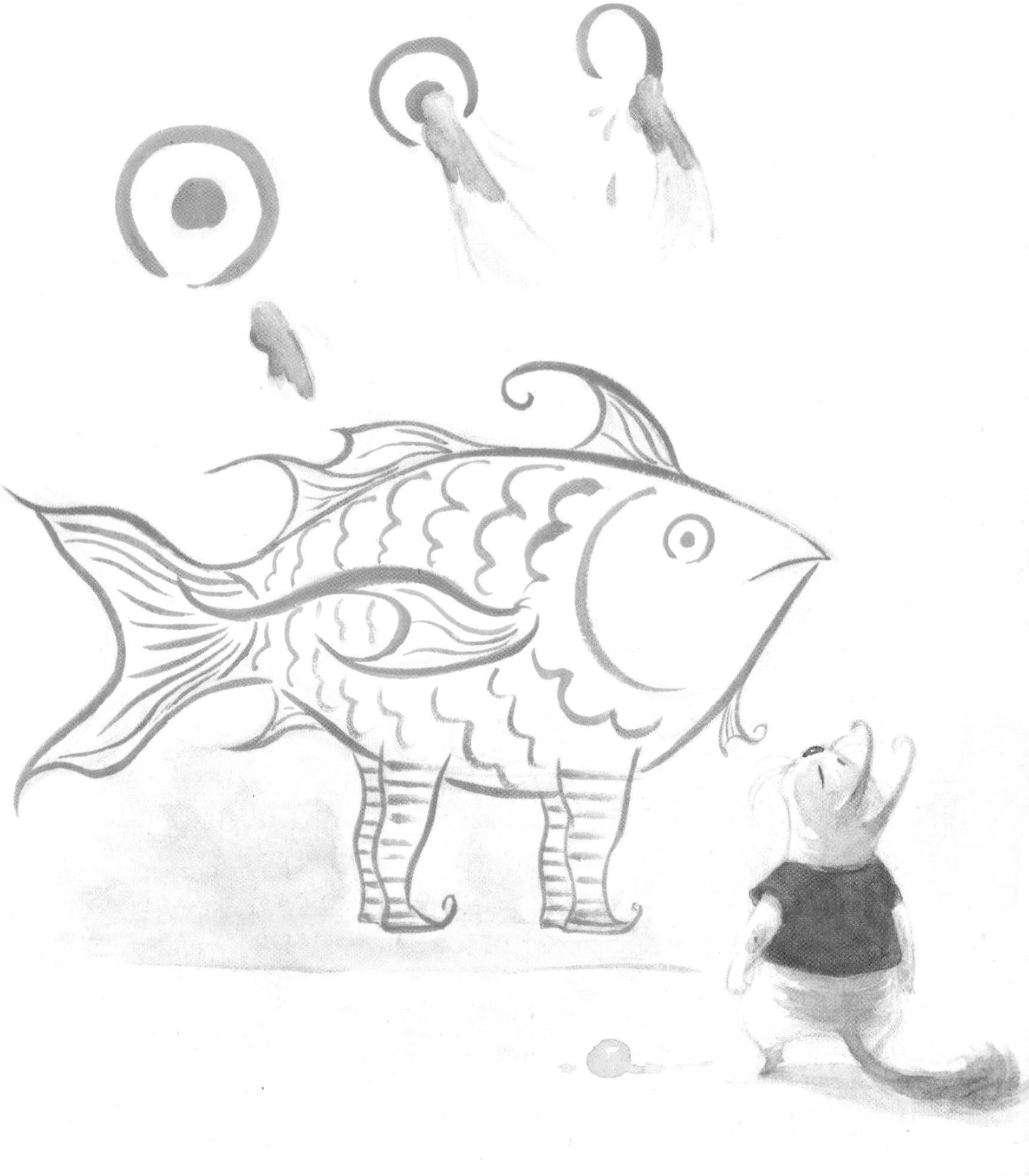

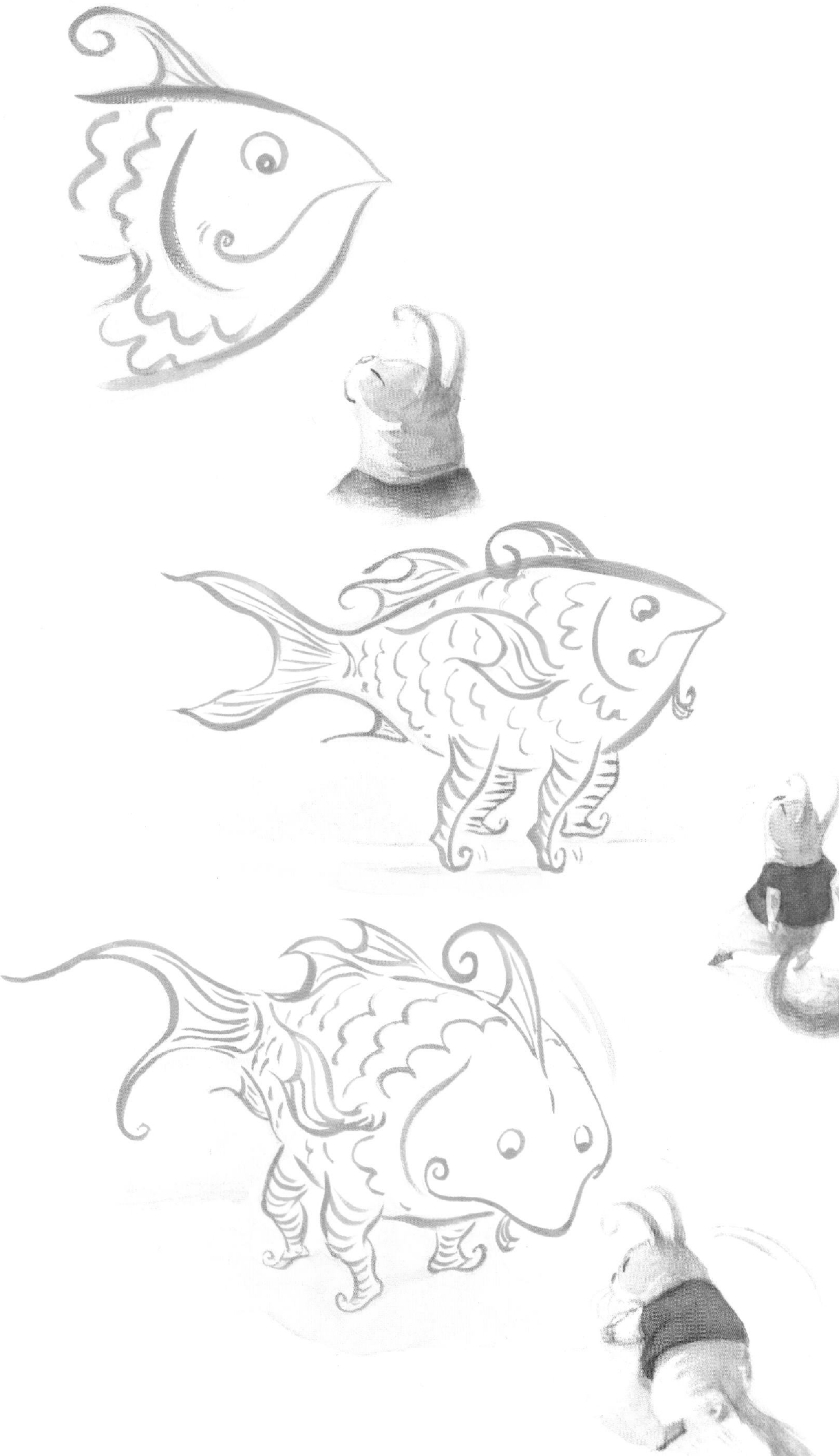

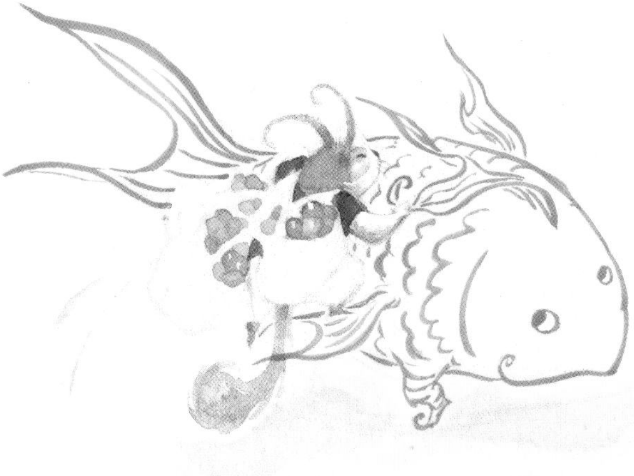

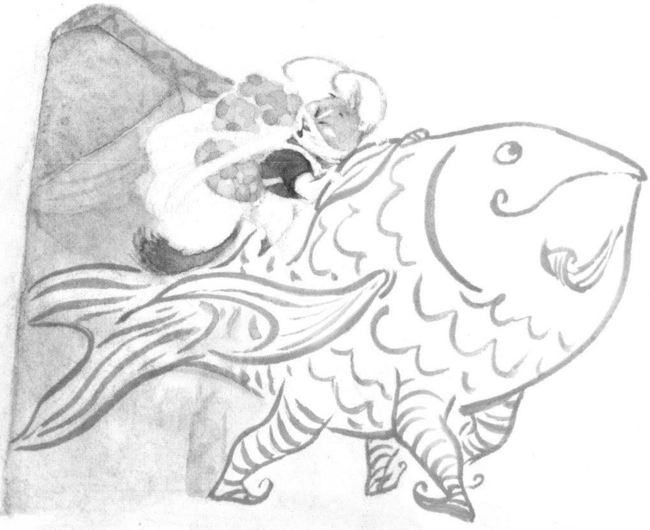

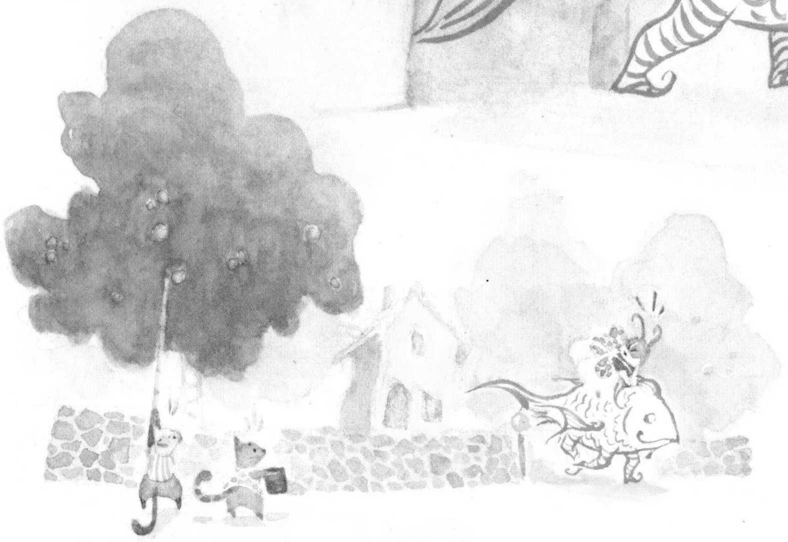

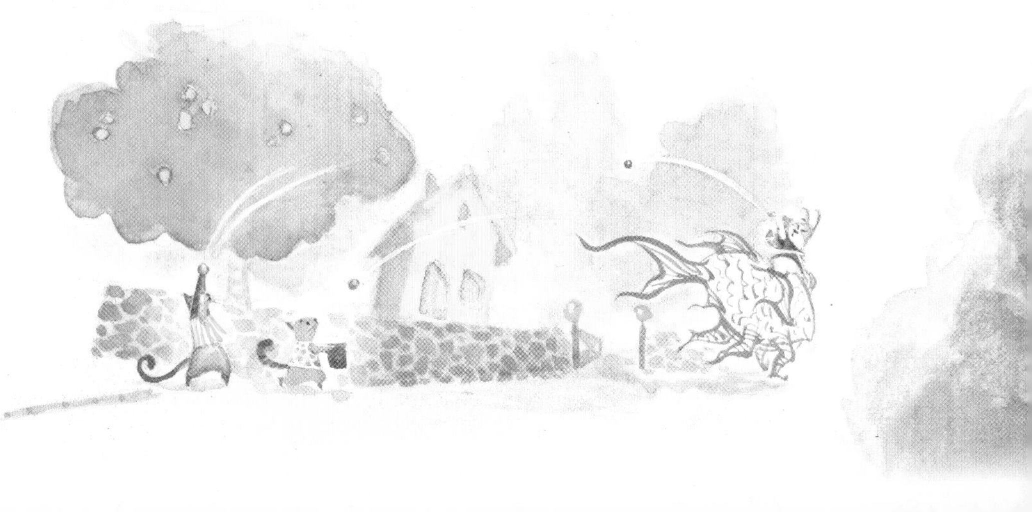

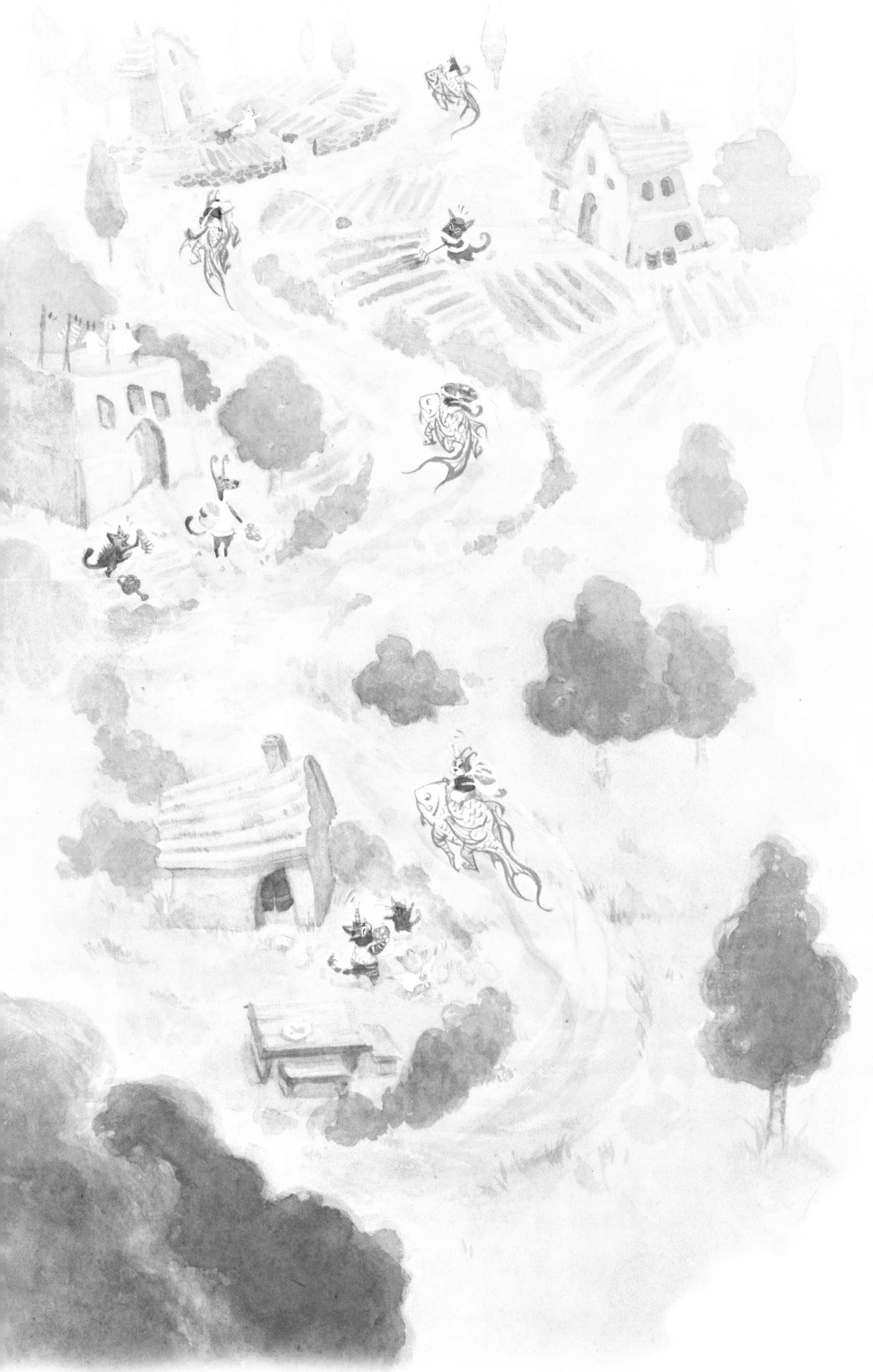

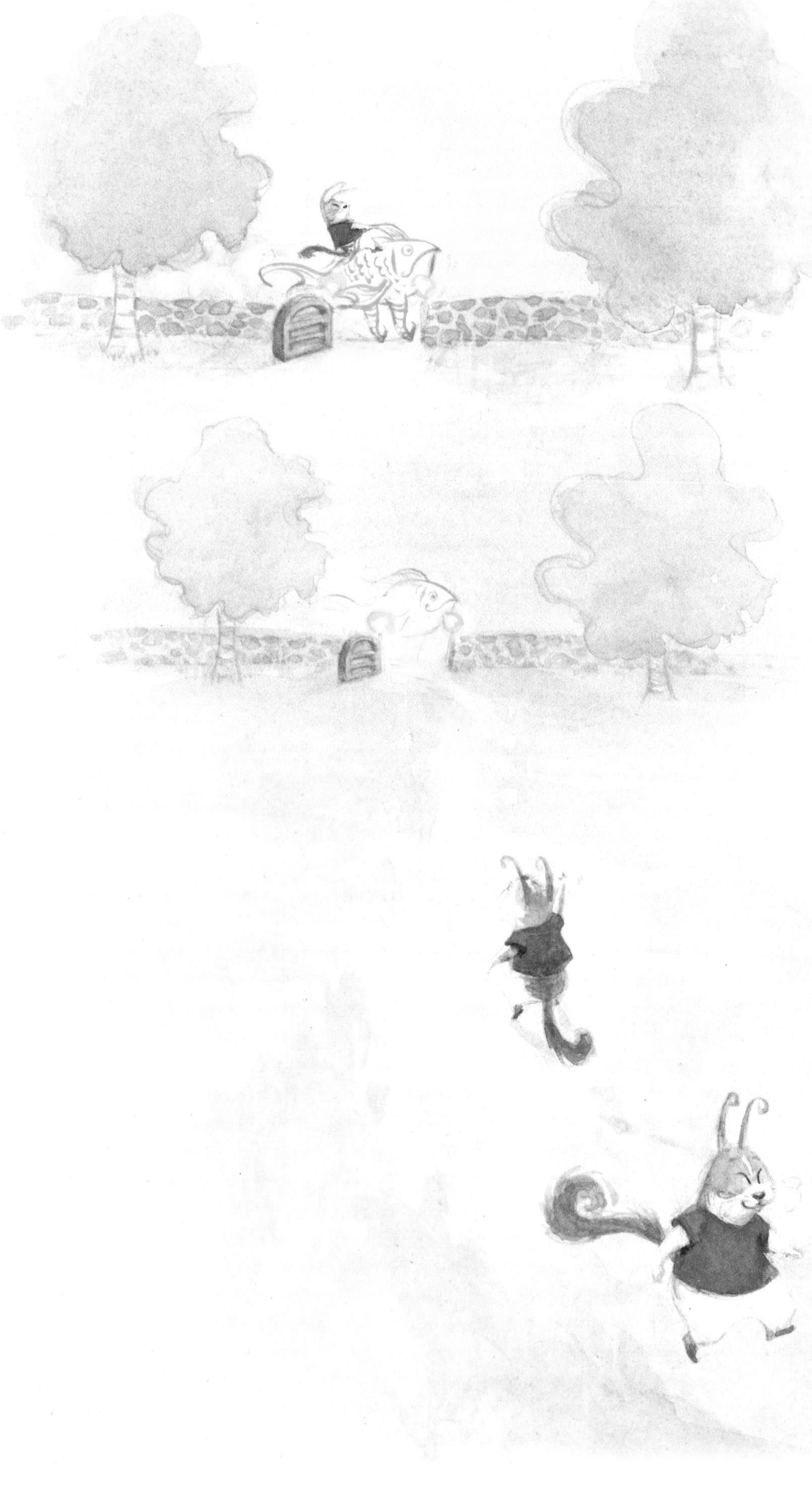

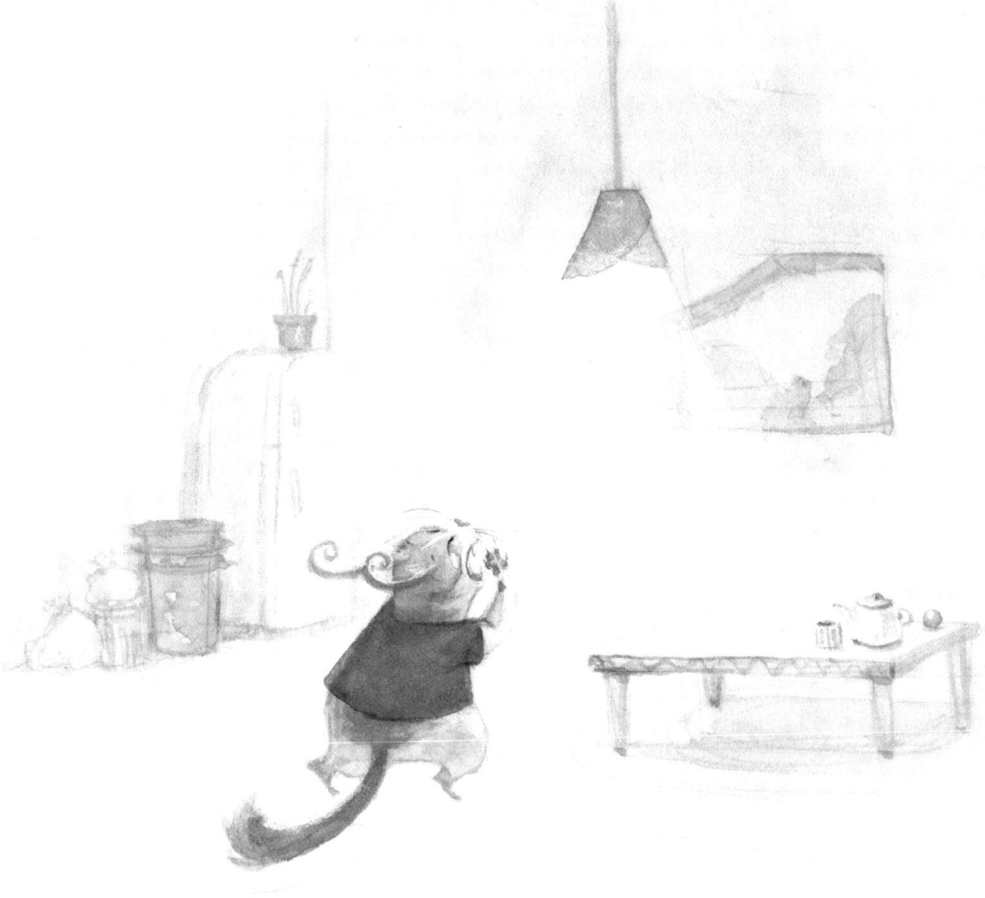

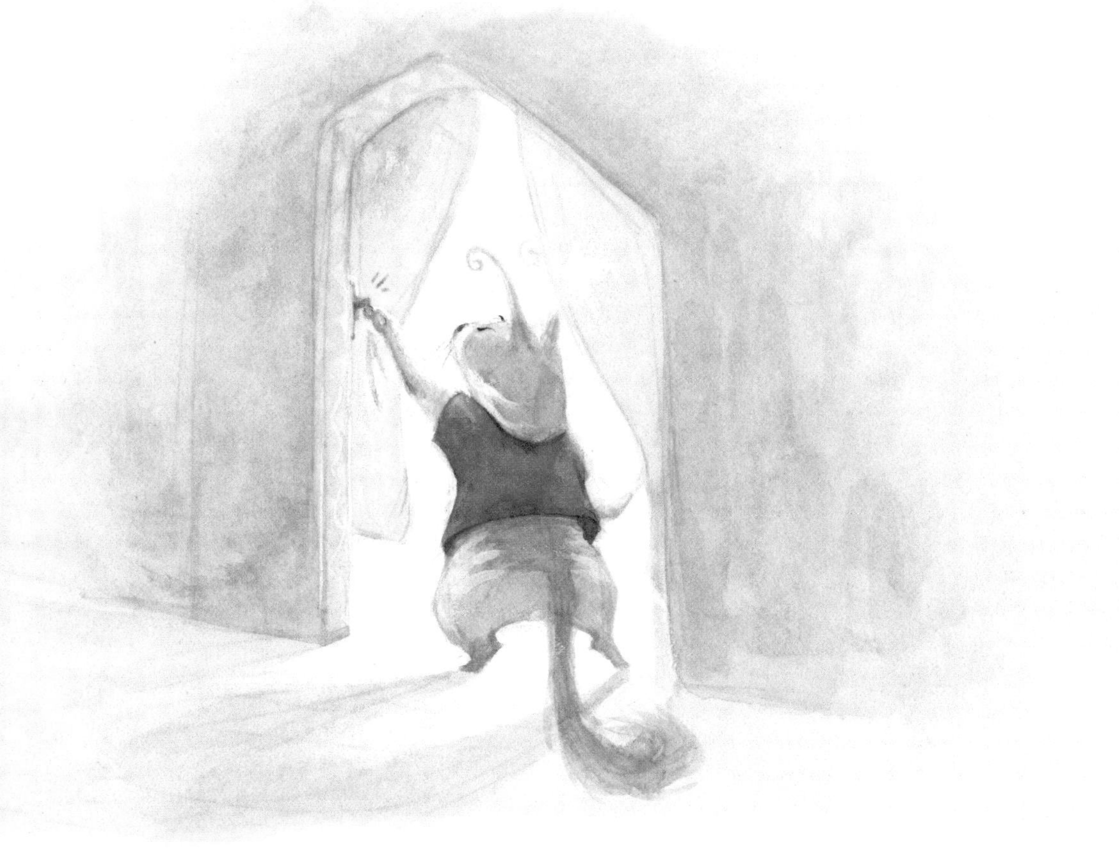

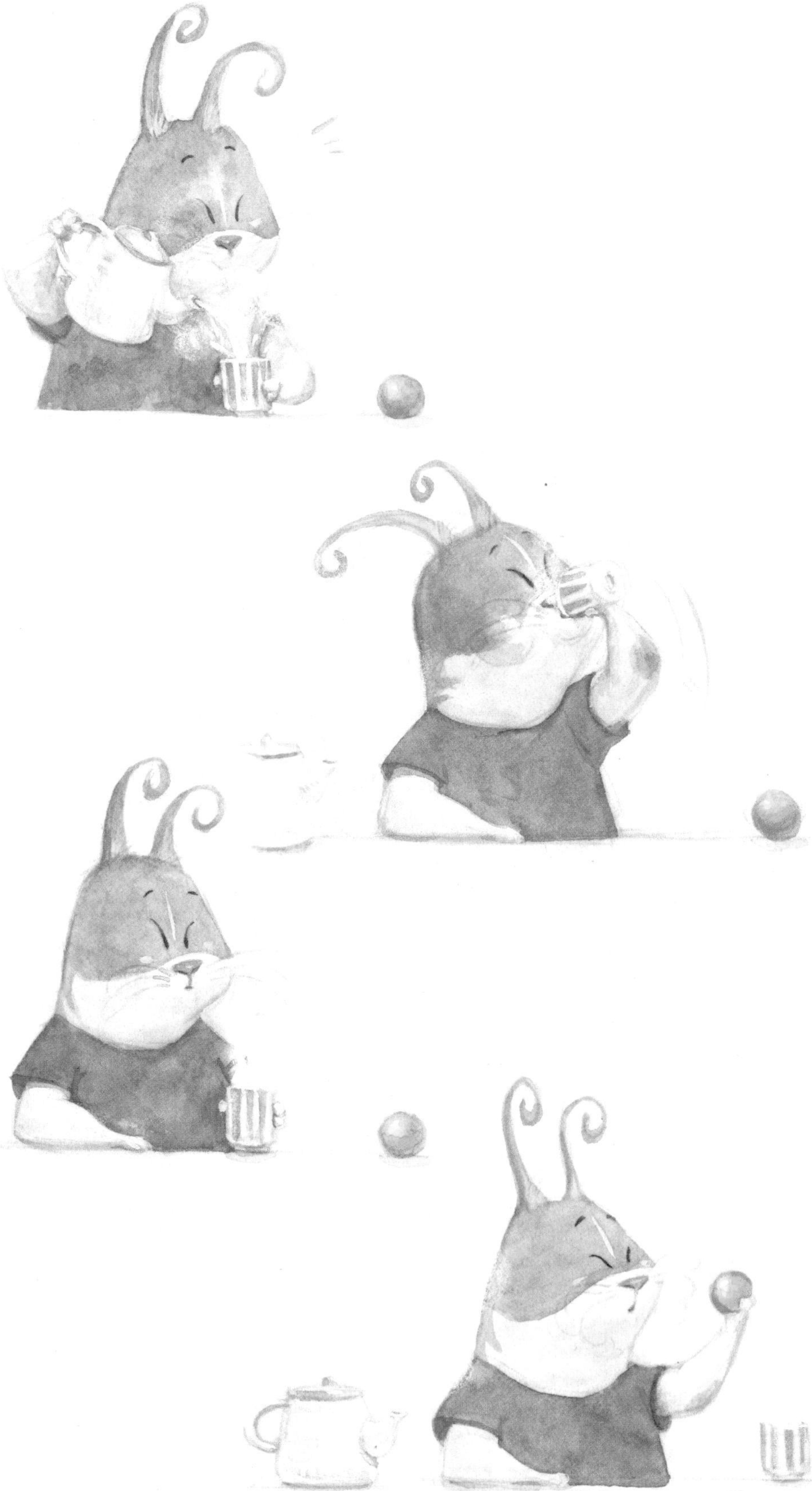

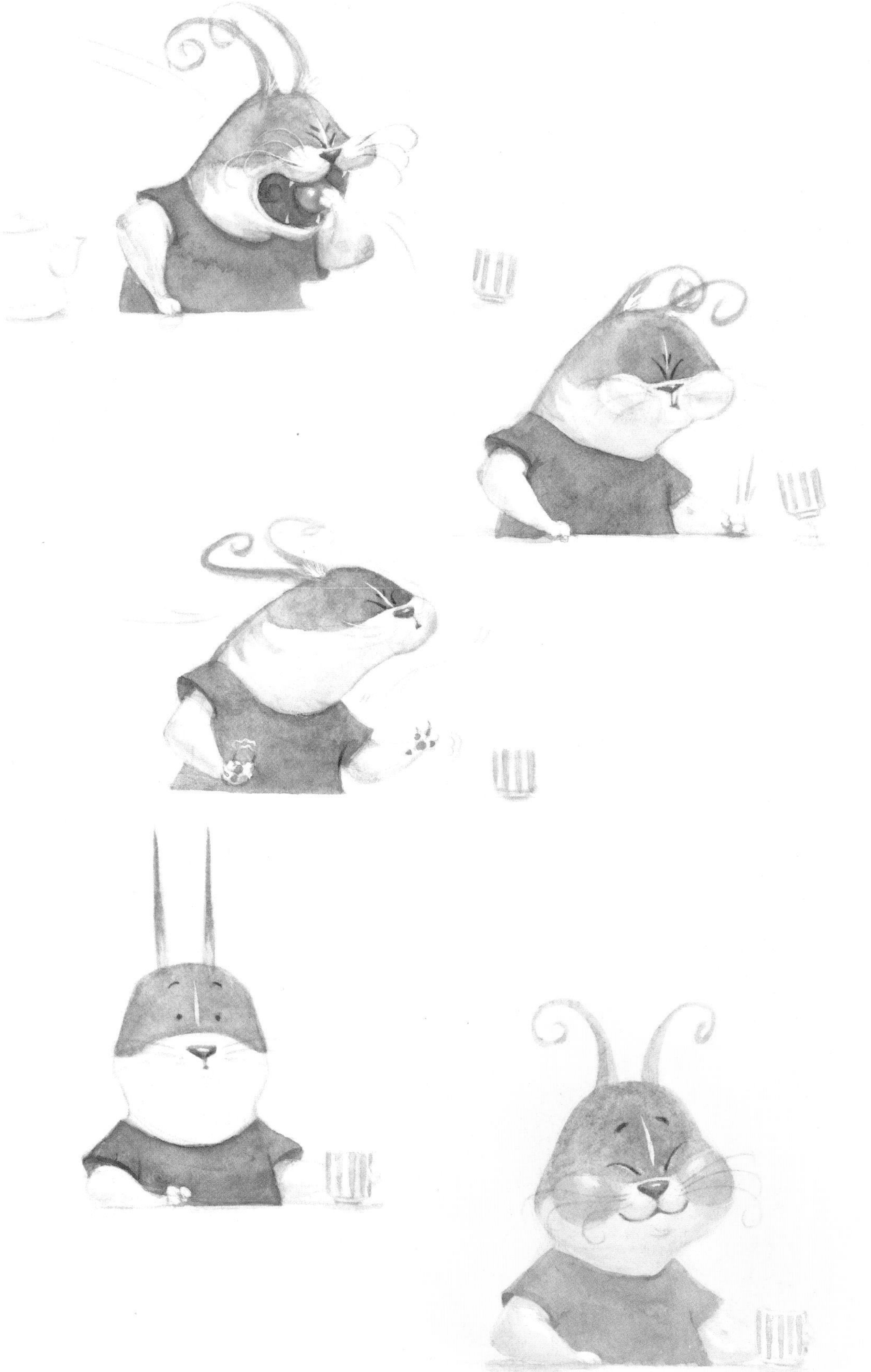

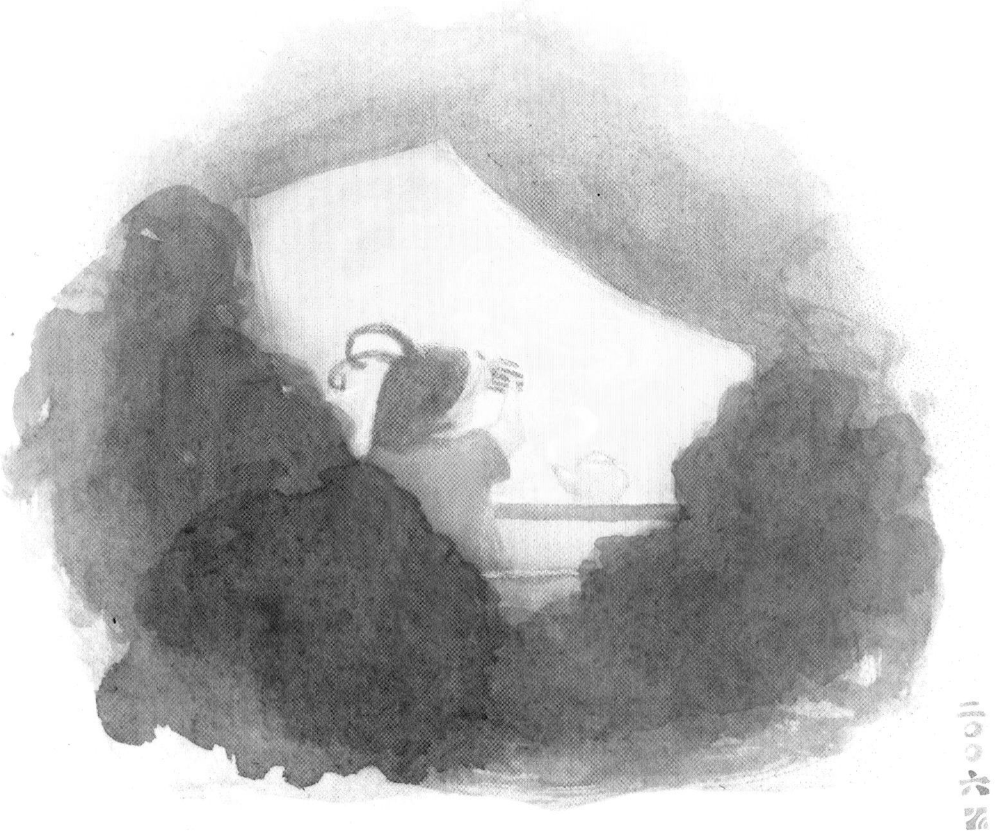
二〇〇六

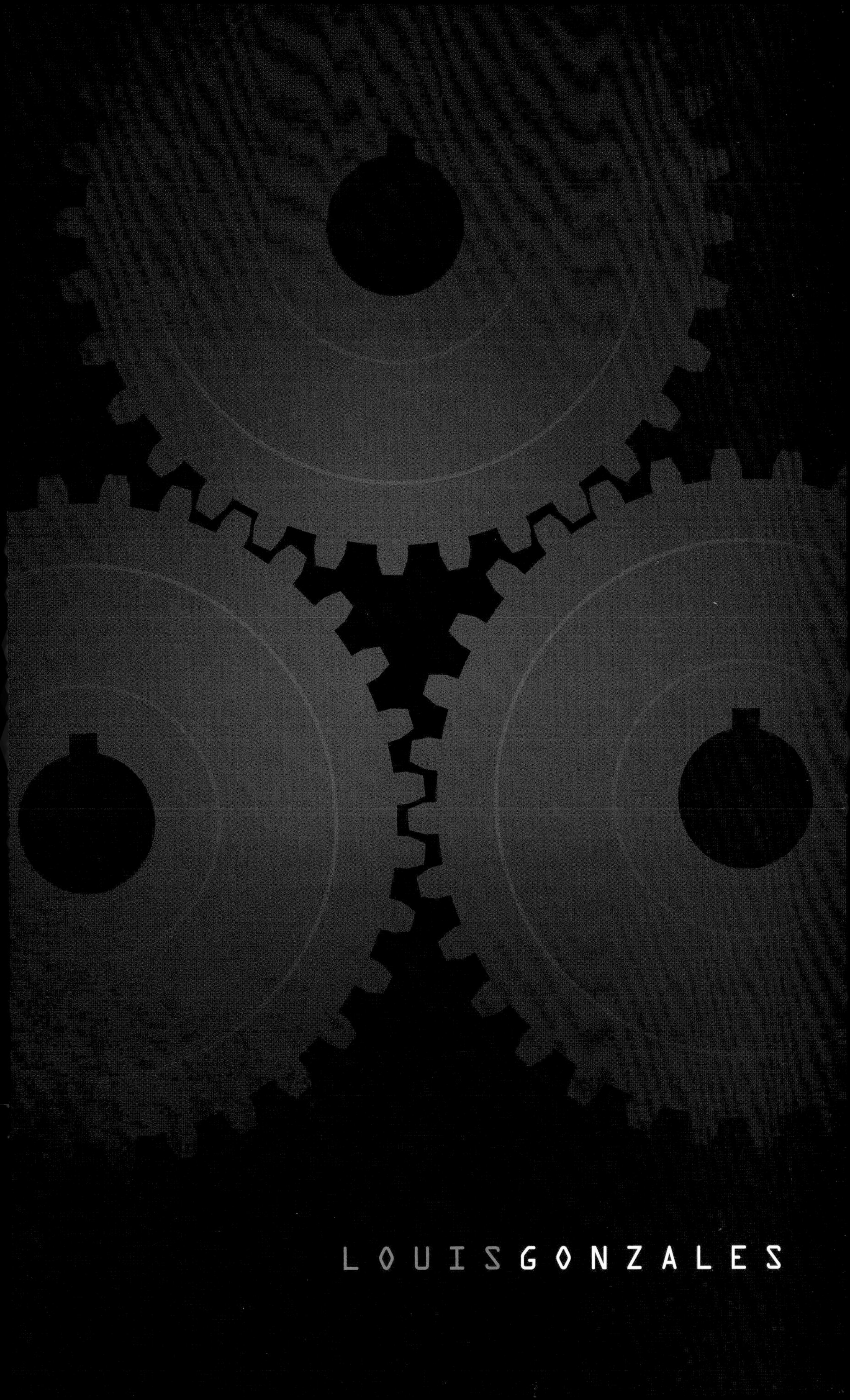
LOUIS GONZALES

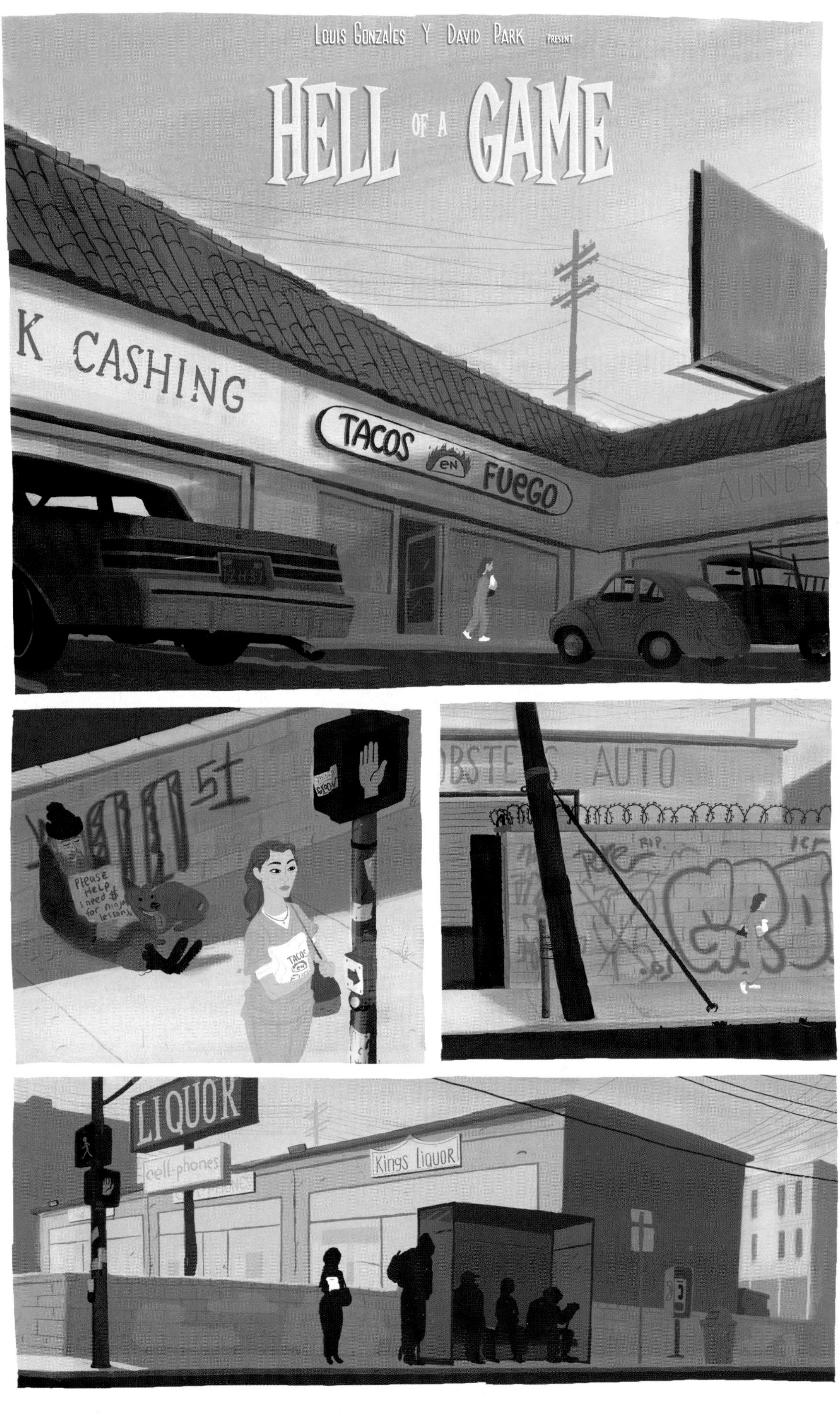
LOUIS GONZALES Y DAVID PARK PRESENT
HELL OF A GAME
K CASHING
TACOS EN FUEGO
LAUNDR
Please help I need $ for ninja lessons
OBSTE S AUTO
R.I.P.
LIQUOR
cell-phones
Kings Liquor

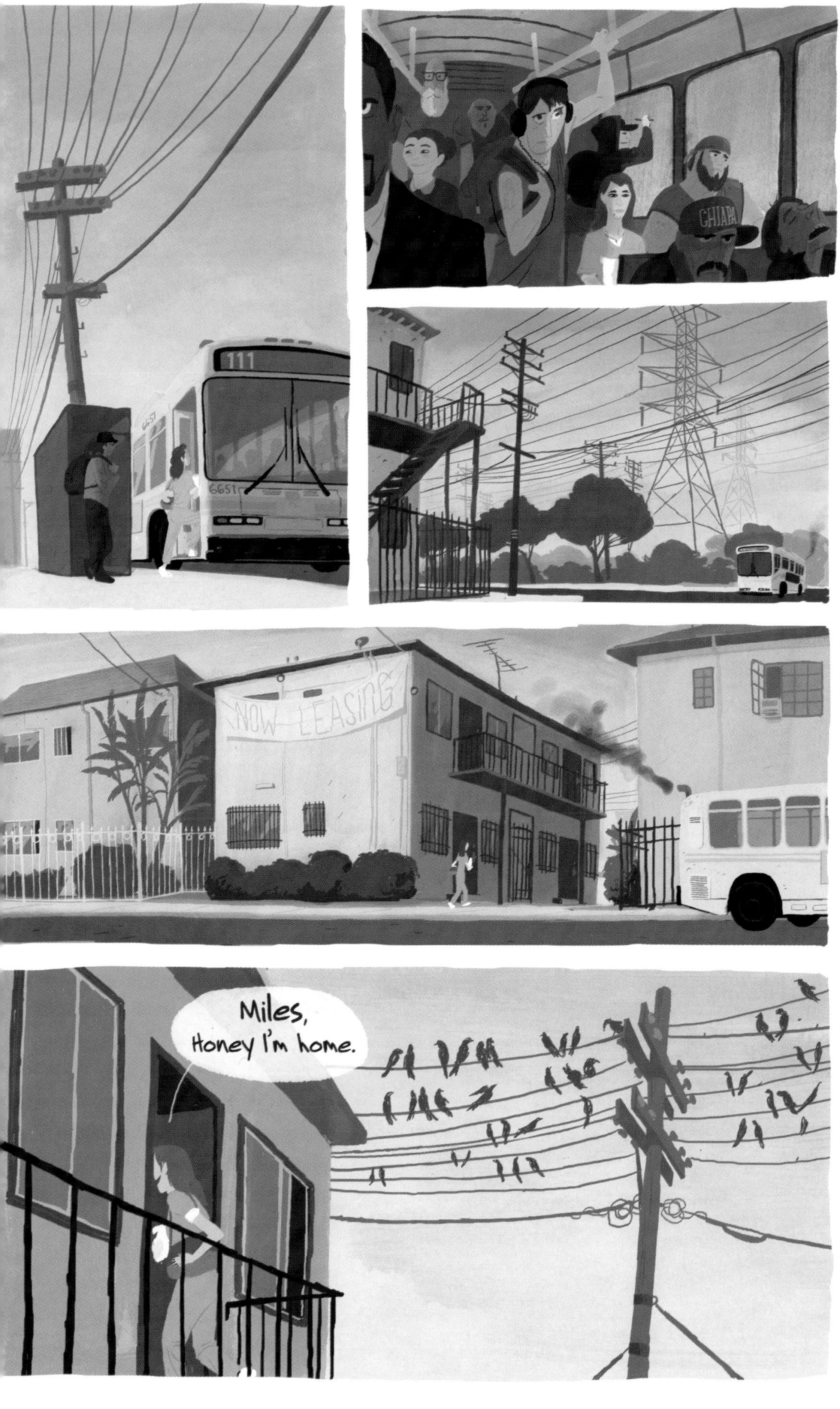

111
6651
CHIAPA
NOW LEASING
Miles, Honey I'm home.

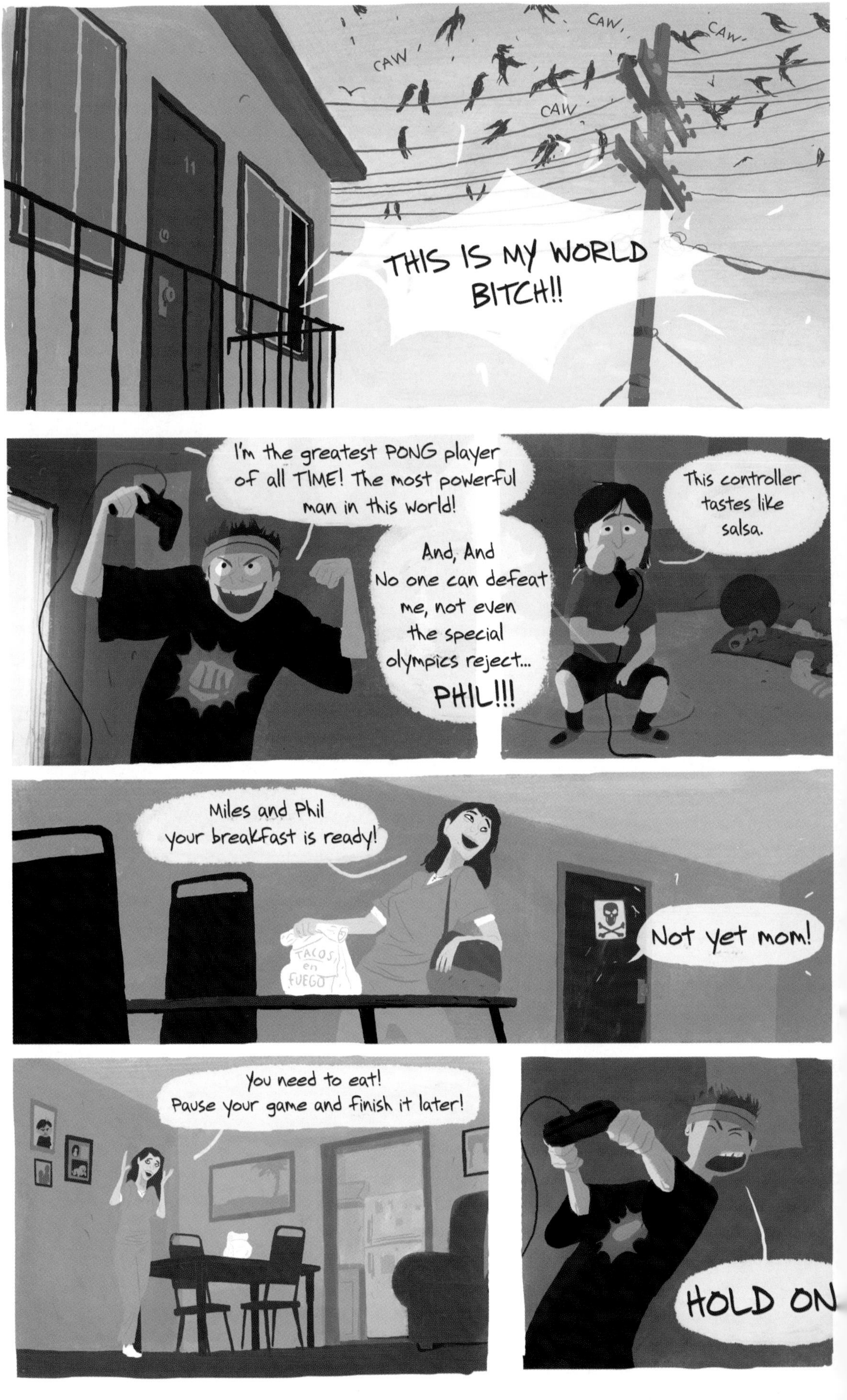
CAW
CAW
CAW
CAW
THIS IS MY WORLD BITCH!!
I'm the greatest PONG player of all TIME! The most powerful man in this world!
And, And No one can defeat me, not even the special olympics reject...
PHIL!!!
This controller tastes like salsa.
Miles and Phil your breakfast is ready!
TACOS en FUEGO
Not yet mom!
You need to eat! Pause your game and finish it later!
HOLD ON

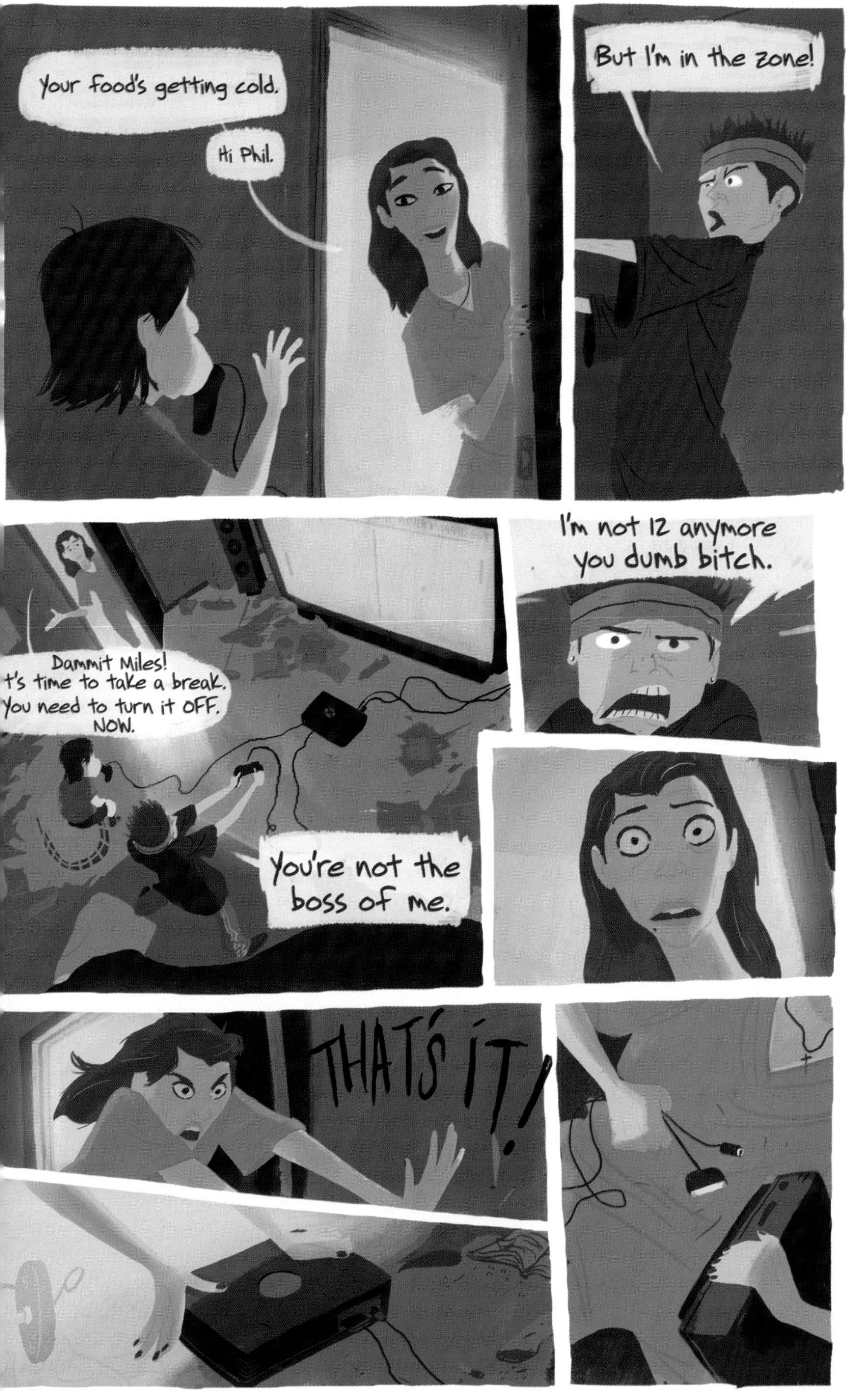
Your food's getting cold.
Hi Phil.
But I'm in the zone!
Dammit Miles! It's time to take a break. You need to turn it OFF. NOW.
You're not the boss of me.
I'm not 12 anymore you dumb bitch.
THAT'S IT!

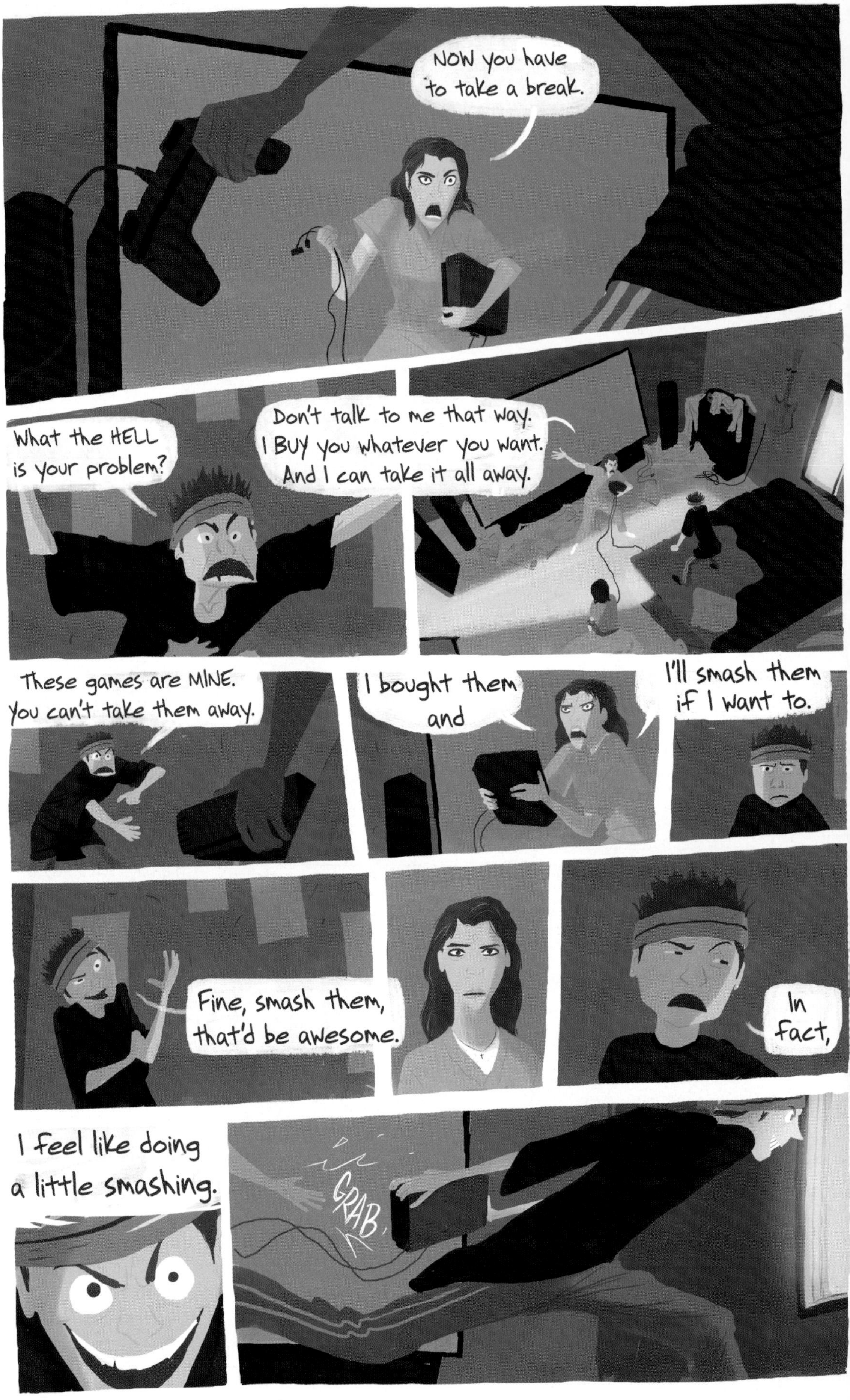
NOW you have to take a break.
What the HELL is your problem?
Don't talk to me that way. I BUY you whatever you want. And I can take it all away.
These games are MINE. You can't take them away.
I bought them and
I'll smash them if I want to.
Fine, smash them, that'd be awesome.
In fact,
I feel like doing a little smashing.
GRAB

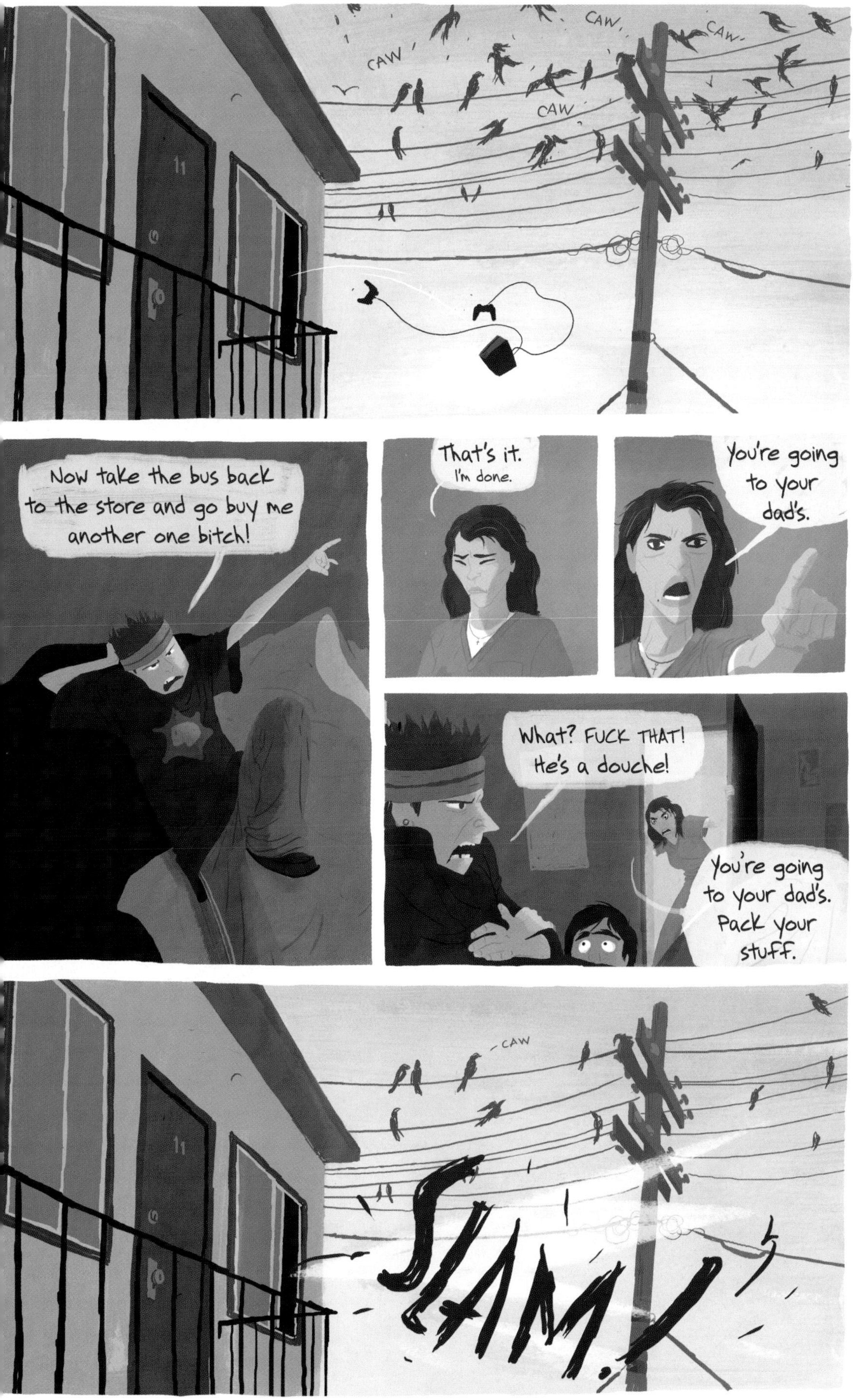
CAW
CAW
CAW
CAW
Now take the bus back to the store and go buy me another one bitch!
That's it. I'm done.
You're going to your dad's.
What? FUCK THAT! He's a douche!
You're going to your dad's. Pack your stuff.
CAW
SLAM!

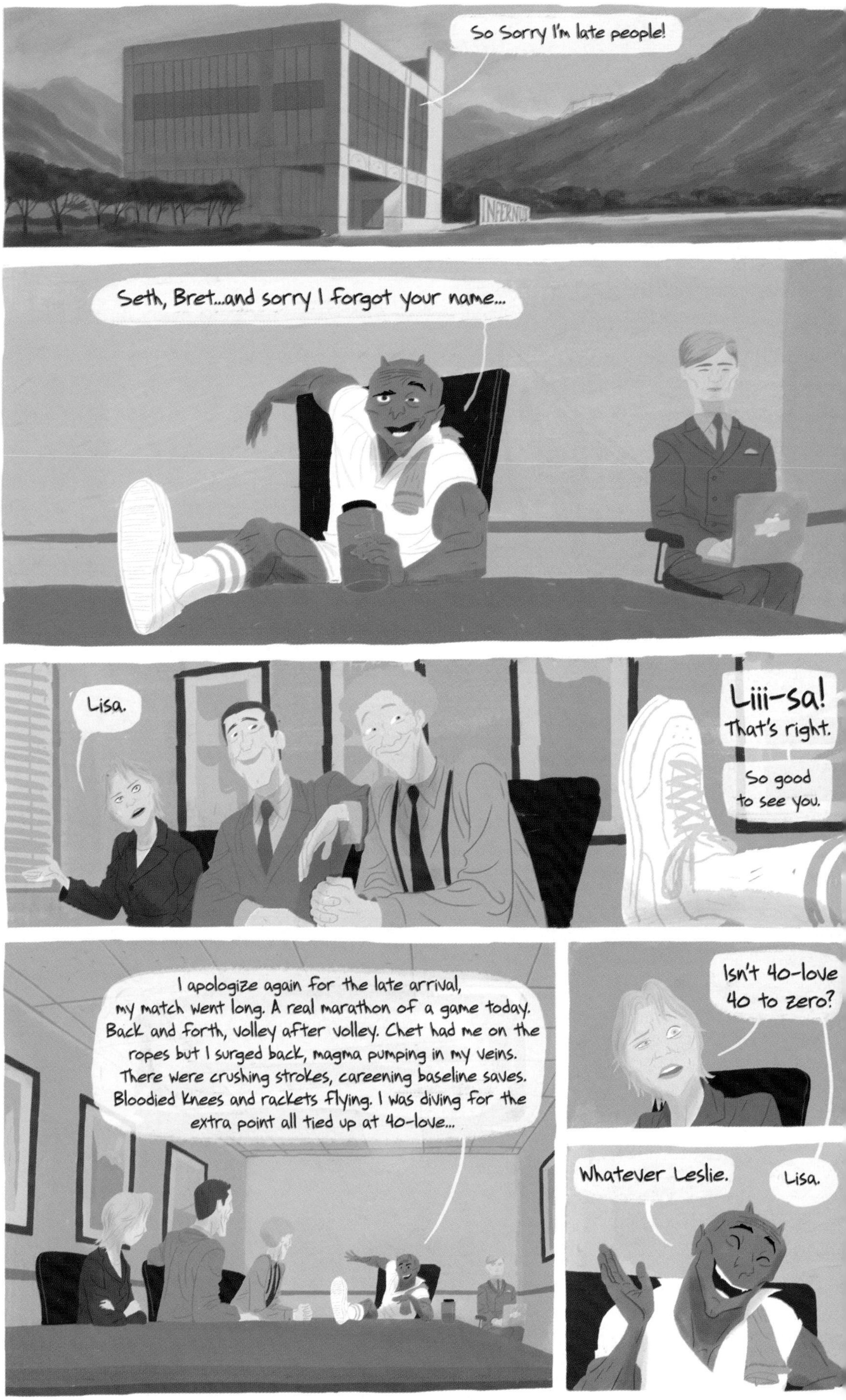

So Sorry I'm late people!
INFERNUS
Seth, Bret...and sorry I forgot your name...
Lisa.
Liii-sa! That's right.
So good to see you.
I apologize again for the late arrival, my match went long. A real marathon of a game today. Back and forth, volley after volley. Chet had me on the ropes but I surged back, magma pumping in my veins. There were crushing strokes, careening baseline saves. Bloodied knees and rackets flying. I was diving for the extra point all tied up at 40-love...
Isn't 40-love 40 to zero?
Whatever Leslie.
Lisa.

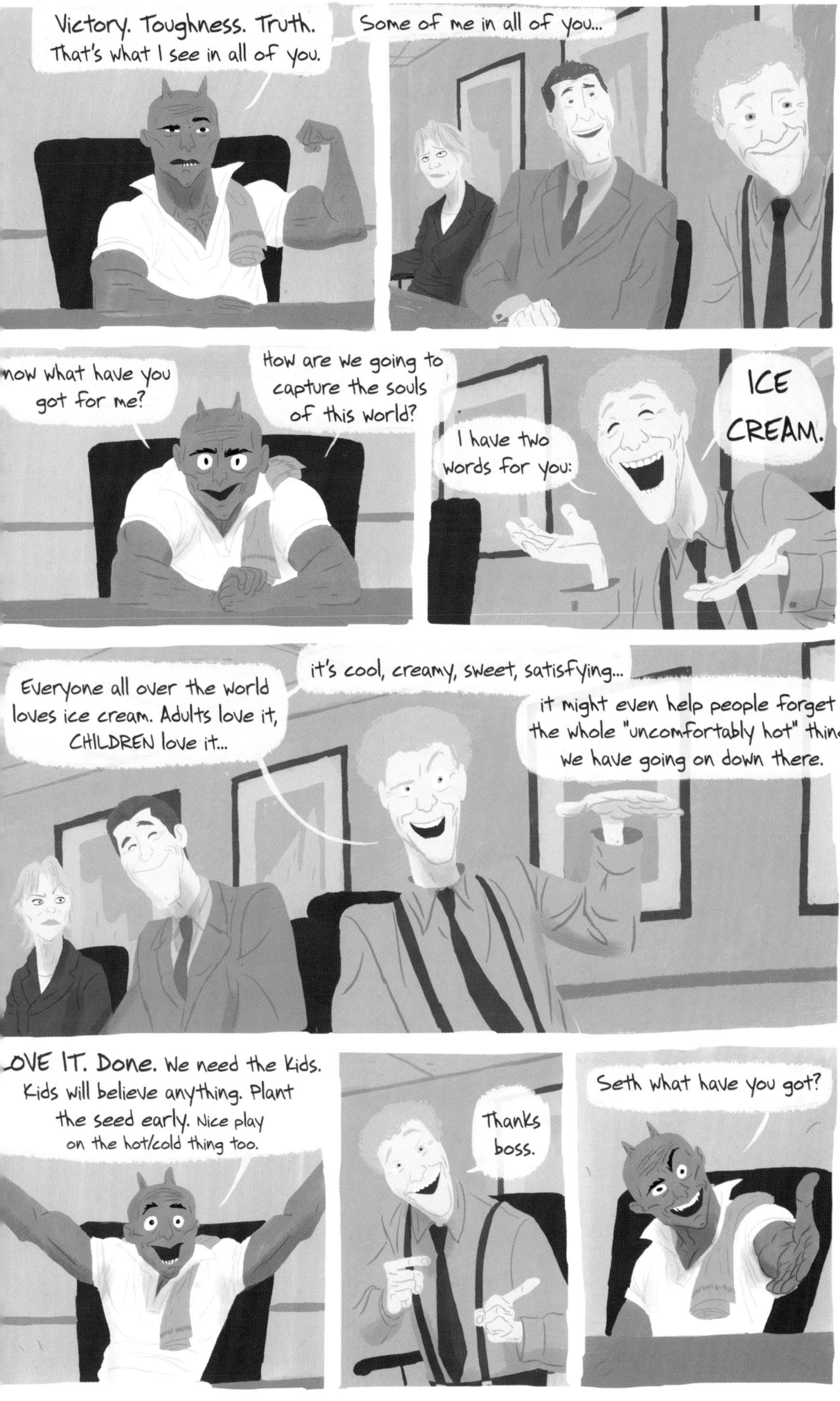
Victory. Toughness. Truth. That's what I see in all of you.
Some of me in all of you...
now what have you got for me?
How are we going to capture the souls of this world?
I have two words for you:
ICE CREAM.
Everyone all over the world loves ice cream. Adults love it, CHILDREN love it...
it's cool, creamy, sweet, satisfying...
it might even help people forget the whole "uncomfortably hot" thing we have going on down there.
OVE IT. Done. We need the kids. Kids will believe anything. Plant the seed early. Nice play on the hot/cold thing too.
Thanks boss.
Seth what have you got?

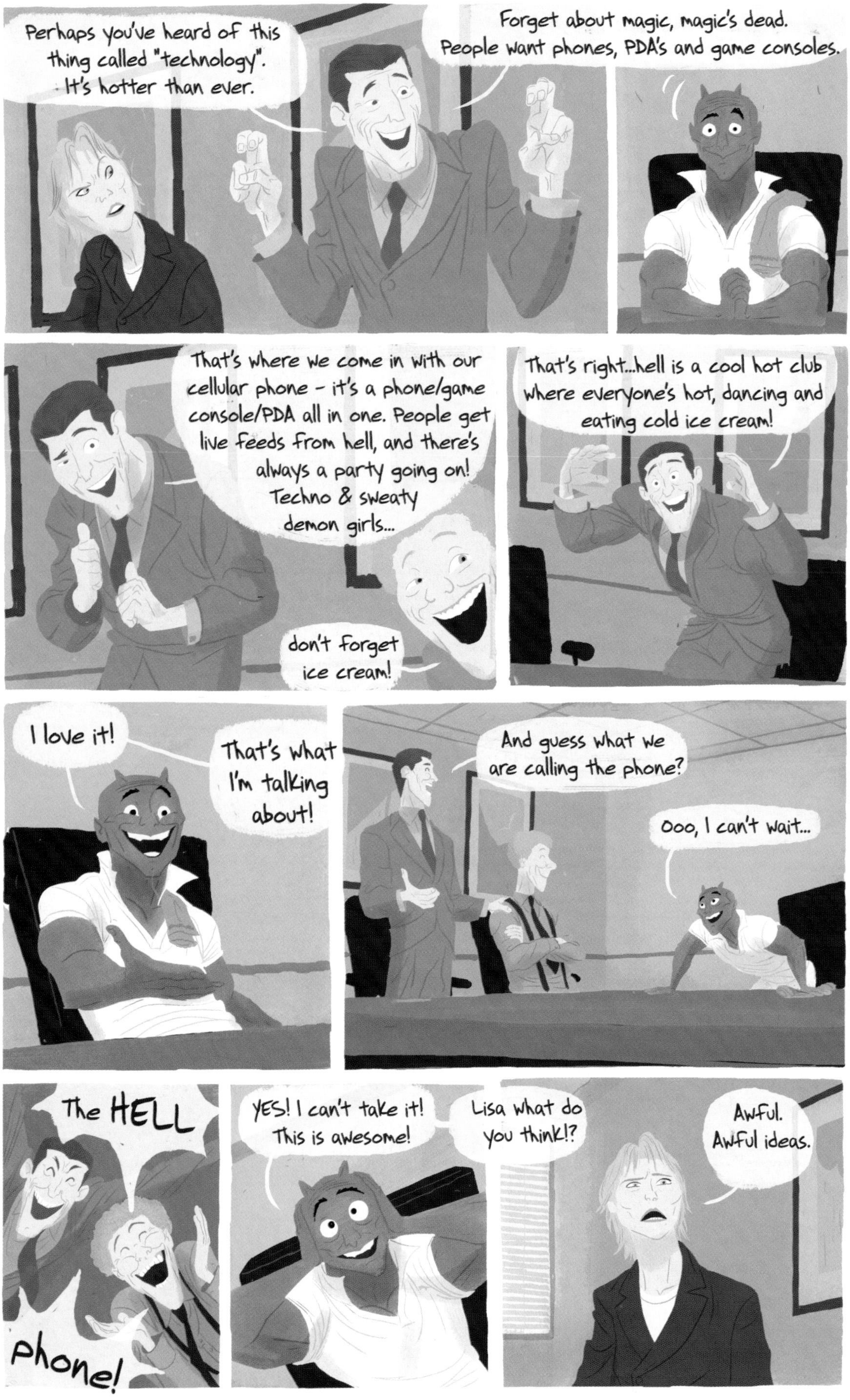
Perhaps you've heard of this thing called "technology". It's hotter than ever.
Forget about magic, magic's dead. People want phones, PDA's and game consoles.
That's where we come in with our cellular phone - it's a phone/game console/PDA all in one. People get live feeds from hell, and there's always a party going on! Techno & sweaty demon girls...
don't forget ice cream!
That's right...hell is a cool hot club where everyone's hot, dancing and eating cold ice cream!
I love it!
That's what I'm talking about!
And guess what we are calling the phone?
Ooo, I can't wait...
The HELL
phone!
YES! I can't take it! This is awesome!
Lisa what do you think!?
Awful. Awful ideas.

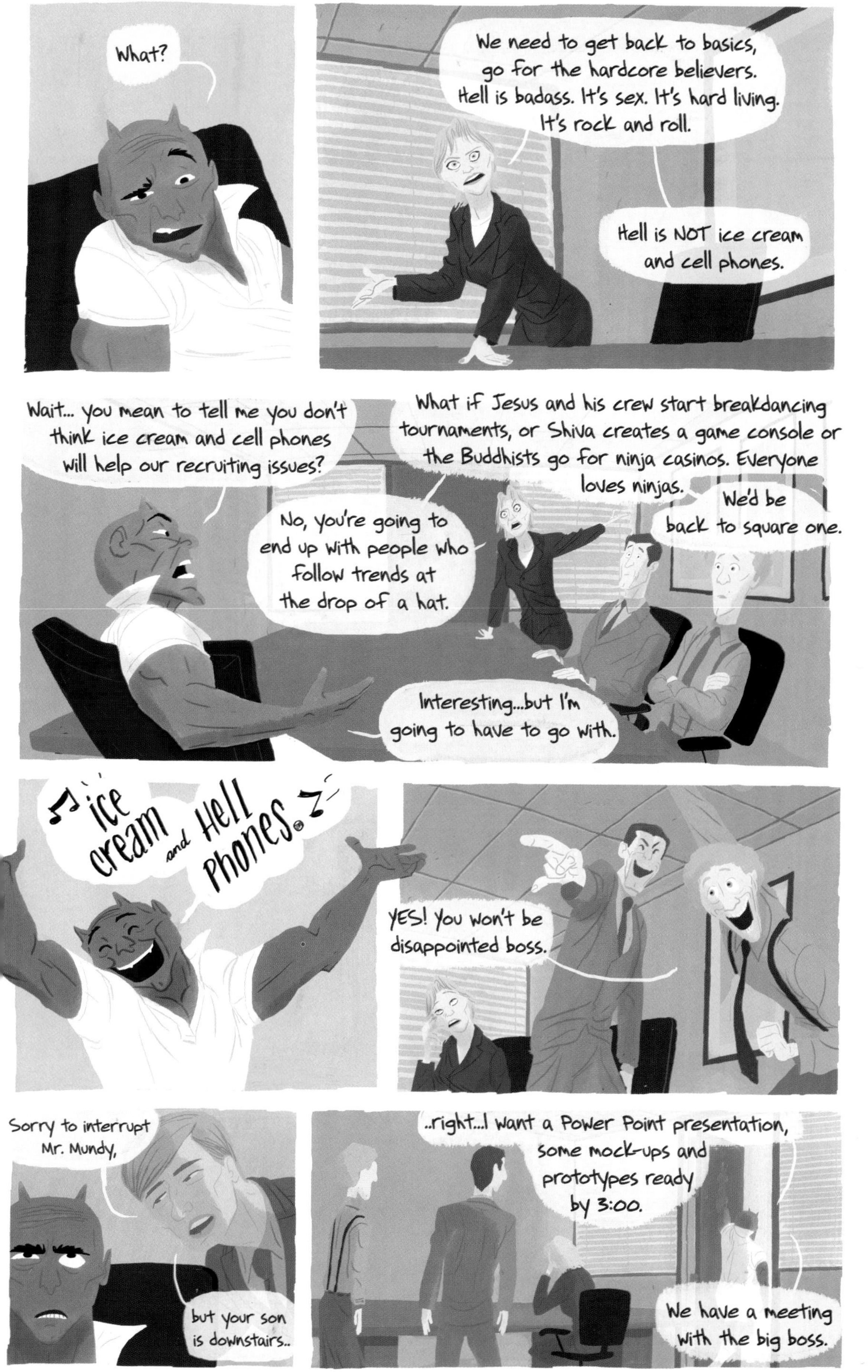
What?
We need to get back to basics, go for the hardcore believers. Hell is badass. It's sex. It's hard living. It's rock and roll.
Hell is NOT ice cream and cell phones.
Wait... you mean to tell me you don't think ice cream and cell phones will help our recruiting issues?
What if Jesus and his crew start breakdancing tournaments, or Shiva creates a game console or the Buddhists go for ninja casinos. Everyone loves ninjas.
No, you're going to end up with people who follow trends at the drop of a hat.
We'd be back to square one.
Interesting...but I'm going to have to go with.
ice cream and Hell phones
YES! You won't be disappointed boss.
Sorry to interrupt Mr. Mundy,
but your son is downstairs..
..right...I want a Power Point presentation, some mock-ups and prototypes ready by 3:00.
We have a meeting with the big boss.

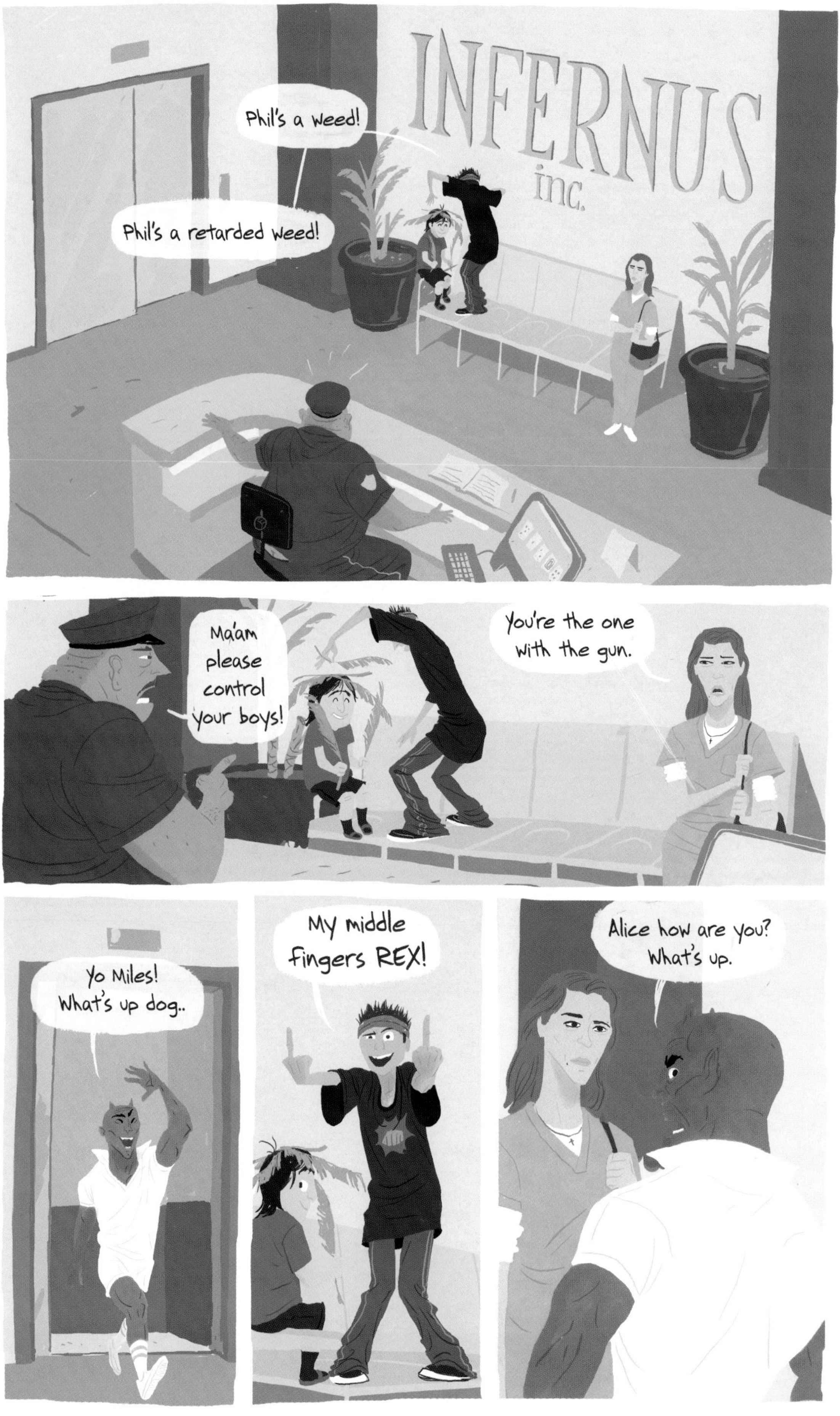
INFERNUS inc.
Phil's a weed!
Phil's a retarded weed!
Ma'am please control your boys!
You're the one with the gun.
Yo Miles! What's up dog..
My middle fingers REX!
Alice how are you? What's up.

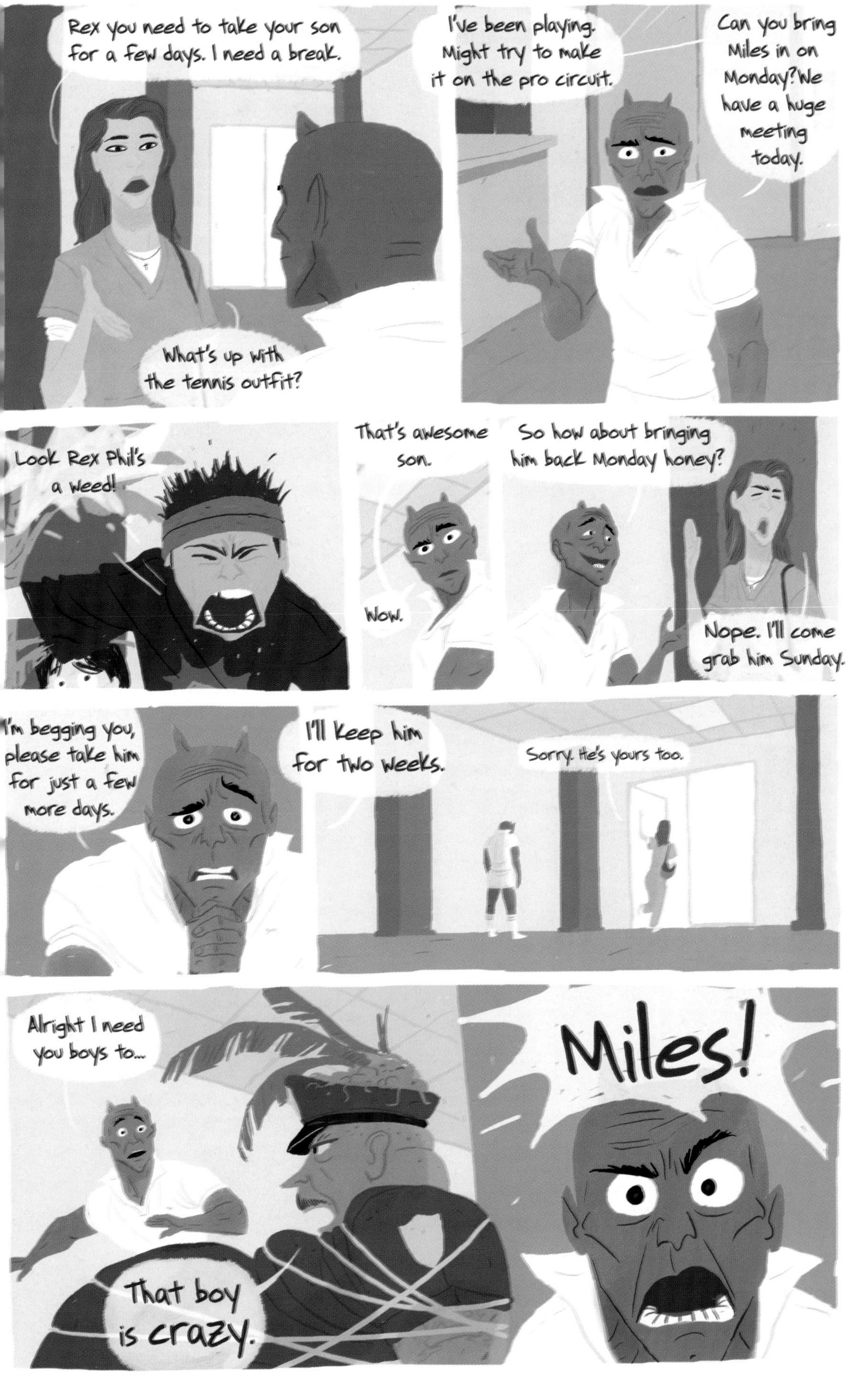
Rex you need to take your son for a few days. I need a break.
What's up with the tennis outfit?
I've been playing. Might try to make it on the pro circuit.
Can you bring Miles in on Monday? We have a huge meeting today.
Look Rex Phil's a weed!
That's awesome son.
Wow.
So how about bringing him back Monday honey?
Nope. I'll come grab him Sunday.
I'm begging you, please take him for just a few more days.
I'll keep him for two weeks.
Sorry. He's yours too.
Alright I need you boys to...
That boy is crazy.
Miles!

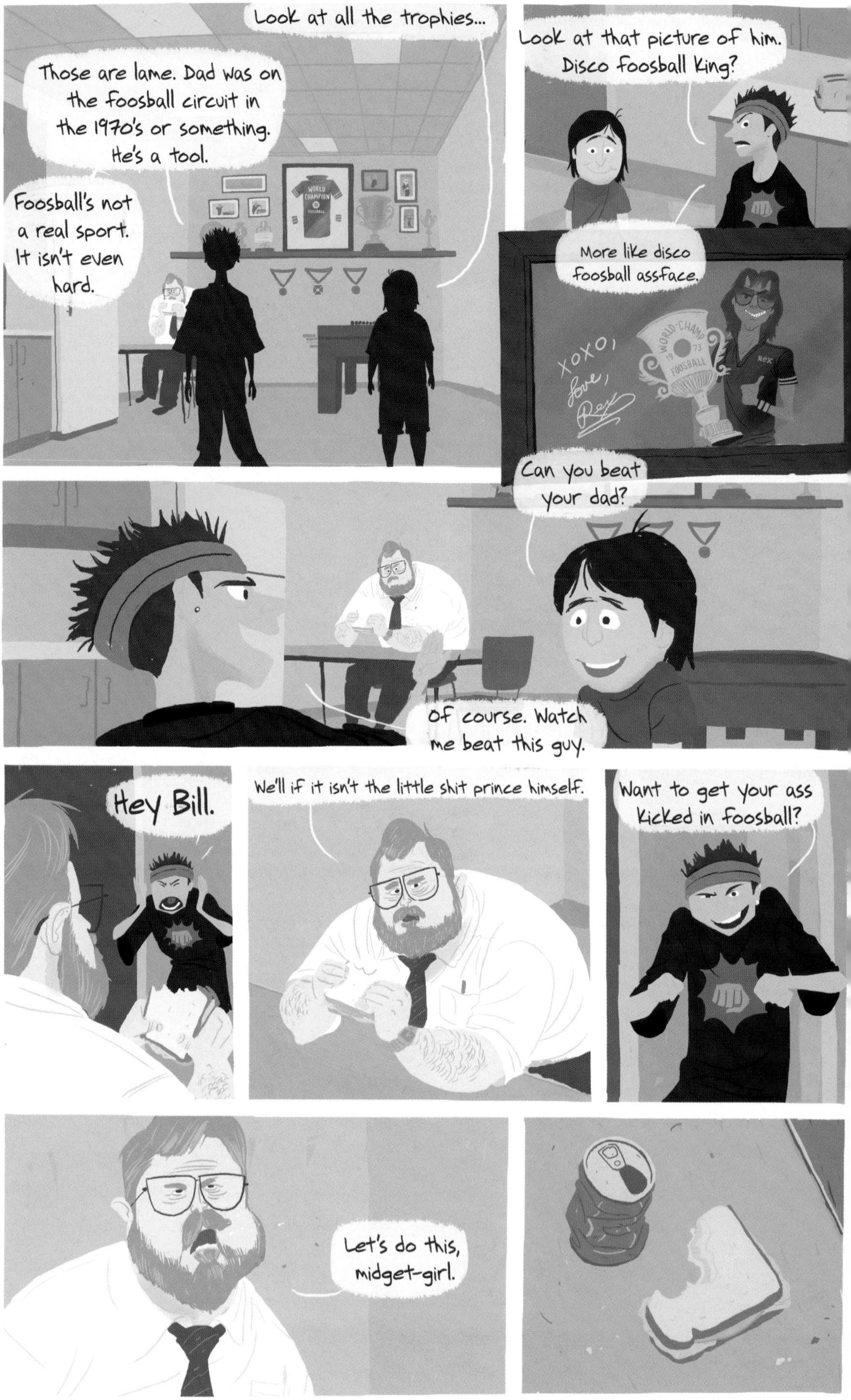
Look at all the trophies...
Those are lame. Dad was on the foosball circuit in the 1970's or something. He's a tool.
Foosball's not a real sport. It isn't even hard.
WORLD CHAMPION FOOSBALL
Look at that picture of him. Disco foosball King?
More like disco foosball assface.
XOXO, Love, Rex
WORLD CHAMP 19 73 FOOSBALL
REX
Can you beat your dad?
Of course. Watch me beat this guy.
Hey Bill.
We'll if it isn't the little shit prince himself.
Want to get your ass Kicked in foosball?
Let's do this, midget-girl.

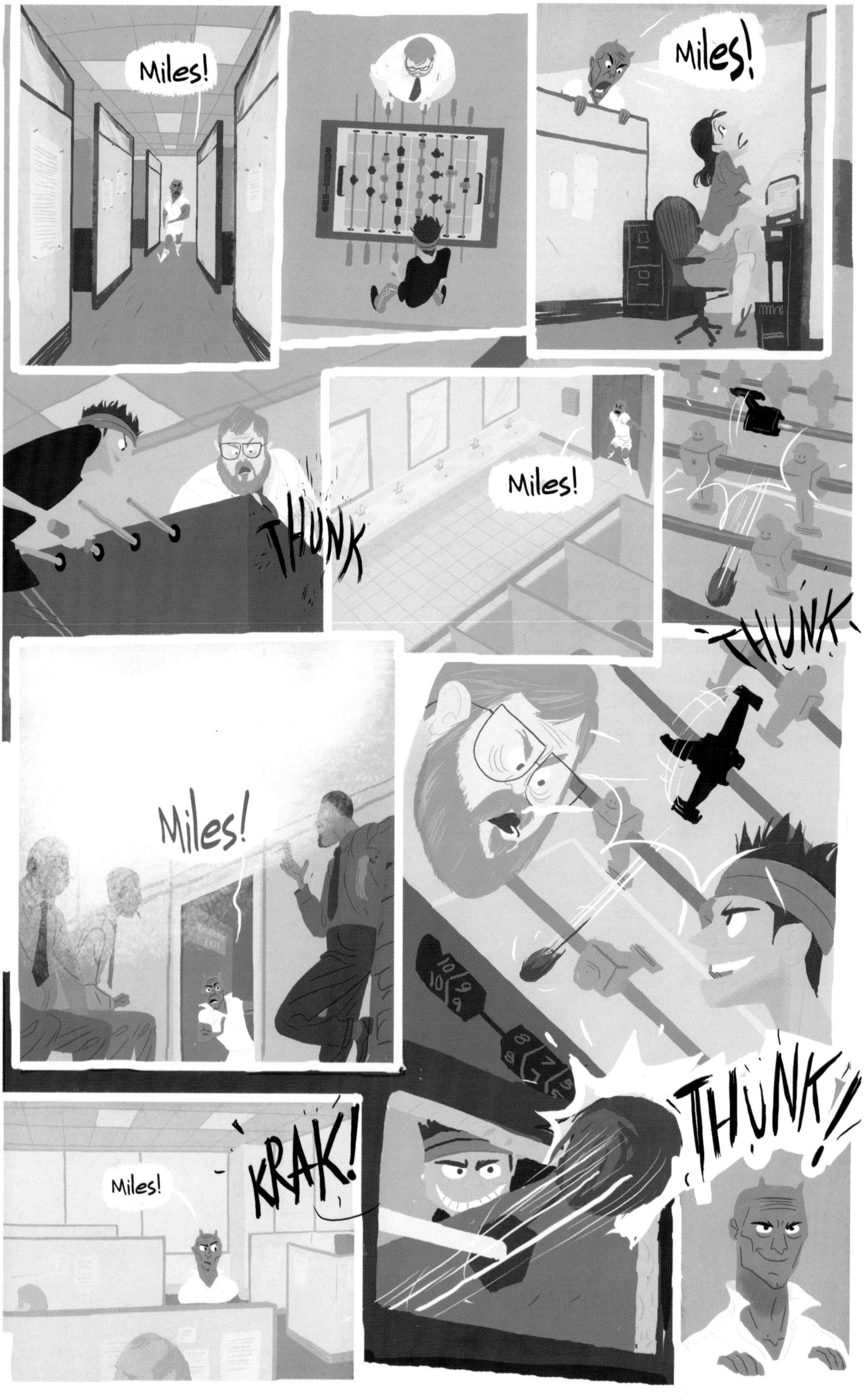

Miles!
Miles!
Miles!
THUNK
THUNK
Miles!
KRAK!
Miles!
THUNK!

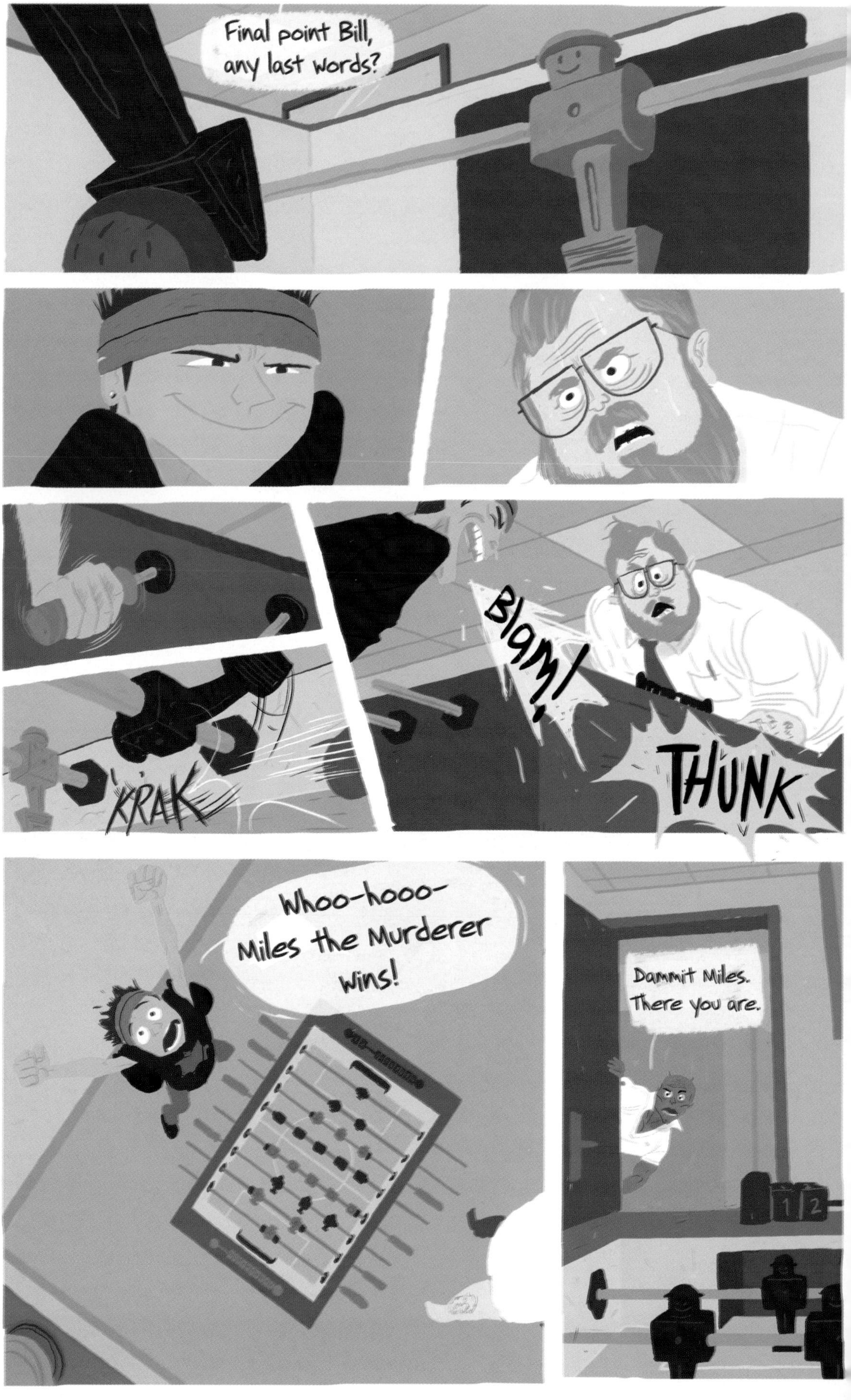
Final point Bill,
any last words?
Blam!
KRAK
THUNK
Whoo-hooo-
Miles the Murderer
wins!
Dammit Miles.
There you are.
1 2

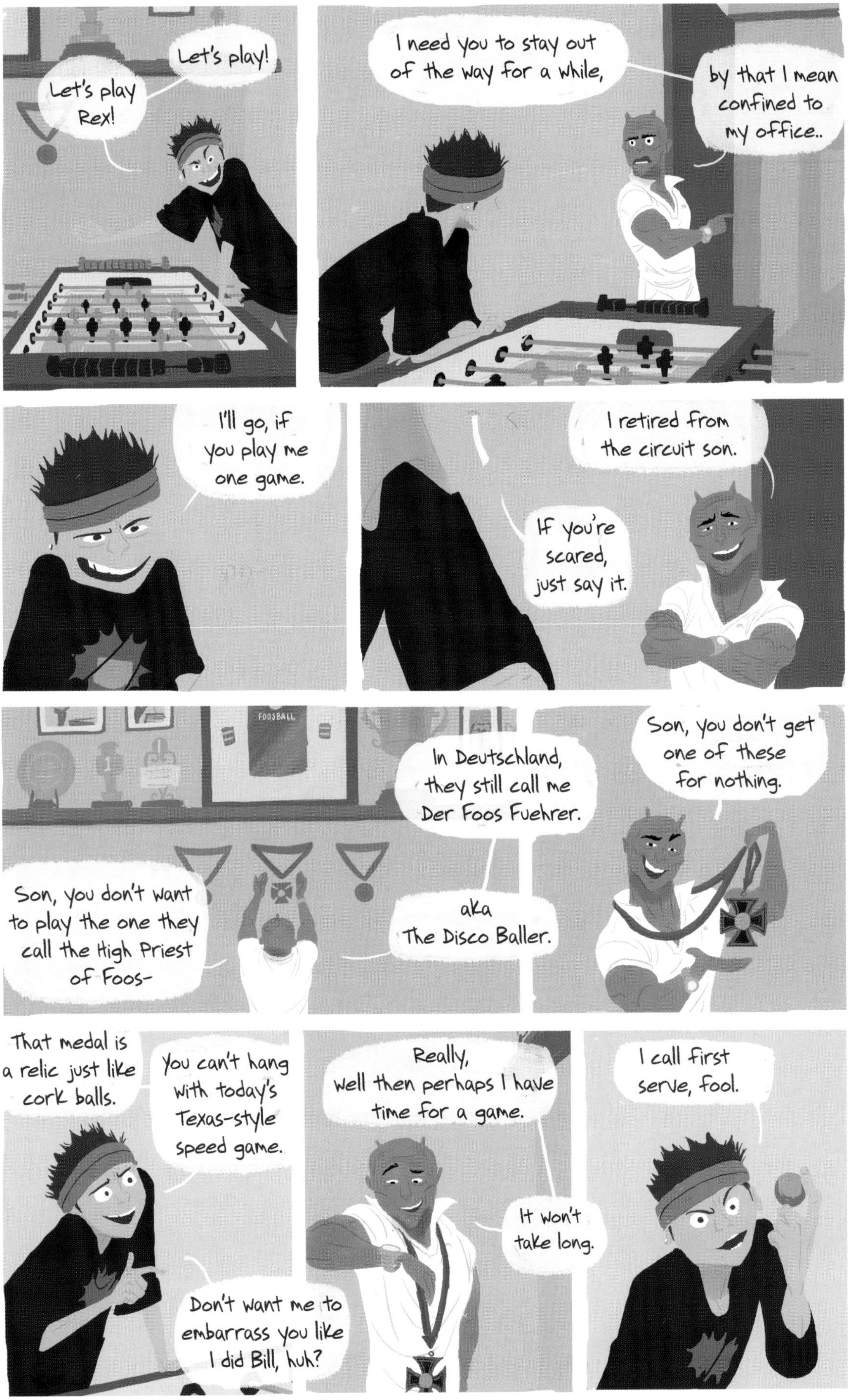
Let's play Rex!
Let's play!
I need you to stay out of the way for a while,
by that I mean confined to my office..
I'll go, if you play me one game.
I retired from the circuit son.
If you're scared, just say it.
FOOSBALL
Son, you don't want to play the one they call the High Priest of Foos-
In Deutschland, they still call me Der Foos Fuehrer.
aka The Disco Baller.
Son, you don't get one of these for nothing.
That medal is a relic just like cork balls.
You can't hang with today's Texas-style speed game.
Don't want me to embarrass you like I did Bill, huh?
Really, well then perhaps I have time for a game.
It won't take long.
I call first serve, fool.

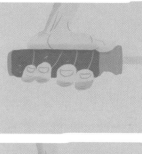

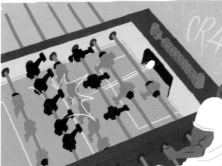

The game is far from over

YOU CAN'T HANDLE MY POWER!

Let me get a basket for your head, because the French nicknamed this—

Le Guillotine!

Can't handle the—

East German Glockenfoos?

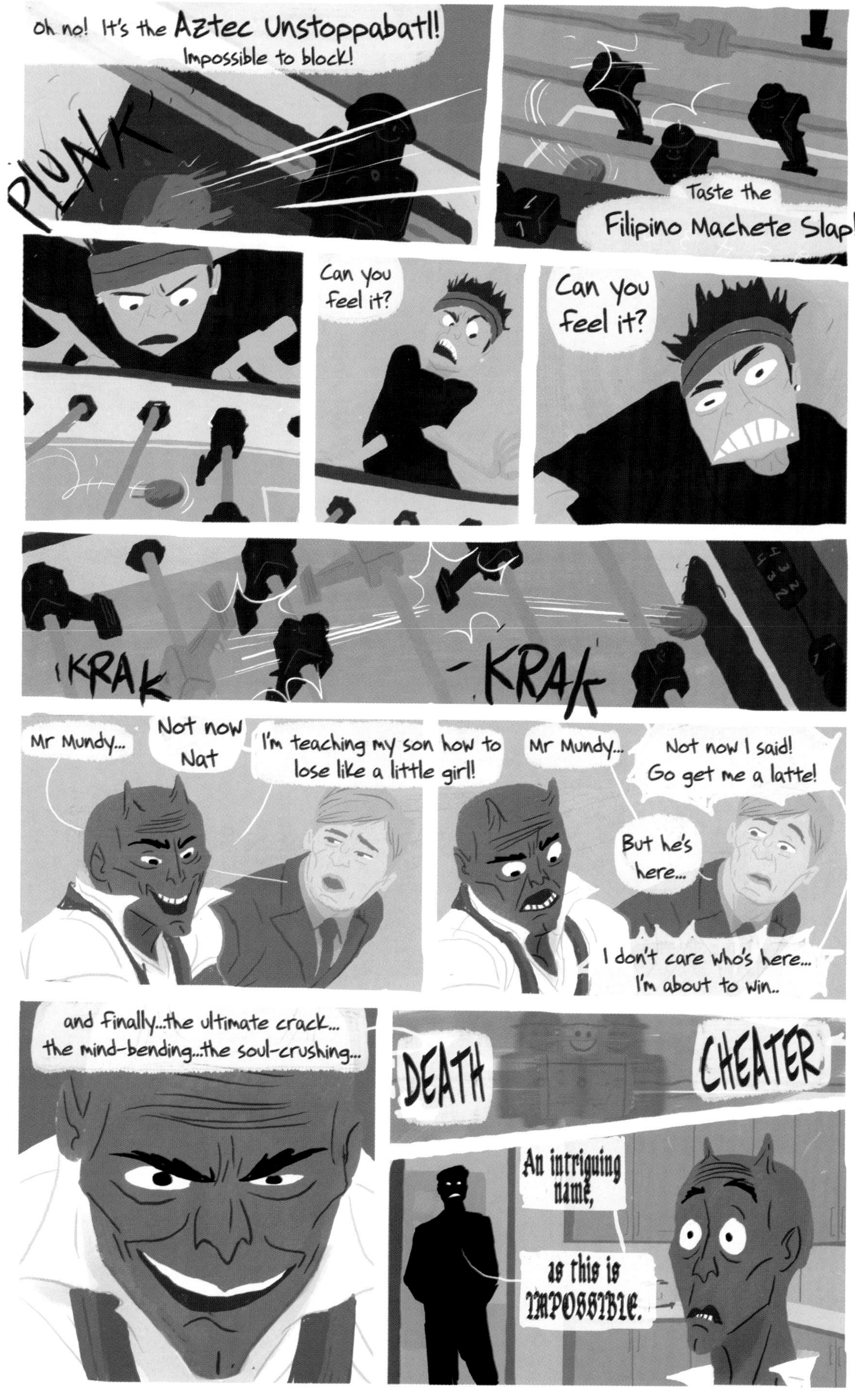

Oh no! It's the Aztec Unstoppabatl! Impossible to block!
PLUNK
Taste the Filipino Machete Slap!
Can you feel it?
Can you feel it?
KRAK
KRAK
Mr Mundy...
Not now Nat
I'm teaching my son how to lose like a little girl!
Mr Mundy...
Not now I said! Go get me a latte!
But he's here...
I don't care who's here... I'm about to win..
and finally...the ultimate crack... the mind-bending...the soul-crushing...
DEATH
CHEATER
An intriguing name,
as this is IMPOSSIBLE.

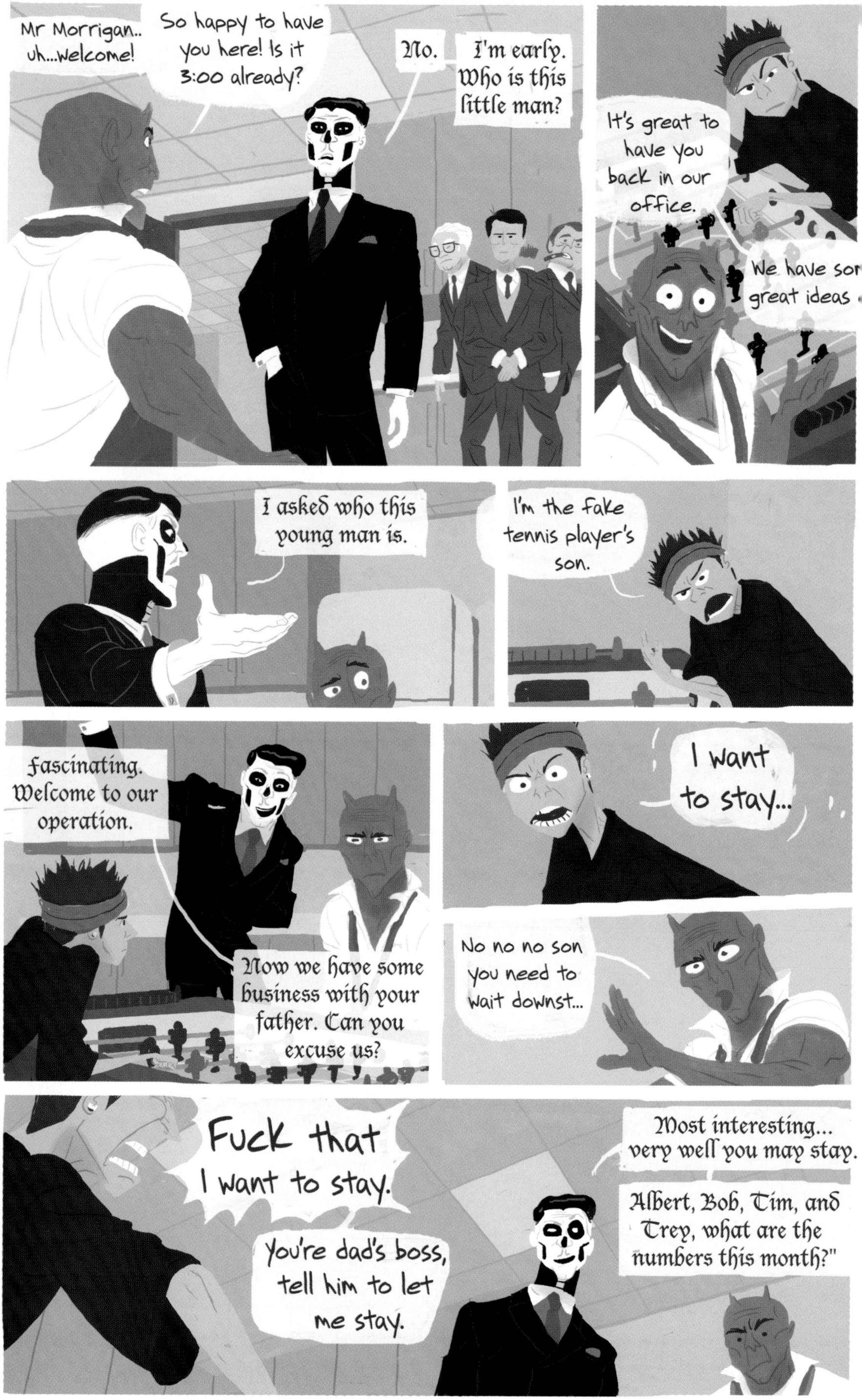
Mr Morrigan.. uh...welcome!
So happy to have you here! Is it 3:00 already?
No.
I'm early. Who is this little man?
It's great to have you back in our office.
We have sor great ideas
I asked who this young man is.
I'm the fake tennis player's son.
Fascinating. Welcome to our operation.
Now we have some business with your father. Can you excuse us?
I want to stay...
No no no son you need to wait downst...
Fuck that I want to stay.
You're dad's boss, tell him to let me stay.
Most interesting... very well you may stay.
Albert, Bob, Tim, and Trey, what are the numbers this month?"

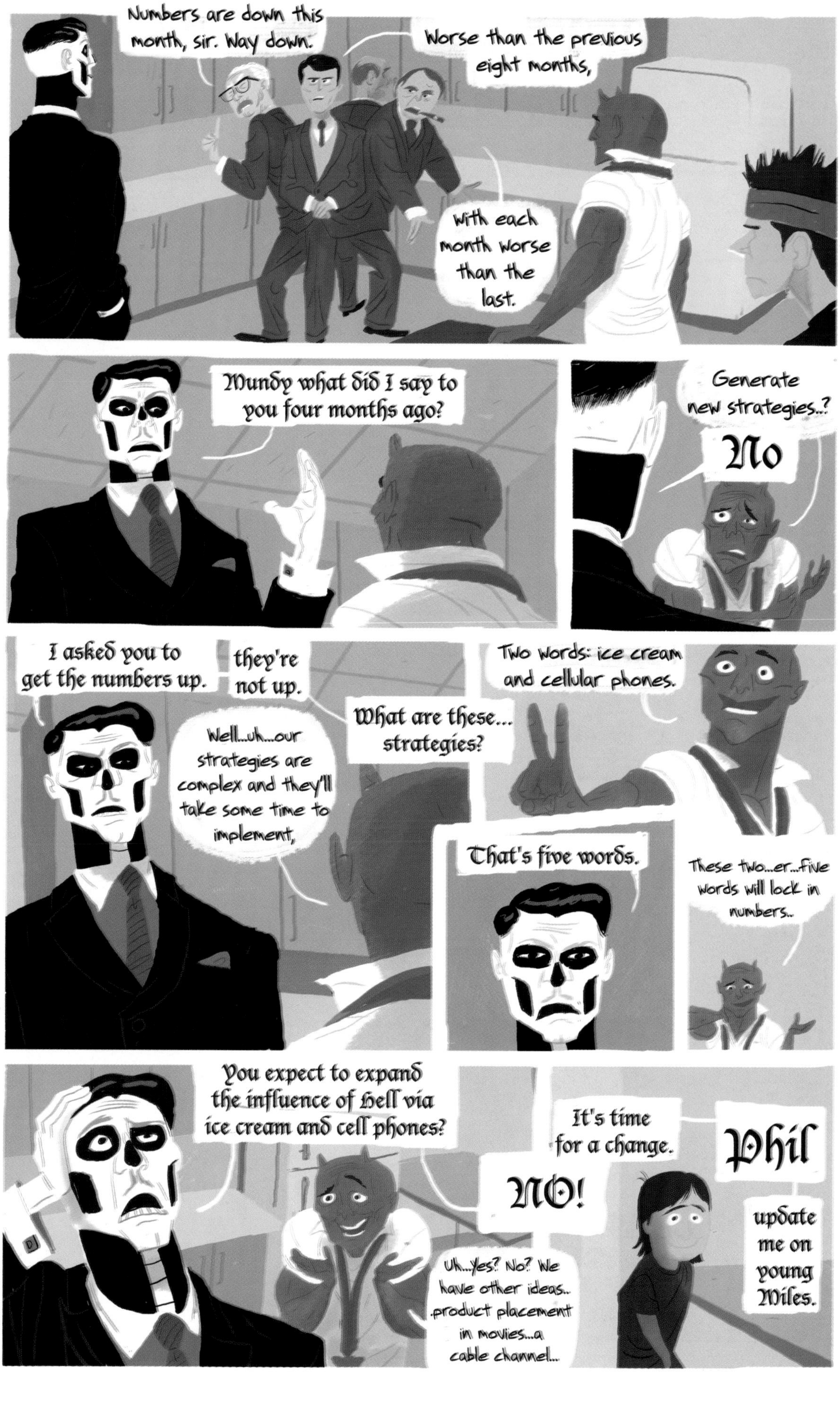
Numbers are down this month, sir. Way down.
Worse than the previous eight months,
With each month worse than the last.
Mundy what did I say to you four months ago?
Generate new strategies..?
No
I asked you to get the numbers up.
they're not up.
What are these... strategies?
Well...uh...our strategies are complex and they'll take some time to implement,
Two words: ice cream and cellular phones.
That's five words.
These two...er...five words will lock in numbers..
You expect to expand the influence of Hell via ice cream and cell phones?
Uh...Yes? No? We have other ideas.. product placement in movies...a cable channel...
NO!
It's time for a change.
Phil
update me on young Miles.

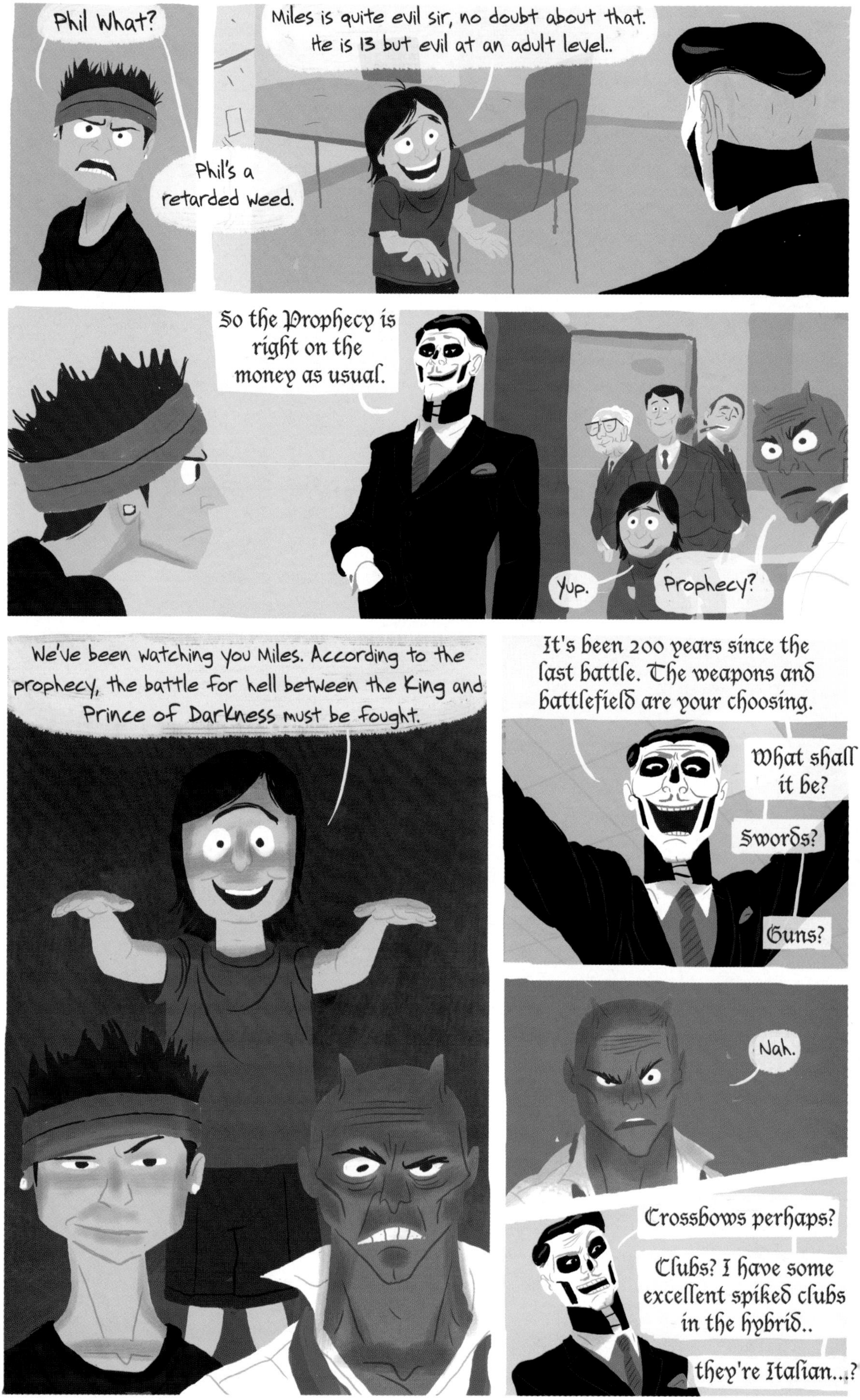

Phil What?
Phil's a retarded weed.
Miles is quite evil sir, no doubt about that. He is 13 but evil at an adult level..
So the Prophecy is right on the money as usual.
Yup.
Prophecy?
We've been watching you Miles. According to the prophecy, the battle for hell between the King and Prince of Darkness must be fought.
It's been 200 years since the last battle. The weapons and battlefield are your choosing.
What shall it be?
Swords?
Guns?
Nah.
Crossbows perhaps?
Clubs? I have some excellent spiked clubs in the hybrid..
they're Italian...?

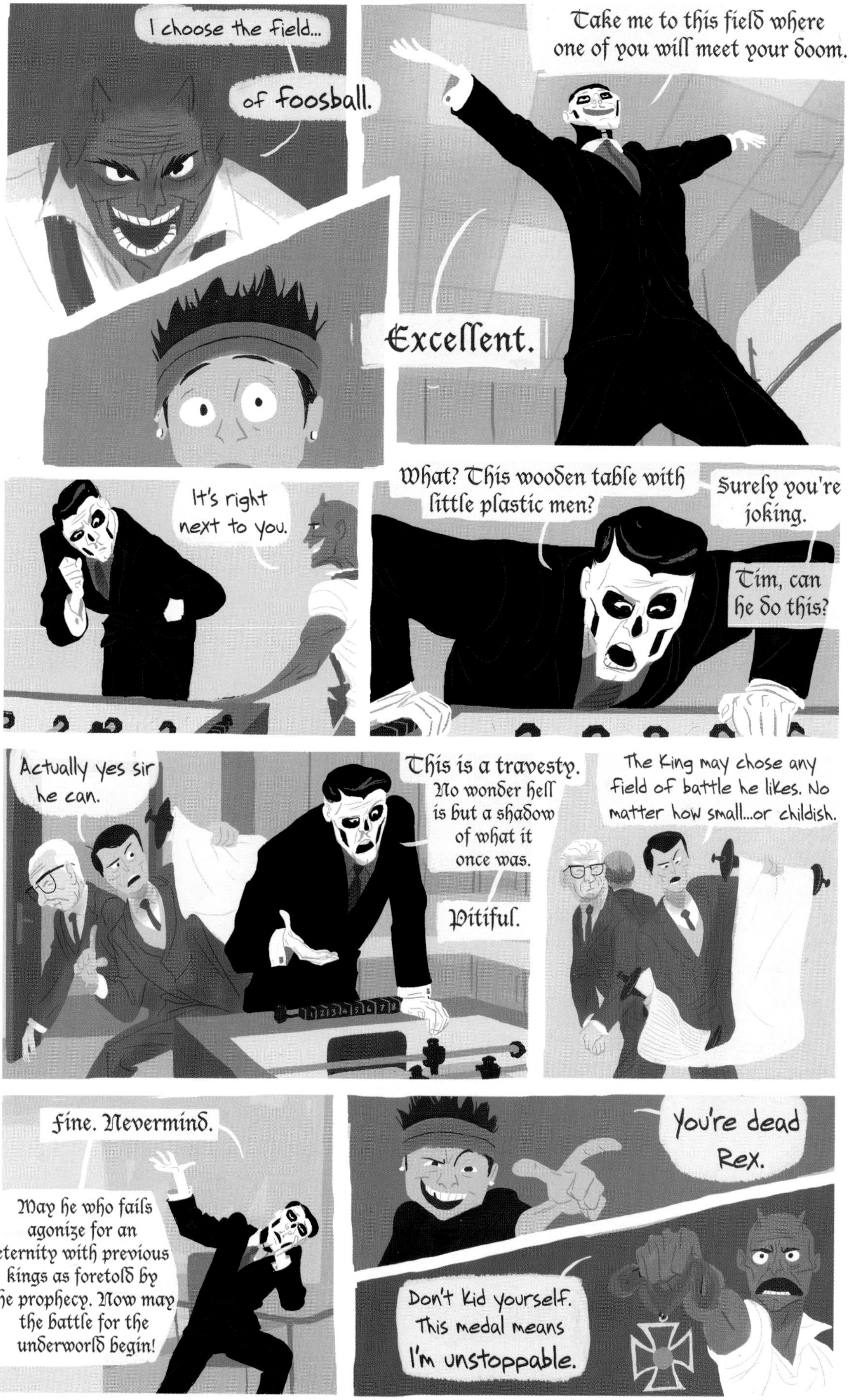
I choose the field...
of foosball.
Take me to this field where one of you will meet your doom.
Excellent.
It's right next to you.
What? This wooden table with little plastic men?
Surely you're joking.
Tim, can he do this?
Actually yes sir he can.
This is a travesty. No wonder hell is but a shadow of what it once was.
Pitiful.
The King may chose any field of battle he likes. No matter how small...or childish.
Fine. Nevermind.
May he who fails agonize for an eternity with previous kings as foretold by the prophecy. Now may the battle for the underworld begin!
You're dead Rex.
Don't kid yourself. This medal means I'm unstoppable.

Alright Rex. I hope you have a clean pair of adult diapers on cause this shot is the shit.

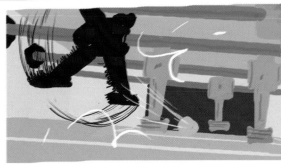

WHAAA!

nice try junior, maybe you should try a different shot. Allow me to demonstrate.

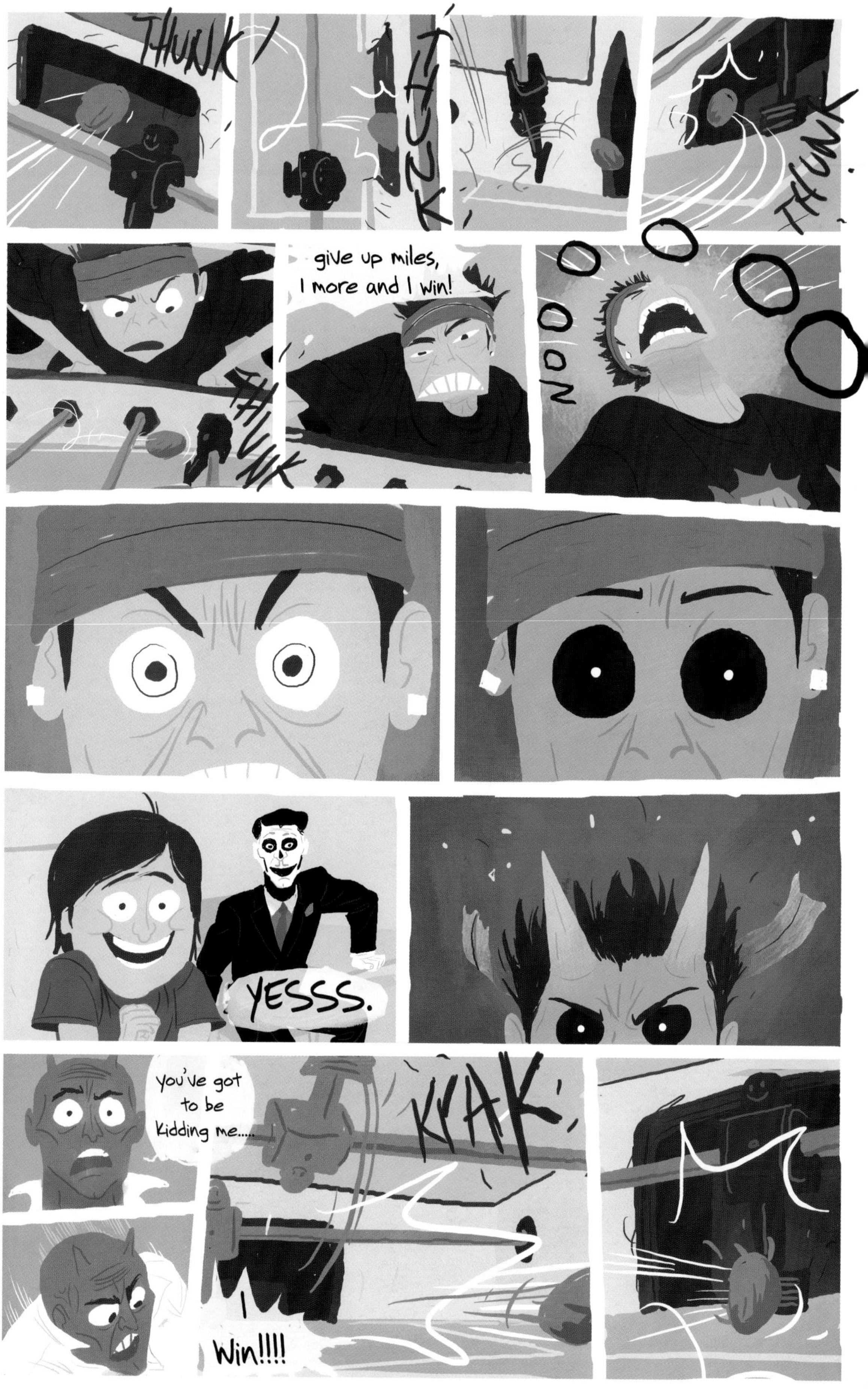
THUNK!
THUNK
THUNK
give up miles,
1 more and I win!
THUNK
NOOOOOOO
YESSS.
you've got
to be
kidding me.....
KRAK!
I
Win!!!!

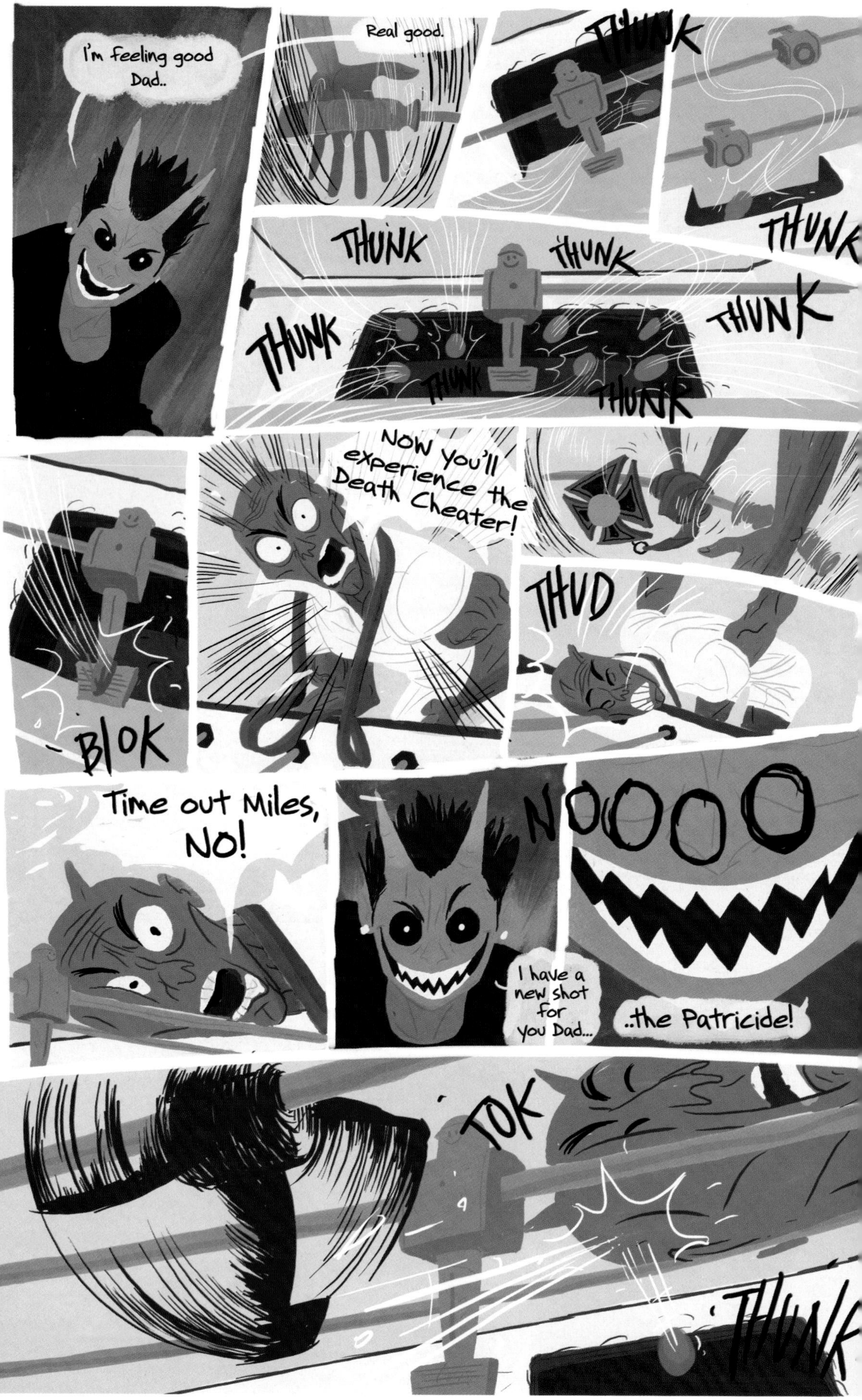
I'm feeling good Dad..
Real good.
THUNK
THUNK
THUNK
THUNK
THUNK
THUNK
THUNK
THUNK
BLOK
NOW you'll experience the Death Cheater!
THUD
Time out Miles, NO!
NOOOOO
I have a new shot for you Dad...
..the Patricide!
TOK
THUNK

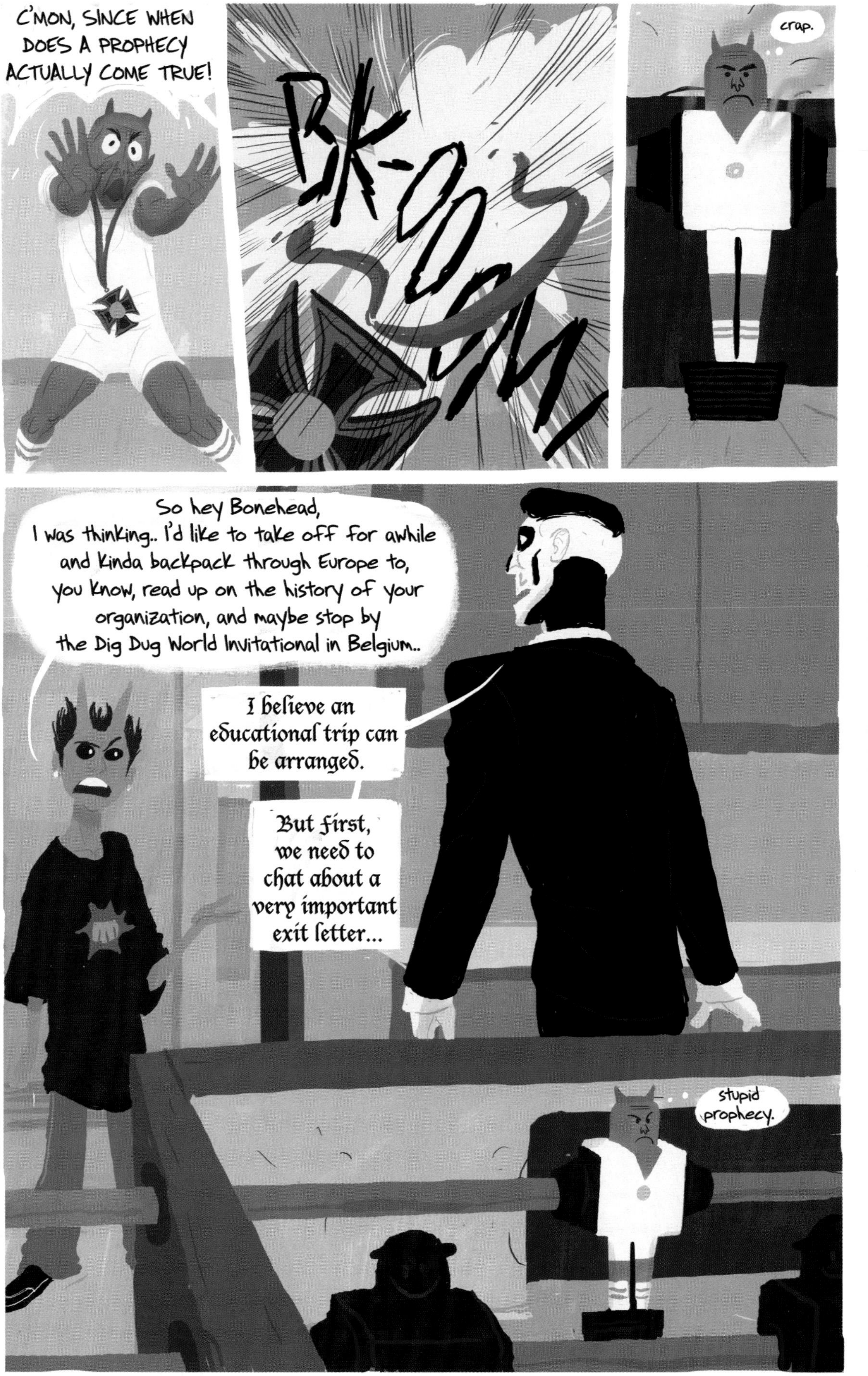
C'MON, SINCE WHEN DOES A PROPHECY ACTUALLY COME TRUE!
BK-OOOM!
crap.
So hey Bonehead, I was thinking.. I'd like to take off for awhile and kinda backpack through Europe to, you know, read up on the history of your organization, and maybe stop by the Dig Dug World Invitational in Belgium..
I believe an educational trip can be arranged.
But first, we need to chat about a very important exit letter...
stupid prophecy.

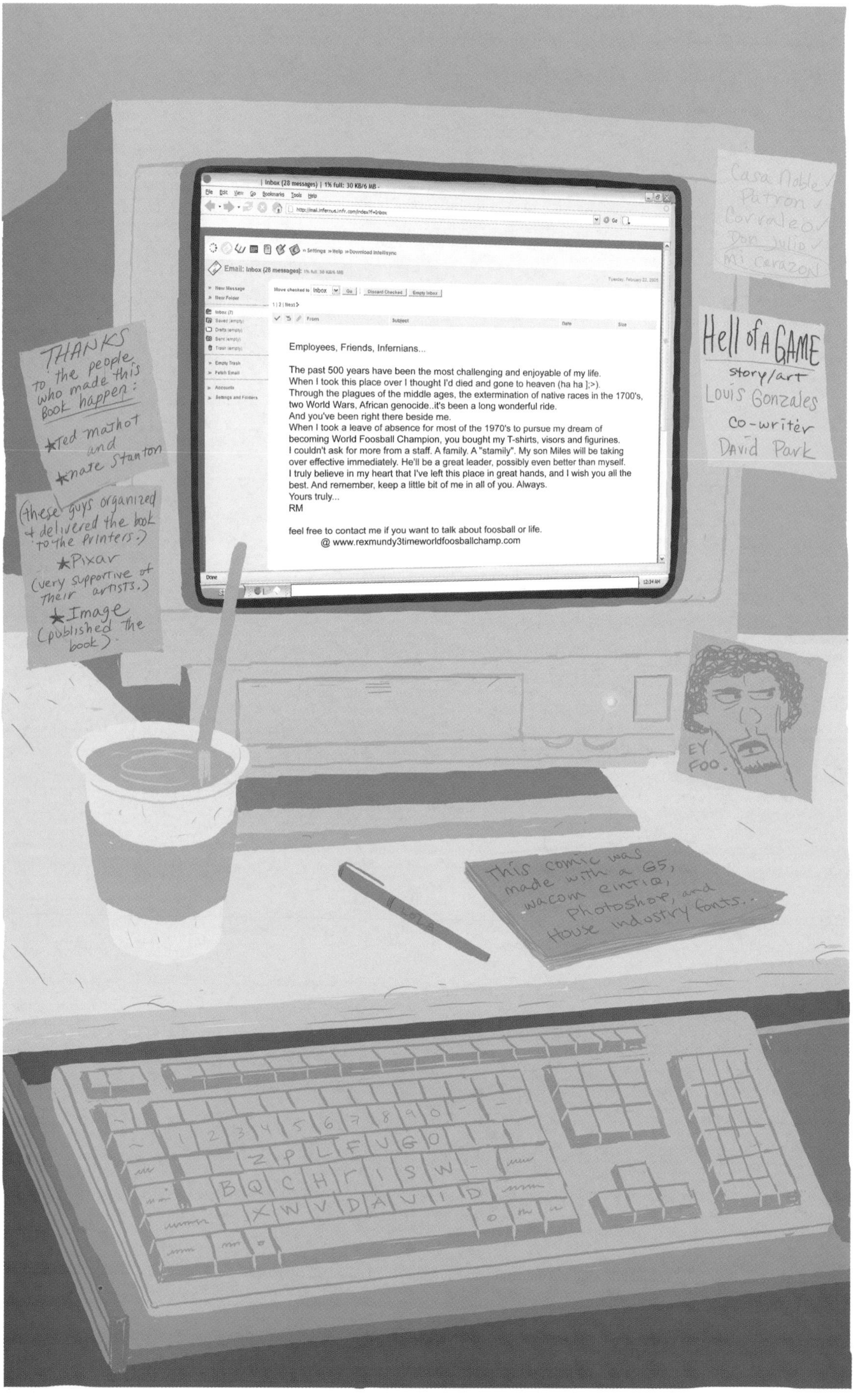
Inbox (28 messages) | 1% full: 30 KB/6 MB
Email: Inbox (28 messages)
Employees, Friends, Infernians...
The past 500 years have been the most challenging and enjoyable of my life.
When I took this place over I thought I'd died and gone to heaven (ha ha];>).
Through the plagues of the middle ages, the extermination of native races in the 1700's, two World Wars, African genocide..it's been a long wonderful ride.
And you've been right there beside me.
When I took a leave of absence for most of the 1970's to pursue my dream of becoming World Foosball Champion, you bought my T-shirts, visors and figurines.
I couldn't ask for more from a staff. A family. A "stamily". My son Miles will be taking over effective immediately. He'll be a great leader, possibly even better than myself.
I truly believe in my heart that I've left this place in great hands, and I wish you all the best. And remember, keep a little bit of me in all of you. Always.
Yours truly...
RM
feel free to contact me if you want to talk about foosball or life.
@ www.rexmundy3timeworldfoosballchamp.com
THANKS to the people who made this book happen:
★Ted mathot and ★nate Stanton
(these guys organized + delivered the book to the printers.)
★Pixar (very supportive of their artists.)
★Image (published the book)
Casa Noble ✓
Patron ✓
Corralejo ✓
Don Julio ✓
Mi Corazon
Hell of a GAME
story/art
Louis Gonzales
co-writer
David Park
EY FOO.
This comic was made with a G5, wacom cintiq, Photoshop, and House industry fonts.
LOLA

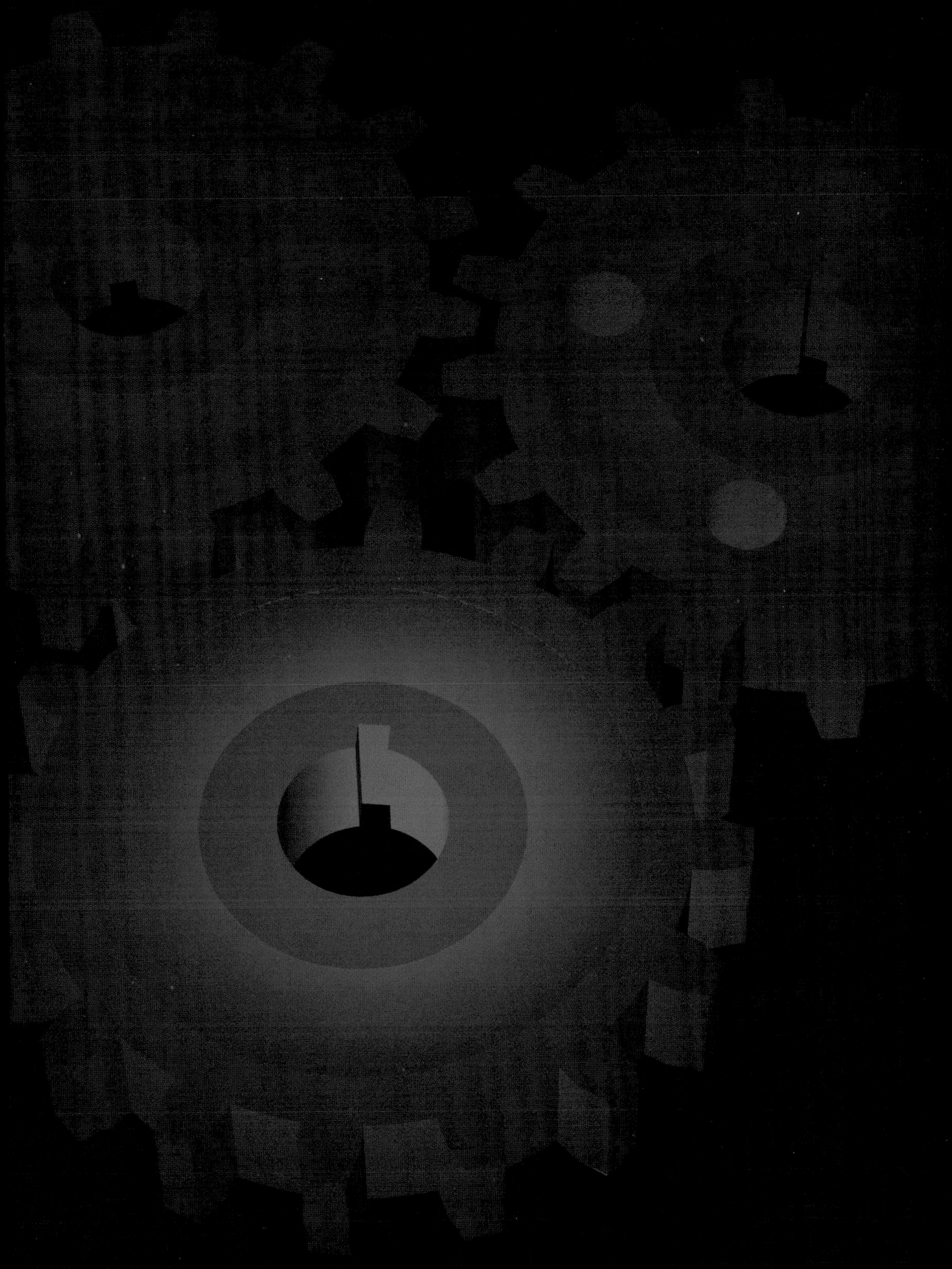

BRIAN LARSEN

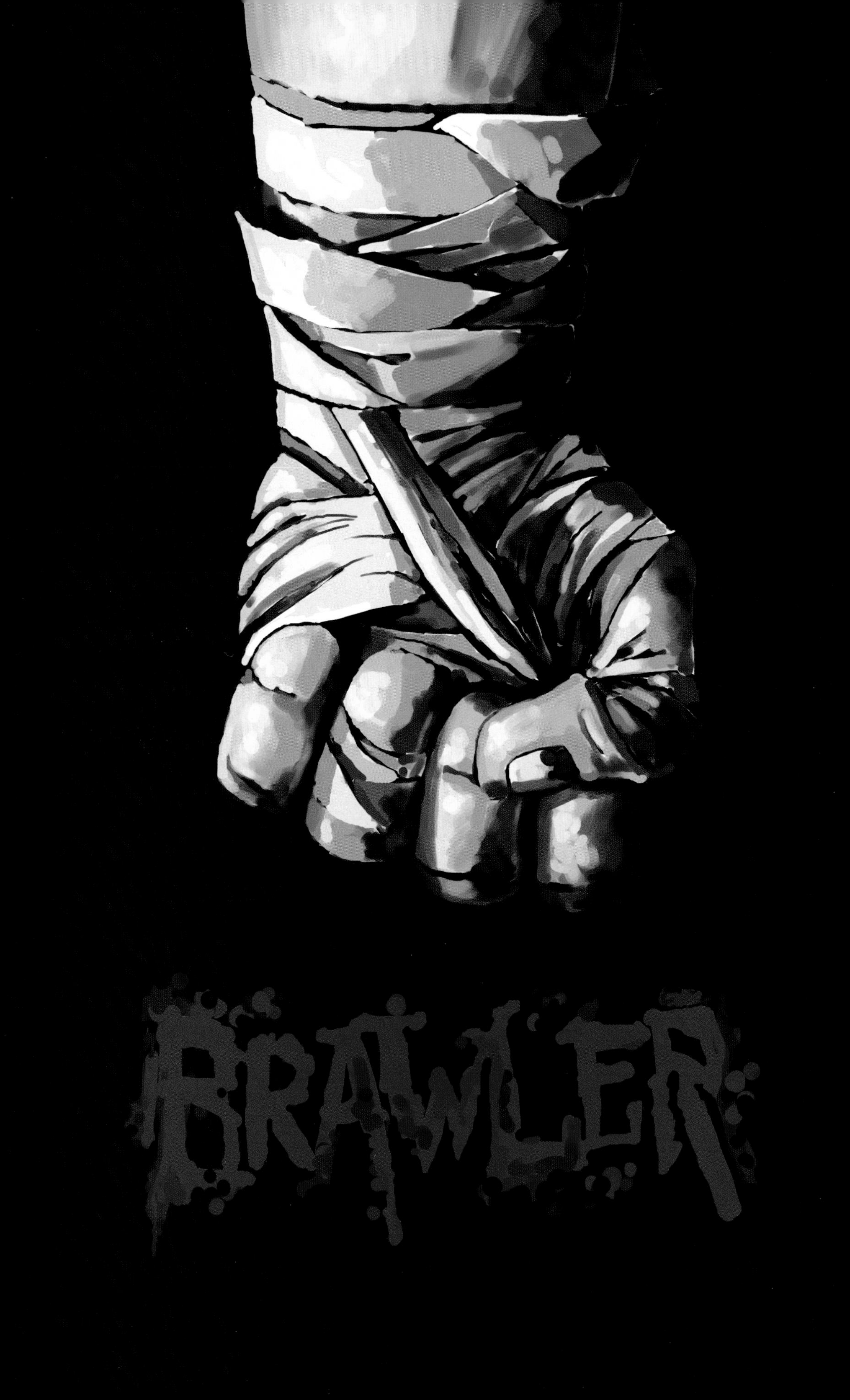
BRAWLER

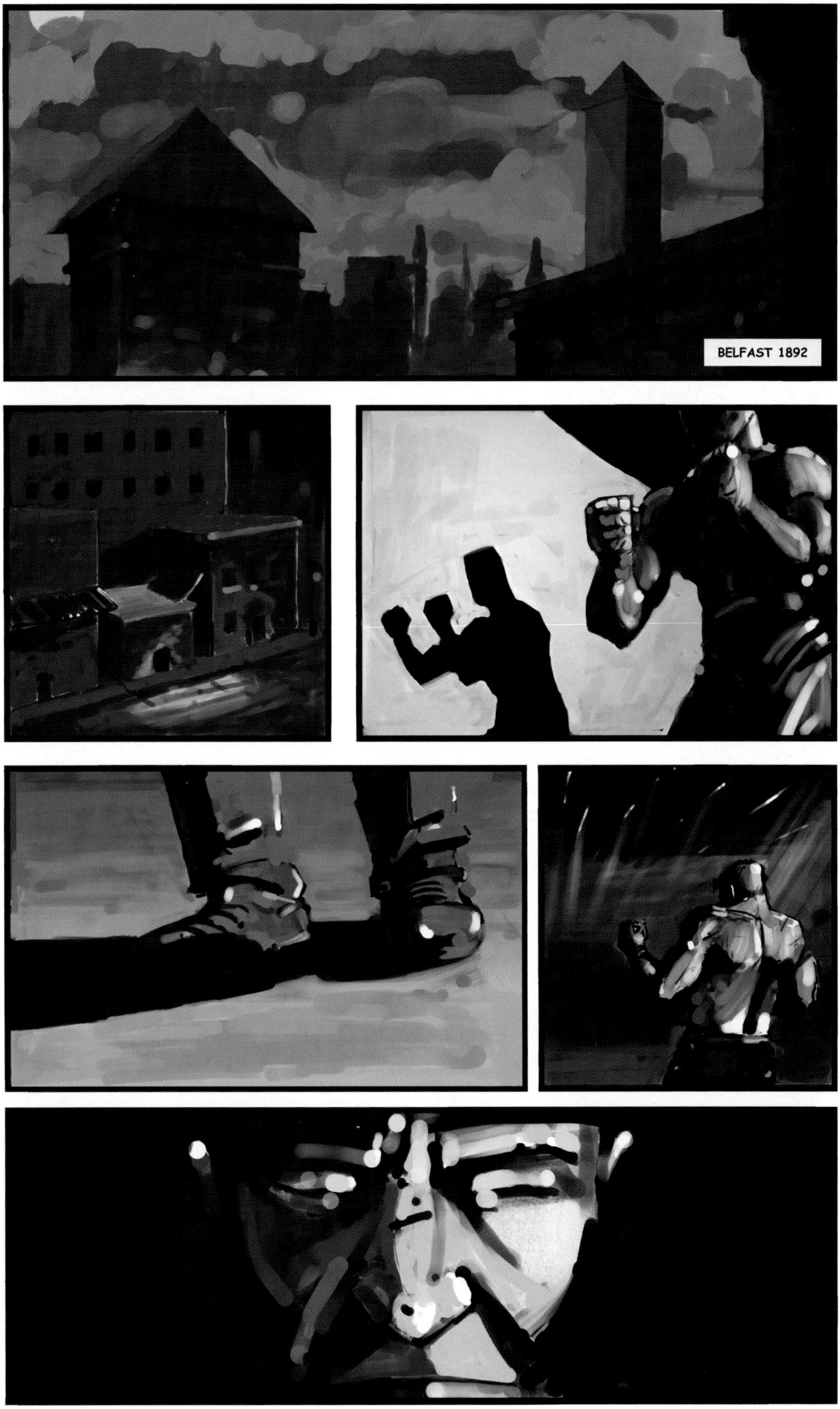
BELFAST 1892

WHY DO YOU CONTINUE TO FIGHT? IT ONLY BRINGS ABOUT MORE PAIN AND SUFFERING. AND WHO DO YOU FIGHT FOR? IT SERVES NO PURPOSE.

IT SERVES THE ANGER WITHIN ME, AND DISTRACTS THE PAIN OF YOUR VOICE IN MY HEAD.

PUNISHING YOURSELF, WILL NOT BRING ME BACK.

I WASN'T STRONG ENOUGH TO SAVE YOU, AND THIS IS MY CURSE. THIS IS ALL I KNOW HOW TO DO ANY MORE.

THEN YOU ARE LOST AND AS DEAD AS I AM...

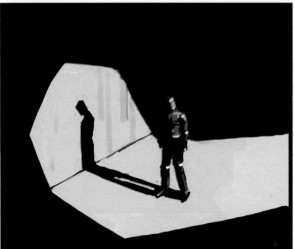

ALL BETS ARE FINAL! READY TO THE LINE LADS!!

FIGHTS GO UNTIL ONE MAN CANNOT STAND AND REACH THE SCRATCH LINE WITH IN 30 SECONDS, OR IF THE MAN IS KNOCKED OUT!

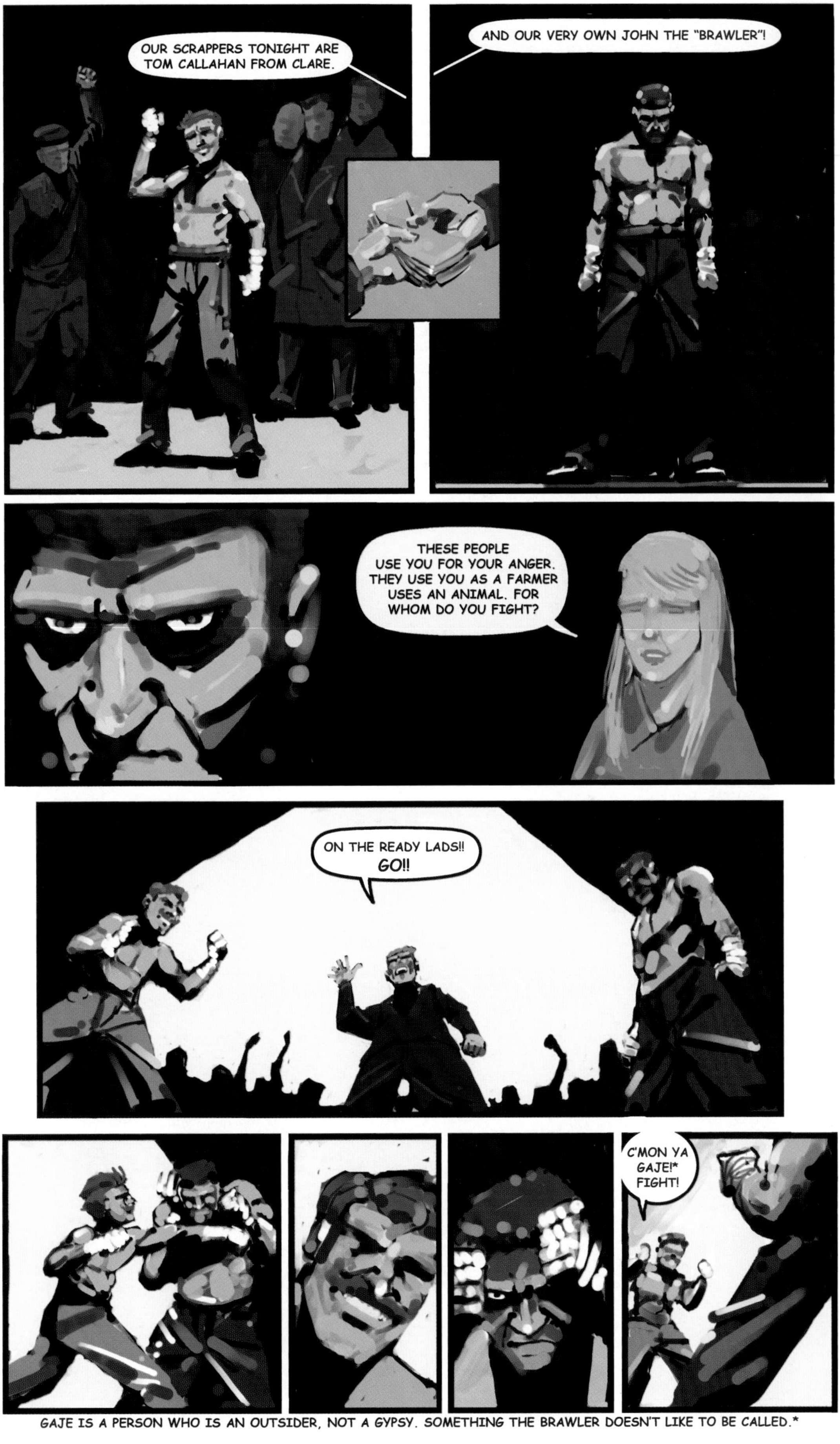
OUR SCRAPPERS TONIGHT ARE TOM CALLAHAN FROM CLARE.
AND OUR VERY OWN JOHN THE "BRAWLER"!
THESE PEOPLE USE YOU FOR YOUR ANGER. THEY USE YOU AS A FARMER USES AN ANIMAL. FOR WHOM DO YOU FIGHT?
ON THE READY LADS!! GO!!
C'MON YA GAJE!* FIGHT!

GAJE IS A PERSON WHO IS AN OUTSIDER, NOT A GYPSY. SOMETHING THE BRAWLER DOESN'T LIKE TO BE CALLED.*

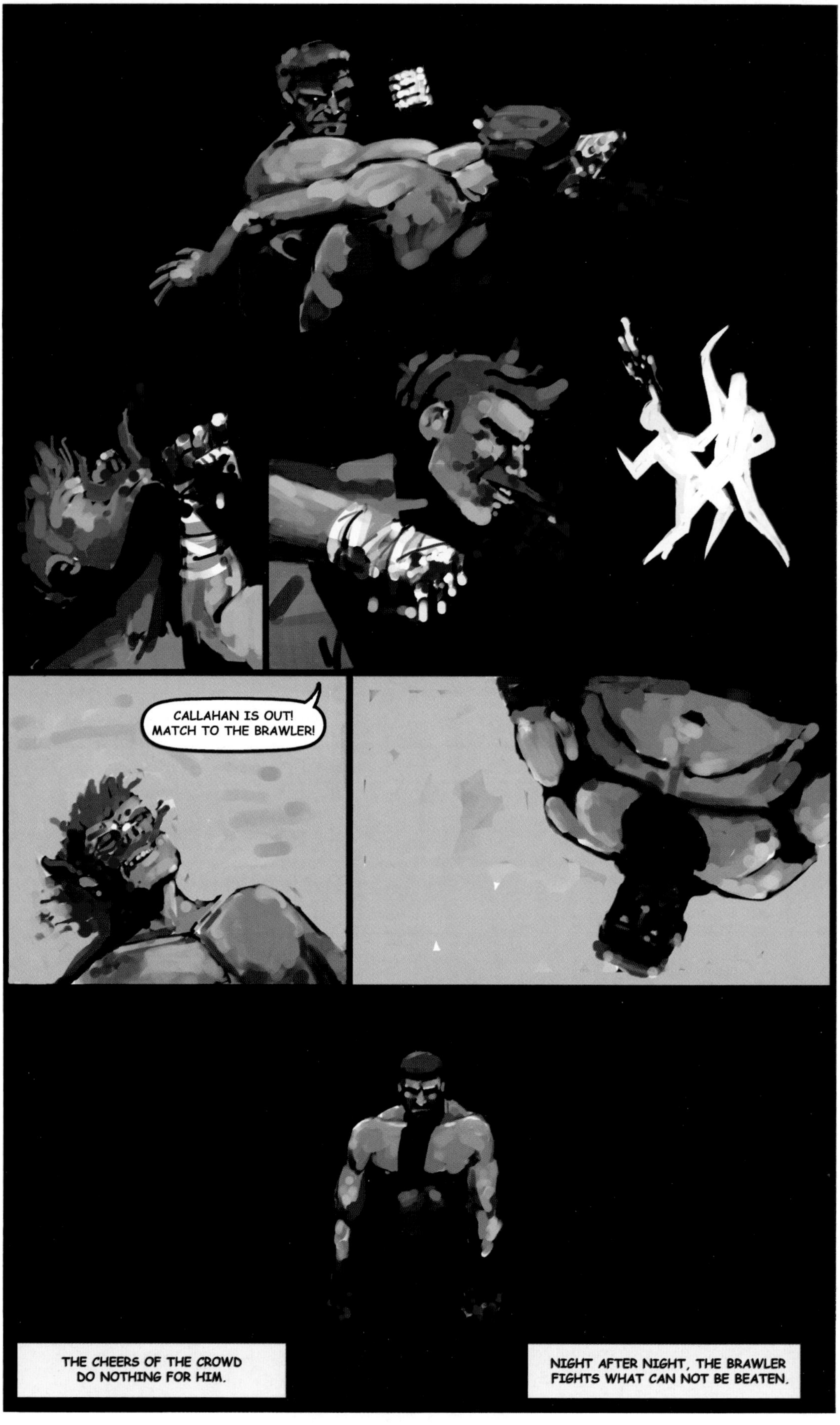
CALLAHAN IS OUT! MATCH TO THE BRAWLER!
THE CHEERS OF THE CROWD DO NOTHING FOR HIM.
NIGHT AFTER NIGHT, THE BRAWLER FIGHTS WHAT CAN NOT BE BEATEN.

JUST WHAT IN THE HELL WAS THAT? CAN YOU NOT UNDERSTAND ME BOY?

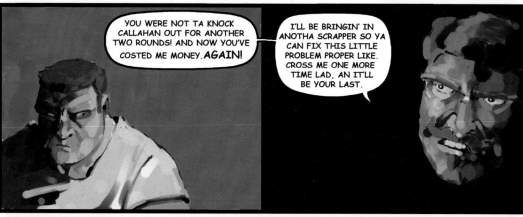

YOU WERE NOT TA KNOCK CALLAHAN OUT FOR ANOTHER TWO ROUNDS! AND NOW YOU'VE COSTED ME MONEY. AGAIN!

I'LL BE BRINGIN' IN ANOTHA SCRAPPER SO YA CAN FIX THIS LITTLE PROBLEM PROPER LIKE. CROSS ME ONE MORE TIME LAD, AN IT'LL BE YOUR LAST.

DON'T YOU EVER FORGET WHO OWNS THIS TOWN, AND EVERYTIN IN IT.

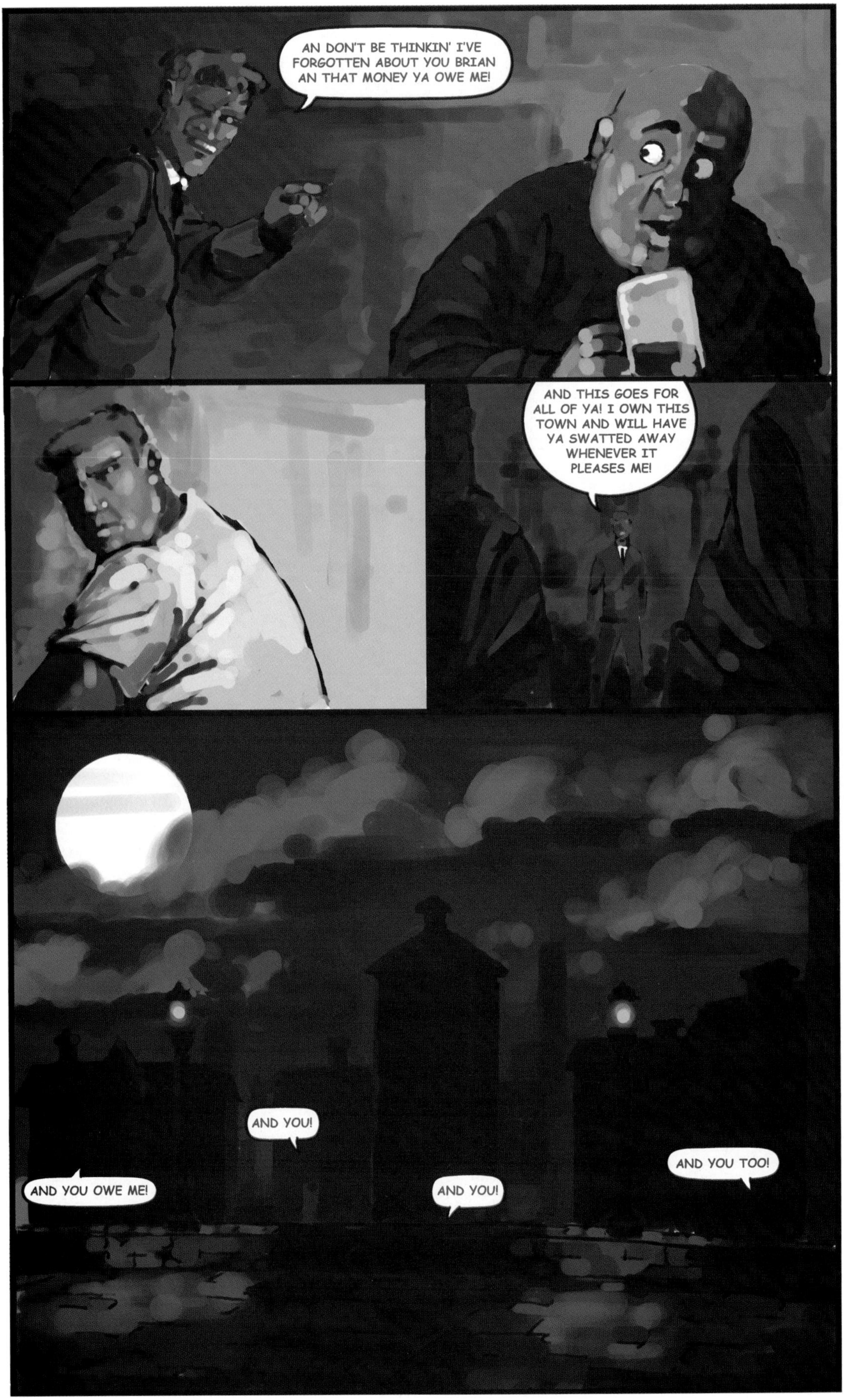
AN DON'T BE THINKIN' I'VE FORGOTTEN ABOUT YOU BRIAN AN THAT MONEY YA OWE ME!
AND THIS GOES FOR ALL OF YA! I OWN THIS TOWN AND WILL HAVE YA SWATTED AWAY WHENEVER IT PLEASES ME!
AND YOU OWE ME!
AND YOU!
AND YOU!
AND YOU TOO!

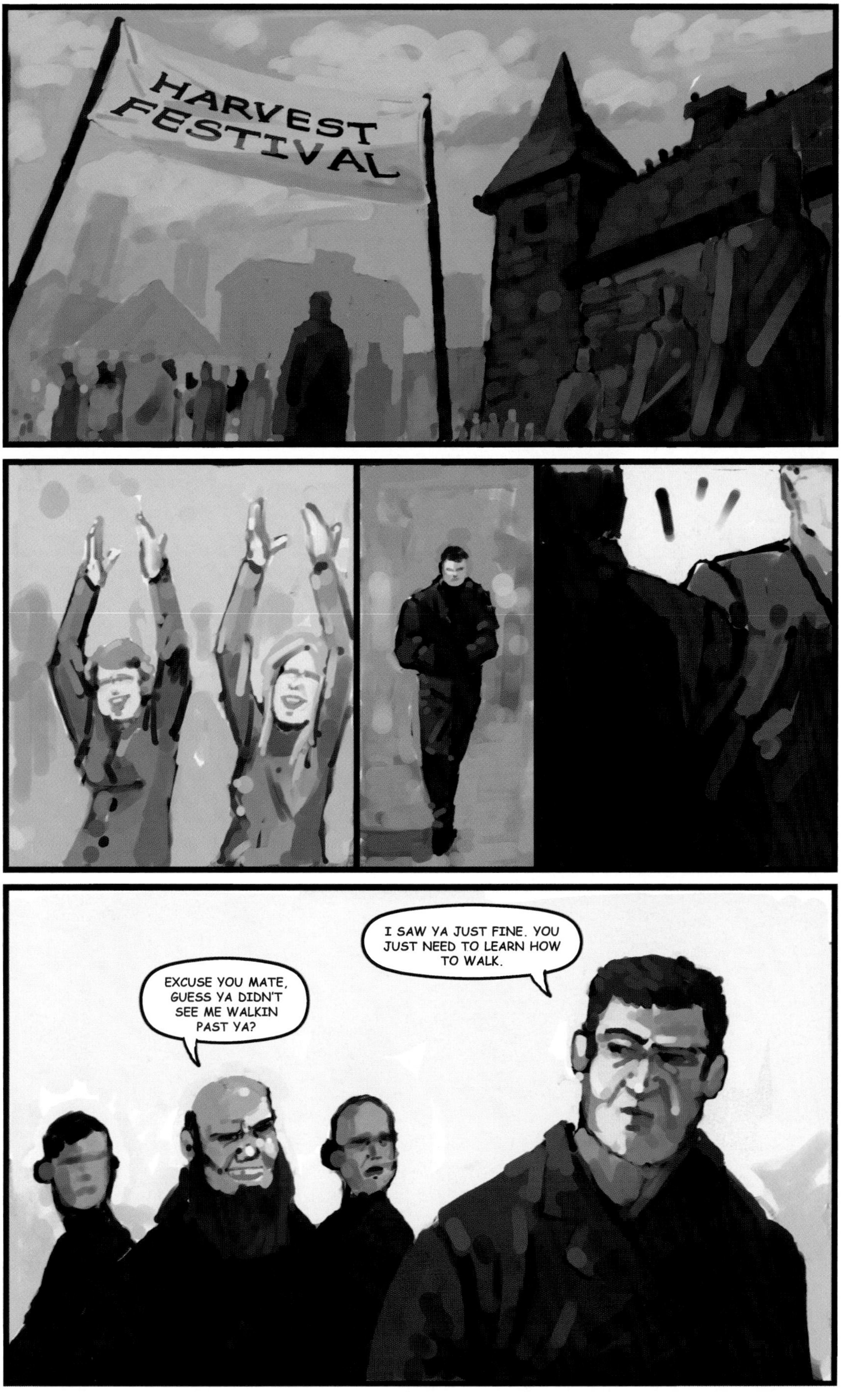
HARVEST FESTIVAL
EXCUSE YOU MATE, GUESS YA DIDN'T SEE ME WALKIN PAST YA?
I SAW YA JUST FINE. YOU JUST NEED TO LEARN HOW TO WALK.

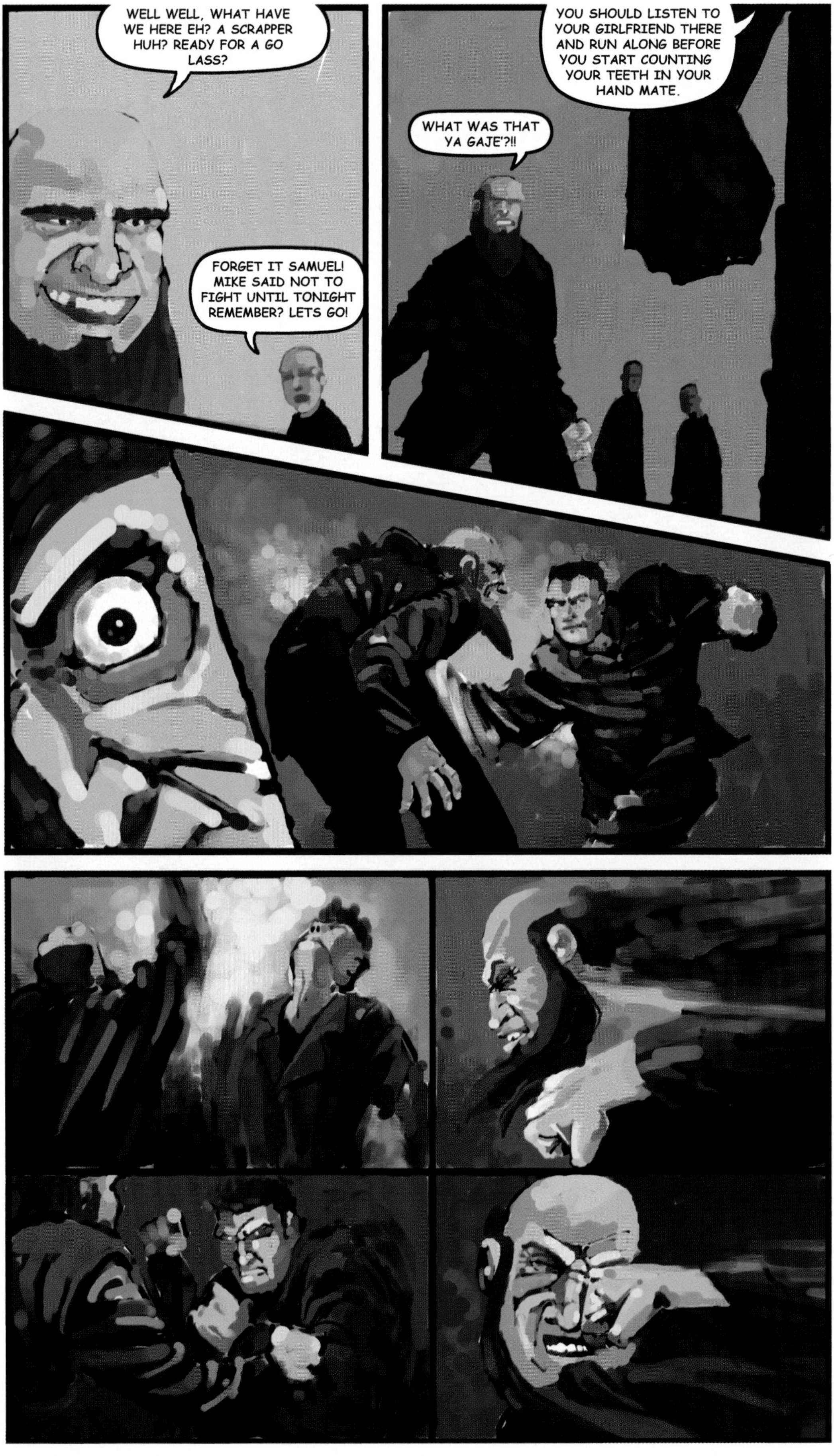
WELL WELL, WHAT HAVE WE HERE EH? A SCRAPPER HUH? READY FOR A GO LASS?
FORGET IT SAMUEL! MIKE SAID NOT TO FIGHT UNTIL TONIGHT REMEMBER? LETS GO!
YOU SHOULD LISTEN TO YOUR GIRLFRIEND THERE AND RUN ALONG BEFORE YOU START COUNTING YOUR TEETH IN YOUR HAND MATE.
WHAT WAS THAT YA GAJE'?!!

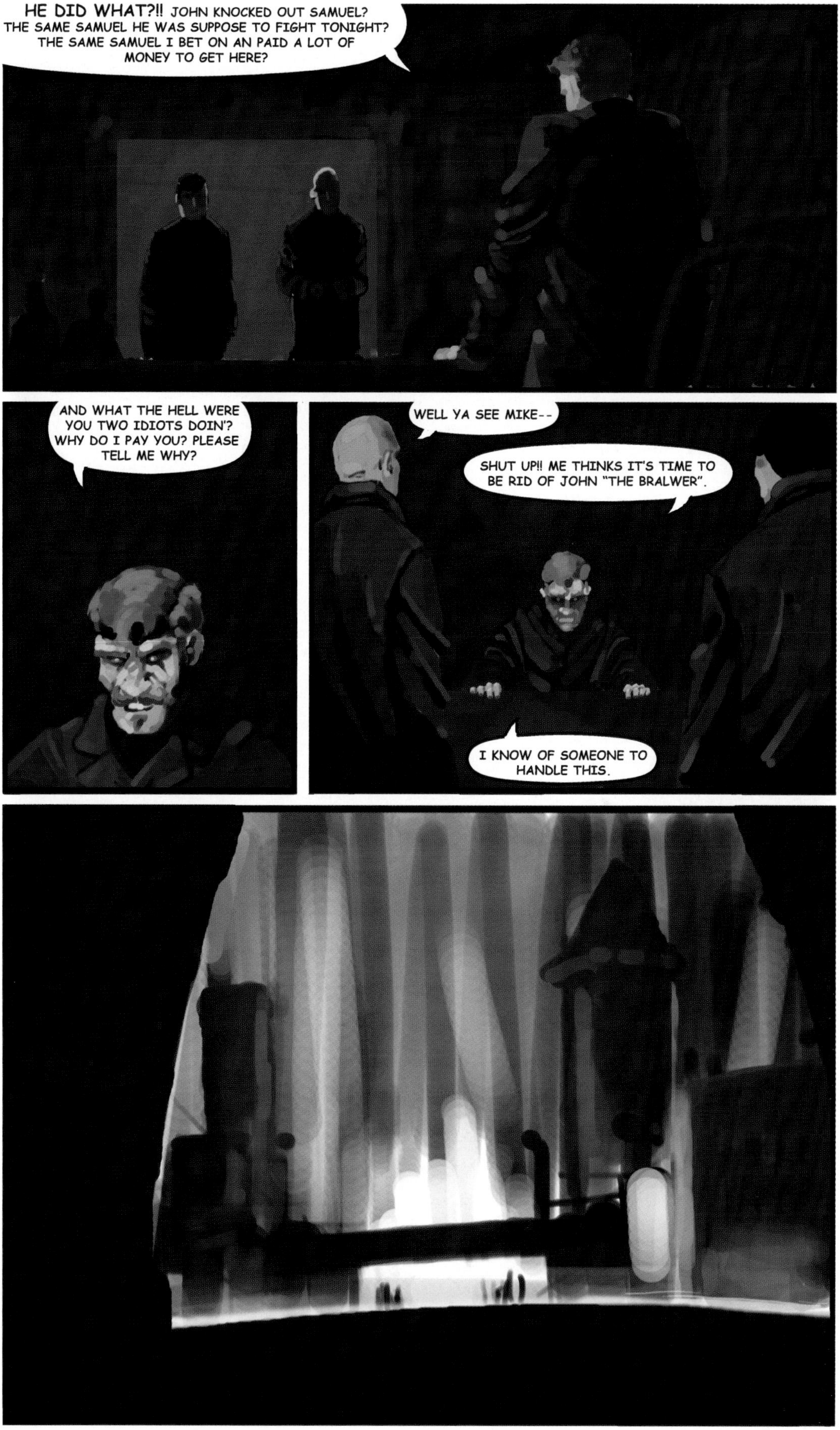
HE DID WHAT?!! JOHN KNOCKED OUT SAMUEL? THE SAME SAMUEL HE WAS SUPPOSE TO FIGHT TONIGHT? THE SAME SAMUEL I BET ON AN PAID A LOT OF MONEY TO GET HERE?
AND WHAT THE HELL WERE YOU TWO IDIOTS DOIN'? WHY DO I PAY YOU? PLEASE TELL ME WHY?
WELL YA SEE MIKE--
SHUT UP!! ME THINKS IT'S TIME TO BE RID OF JOHN "THE BRALWER".
I KNOW OF SOMEONE TO HANDLE THIS.

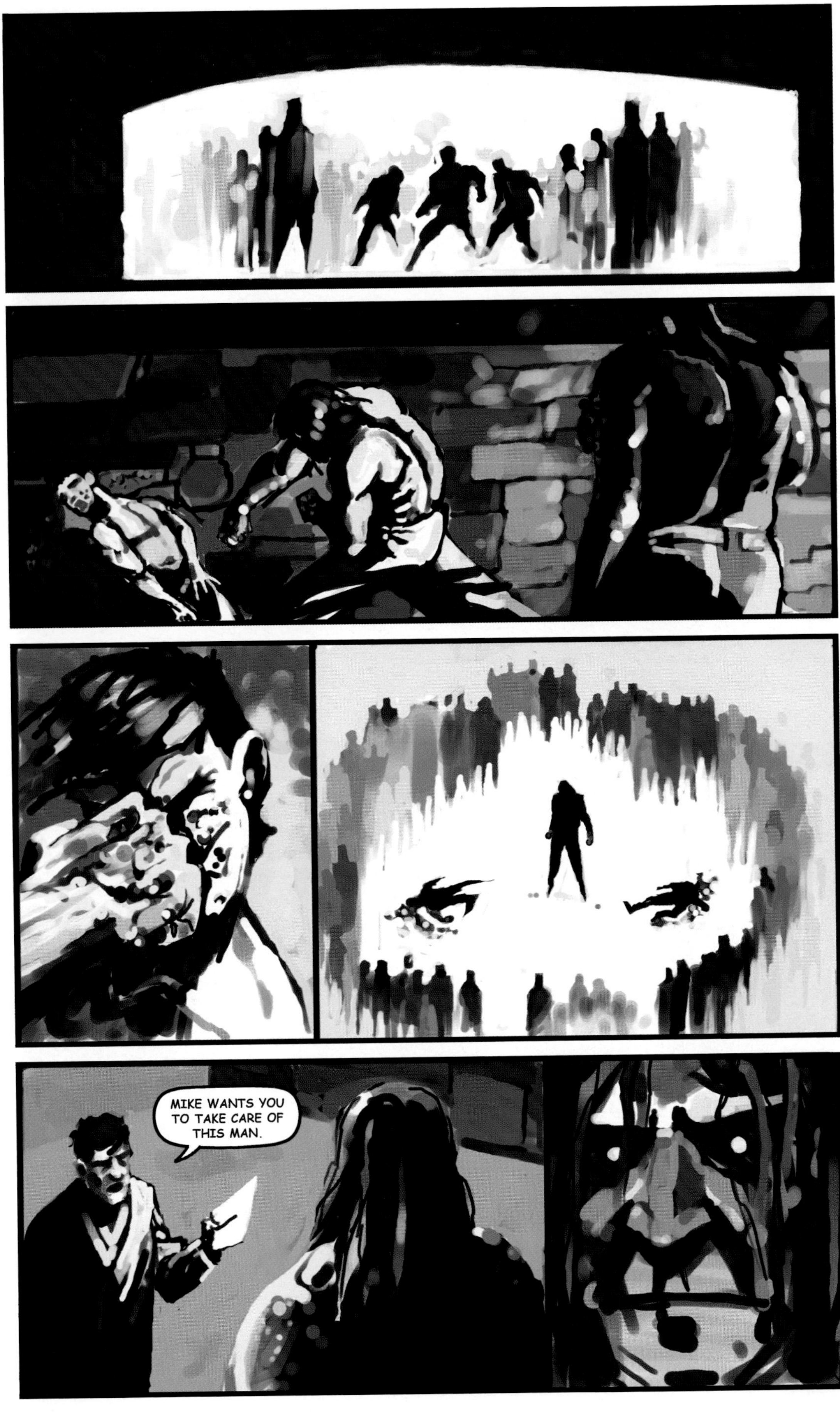
MIKE WANTS YOU TO TAKE CARE OF THIS MAN.

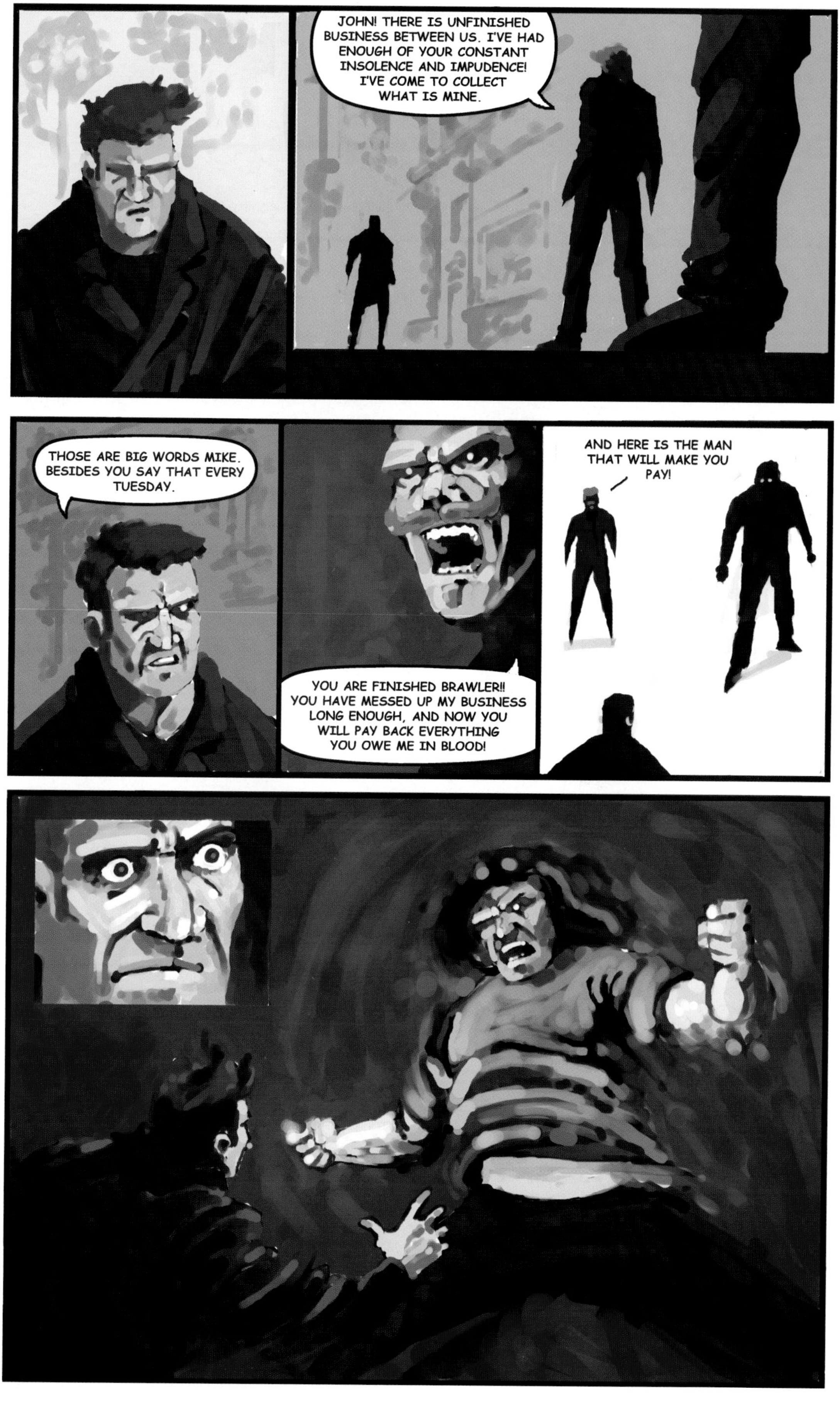
JOHN! THERE IS UNFINISHED BUSINESS BETWEEN US. I'VE HAD ENOUGH OF YOUR CONSTANT INSOLENCE AND IMPUDENCE! I'VE COME TO COLLECT WHAT IS MINE.
THOSE ARE BIG WORDS MIKE. BESIDES YOU SAY THAT EVERY TUESDAY.
YOU ARE FINISHED BRAWLER!! YOU HAVE MESSED UP MY BUSINESS LONG ENOUGH, AND NOW YOU WILL PAY BACK EVERYTHING YOU OWE ME IN BLOOD!
AND HERE IS THE MAN THAT WILL MAKE YOU PAY!

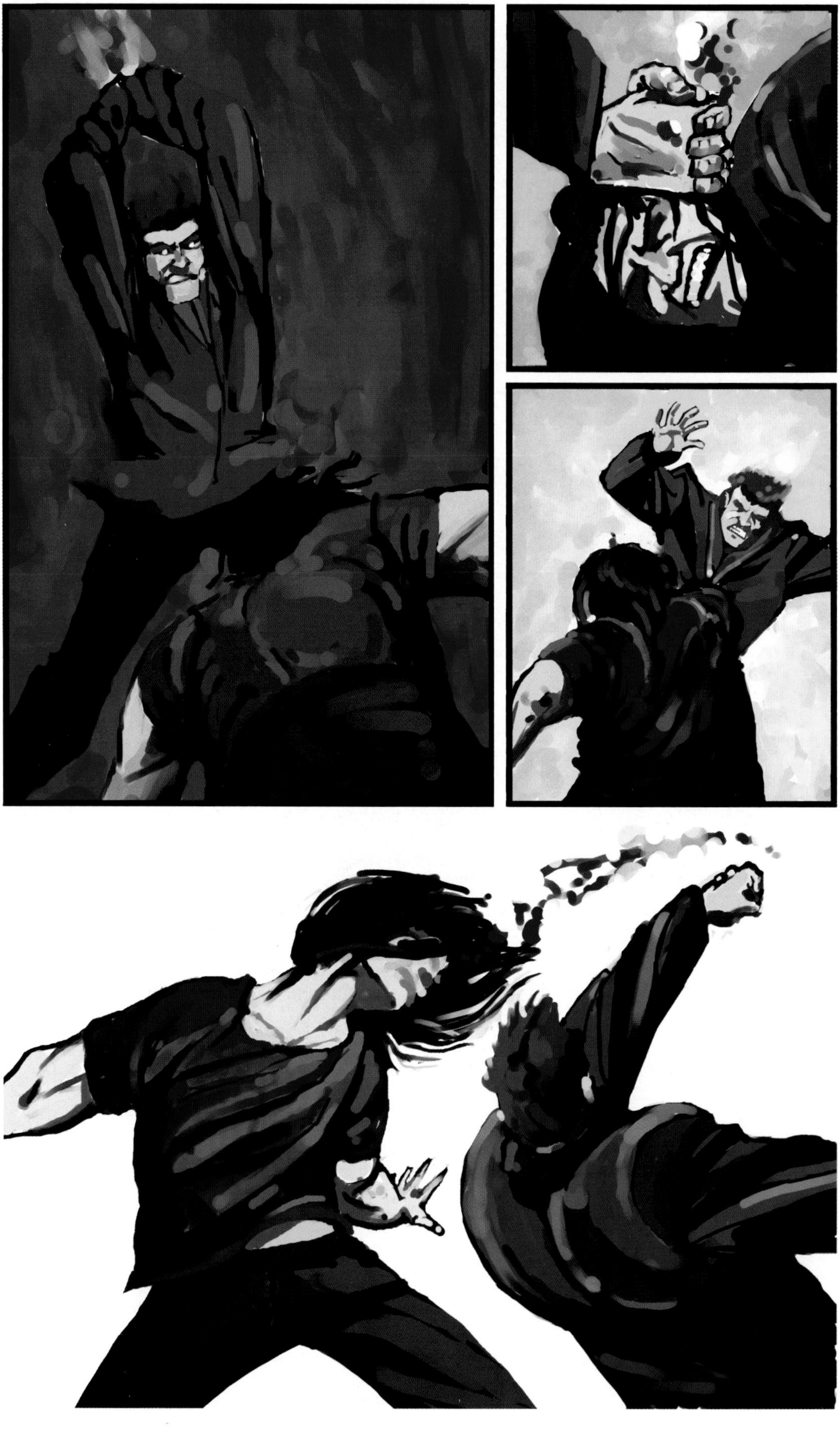

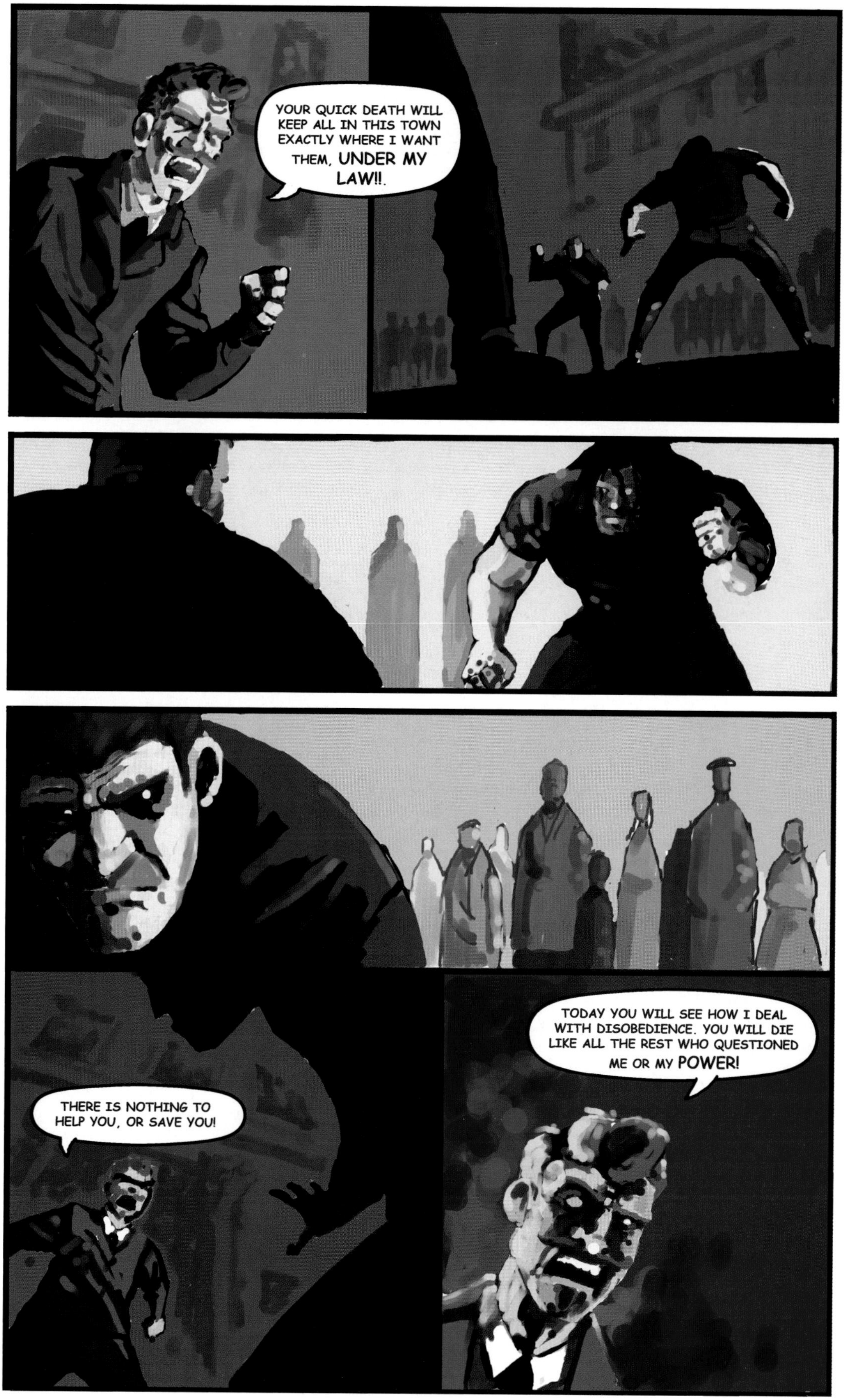
YOUR QUICK DEATH WILL KEEP ALL IN THIS TOWN EXACTLY WHERE I WANT THEM, UNDER MY LAW!!.
THERE IS NOTHING TO HELP YOU, OR SAVE YOU!
TODAY YOU WILL SEE HOW I DEAL WITH DISOBEDIENCE. YOU WILL DIE LIKE ALL THE REST WHO QUESTIONED ME OR MY POWER!

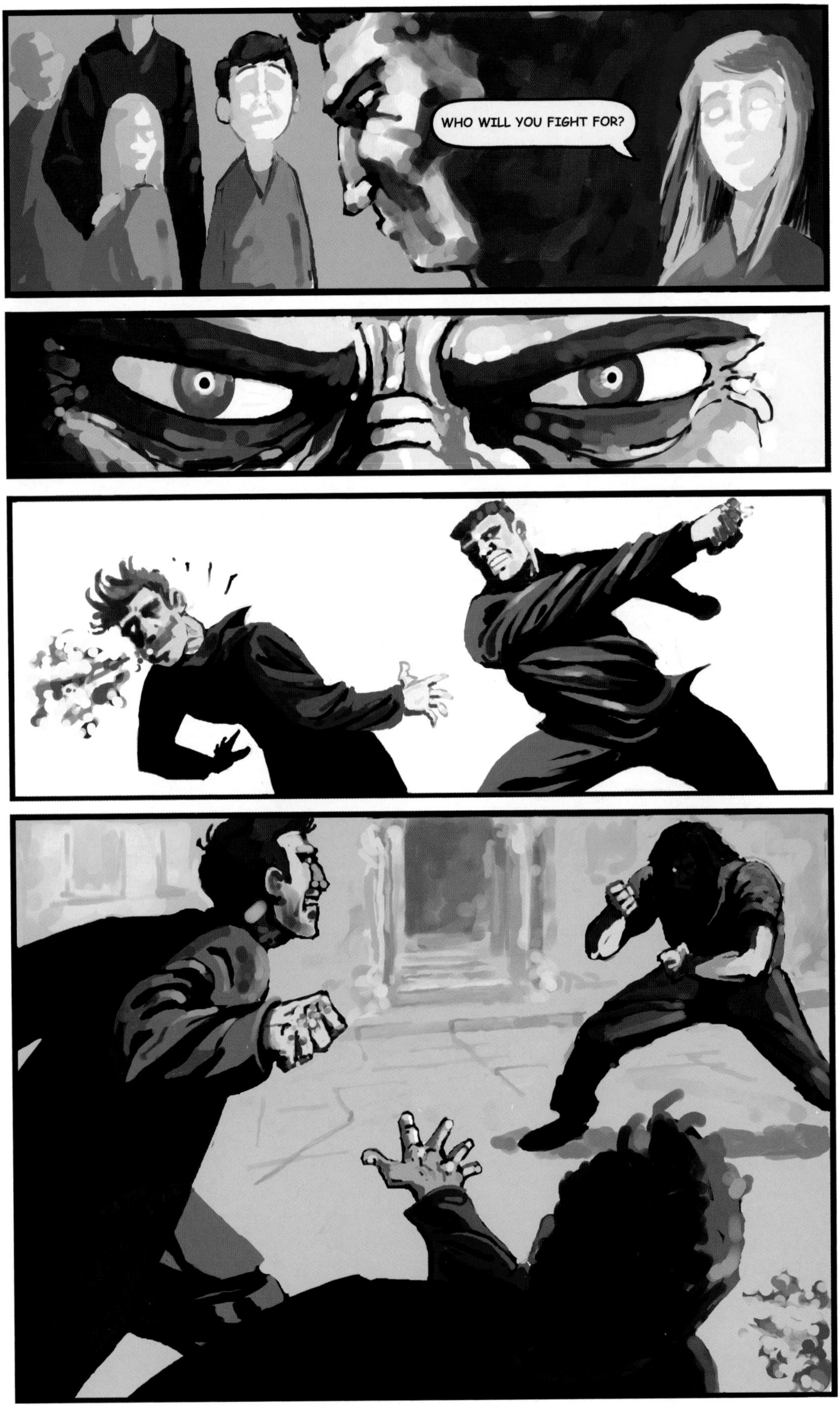
WHO WILL YOU FIGHT FOR?

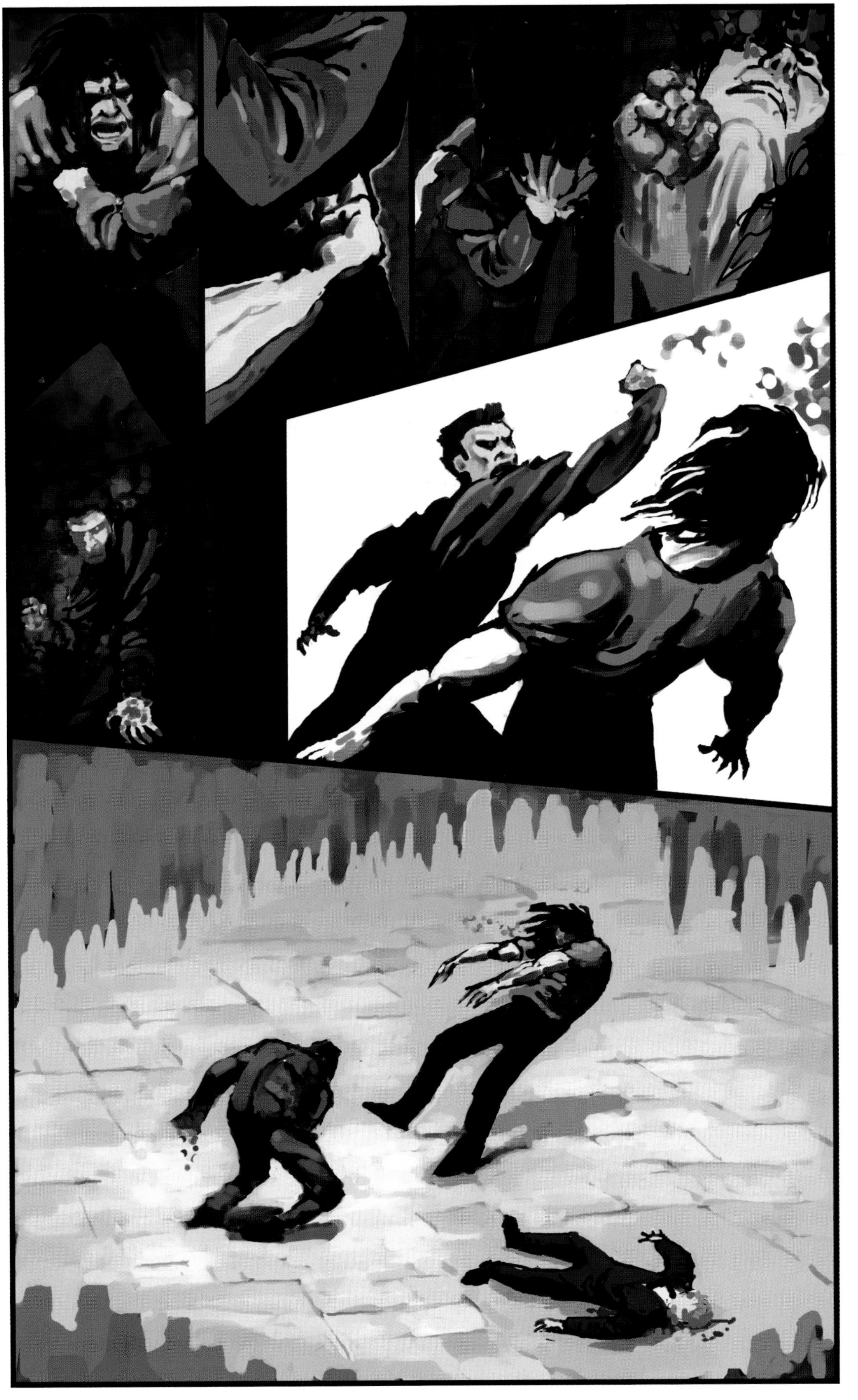

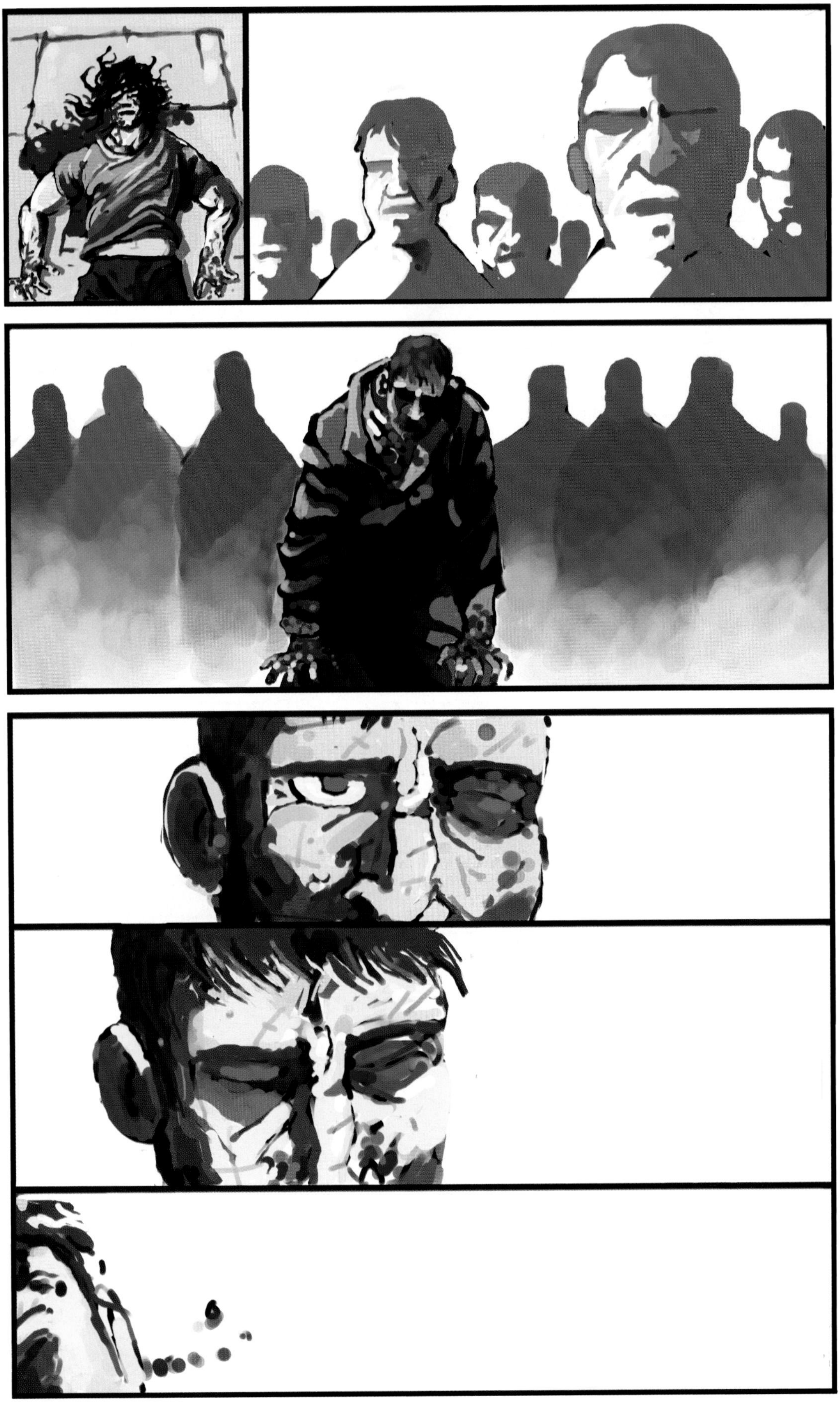

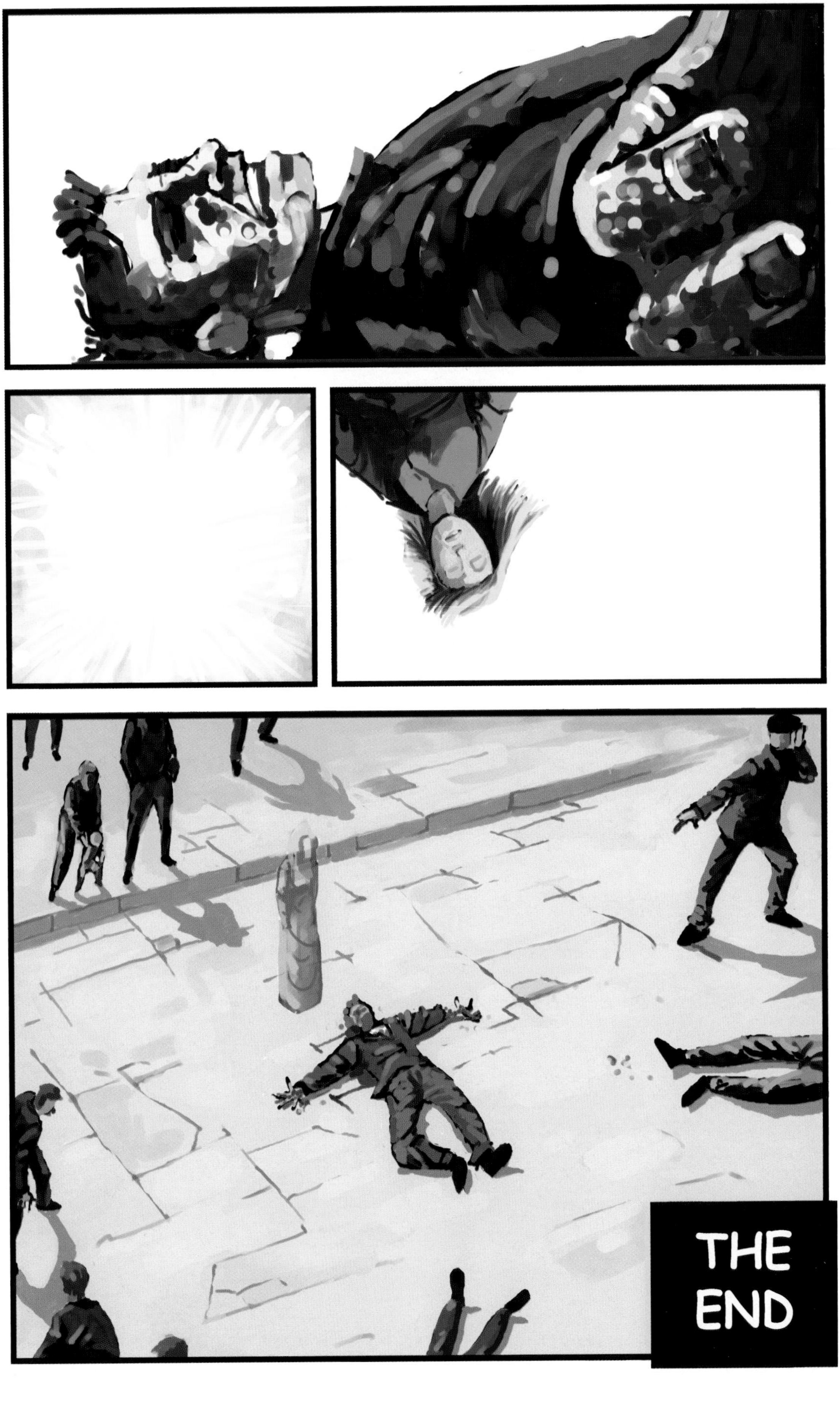
THE
END

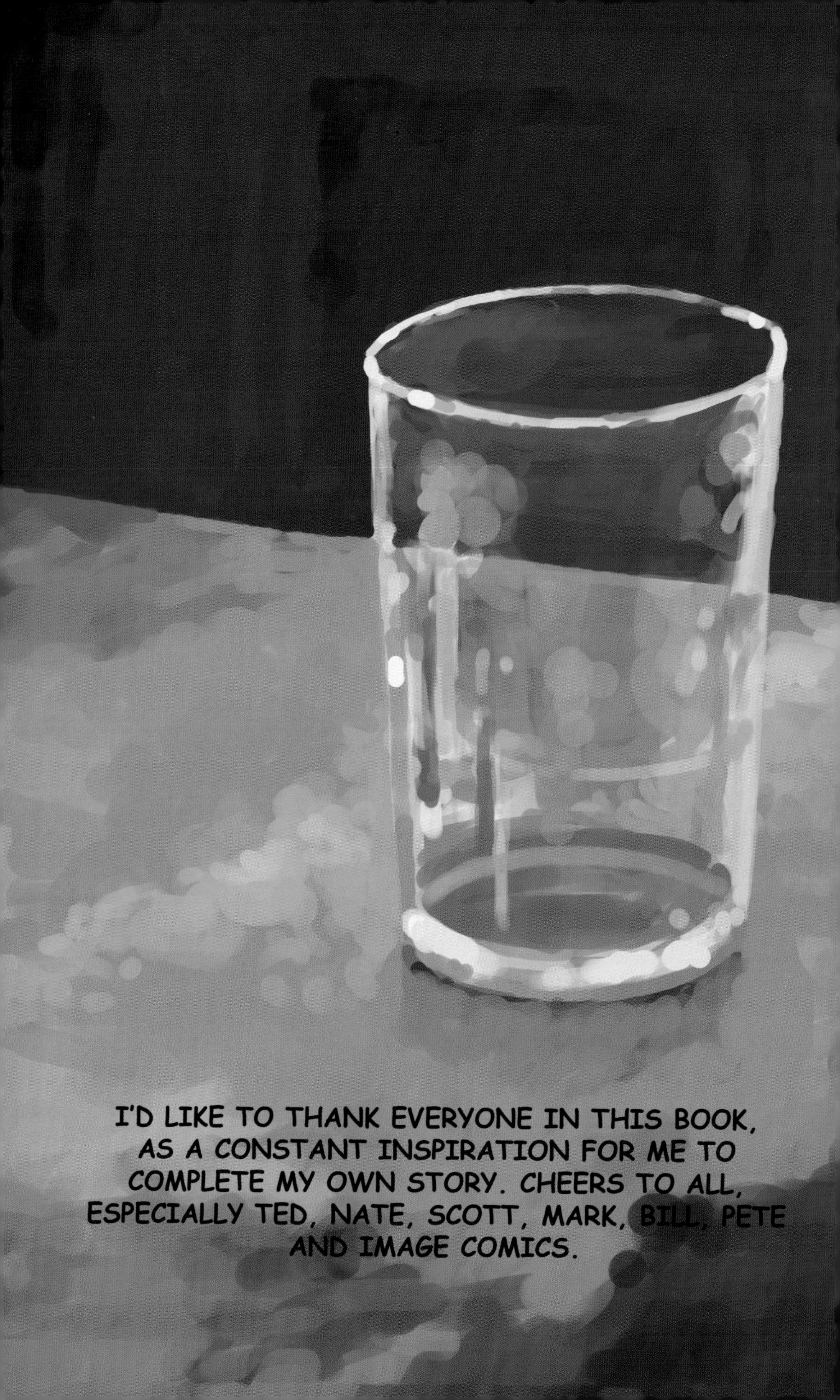
I'D LIKE TO THANK EVERYONE IN THIS BOOK,
AS A CONSTANT INSPIRATION FOR ME TO
COMPLETE MY OWN STORY. CHEERS TO ALL,
ESPECIALLY TED, NATE, SCOTT, MARK, BILL, PETE
AND IMAGE COMICS.

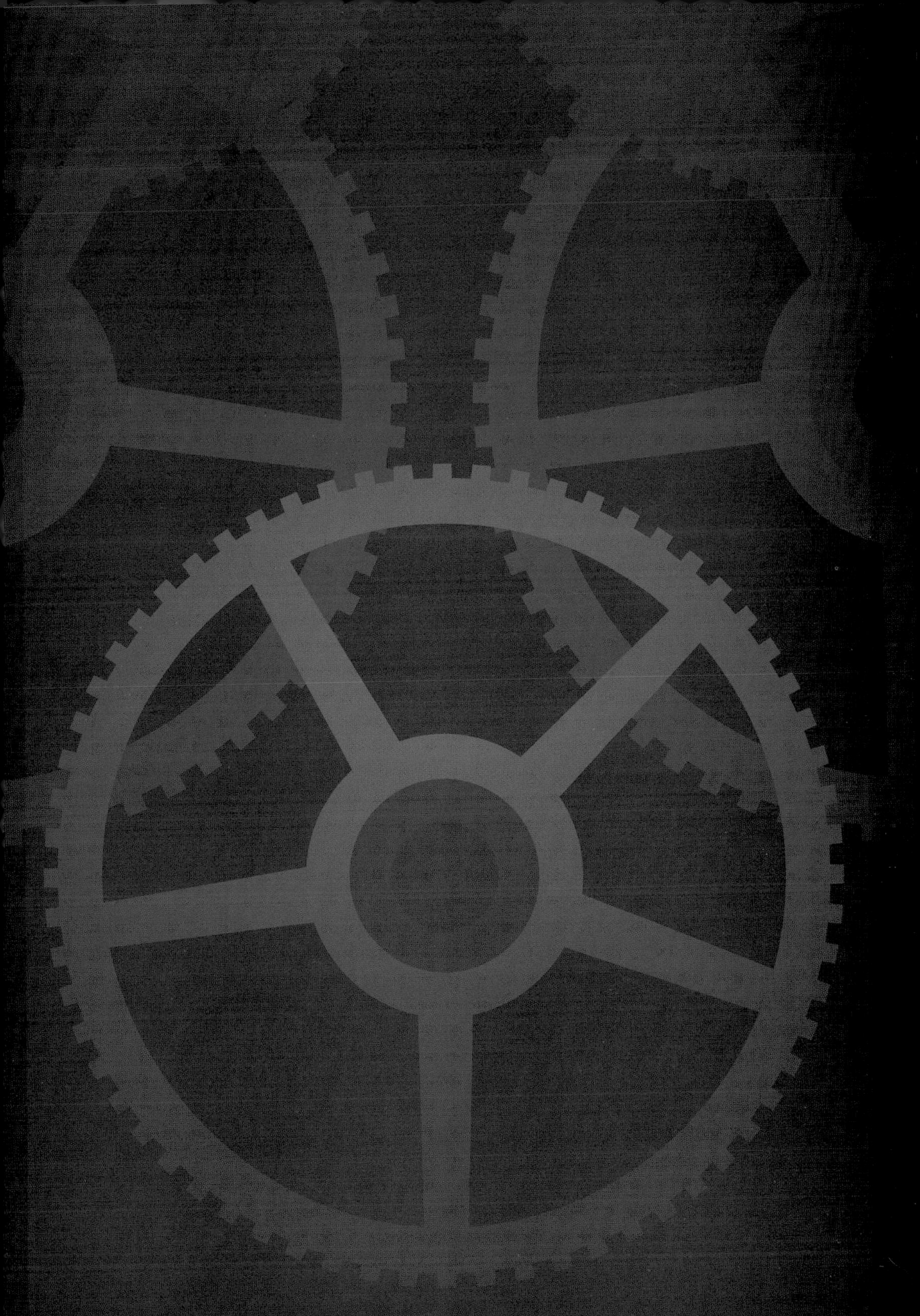

ROB GIBBS

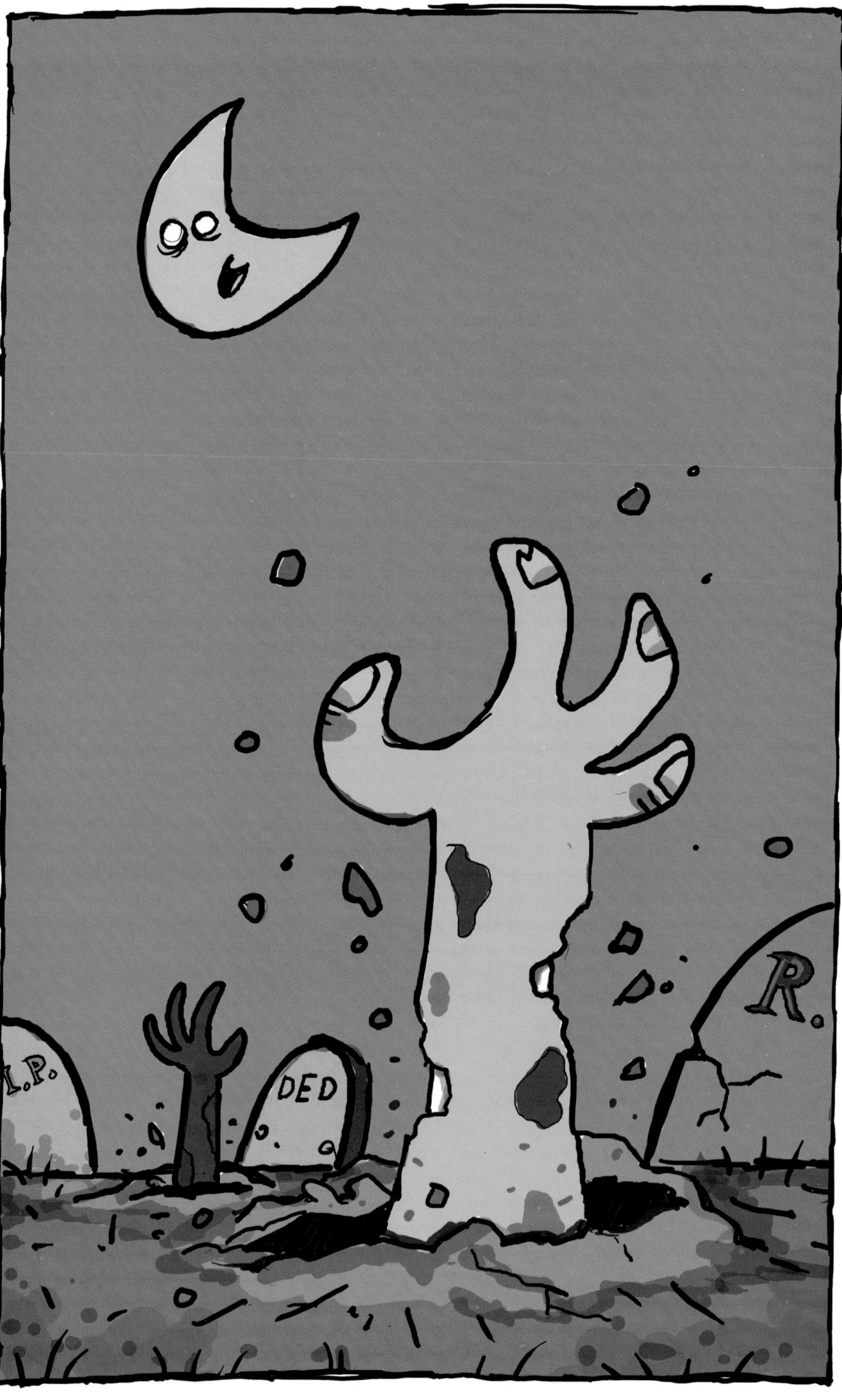
I.P.
DED
R.

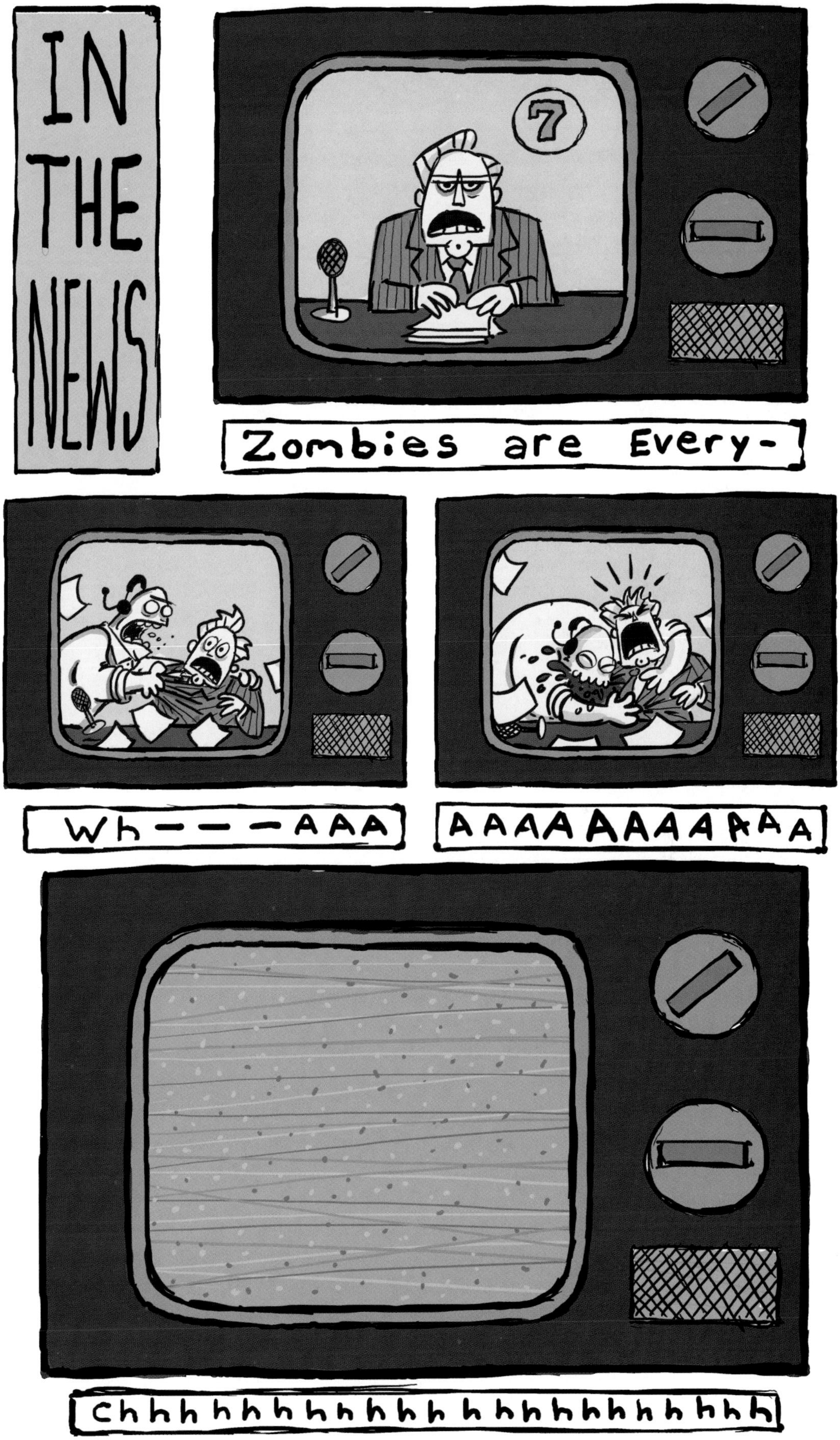
IN THE NEWS
7
Zombies are Every-
Wh----AAA
AAAAAAAAAAAA
Chhhhhhhhhhhhhhhhhhhhhhh

DATE OF THE DEAD

Our Story Begins... at

the mall

One of those Big indoor Shopping Centers

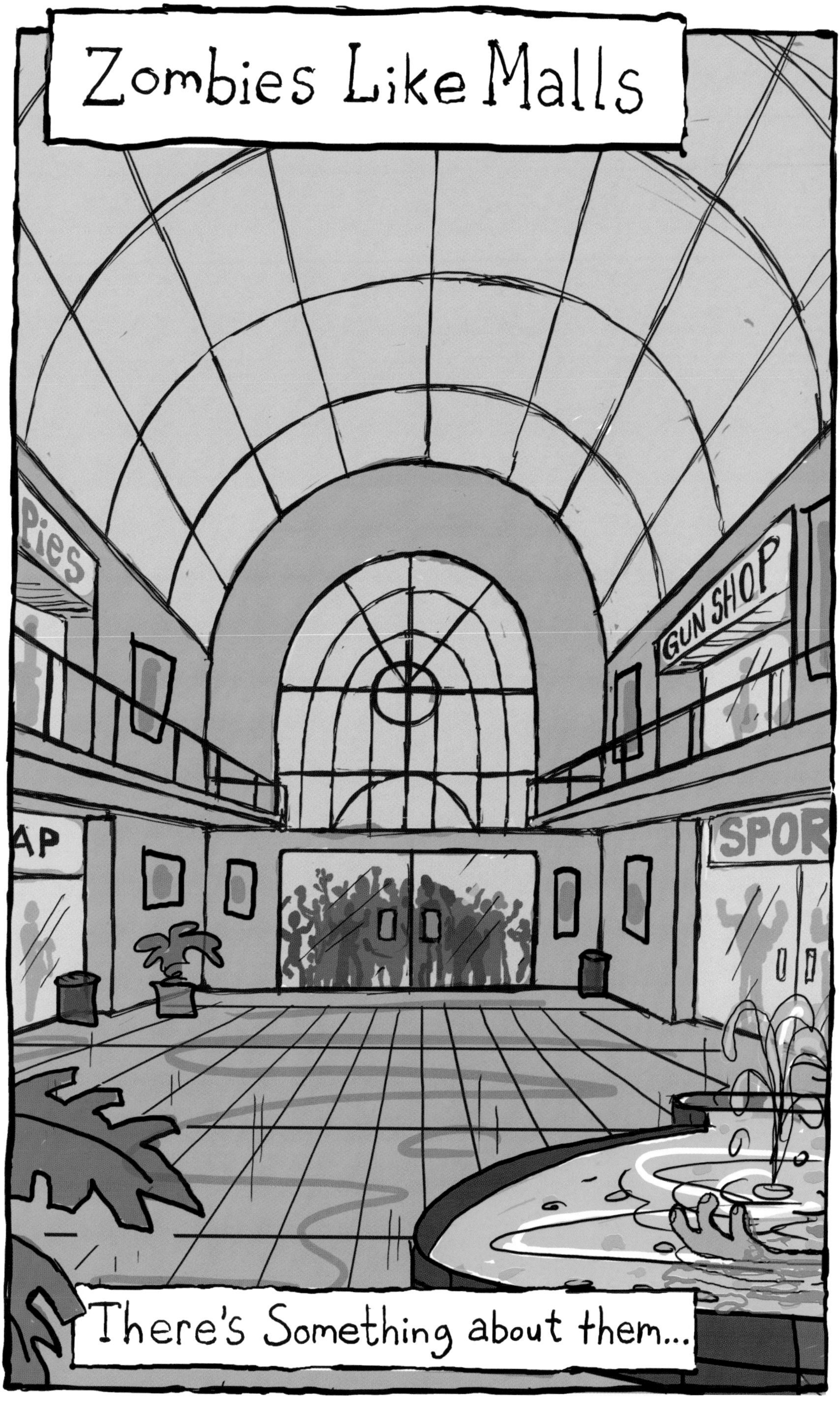
Zombies Like Malls
Pies
GUN SHOP
AP
SPOR
There's Something about them...

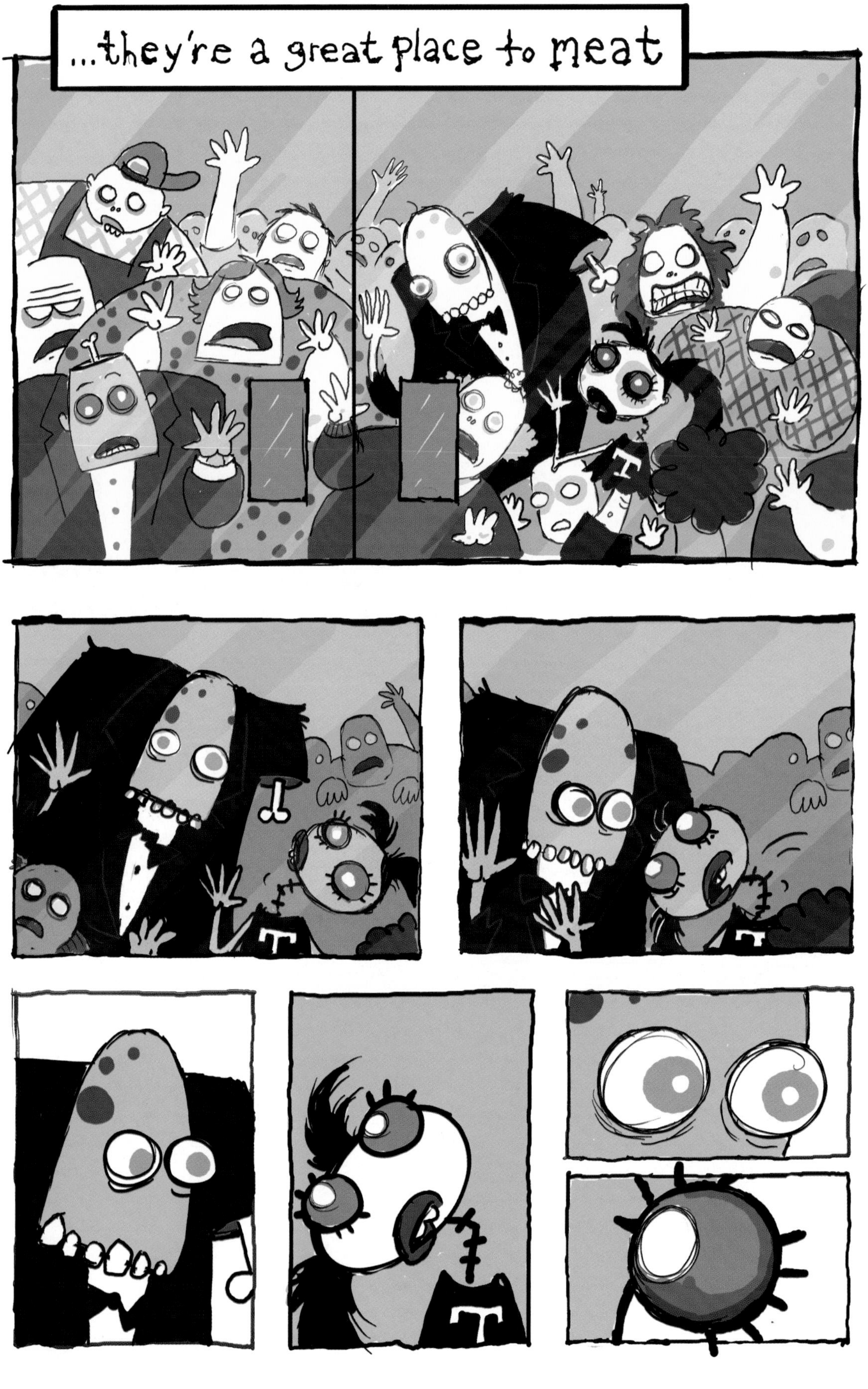
...they're a great place to meat

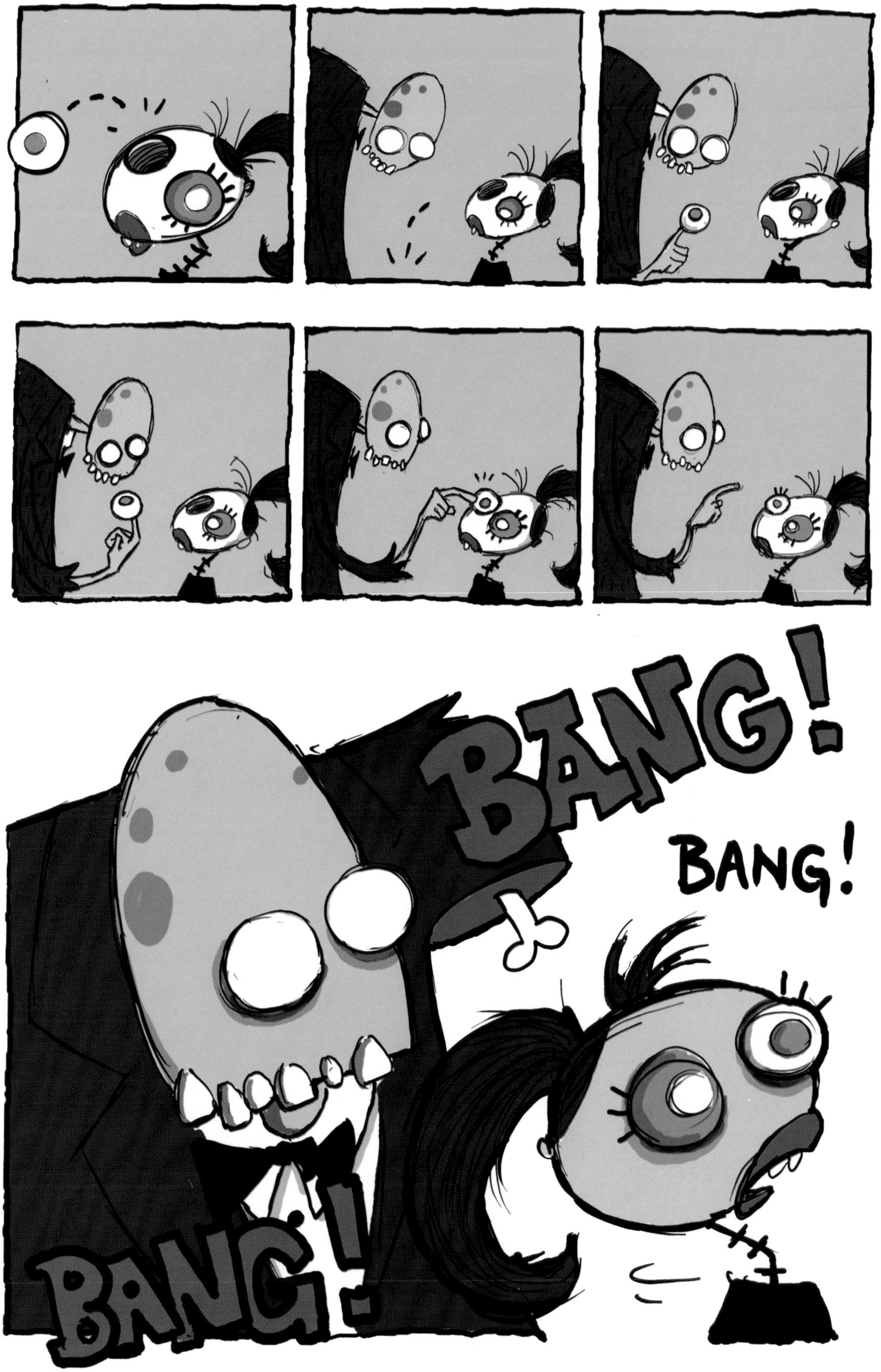
BANG!
BANG!
BANG!

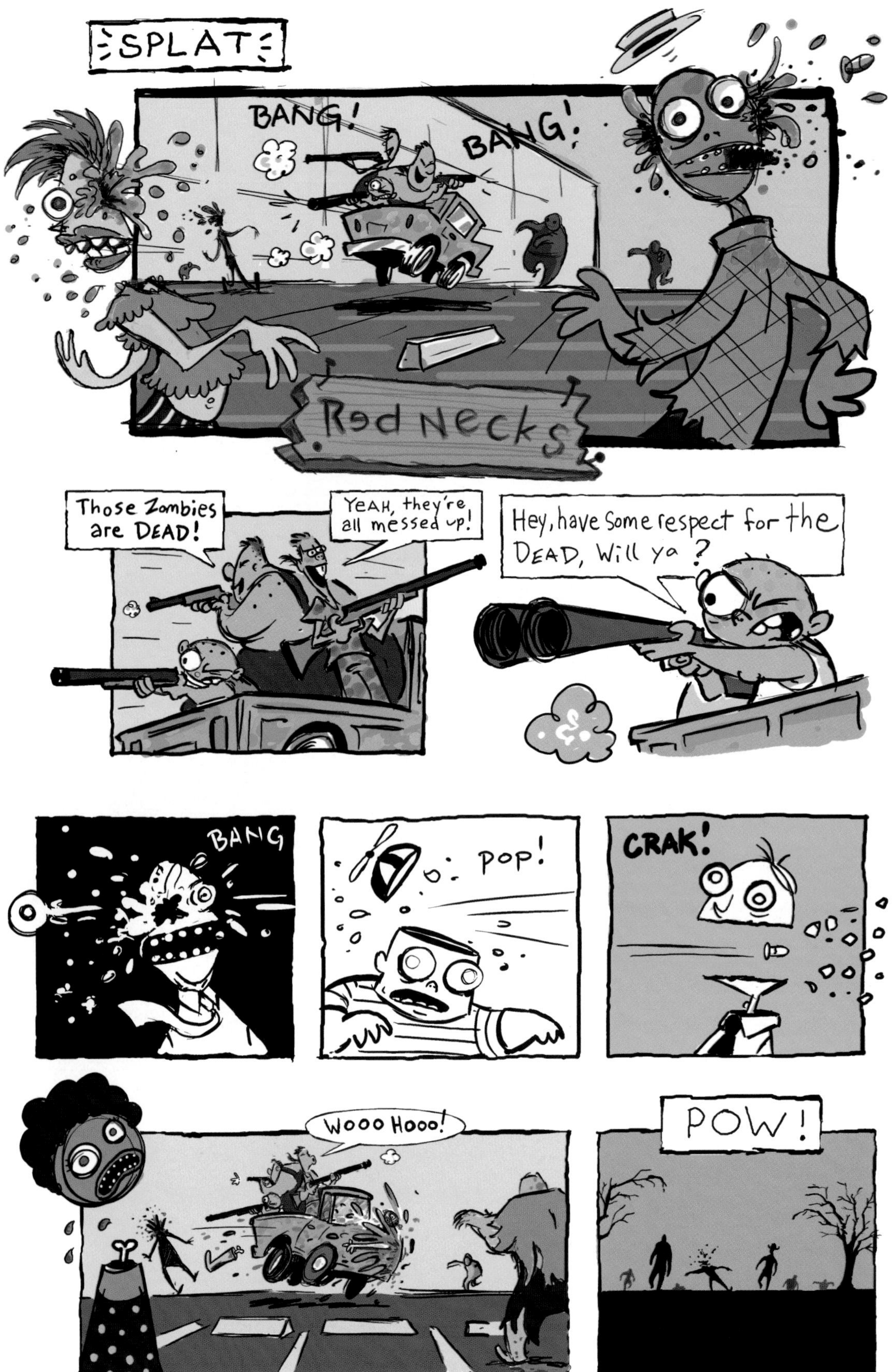
SPLAT
BANG!
BANG!
Red Necks
Those Zombies are DEAD!
YEAH, they're all messed up!
Hey, have some respect for the DEAD, Will ya?
BANG
pop!
CRAK!
WOOO HOOO!
POW!

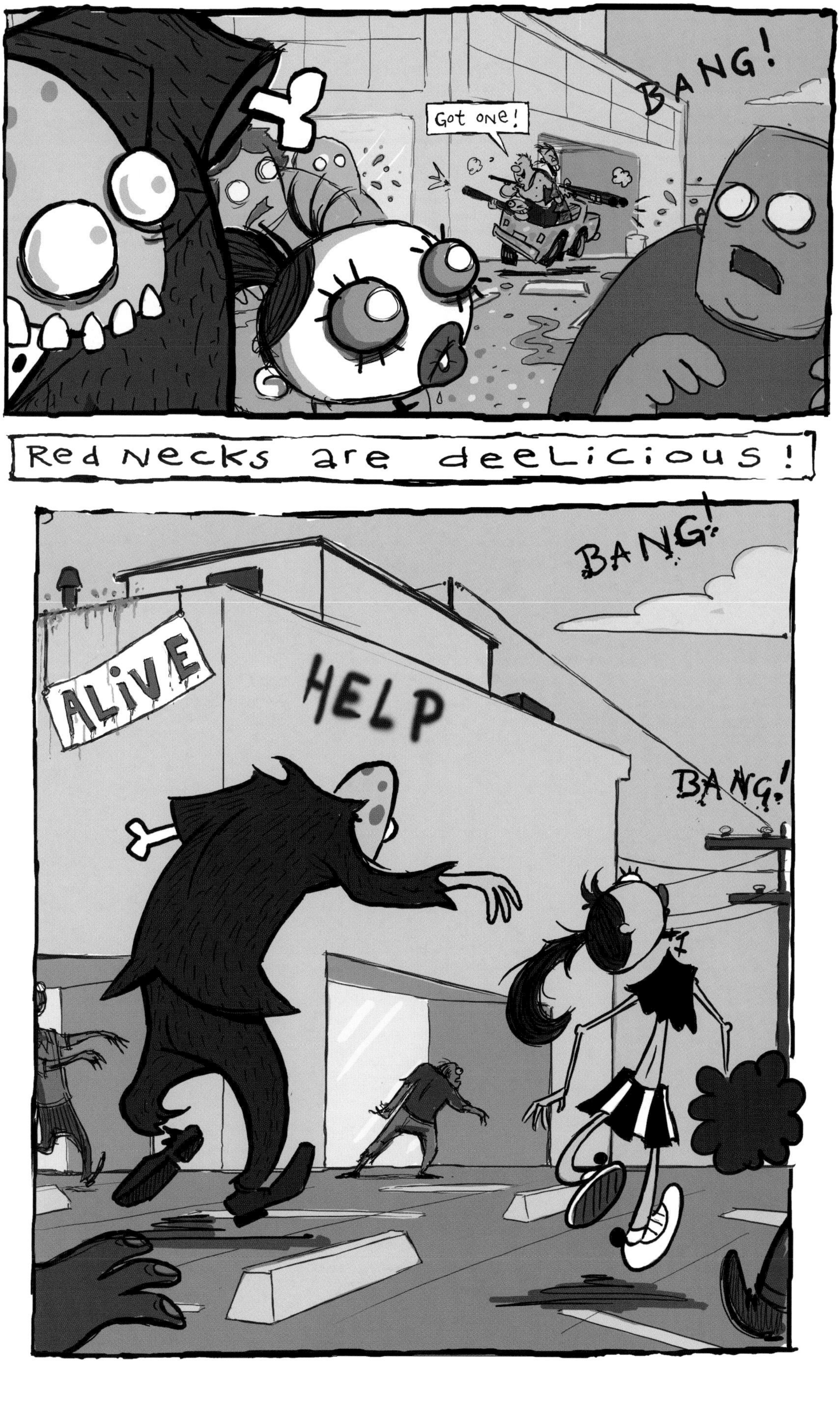
Got one!
BANG!
Rednecks are deelicious!
BANG!
ALIVE
HELP
BANG!

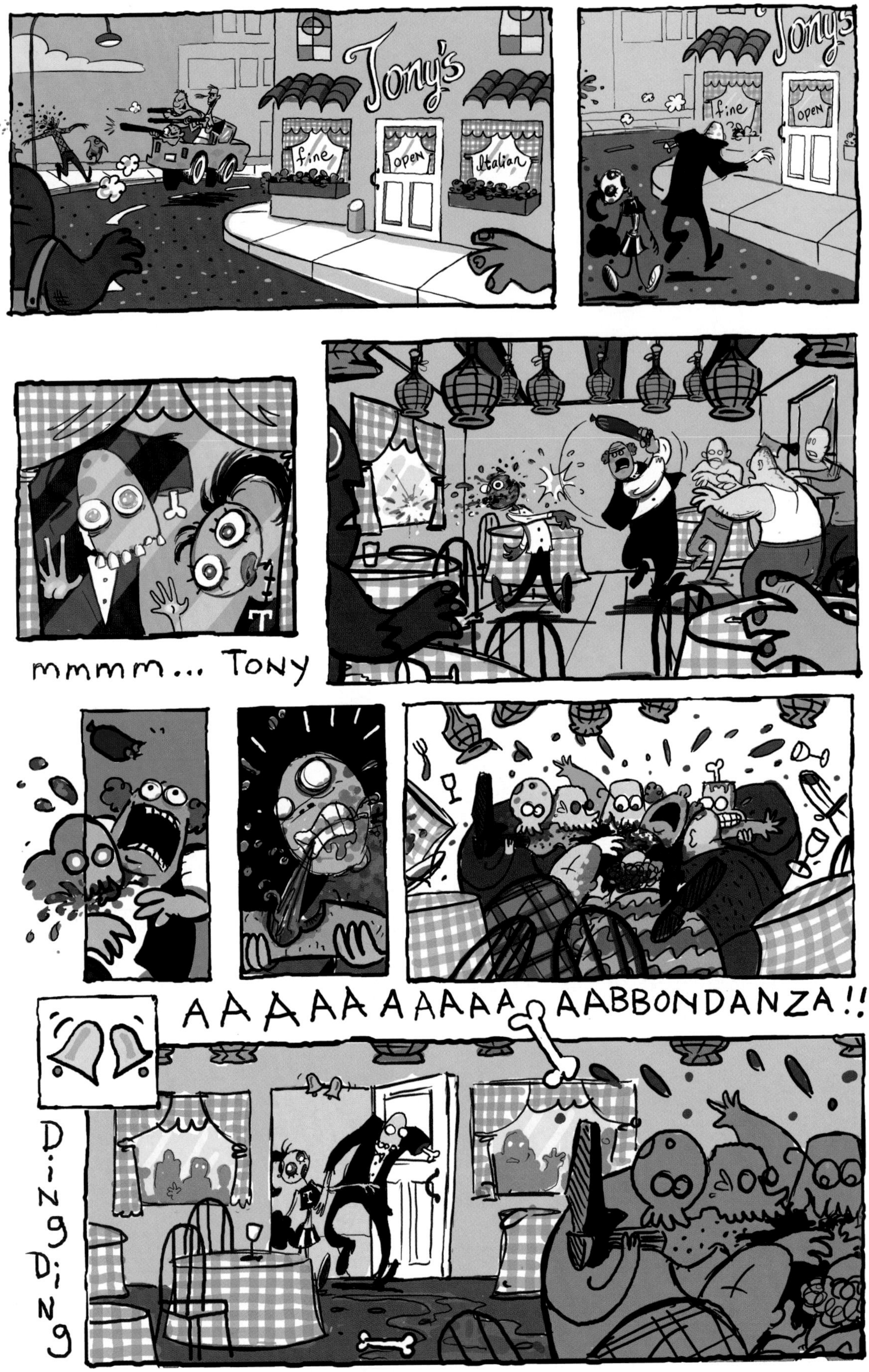
Tony's
fine
open
Italian
Tony's
fine
open
mmmm... TONY
AAAAAAAAAA AABBONDANZA!!
DINGDING

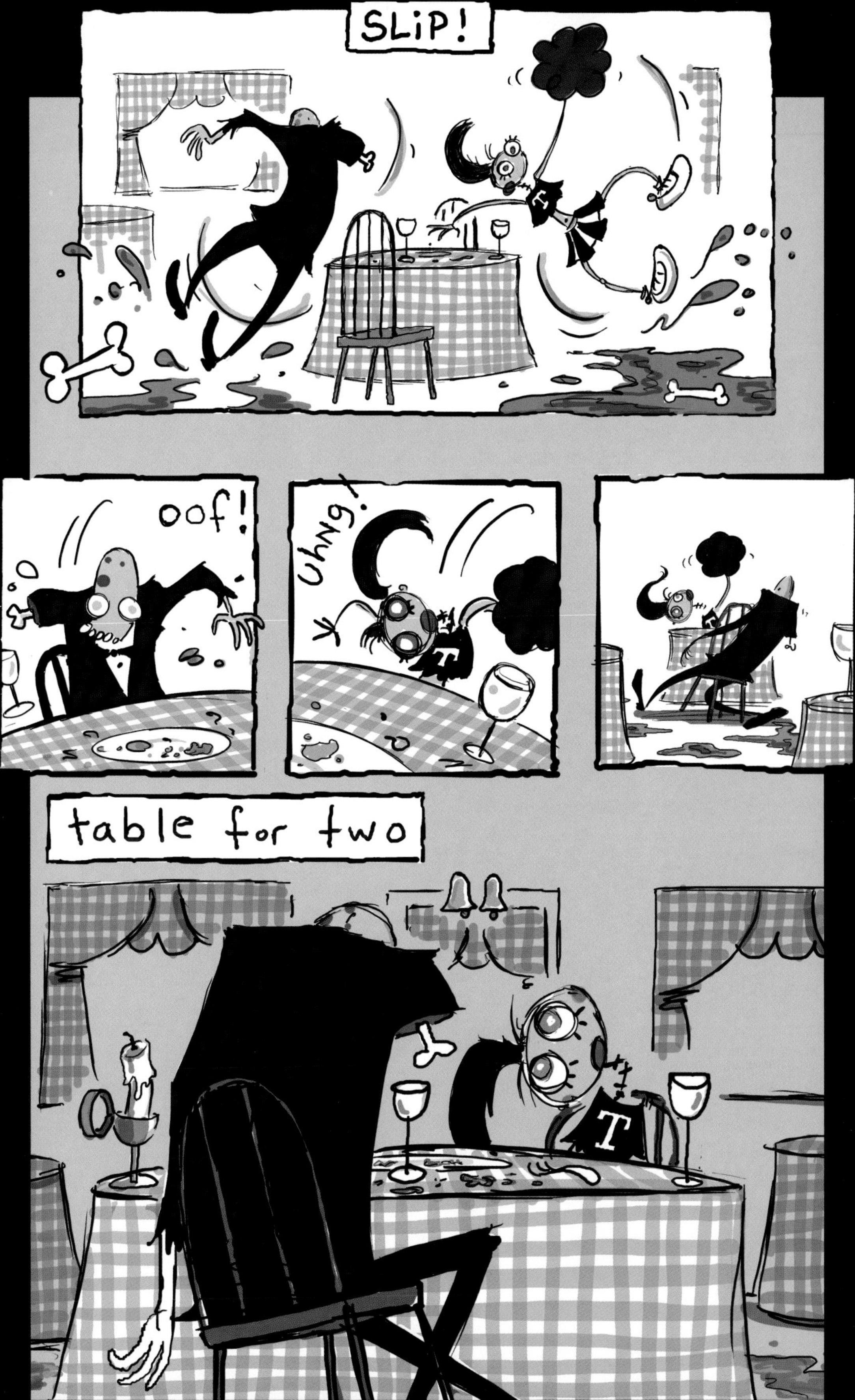
SLIP!
oof!
Uhng!
table for two

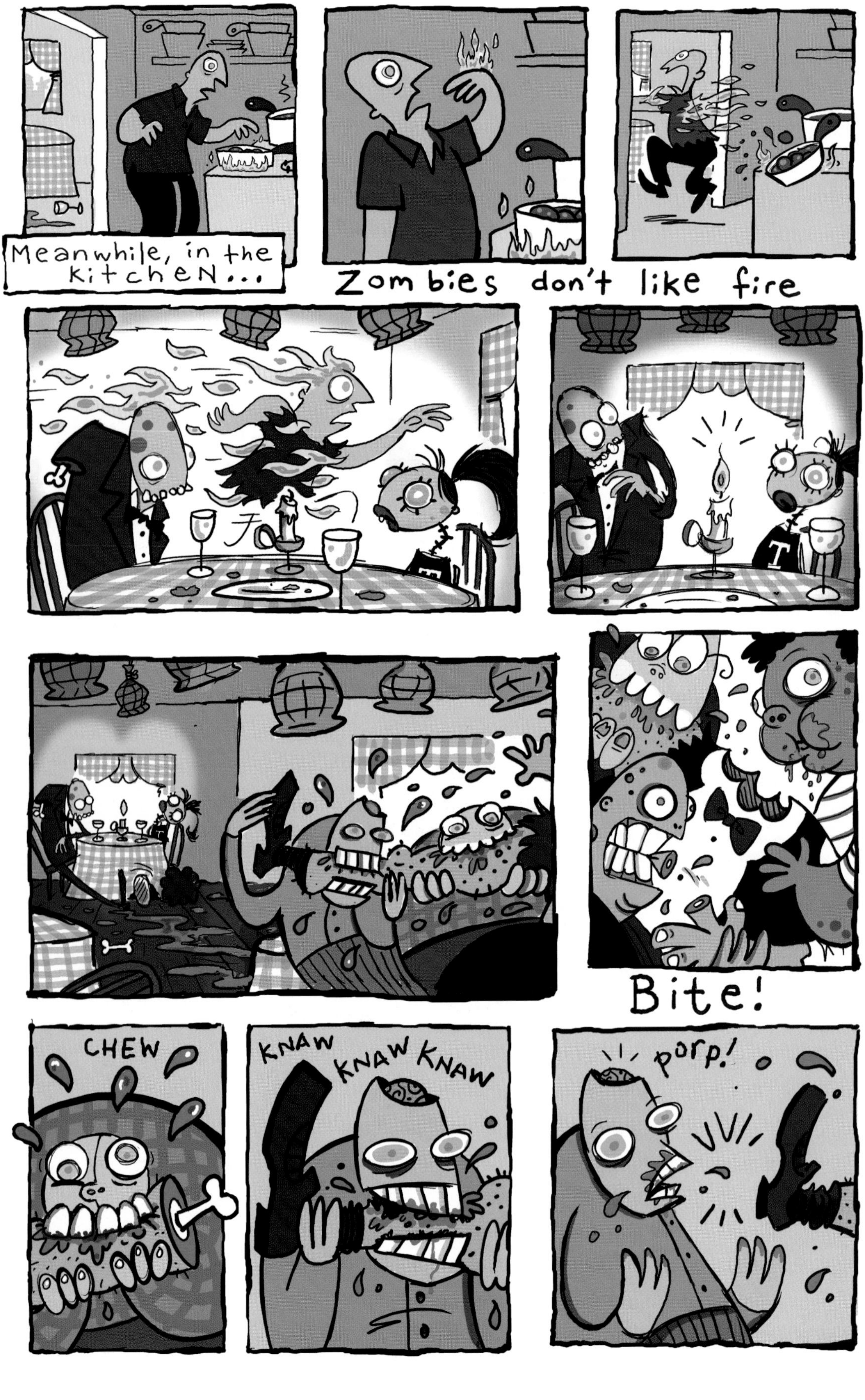
Meanwhile, in the kitchEN...
Zombies don't like fire
Bite!
CHEW
KNAW KNAW KNAW
porp!

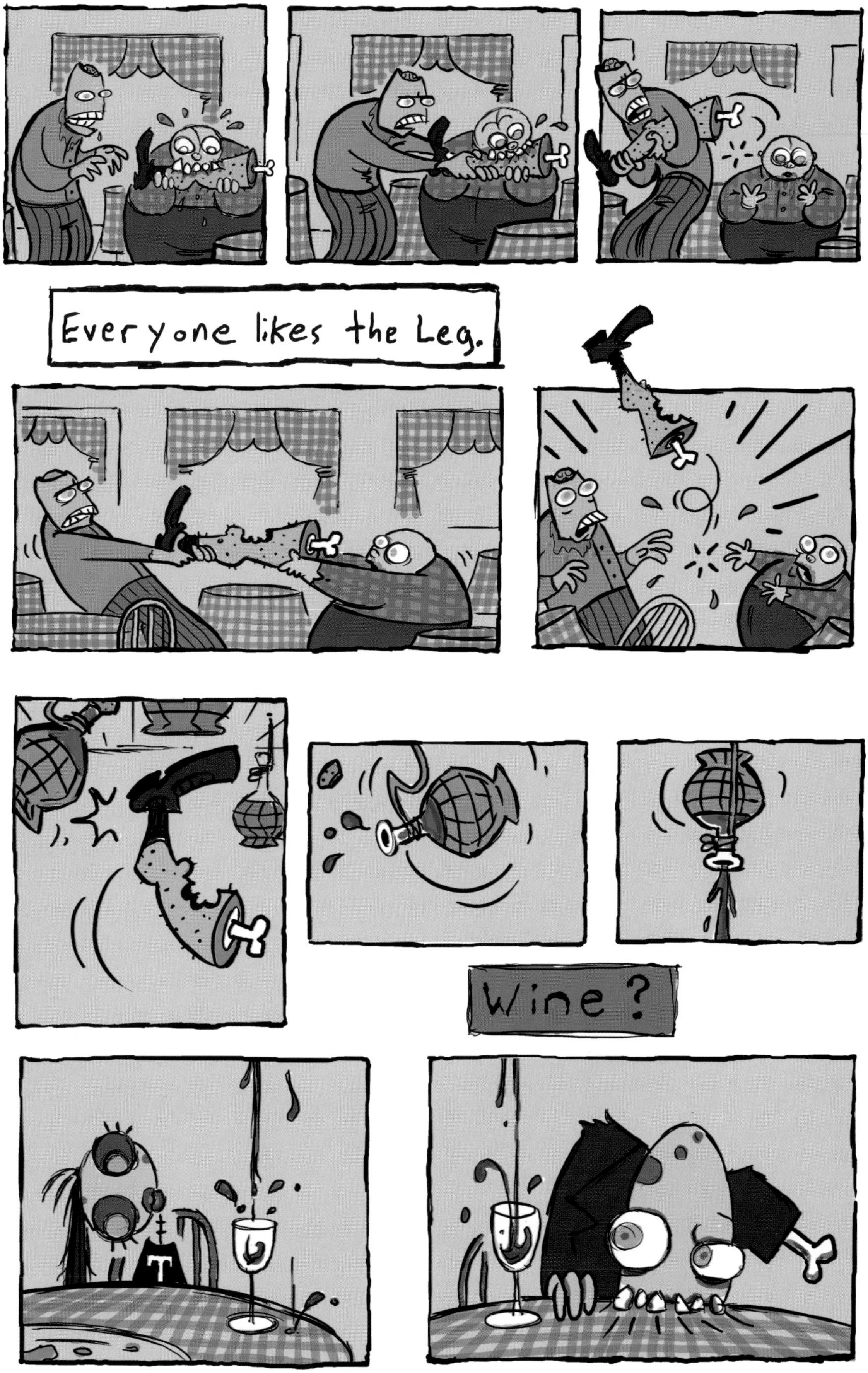
Everyone likes the Leg.
Wine?

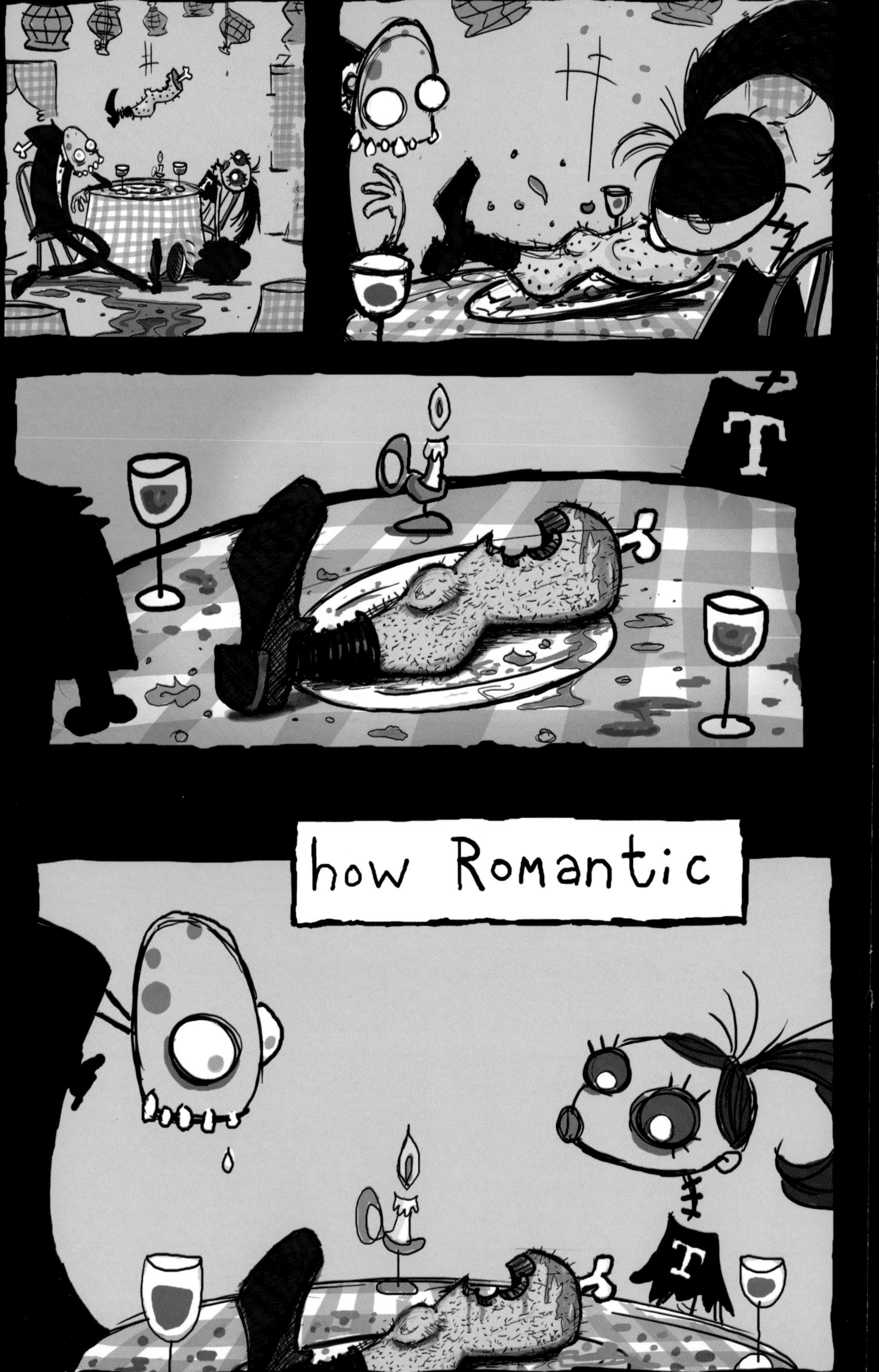
T
how Romantic
T

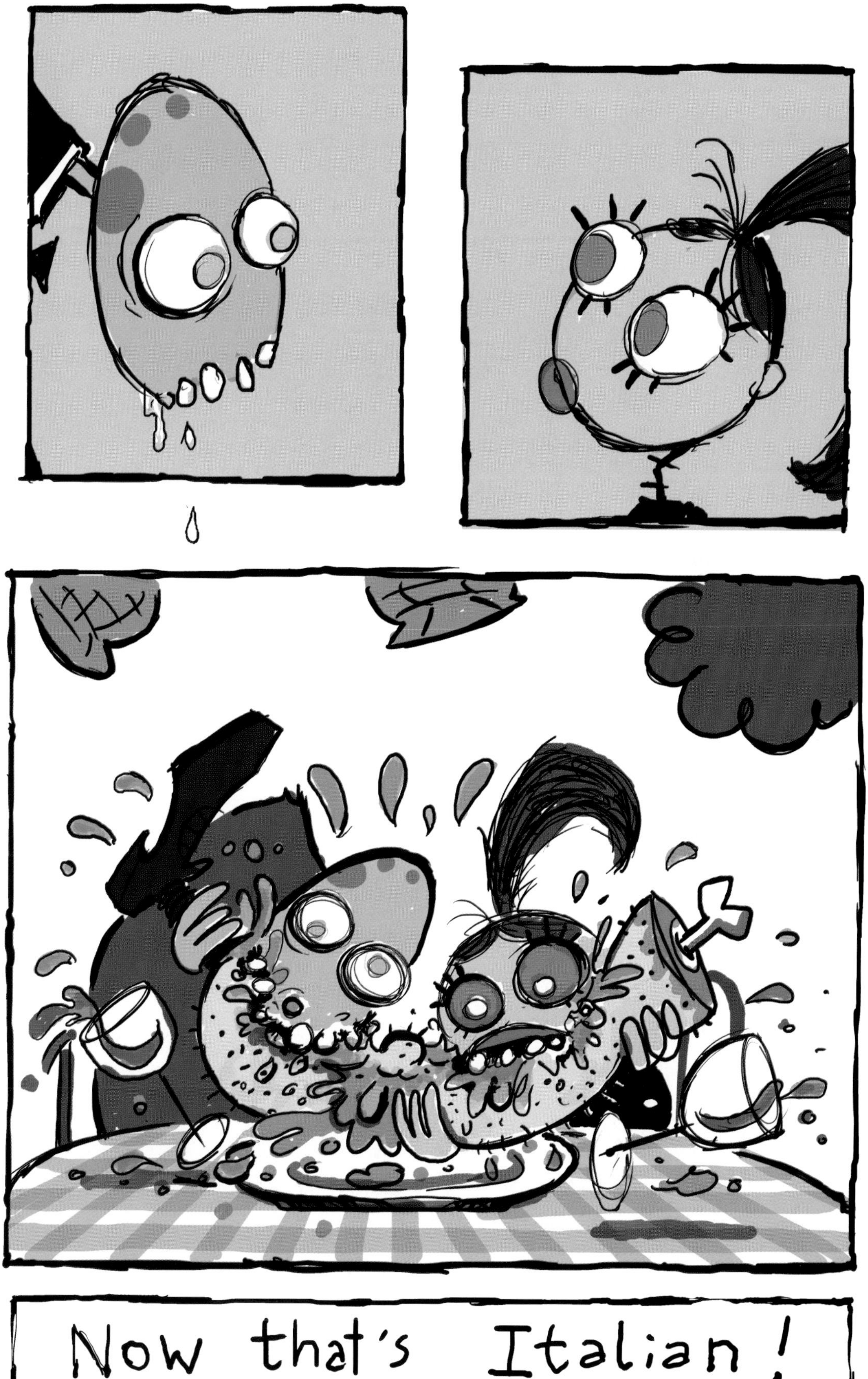
Now that's Italian!

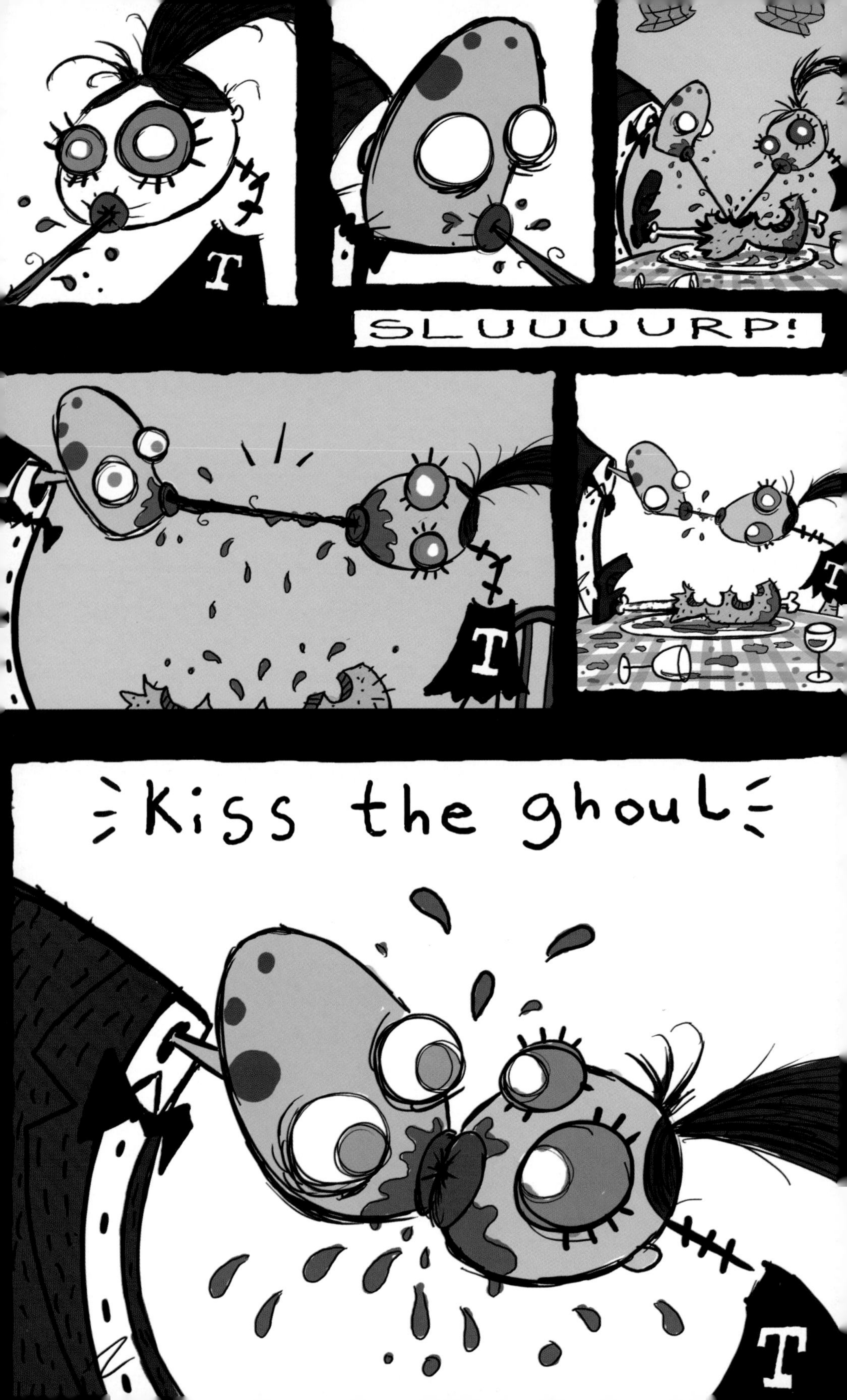
SLUUUURP!
Kiss the ghoul

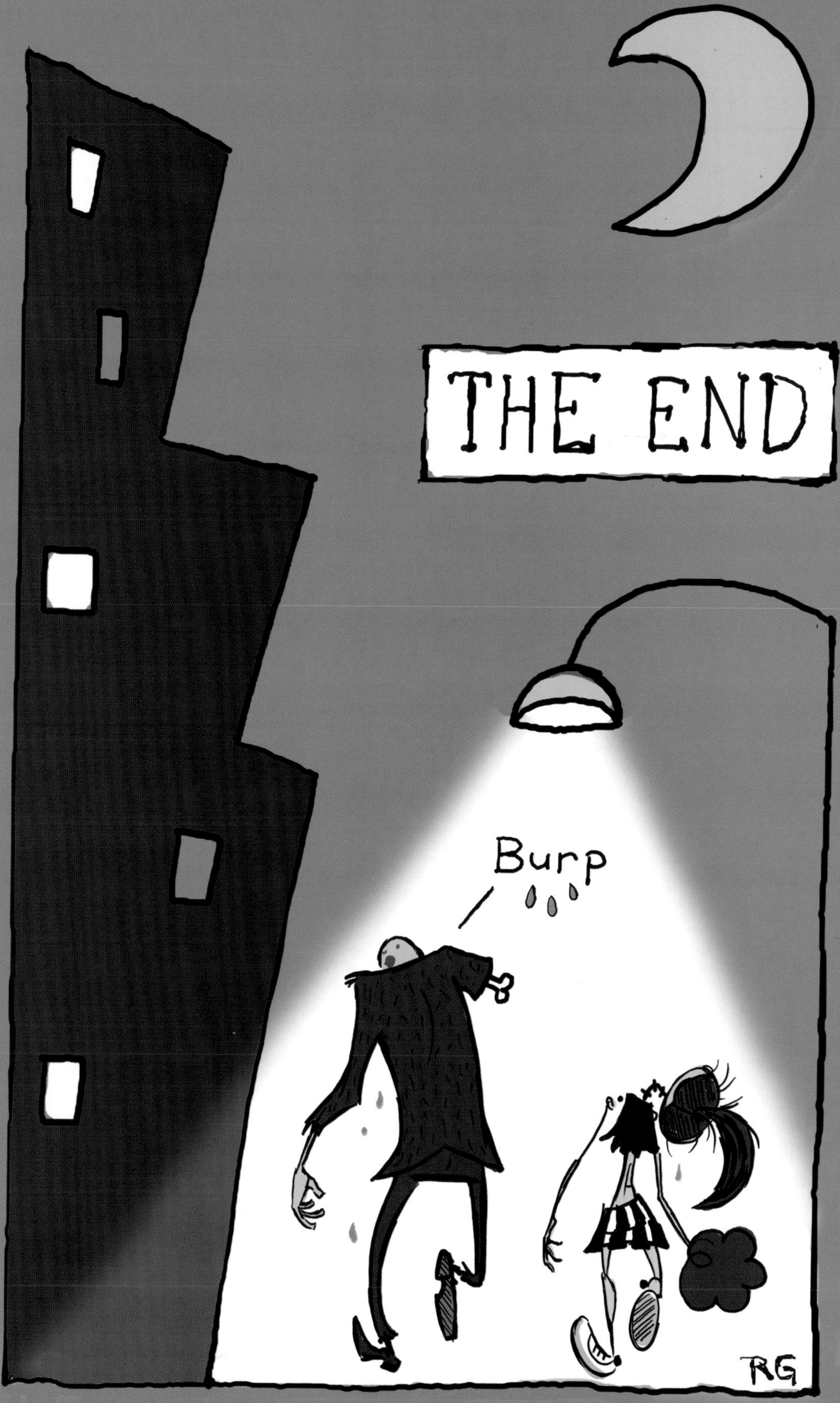
THE END
Burp
RG

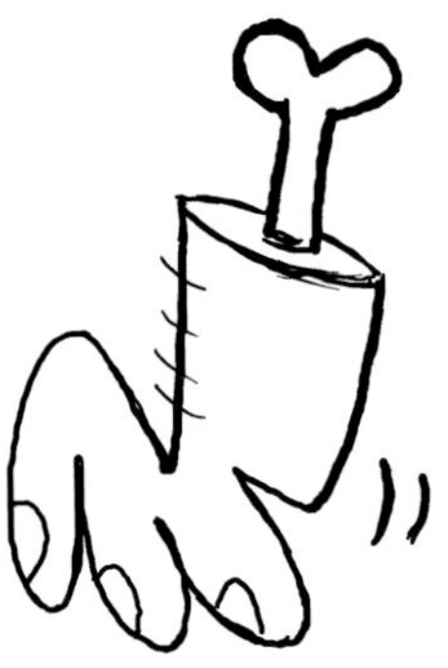

PINUPS BY

NATE STANTON
STEVE PURCELL

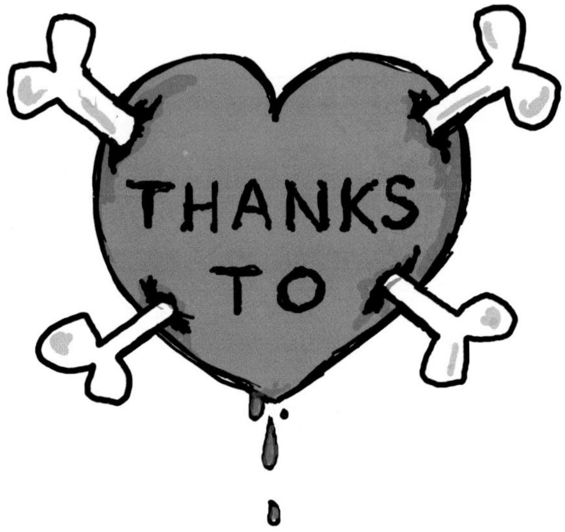
THANKS
TO

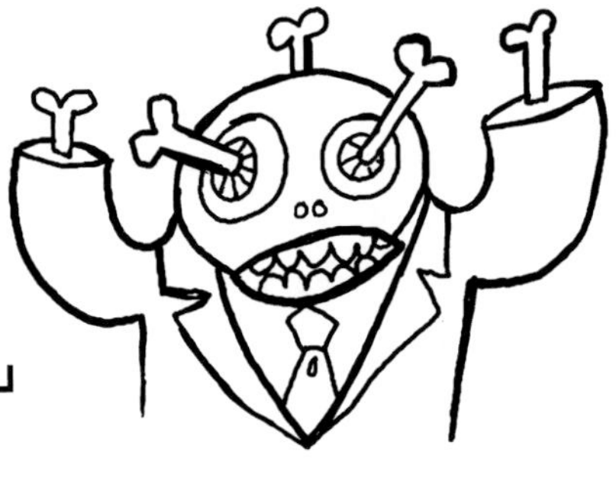

NATE STANTON
TED MATHOT
STEVE PURCELL
DAN SCANLON
DEREK THOMPSON
JAMIE BAKER
RYAN LYNCH
JOSH COOLEY

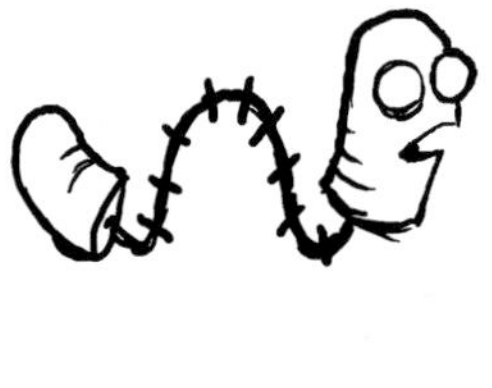

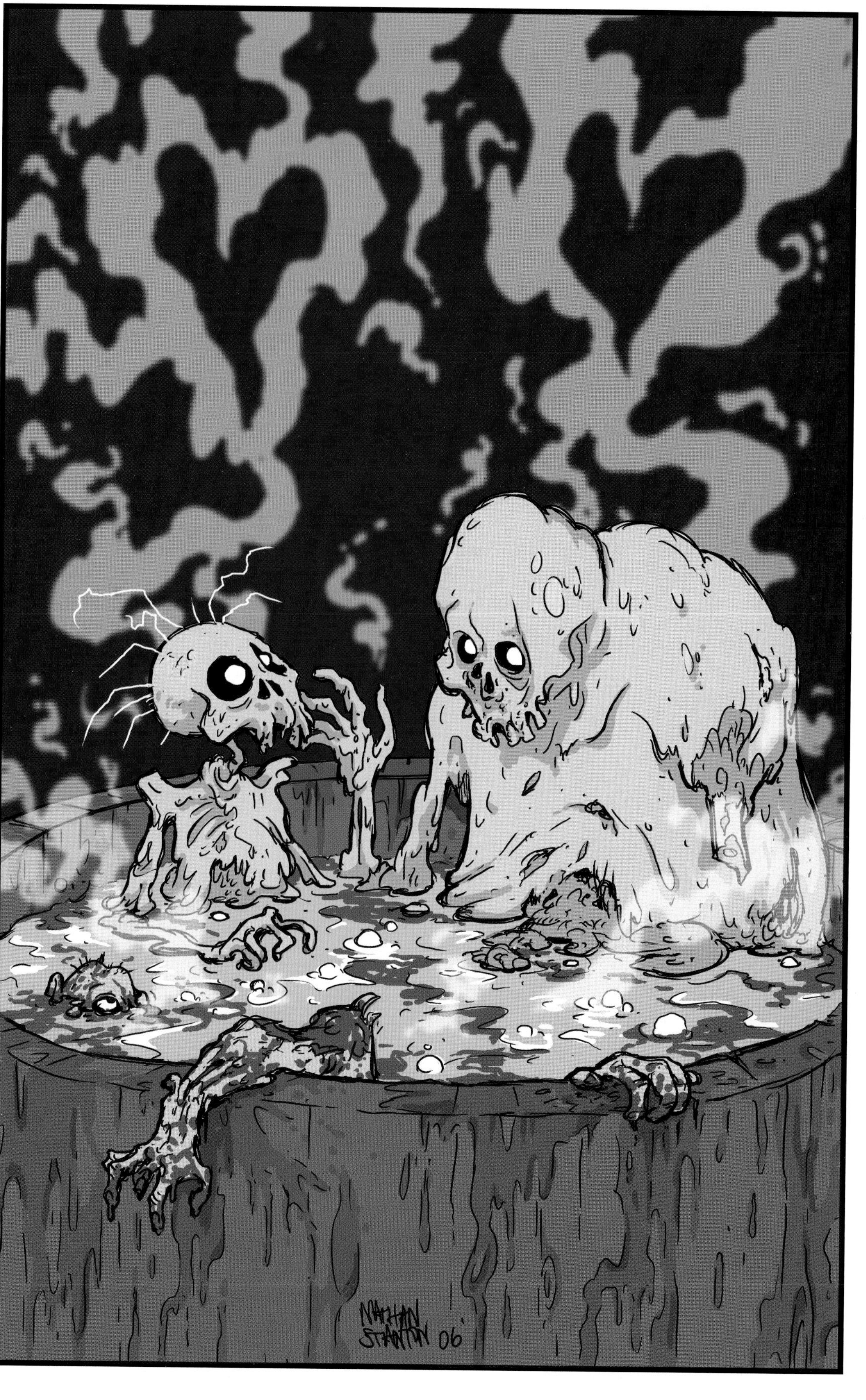
NATHAN STANTON 06'

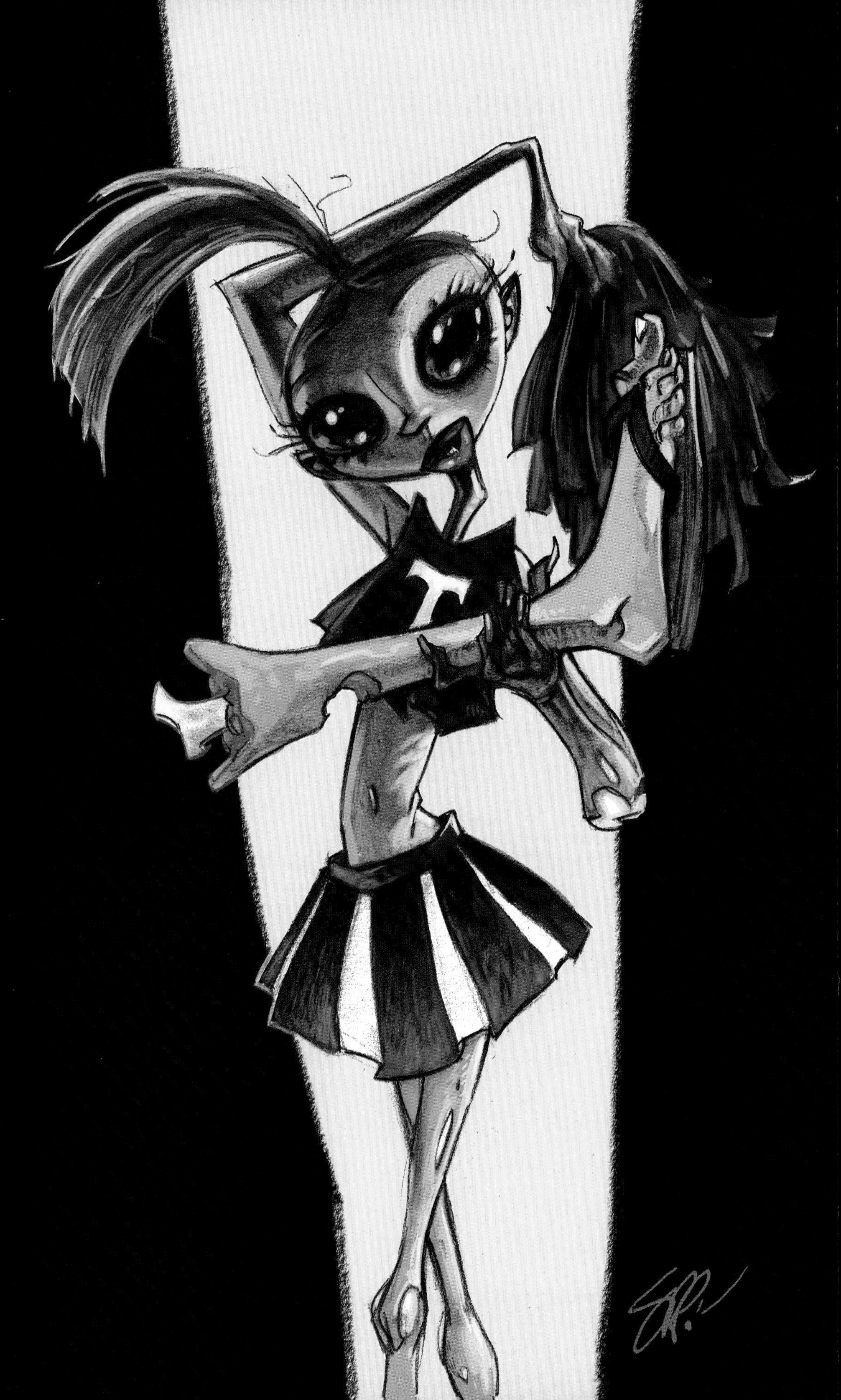

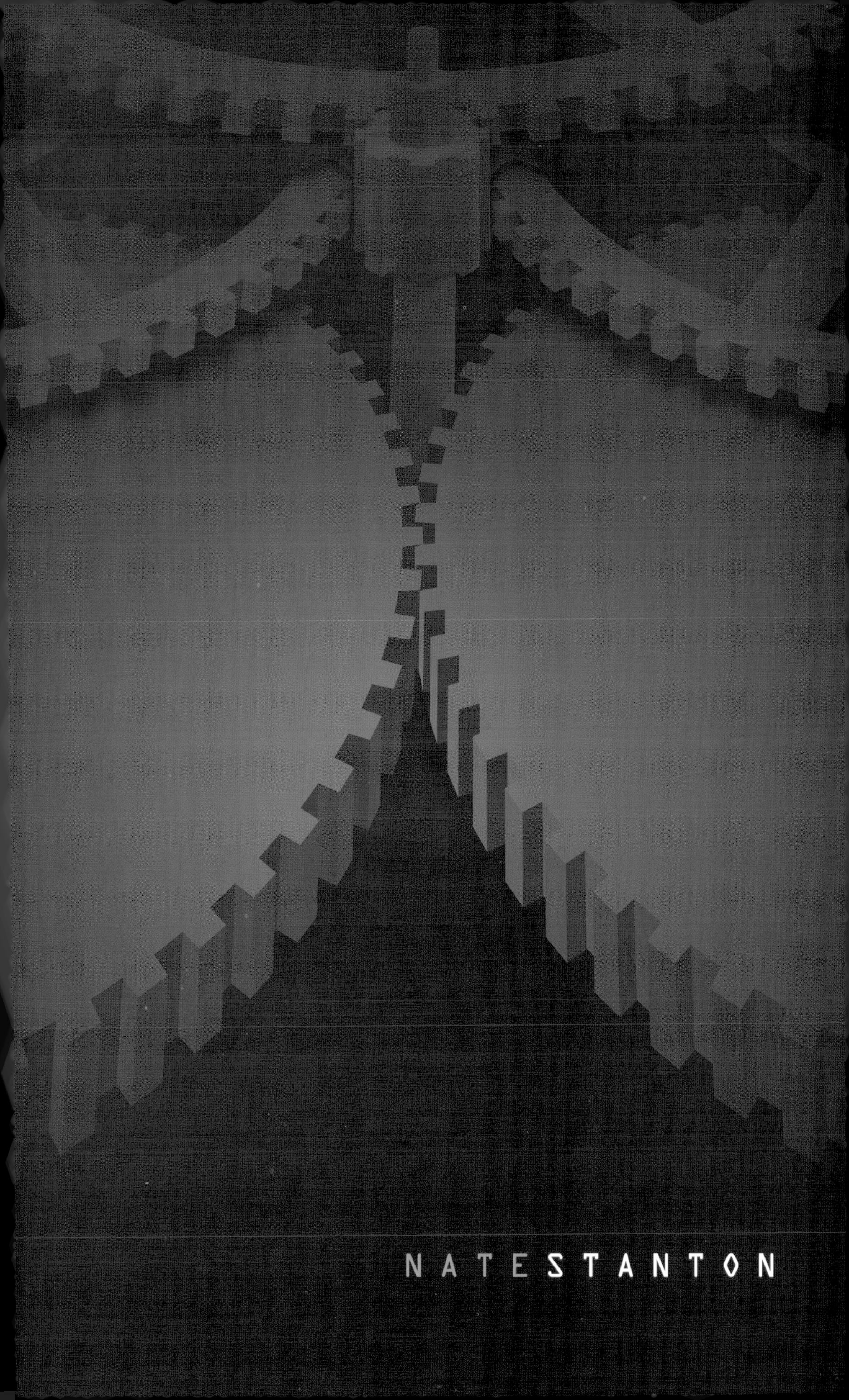
NATESTANTON

DEDICATED TO

my lovely and amazing wife Esther Pearl
and my beautiful daughter
Lotus Maria Stanton-Pearl

THANKS TO

Robert Kondo
Simon Dunsdon
Ted Mathot
Max Brace
Sanjay Patel
Sam Hiti
Ronnie Del Carmen
James S. Baker
Derek Thompson
Matthew Stanton
Andrew Stanton
my parents Ron & Gloria Stanton

and the whole AFTERWORKS 2 crew

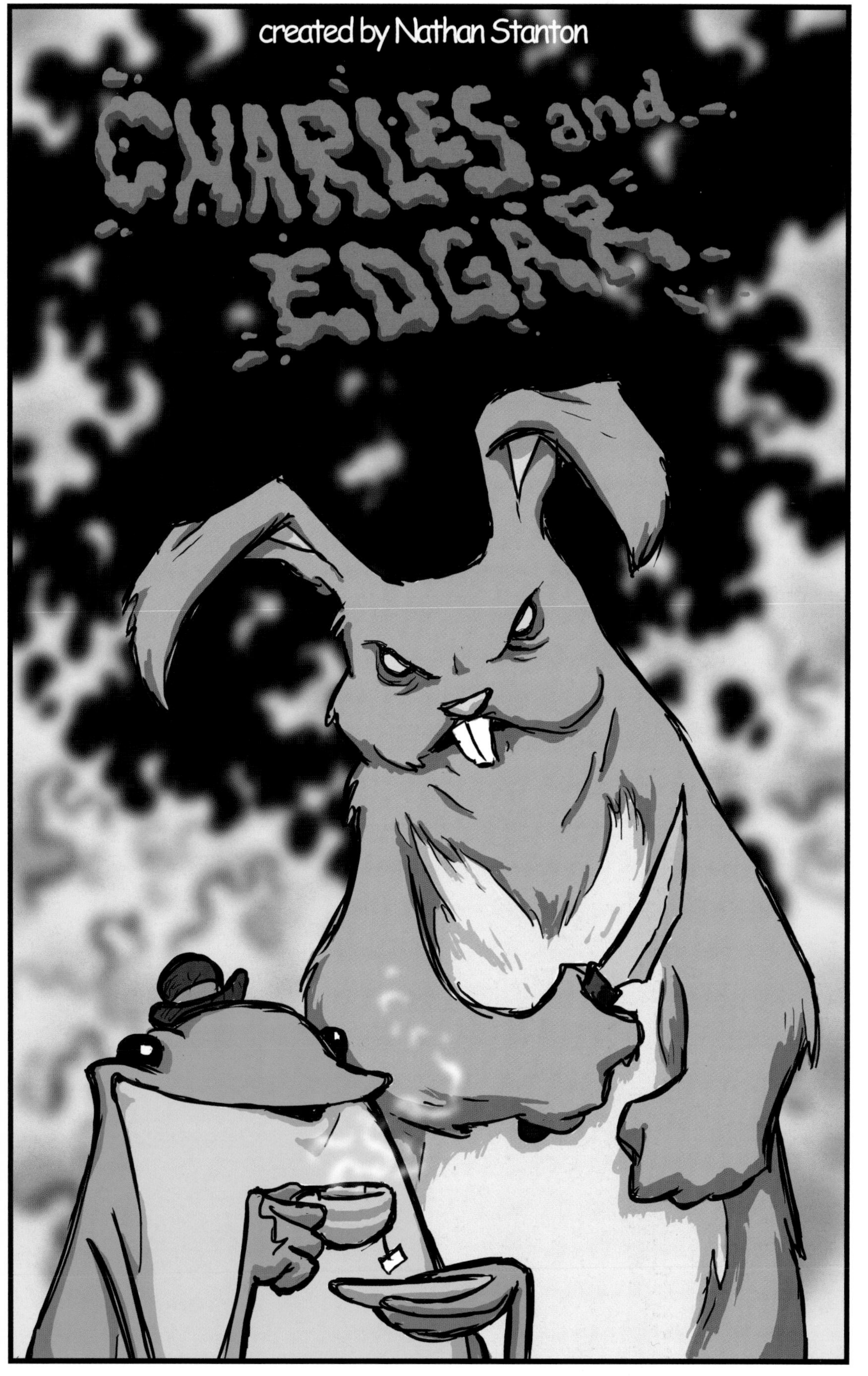
created by Nathan Stanton
CHARLES and EDGAR

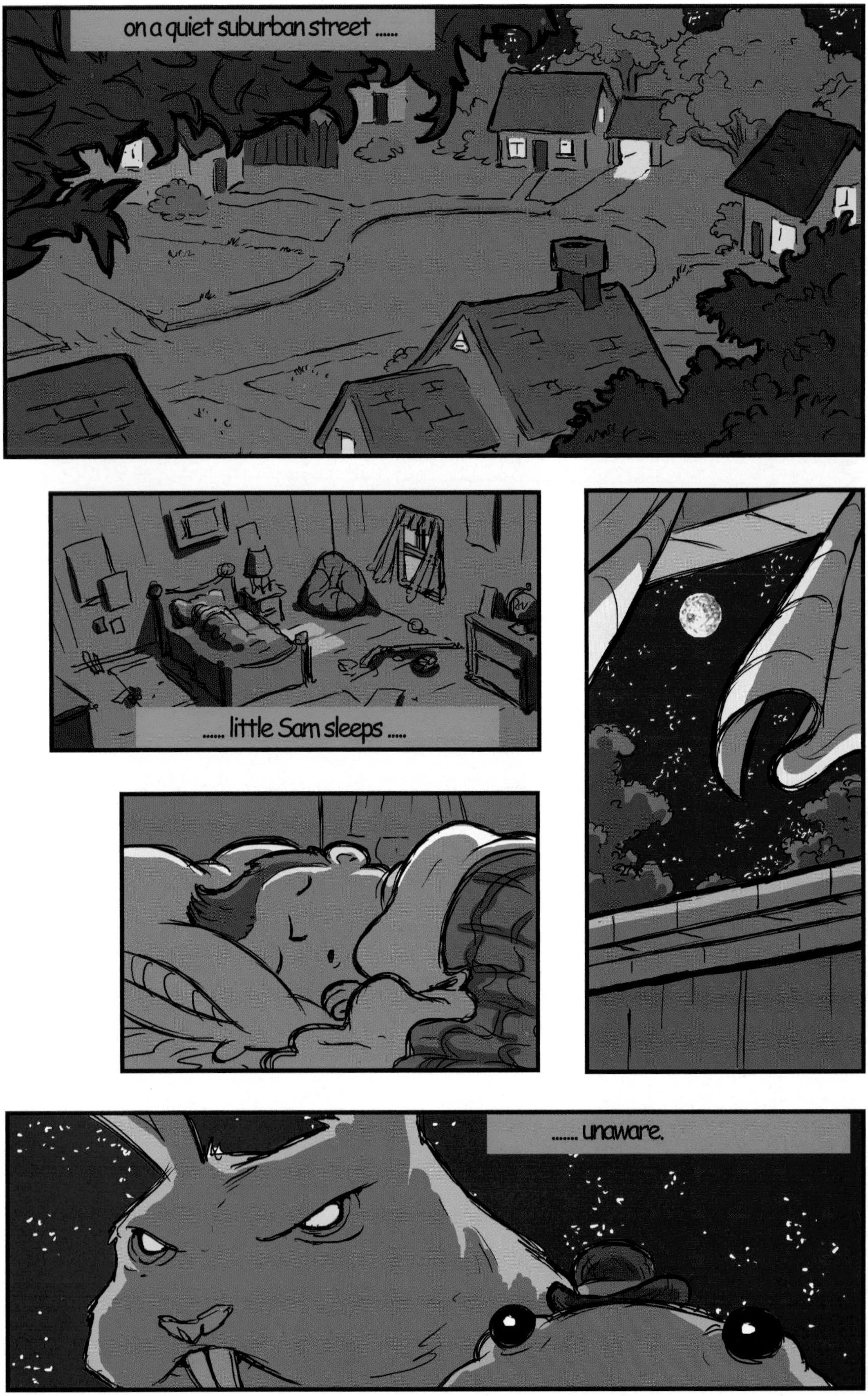
on a quiet suburban street ......
...... little Sam sleeps .....
.... unaware.

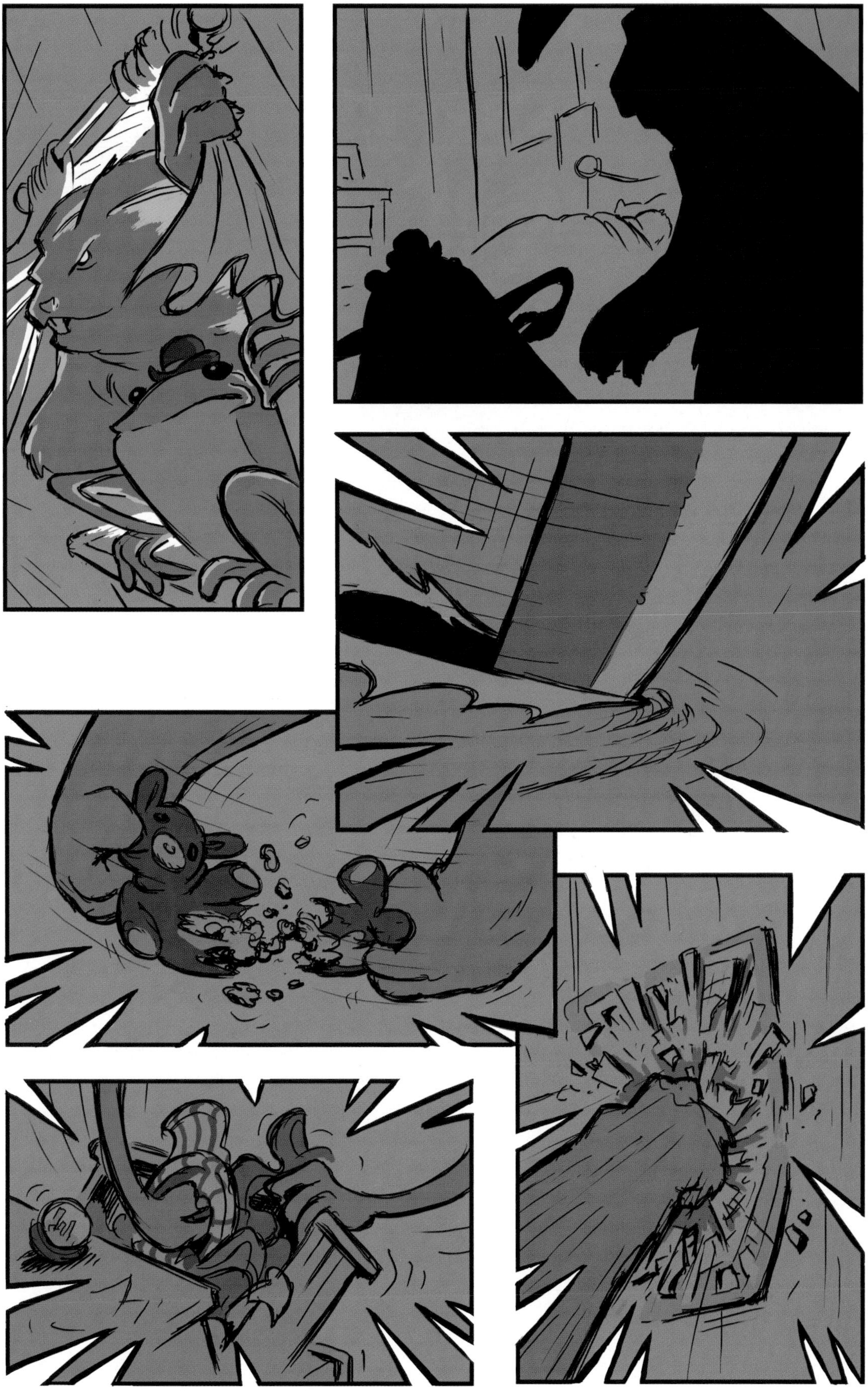

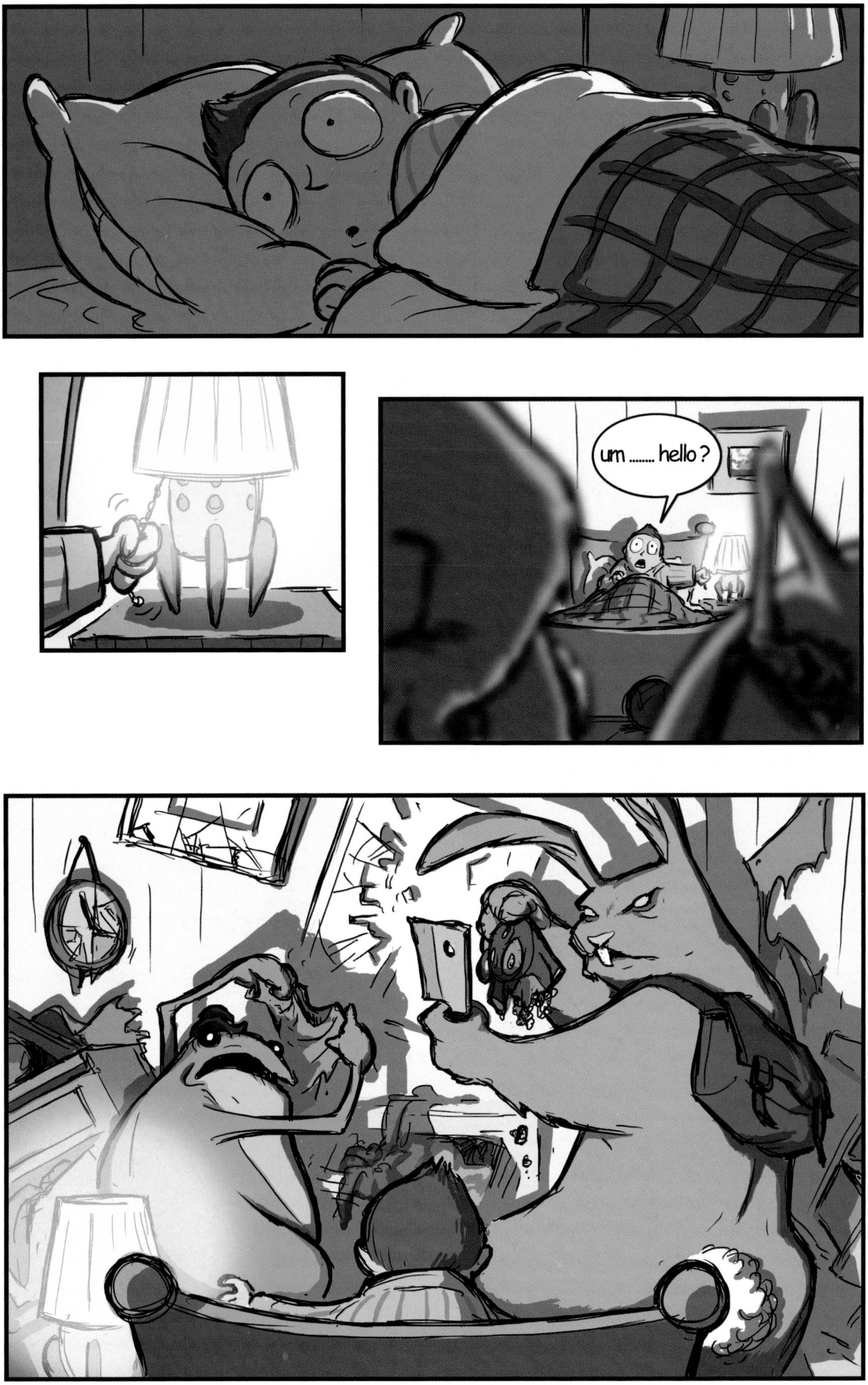
um .... hello ?

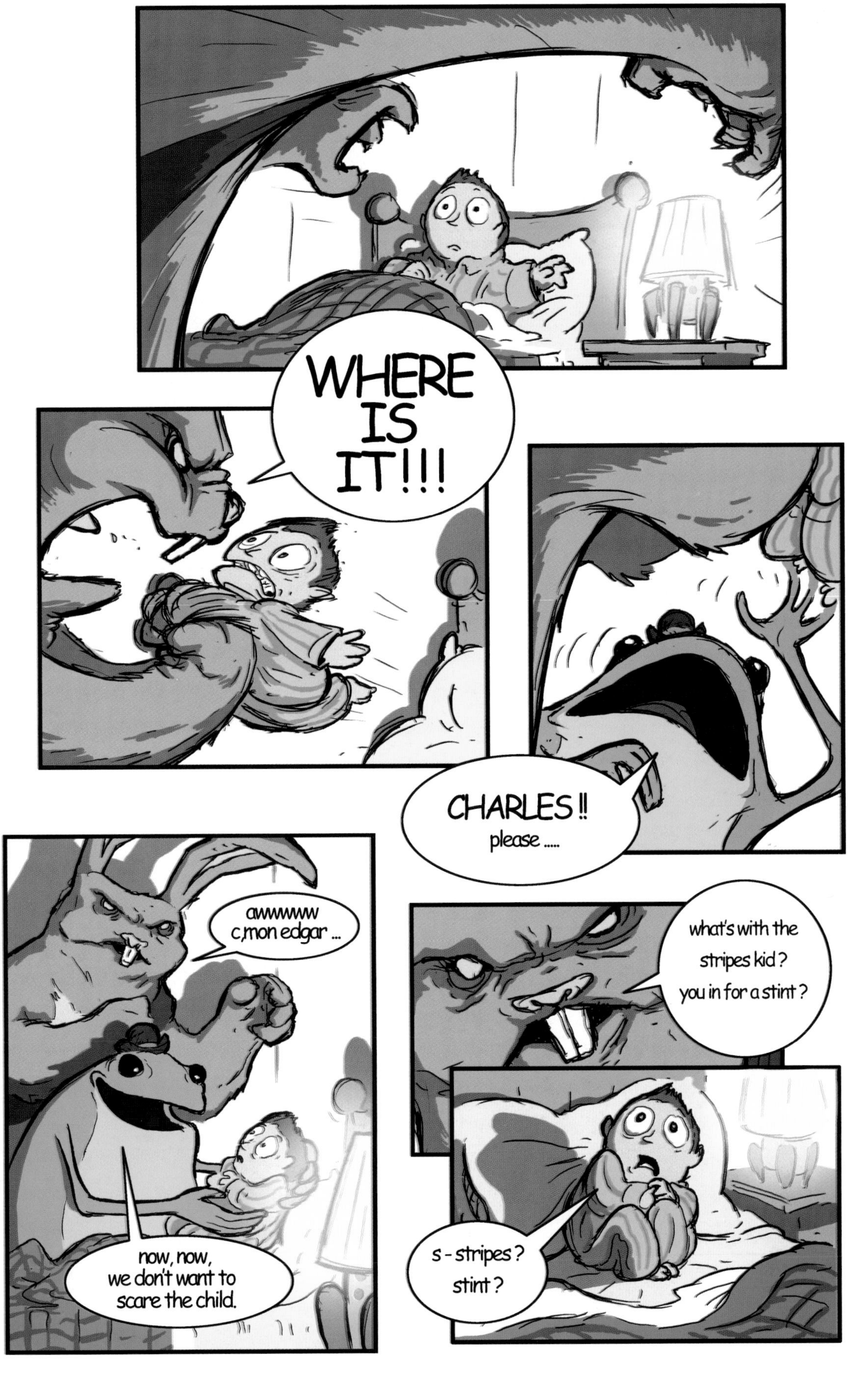
WHERE IS IT!!!
CHARLES!! please .....
awwwww c,mon edgar ...
now, now, we don't want to scare the child.
what's with the stripes kid? you in for a stint?
s - stripes? stint?

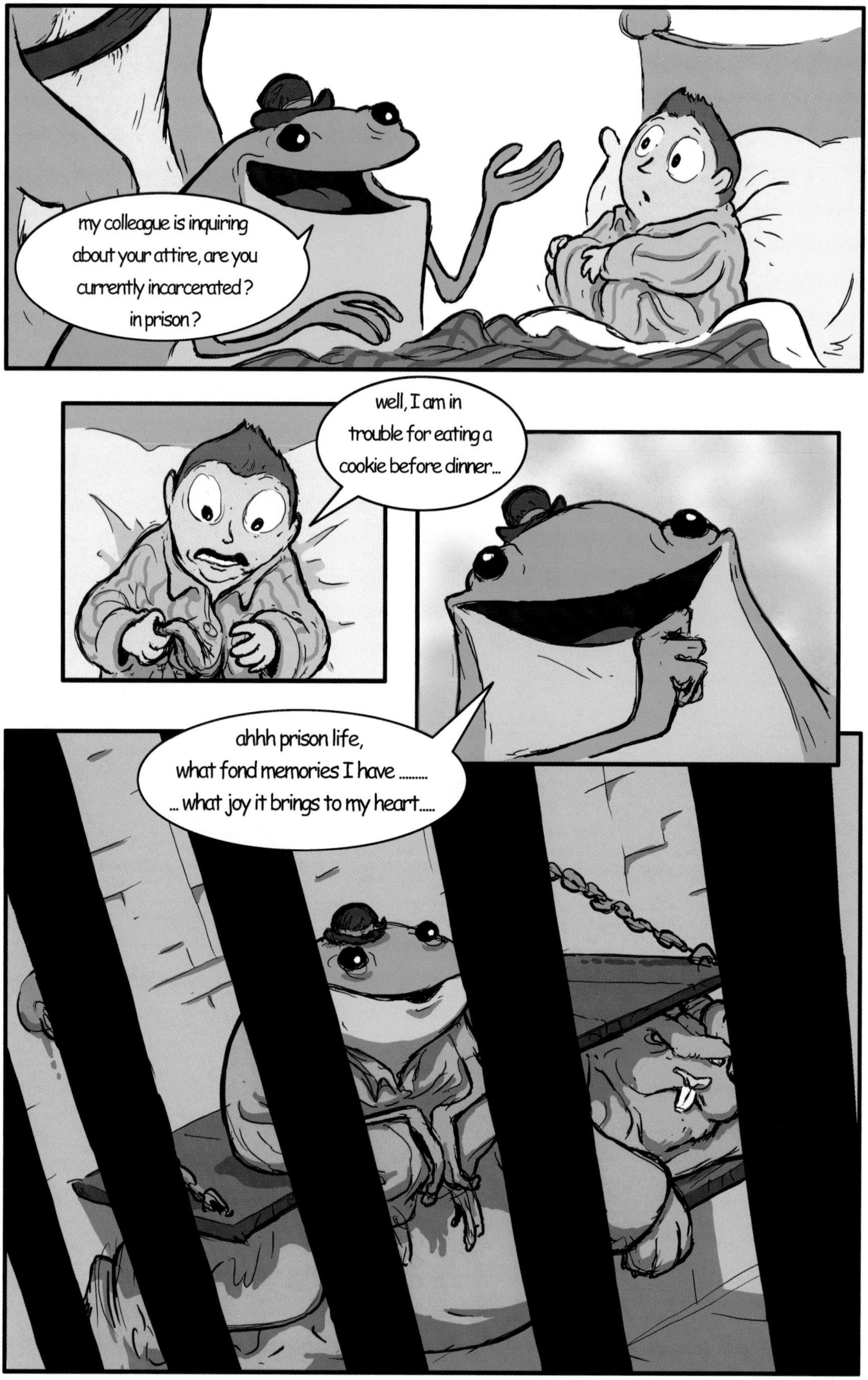
my colleague is inquiring about your attire, are you currently incarcerated? in prison?
well, I am in trouble for eating a cookie before dinner...
ahhh prison life, what fond memories I have ....
... what joy it brings to my heart.....

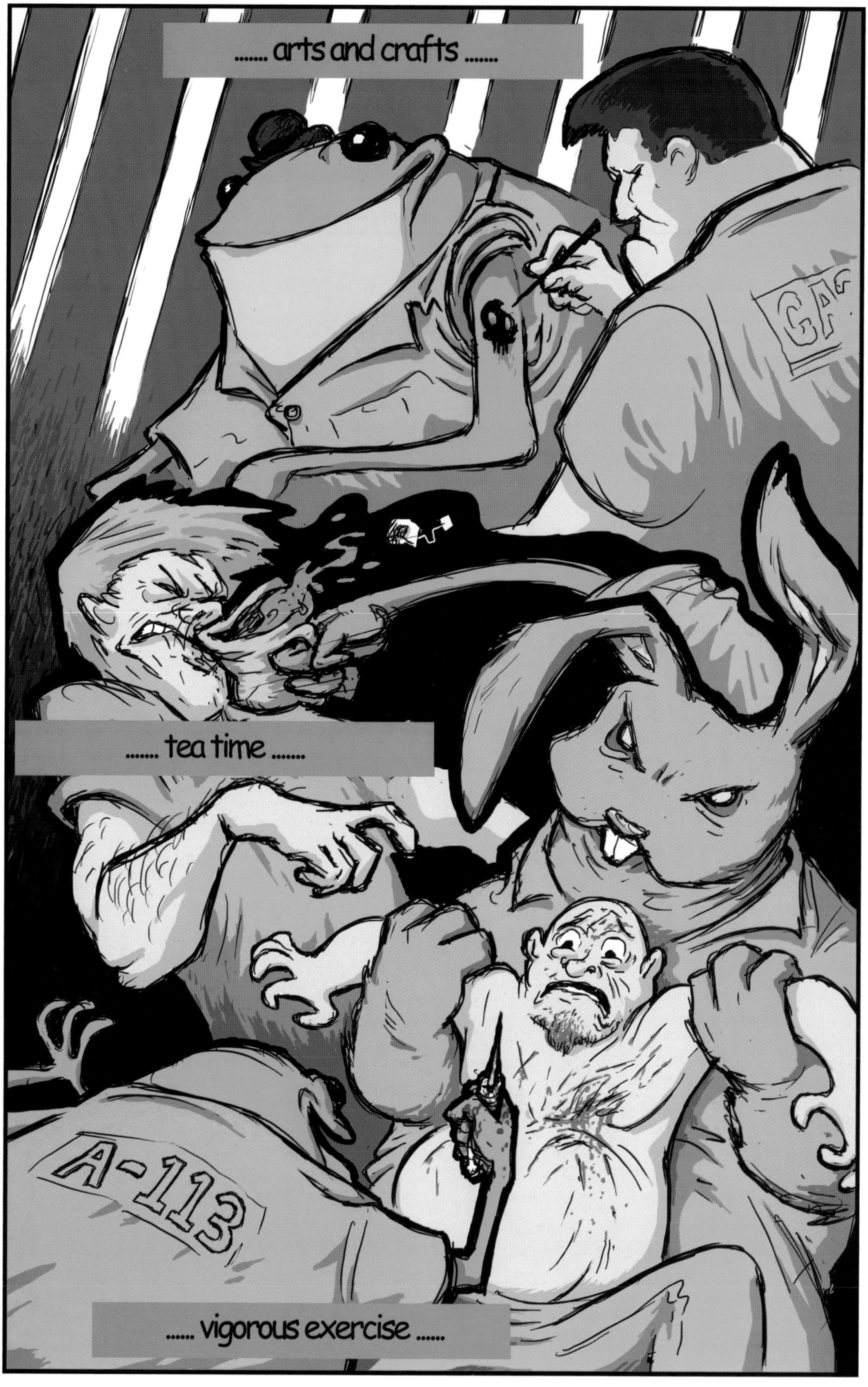
.... arts and crafts ....
GAS
.... tea time ....
A-113
...... vigorous exercise ......

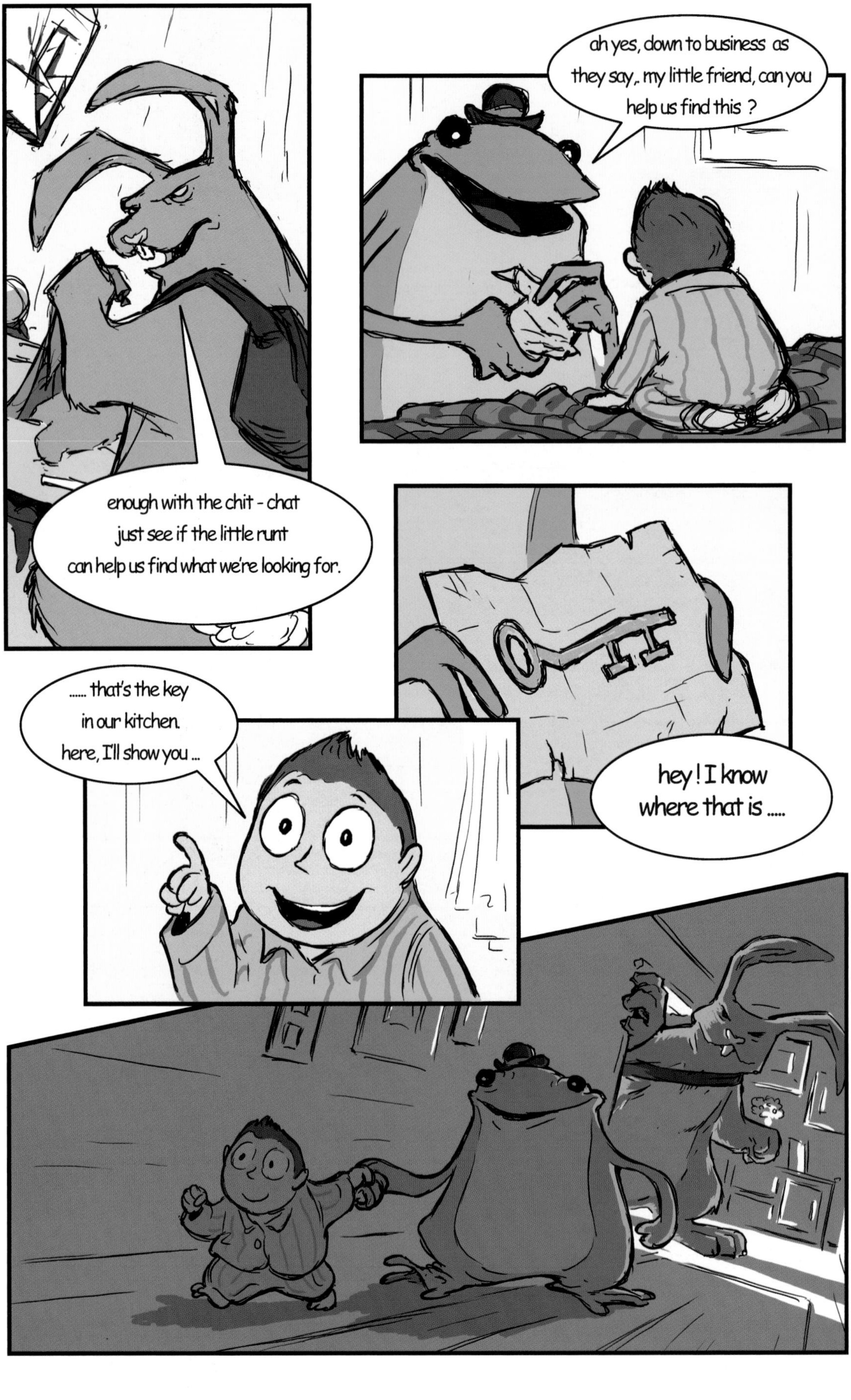
enough with the chit - chat just see if the little runt can help us find what we're looking for.
ah yes, down to business as they say,. my little friend, can you help us find this ?
hey ! I know where that is .....
...... that's the key in our kitchen. here, I'll show you ...

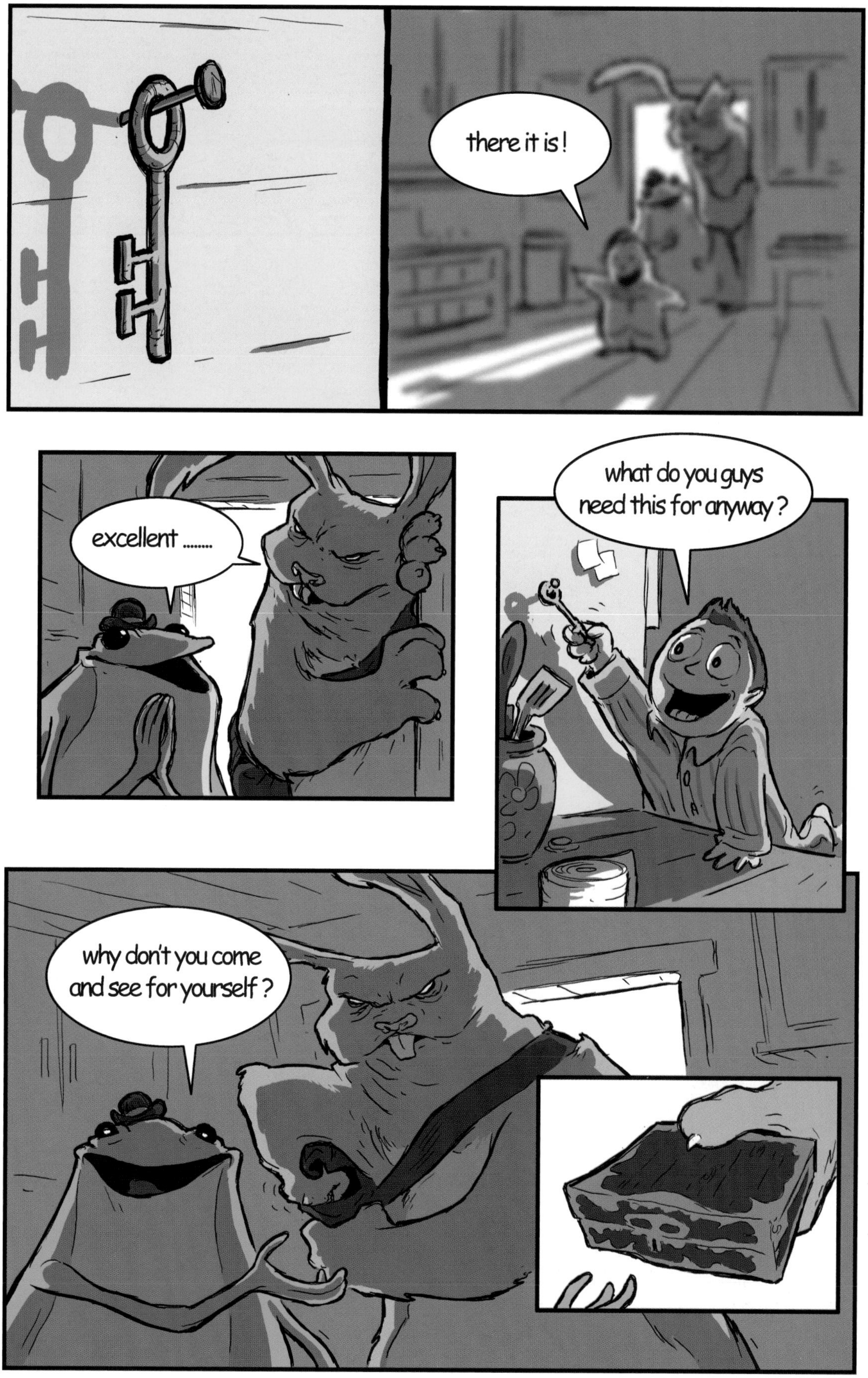
there it is!
excellent ....
what do you guys need this for anyway?
why don't you come and see for yourself?

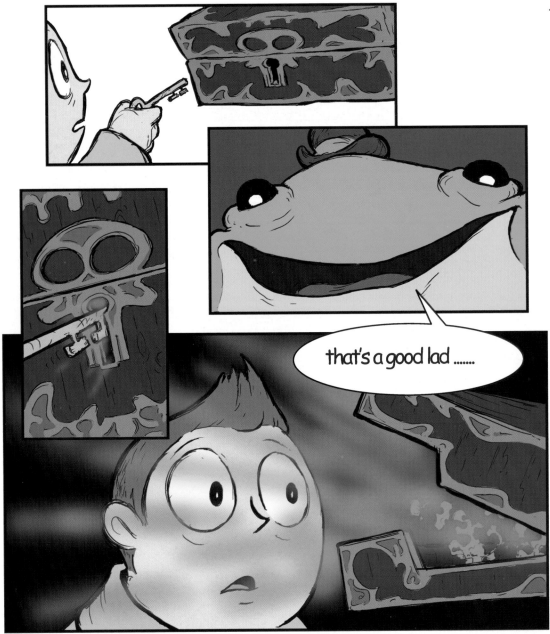

that's a good lad ....

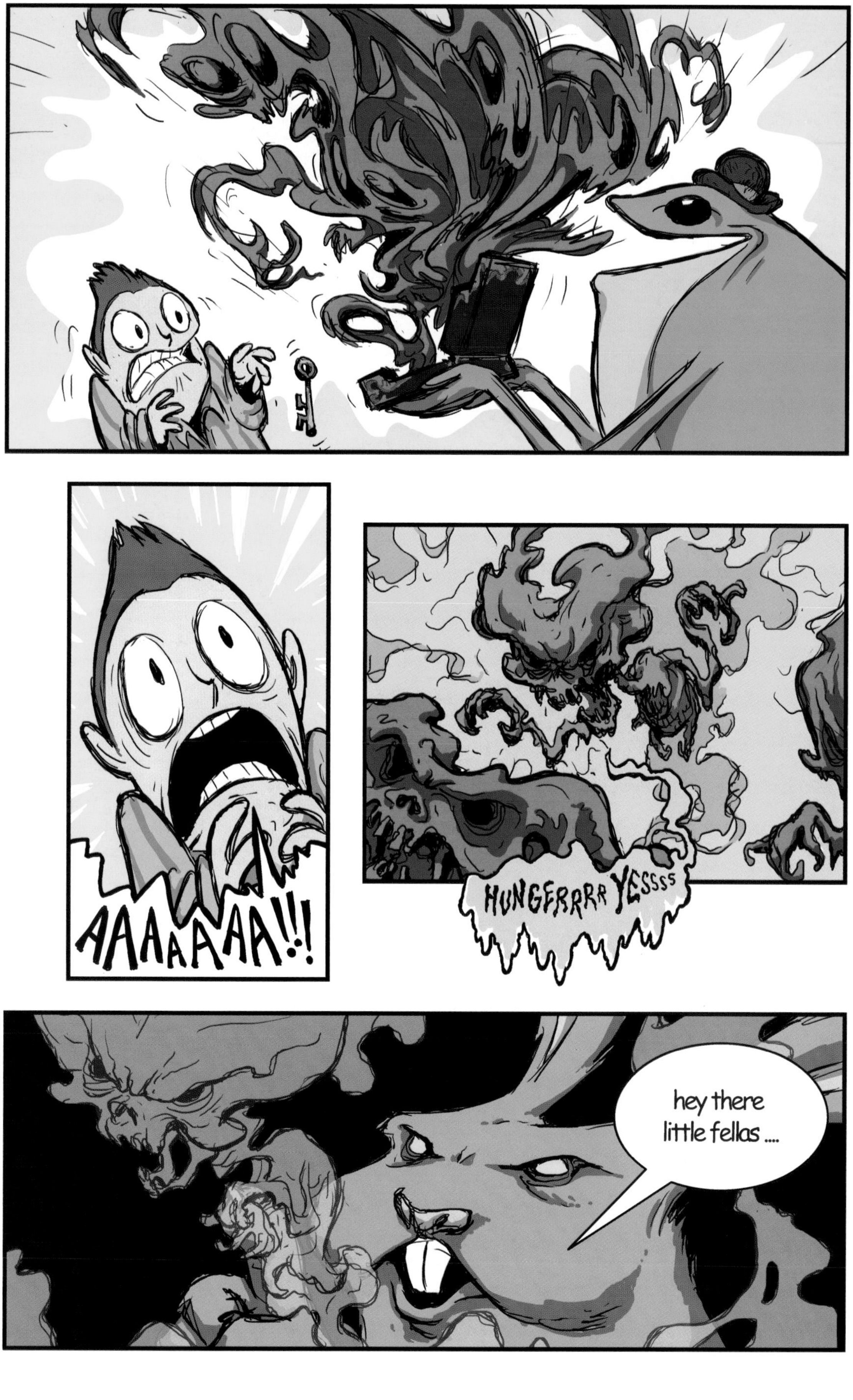
AAAAAAA!!!
HUNGERRRR YESSSS
hey there little fellas ....

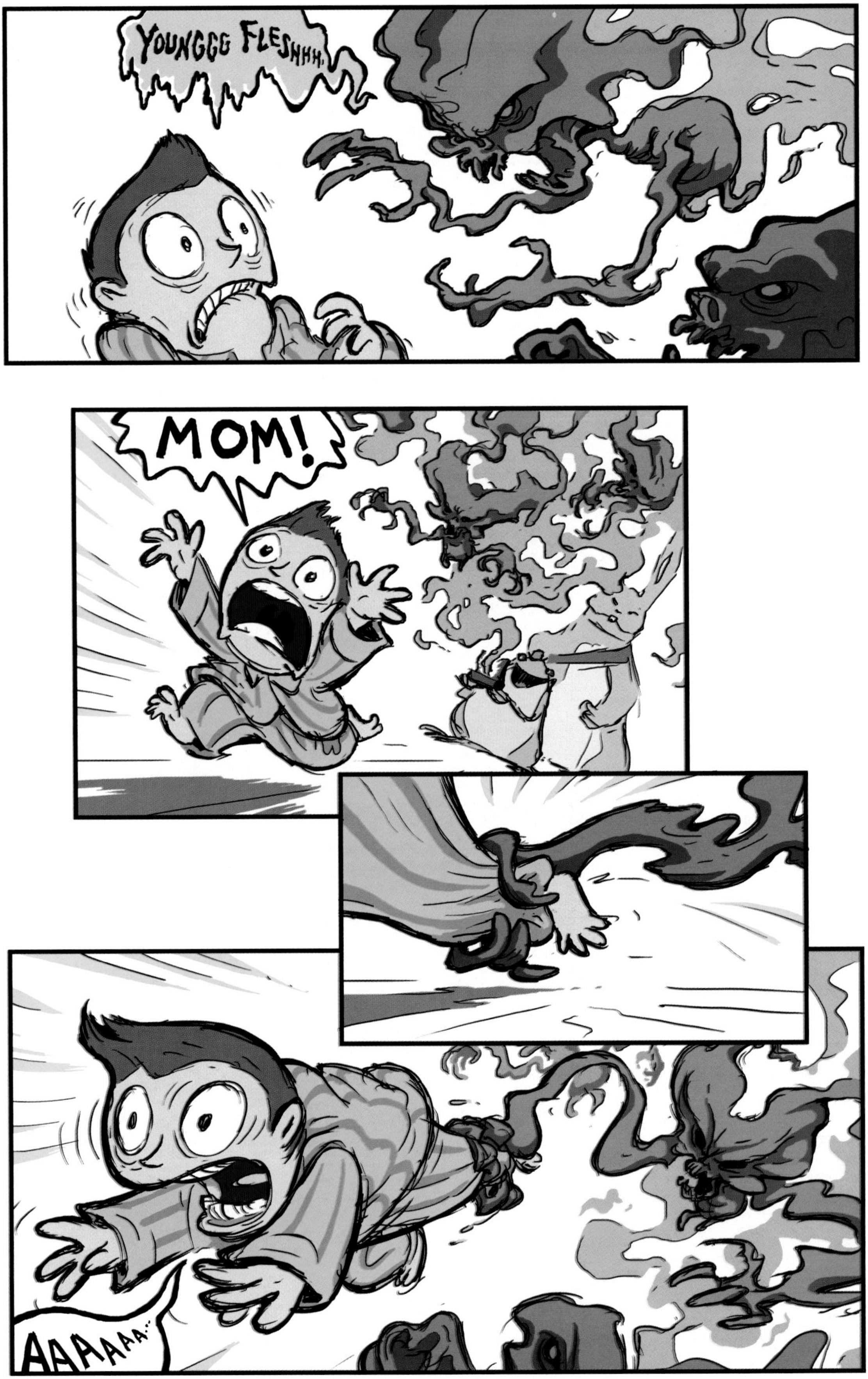
YOUNGGG FLESHHH.
MOM!
AAAAAA...

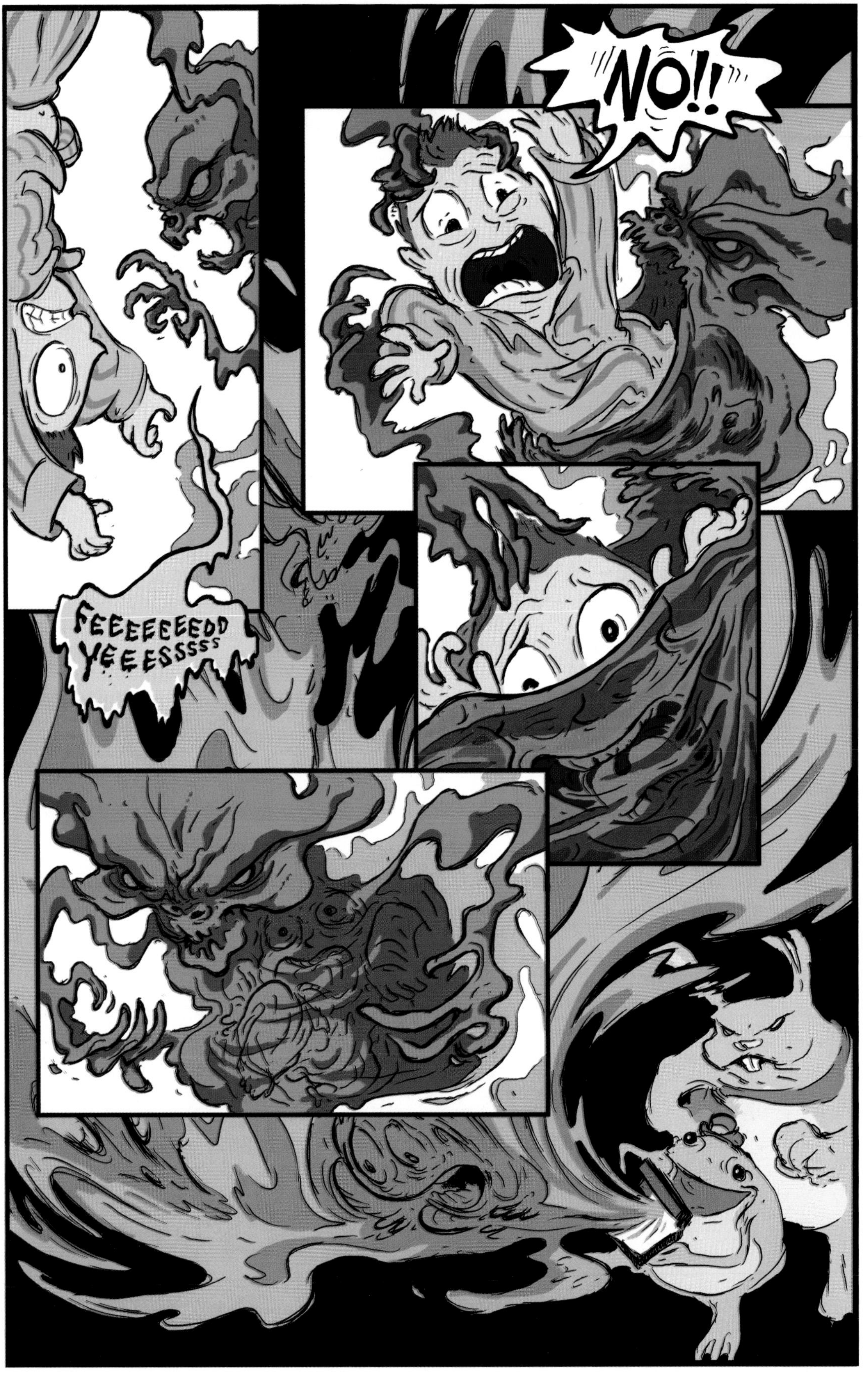
NO!!
FEEEEEEEDD YEEESSSSS

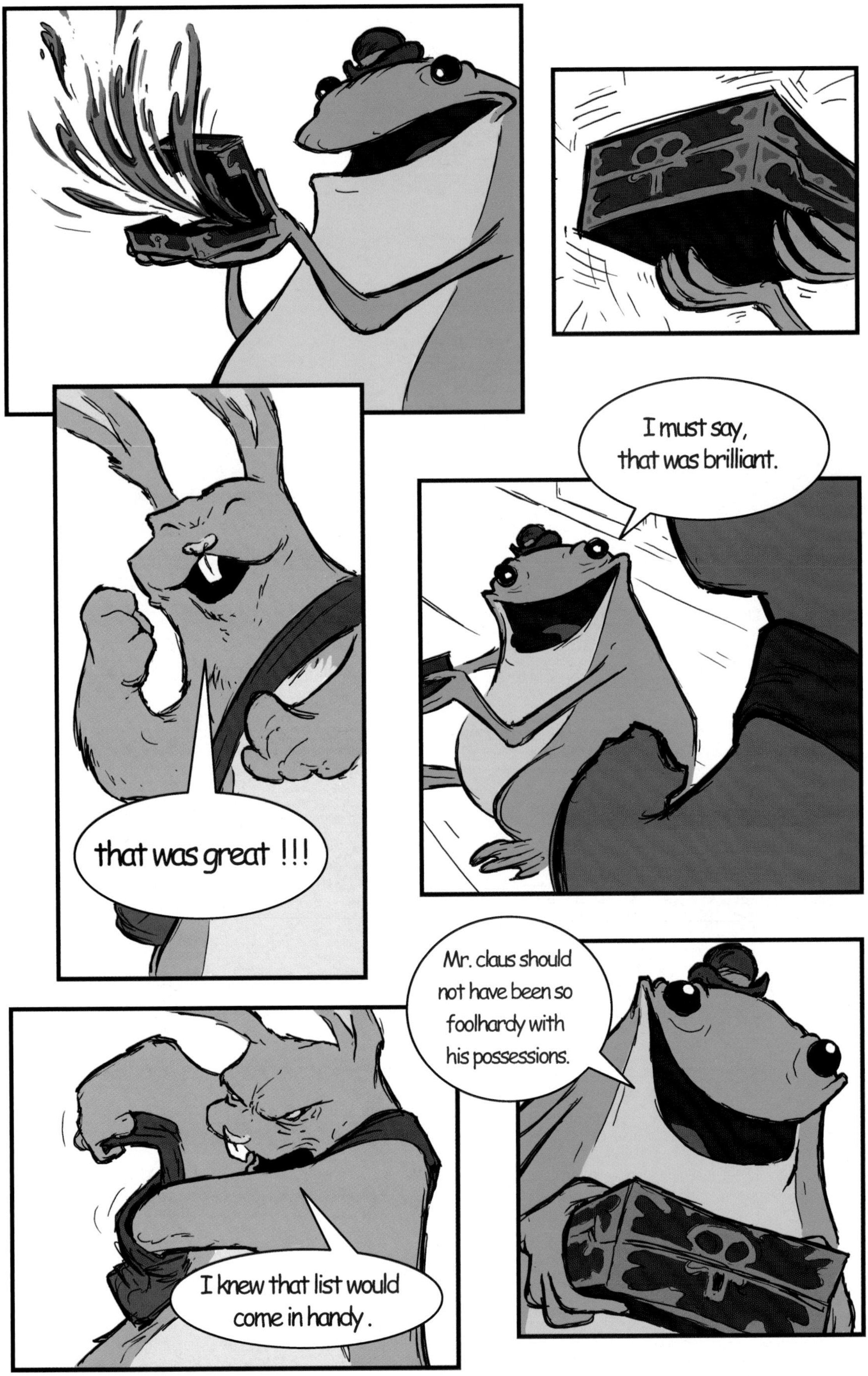
that was great !!!
I must say,
that was brilliant.
Mr. claus should
not have been so
foolhardy with
his possessions.
I knew that list would
come in handy.

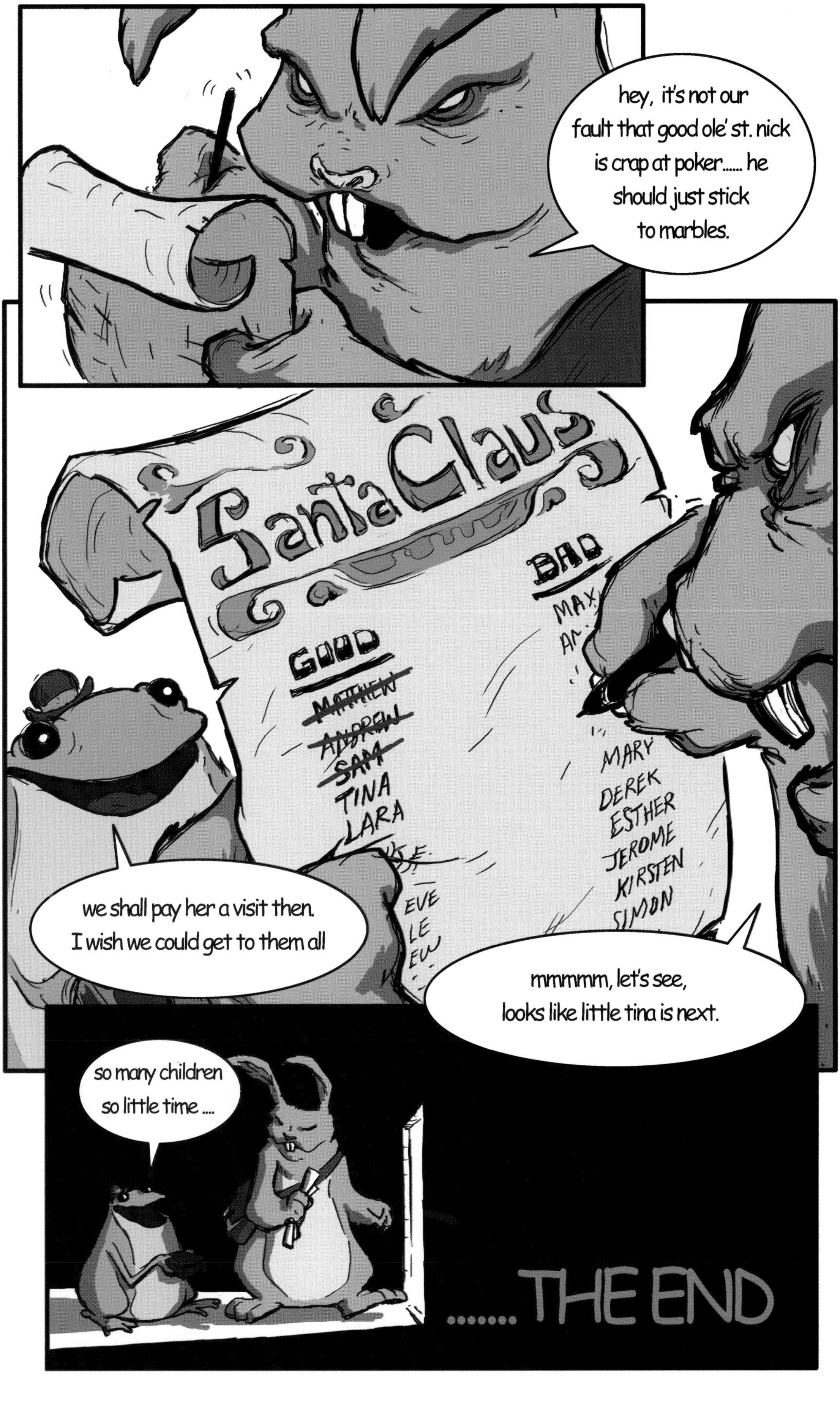

hey, it's not our fault that good ole' st. nick is crap at poker...... he should just stick to marbles.
Santa Claus
BAD
MAX
GOOD
MATTHEW
ANDREW
SAM
TINA
LARA
MARY
DEREK
ESTHER
JEROME
KIRSTEN
SIMON
EVE
we shall pay her a visit then. I wish we could get to them all
mmmmm, let's see, looks like little tina is next.
so many children so little time ....
.... THE END

GUEST GALLERY

Max Brace
Sanjay Patel
Simon Dunsdon
Sam Hiti
Ronnie Del Carmen
James S. Baker

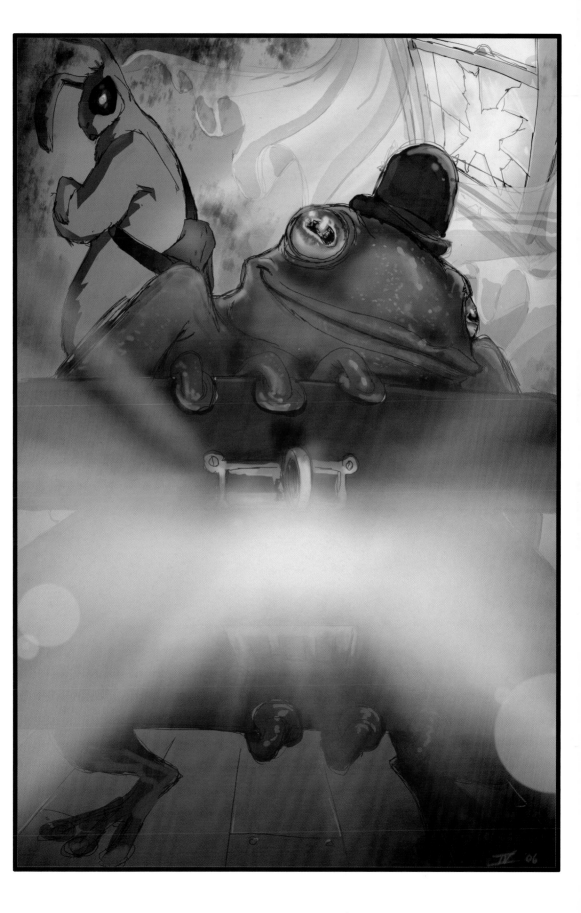

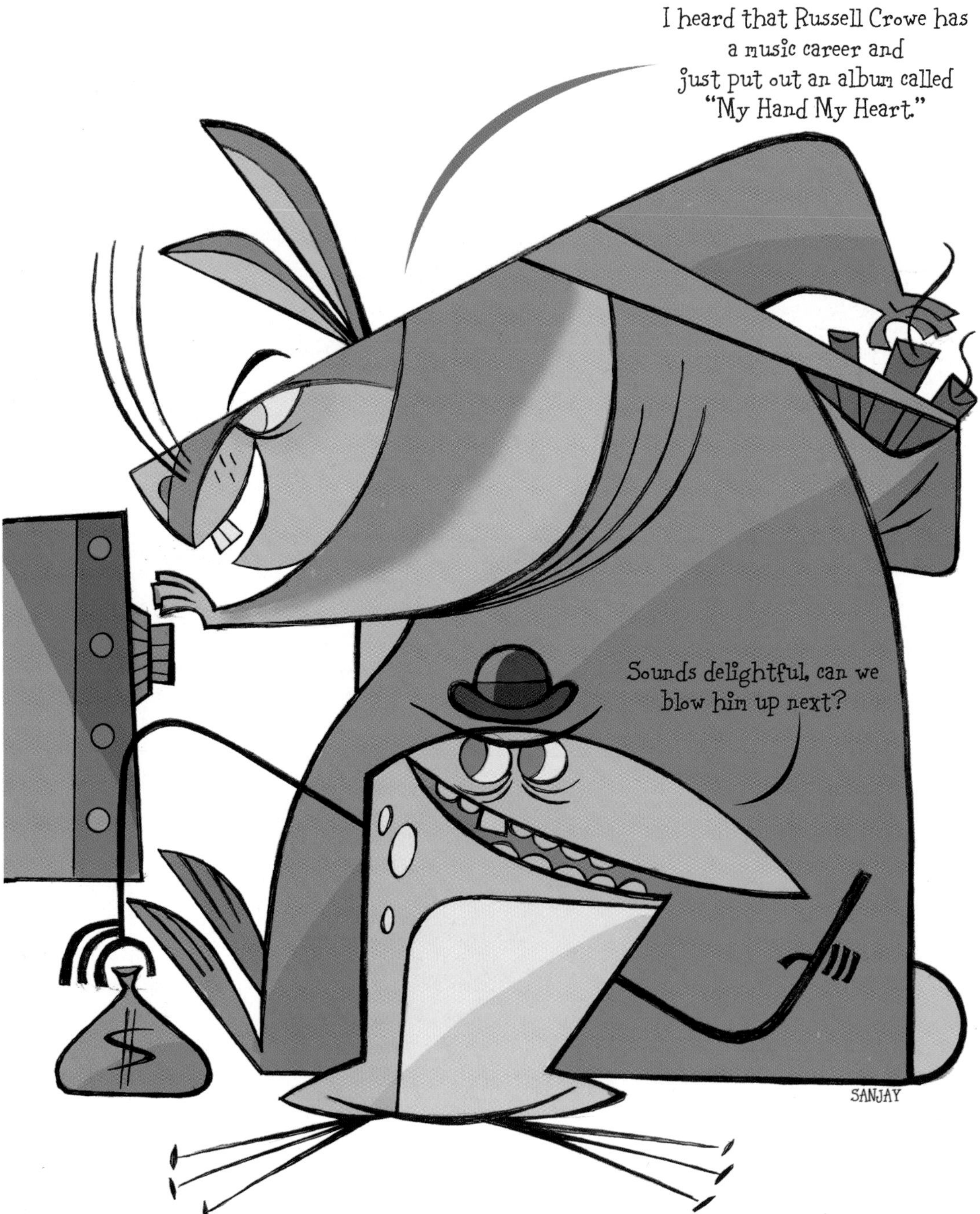
I heard that Russell Crowe has a music career and just put out an album called "My Hand My Heart."
Sounds delightful, can we blow him up next?
SANJAY

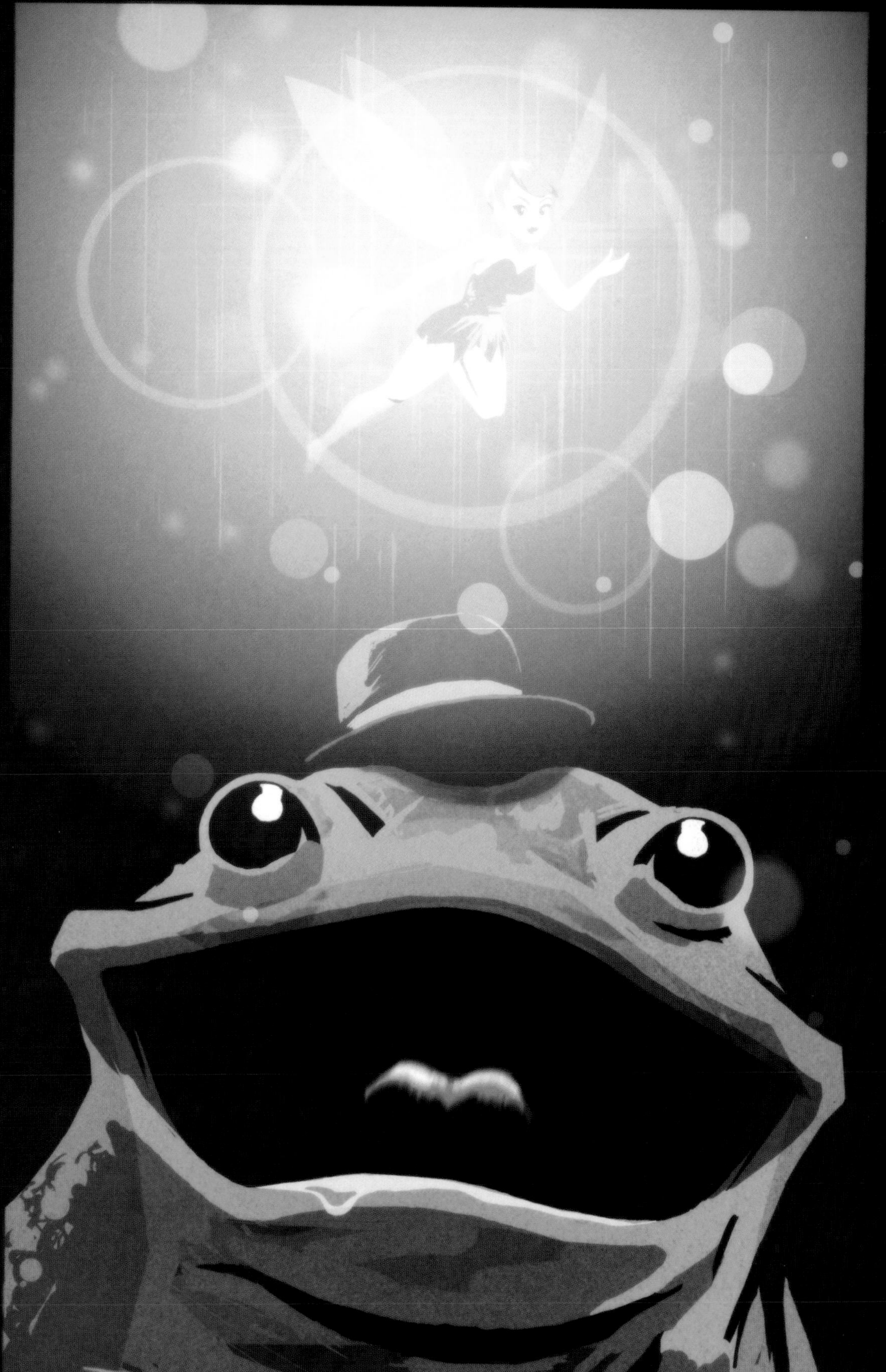

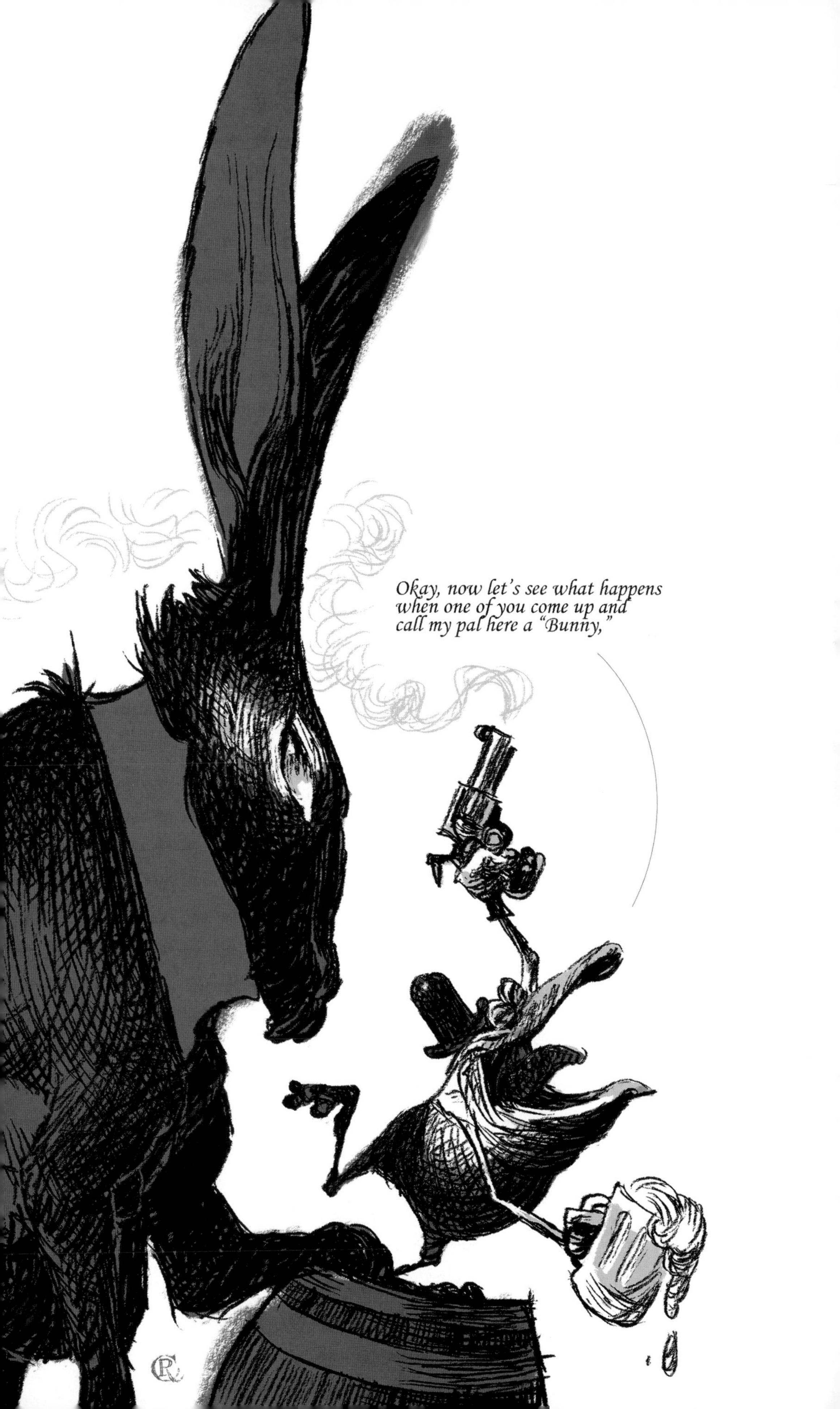

Okay, now let's see what happens when one of you come up and call my pal here a "Bunny,"

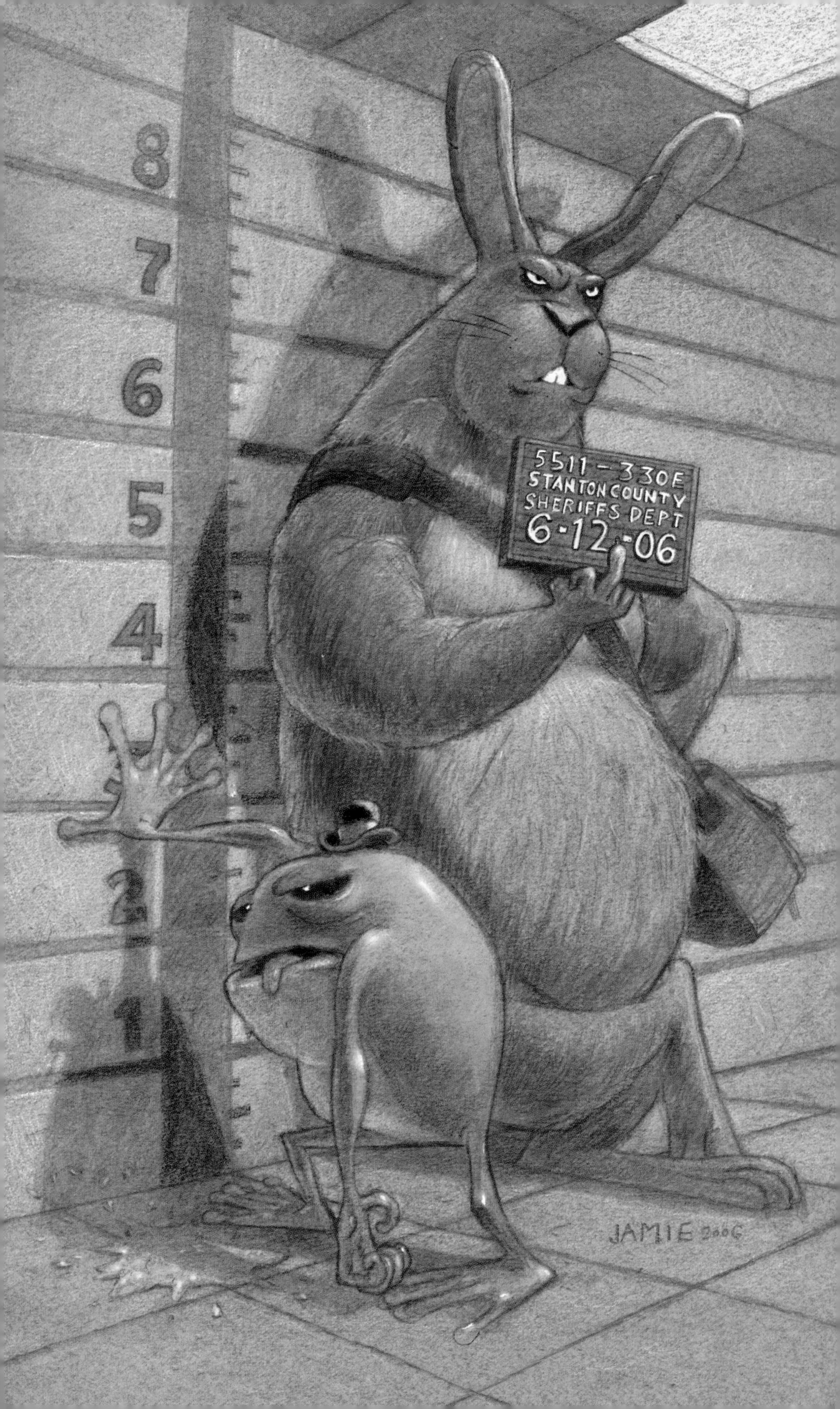

8
7
6
5
4
2
1
5511 - 330E
STANTON COUNTY
SHERIFFS DEPT
6-12-06
JAMIE 2006

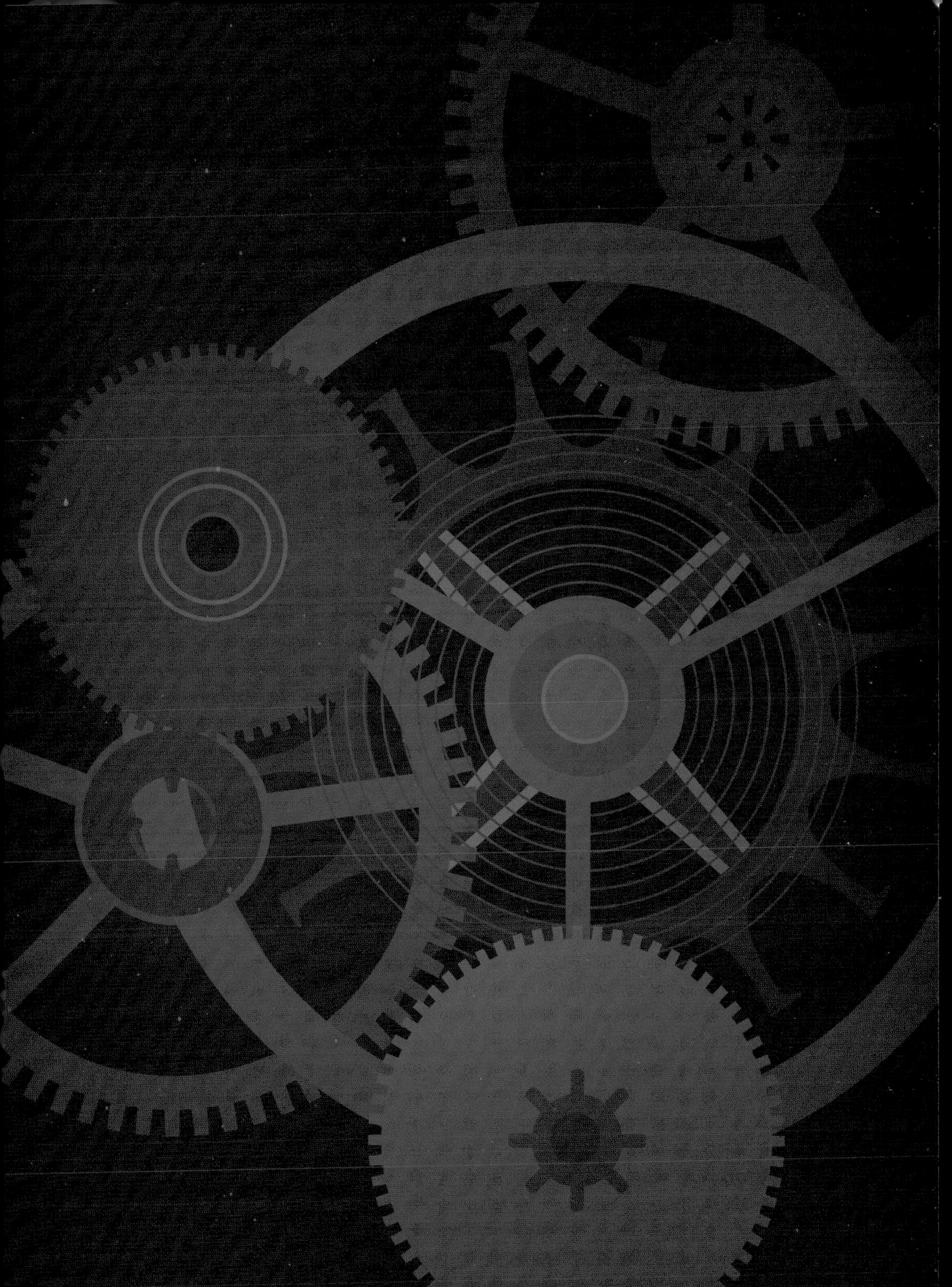

SANJAY PATEL

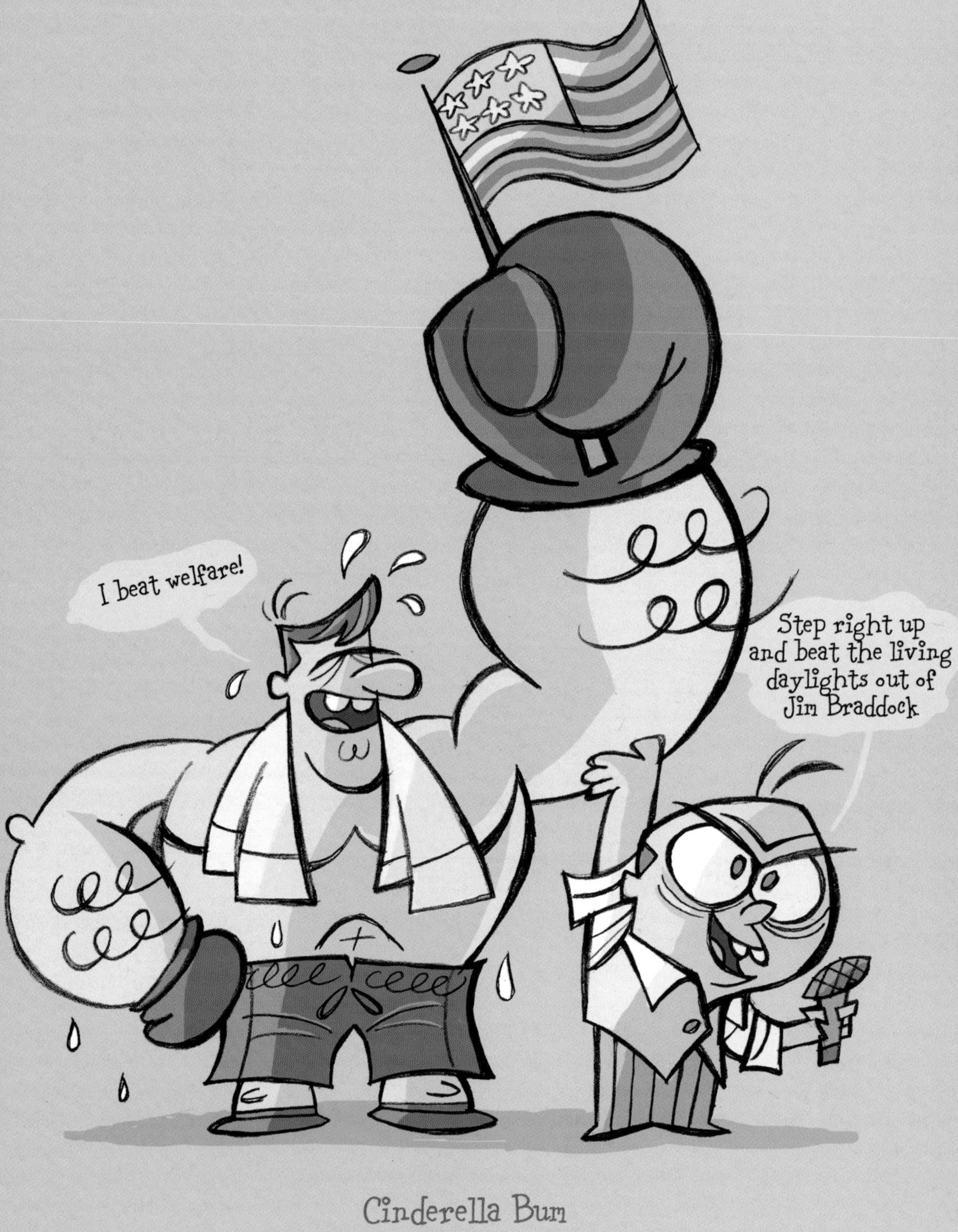
I beat welfare!
Step right up and beat the living daylights out of Jim Braddock

Cinderella Bum

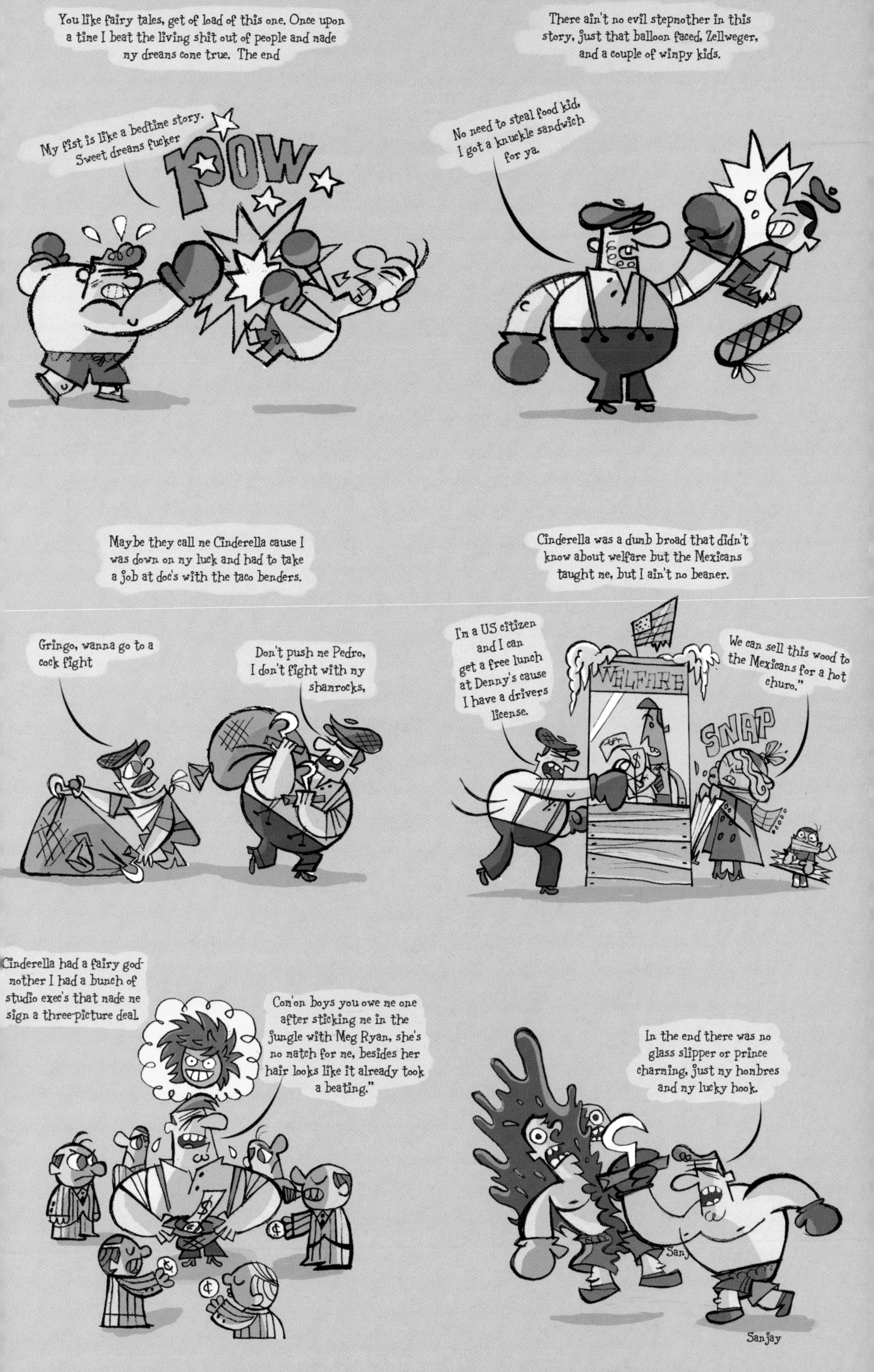

You like fairy tales, get of load of this one. Once upon a time I beat the living shit out of people and made my dreams come true. The end
My fist is like a bedtime story. Sweet dreams fucker
POW
There ain't no evil stepmother in this story, just that balloon faced, Zellweger, and a couple of wimpy kids.
No need to steal food kid, I got a knuckle sandwich for ya.
Maybe they call me Cinderella cause I was down on my luck and had to take a job at doc's with the taco benders.
Gringo, wanna go to a cock fight
Don't push me Pedro, I don't fight with my shamrocks,
Cinderella was a dumb broad that didn't know about welfare but the Mexicans taught me, but I ain't no beaner.
I'm a US citizen and I can get a free lunch at Denny's cause I have a drivers license.
WELFARE
SNAP
We can sell this wood to the Mexicans for a hot churo."
Cinderella had a fairy godmother I had a bunch of studio exec's that made me sign a three-picture deal.
Com'on boys you owe me one after sticking me in the jungle with Meg Ryan, she's no match for me, besides her hair looks like it already took a beating."
In the end there was no glass slipper or prince charming, just my hombres and my lucky hook.
Sanjay

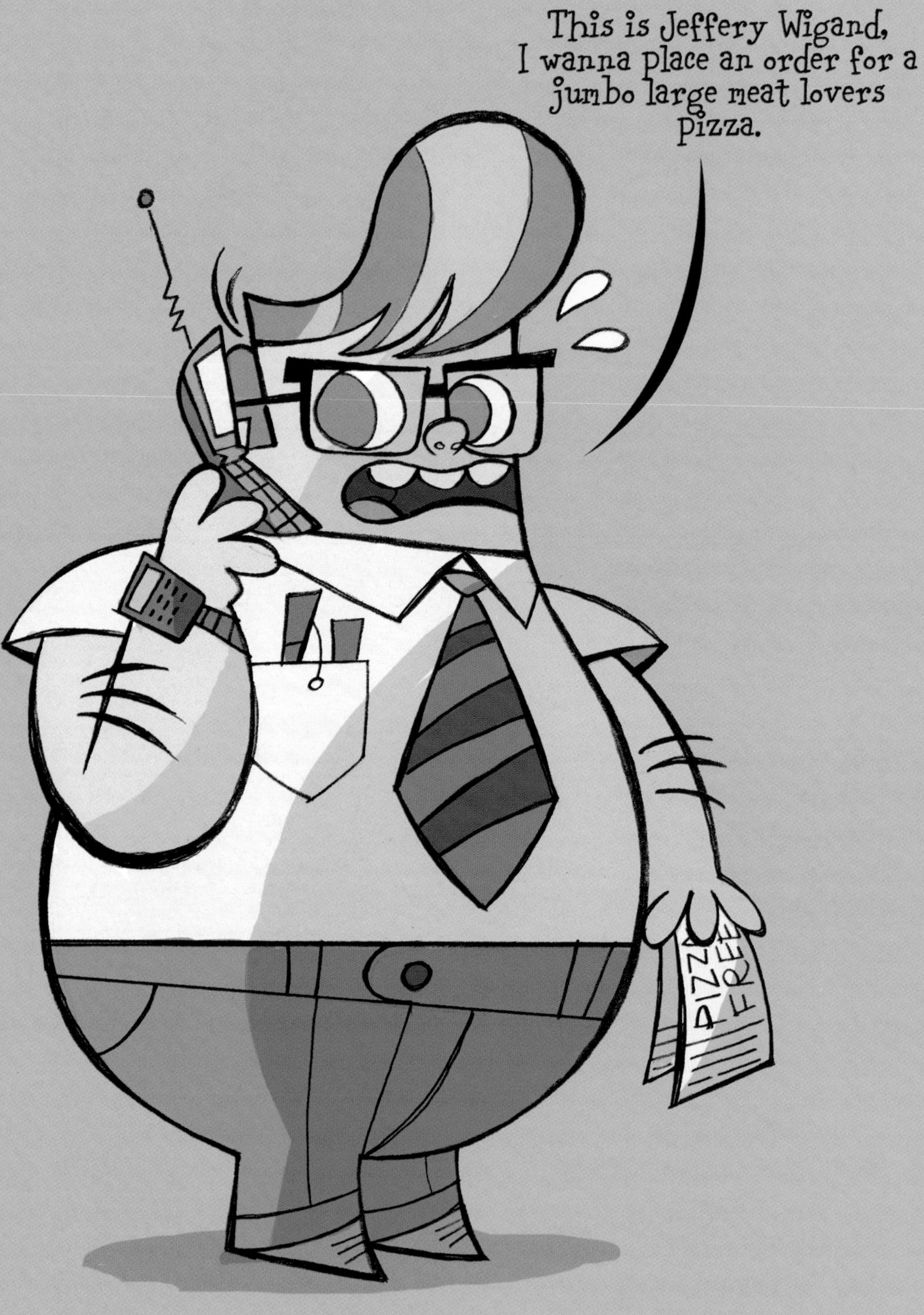
This is Jeffery Wigand, I wanna place an order for a jumbo large meat lovers pizza.

The Outsider

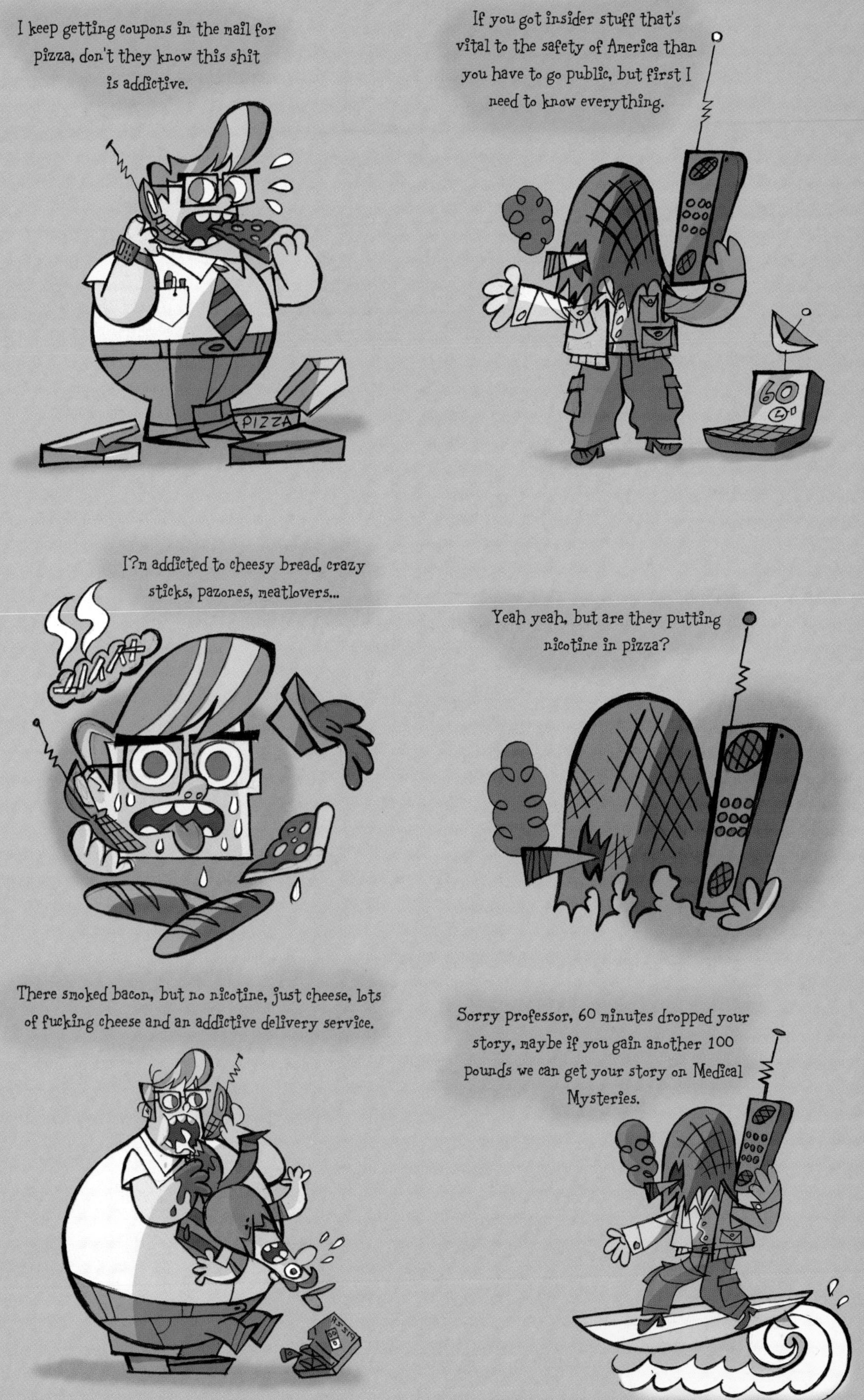

I keep getting coupons in the mail for pizza, don't they know this shit is addictive.
PIZZA
If you got insider stuff that's vital to the safety of America than you have to go public, but first I need to know everything.
60
I?m addicted to cheesy bread, crazy sticks, pazones, meatlovers...
Yeah yeah, but are they putting nicotine in pizza?
There smoked bacon, but no nicotine, just cheese, lots of fucking cheese and an addictive delivery service.
Sorry professor, 60 minutes dropped your story, maybe if you gain another 100 pounds we can get your story on Medical Mysteries.
Sanjay

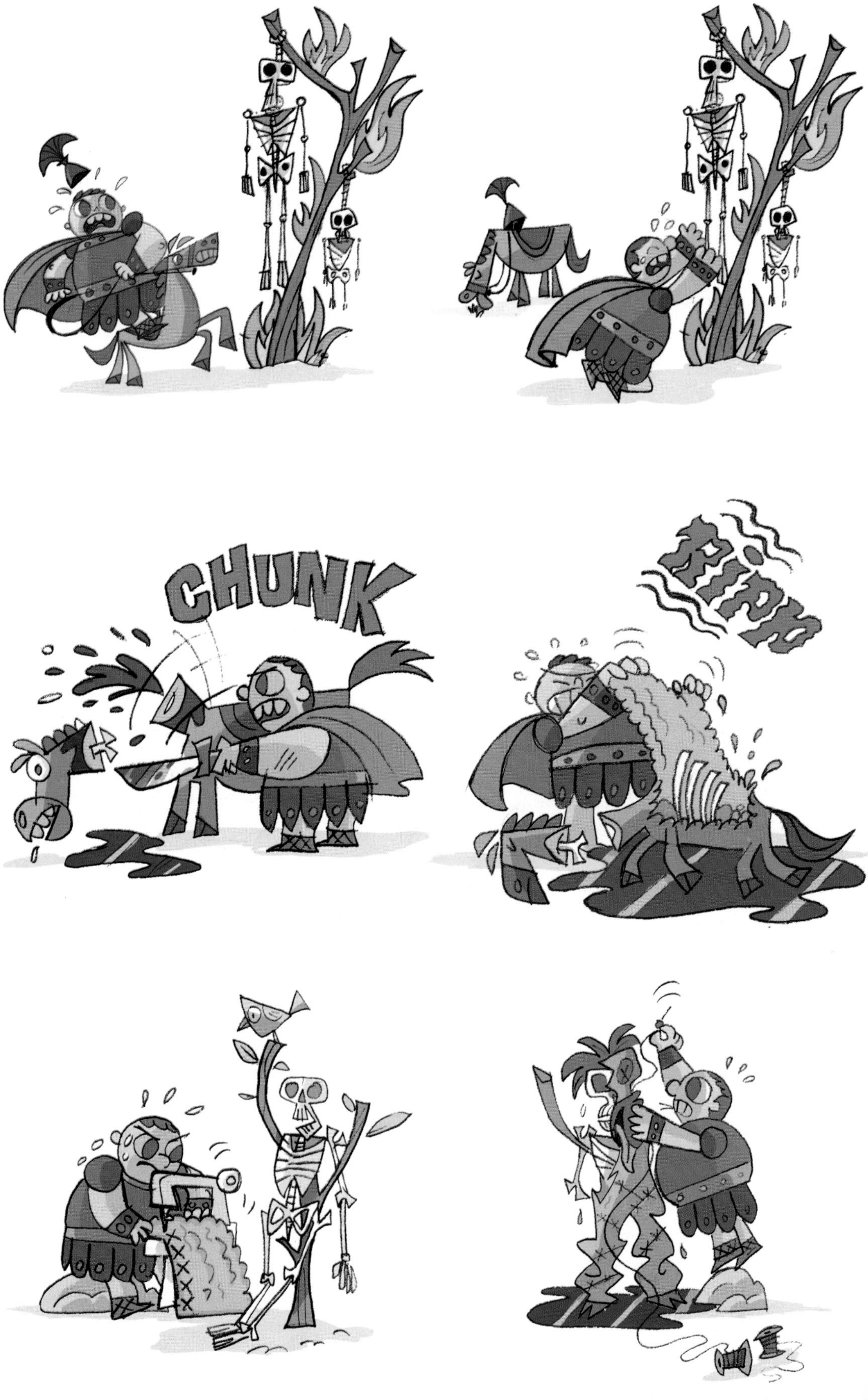
CHUNK
RIPP

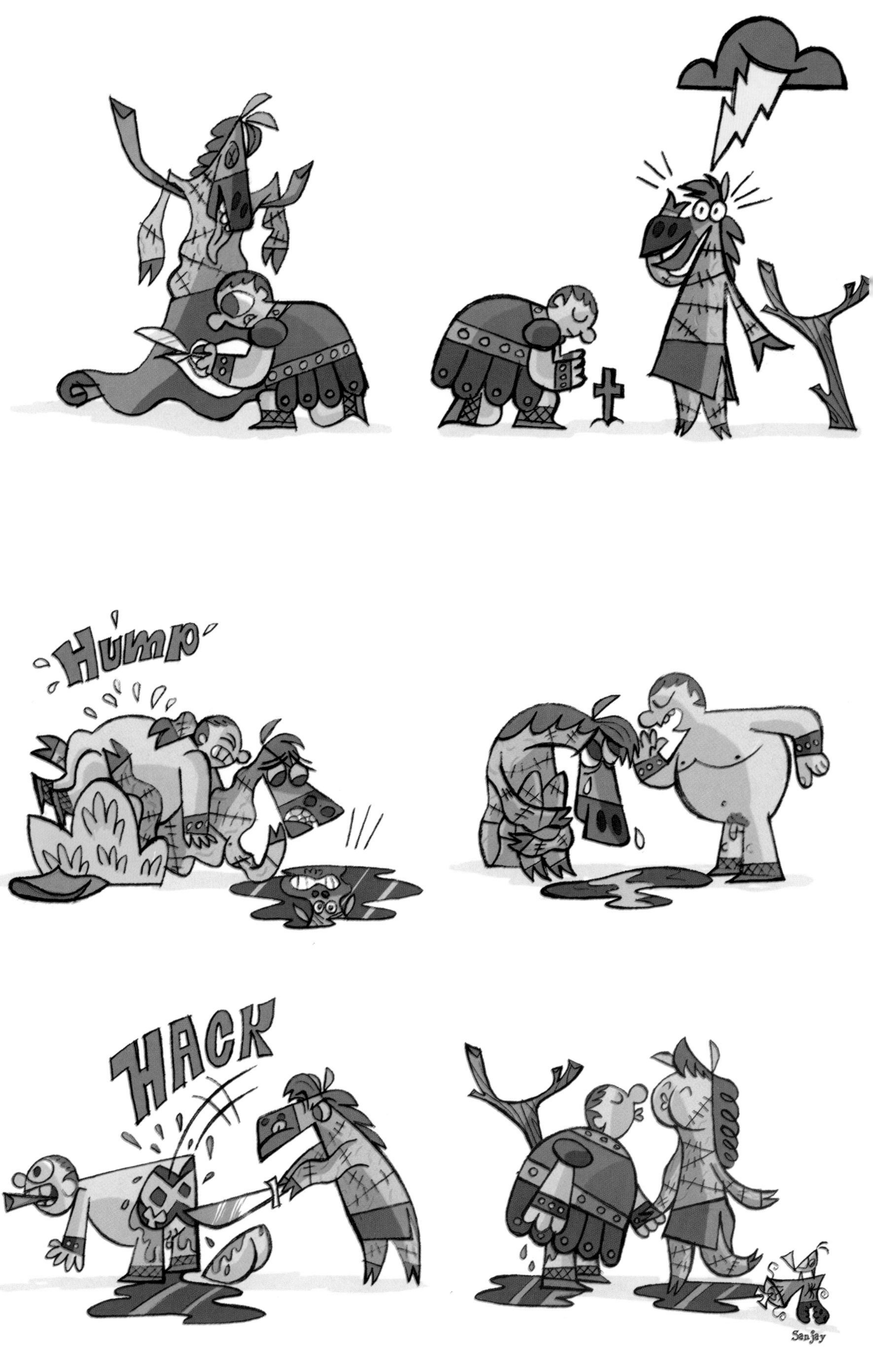
HUMP
HACK
Sanjay

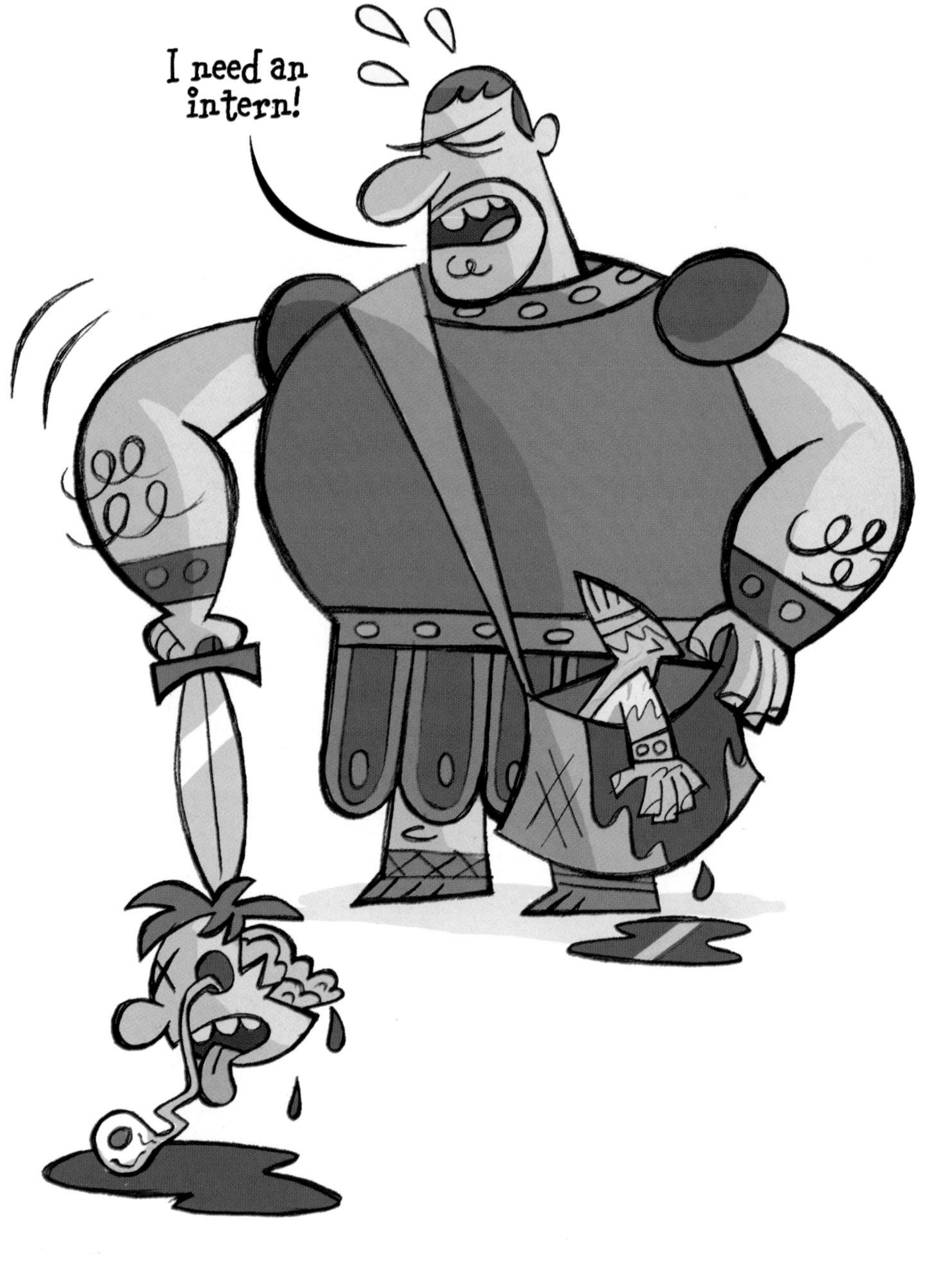
I need an intern!

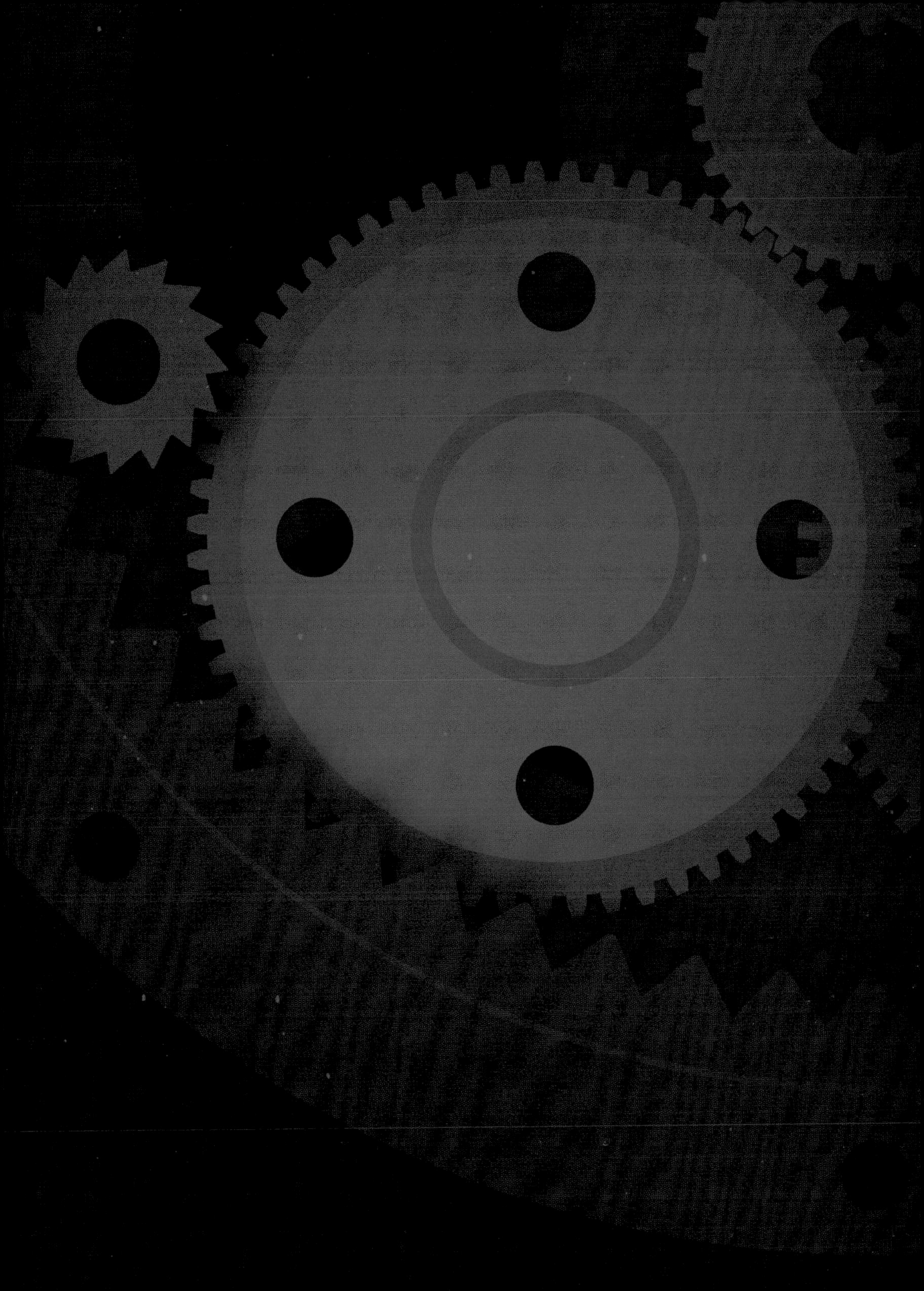

TED MATHOT

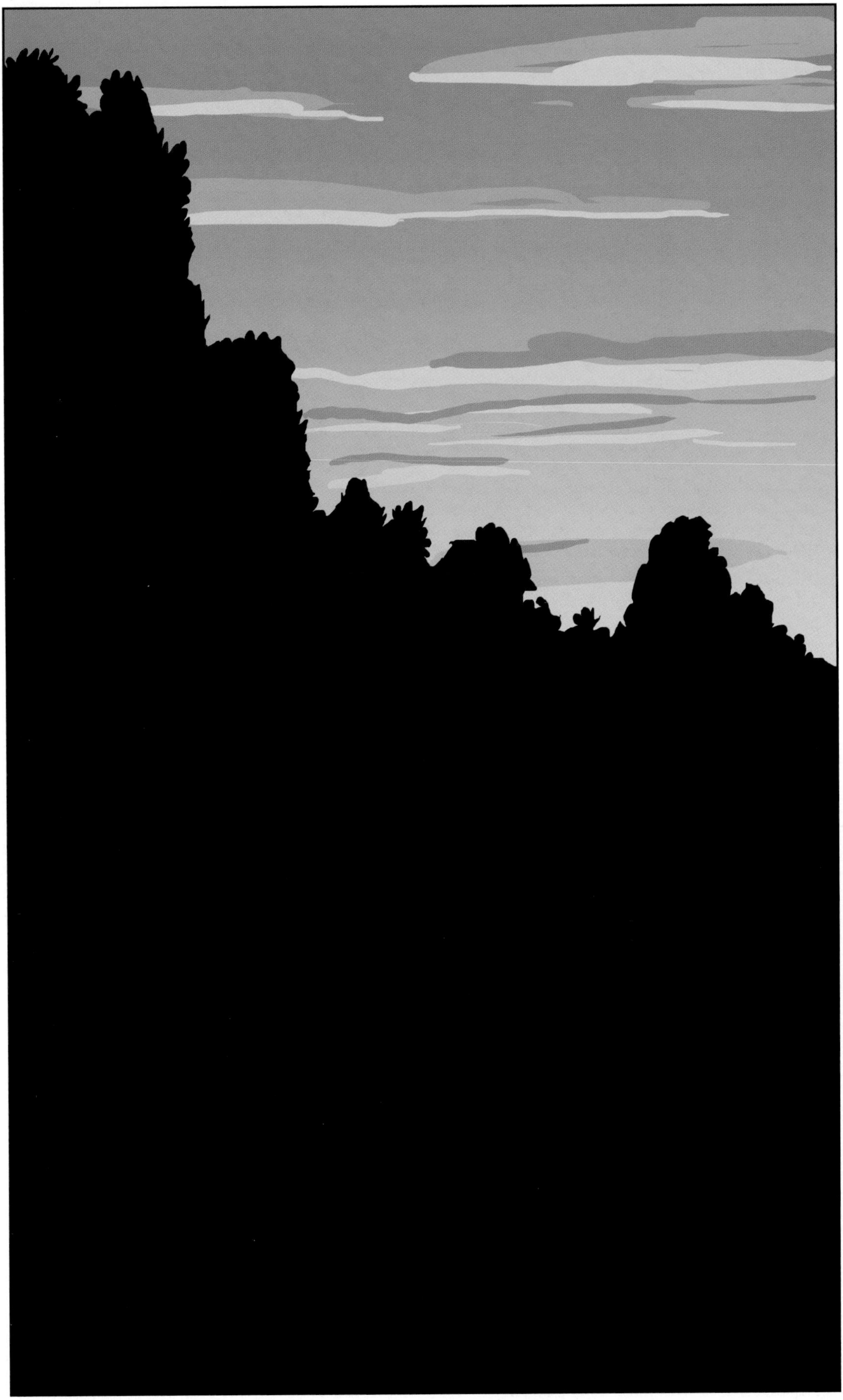

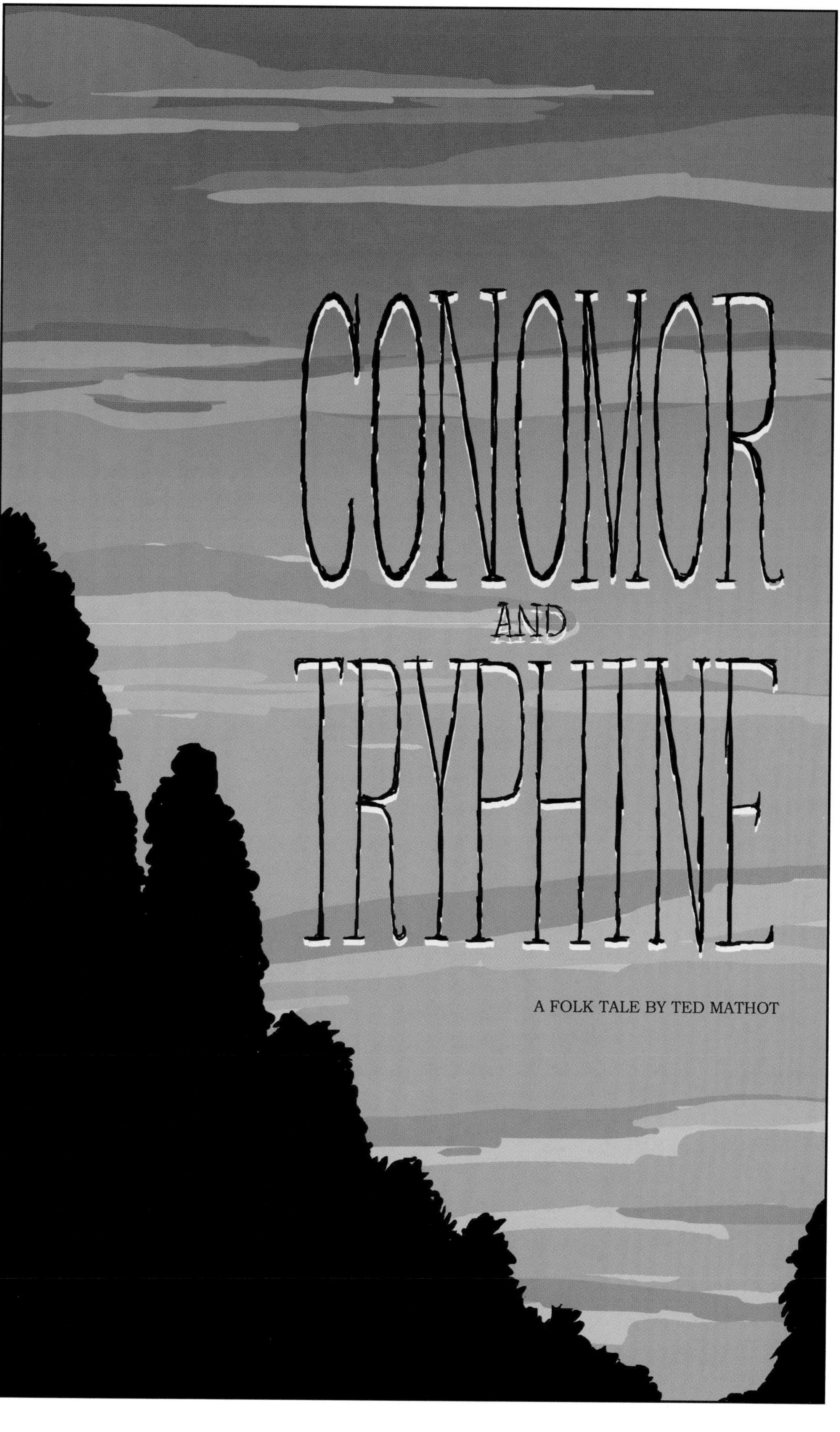
CONOMOR
AND
TRYPHINE
A FOLK TALE BY TED MATHOT

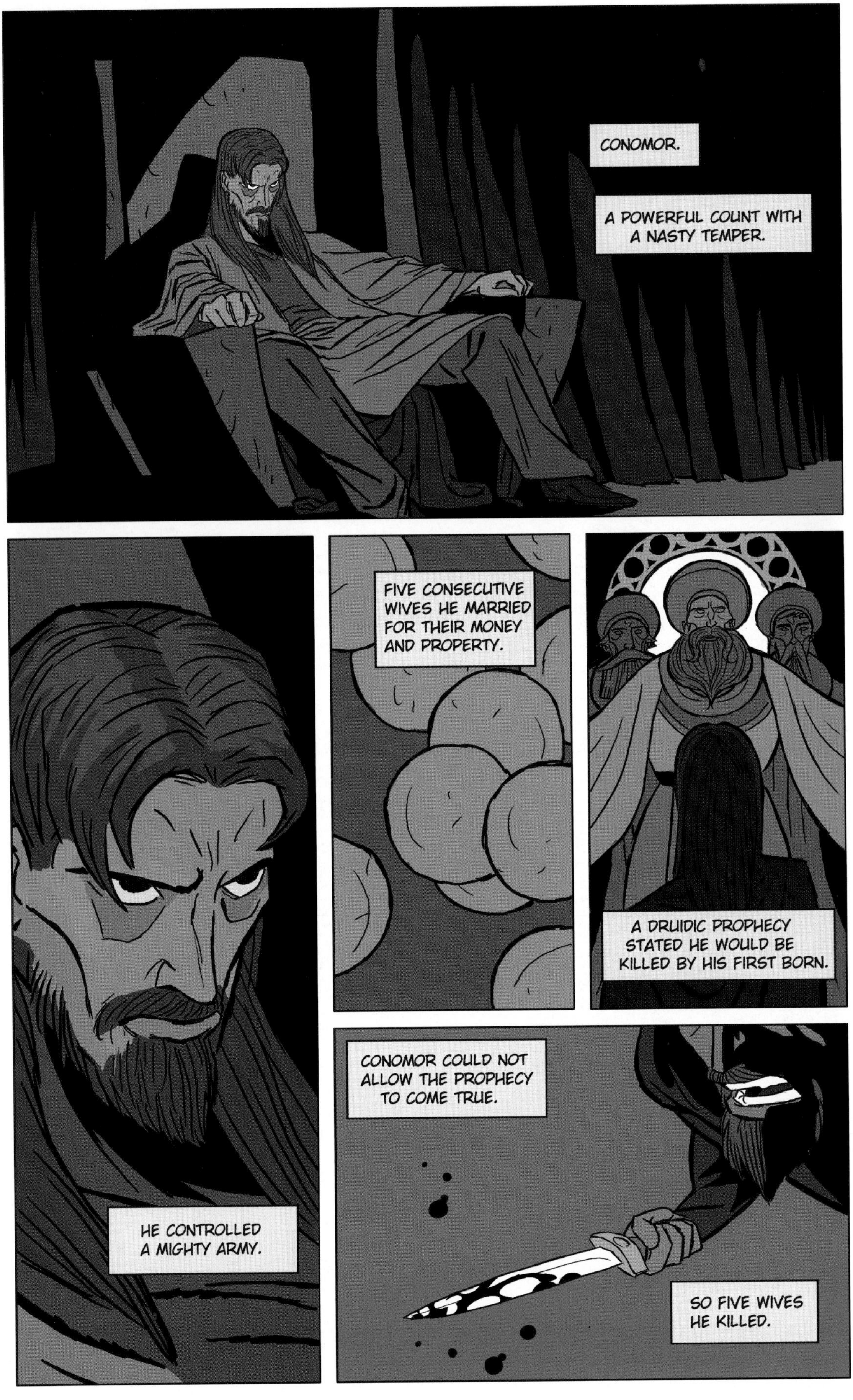
CONOMOR.
A POWERFUL COUNT WITH A NASTY TEMPER.
HE CONTROLLED A MIGHTY ARMY.
FIVE CONSECUTIVE WIVES HE MARRIED FOR THEIR MONEY AND PROPERTY.
A DRUIDIC PROPHECY STATED HE WOULD BE KILLED BY HIS FIRST BORN.
CONOMOR COULD NOT ALLOW THE PROPHECY TO COME TRUE.
SO FIVE WIVES HE KILLED.

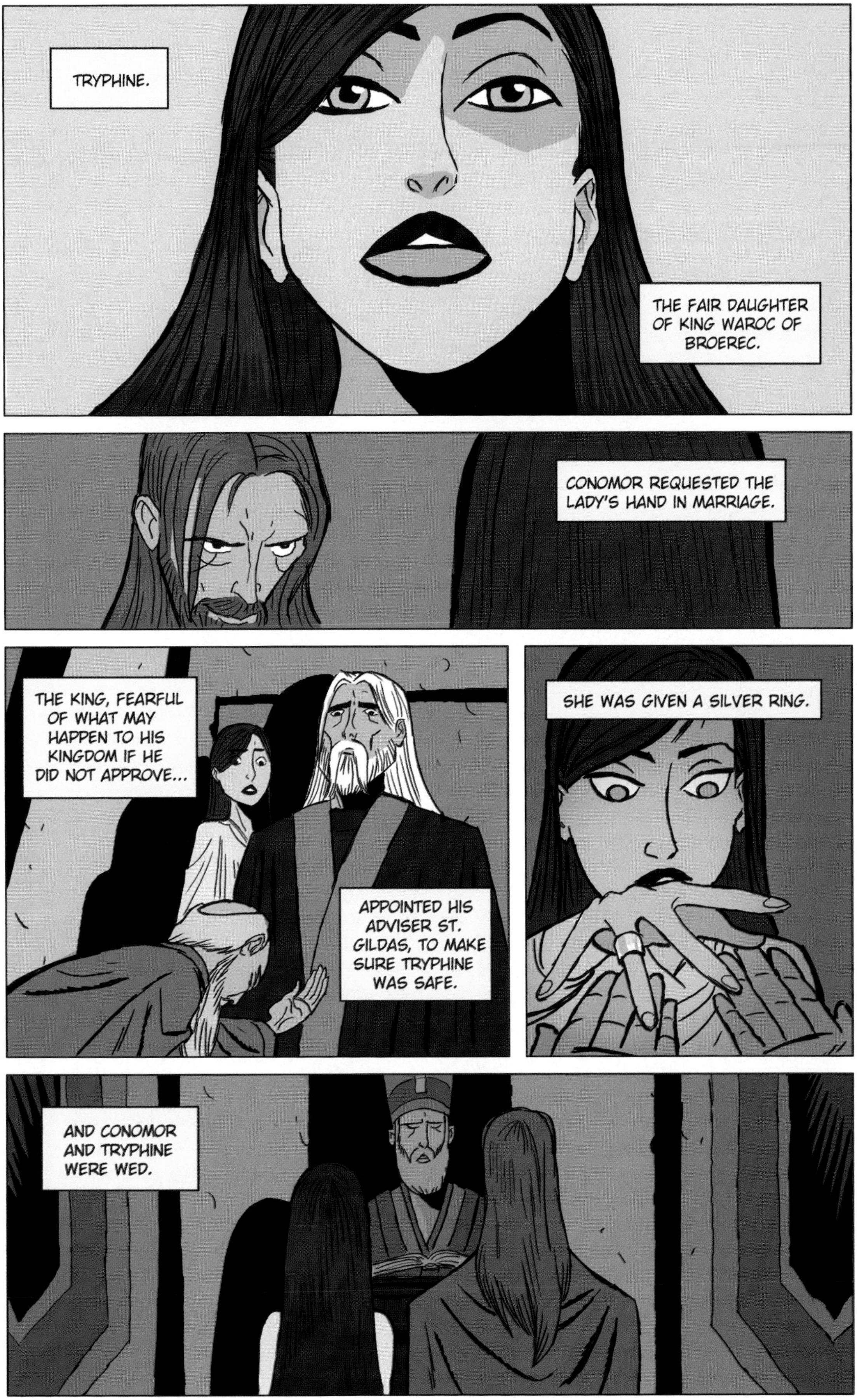
TRYPHINE.
THE FAIR DAUGHTER OF KING WAROC OF BROEREC.
CONOMOR REQUESTED THE LADY'S HAND IN MARRIAGE.
THE KING, FEARFUL OF WHAT MAY HAPPEN TO HIS KINGDOM IF HE DID NOT APPROVE...
APPOINTED HIS ADVISER ST. GILDAS, TO MAKE SURE TRYPHINE WAS SAFE.
SHE WAS GIVEN A SILVER RING.
AND CONOMOR AND TRYPHINE WERE WED.

FOR TWO YEARS, THE COUPLE LIVED A NORMAL, ALBEIT SPIRITLESS EXISTENCE.

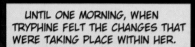

UNTIL ONE MORNING, WHEN TRYPHINE FELT THE CHANGES THAT WERE TAKING PLACE WITHIN HER.

CONOMOR WAS NO STRANGER TO THIS.

THEN TRYPHINE NOTICED SOMETHING THAT SHE HAD BEEN WARNED ABOUT.

THE RING BESTOWED BY ST. GILDAS HAD TURNED BLACK.

SHE WAS IN GRAVE DANGER.

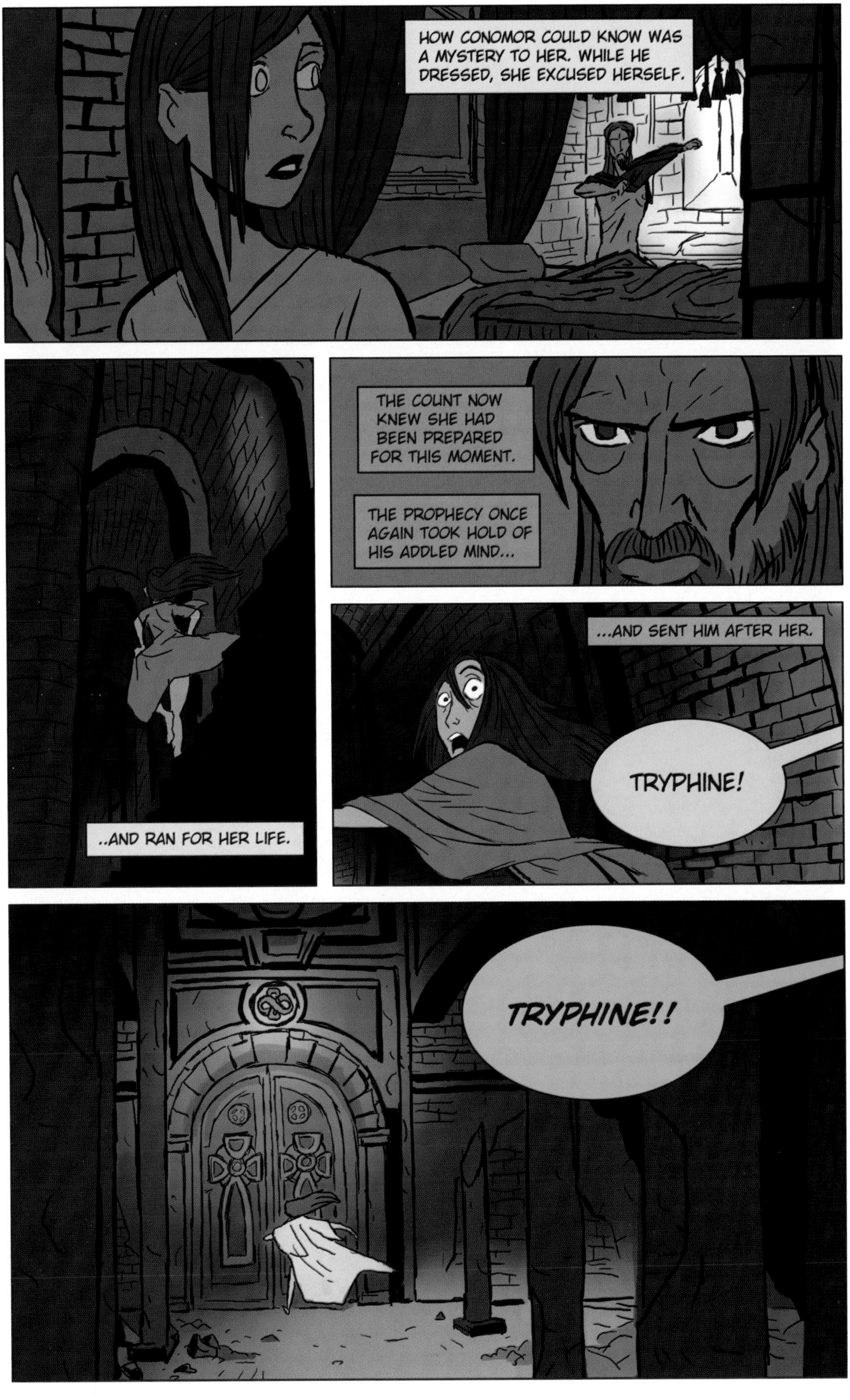
HOW CONOMOR COULD KNOW WAS A MYSTERY TO HER. WHILE HE DRESSED, SHE EXCUSED HERSELF.
..AND RAN FOR HER LIFE.
THE COUNT NOW KNEW SHE HAD BEEN PREPARED FOR THIS MOMENT.
THE PROPHECY ONCE AGAIN TOOK HOLD OF HIS ADDLED MIND...
...AND SENT HIM AFTER HER.
TRYPHINE!
TRYPHINE!!

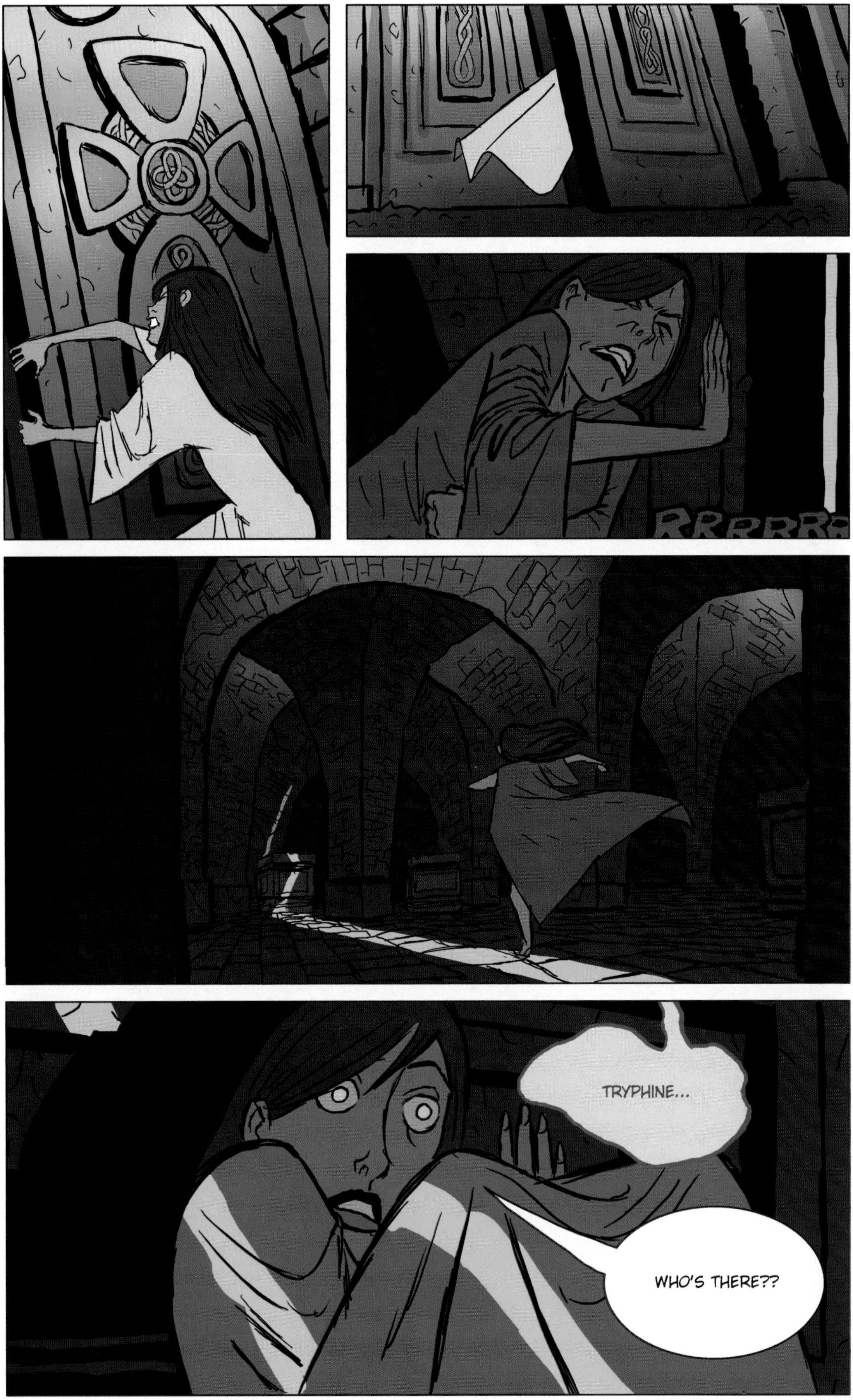
RRRRRR
TRYPHINE...
WHO'S THERE??

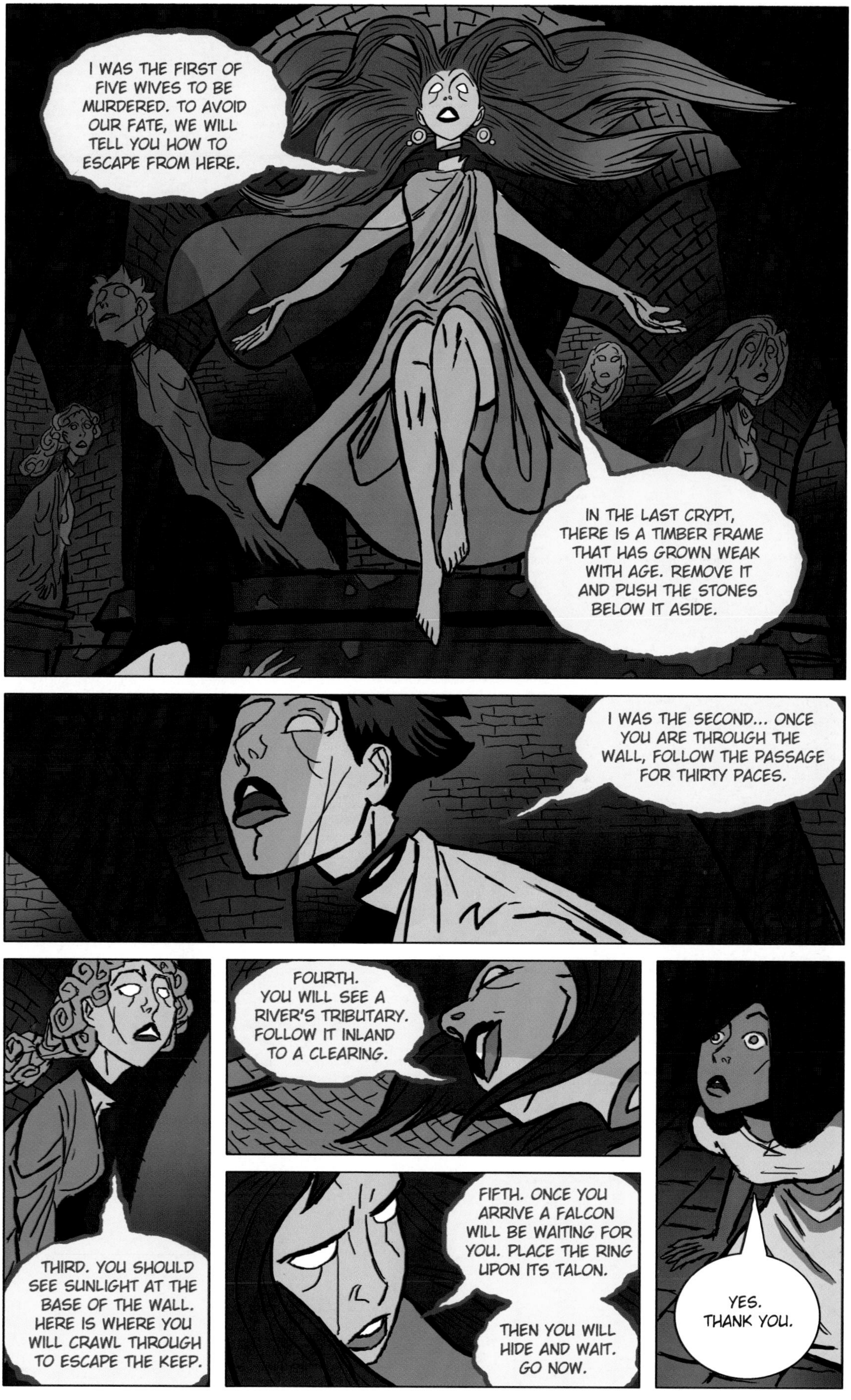
I WAS THE FIRST OF FIVE WIVES TO BE MURDERED. TO AVOID OUR FATE, WE WILL TELL YOU HOW TO ESCAPE FROM HERE.
IN THE LAST CRYPT, THERE IS A TIMBER FRAME THAT HAS GROWN WEAK WITH AGE. REMOVE IT AND PUSH THE STONES BELOW IT ASIDE.
I WAS THE SECOND... ONCE YOU ARE THROUGH THE WALL, FOLLOW THE PASSAGE FOR THIRTY PACES.
THIRD. YOU SHOULD SEE SUNLIGHT AT THE BASE OF THE WALL. HERE IS WHERE YOU WILL CRAWL THROUGH TO ESCAPE THE KEEP.
FOURTH. YOU WILL SEE A RIVER'S TRIBUTARY. FOLLOW IT INLAND TO A CLEARING.
FIFTH. ONCE YOU ARRIVE A FALCON WILL BE WAITING FOR YOU. PLACE THE RING UPON ITS TALON.
THEN YOU WILL HIDE AND WAIT. GO NOW.
YES. THANK YOU.

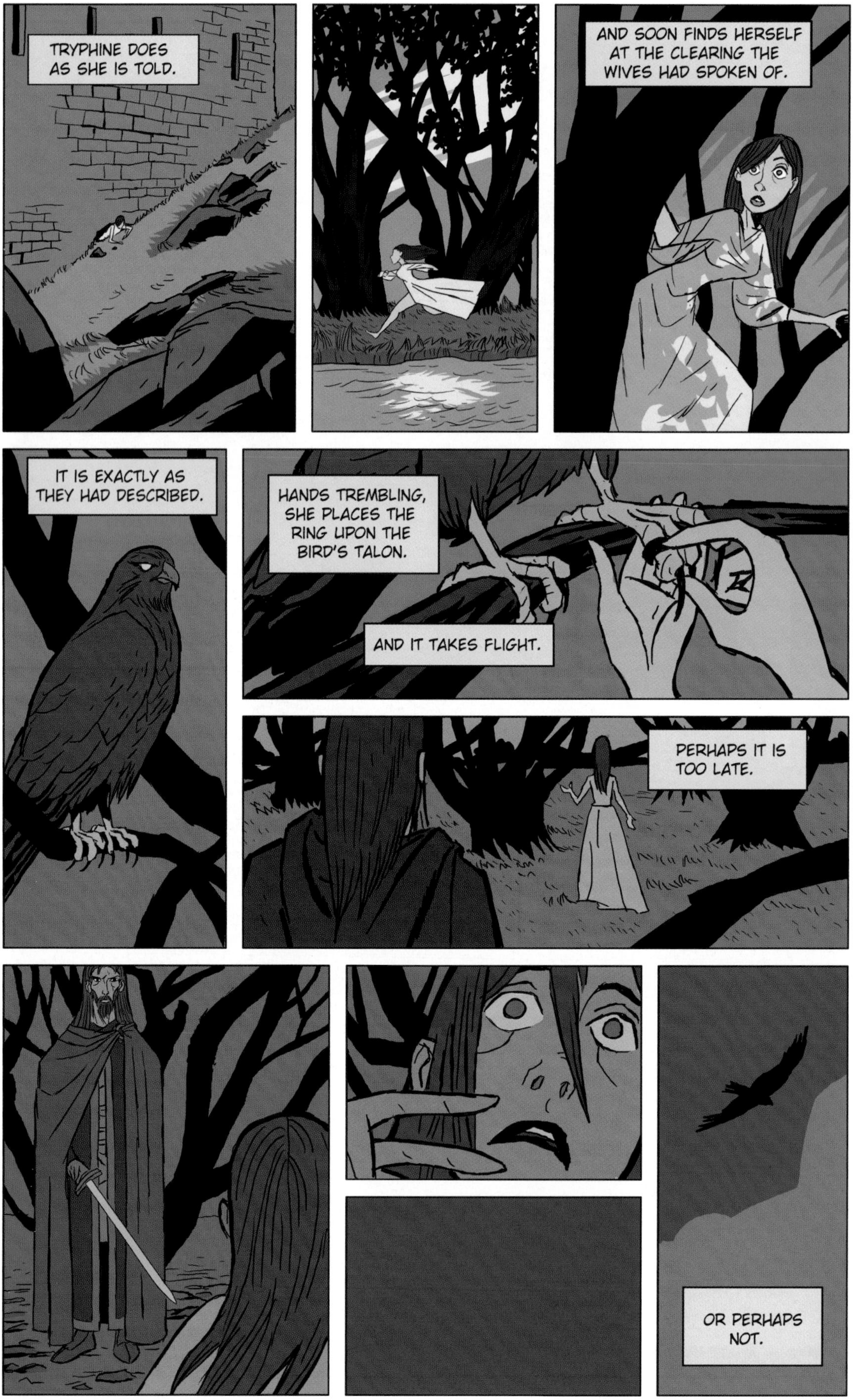
TRYPHINE DOES AS SHE IS TOLD.
AND SOON FINDS HERSELF AT THE CLEARING THE WIVES HAD SPOKEN OF.
IT IS EXACTLY AS THEY HAD DESCRIBED.
HANDS TREMBLING, SHE PLACES THE RING UPON THE BIRD'S TALON.
AND IT TAKES FLIGHT.
PERHAPS IT IS TOO LATE.
OR PERHAPS NOT.

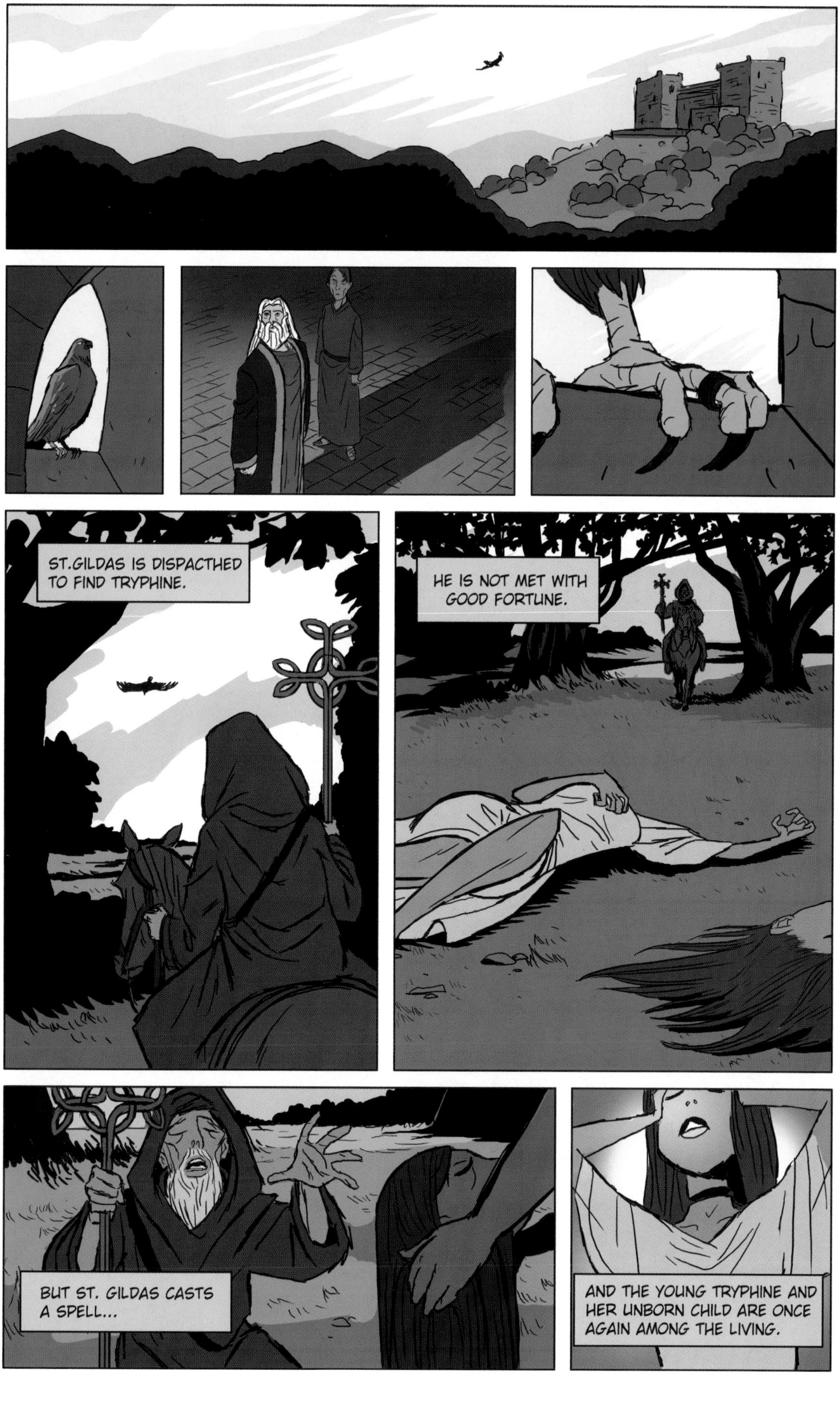
ST.GILDAS IS DISPACTHED TO FIND TRYPHINE.
HE IS NOT MET WITH GOOD FORTUNE.
BUT ST. GILDAS CASTS A SPELL...
AND THE YOUNG TRYPHINE AND HER UNBORN CHILD ARE ONCE AGAIN AMONG THE LIVING.

TRYPHINE WAS RETURNED TO HER FATHER'S CASTLE.

SHE WAS KEPT HIDDEN AND UNDER CLOSE WATCH.

IT WAS THERE THAT SHE BORE AND RAISED A SON.

AFTER HEARING OF THE BIRTH, CONOMOR SEARCHED THE LAND FOR THE BOY.

FOR THREE YEARS HE LOOKED, BEFORE CONCLUDING THAT THE PROPHECY WAS A LIE.

WHEN THE BOY WAS OLD ENOUGH, TRYPHINE TOLD HIM OF HIS FATHER.

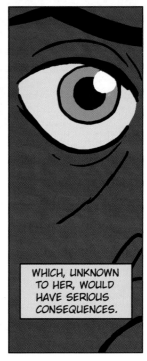

WHICH, UNKNOWN TO HER, WOULD HAVE SERIOUS CONSEQUENCES.

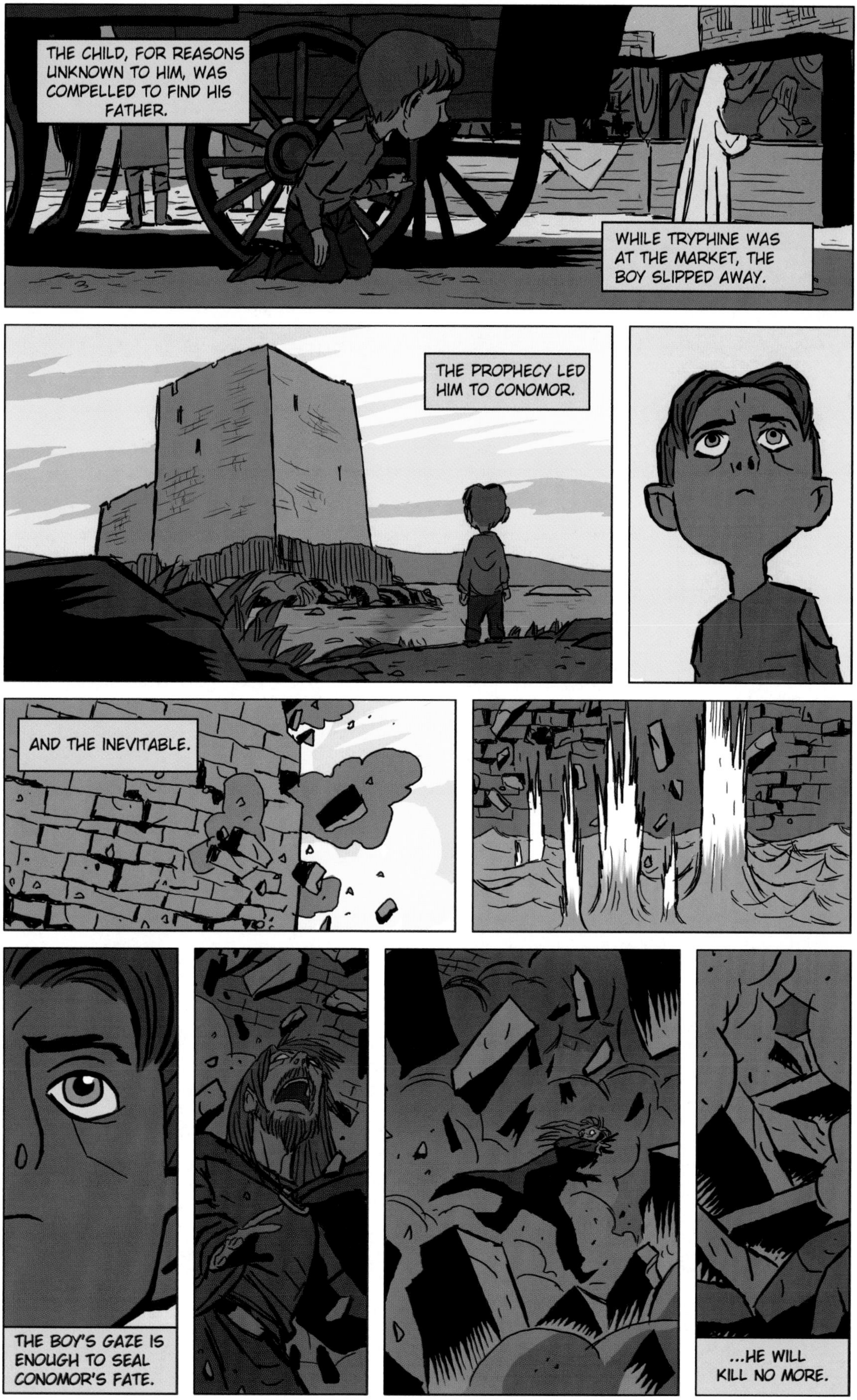
THE CHILD, FOR REASONS UNKNOWN TO HIM, WAS COMPELLED TO FIND HIS FATHER.
WHILE TRYPHINE WAS AT THE MARKET, THE BOY SLIPPED AWAY.
THE PROPHECY LED HIM TO CONOMOR.
AND THE INEVITABLE.
THE BOY'S GAZE IS ENOUGH TO SEAL CONOMOR'S FATE.
...HE WILL KILL NO MORE.

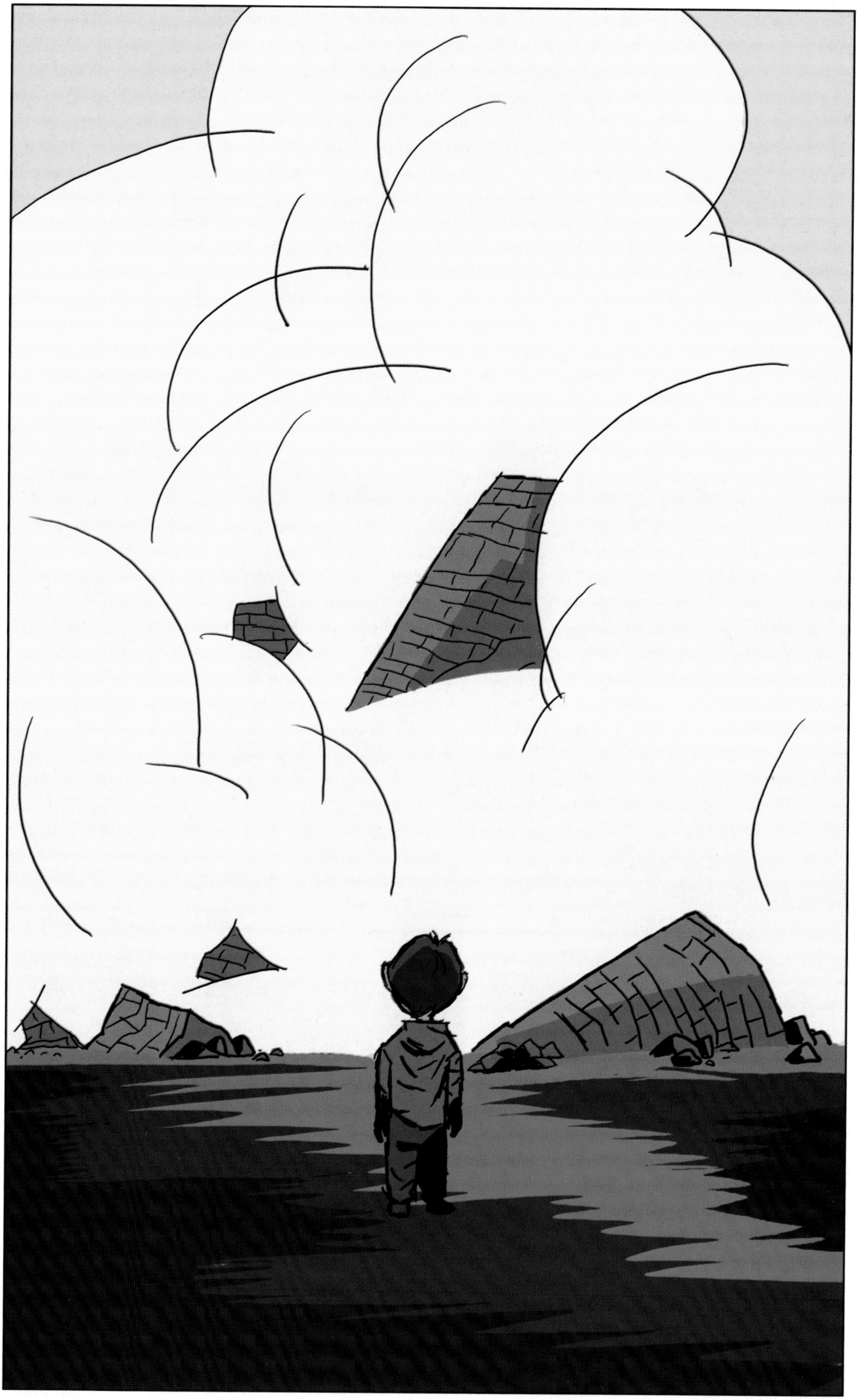

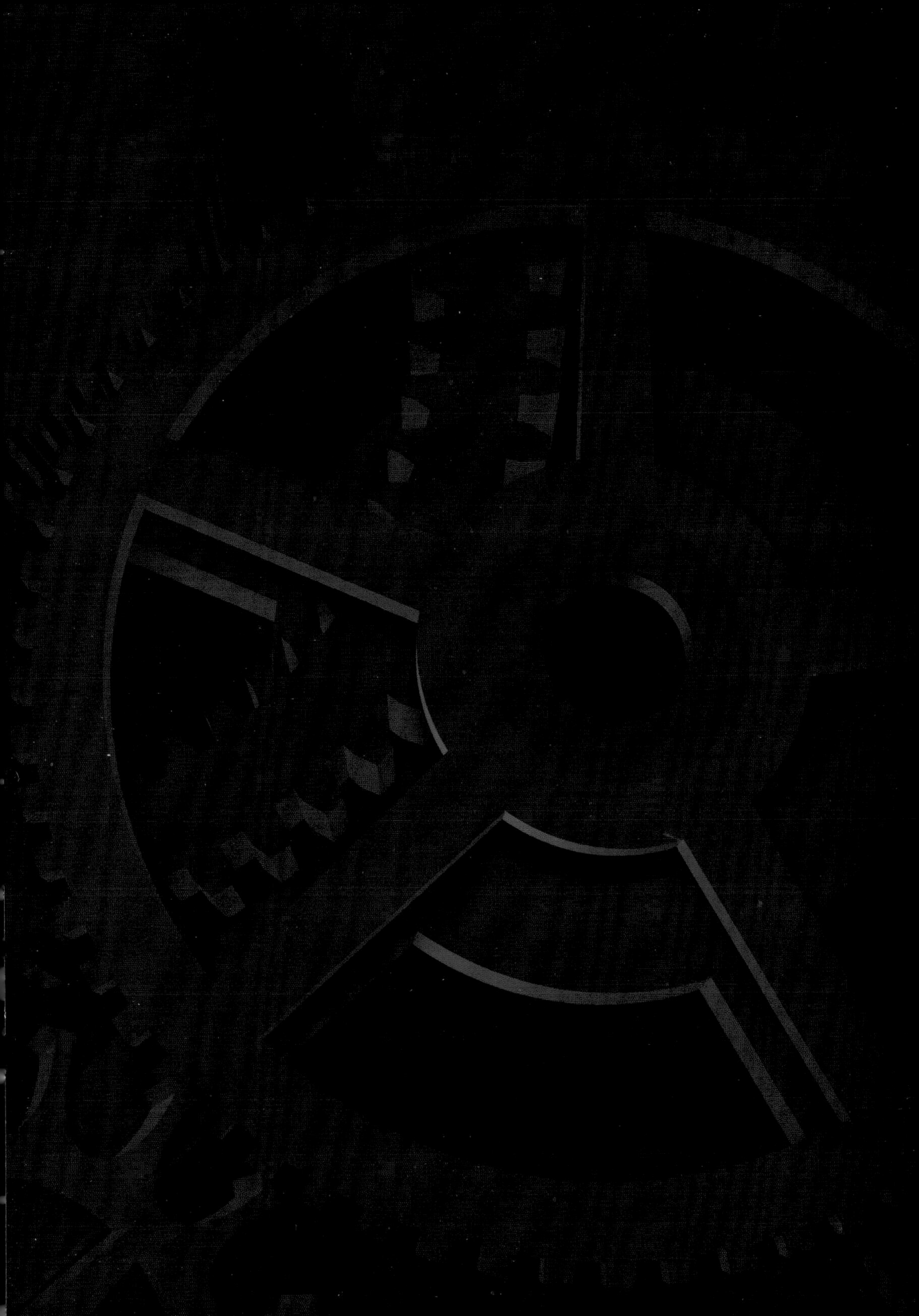

DEREK THOMPSON

eggsucker

derek thompson

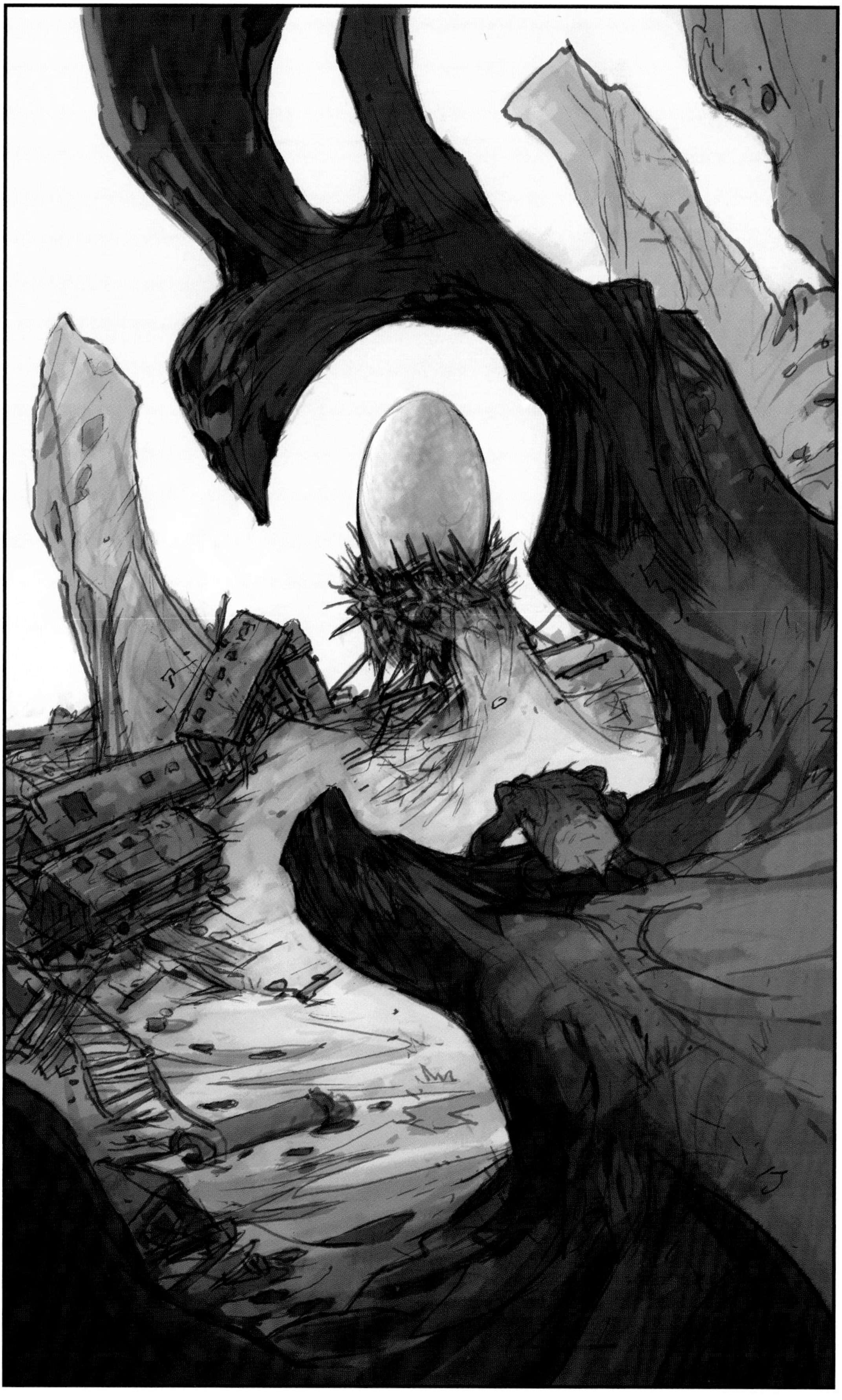

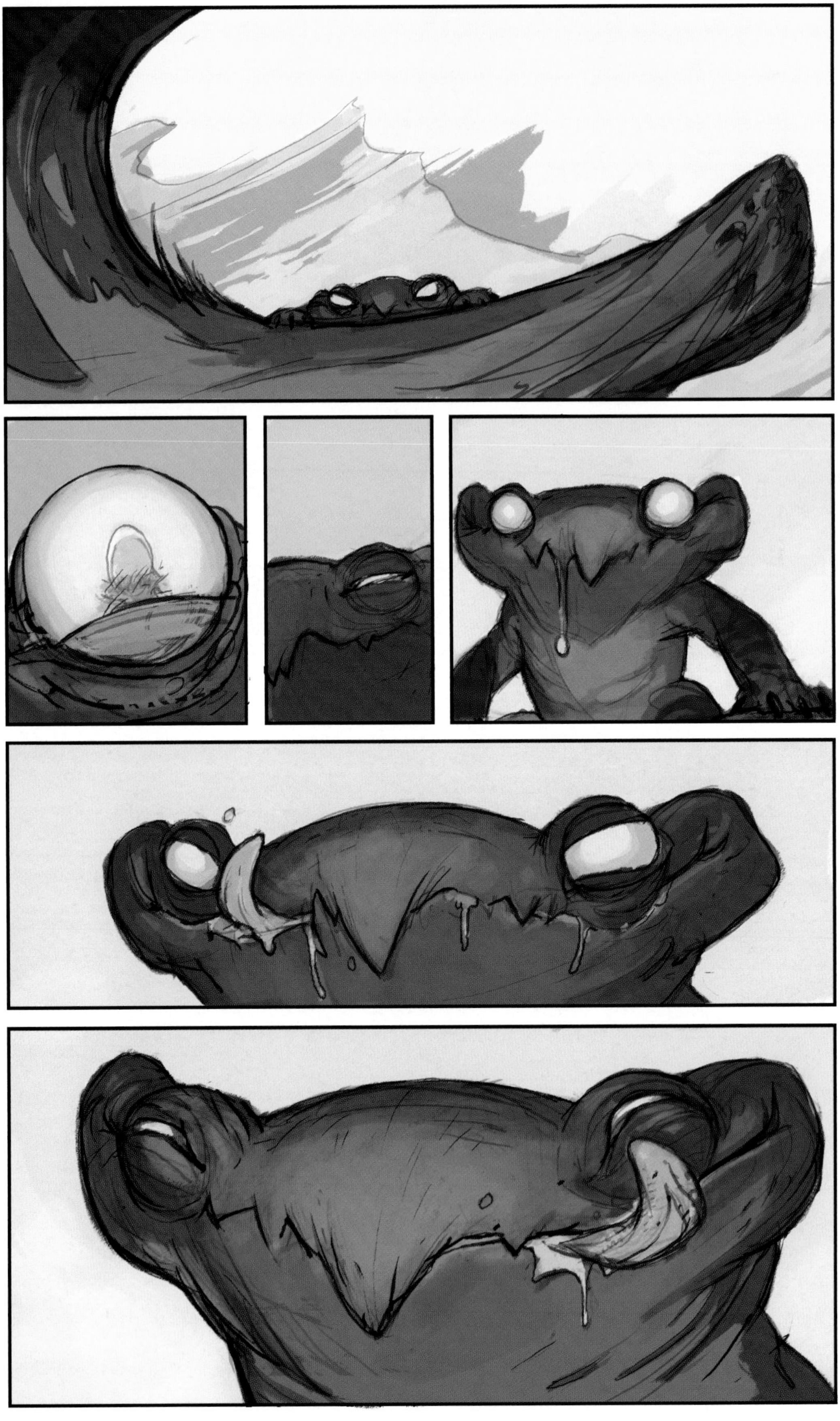

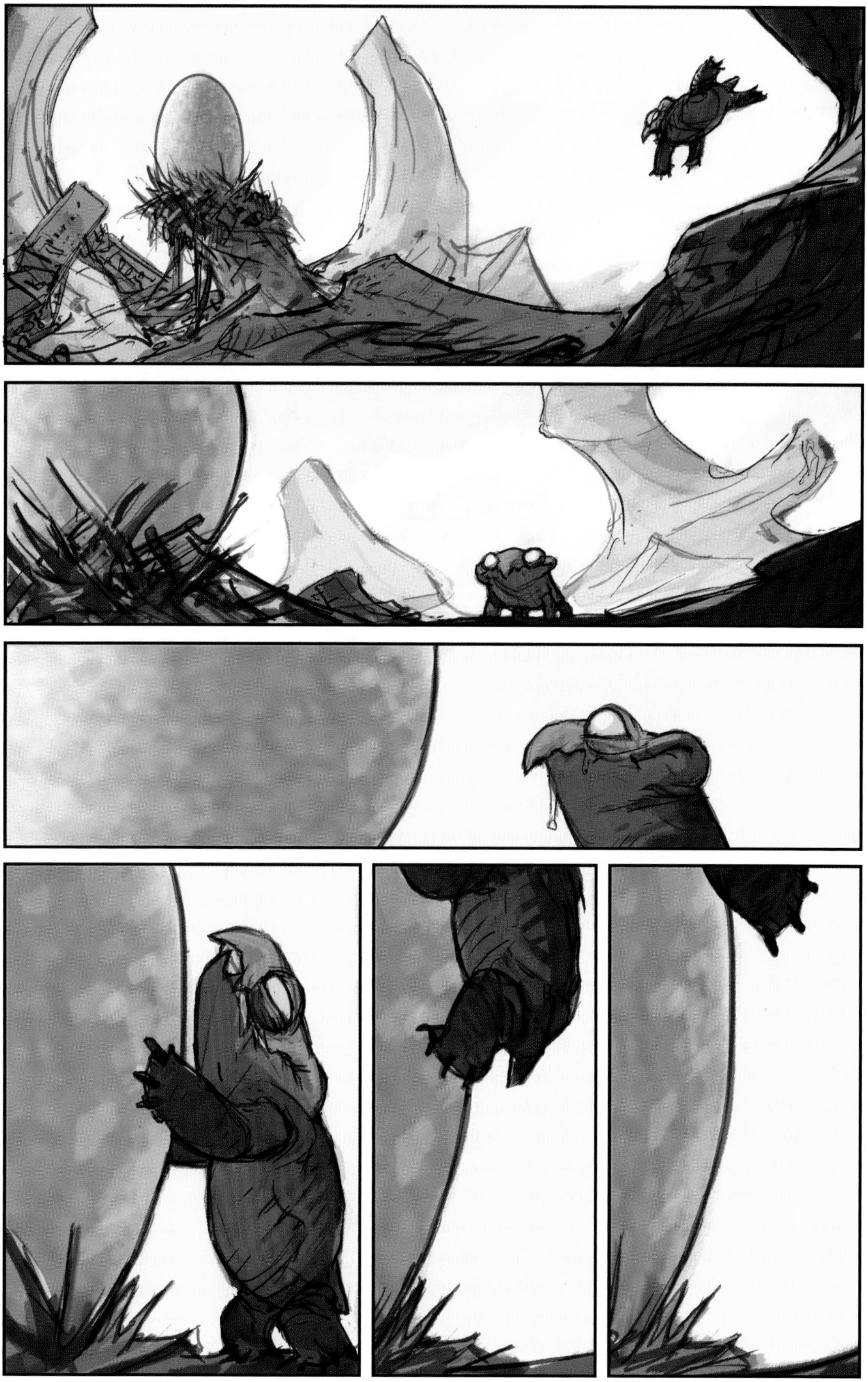

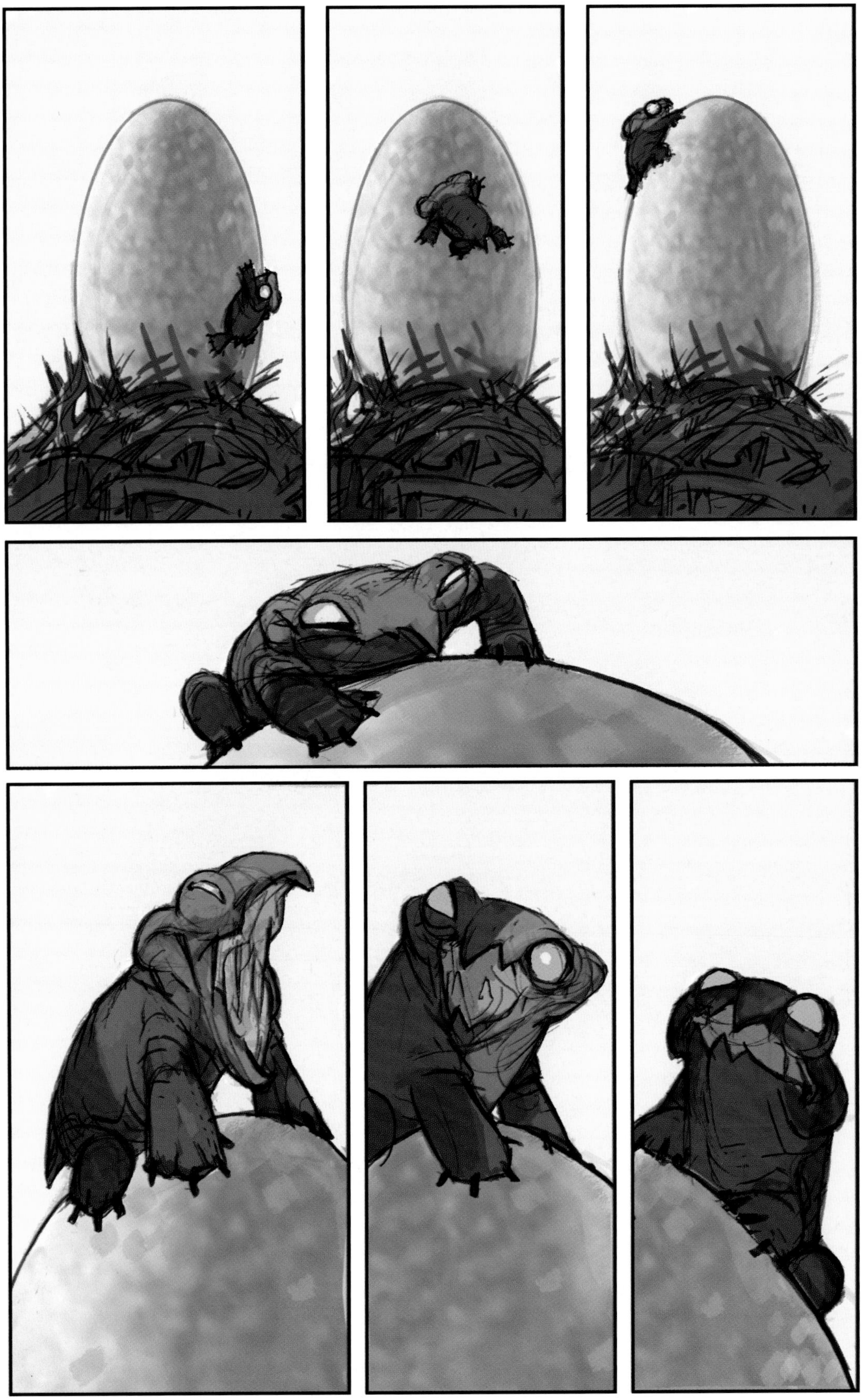

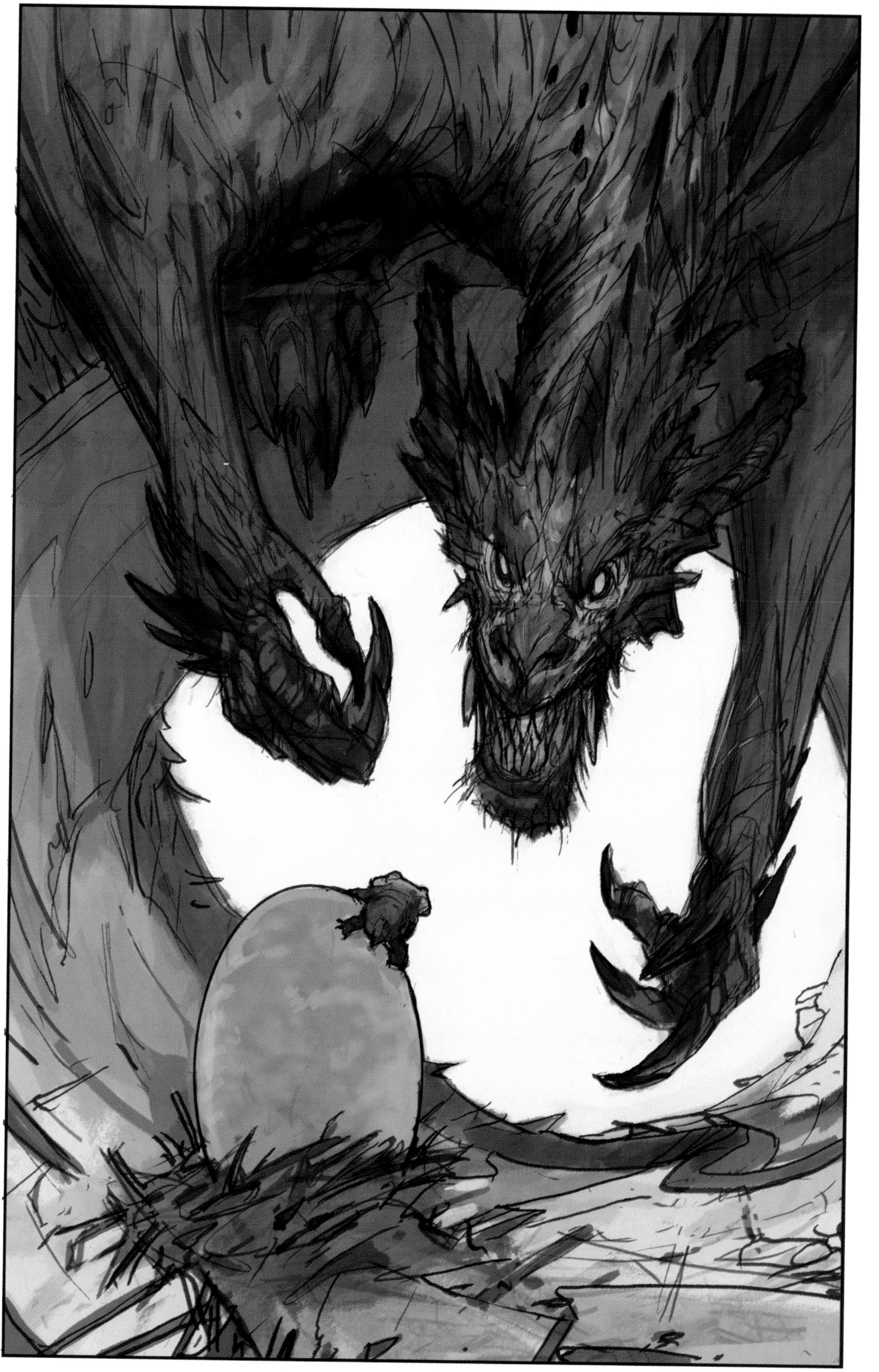

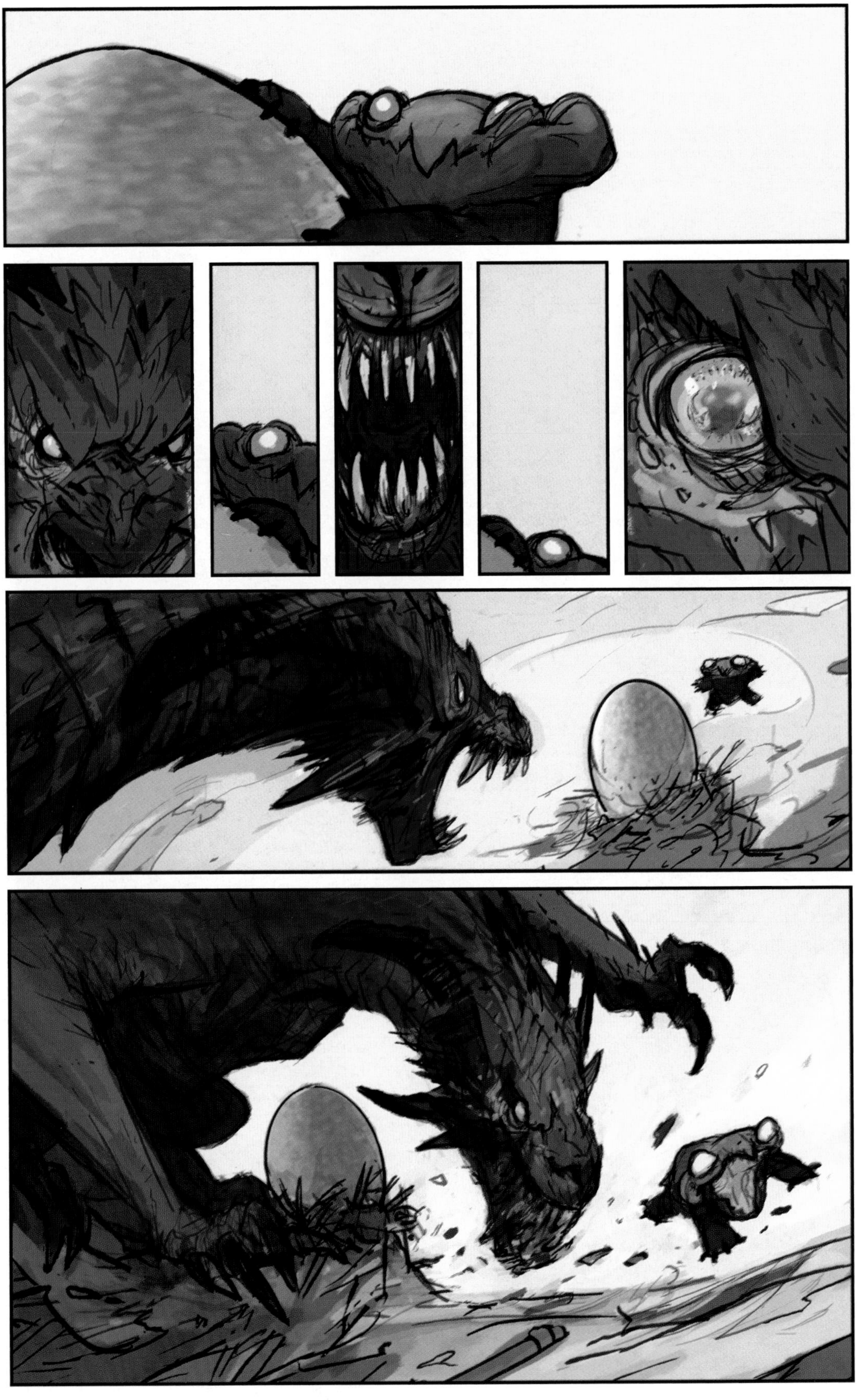

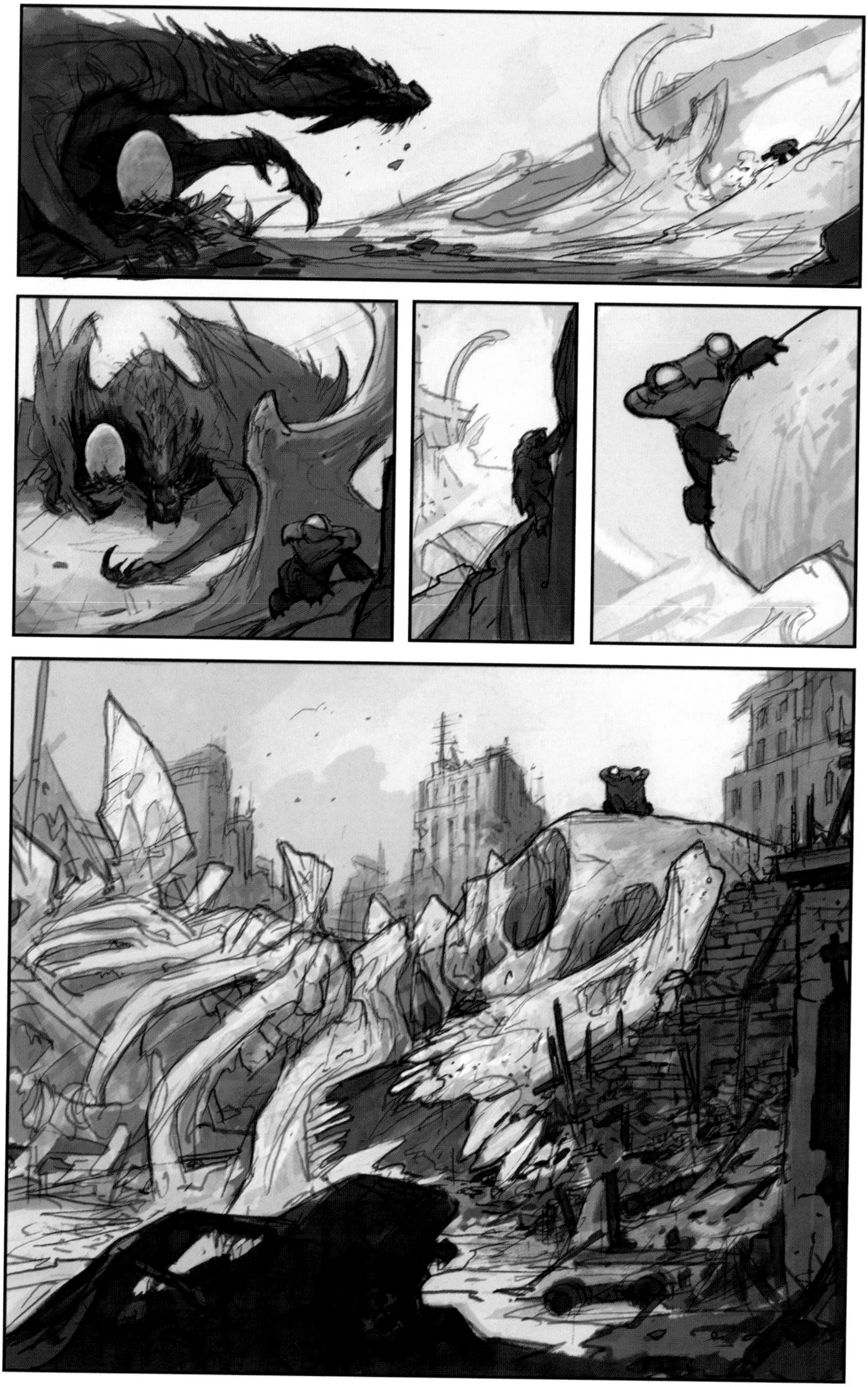

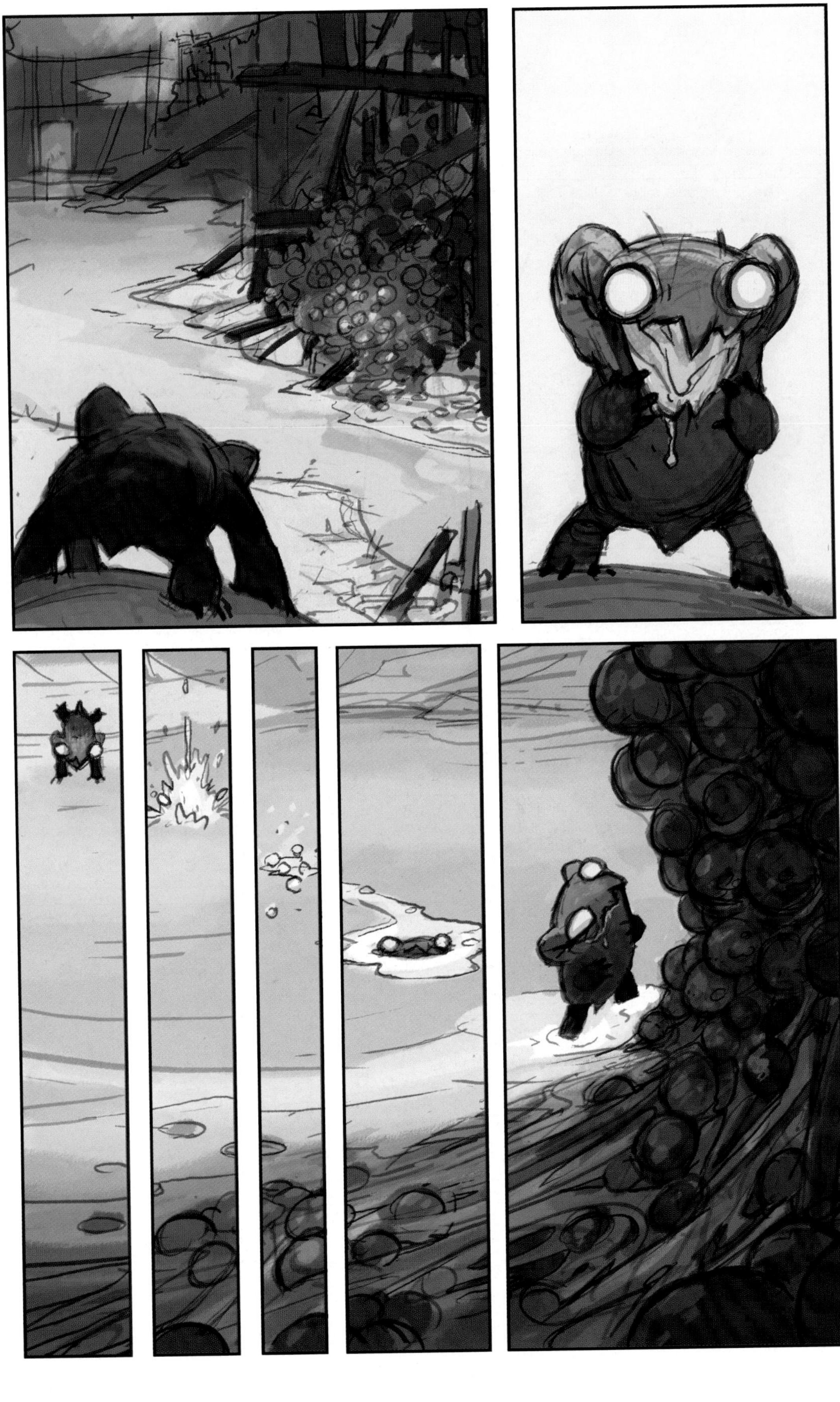

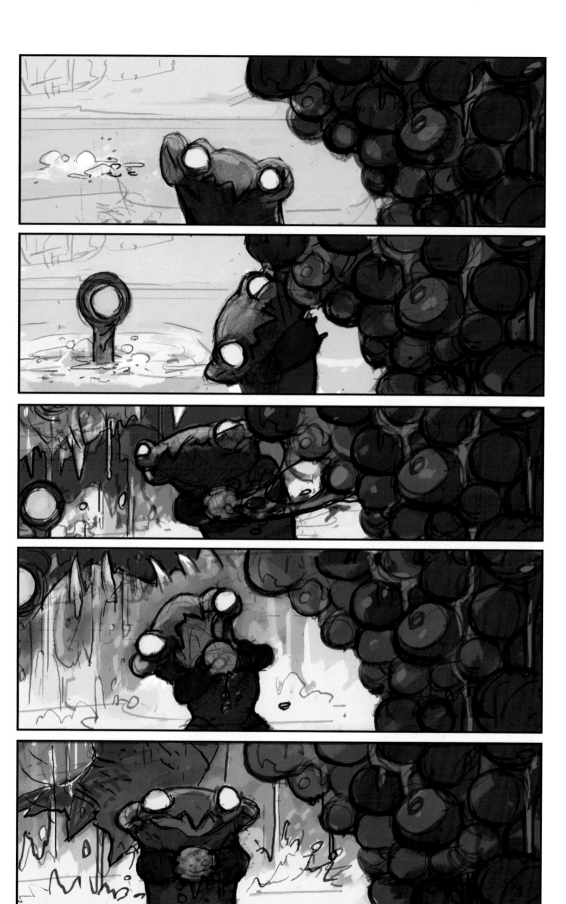

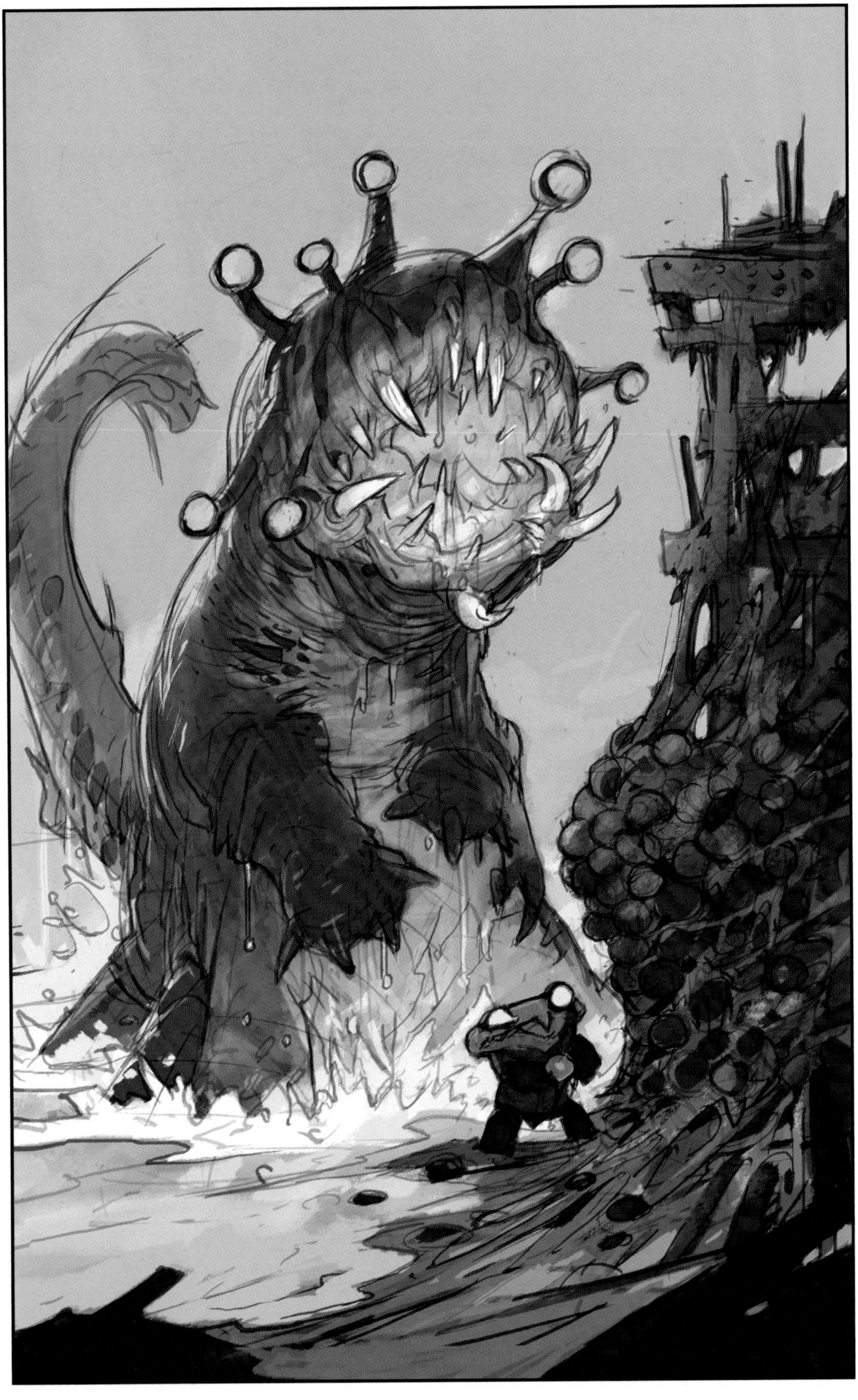

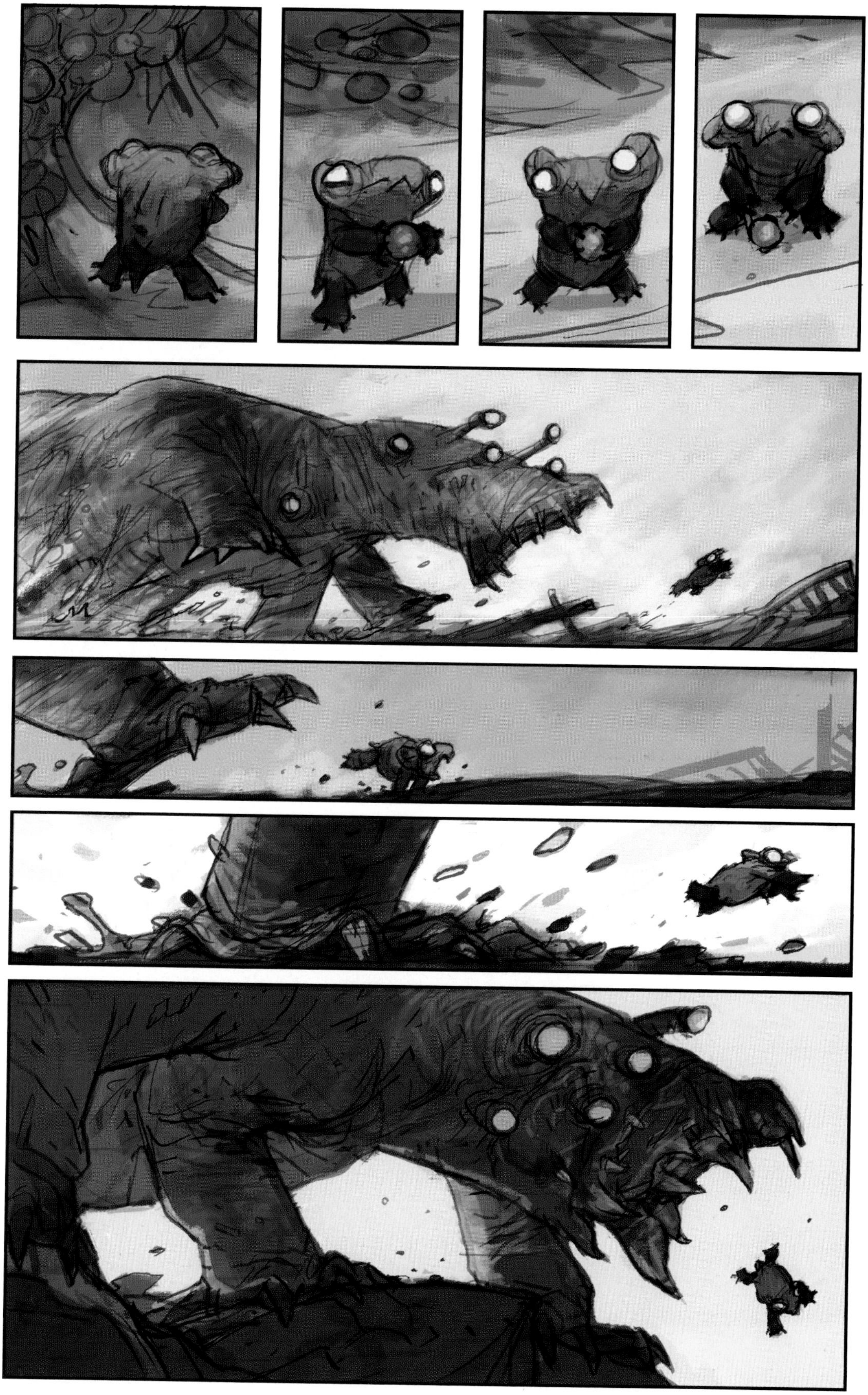

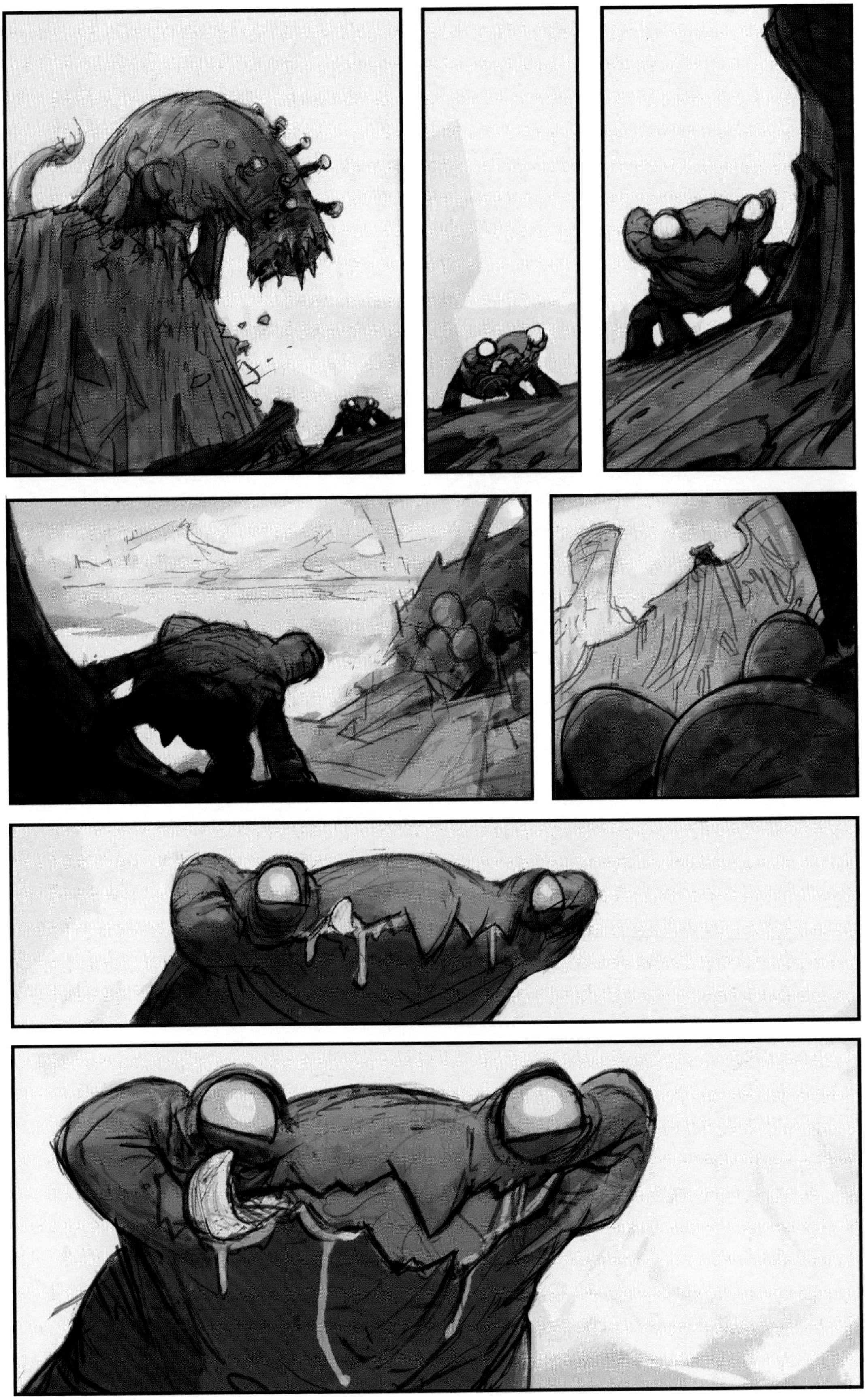

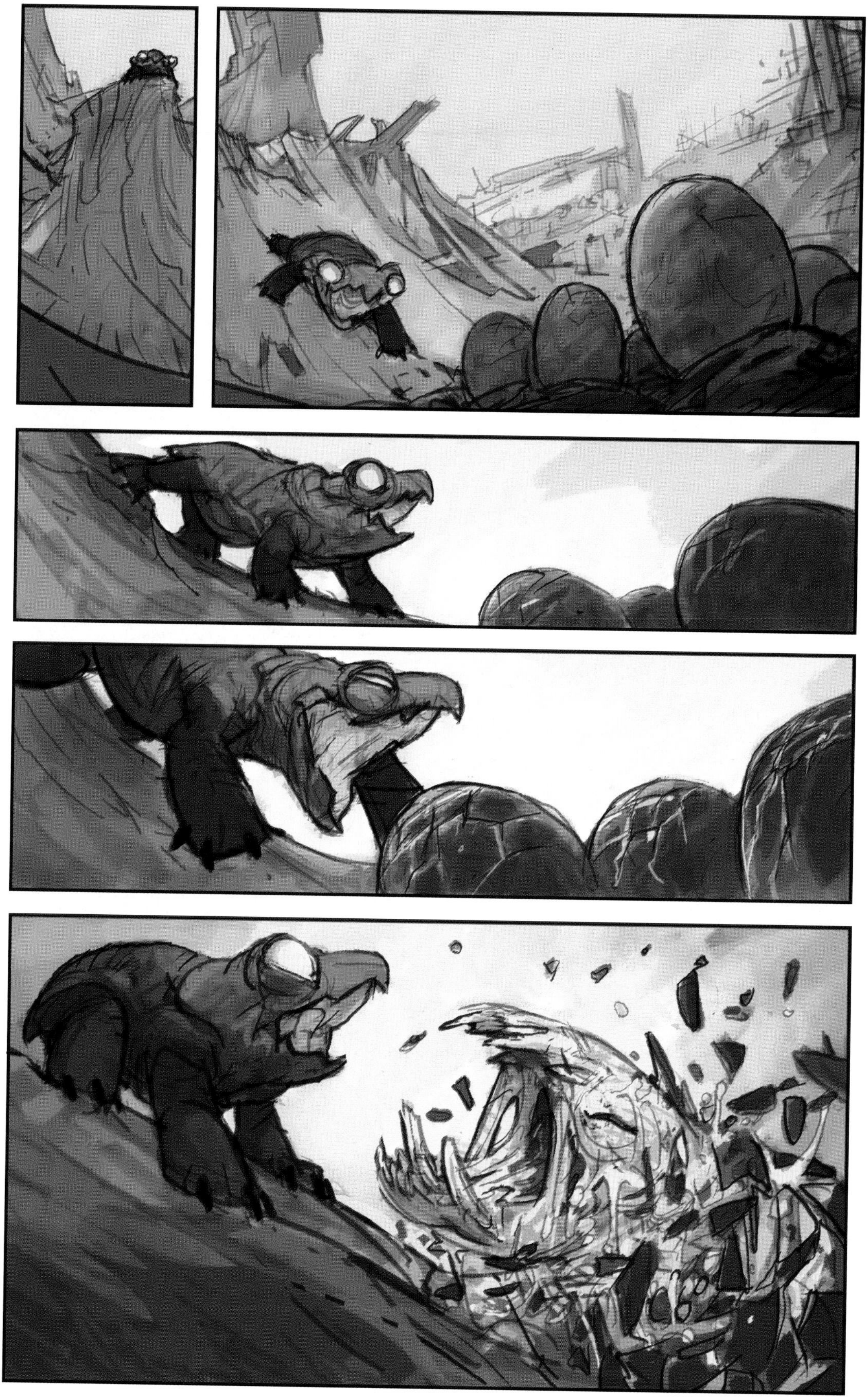

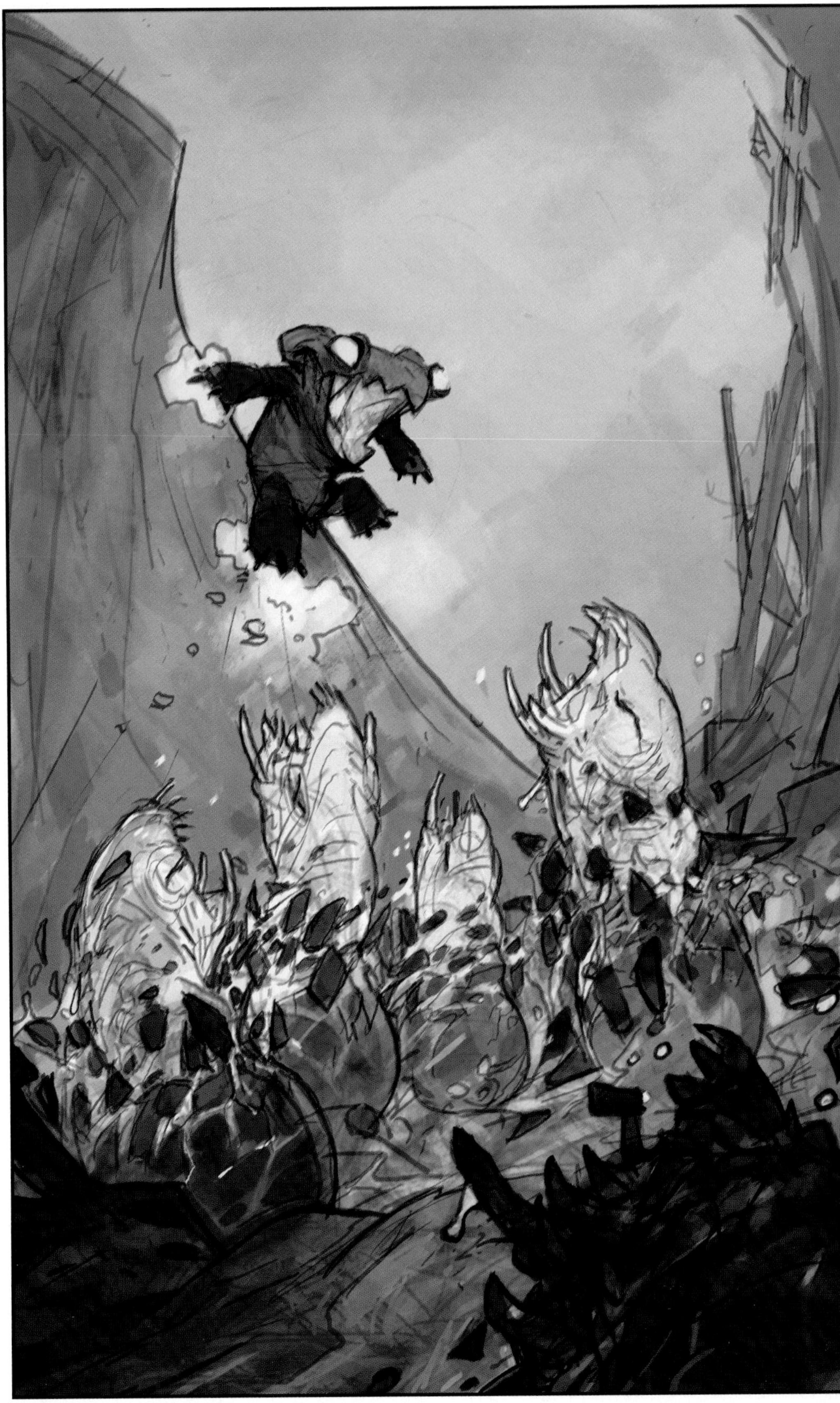

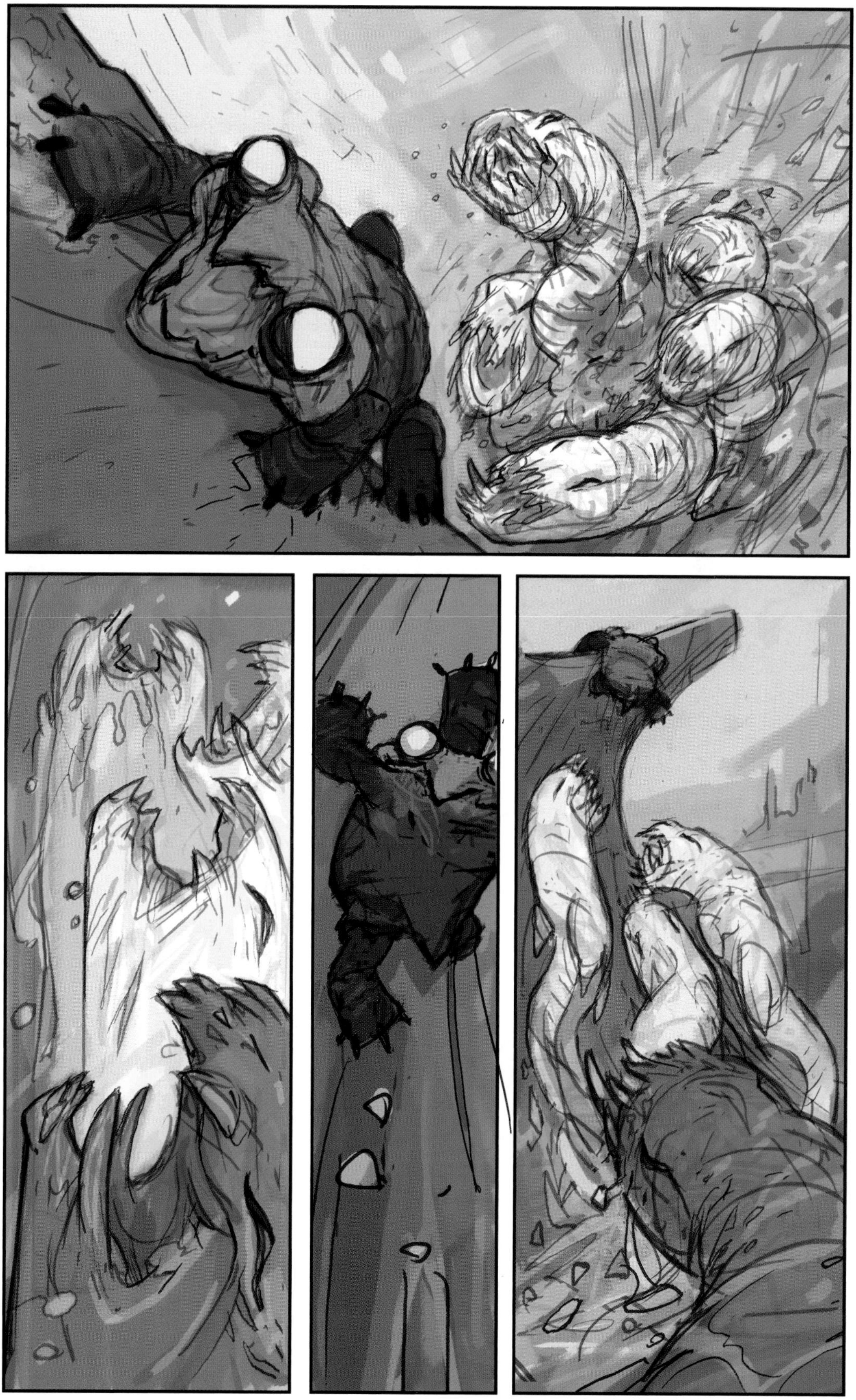

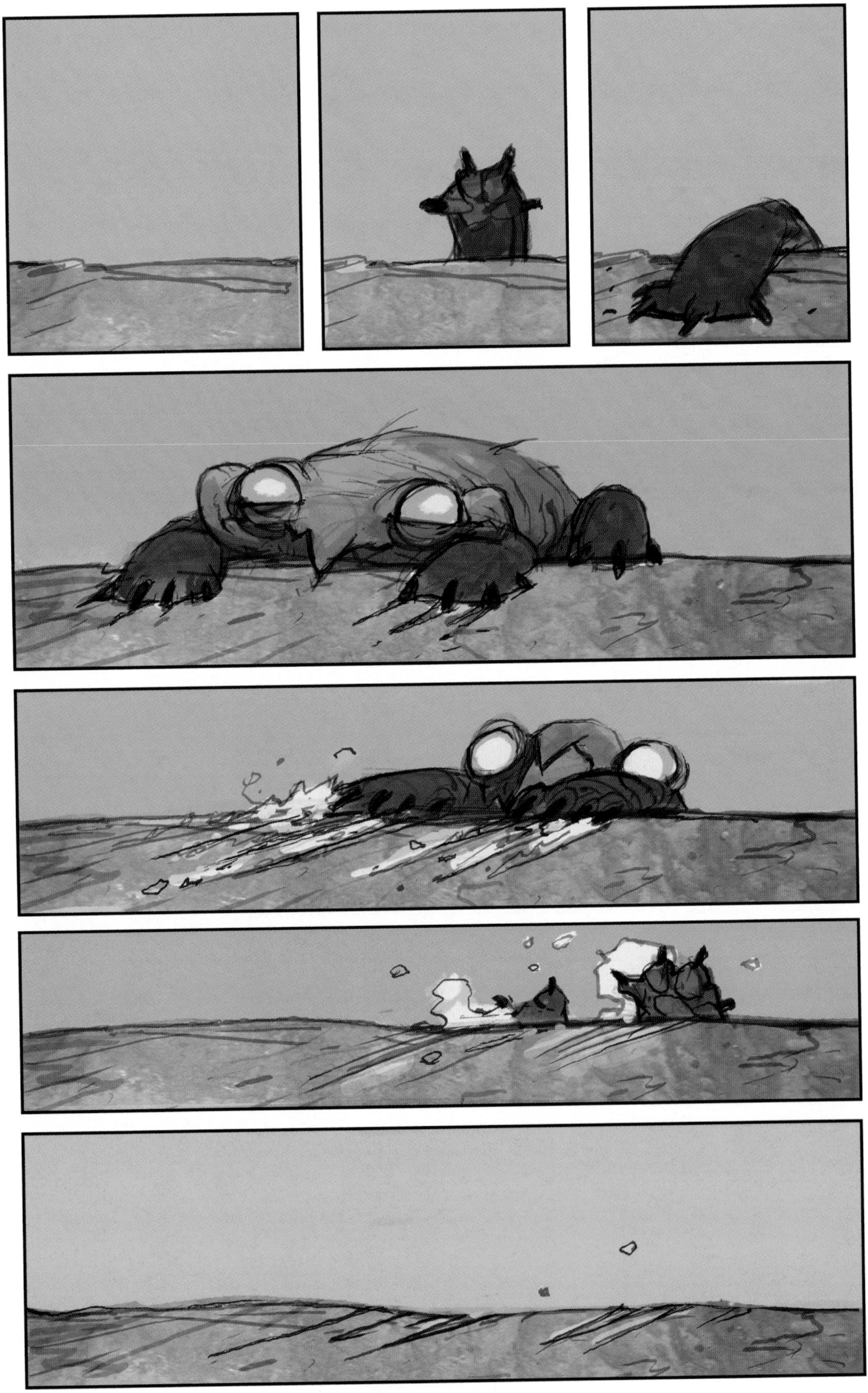

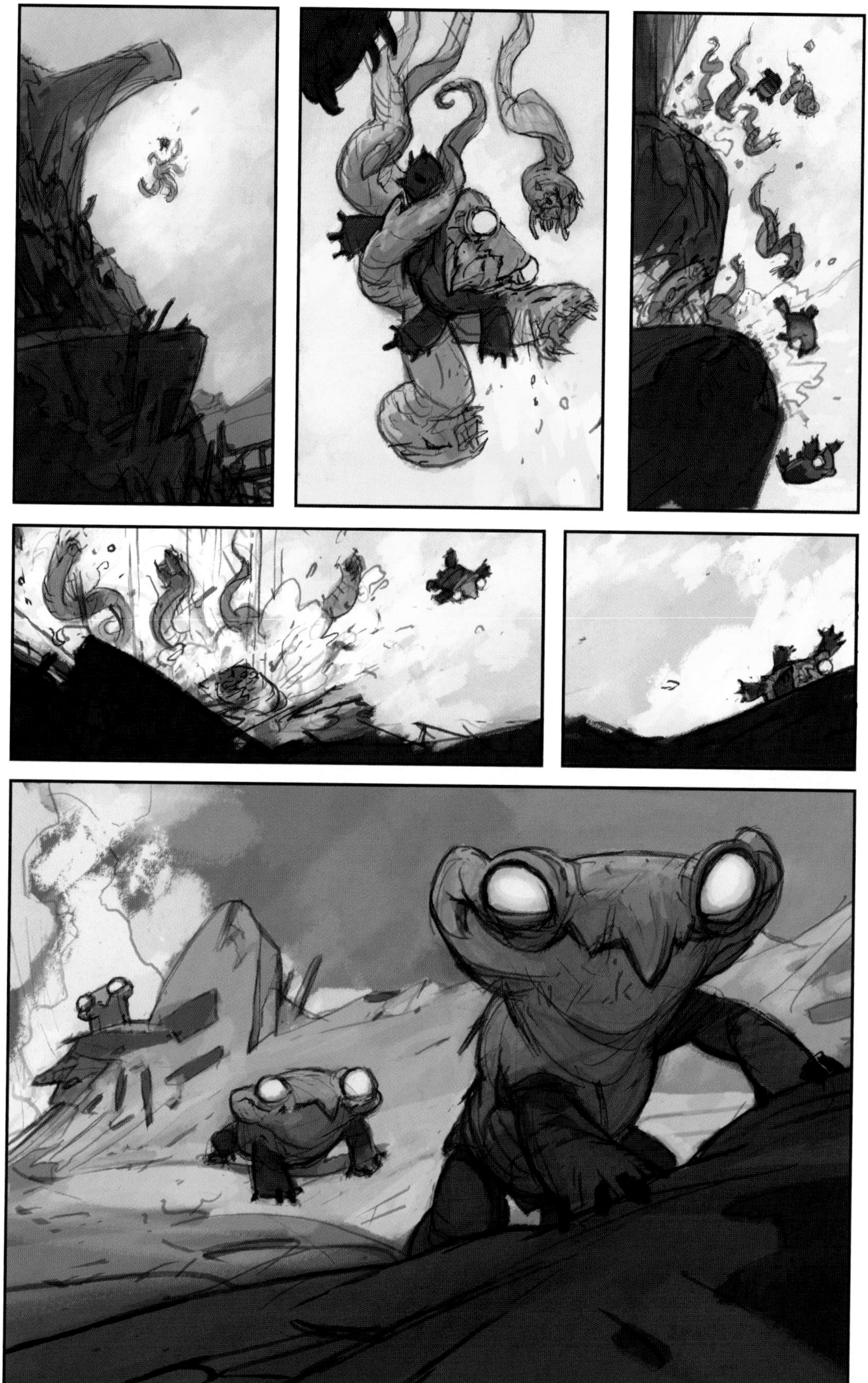

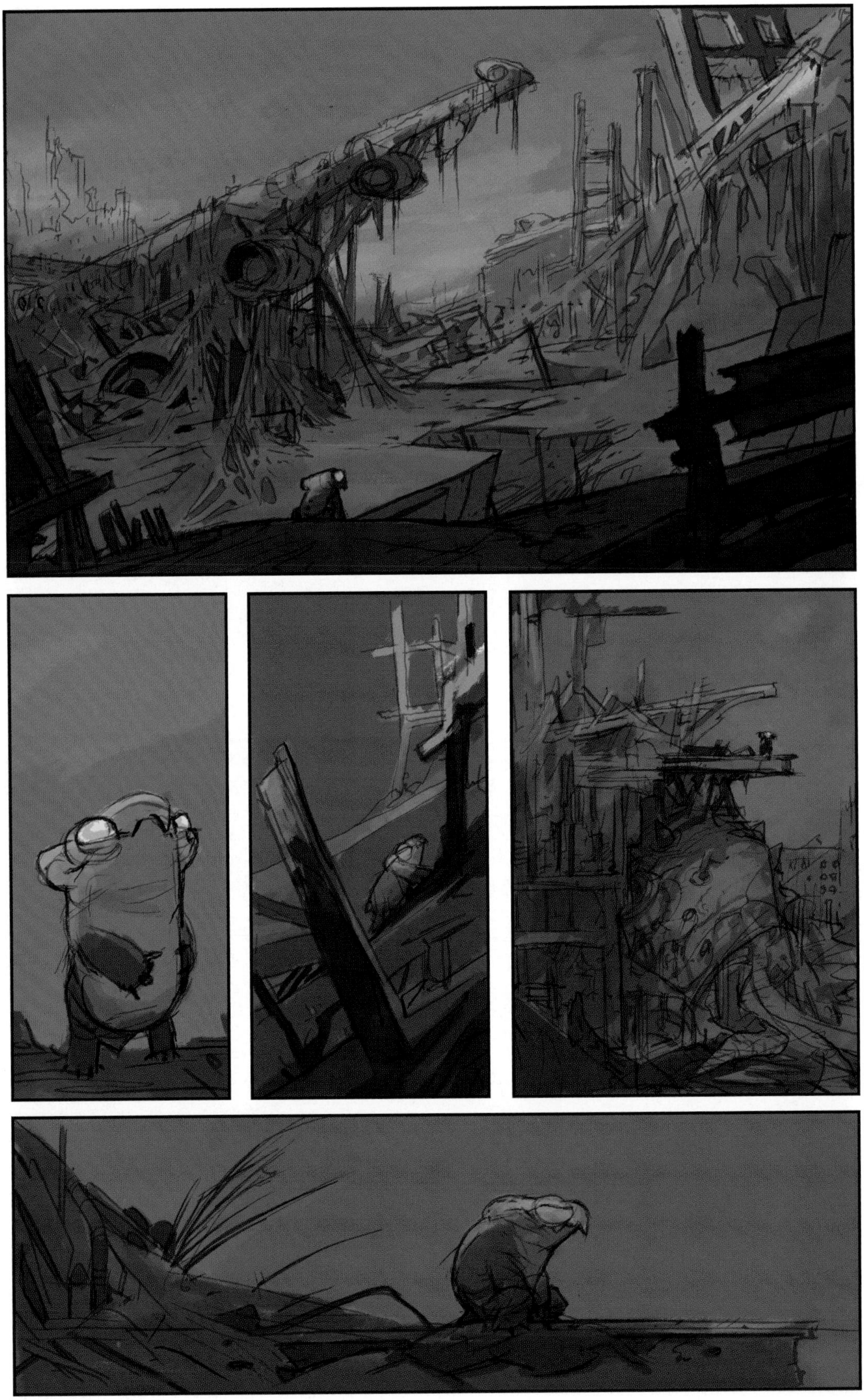

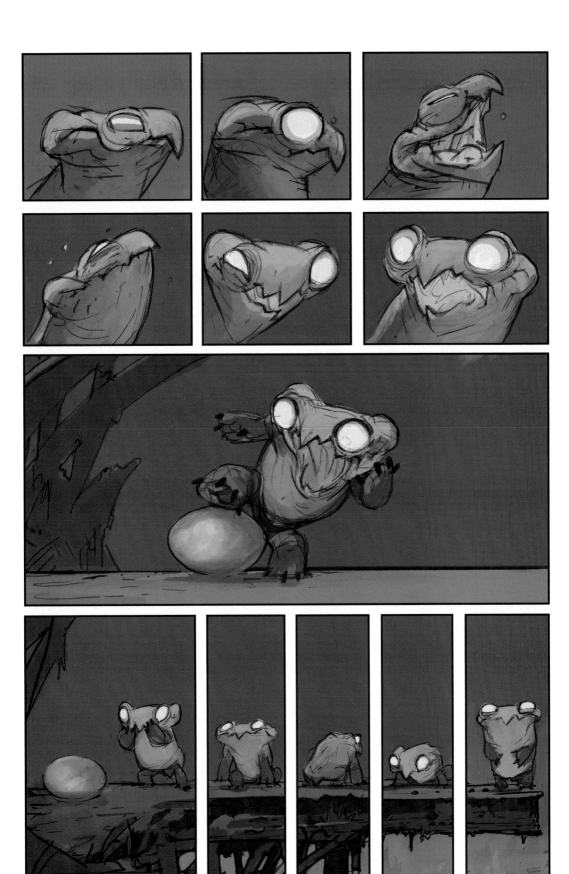

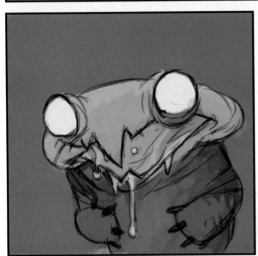

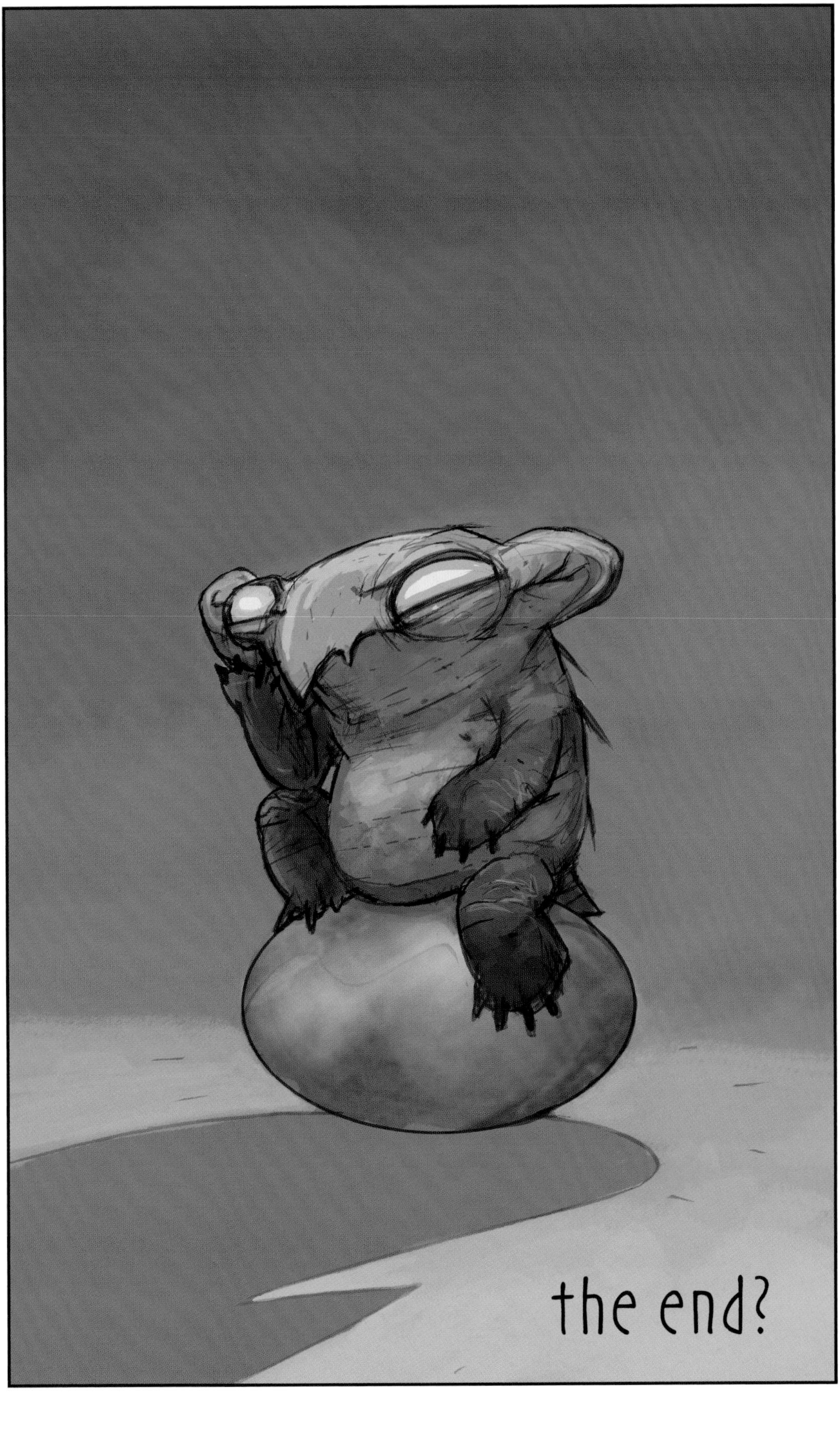
the end?

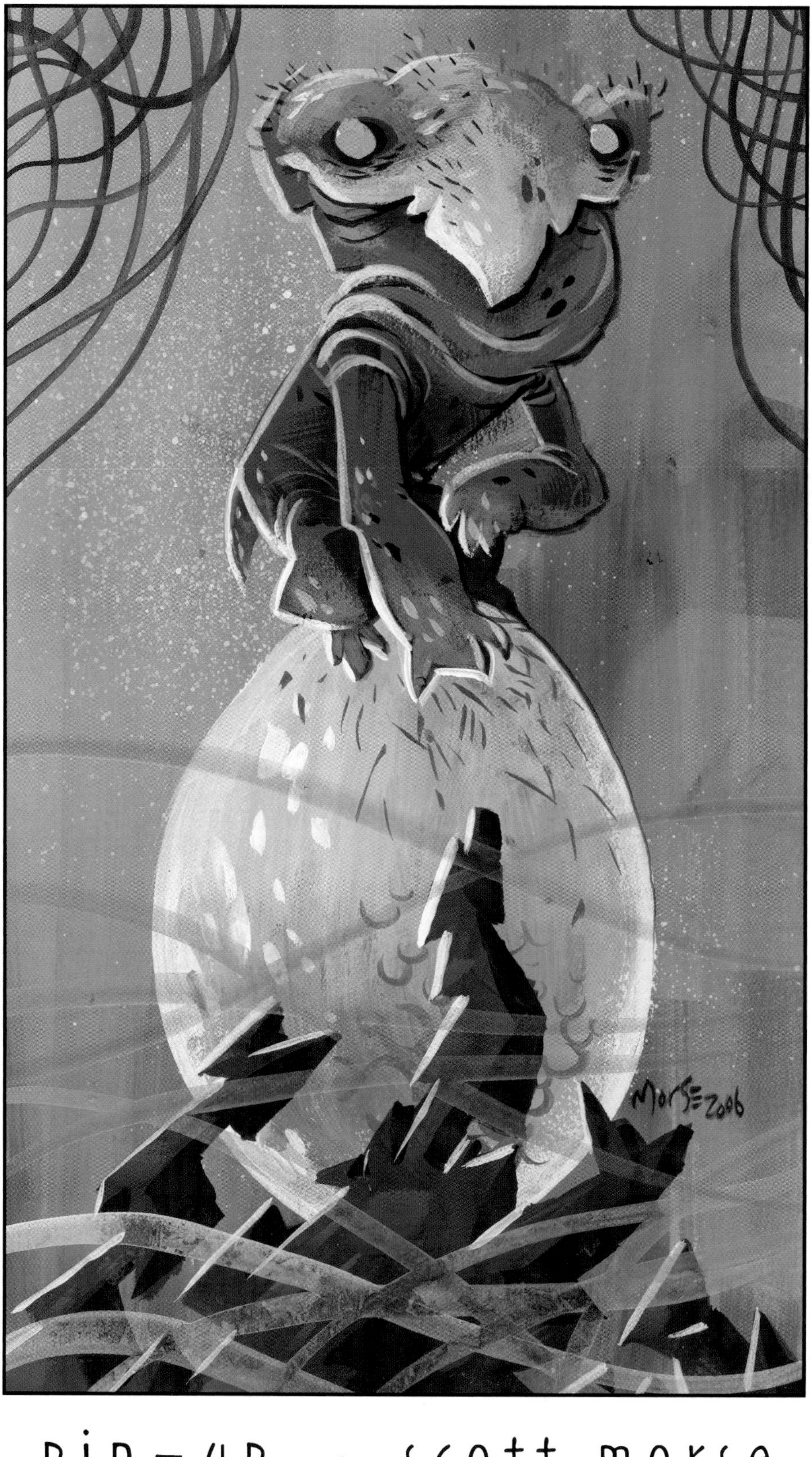
MORSE 2006

pin-up · scott morse

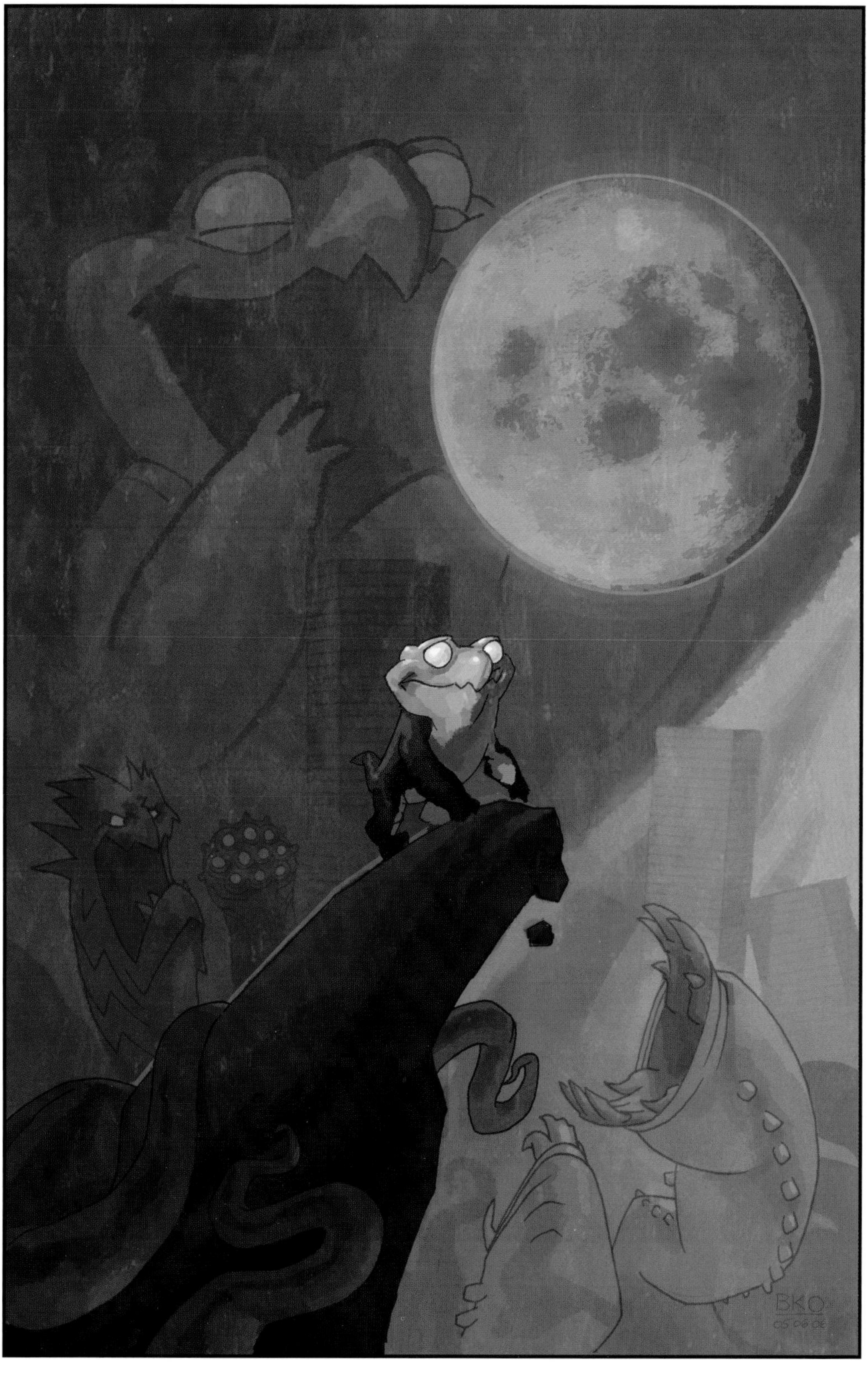

pin-up · brian kalin o'connell

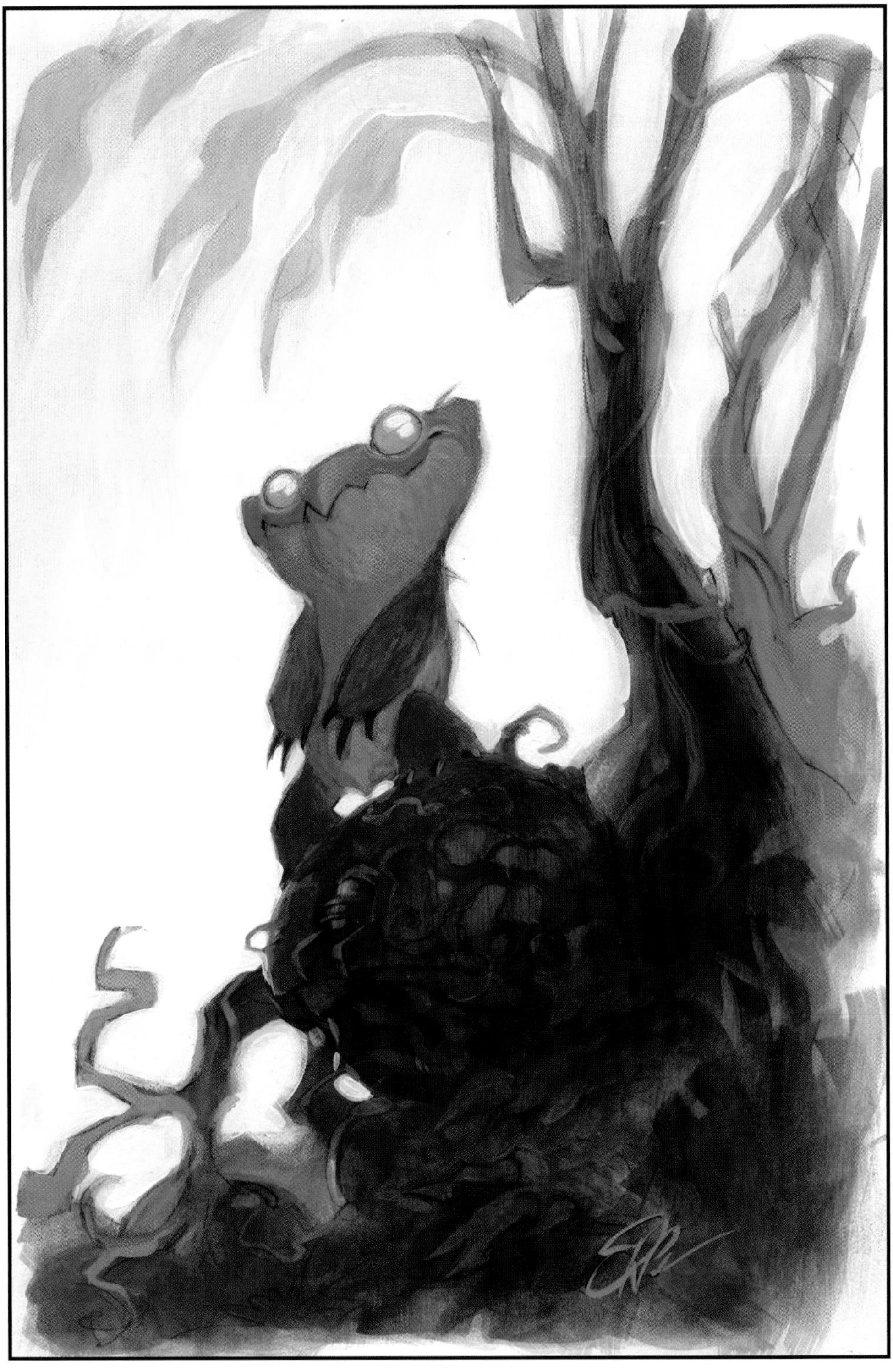

pin-up · steve purcell

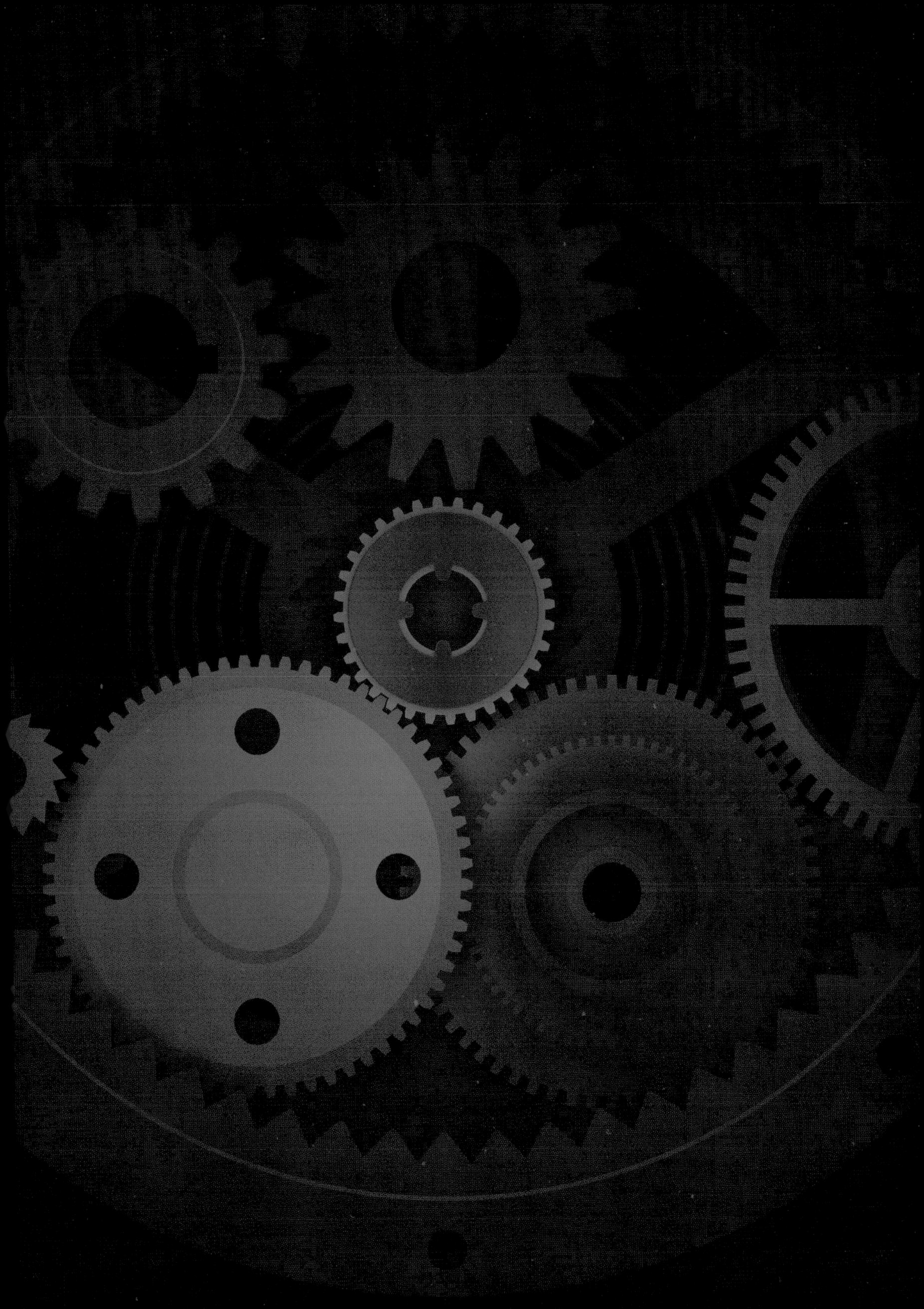

PETER SOHN

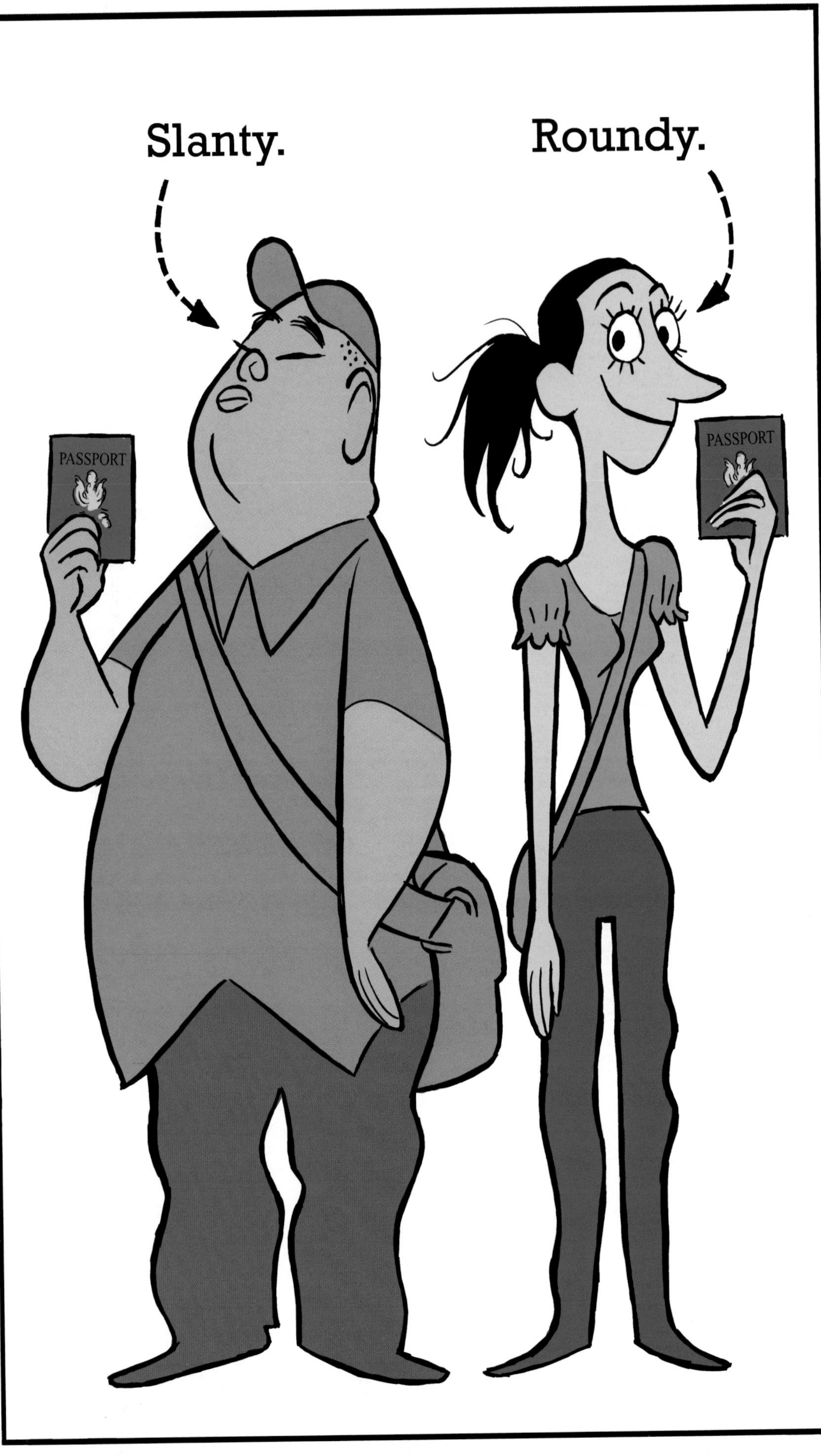
Slanty.
Roundy.
PASSPORT
PASSPORT

The following story takes place in
TOKYO, JAPAN and PARIS, FRANCE.

This is a true story.

Illustrations-   Peter Sohn

Color-   Nate Wragg

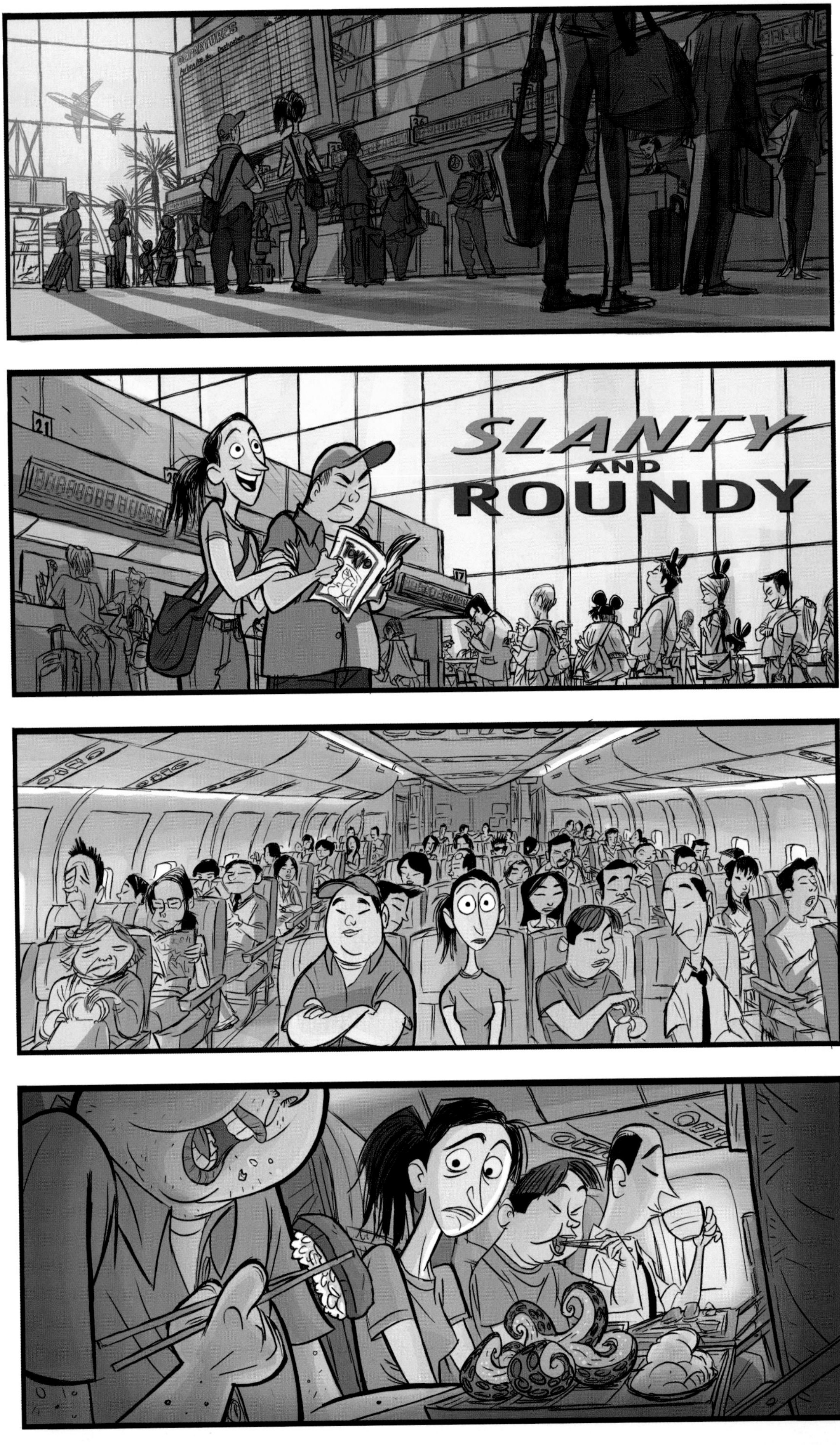
DEPARTURES
SLANTY
AND
ROUNDY

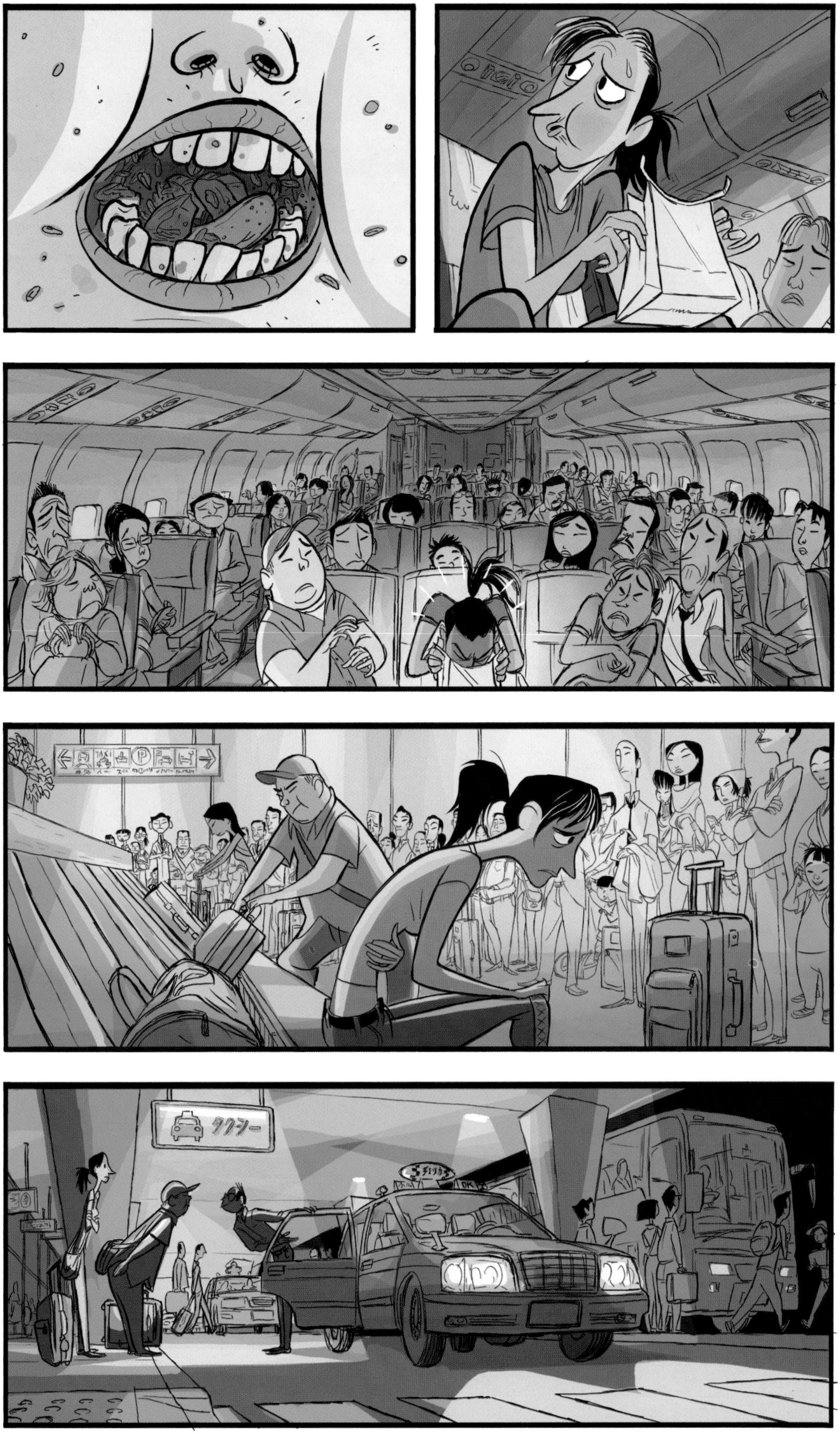
TAXI
タクシー
OK

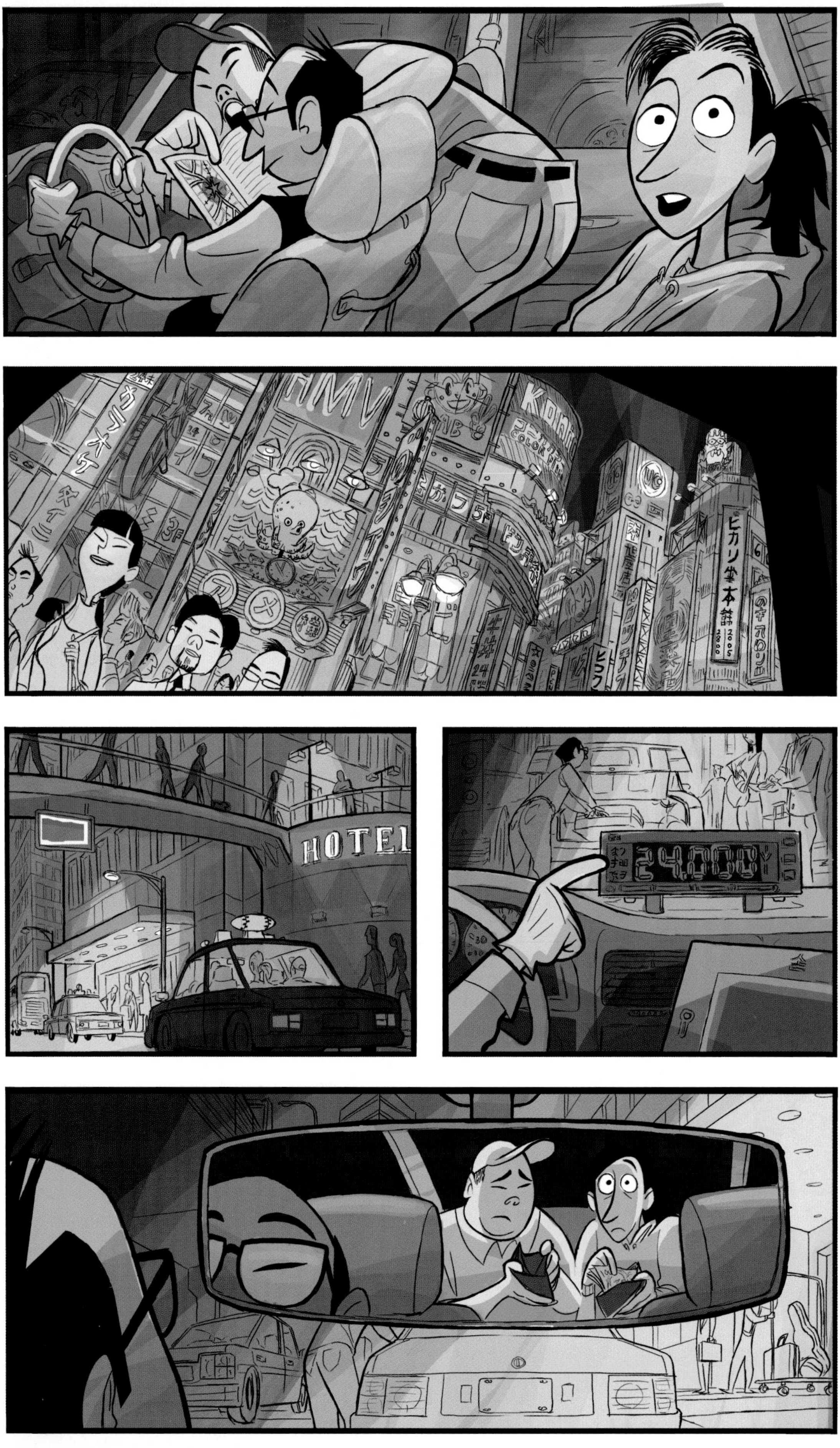
HMV
HOTEL

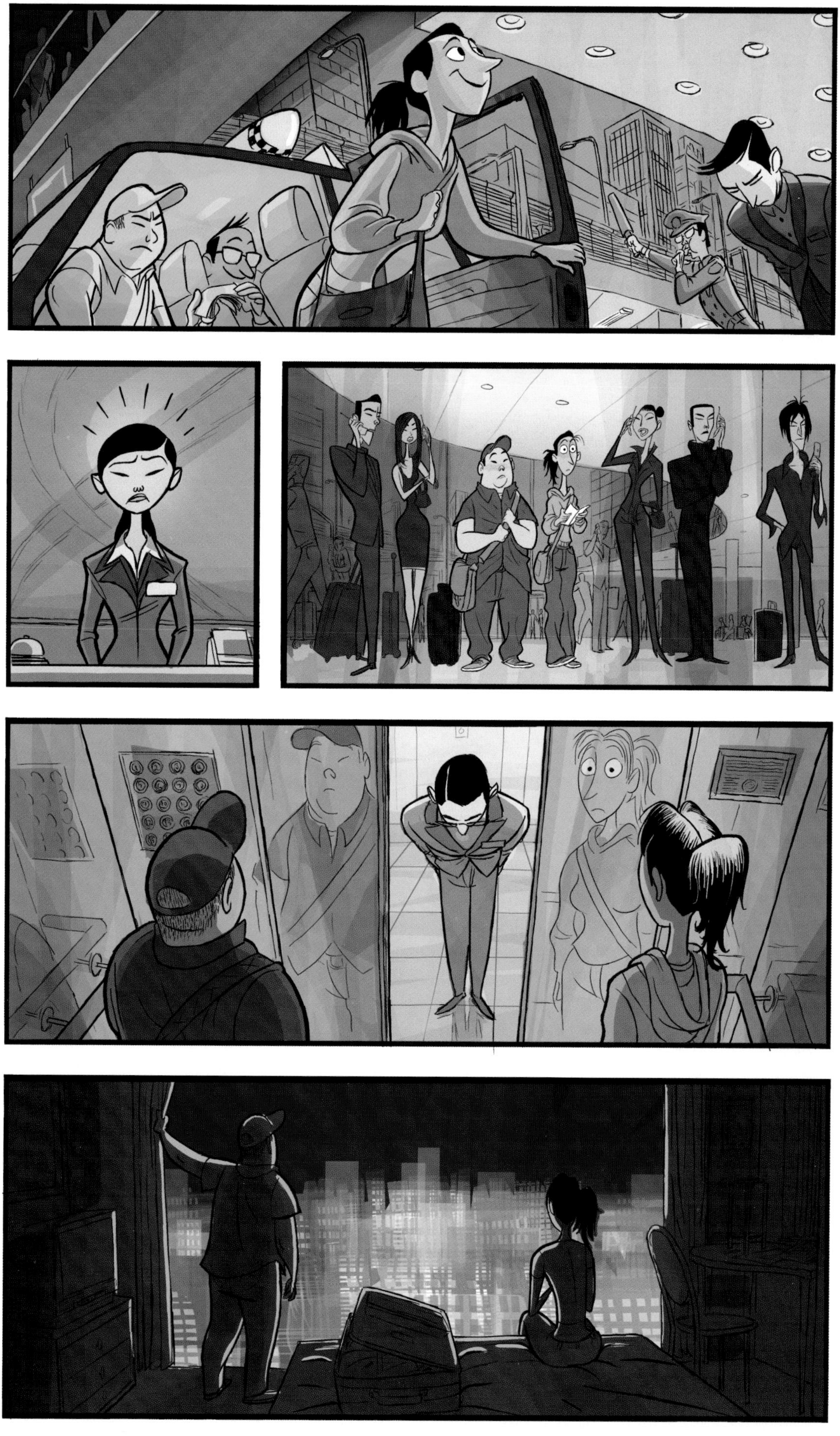

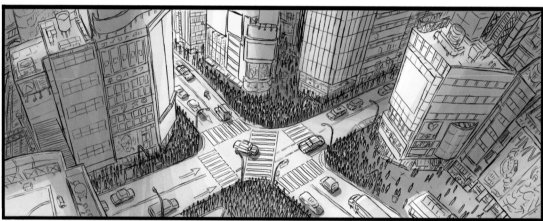

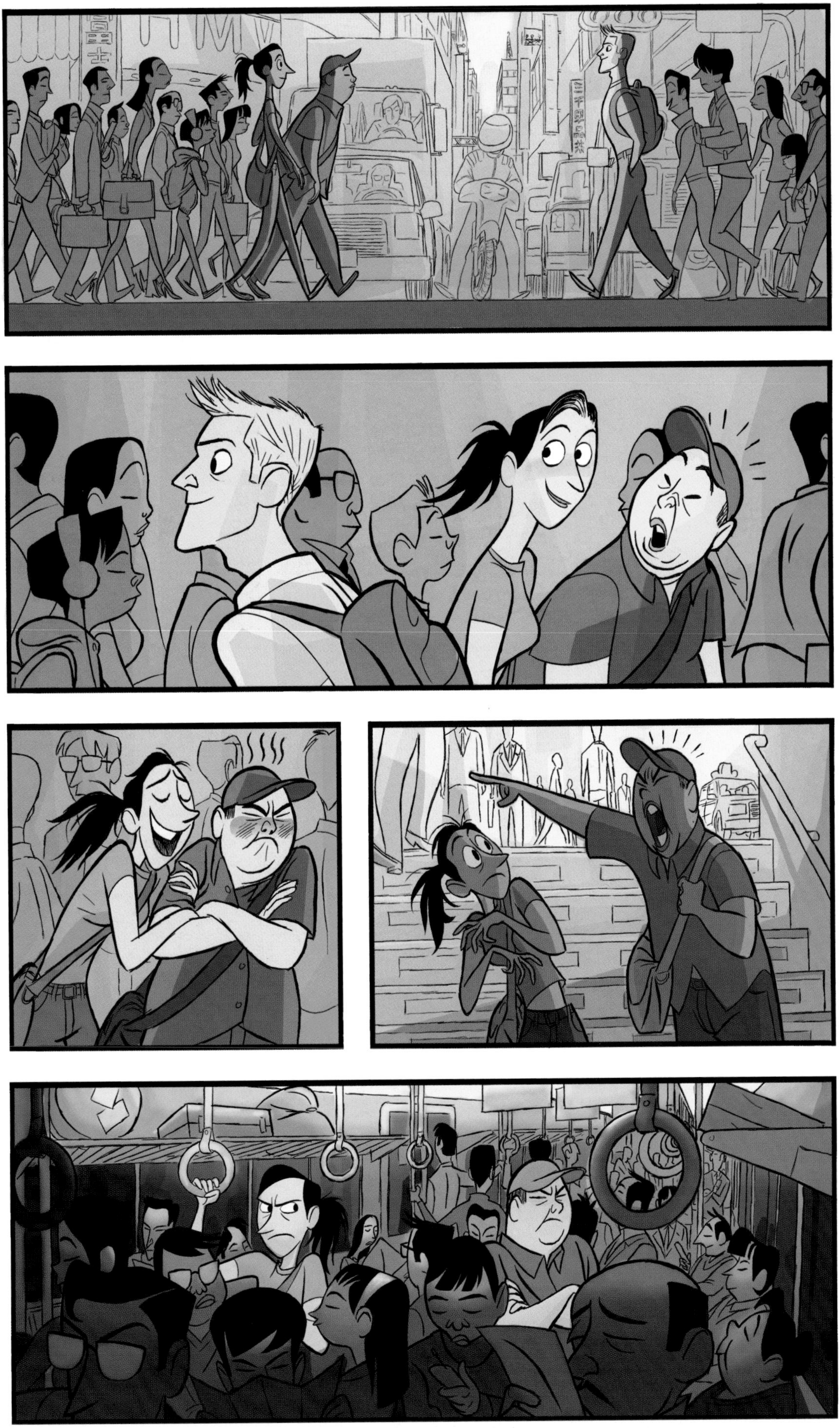

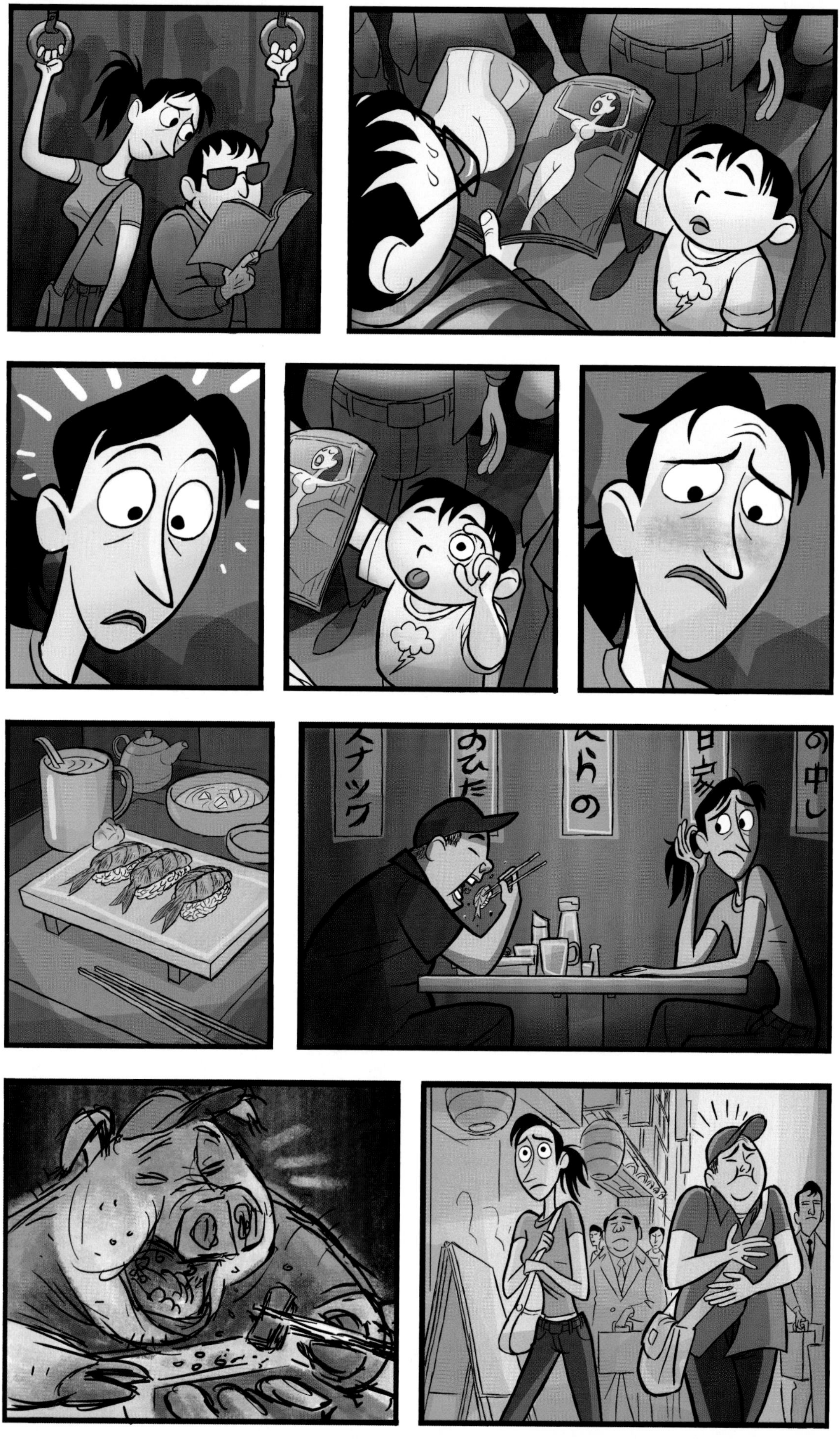

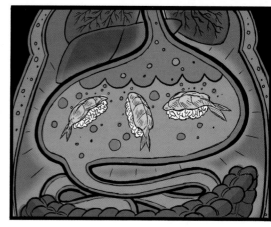

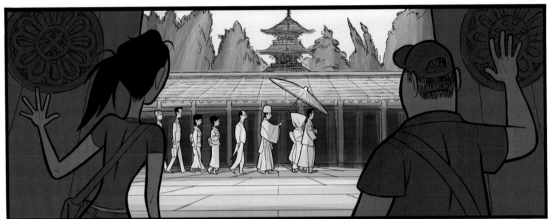

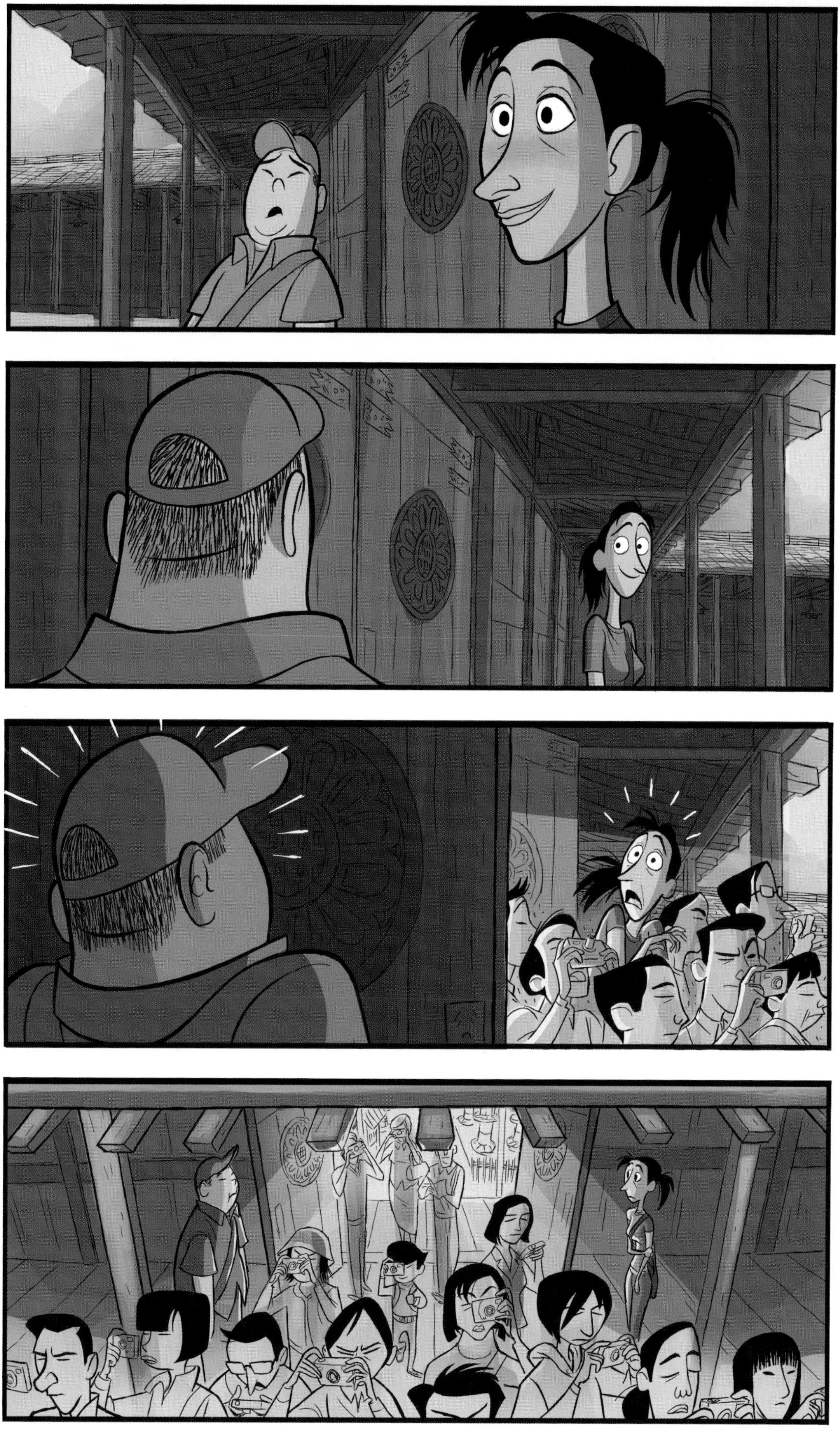

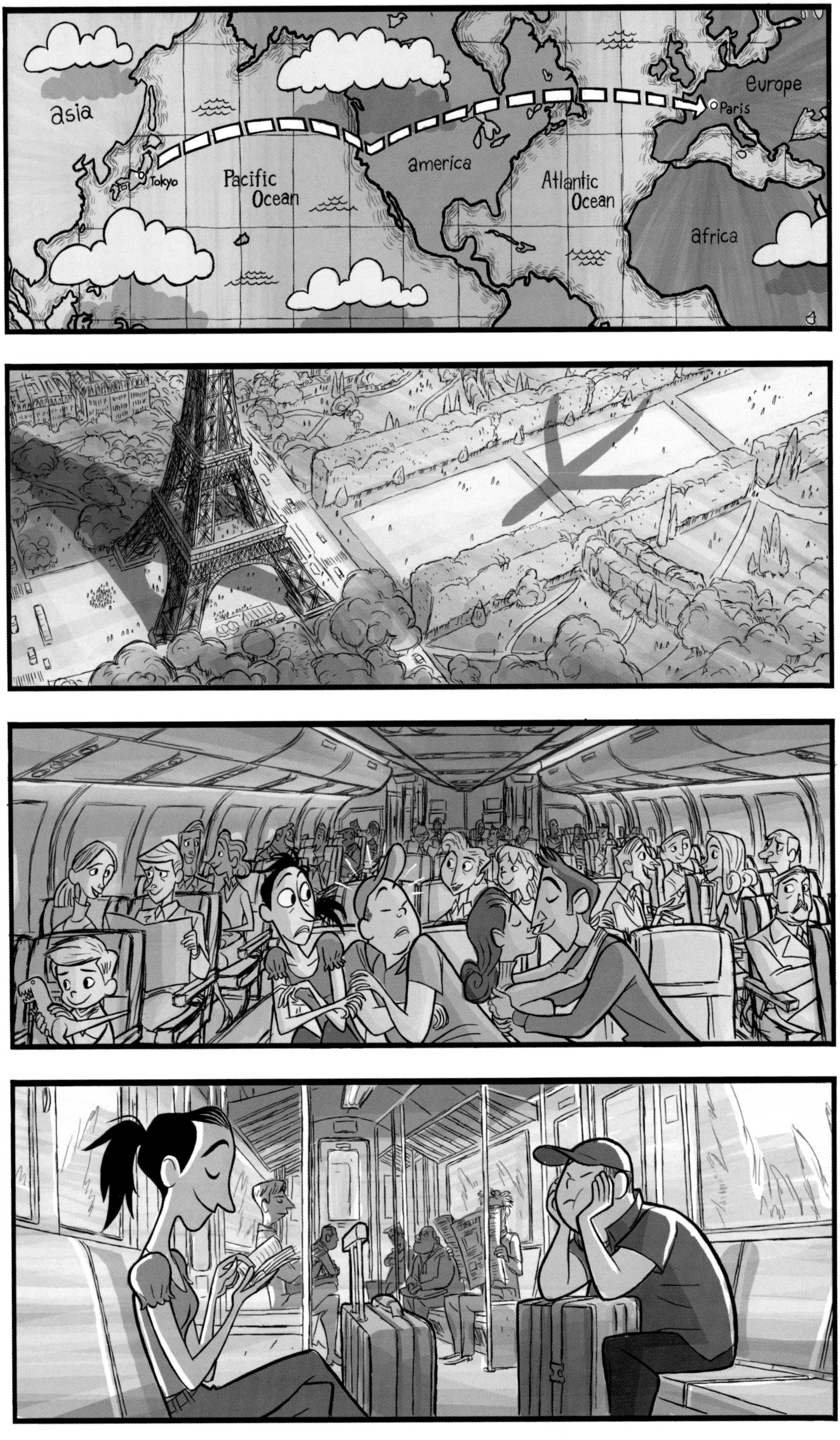
asia
Tokyo
Pacific Ocean
america
Atlantic Ocean
europe
Paris
africa

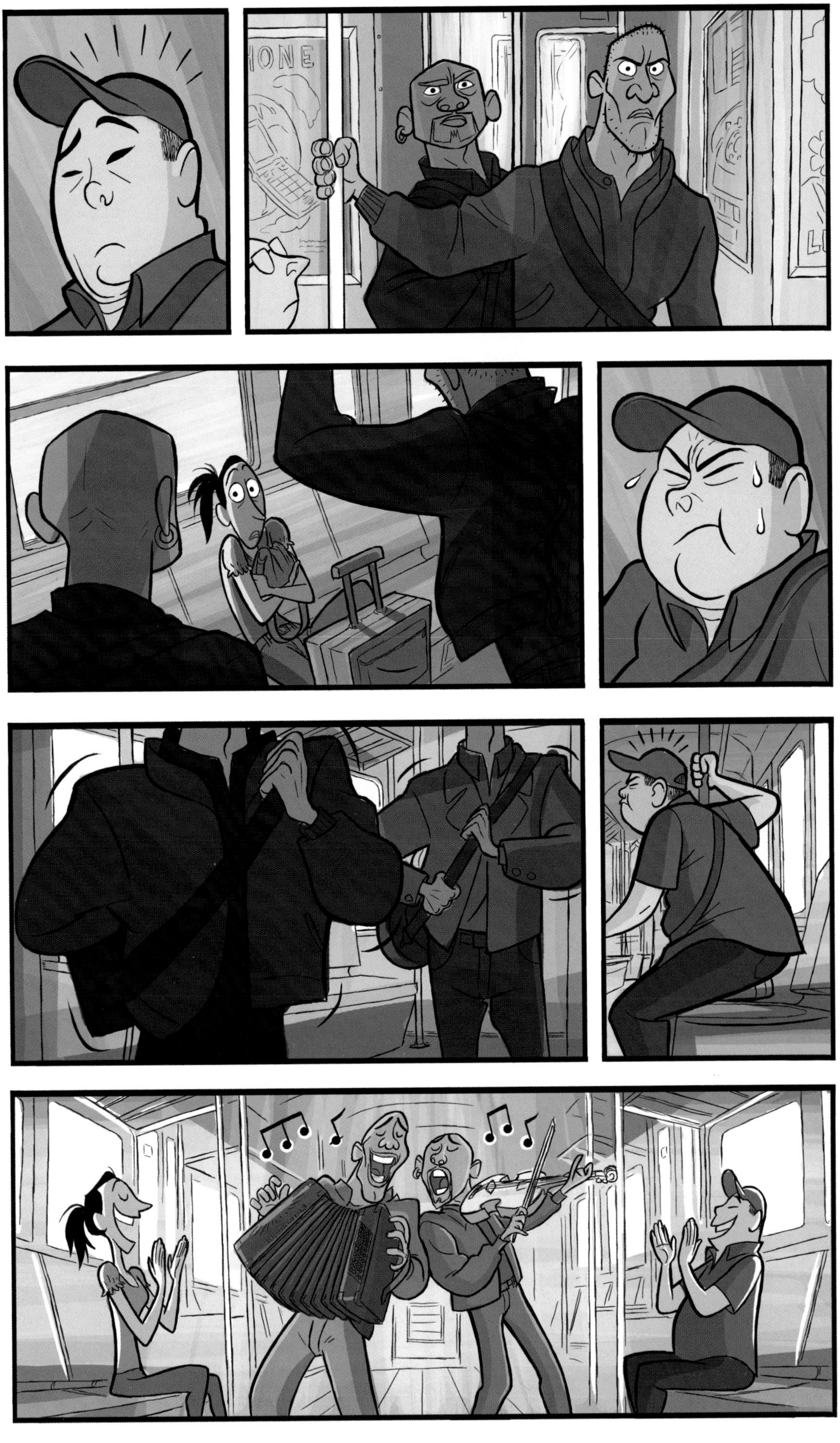

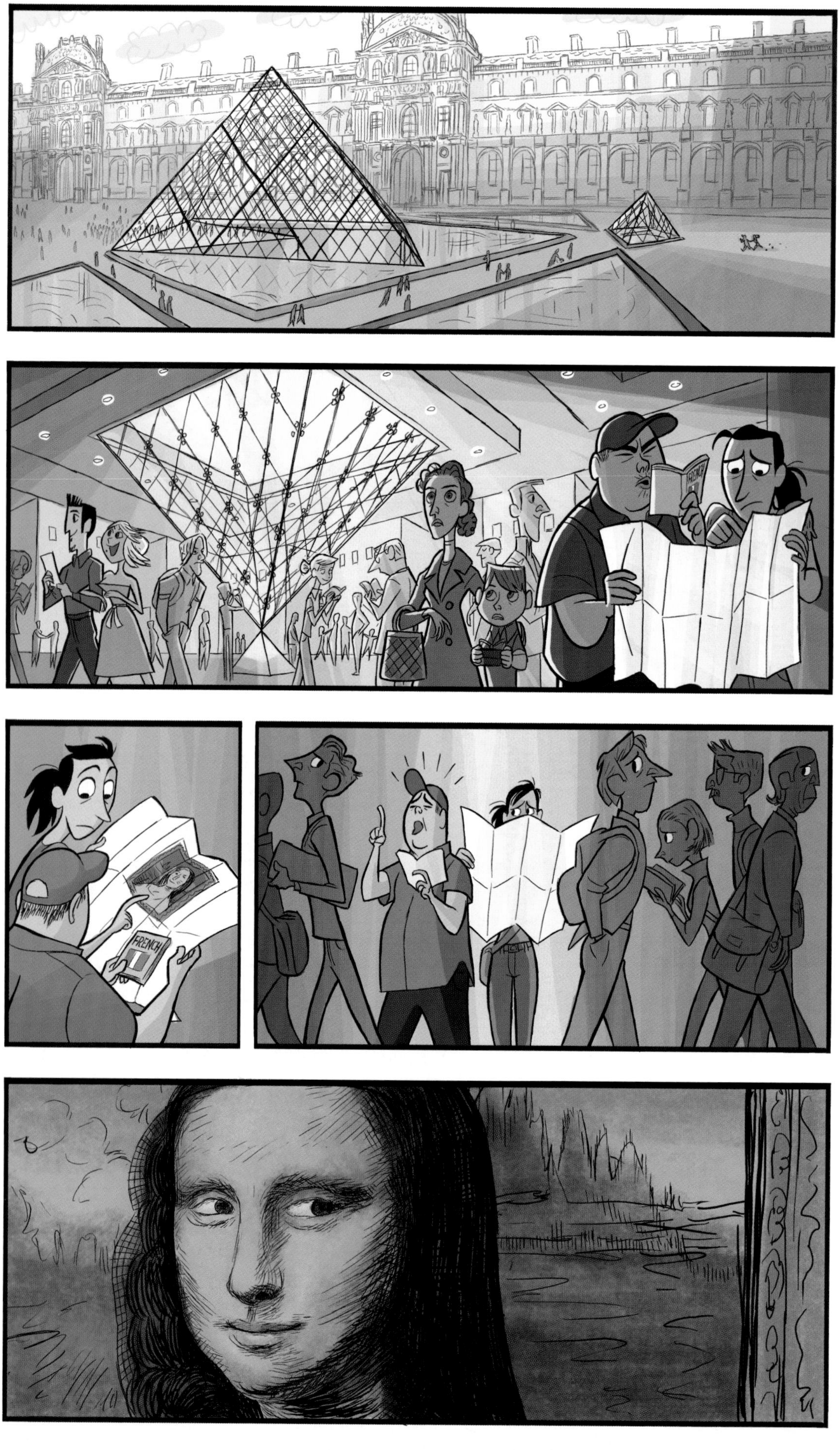
FRENCH

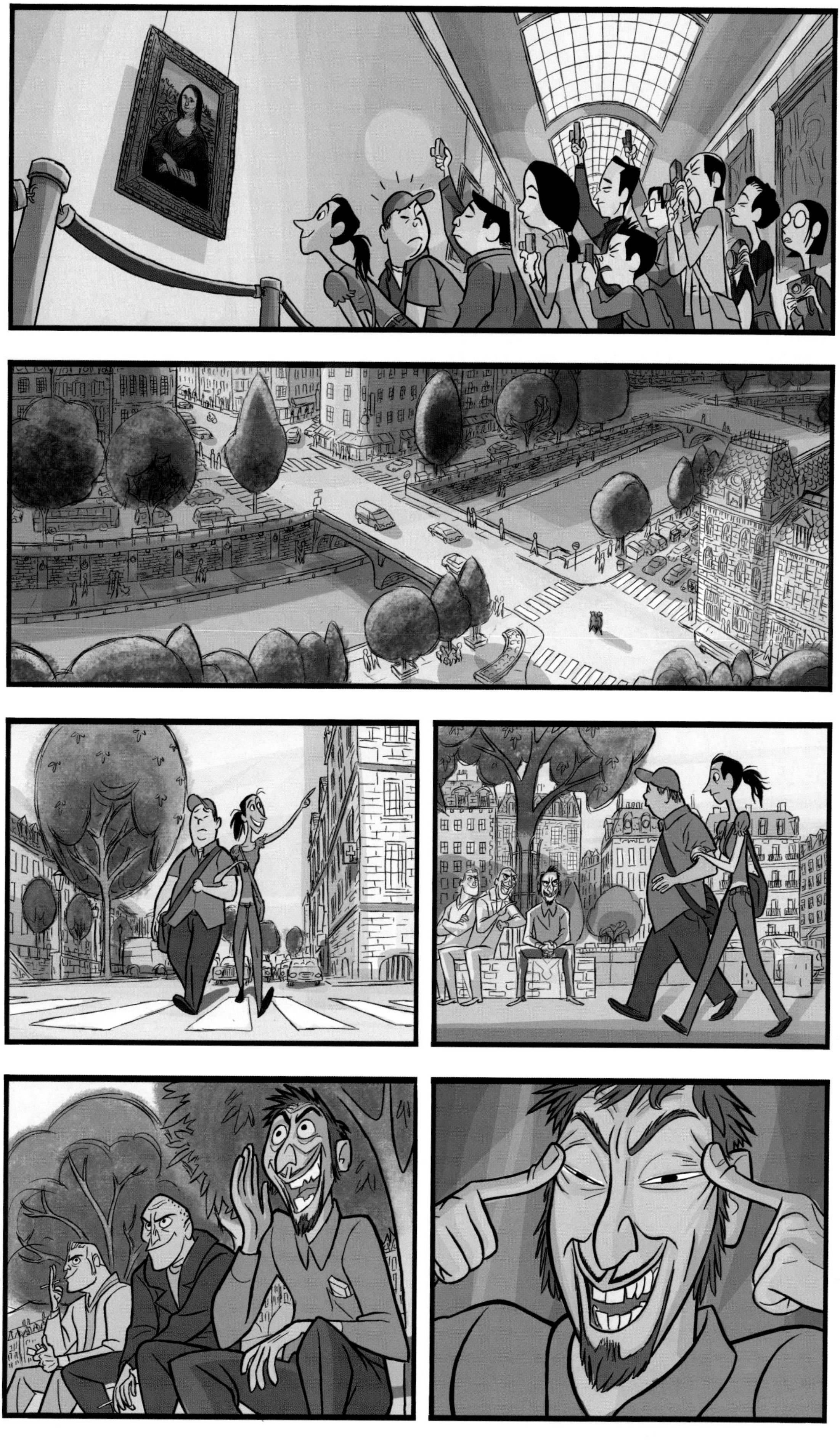

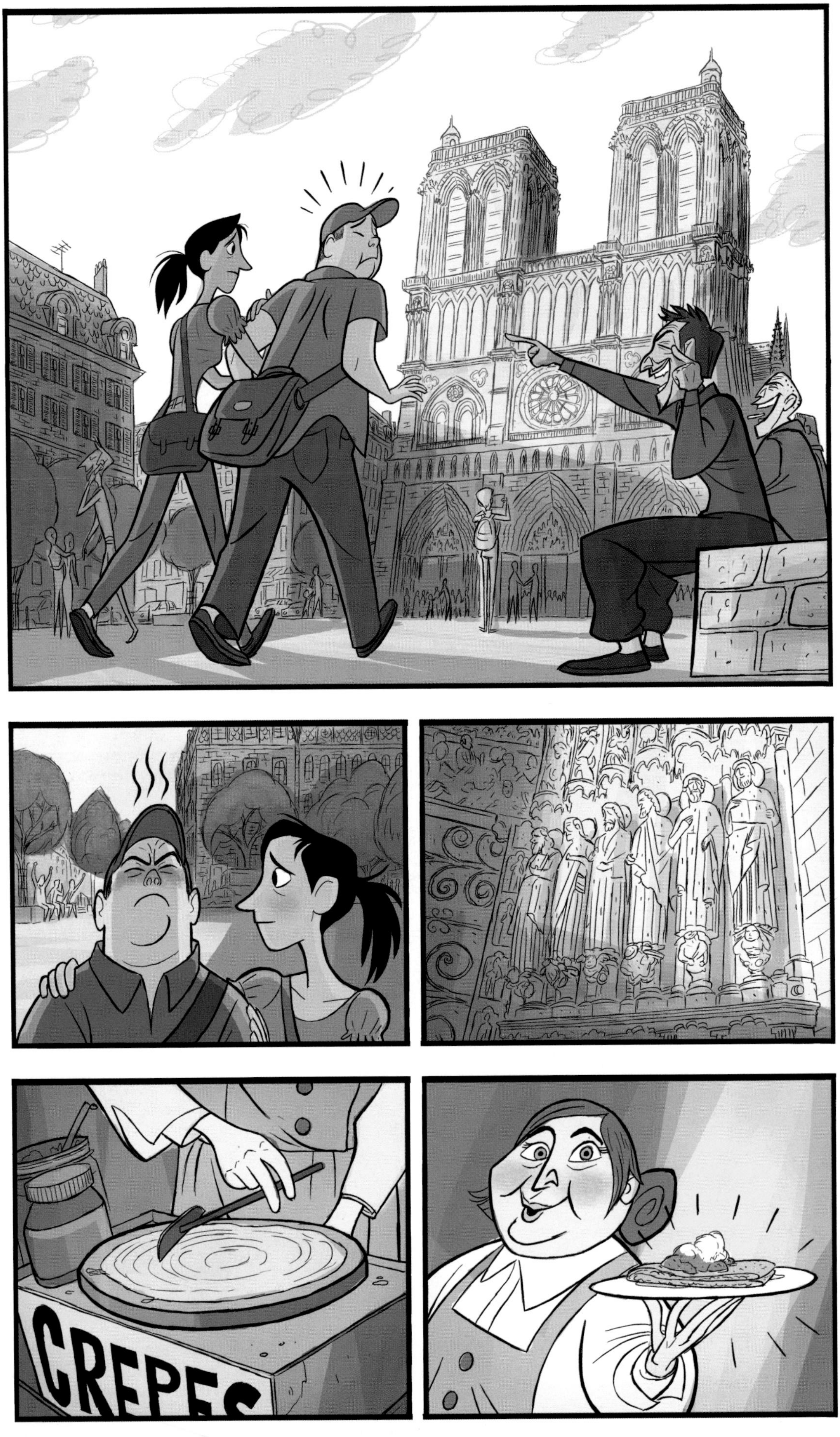
CREPES

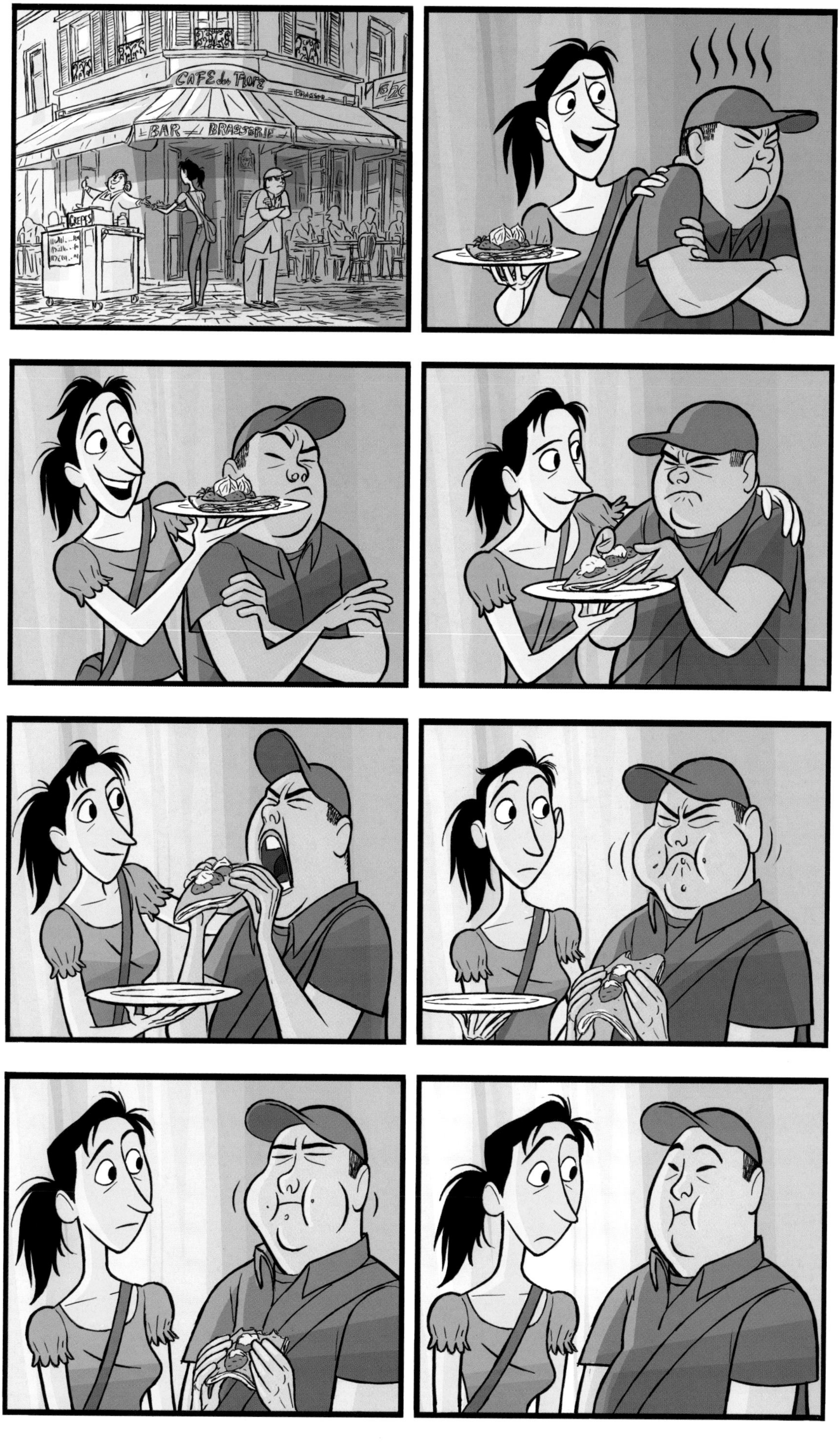
CAFE des Flore
BAR
BRASSERIE
CREPES

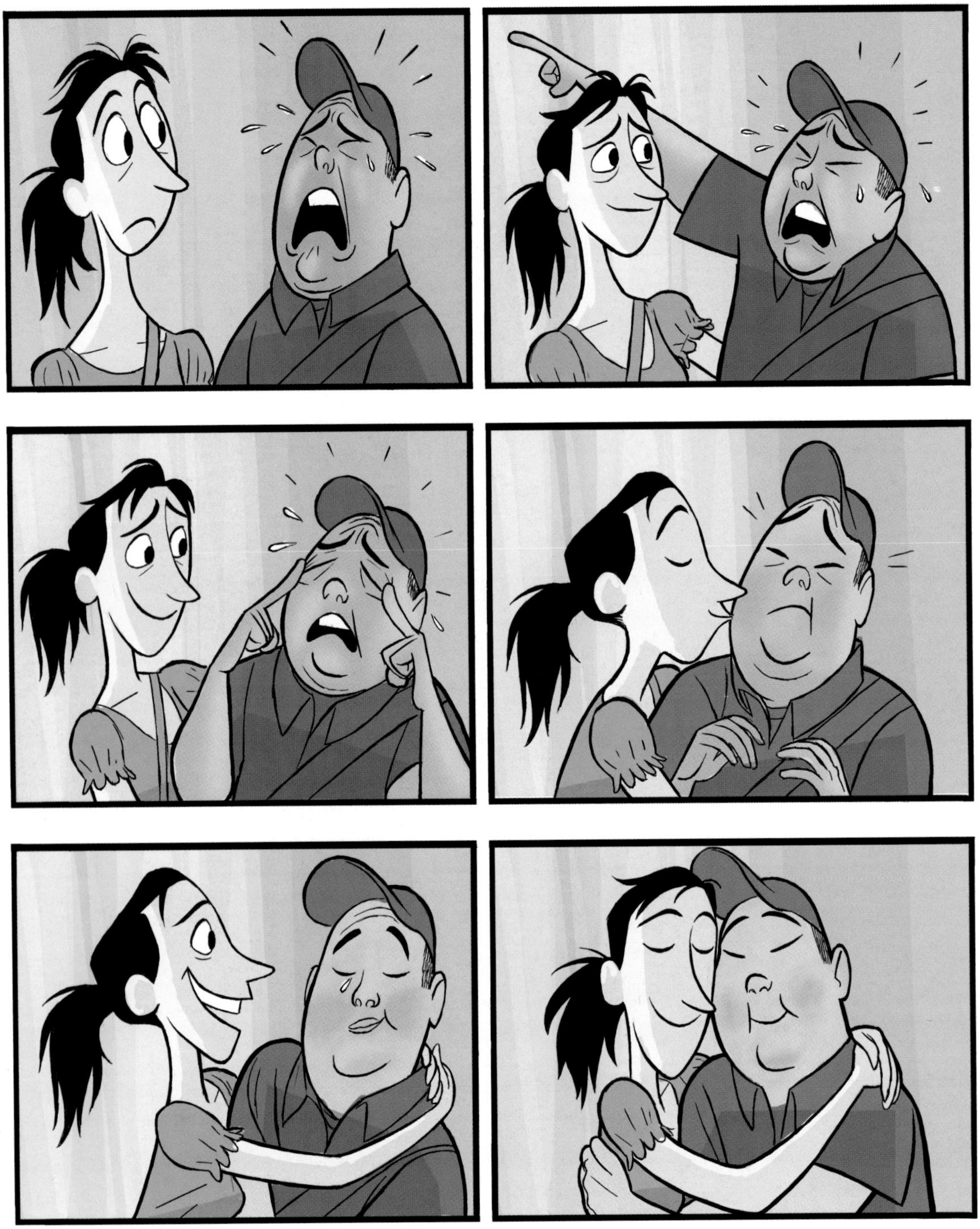

Fin

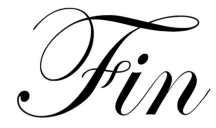

Dear Roundy,

In times of humiliation, and in times of harmony, you have always been there to help. Thanks for taking care of me.

With all my love,
Slanty

MARK ANDREWS IS THE AWARD-WINNING AUTHOR OF TALES OF COLOSSUS. IN ANIMATION, ANDREWS HAS ACTED AS HEAD OF STORY ON MULTIPLE CRITICALLY ACCLAIMED FILMS, INCLUDING THE IRON GIANT AND THE INCREDIBLES. HE'S WON AN EMMY FOR HIS WORK ON STAR WARS: CLONE WARS AND HIS PIXAR SHORT FILM, ONE MAN BAND, WAS NOMINATED FOR A 2005 ACADEMY AWARD FOR HIS DIRECTORIAL DEBUT (WITH CO-DIRECTOR ANDREW JIMENEZ) . HE POUNDS DRUMS AND SWINGS SWORDS IN NORTHERN CALIFORNIA WITH HIS WIFE AND CHILDREN. HTTP://TALESOFCOLOSSUS.BLOGSPOT.COM/

JAY BOOSE WAS BORN AND RAISED IN THE TUNDRA OF ONTARIO, CANADA WHERE HE STUDIED CLASSICAL ANIMATION. IN 1995 HE GOT HIS BIG BREAK AND MOVED SOUTH OF THE BORDER WHERE HE LANDED HIS FIRST JOB AS AN ASSISTANT ANIMATOR ON FOX ANIMATION'S "ANASTASIA". SOON, WALT DISNEY FEATURE ANIMATION BECKONED AND HIS ADVENTURE IN SUNNY FLORIDA BEGAN. HE WORKED ON DISNEY'S "MULAN" AS AN ASSISTANT ANIMATOR AND ON "LILO & STITCH" AND "BROTHER BEAR" AS AN ANIMATOR. SINCE THE UNTIMELY DEATH OF 2-D ANIMATION HE HAS BEEN BLISSFULLY WORKING AS AN ANIMATOR IN A HAPPY LAND CALLED PIXAR. TO SEE MORE VISIT: WEB.MAC.COM/JAYBOOSE/IWEB

JENNIFER CHANG GRADUATED FROM ACADEMY OF ART UNIVERSITY IN SAN FRANCISCO, AND IS CURRENTLY WORKING AS A SKETCH ARTIST AT PIXAR. SHE ENJOYS EXPERIMENTING IN PAINTINGS AND DRAWINGS AND READING SHORT STORIES/COMICS, AND WISHES TO DRAW AS FAST AS HER BITS AND PIECES OF IDEAS FLASHING THROUGH HER MIND. WWW.JENNIFER-CHANG.COM

JOSH COOLEY WAS SENT TO DOWN TO EARTH FROM A DISTANT WORLD AT A VERY YOUNG AGE TO HELP MANKIND AND SPREAD PEACE ACROSS THE PLANET. INSTEAD, HE DECIDED TO GO TO ART SCHOOL IN SAN FRANCISCO, CA AND STUDY CARTOONS. JOSH ENJOYS GOING TO THE MOVIES WITH HIS WIFE, ERIN, PLAYING WITH HIS 2 DOGS - TRIXIE AND JACK BAUER, AND EATING CUPCAKES. HE CURRENTLY LIVES IN BEAUTIFUL OAKLAND, CA, AND IS WORKING AS A STORYBOARD ARTIST AT PIXAR ANIMATION STUDIOS. SOMEDAY HE'LL GET AROUND TO HELPING MANKIND.

ROB GIBBS IS A STORY ARTIST AT PIXAR. ROB WENT TO SCHOOL AT CAL ARTS FROM '89 TO '90, WORKED ON THE INFAMOUS MOVIE: COOL WORLD, BEFORE SPENDING A FIVE YEAR SENTENCE AT DISNEY. COINCIDENTALLY, ROB LIKES ZOMBIES.

LOUIS GONZALES, HAVING RECEIVED NO AWARDS FOR HIS 6 PAGES SHORT STORY IN AFTERWORKS 1, CONTINUES TO DRAW STORIES AND DRINK TEQUILA TRYING TO FILL THE VOID IN HIS HEART. HE IS TAKEN CARE OF BY HIS FAMILY CONSISTING OF ONE WIFE AND 3 WELL ADJUSTED KIDS. TO LEARN MORE ABOUT LOUIS VISIT HIS BLOG AT WWW.LOUISGONZALES.COM/BLOG.

MARK CORDELL HOLMES HAS MEDDLED ON MANY PIXAR FILMS OVER THE LAST 10 YEARS. WHEN NOT AT WORK, MARK PASSES HIS COPIOUS SPARE TIME WRITING, SHOOTING PICTURES, TAKING ART DIRECTION FROM HIS TWIN SONS AND OCCASSIONALLY MEDDLING IN OTHER PEOPLES' COMICS. WWW.LUNAVILLA.COM

BRIAN LARSEN IS A LOS ANGELES NATIVE WHO HAS WORKED ON "THE IRON GIANT", "SKY HIGH" AND A FEW YEARS ON "SAMURAI JACK". LARSEN IS CURRENTLY WORKING AS A STORYBOARD ARTIST AT PIXAR. THIS IS HIS FIRST COMIC.

ANGUS MACLANE GREW UP IN PORTLAND, OREGON AND GRADUATED WITH A BACHELOR OF FINE ARTS FROM RHODE ISLAND SCHOOL OF DESIGN IN 1997. AS AN ANIMATOR, ANGUS HAS CONTRIBUTED TO SUCH AWARD-WINNING PIXAR FILMS AS GERI'S GAME, A BUG'S LIFE, TOY STORY 2, FOR THE BIRDS, MONSTERS, INC., AND FINDING NEMO. FOR HIS WORK ON THE INCREDIBLES, ANGUS RECEIVED THE ANNIE AWARD FOR "OUTSTANDING ACHIEVEMENT IN CHARACTER ANIMATION". RECENTLY, ANGUS SUPERVISED THE ANIMATION ON PIXAR'S ACADEMY AWARD NOMINATED ANIMATED SHORT FILM, ONE MAN BAND. ANGUS CURRENTLY RESIDES IN SAN FRANCISCO.

TED MATHOT HAS WORKED ON ANIMATED TV SHOWS, GAMES, AND FEATURES FOR THE PAST 13 YEARS INCLUDING REN & STIMPY, THE SIMPSONS, AND PIXAR'S MONSTER'S INC AND THE UPCOMING CARS. IN 2005, HE WAS NOMINATED FOR AN ANNIE AWARD FOR HIS STORYBOARD WORK ON THE THE INCREDIBLES. HE IS CURRENTLY WORKING AT PIXAR AND ON HIS OWN GRAPHIC NOVEL, ROSE AND ISABEL. HTTP://ROSEANDISABEL.BLOGSPOT.COM/

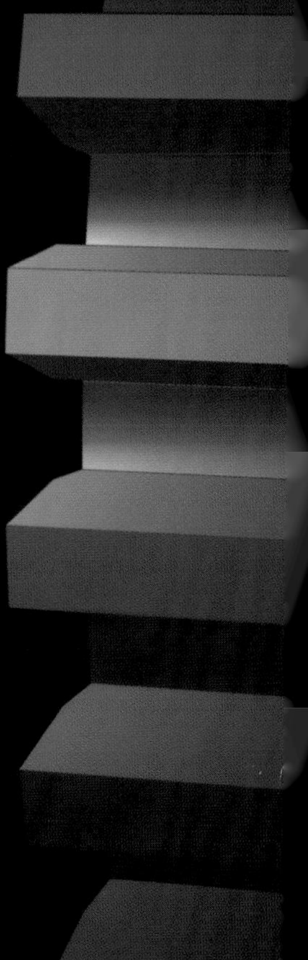

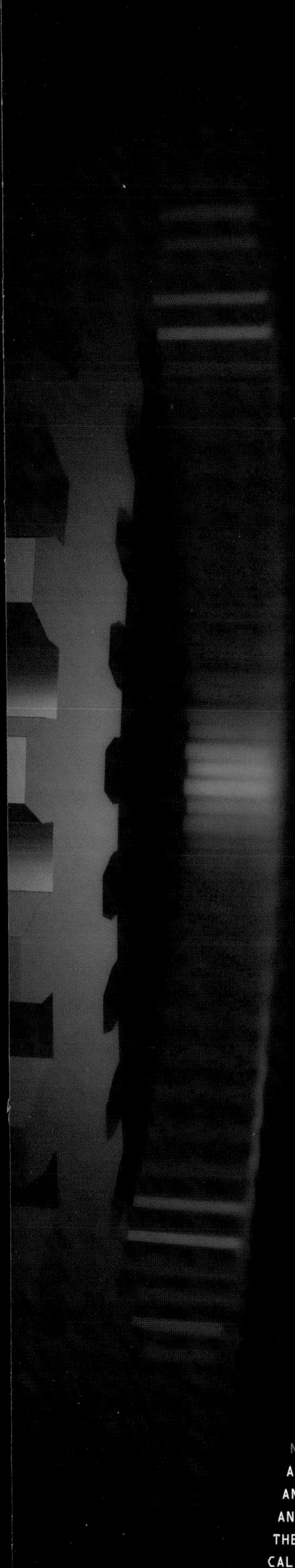

SCOTT MORSE IS THE AWARD-WINNING AUTHOR OF OVER 10 GRAPHIC NOVELS, INCLUDING NOBLE BOY, SOULWIND, THE BAREFOOT SERPENT, SPAGHETTI WESTERN, MAGIC PICKLE, AND SOUTHPAW. IN ANIMATION, HE'S WORKED AS A DESIGNER, ART DIRECTOR, WRITER, PRODUCER, AND STORY MAN FOR CARTOON NETWORK, UNIVERSAL, NICKELODEON, AND DISNEY. HE CURRENTLY RESIDES IN NORTHERN CALIFORNIA WITH HIS WIFE AND SON, WORKING AT PIXAR. WWW.SCOTTMORSE.CO SCOTTMORSE.BLOGSPOT.COM

SANJAY PATEL HAS NO ORIGINAL IDEAS AND RESORTS TO LOW BLOWS ON QUALITY FILMS STARING RUSSELL CROWE. WHEN HE'S NOT ANIMATING OR STORYBOARDING AT PIXAR HE SPENDS HIS TIME DRAWING HINDU GODS AND GODDESSES FOR WWW.GHEEHAPPY.COM

MATT PETERS WENT TO THE JOE KUBERT SCHOOL OF CARTOON AND GRAPHIC ART WHERE HE MET BILL AND TOGETHER CREATED REX STEELE AS A JOKE ON OLD MOVIE SERIALS. NOW WITH ONE SHORT FILM AND SIX COMIC STORIES UNDER HIS BELT, MATT HAD BETTER START TAKING REX SERIOUSLY.

JEFF PIDGEON HAS WORKED IN ANIMATION SINCE 1987, ON SUCH PROJECTS AS "MIGHTY MOUSE: THE NEW ADVENTURES", "THE SIMPSONS", AND "TOY STORY". HE IS CURRENTLY A STORY ARTIST, AND LIVES IN BERKELEY WITH HIS WIFE ANITA. THIS IS HIS FIRST COMIC. WWW.JEFFPIDGEON.COM

BILL PRESING WAS TRAINED TO BE A COMIC BOOK ARTIST IN THE MID 90'S. DURING WHICH THE VARIANT COVER/COLLECTORS MARKET DISASTER LEFT THE COMIC INDUSTRY IN SHAMBLES. AFTER REALIZING THE MINIMAL JOB OPPORTUNITY, LOW PAY, MURDEROUS HOURS, AND DEMORALIZING SOLITUDE THAT AWAITED BILL, HE QUICKLY CHANGED HIS CAREER PATH TO THE HAPPY CANDYLAND THAT IS ANIMATION. WHERE HE REMAINS TODAY.

PETER SOHN WAS BORN AND RAISED IN NEW YORK AND THROUGH A LOT OF LUCK GOT A JOB IN ANIMATION IN CALIFORNIA. THIS IS HIS FIRST COMIC AND IF YOU LIKED IT, YOU CAN REACH HIM AT SOHNPETER@HOTMAIL.COM. IF YOU DIDN'T LIKE IT, I DON'T THINK THERE IS AN EMAIL ADDRESS FOR THAT. AND IF YOU LIKE THE DOLLS IN THE PHOTOS, YOU CAN GET ONE AT WWW.ANNACHAMBERS.COM.

NATHAN STANTON WAS BORN AND RAISED IN ROCKPORT, MA., AFTER GRADUATING FROM HIGH SCHOOL HE MADE HIS WAY TO THE WEST COAST TO ATTEND THE CALIFORNIA INSTITUTE OF THE ARTS FROM 1988 TO 1992 WHERE HE RECEIVED HIS TRAINING IN ANIMATION. FROM THERE HE MOVED TO SAN FRANCISCO AND GOT HIS FIRST JOB IN THE ANIMATION INDUSTRY ON THE NIGHTMARE BEFORE CHRISTMAS IN 1993, AND AFTER SEVERAL YEARS OF FREELANCE ON VARIOUS COMMERCIALS AND SUCH, HE LANDED A JOB AT PIXAR ANIMATION STUDIOS IN 1996, STORYBOARDING ON A BUGS LIFE. HE CONTINUES TO WORK AWAY IN THE STORY TRENCHES TO THIS DAY AT PIXAR, AND HOPES TO CONTINUE IN THE WORLD OF COMICS WITH MANY MORE STORIES TO COME......

DEREK THOMPSON HAS WORKED PROFESSIONALLY IN COMIC BOOKS, VIDEO GAMES, AND FEATURE FILMS FOR OVER 13 YEARS. HE HAS CONTRIBUTED TO PROJECTS FOR DARK HORSE COMICS, RHYTHM & HUES, ELECTRONIC ARTS, AND LUCASFILM LTD. HE IS CURRENTLY WORKING AS A STORY ARTIST FOR PIXAR ANIMATION STUDIOS. YOU CAN CHECK OUT SOME OF HIS WORK AT WWW.DEREKMONSTER.COM.

ANTHONY WONG WAS BORN AND RAISED IN HONG KONG. AFTER GRADUATING FROM UC IRVINE WITH A COMPUTER SCIENCE DEGREE, HE CONTINUED HIS EDUCATION AT CAL ARTS. THE 4 SEMESTERS HE SPENT AT CAL ARTS REALLY ALTERED HIS LIFE. FOR 10 GOOD YEARS, HE WORKED FOR DISNEY FEATURE ANIMATION AS AN ANIMATOR. CURRENTLY, ANTHONY IS FORTUNATE ENOUGH TO WORK FOR PIXAR AS AN ANIMATOR, AND IS JUMPING UP AND DOWN BECAUSE HE IS DRAWING COMICS FOR AFTERWORKS2. HE ENJOYS LIVING IN NORTHERN CALIFORNIA WITH HIS WONDERFUL WIFE, ELLEN, AND 2 FAT CATS.

NATE WRAGG WAS BORN AND RAISED IN THE SMALL TOWN OF DAVIS, CALIFORNIA. AFTER GRADUATING HIGH SCHOOL, HIS LOVE FOR ART AND ANIMATION TOOK HIM SOUTH AND FAR FROM HOME TO CAL ARTS. AFTER THREE YEARS OF LEARNING CHARACTER ANIMATION IN SCHOOL, A HOSTILE ZOMBIE TAKEOVER, AND A SUMMER INTERNSHIP AT THE JAMES BAXTER ANIMATION STUDIO, NATE FINDS HIMSELF BACK UP IN NORTHERN CALIFORNIA CLOSE TO HOME, WORKING AS AN ARTIST HERE AT PIXAR.

THE AFTERWORKS 2 CREW
WOULD LIKE TO THANK
JIM DEMONAKOS, IMAGE COMICS,
PIXAR ANIMATION STUDIOS,
SIMON DUNSDON, ROBERT KONDO
AND THE CREW OF AFTERWORKS 1
FOR SETTING A GREAT PRECEDENT.

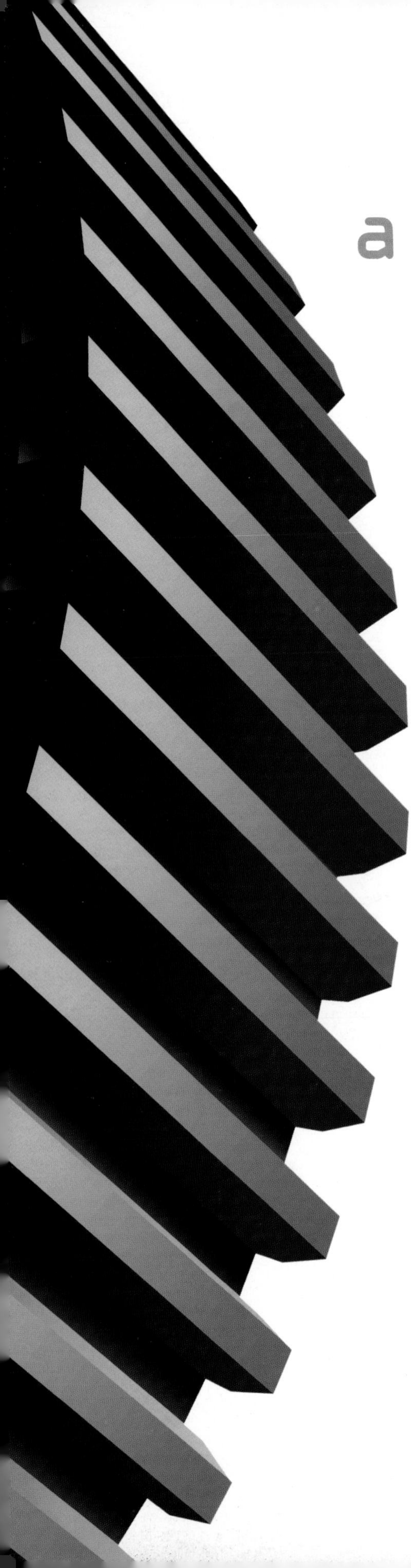

afterworks

AFTERWORKS
VOL. 1 TP

152 PAGES
BLACK & WHITE
ISBN# 1-58240-626-X
$17.99

"...this is a strong
anthology. There are tons of
animators spilling over into
comics these days, but if
they're as varied in style
and content as this bunch,
comics'll be all the better
for it."

—Nashville City Paper

ONLY
FROM
IMAGE
COMICS